EYES OF ARTILLERY

INSIGNIA OF THE FIFTH ARMY ARTILLERY AIR SECTIONS

ARMY HISTORICAL SERIES

EYES OF ARTILLERY

THE ORIGINS OF MODERN U. S. ARMY AVIATION IN WORLD WAR II

by
Edgar F. Raines, Jr.

Center of Military History
United States Army
Washington, D.C., 2000

Library of Congress Cataloging-in-Publication Data

Raines, Edgar F.
    Eyes of artillery : the origins of modern U.S. Army aviation in World War II / Edgar F. Raines, Jr.
       p. cm. — (Army historical series)
    Includes bibliographical references and index.
    1. World War, 1939–1945—Artillery operations, American. 2. United States. Army—Aviation—History. 3. Aerial observation (Military science)—United States—History.   I. Title.   II. Series.
D790.R25   1999
940.54'4973—dc21   99–13019
                                                                                      CIP

CMH Pub 70–31–1

Army Historical Series
Jeffrey J. Clarke, General Editor

Advisory Committee

(As of October 1999)

Gerhard L. Weinberg University of North Carolina	John H. Morrow, Jr. University of Georgia
Lawrence R. Atkinson IV The *Washington Post*	Lt. Gen. David H. Ohle Deputy Chief of Staff for Personnel
Linda S. Frey University of Montana	Carol A. Reardon Pennsylvania State University
Michael J. Kurtz National Archives and Records Administration	Mark A. Stoler University of Vermont
Brig. Gen. Fletcher M. Lamkin, Jr. U.S. Military Academy	Maj. Gen. Charles W. Thomas U.S. Army Training and Doctrine Command
Peter Maslowski University of Nebraska–Lincoln	Brig. Gen. John R. Wood U.S. Army Command and General Staff College
Col. Charles C. Ware U.S. Army War College	

U.S. Army Center of Military History

Brig. Gen. John S. Brown, Chief of Military History

Chief Historian	Jeffrey J. Clarke
Chief, Histories Division	Richard W. Stewart
Editor in Chief	John W. Elsberg

Foreword

Warfare has had its third dimension, air, for so long that no soldier or airman now serving has a personal memory of the expectations, adaptations, or debate that accompanied its early years. Air enthusiasts too often appear to forget that the most effective applications of air power have been in concert with ground forces. Indeed, for three wars running—World War II, Korea, and Vietnam—the close support technique of choice featured airborne eyes and ground artillery. This volume examines the institutional origins of modern Army Aviation by recounting the experiences of the men who flew observed fire missions in light aircraft for the Field Artillery during World War II. The War Department designated these aircraft "air observation posts," but the ground troops they supported affectionately referred to them by such names as "Maytag Messerschmidts" and "biscuit bombers" instead. Aircraft served as a key component of the Field Artillery indirect fire system—and also played a crucial role in the command and control of armored divisions during mobile operations. The author takes care to delineate how air observation posts interacted with each element of the combined arms team.

Eyes of Artillery identifies the circumstances and debate that gave rise to the Air-Observation-Post Program. The development of military aviation generated an extended struggle within the Army for the control of aerial observation and posed related questions concerning how air and ground elements should interact with one another. The author gives primary emphasis to the period from January 1939, when the Field Artillery began to actively seek control of its own observation aircraft, until September 1945, when Japan surrendered and the War Department prepared to expand the organic light aircraft program to the other ground combat arms. Many of the traditions, concepts, and disputes that still characterize Army Aviation originated during these critical years.

Eyes of Artillery is the first archive-based, in-depth study of the origins of modern Army Aviation in the United States. It makes a genuine and unique contribution to the literature of World War II and to the institutional history of the Army. The U.S. Army Center of Military History is proud to publish this valuable work.

Washington, D.C.
10 March 2000

JOHN S. BROWN
Brigadier General, USA
Chief of Military History

The Author

   Edgar Frank Raines, Jr., was born and raised in Murphysboro, Illinois. He attended Southern Illinois University, where he received his B.A. in history in 1966 and his M.A. in the same subject in 1968. He obtained his Ph.D. in history from the University of Wisconsin in 1976. From 1976 until 1979 he was the assistant academic dean at Silver Lake College in Manitowoc, Wisconsin. He spent the next fourteen months as a historian with the Office of Air Force History, Washington, D.C. Employed as a historian at the Center of Military History since November 1980, Dr. Raines is currently assigned to the General History Branch. In 1986 he coauthored (with Maj. David R. Campbell) *The Army and the Joint Chiefs of Staff: Evolution of Army Ideas on the Command, Control, and Coordination of the U.S. Armed Forces, 1942–1985*. Dr. Raines has written numerous unpublished special studies as well as several articles in military and social history. In 1985 his "The Ku Klux Klan in Illinois, 1867–1875" won the Harry E. Pratt Award for the best article on Illinois history.

Preface

On 24 February 1991, some two hundred helicopters, UH–60 Blackhawks, AH–64 Apaches, CH–47 Chinooks, OH–58 Kiowas, and a few UH–1 Hueys, carried the 1st Brigade, 101st Airborne Division, ninety-five miles into Iraqi territory—the longest air assault heretofore attempted. It was a striking display of operational mobility during the short, sharp ground combat portion of the Gulf War and an indication of why some military analysts, most notably Richard E. Simpkin, used the phrase "rotary-wing revolution" to describe warfare in the late twentieth century. The helicopters that made possible the 1st Brigade's assault into Forward Operating Base Cobra were operated and supported by members of the U.S. Army. The Department of the Army had organized the Aviation branch in 1983, but the origins of Army Aviation go back much earlier—to World War II.[1]

This monograph discusses the institutional beginnings of Army Aviation in the Field Artillery's Air-Observation-Post Program of World War II. It seeks to explain why the Army turned to organic aviation as a solution to the doctrinal and tactical problems it faced in 1942 and how it implemented this change. In essence, this study argues that transformations in the art of war created the necessity for reform, while new technologies provided the means that previously had not existed. The *how* is also important. A loose coalition of senior officer mentors and mid-level and junior officer reformers maneuvered to organize a test of the organic aviation concept, demonstrate its efficacy for the Field Artillery, set up a training program, use light aircraft effectively in combat, and expand the program to the other combat arms. In the process the center of innovation shifted from the Office of the Chief of Field Artillery in the War Department to Headquarters, Army Ground Forces, to the Department of Air Training at the Field Artillery School, to the air sections in field artillery battalions overseas, and back again to the War Department. Depending on the issue and the circumstances, senior officers, mid-level officers, junior officers, or some combination of the above were most important at any particular time.

Although the increasing importance of Army Aviation amply justifies a study of its institutional origins, it also provides a means of examining the dominant tactical philosophy of the U.S. Army in the twentieth century—combined arms. The *Army Dictionary* defines this concept as "more than one tactical branch of the Army used together in operations." The combined arms approach assumes that, if a commander can effectively coordinate all his assets in a blend of fire and maneuver adapted to the particular situation he faces, he will achieve a synergy that makes the effectiveness of the whole greater than the sum of its individual components. How the ground Army attempted to integrate aircraft

---

[1] Edward M. Flanagan, Jr., *Lightning: The 101st in the Gulf War* (Washington, D.C.: Brassey's, 1994), pp. 165–77; Richard E. Simpkin, *Race to the Swift: Thoughts on Twenty-First Century Warfare* (Washington, D.C.: Brassey's Defence Publishers, 1985), pp. 117–32.

into its operations, so different in approach from the principles espoused by the Army Air Forces, says something about the larger institution and its approach to war. This study also provides a new angle of vision about the conduct of operations in World War II. Finally, in some sense it is an extended essay on the theme of the difficulty of introducing a low-technology solution to a military problem when powerful vested interests desire a high-technology resolution.[2]

Eyes of Artillery is unabashedly an institutional history. It seeks to identify the collection of ideas at the institution's core and how they worked out in organizational arrangements, doctrinal changes, and combat actions. Seen from this vantage point, an inquiry into the origins of Army Aviation is an exercise in intellectual history. As such, I am deeply indebted to three scholars whom I have never met. Graham Allison and Morton Halperin pioneered the concept of "bureaucratic politics," while the late Elting E. Morison did equally significant work on the subject of military cultures.

I have also incurred a host of obligations to people I met while preparing this study. Unfortunately, the vagaries of memory and note taking render the acknowledgements that follow only a partial account of all who assisted. I am deeply indebted to the successive Chiefs of Military History of the U.S. Army for their approval and support: Brig. Gen. (Ret.) James L. Collins, Brig. Gen. (Ret.) Douglas Kinnard, Maj. Gen. (Ret.) William A. Stofft, Brig. Gen. (Ret.) Harold W. Nelson, Brig. Gen. (Ret.) John W. Mountcastle, and Brig. Gen. John S. Brown, as well as consecutive Chief Historians who influenced this effort: the late Dr. Maurice Matloff, Dr. David F. Trask, Mr. Morris J. MacGregor, and Dr. Jeffrey J. Clarke.

Although writing is a solitary experience, good historical writing depends heavily on the author's interaction with his peers. Present and former colleagues, librarians, archivists, and just plain friends by their support, encouragement, and insightful criticisms made this a far better study than otherwise would have been the case. These include: at the U.S. Army Center of Military History, Dr. Graham A. Cosmas, the late Mr. Billy C. Mossman, Dr. Charles A. Kirkpatrick, Mrs. Rebecca C. Raines, Ms. Diane Arms, Ms. Romana Danysh, Mr. John B. Wilson, Ms. Janice E. McKenney, Dr. David W. Hogan, Jr., the late Dr. James E. Hewes, Col. (Ret.) William T. Bowers, Col. (Ret.) Robert H. Sholly, Col. (Ret.) James W. Dunn, Col. (Ret.) Clyde L. Jonas, Dr. Richard W. Stewart, the late Col. (Ret.) John A. Cash, Dr. Paul J. Scheips, Mr. William G. Bell, Lt. Col. (Ret.) George L. MacGarrigle, Mr. Vincent H. Demma, Dr. Terrence J. Gough, Dr. John M. Carland, Mr. Wayne M. Dzwonchyk (now with the Joint Chiefs of Staff Historical Division), Dr. Russell J. Parkinson, Dr. Joel D. Meyerson, Mr. Dwight D. Oland, Mr. Stephen E. Everett, Dr. Norman M. Cary, Mr. Walter H. Bradford, Mr. David C. Cole, Mr. James A. Speraw, Ms. Hannah M. Zeidlik, Mrs. Wanda R. Radcliffe, Ms. Geraldine K. Harcarik, Mr. James B. Knight, Mrs. Mary L. Sawyer, Dr. Donald Carter, the late Ms. Carol I. Anderson, the late Mr. Ronald E. Dudley, Mr. Jefferson Powell, Ms. Cathleen Armstrong, and Ms. Mildred Gee; at the Air Force History Support Office, Washington, D.C., Dr. Walton S. Moody, Mr. William C. Heimdahl, Dr. Wayne S. Thompson, Dr. Daniel R. Mortensen, Mr. Herman S. Wolk, and Ms. Yvonne Kinkaid; at

---

[2] Department of the Army, Special Regulation 320–5–1, *Dictionary of United States Army Terms* (Washington, D.C.: Department of the Army, 1950), p. 52.

the Federal Aviation Administration, Washington, D.C., Dr. Teresa L. Krause, Mr. Thomas Haggerty, and Ms. Amy Tursky; at the National Archives and Records Administration, Washington, D.C., the late Mr. Edward J. Reese, Mr. Wilbert B. Mahoney, Mr. George C. Chalou, Mr. Gibson Smith, Mr. John E. Taylor, Ms. Teresa Hamett, Ms. Jo Ann Williamson, Mr. William H. Cunliffe, Dr. Timothy K. Nenninger, Mr. Richard L. Boylan, Mr. Fred Reason, and Ms. Angela Fernandez; at the National Personnel Records Center, St. Louis, Missouri, Ms. Thelma J. Martin; at the Library of Congress, Washington, D.C., Mr. Frederick Bauman; at the Robert Frost Library, Amherst College, Amherst, Massachusetts, Ms. Janet Poirrier, Ms. Carol Trabulsi, Ms. Donna Skibel, and Mr. Peter Weis; at the U.S. Army Training and Doctrine Command, Fort Monroe, Virginia, Dr. Henry O. Malone, the late Mr. Richard P. Weinert, and Mr. John L. Romjue; at the U.S. Army Military History Institute, Carlisle Barracks, Pennsylvania, Mr. John Slonaker, Dr. Richard J. Sommers, Dr. David Keogh, Ms. Pamela Cheney, Ms. Louise Arnold-Friend, and Mr. Dennis Vetock; at the U.S. Army Aviation Center and School, Fort Rucker, Alabama, the late Lt. Col. (Ret.) James C. Craig, Lt. Col. (Ret.) Thomas J. Sabiston, Mr. R. Steven Maxham, Mrs. Regina Burns, Mr. Harford T. Edwards, Dr. John W. Kitchens, Ms. Lucille Durkin, Ms. Mary Nell Durant, Dr. Burton Wright III, and Mr. James P. Finley; at the U.S. Army Aviation Systems Command, St. Louis, Missouri, Dr. Howard K. Butler; at the U.S. Air Force Military Airlift Command, Scott Air Force Base, Illinois, Mr. Laurence Epstein; at the Field Artillery School, Fort Sill, Oklahoma, Dr. Boyd L. Dastrup, Dr. L. Martin Kaplan (now at the Center of Military History), Mr. Les Miller, Ms. Martha Relp, Ms. Vicki Armstrong, and Col. (now Maj. Gen.) Robert H. Scales, Jr. (currently commandant of the Army War College); at the Combined Arms Research Library, U.S. Army Command and General Staff College, Fort Leavenworth, Kansas, Ms. Elizabeth Snoke; at the University of Kansas, Lawrence, Dr. Theodore J. Wilson; and at the Indiana Historical Society, Indianapolis, Mr. Douglas E. Clanin.

A number of people read and commented on the entire manuscript. I am very grateful to them for both their insights and their perseverance. They include: at the Center of Military History, Dr. Clarke, Colonel Bowers, Dr. Cosmas, Dr. Kaplan, Mrs. Raines, and Ms. Arms; at the Air Force History Support Office, Dr. Thompson and Dr. Mortensen; at Southern Illinois University, Carbondale, Dr. John Y. Simon; at the University of Cincinnati, Ohio, Dr. Daniel R. Beaver; at the University of Wisconsin, Madison, Dr. Edward M. Coffman (now retired to Lexington, Kentucky); an independent scholar, Lt. Col. (Ret.) Carlo D'Este; and three veterans of World War II, Lt. Gen. (Ret.) Robert R. Williams, the late Col. (Ret.) Michael J. Strok, and Col. (Ret.) William R. Mathews.

Although I was able to find a few photographs interspersed among the textual records, I located the vast majority only after a special search. Once again, the final result was greatly improved through the generous assistance of individuals with specialized knowledge. These include: at the National Archives Still Picture Branch, College Park, Maryland, Ms. Mary Ilario, Ms. Holly Reed, Ms. Sharon Culley, Ms. Nikia Breedlove, Ms. Cabbie Smith, Ms. Janita Dixon, Ms. Kate Flaherty, Mr. Kevin Morrow, Ms. Theresa Roy, and Ms. Rutha Dicks; at the National Air and Space Museum Library, Washington, D.C., Mr. Brian Nicklas, Ms. Kristine Daske, Mr. Phil Edwards, and Ms. Melissa Kaiser; at the National Guard Bureau, Falls Church, Virginia, Lt. Col. Leonid E. Kondratiuk; at the National Guard

Association Museum Library, Washington, D.C., Mr. Thomas Weaver; at Nappanee, Indiana, Mr. John Stahly, former editor of the *L–4 Grasshopper Newsletter*; at Remus, Michigan, Mr. John Bergeson, publisher and editor of the *Cub Club*; at Sentimental Journeys, Lock Haven, Pennsylvania, Ms. Madeline Blesch; at the Piper Aviation Museum, Lock Haven, Pennsylvania, Mr. Harry P. Mutter and Mrs. Anna Wallace; and at the U.S. Army Aviation Museum Library, the ever efficient Mrs. Burns and Mr. Tierney, who came out of retirement to help see this project through to completion.

I am also greatly obligated to all the Field Artillery air-observation-post pilots with whom it was my good fortune to correspond and conduct interviews. They invited me into their homes, patiently explained what were to them obvious points, talked with me at length on the telephone, and were most kind and forthcoming. They made my research much less tedious and helped me avoid many errors. They are listed in the bibliographical note. A number of aviators saved documents and photographs as well as memories, which they and their families also shared with me. I am particularly indebted to the following: in Florissant, Missouri, Mrs. Vivian Bristol, who allowed me to borrow the papers of her late husband, Col. (Ret.) Delbert L. Bristol, for an extended period; at Edgewater, Maryland, Mrs. Marcia Strok, who located materials on Fifth Army Air Observation Post losses, and her late husband, Colonel Strok, who let me use his papers, books, and photographs; at Fort Worth, Texas, General Williams, who contributed two wartime photographs and suggested other possible sources, and Col. (Ret.) John W. Oswalt, who loaned me personal papers; in Austin, Texas, the late Col. (Ret.) Gordon J. Wolf, who provided a sizable body of documents and many photographs, which he allowed me to copy; in San Antonio, Texas, Colonel Mathews, who lent me a photograph; at the Army Aviation Association of America, Westport, Connecticut, Mr. Arthur Kesten, who allowed me to copy photographs and documents; at Lawton, Oklahoma, Lt. Col. (Ret.) Robert R. Yeats, who permitted me to examine his personal papers and make copies of photographs from his extensive collection; and in Agoura Hills, California, Lt. Col. (Ret.) Charles W. Lefever, who permitted me to borrow his World War II photographic album. The images in the Lefever and Wolf collections proved particularly valuable for this volume. I am also indebted to the late Maj. Gen. (Ret.) William A. Harris. Although not an Army aviator, he thought that Army Aviation deserved a history. He made arrangements for me to examine the papers of the late Brig. Gen. (Ret.) Rex Chandler and Colonel Wolf and conducted an interview with Colonel Wolf for me. This history is the richer for General Harris' efforts.

Once an author completes research and writing, his manuscript requires the ministrations of many talented professionals before it can become a book. To my editor at the Center of Military History, Ms. Diane M. Donovan, I extend my thanks for working with my prose and bringing system to my footnotes. The chief of the Editorial Branch, Ms. Catherine A. Heerin, has guided the manuscript through all the steps of the editorial process and provided sound advice on more than one occasion. Graphics support at the Center of Military History is also of a very high order. I am under particular obligation to Mr. Arthur S. Hardyman, Mr. Howell C. Brewer, Jr., Ms. Beth F. MacKenzie, and Mr. Roger S. Wright for their invaluable assistance. Mr. John A. Birmingham designed the cover. The editor in chief, Mr. John W. Elsberg, has overseen the production of this volume in all its phases.

Family members provided essential support, both before and during the writing of this book. The stories of my maternal grandfather, Herman H. Mohlenbrock, and my fraternal grandmother, Iva B. Raines, awakened an interest in and a love for history that date from my earliest recollections. My parents, Edgar F. and Mary B. Raines, gave me the opportunity to pursue both my undergraduate and graduate education, which ultimately made this study possible. Finally, I am greatly indebted to my son, Edgar, and my wife, Rebecca. They have provided the reasons for persevering during the low moments that befall all books. My wife, also my colleague, ensured that this account is both more literate and error free than would have otherwise been the case. She read and reread more drafts than should be the lot of any human being. It goes without saying, however, that any errors of fact or interpretation that remain are the sole responsibility of the author.

Washington, D.C. EDGAR F. RAINES, JR.
10 March 2000

Contents

Chapter	Page
PROLOGUE: AERIAL OBSERVATION TO 1938	3
The Origins of Aerial Observation in the U.S. Army, 1861–1917	5
Aerial Observation in a War of Position, 1917–1918	10
Aerial Observation in Flux, 1919–1938	14
Conclusion	28
1. THE GROUND ARMS SEEK THEIR OWN AIRCRAFT, 1939–1941	31
The Field Artillery and the Aerial Observation Problem, 1939–1940	31
Air Observation for the Cavalry, Armor, and Infantry, 1939–1940	43
The Fight for Organic Air, January–September 1941	47
Conclusion	55
2. THE FIELD ARTILLERY ACQUIRES ITS OWN AIRCRAFT, JULY 1941–JUNE 1942	57
The War Department and Aerial Observation, July 1941–January 1942	57
Testing the Concept	66
Approving the Concept	75
Light Aircraft for the Other Combat Arms	79
Conclusion	80
3. CREATING THE AIR-OBSERVATION-POST PROGRAM, JUNE–DECEMBER 1942	85
Writing the Charter	85
Establishing the Training and Logistical Base, June–July 1942	87
Pilot, Mechanic, and Observer Training, July–November 1942	95
A Reexamination of Mission	102
Conclusion	106
4. DEVELOPING THE AIR-OBSERVATION-POST PROGRAM, JANUARY–DECEMBER 1943	109
Aircraft Procurement for 1943	109
Creating an Air-Observation-Post Logistical System	112
Research and Development, Force Development, and Combat Development	116
The Department of Air Training	122
Unit Training	129
Conclusion	137

Chapter	Page

5. INITIAL DEPLOYMENT AND COMBAT IN THE NORTH AFRICAN AND MEDITERRANEAN THEATERS 145
The European Theater of Operations and North Africa............ 145
Sicily.. 161
Italy: Salerno to Rome.. 166
North of Rome.. 182
Conclusion... 188

6. THE EUROPEAN THEATER OF OPERATIONS, JUNE 1944–SEPTEMBER 1945 189
The European Theater of Operations: Administration and Logistics... 189
Normandy: Planning and Invasion............................... 203
The Battle for the Hedgerows................................. 208
Pursuit and the Landing in Southern France 212
The Border Battles... 226
The German Counteroffensive 228
The Final Battles 231
Conclusion 234

7. THE PACIFIC, JUNE 1943–SEPTEMBER 1945 237
Personalities, Command Arrangements, Terrain, and Water 237
Southwest Pacific Area: New Guinea, June 1943–June 1944 241
South Pacific Area: Bougainville 245
Central Pacific Area, 1944................................... 251
Southwest Pacific Area, June 1944–September 1945 252
Central Pacific Area: Okinawa, 1945........................... 266
Conclusion 271

8. CREATING ARMY GROUND FORCES LIGHT AVIATION 273
War Department Policy and the Air-Observation-Post Program, September 1943–October 1944 273
Air-Observation-Post Logistics 280
Training 282
Research and Development 284
Department of Air Training 288
Final Steps to a Permanent Program, September 1944–January 1945 . 294
The Creation of the Army Ground Forces Light Aviation Program, February–August 1945... 296
Conclusion 304

Chapter	Page
EPILOGUE: AIR OBSERVATION POSTS, WORLD WAR II, AND ARMY AVIATION	307
The Air-Observation-Post Program, 1945	307
Wartime Casualties	308
Conclusion	315
APPENDIXES	
A. Selected U.S. Army Field Artillery and U.S. Army Air Forces Liaison Aircraft and Helicopters, 1942–1945	327
B. Letter From the Chief of Field Artillery Proposing Organic Air Observation for the Field Artillery, 15 July 1940	335
BIBLIOGRAPHICAL NOTE	339
INDEX	351

Charts

No.		Page
1.	Field Artillery School, Department of Air Training, October 1942	91
2.	Organization of U.S. Infantry Division, July 1943–May 1945	138
3.	Organization of U.S. Armored Division, October 1942–September 1943	139
4.	Organization of U.S. Armored Division, September 1943–February 1944	140
5.	Organization of U.S. Armored Division, February 1944–November 1945	141
6.	Organization of U.S. Airborne Division, February–August 1944	142
7.	Organization of U.S. Airborne Division, August–December 1944	143
8.	Organization of U.S. Airborne Division, December 1944–December 1945	144
9.	Organization of a Field Army Artillery Section, 1945	154
10.	Coordination Responsibilities of a Field Army Artillery Air Officer, 1945	155
11.	Field Artillery Air Officers in the European Theater of Operations, 1944–1945	191
12.	Organization of Army Air Forces Logistical Support for Field Artillery Air Observation Posts in the 12th Army Group, 24 November 1944	194
13.	Organization of Army Air Forces Logistical Support for Field Artillery Air Observation Posts in the 12th Army Group, 8 May 1945	195
14.	Organization of Army Air Forces Logistical Support for Field Artillery Air Observation Posts in the 6th Army Group, 11 March 1945	196
15.	Field Artillery School, Department of Air Training, 6 November 1944	289

Figures

No.		Page
1.	Cross-Sectional Diagram of a Piper Cub	24
2.	Instrument Panel of a Piper Cub	25
3.	Organization of a Landing Field in Combat	131
4.	Land Installation of the Brodie Device	268

Tables

1.	Statistical Analysis of Air-Observation-Post Activities in U.S. First Army, June 1944–April 1945	310
2.	Air-Observation-Post Operations in U.S. Fifth Army, 1944	312
3.	Ratio of Air-Observation-Post Pilot Losses to Aircraft Losses in U.S. First and Fifth Armies, January 1944–April 1945	314
4.	Air-Observation-Post Losses in U.S. Tenth Army During the Okinawa Campaign, 1 April–30 June 1945	315

Maps

1.	Operation TORCH, November 1942	148
2.	Assault on Sicily, 10 July 1943	164
3.	Italian Campaign, 9 September–15 November 1943	168
4.	German Counterattacks on the Anzio Beachhead, 16 February–3 March 1944	179
5.	The Final OVERLORD Plan	206
6.	Drive to the Seine River, 16–25 August 1944	216
7.	The Pacific Theater and Adjacent Regions, 1942	238
8.	New Guinea Operations, June 1943–July 1944	242
9.	The Northern Solomons and Bismarck Archipelago, 1943	248
10.	The Philippines, 1944	255

Illustrations

Insignia of the Fifth Army Artillery Air Sections	*Frontispiece*
Professor Thaddeus S. C. Lowe and Ground Crew at the Battle of Fair Oaks, Virginia	6
Orville Wright Stands before a U.S. Production Model De Havilland DH–4	12
Formation of North American O–47s	19
Kellett YG–1A Autogiro	21
Focke-Achgelis Fw–61	21
Continental A–65 Opposed Engine	26
Fieseler Storch Fi–156	27
Maj. Gen. Robert M. Danford	32

	Page
Stinson O–49	34
Col. Rex E. Chandler	37
Igor I. Sikorsky in the VS–300	41
Maj. Gen. John K. Herr and Brig. Gen. Adna R. Chaffee, Jr.	45
William T. Piper and Members of the Grasshopper Squadron During the Louisiana Maneuvers	50
"Gas Stop"	51
Measuring Takeoff and Landing Distances During the Stinson Model 76 Tests	61
John J. McCloy	62
Col. William W. Ford and Lt. Col. Gordon J. Wolf	65
The SCR–610 Mounted in an L–4	66
Members of Flight A Refuel an O–59 in the Field	71
Overhead Photograph of the YO–59A	73
Aircraft of Flight B Pass in Review with Elements of the 2d Division at Fort Sam Houston	78
World War II Aerial View of Post Field	89
Capt. Theodore F. Schirmacher and Capt. Thomas S. Baker	92
Maj. Robert M. Leich, 1st Lt. L. M. Bornstein, and 1st Lt. Marion J. Fortner	93
Maj. Gen. Idwal H. Edwards	97
Contour Flying at Fort Sill	101
An O–59 Loaded on an Army Truck for Cross-Country Movement	105
The Piper Aircraft Corporation's Plant at Lock Haven	111
Field Assembly of an L–4	113
Sikorsky XR–4 Helicopter	117
Taylorcraft L–2	119
Rawdon T–1	121
Maj. Victor E. Frazier Helps Load a Simulated Casualty Aboard a Navy NE–1	128
An L–4 of the 29th Infantry Division Flies over a Battery of 105-mm. M2 Howitzers	130
Second Lt. Charles M. Brown in the Cockpit of an L–4	135
Lt. Delbert L. Bristol	147
Second Lt. William H. Butler and Capt. Breton A. Devol Prepare To Take Off from the USS *Ranger*	150
Mark III Auster with Royal Air Force Markings	152
S. Sgt. Frank A. Perkins, 1st Armored Division, With the L–4 "Super Snooper"	159
An L–4 Cub Takes Off from a Runway Built on a Landing Ship, Tank	162
Lt. Col. John T. Walker, Lt. Gen. Mark W. Clark, Robert P. Patterson, and Lt. Gen. Brehon B. Somervell	167
Capt. Michael J. Strok	169
An L–4 With a Fairchild K–24 Aerial Camera Mounted for Oblique Photographs	176
An Oblique-Angle Aerial Photograph Shows German Artillery Positions Destroyed by Artillery	177
Capt. John W. Oswalt	181

	Page
Maj. Jack L. Marinelli	185
U.S. Fifth Army's "Ski Jump" Airstrip at Futa Pass, Italy	187
Brig. Gen. H. B. Lewis Presents the Bronze Star to Lt. Col. Charles W. Lefever	190
Maj. Bryce Wilson as a Lieutenant in 1942	198
An Air Observation Post Flies over an M3A1 Stuart Light Tank	214
Some L–4s Temporarily Grounded by a Flood near the German Frontier	227
An L–4 Lands on Skis in France	230
Tech. 5 William E. Huddleston Tunes the Engine of an L–4	230
A Section of German Autobahn Serves as an Airstrip for Army L–4s	233
An L–4 on Patrol along the Beach at Aitape, Dutch New Guinea	245
A K–20 Aerial Camera Mounted on an L–4H for Vertical Photography	247
An L–4 Lands at Morotai Island, Dutch East Indies, After Observing Japanese Positions	254
Eleventh Airborne Division L–4s Transport Christmas Dinners for the Troops	258
Col. Robert F. Cassidy	265
The USS *Brodie* with the Brodie Device Installed	269
Maintenance Specialists of the 1st Depot Unit, Army, Examine a Battle-Damaged L–4	270
Col. Claude L. Shepard	274
Lt. Gen. Mark W. Clark, General Henry H. Arnold, and Lt. Gen. George S. Patton, Jr.	279
A Piper L–14	287
An L–4 Nears the End of Its Takeoff Run on a Lake at Fort Sill	292
An L–4 on the Land-Rig Version of the Brodie Device	293
An L–5 Outfitted with Six Rocket Launchers and One Navy High-Velocity Aerial Rocket	297
Lt. Col. Robert R. Williams	301
Maj. Gen. Gilbert R. Cook	303
Aftermath of an L–4 Accident on Lucca Air Strip, Italy	313
Some L–4s at an Airport on Saipan	318
Troops Inspect an L–5 Damaged by Japanese Raiders	319
An L–4 Takes Off From Itibashi-Ku Airfield, Tokyo, Japan	325

Illustrations courtesy of the following sources: pp. 12, 19, 21 (*bottom*), 26, 27, 34, 41, 51, 121, 152, 214, 279, Smithsonian Institution, Washington, D.C.; 32, 37, 45, 61, 62, 66, 71, 73, 97, 119, 128, 130, 150, 159, 162, 167, 169, 185, 245, 247, 254, 279, 297, 313, 325, National Archives and Records Administration, College Park, Md.; 6, 50, 78, 93, 105, 113, 117, 135, 147, 176, 177, 187, 198, 227, 230 (*top*), 233, 269, 274, 318, 319, U.S. Army Aviation Museum Library, Fort Rucker, Ala.; 181, U.S. Army Center of Military History, Washington, D.C.; 327, 328, 329, 330, 331, 332, 333, *Aviation Digest*, Fort Rucker; 111, Piper Aviation Museum, Lock Haven, Pa.; 258, 270, Commonwealth Books, New York, N.Y.; 265, Army Aviation Association of America, Westport, Conn.; 303, XII Corps History Association; 301, Lt. Gen. (Ret.) Robert R. Williams; 292, 293, the late Col. (Ret.) Gordon J. Wolf; 65, 89, 92, 101, 190, 230 (*bottom*), 287, Lt. Col. (Ret.) Charles W. Lefever; 21 (*top*), Lt. Col. (Ret.) Robert R. Yeats.

EYES OF ARTILLERY

PROLOGUE

Aerial Observation to 1938

"The little two-seater Piper Cub planes," observed an American war correspondent at Anzio in the spring of 1944, "are all over the beachhead like smoke over Pittsburgh." The aircraft were militarized versions of a light plane, the Cub J-3 produced by the Piper Aircraft Corporation. Officially designated L-4, they were better known to ground troops by a variety of affectionate nicknames—"flivver planes," "grasshoppers," "flying jeeps," "doodlebugs," "Maytag Messerschmidts," "biscuit bombers," "puddle jumpers," and sometimes with irony as "our air force." The pilots who flew them and the mechanics who maintained them were field artillerymen. Each firing battalion of field artillery in the U.S. Army had its own air section with two aircraft. By the end of the war the number of such planes assigned to the ground forces totaled well over fifteen hundred. They were part of the U.S. Army Field Artillery's Air-Observation-Post Program and as such represented the institutional beginnings of today's Army Aviation.[1]

Army Aviation is simply the aerial component of the U.S. Army. It consists of aircraft deemed so essential to the conduct of ground forces that they must come under the operational control of a ground forces commander. Because these aerial vehicles are intrinsic to the ground forces, they are sometimes referred to as "organic aviation." The *Army Dictionary* provides a purely descriptive definition of Army Aviation: "Personnel, aircraft, and allied aircraft equipment organically assigned to Army organizations by appropriate tables of organization and equipment, tables of distribution, tables of

---

[1] Sid Felder, "Article by Sid Felder in the New Britain (Conn.) Herald," reprinted in Memo, Lt Col Gordon J. Wolf, Director (Dir), Field Artillery School (FAS), Department of Air Training (DAT), 29 May 44, sub: Informal Info, in DAT, "Training Memoranda" (Bound Manuscript [Ms], Morris Swett Technical Library, FAS, Fort Sill, Okla. [hereafter cited as Morris Swett Tech Lib], 1944–1945); Memo, Col C. H. Day, Assistant Ground Adjutant General (AGAG), for The Adjutant General (TAG), 26 Sep 42, sub: Changes in Field Artillery (FA) Tables of Organization (TOs), Headquarters, Army Ground Forces (HQ, AGF), General Correspondence (Gen Corresp), 1942–1948, 320.3/60 (FA), Record Group (RG) 337, National Archives and Records Administration, Washington, D.C. (hereafter cited as NARA); War Department (WD), Field Manual (FM) 6–150, *Organic Field Artillery Air Observation* (Washington, D.C.: Government Printing Office, 1944), pp. 2–3. For a technical description of the L-4, see Frederick G. Swanborough and Peter M. Bowers, *United States Military Aircraft Since 1909* (Washington, D.C.: Smithsonian Institution Press, 1989), pp. 516–19; Devon Francis, *Mr. Piper and His Cubs* (Ames: Iowa State University Press, 1973), pp. 23–25. Maj. Edward M. Flanagan, Jr., "Biscuit Bombers (Leyte Style)," *Field Artillery Journal (FAJ)* 38 (March–April 1948):73–75; Francis, *Mr. Piper and His Cubs,* pp. 22, 106–07; and Felder, "Article," give some of the many nicknames by which these aircraft were known.

allowances, or other competent authority." In World War II the term *air observation post* identified a Field Artillery aircraft (and differentiated it from similar light planes assigned to the Army Air Forces) by referring to its primary mission, directing artillery fire on targets out of sight of the gunners. In the Field Artillery lexicon it complemented a *ground observation post*, where observers did the same thing using a terrain feature or structure for a vantage point. Other than the Army Air Forces, only the Field Artillery possessed its own organic aircraft before the summer of 1945. The phrase Air-Observation-Post Program, consequently, is the best, in fact the only, descriptor for this organization. At times during the war, Army Air Forces liaison squadrons were attached to higher-level ground forces headquarters. They thus came under the operational control of the supported ground forces headquarters, although all the other command functions, such as personnel replacement and logistical support for aviation equipment, continued to be performed through an Army Air Forces chain of command. They also constituted organic aviation in these instances. The official Army view, whether in 1944 or 1999, is that an organic airplane is just another piece of equipment like a jeep, a 2 1/2–ton truck, or a 105-mm. howitzer. Such a notion is a very traditional way of conceiving a military role for an aerial vehicle.[2]

Although the Air-Observation-Post Program was only two years old in 1944, the principles governing its organization dated back to the first employment of military balloons in the eighteenth century. Military aviation was considered an integral part of the ground forces it supported, from the invention of balloons in 1783 until World War I. The earliest attempts in military aeronautics foundered, however, on a combination of technical and administrative shortcomings, military conservatism, and the nature of battle in the late eighteenth and early nineteenth centuries. The relatively short range of weapons and the correspondingly small size of battlefields permitted effective reconnaissance by mounted units, either light cavalry or dragoons, and limited the demand for aerial observers. From a hill, an army commander equipped with a telescope could easily survey the positions of his own army and those of the enemy. During the French Revolution, the French Army formed two balloon companies. The inability of the aeronauts to generate hydrogen in the field, coupled with the lack of mobility of the ground support element, dubbed the balloon train, led to the disbandment of the companies in 1799 after five years of generally indifferent service.[3]

---

[2] Department of the Army (DA), Army Regulation (AR) 310–25, *Dictionary of United States Army Terms* (Washington, D.C.: Department of the Army, 1986), p. 18. This study was written at a time of considerable intellectual ferment in American joint doctrine. Specifically, the chairman of the Joint Chiefs of Staff has adopted new, very precise meanings for the terms "role," "mission," and "function." One of the meanings of mission in the new formulation is "a task." Currently, U.S. Army tables of organization and equipment retain statements of "unit missions," that is, the types of tasks a unit is capable of performing during military operations. Consequently, in this study, "mission" used in conjunction with a branch or unit adheres to this traditional usage. See United States, Office of the Chairman, Joint Publication 1–02, *Department of Defense Dictionary of Military Terms* (Washington, D.C.: Information Management Division, 1994), p. 245.

[3] F. Stansbury Haydon, *Aeronautics in the Union and Confederate Armies with a Survey of Military Aeronautics Prior to 1861* (Baltimore, Md.: Johns Hopkins University Press, 1941), pp. 3–4; Tom D. Crouch, *The Eagle Aloft: Two Centuries of the Balloon in America* (Washington, D.C.: Smithsonian Institution Press, 1983), pp. 1–38; Charles Christienne and Pierre Lissarague, *A History of French Military Aviation*, trans. Francis Kianka (Washington, D.C.: Smithsonian Institution Press, 1986), pp. 4–13; John R. Elting, *Swords Around a Throne: Napoleon's Grande Armée* (New York: Free Press, 1988), p. 277.

The Origins of Aerial Observation in the U.S. Army, 1861–1917

In the United States, the Union Army used balloons during the first two years of the Civil War, largely in the eastern theater. The development of a domestic gas industry for illumination in the decades after the War of 1812 provided the technical environment that made these experiments possible. Benefiting from the scientific advances of the previous seventy years, the Americans enjoyed greater technical success than had the French. The Army of the Potomac's chief aeronaut, Prof. Thaddeus S. C. Lowe, even developed an apparatus for generating hydrogen in the field. Lowe, like the French before him, favored positioning tethered balloons behind friendly lines. The observer often took a telegraph key with him into the basket and thus could transmit his reports directly to army headquarters through a wire linked to land lines. The Army of the Potomac used balloons for protecting the flanks of Federal forces, collecting information about the number and composition of the Confederate units to their front, producing maps, acquainting general officers with the terrain, and, in certain rare instances, observing indirect fire by field artillery.[4]

Cavalry could still perform its traditional reconnaissance and screening mission, but with greater difficulty given the widespread use of rifles by both Union and Confederate infantry. The mounted units, moreover, had much greater tactical mobility than the balloon train. Signal parties from the newly formed U.S. Army Signal Corps supplemented the efforts of Federal cavalry. Equipped with telescopes and binoculars to read signal flags at a distance, signal officers stationed at vantage points close behind friendly battle lines could and did routinely scan Confederate positions for any signs of activity and then passed the information along to higher headquarters. Aerial observers in the 1860s still did not perform a unique mission for a field army.[5]

Throughout its existence the Balloon Corps was an emergency organization with no legal basis. Lowe and the other balloonists were civilians paid by the War Department. Despite the technical accomplishments—though the mobility of the balloon train remained a problem—the successive commanders of the Army of the Potomac were never able to translate the information that the aeronauts generated into operational successes. Practical soldiers thus could find less justification for the corps as the war progressed. Long simmering civilian-military tensions erupted during the Chancellorsville campaign and ultimately led to Lowe's resignation. Lacking both the patina of victory and a well-defined place in the military hierarchy, the Balloon Corps expired soon afterward.[6]

Aerial observation made at least one unqualified contribution to a Union victory, but it was unheralded and largely ignored at the time. The lone balloonist assigned to the Department of the Missouri, Jacob Steiner, succeeded during the battle of Island Number 10 (3 March–9 April 1862) in directing the fire of mortar boats onto the Confederate water

---

[4] Crouch, *Eagle Aloft*, pp. 267–70; Eugene B. Block, *Above the Civil War: The Story of Thaddeus Lowe, Balloonist, Inventor, Railway Builder* (Berkeley, Calif.: Howell-North Books, 1966).

[5] Rebecca R. Raines, *Getting the Message Through: A Branch History of the U.S. Army Signal Corps,* Army Historical Series (Washington, D.C.: U.S. Army Center of Military History, 1996), pp. 13–16, 24–29.

[6] Haydon, *Aeronautics in the Union and Confederate Armies*, pp. 168–98; Block, *Above the Civil War*, pp. 54–59. For Lowe's report of his entire war service, see Report (Rpt), T. S. C. Lowe to E. M. Stanton, 26 May 63, in WD, *The War of the Rebellion: Official Records of the Union and Confederate Armies*, 4 ser., 130 vols. (Washington, D.C.: Government Printing Office, 1880–1901), ser. 4, 3:252–319.

Professor Lowe and Ground Crew at the Battle of Fair Oaks, Virginia, May 1862

battery. Its destruction permitted a Union gunboat to run by the fortifications, the essential first step in isolating and forcing the surrender of the garrison. Steiner's accomplishment did not translate well to operations in the open field. The state of the art in both metallurgy and powder manufacture did not permit consistently accurate delivery of long-range fire, an essential prerequisite for effective observed indirect fire. The butt of ridicule by his military superiors for his ethnicity as well as his calling, Steiner left military employment even before Lowe.[7]

In the immediate postwar period, the head of the U.S. Army Signal Corps, Col. (later Brig. Gen.) Albert J. Myer, sought to justify the peacetime existence of his organization by expanding its mission. Specifically, the Signal Corps assumed responsibility for the systematic collection of meteorological information and the preparation of forecasts. In the process, the Signal Corps hired a balloonist, Samuel Archer King, who made a series of flights with Signal Corps personnel aboard to obtain data. After Congress shifted the Weather Bureau to the Department of Agriculture in 1891, the Signal Corps became a logical home for military ballooning, once more gaining popularity in European armies. One of Myer's successors, Brig. Gen. (later Maj. Gen.) Adolphus W. Greely, purchased a balloon in 1892 and subsequently established a detachment at Fort Logan, Colorado.[8]

The Army once again had an aerial component, but only a pale shadow of the balloon detachments of the armies of the major Continental powers. Underfunded by Congress—a reflection of a general lack of public support for the military as a whole—and possibly hampered by an overly strong sense of branch consciousness, the balloon detachment did not exercise with infantry, cavalry, or field artillery units. The Signal Corps also failed to develop and promulgate doctrine to guide the employment of balloons in battle. This deficiency became glaringly apparent during the War with Spain in 1898. Lack of shipping space prevented V Corps from transporting more than a handful of cavalry mounts to Cuba, making the expeditionary force peculiarly dependent for reconnaissance on its single observation balloon. During the battle of San Juan Hill on 1 July 1898, the Signal Corps balloon detachment, commanded by Maj. Joseph E. Maxfield, succeeded in detecting a heretofore undiscovered lane that permitted the troops to deploy more rapidly, a crucial element in the successful assault. At the same time, however, an officer on the corps staff ordered the balloon so far forward that it served as an admirable target marker for the Spanish guns as they pounded the American infantry and dismounted cavalry at a place the troops called Bloody Ford. Lack of widespread knowledge about how to employ balloons led to this disaster.[9]

These mixed results ensured that military balloons survived but did not prosper in the postwar period. The Signal Corps retained but did not expand its balloon train. Nevertheless,

---

[7] Haydon, *Aeronautics in the Union and Confederate Armies*, pp. 262–63, 386–97; Crouch, *Eagle Aloft*, pp. 372–74; Robert V. Bruce, *Lincoln and the Tools of War* (Indianapolis, Ind.: Bobbs-Merrill, 1956), pp. 156–66.

[8] Crouch, *Eagle Aloft*, pp. 215, 451–63; Raines, *Getting the Message Through*, pp. 41–88; Russell J. Parkinson, "Politics, Patents, and Planes: Military Aeronautics in the United States, 1863–1907" (Ph.D. diss., Duke University, 1963), pp. 24–35. Parkinson's dissertation is the best single account of military aeronautics in the United States from 1863 to 1907 and has long deserved publication.

[9] Parkinson, "Politics, Patents, and Planes," pp. 106–33. Graham A. Cosmas, "San Juan Hill and El Caney, 1–2 July 1898," in *America's First Battles*, ed. Charles E. Heller and William A. Stofft (Lawrence: University Press of Kansas, 1986), pp. 104–48, gives the standard modern account of the battle. See pages 133–34 for a succinct account of balloon operations.

the employment of balloons received serious attention at high levels. The new War Department General Staff worked out a doctrine for using balloons in combat, drawing upon the aeronauts' experience in both the Civil War and the War with Spain.[10]

By the time the War Department purchased its first airplane, a Wright Flyer, in 1909, a number of officers had given considerable thought to aerial observation. *Field Service Regulations, 1910*, published within months of the Flyer's successful acceptance tests at Fort Myer, Virginia, specified the formation of an aerial company in each corps-size unit upon mobilization but left the question of mission open until the Aviation Section of the Signal Corps had acquired experience with the new machine. Four years later the Army's first table of organization increased the number of companies to two per mobilized corps. The new edition of the *Field Service Regulations*, published just before the outbreak of World War I in Europe, promulgated three missions—strategic reconnaissance, tactical reconnaissance, and artillery observation—and implied a fourth, the use of armed airplanes to defend friendly observation.[11]

Pilots in the fledgling Aviation Section had experimented even more widely than the statement of missions implied in the 1914 edition of the *Field Service Regulations*. Limitations of equipment and doctrine, however, imposed severe constraints on what they could accomplish. Airplanes fell out of the sky with distressing regularity. Piloting techniques were in their infancy—pilots gained knowledge at the cost of injury and death. American airplane designers, with less excuse, followed the same untheoretical and blindly empirical approach, inadvertently producing some service models that were little better than death traps. Poorly designed American airplanes were also underpowered, which limited the amount of additional weight they could carry, whether machine guns, bombs, cargo, or an observer. Their inability to haul such loads hampered experimentation. American engine manufacturers remained years behind their European counterparts in the development of powerful, lightweight engines. In addition, the use of airplanes to direct artillery fire suffered from the lack of a large cadre of Field Artillery officers trained to deliver indirect fire. The War Department had adopted a family of rapid-fire guns beginning in 1902 with the M1902 3-inch gun (first fielded in 1905) and had revised Field Artillery doctrine, beginning with *Field Artillery Drill Regulations, 1907*, to give more emphasis to indirect fire and to refine technique. Lack of training funds limited most officers' practice in the new techniques.[12]

Experiments in aerial observation at Fort Riley in 1912 and Fort Sill in 1915–1916 foundered on these realities. In contrast to these practical difficulties, at least some

---

[10] WD, Office of the Chief of Staff, Army (OCSA), *Field Service Regulations [FSR], 1905*, WD Document (Doc) 241 (Washington, D.C.: Government Printing Office, 1905), pp. 46–47.

[11] WD, OCSA, *FSR, 1910*, WD Doc 363 (Washington, D.C.: Government Printing Office, 1910), p. 53; WD, Table of Organization (TO), 25 Feb 14, p. 39; WD, OCSA, *FSR, 1914*, WD Doc 462 (Washington, D.C.: Government Printing Office, 1914), pp. 19–20; WD, OCSA, *FSR, 1914, Corrected to April 15, 1917 (Change Nos. 1–6)*, WD Doc 475 (Washington, D.C.: Government Printing Office, 1917), p. 20.

[12] Juliette A. Hennessy, *The United States Army Air Arm, April 1861 to April 1917*, U.S. Air Force (USAF) General Histories (Washington, D.C.: Office of Air Force History, 1985), pp. 40–71; Herschel Smith, *Aircraft Piston Engines: From the Manly Baltzer to the Continental Tiara* (New York: McGraw-Hill, 1981), pp. 11–25; Boyd L. Dastrup, *King of Battle: A Branch History of the U.S. Army's Field Artillery*, U.S. Army Training and Doctrine Command Branch Histories Series (Washington, D.C.: U.S. Army Training and Doctrine Command and U.S. Army Center of Military History, 1993), pp. 148–55.

American officers possessed considerable knowledge of European developments. Early in 1915 the chief signal officer, Brig. Gen. George P. Scriven, published a very sophisticated analysis of the use of aviation in the opening campaigns of World War I. Toward the end of 1915, as part of the War Department's efforts to encourage preparedness, the War College Division of the General Staff prepared a study of aerial developments in the European war based on attaché reports, subsequently published in 1916 both as a separate pamphlet and as an article in the *Field Artillery Journal*. More descriptive than analytical, it nevertheless noted the introduction of specialized "bombing aircraft." By 1915, in the event of mobilization, the Signal Corps planned to equip each aero squadron attached to a division with 8 observation planes for battlefield observation and artillery spotting, 2 "high speed machines" with counterair and long-range reconnaissance responsibilities, and 2 "battle planes" for bombardment missions. The Aeronautical Division in the Office of the Chief Signal Officer did not fail to understand or appreciate European aviation developments, but detailed engineering data were often lacking.[13]

American pilots knew their airplanes were technically inferior to those of their European counterparts. The aviators blamed their predicament on a shortage of funds and the lack of understanding by senior ground officers of the new medium of the air, rather than on the general lack of knowledge of the engineering problems shared by aviators and nonaviators alike. On the other hand, senior officers, survivors of the Indian Wars and extensive tropical service at the turn of the century, tended to minimize the perils the pilots faced as no greater than those they had faced as young officers. The pilots naturally contrasted their experiences with those of their peers in the other branches, where the hazards were far fewer. The pilots, all young men, focused on the potential of military aviation for the next generation. The senior officers, all older men, focused on its current capabilities. The origins of the estrangement between the U.S. Army and its air component thus preceded the American entry into World War I.[14]

---

[13] Army War College (AWC), Historical Section, *The Signal Corps and the Air Service: A Study of Their Expansion in the United States, 1917–1918*, Monograph no. 16 (Washington, D.C.: Government Printing Office, 1922), p. 34. The War College Division (WCD) study is reprinted in toto in Maurer Maurer, ed., *The U.S. Air Service in World War I*, 4 vols. (Washington, D.C.: Office of Air Force History, 1978), 2:41–53. Memo for [WCD], 16 Mar 17, sub: Aerial Observation (Obsn) in Liaison with Artillery (Arty), WCD, Gen Corresp, 1903–1919, file 1056–43, RG 165, NARA, contains a translation of French aerial observation doctrine. The distribution list is most suggestive. Unfortunately, this is the only document in the file. All the other materials were "weeded" by The Adjutant General in the 1920s. Paul W. Clark, "Major General George Owen Squier: Military Scientist" (Ph.D. diss., Case Western University, 1974), pp. 219–49, recounts Squier's efforts as military attaché in Great Britain and on the Western Front. WD, Office of the Chief Signal Officer (OCSO), *The Service of Information, United States Army*, by George P. Scriven (Washington, D.C.: Government Printing Office, 1915), pp. 21–23, 61. The counterview of contemporary ignorance of European developments, the interpretation that has dominated the historical literature, is most brilliantly stated by Irving B. Holley, Jr., *Ideas and Weapons: Exploitation of the Aerial Weapon by the United States During World War I; A Study in the Relationship of Technological Advance, Military Doctrine, and the Development of Weapons*, USAF Special Studies (Washington, D.C.: Office of Air Force History, 1983), pp. 36–38, a reprint of the original Yale University Press edition of 1953. An examination of Holley's footnotes reveals that he depended heavily on postwar testimony of senior Air Service officers who found prewar ignorance a convenient explanation for their own wartime failures.

[14] Hennessy, *United States Army Air Arm*, pp. 40–71. For the "generational approach" to studying the U.S. Army officer corps, see Allan R. Millett, *The General: Robert L. Bullard and Officership in the United States Army, 1881–1925* (Westport, Conn.: Greenwood Press, 1975), pp. 475–91.

Aerial Observation in a War of Position, 1917–1918

By European standards the Aviation Section of the Signal Corps in early 1917 was very small and technically backward, with only sketchy doctrine. With America's entry into World War I and the dispatch of an expeditionary force to France, the Army rapidly expanded its air arm. Lacking time to develop their own doctrine for the employment of balloons and airplanes, General John J. Pershing and his staff adopted wholesale the methods of the Allies, which by this time were very sophisticated. The new American aerial observation doctrine came directly from the French Army; it did not displace prewar American doctrine so much as it elaborated the concepts of the latter in vast detail.[15]

Both the Allied and German armies used balloons and fixed-wing observation aircraft to collect information about their opponents and to serve as aerial sentries, warning of increased enemy ground activity and monitoring the location of enemy aircraft. A line of balloons paralleled the front, a maze of trenches stretching from the Swiss border to the Belgian coast. Connected to the ground by field telephones and stationed just far enough behind the fighting positions to remain safe from enemy long-range artillery, each balloon provided an overwatch of a sector about ten miles in radius. As early as 1915 the chief signal officer, General Scriven, commented that the primary effect of these efforts was to rob both sides of surprise at the strategic and operational (he used the contemporary term "grand tactical") levels.[16]

While aerial observation markedly strengthened the power of the defense between 1914 and 1918, its contributions to the attack were much more limited. During offensives, balloon observers could monitor the progress of friendly infantry for at least a short distance. But the balloon observer's oblique angle of vision, coupled with the irregularities of the ground and the thick clouds of dust thrown up by concentrated shelling, soon masked the advance from clear view. Observers in fixed-wing aircraft could overcome some of the deficiencies in balloon observation by flying directly above enemy positions. Primitive air-ground communications, however, limited their utility and hampered timely and effective communication between an airborne observer and the radio listening stations that dotted the front.[17]

---

[15] Edward M. Coffman, *The War To End All Wars: The American Military Experience in World War I* (New York: Oxford University Press, 1968), pp. 121–41; General Headquarters (GHQ), American Expeditionary Forces (AEF), *Instructions on Liaison for Troops of All Arms* (Paris: Imprimerie Nationale, 1917); GHQ, AEF, *Liaison for All Arms* (Chaumont, France: General Headquarters, American Expeditionary Forces, 1918).

[16] Christienne and Lissarague, *A History of French Military Aviation*, pp. 69–82; Peter Mead, *The Eye in the Air: History of Air Observation and Reconnaissance for the Army, 1785–1945* (London: Her Majesty's Stationery Office, 1983), pp. 51–58; WD, *America's Munitions, 1917–1918: Report of Benedict Crowell, The Assistant Secretary of War, Director of Munitions* (Washington, D.C.: Government Printing Office, 1919), pp. 332–33; Lt. Col. William C. Sherman, "Tentative Manual for the Employment of Air Service" in Maurer, *Air Service in World War I*, 2:313, 329; WD, OCSO, *The Service of Information*, pp. 21–23, 61. See also Lee B. Kennett, *The First Air War, 1914–1918* (New York: Free Press, 1991); John H. Morrow, *The Great War in the Air: Military Aviation from 1909 to 1921* (Washington, D.C.: Smithsonian Institution, 1993). Morrow is particularly good on European developments. These can be supplemented by James J. Cooke, *The U.S. Air Service in the Great War, 1917–1919* (Westport, Conn.: Praeger, 1996) and Eileen F. Lebow, *A Grandstand Seat: The American Balloon Service in World War I* (Westport, Conn.: Praeger, 1998).

[17] WD, *America's Munitions*, pp. 331–42; Harold E. Porter, *Aerial Observation: The Airplane Observer, the Balloon Observer, and the Army Corps Pilot* (New York: Harper and Brothers, 1921), pp. 133–57.

Each American corps on the Western Front normally contained a "corps air service," consisting of one balloon group and one observation group, although balloon companies usually were attached directly to the divisions at the front. The size of the observation component within the U.S. Army Air Service was thus, at least in part, a function of the size of the ground army. By the last six weeks of the war, most Air Service observation units possessed the technical competence to conduct the four missions already standard in Allied air services when the American Expeditionary Forces arrived in France in 1917.

In addition to general intelligence gathering, observation aircraft performed contact, aerial fire, and photographic reconnaissance missions. In general, the contact mission involved aircrew monitoring and reporting on the progress of friendly infantry in the attack to both division artillery and higher headquarters. Aerial fire missions required meticulous planning and careful briefing of the pilot and observer. Photographic reconnaissance, using vertical shots instead of oblique photographs from balloons, permitted intelligence officers to monitor changes in the German position and to produce detailed maps. Since virtually all massed indirect fire during the war was map fire (fire directed on a previously surveyed location) and hence unobserved, photographic reconnaissance became observation's most important contribution to the conduct of artillery operations during the war.[18]

During America's involvement in the war, standard Air Service observation aircraft, such as the De Havilland DH–4 and the Spad XI, were sturdy two-seater, externally braced, fabric-covered biplanes with fixed landing gear. Capable of top speeds approaching 120 miles per hour, they were armed with one or more machine guns firing forward and two machine guns on a swivel mount manned by the observer. The aircraft could operate off rough, partially improved fields close to the front, which facilitated coordination between Air Service squadrons and the supported ground elements. The same aircraft could perform all observation missions at corps, field army, army group, and theater levels.[19]

The primary limitations on effective aerial observation were those imposed by the capabilities of existing radios and American artillery doctrine. Aerial observers used spark-gap transmitters without receivers because of their weight. The transmitters sent bursts of static in Morse Code over a wide range of frequencies but were sometimes masked by the static produced by aircraft engines. The Allied armies responded to this technological limitation by covering the front with masses of observation airplanes. In an emergency an aviator could shoot a flare meaning "Fire on my position." A ground observer, however, had to be looking directly at the aircraft the moment the flare ignited to deliver fire accurately. Division and corps artilleries maintained watch posts behind the front to allow them to

---

[18] GHQ, AEF, *Instructions for the Employment of Aerial Observation*, pp. 27–34; Memo, Lt Col H. A. Drum, G–3 Section, GHQ, for Assistant Chief of Staff (ACS), G–3, 18 May 18, in DA, *United States Army in the World War, 1917–1918*, 17 vols. (Washington, D.C.: U.S. Army Center of Military History, 1989–1990), 2:406–10; General Orders (GO) 8, GHQ, AEF, 10 Aug 18, sub: Instructions in Regard to Air Service (AS), First Army, in Maurer, *Air Service in World War I*, 3: 9–10; An. 4, Field Order (FO) 20, HQ, AS, First Army, 17 Sep 18, sub: Plan of Employment of AS Units, First Army, in Maurer, *Air Service in World War I*, 2:232–34; John B. Wilson, *Maneuver and Firepower: The Evolution of Divisions and Separate Brigades,* Army Lineage Series (Washington, D.C.: U.S. Army Center of Military History, 1998), pp. 23–45.

[19] Walter J. Boyne, *de Havilland DH–4: From Flaming Coffin to Living Legend*, Famous Aircraft of the National Air and Space Museum 7 (Washington, D.C.: Smithsonian Institution Press, 1984); Swanborough and Bowers, *Military Aircraft Since 1909*, pp. 241–48.

ORVILLE WRIGHT (*left*) STANDS BEFORE A U.S. PRODUCTION MODEL DE HAVILLAND DH–4, MAY 1918.

do just that. Given the vagaries of the human attention span and the fact that there were often more than one aircraft in a sector at any time, whether a ground observer actually saw the flare at the crucial instant remained a matter of chance.[20]

Air-ground communications difficulties explained only in part the low standard of observed fire technique that the U.S. Army Field Artillery attained on the Western Front. The American Field Artillery also borrowed its fire control procedures for indirect fire from the French. While less cumbersome than the prewar American doctrine, the new system remained rather primitive compared to either British or German artillery. To call fire on a target, an observer had to have both the target and the firing battery in view, which significantly limited the ability to mass the fire from several batteries on the same target.[21]

One aspect of the fire control system provoked controversy in both the United States and France: the selection, training, and rating of aerial observers, that is, the formal cer-

---

[20] Rpt, Maj Gen George O. Squier, Chief Signal Officer (CSO), to Newton D. Baker, Secretary (Sec) of War, 15 Oct 19, sub: Annual Rpt for Fiscal Year (FY) Ended 30 June 1919, in WD, *Report of the Chief Signal Officer, 1919* (Washington, D.C.: Government Printing Office, 1919), p. 314; WD, *America's Munitions*, pp. 323–30; GHQ, AEF, *Employment of Aerial Observation*, pp. 27–34.

[21] Richard L. Pierce, "A Maximum of Support: The Development of U.S. Field Artillery Doctrine in World War I" (M.A. thesis, Ohio State University, 1983), pp. 52–54; Dastrup, *King of Battle*, pp. 145–75. See also Steven A. Stebbins, "Indirect Fire: The Challenge and Response in the U.S. Army, 1907–1917" (M.A. thesis, University of North Carolina–Chapel Hill, 1993). For developments in the German Army, see David T. Zabecki, *Steel Wind: Colonel Georg Bruchmüller and the Birth of Modern Artillery* (Westport, Conn.: Praeger, 1994). The British Army is covered by Shelford Bidwell and Dominick Graham, *Fire-Power: British Army Weapons and Theories of War, 1904–1945* (Boston: Allen and Unwin, 1982), pp. 7–146.

tification that a soldier could perform the required duties of the position (and in this case receive flight pay). Until August 1918 observers were detailed from infantry and artillery units. These officers, remarked a postwar chief of Field Artillery, "were young and inexperienced, knew little or nothing of the tactics and technique of their branches, and were representatives of their arm in name only." The Field Artillery observers first trained at Fort Sill. They then went into replacement pools and retained their commissions in their original branch until they actually began functioning as aerial observers. At that time they automatically transferred to the Aviation Section of the Signal Corps (later the Air Service). Not all officers wanted to lose their original branch association. The wartime chief of Field Artillery, Maj. Gen. William J. Snow, obtained a ruling from the judge advocate general that officers could retain their original commissions and be detailed to the Signal Corps. The new director of military aeronautics, Maj. Gen. William L. Kenly, ironically a field artilleryman by training, did not approve of these arrangements. In August 1918 he convinced the War Department to set them aside and to require that all aerial observers receive their commissions from the Signal Corps, effectively placing the observers under his control. This remained War Department policy through the end of the war. In the American Expeditionary Forces field artillerymen blamed the aerial observers' lack of continuing association with field artillery units for much of the inefficiency in observed fire. The chief of the Air Service, American Expeditionary Forces, Maj. Gen. Mason M. Patrick, on the other hand, suggested that not all the Field Artillery officers selected to train as aerial observers possessed the intense interest in flying required to succeed.[22]

The expansion of the wartime Army was so great, the conditions on the Western Front so unique, and the quantity of new information that officers had to absorb so immense that American artillerymen made no attempt to improve on the procedures they had inherited from the French Army. They may not have even identified their technique as a problem, given the relatively short duration of the American Expeditionary Forces' commitment to close combat.

Conversely, from the beginning the Signal Corps realized that it had a radio problem. Scriven's successor as chief signal officer, Brig. Gen. George O. Squier, emphasized experimentation to reduce the weight and increase the range of the Army's radios. When the Americans began arriving in France in 1917, their 500-pound radios were allocated to division headquarters and higher echelons. By November 1918 U.S. divisions had 50-pound radios as the primary communications link from the battalion to higher echelons. Work on airborne radios proceeded apace. In November 1918 American observation squadrons were beginning to obtain spark-gap radios that could both send and receive. None were actually used at the front because of lack of time to instruct the operators. All the sets were still undamped, which meant that they still picked up the electrical discharges of spark plugs in the engines. Squier took a personal interest in the development of what he saw as the solution to the flexibility, if not the static, problem: voice radio, field-tested on 30

---

[22] William J. Snow, *Signposts of Experience* (Washington, D.C.: U.S. Field Artillery Association, 1941), pp. 158–59; Memo, Office of the Chief of Field Artillery (OCFA), [7 Jun 32], sub: Air Obsn for Ground Troops, in OCFA, "Air Observation for Ground Troops," (Unpublished [Unpubl] Ms, Morris Swett Tech Lib, 1932). The latter is the source of the quote. For the Air Service view, see Rpt, Maj Gen Mason W. Patrick, n.d., sub: Final Rpt of Chief (Ch) of AS, AEF, in Maurer, *Air Service in World War I*, 1:104–06.

September 1918 at an airfield near Paris. In airborne communications the Americans were far in advance of any other nation at the end of the war, but many problems remained before radio could become the flexible instrument of control that Squier envisioned.[23]

Despite the limitations of the equipment actually in observation units, during the closing days of the conflict the 3d Observation Group in U.S. III Corps pioneered yet another mission, what the III Corps chief of Air Service, Maj. Kenneth P. Littauer, referred to as "cavalry reconnaissance." Using message drops, 3d Group airplanes informed attacking U.S. infantry of the location of the nearest German positions. Occasionally, the aircraft assisted closely engaged infantry with direct fire support. Although these techniques worked well, they had not yet spread beyond III Corps when the war ended.[24]

Aerial Observation in Flux, 1919–1938

Following the war, a rich confluence of factors—the novelty of the aerial weapon, the promise of its potential contrasted to the limits of its existing power, the personalities involved, and the interjection of the question of an independent air force into the debate over national defense policy—kept Air Service organization and doctrine under almost perpetual debate and scrutiny until 1926. In the process the perceived importance of aerial observation changed dramatically in Air Service circles. In 1919 General Patrick, the wartime chief of the Air Service in the American Expeditionary Forces, held that an air service in a theater of war ought to consist of 80 percent observation and 20 percent other aircraft, mirroring the wartime experience. Seven years later he reversed these ideal proportions. And Patrick represented the conservative wing of the Air Service, the officers most inclined to take seriously the concerns of the ground combat arms. In 1919 Patrick's sometime assistant, Brig. Gen. William Mitchell, considered observation the least important Air Service mission. By 1926 he argued that it simply represented a phase in the early development of the air arm. It had no role in the future. Mitchell's apotheosis as a "martyr for air power" in 1926 and the passage of the Air Corps Act that same year accelerated observation's decline into orphan status and an intellectual and professional backwater within the Air Corps.[25]

---

[23] Saumur Artillery School, [AEF], *Artillery Lines of Information: Means of Liaison, Duties of Specialists, Standard Codes*, Manual of Artillery, 5 vols. (Paris: General Headquarters, American Expeditionary Forces, G–5, 1918), 3:102–08; Rpt, Capt H. Hardinge, Radio Division (Div), OCSO, Services of Supply (SOS), AEF, in Maurer, *Air Service in World War I*, 4:251–52; Clark, "George Owen Squier," pp. 343–85; Mason M. Patrick, *The United States in the Air* (Garden City, N.Y.: Doubleday, Doran, and Co., 1928), p. 33; Pierce, "A Maximum of Support," p. 48.

[24] Lessons Learned, 2d Lt H. L. Borden, 90th Aero Squadron, in Maurer, *Air Service in World War I*, 4:190–93.

[25] Ltr, Maj Gen M. M. Patrick to Gen J. J. Pershing, 19 May 19, sub: AS Organization, in Congress, House, *Department of Defense and the Unification of the Air Service: Hearings Before the Committee on Military Affairs, House of Representatives*, 69th Cong., 1st sess. (Washington, D.C.: Government Printing Office, 1926), pp. 671–76; William Mitchell, *Winged Defense: The Development and Possibilities of Modern Air Power, Economic and Military* (New York: Dover, 1988), pp. 11, 18–19, 140–41; Alfred F. Hurley, *Billy Mitchell: Crusader for Air Power* (Bloomington: Indiana University Press, 1975), a model intellectual biography. See in particular pages 30, 37–108. See also Robert F. Futrell, *Ideas, Concepts, Doctrine: A History of Basic Thinking in the United States Air Force, 1907–1964*, Air University (AU)–19 (Maxwell Air Force Base [AFB], Ala.: Air University, 1974), pp. 15–30; Mark A. Clodfelter, "Molding Airpower Convictions: Development and Legacy of William Mitchell's Strategic Thought," in *The Paths of Heaven: The Evolution of Airpower Theory*, ed. Philip S. Meilinger (Maxwell AFB, Ala.: Air University Press, 1997), pp. 79–114.

In effect the Air Corps Act represented the final statement of the lessons of World War I for the Army's air arm. The act changed the name of the Air Service to the Air Corps and thus by implication suggested that aviation had an independent role in war in addition to supporting the ground arms. Furthermore, the law called for Congress to progressively increase the size of the Air Corps to some eighteen hundred aircraft over a five-year period, provided for Air Corps representation in all the agencies of the General Staff, and reestablished the post of assistant secretary of war for air that had lapsed at the end of the war. The onset of the Great Depression prevented the full attainment of some of these goals, but the act did succeed in making the chief of the Air Corps first among his statutory equals, the branch chiefs of the War Department.[26]

During the years between the world wars, responsibility for the organization, doctrine, and training of the combat arms rested in the first instance with their respective branch chiefs. They achieved their goals in these areas in part by shepherding funding requests for their branches through the War Department, the Bureau of the Budget, and the Congress. The equipment category of the War Department budget provides eloquent testimony to the Air Corps' favored status. In 1931, one of the few years for which detailed figures survive, the Air Corps received $35,823,473. By way of contrast the Infantry received $65,623, the Field Artillery $20,610, and the Cavalry $26,685. This was not autonomy—the Air Corps portion of the budget was still subject to General Staff control—but its size in comparison to the other branches did represent a substantial measure of power within the narrow confines of the War Department.[27]

The Air Corps Act and its consequences also reflected a political reality: The Air Corps benefited from a constituency in the country at large in a way denied all other portions of the Army and, for that matter, the Army as a whole. To a substantial segment of the public, including some of its most literate and articulate members, the Air Corps represented the cutting edge of modernity. Such a belief guaranteed Air Corps spokesmen ready public attention and a certain level of almost automatic support for their ideas.[28]

The Field Artillery enjoyed no such popular esteem. Immediately after the war the chief of artillery, American Expeditionary Forces, Maj. Gen. Ernest Hines, established the Hero Board, named for its president, Brig. Gen. Andrew Hero, Jr., to determine the Field Artillery lessons of the war. After extensive interviews with Field Artillery commanders and staffs still in France, the board bluntly concluded that "adjustment by aerial observation was unsatisfactory." Aerial observers obtained good results only in "isolated cases." The board believed that five factors were at work. The artillery lacked effective control over observers, who also lacked sufficient artillery training. Coordination "was imperfect" between corps observation aviation and division artillery. Airfields were simply too distant

---

[26] Rpt, Dwight W. Morrow, et al., to President Calvin Coolidge, 30 Nov 25, sub: A Study of the Best Means of Developing and Applying Aircraft in National Defense, in Congress, House, *Unification of the Air Service*, pp. 83–120.

[27] Table, WD General Staff, Statistics Branch (Br), 15 Jul 31, sub: WD Appropriations, FY 1931, WD General Staff Statistics Br, Weekly Rpts, 1917–1945, file 290, RG 165, NARA. I am indebted to Dr. Charles E. Kirkpatrick for calling this document to my attention.

[28] For a discussion of the cultural impact of aviation, see Joseph J. Corn, *The Winged Gospel: America's Romance with Aviation, 1900–1950* (New York: Oxford University Press, 1983); Michael J. Sherry, *The Rise of American Air Power: The Creation of Armageddon* (New Haven, Conn.: Yale University Press, 1987), pp. 1–75.

from the front lines. The Air Service was undisciplined, "which resulted in absolute undependability for results obtained." Finally, the Air Service failed to provide adequate pursuit protection for observation flights; German pursuits, that is, fighter aircraft, had often attacked them.[29]

The Hero Board proposed a variety of remedies. The foremost was that the artillery commander should have sufficient control over the aviation unit to ensure that it completed its assigned missions. The board recommended that the War Department make one observation squadron, size unspecified, organic to each division. Better liaison between aerial observers and artillery brigades required more detailed doctrine and ample training time. The aerial observers should be artillerymen who lived with the artillery units they supported and left only when on an actual mission. The pilots should also train with the artillery units they supported. Pursuit units to protect observation flights, however, ought to be organic at corps or field army level.

The American Expeditionary Forces Air Service and Infantry Boards, meeting at the same time as the Hero Board, agreed with the wisdom of returning some observation elements to division control. Most important, so did the American Expeditionary Forces Superior Board, which General Pershing had established to collate the results of these inferior boards and prepare a single American Expeditionary Forces position on organizational and doctrinal issues. In the postwar reorganization of the Army, the War Department attached a balloon squadron and a nineteen-plane observation squadron to each division. The balloons returned to corps control in 1926, the observation squadron in the early 1930s. The Field Artillery was denied even this degree of fleeting success with regard to the branch assignment of aerial observers. Through 1932 the question remained a perennial topic of controversy between the Office of the Chief of Field Artillery and the Office of the Chief of Air Service (after 1926, the Air Corps).[30]

In the 1930s many innovative Air Corps officers became increasingly focused on the concept of strategic bombardment. It offered a means of avoiding the stalemate and mass slaughter that had characterized close combat on the Western Front. Theorists at the Air Corps Tactical School at Maxwell Field, Alabama, believed that large formations of modern heavy bombers would always reach their targets. There, they would deliver a "knockout blow," not just to the enemy army or the enemy air force, but to the enemy nation as a whole. By attacking certain choke points they would so disrupt its economy that it would have to sue for peace. Some of the more radical air power exponents believed that

---

[29] Memo Order, Office of the Chief of Artillery (OCA), AEF, 8 Dec 18; Brig Gen Andrew Hero, Jr., et al., "Report of Field Artillery Board, AEF, on Organization and Tactics" (Unpubl Ms, Morris Swett Tech Lib, c. 1919).

[30] Rpt, Maj Gen E. M. Lewis, sub: Rpt of the Infantry (Inf) Board, AEF, on Organization and Tactics; Rpt, Brig Gen B. D. Foulois, et al., sub: Rpt of AS Board, AEF, on Organization and Operation (Opn) of the Service; both in GHQ, AEF, Rpts and Proceedings of Boards of Officers, RG 120, NARA; Rpt, Maj. Gen. J. T. Dickman, et al., 1 Jul 19, sub: Rpt of the Superior Board, AEF, on Organization and Tactics, in Congress, House, *Unification of the Air Service,* pp. 917–94; WD, Table 70W, 5 Apr 26, sub: Div AS. Memo, Maj Gen A. J. Booth, TAG, for Maj Gen J. O. Fechet, Chief of Air Corps (CAC), 17 Jan 29, sub: Principles To Be Followed in Assignment of Air Corps Troops to Higher Tactical Organizations; Memo, Maj Gen J. O. Fechet, CAC, for Maj Gen A. J. Booth, 10 Feb 28, sub: TOs; both in Microfilm A2765, U.S. Air Force Historical Research Agency, Maxwell AFB, Ala. (hereafter cited as AFHRA). Wilson, *Maneuver and Firepower,* pp. 79–108. Memo, OCFA, [7 Jun 32], provides a detailed account of the controversy over aerial observers from 1919 until 1932.

intelligently delivered air raids might so interfere with a country's mobilization that ground armies might never come into contact. Modern war—air war—would be short, sharp, and decisive.[31]

The theory carried certain organizational implications. Since decision was possible only in the air and could come with frightening suddenness, the best protection was to maintain a large standing air force capable of launching an overwhelming attack on the opening day of any conflict. Mitchell, the assistant chief of the Air Service from 1919 until 1925, proposed to finance such a force by shifting money from the Navy and the ground forces, which in his view were archaic holdovers from the primitive age of warfare. As a practical matter, military aviation would obtain adequate funding only if it escaped the control of the older services and became independent. As early as 1919 Mitchell had called for the creation of an air department coequal to the War and Navy Departments.[32]

The strategy of the senior Army officers was to grant the aviators increasing autonomy but not independence. These high-ranking officers were impressed by the flexibility and power of modern aircraft and their ability to intervene in the ground battle. The chiefs of staff of the Army in the 1930s, Generals Douglas MacArthur (1930–1935) and Malin Craig (1935–1939), sought to ensure that American ground commanders in future wars would have that capacity available to them. In this they stood squarely in the combined arms tradition that had dominated the thinking of the American officer corps since the period of professional reform that started in the 1880s. In this view, victory in combat went to the army that could most effectively blend the combat power generated by all the arms and services working in close conjunction, rather than depending on a single arm operating alone. In contrast, air power theorists emphasized the need to centralize most air assets under a single air commander acting independently of any ground commander. Command and control became a focal point of tension between ground and air officers.[33]

The rise of strategic bombardment theory to a position of intellectual dominance within the Air Corps virtually ensured the stagnation of observation doctrine. The very existence of observation aviation presumed the continued importance of ground armies in future conflicts. Since the observation establishment was proportional in size to the ground forces, and the ground forces were small, observation aviation would be ready for combat only after an extended period of mobilization—in the same manner as the ground forces. Thus, while strategic bombardment theory carried to its extreme assumed a wartime role for ground troops no more strenuous than guarding air bases, the very existence of observation aviation suggested that victory in the next war would come only after a long, grinding, brutal ground campaign. General Mitchell was not obtuse when he relegated observa-

---

[31] Thomas H. Greer, *The Development of Air Doctrine in the Army Air Arm* (Washington, D.C.: Office of Air Force History, 1985), pp. 44–106; Sherry, *The Rise of American Air Power*, pp. 47–75.

[32] Brig. Gen. W. Mitchell, Dir, Military (Mil) Aeronautics, "Testimony Before the Committee on Military Affairs, House of Representatives, 7 Oct 19," in Congress, House, *Army Reorganization: Hearings Before the Committee on Military Affairs*, 61st Cong., 1st sess., 2 vols. (Washington, D.C.: Government Printing Office, 1919), 1:907.

[33] On the development of combined arms doctrine, see Timothy K. Nenninger, *The Leavenworth Schools and the Old Army: Education, Professionalism, and the Officer Corps of the United States Army, 1881–1918* (Westport, Conn.: Greenwood Press, 1978); Harry P. Bell, *Of Responsible Command: A History of the Army War College* (Carlisle Barracks, Pa.: Alumni Assoc. of the U.S. Army War College, 1983), pp. 41–46. On the Air Corps in the 1930s, see Jeffery S. Underwood, *The Wings of Democracy: The Influence of Air Power on the Roosevelt Administration, 1933–1941* (College Station: Texas A&M University Press, 1991).

tion to an earlier phase of the evolution of air power. It was a logical and political necessity given his view of the future of war.

No theorist of aerial observation arose to spell out these implications, but then the whole philosophy of combined arms remained restricted to the field manuals and textbooks of the professionals. Meanwhile, Mitchell and other publicists ensured that air power doctrine reached as wide an audience as possible. What passed for aerial observation doctrine—it hardly rose above the level of tactics and technique—continued in the well-worn grooves of 1918. In part this indicated bombardment doctrine's magnetic attraction for some of the brightest young air officers in terms of both intellectual excitement and possible professional advancement. It also reflected the sad state of the U.S. Army's ground elements, undermanned and underfunded, still equipped with the decaying weapons of the last war. Such conditions encouraged Air Corps officers—and not just specialists in observation—to continue to think of the capabilities of the ground arms as they had been in World War I. The War Department—primarily for budgetary reasons—waited until 1927 to stage combined air-ground exercises involving an infantry division and a cavalry brigade (both at less than half strength) and some two hundred Air Corps aircraft. The result was little more than an affirmation of the status quo. Not until 1935 did the Army make a feeble attempt at large-scale ground maneuvers, the first since 1916. No matter what their intellectual attainments, Air Corps officers specializing in observation received very little stimulation for innovative thinking.[34]

The Air Corps doctrinal changes of the 1930s reflected a veritable revolution in aircraft performance capabilities that stemmed from a series of incremental changes in aircraft design in the late 1920s and early 1930s. Aircraft engines became much more powerful, lighter in weight, and more reliable. Monoplanes with cantilevered wings, stressed aluminum skin that carried most of the structural load, internal bracing, closed cockpits, retractable landing gear, and a design approach that placed greater emphasis on streamlining replaced the fabric-covered, externally braced biplanes of World War I and the early 1920s. For bombers and pursuits, where the designers understood the primary function of the aircraft type and could emphasize the relevant characteristics, these changes were an unalloyed benefit. By the late 1930s the most advanced American bombers and pursuits had maximum speeds in excess of 290 miles per hour for bombers and 300 miles per hour for pursuits, operational altitudes in excess of 30,000 feet, and ranges of 2,400 miles for heavy bombers and 1,000 miles for pursuits.[35]

The design revolution also affected observation aircraft, but with less positive results. The Air Service/Air Corps development strategy after 1918 emphasized the production of

---

[34] Robert F. Futrell, *Command of Observation Aviation: A Study in Control of Tactical Airpower* (Maxwell AFB, Ala.: U.S. Air Force Historical Division, 1956), pp. 1–5; Jean R. Moenk, *A History of Large-Scale Army Maneuvers in the United States, 1935–1964* (Fort Monroe, Va.: U.S. Continental Army Command, 1969), pp. 21–70; Charles D. McKenna, "The Forgotten Reform: Field Maneuvers in the Development of the U.S. Army, 1902–1920" (Ph.D. diss., Duke University, 1981), pp. 152–76, William O. Oden, *After the Trenches: The Transformation of U.S. Army Doctrine, 1918–1939,* Texas A&M University Military History Series, no. 64 (College Station: Texas A&M University Press, 1999), pp. 204–05.

[35] Robert Perry, "The Interaction of Technology and Doctrine in the USAF," in *Air Power and Warfare: Proceedings of the Eighth Military History Symposium, United States Air Force Academy, 18–20 October 1978,* ed. Alfred F. Hurley and Ronald C. Ehrhart (Washington, D.C.: Office of Air Force History and U.S. Air Force Academy, 1979), pp. 386–401; Benjamin S. Kelsey, *The Dragon's Teeth: The Creation of United States Air Power for World War II* (Washington, D.C.: Smithsonian Institution Press, 1982); Swanborough and Bowers, *Military Aircraft Since 1909,* pp. 103–12, 227–37.

Formation of North American O-47s, April 1941

multimission observation aircraft just as during the war. The Air Materiel Division at Wright Field, Ohio, gave equal emphasis to such characteristics as speed, maneuverability, weight-carrying capacity, and durability and as a result developed observation planes that exhibited mediocre performance in these areas. The exclusion of ground officers from preparing military characteristics for such craft for much of the period and the absence of effective large-scale maneuvers before 1939 combined to produce planes ill fitted for the role ground officers envisioned for them. As a consequence, the evolution of the standard type of observation aircraft helped separate observation from its natural constituency, the ground arms, at the same time that institutional and doctrinal developments increasingly isolated observation aviation from the rest of the Air Corps.[36]

The standard observation aircraft of the late 1930s, the three-place North American O-47, was modern in appearance and design. Unfortunately, it was large, heavy, and complicated to maintain, and it required bases far to the rear where prepared, preferably hard-surface, landing fields and ample maintenance facilities were available. (It required a 1,200-foot takeoff roll on sod.) An O-47 could not operate out of a forward area, which meant that the aircrew would not have the opportunity to gain an intimate knowledge of conditions at the front or to interact much with the men they supported. In the air, it was sluggish to maneuver. While much faster than its World War I counterparts, with a top

---

[36] Irving B. Holley, Jr., *Evolution of the Liaison-Type Airplane, 1917–1944*, Army Air Forces (AAF) Historical Studies 44 [Washington, D.C.: Headquarters, Army Air Forces, 1945], p. 60; Howard K. Butler, *Army Air Corps Airplanes and Observation, 1935–1941* (St. Louis, Mo.: U.S. Army Aviation Systems Command, 1990), pp. 160–61, 170, 174–75; WD, FM 100–5, *Tentative FSR, 1939* (Washington, D.C.: Government Printing Office, 1939), pp. 15–22, 42–52.

speed of 221 miles per hour, the O–47's gain in speed increased the difficulty of making observations. Furthermore, the O–47 still appeared very vulnerable, even to the aviators. It was almost 100 miles per hour slower than the latest American pursuits. In 1939 the Air Corps assigned long-range reconnaissance, heretofore a mission for observation squadrons, to light bombardment units.[37]

Concern about the efficacy of the existing arrangements for aerial observation existed at the highest levels of the Army. In June 1938 the chief of staff, General Craig, enjoined the chief of the Air Corps, Maj. Gen. Oscar Westover, to put more effort into aerial fire control. In Craig's view practice and instruction in this technique was "at a low ebb." Craig wanted Westover to quickly make available "modern planes suitable for this purpose." In the context of June 1938 this meant O–47s, at least as far as the Air Corps was concerned.[38]

Observation balloons still lingered in the force structure, but in steadily decreasing numbers. Almost no one took them seriously. Air officers regarded balloons as even more vulnerable to air attack than fixed-wing observation aircraft; ground officers expected that the next war would involve much more maneuver. Still, the officers who remained in the lighter-than-air specialty, very much the stepchildren of the Air Corps, were enthusiasts. On very minimal funds, at times no more than $5,000 annually for research, they produced a motorized helium balloon that could travel across country at ten miles per hour. A Field Artillery officer who inspected it at Fort Bragg, North Carolina, found the balloon a wonderful observation platform "but of course terribly vulnerable as such things are." The German campaign in Poland beginning 1 September 1939—more mobile, violent, and decisive than even most of the American interwar proponents of mobility anticipated—effectively ended the lighter-than-air program in the Air Corps, although the units remained in existence for a short time longer.[39]

The development of rotary-wing aircraft appeared to provide one solution to the observation problem. During the 1930s pressure from the ground arms and reform-minded congressmen led the Air Corps to experiment with autogiros. The autogiro, the invention of Don Juan de la Cierva Codorníu of Spain, consisted of a conventional aircraft fuselage and a tractor engine, with rotary wings not connected to a motor substituting for traditional fixed wings. The movement of air past the blades caused them to rotate, generating lift. Unfortunately, the almost decade-long tests revealed what Air Corps engineers had

---

[37] Memo, Ch, Training and Opns Div, Office of the Chief of Air Corps (OCAC), 22 Jul 38, sub: Designation of Observation Squadron and Equipment, in Microfilm A1409, AFHRA; Memo, Maj Gen E. S. Adams for Chiefs of Arms and Services and Commandants of General and Special Service Schools, 15 Sep 39, sub: Air Board Rpt, Microfilm A2765, AFHRA; WD, FM 100–5, *Tentative FSR, 1939*, pp. 15–22, 42–52; Holley, *Evolution of the Liaison-Type Airplane*, pp. 23–26; Swanborough and Bowers, *Military Aircraft Since 1909*, pp. 452–53. The Army Air Forces began replacing the O–47 in 1940–1941 with the O–52, which was lighter, had better visibility, and was slightly slower. James C. Fahey, *U.S. Army Aircraft, 1908–1946* (Falls Church, Va.: Ships and Aircraft, 1946), p. 31.

[38] Memo, Gen Malin M. Craig, Chief of Staff, Army (CSA), for Deputy CSA, 18 Jun 38, sub: Fire Control for FA from the Air, in FA Aerial Obsn, 1938–1941, file, FAS Archives, Morris Swett Tech Lib. Dr. L. Martin Kaplan located this document for me.

[39] Table, sub: General Characteristics and Purpose, Aviation (Avn): Minimum Requirements, Incl in Memo, Adams for Chiefs of Arms and Services, Commandants of General and Special Schools, 15 Sep 39; Ltr, Lt Col I. T. Wyche, Commanding Officer (CO), 2d Battalion (Bn), 4th FA, to Col F. C. Wallace, OCFA, 19 Dec 39, OCFA, Gen Corresp, 1917–1941, 452.3/A–1, RG 177, NARA; Holley, *Evolution of the Liaison-Type Airplane*, pp. 36–39.

Kellett YG–1A Autogiro; *below,* Focke-Achgelis Fw–61

suspected all along: The autogiro at its current stage of development lacked sufficient lift to carry aloft a pilot, an observer, and a service radio, which made it impracticable for field use. Disappointing as this result was for the ground arms, the autogiro tests did confer at least two positive benefits. By demonstrating the feasibility of short takeoffs and landings on unprepared fields close to the front, autogiros increased the constituency in the ground arms for an aircraft of more conventional design but with similar capabilities. Second, they stimulated Congress to appropriate funds for further development of rotary-wing aircraft. The legislative language was broad enough to encompass helicopters as well as autogiros.[40]

Two Frenchmen, Louis Bréguet and Réne Dorland, developed the first practical helicopter, the Bréguet-Dorland 314 Gyroplane Laboratoire, which first flew on 26 June 1935. It featured two coaxial, counterrotating, two-blade rotors to neutralize torque. Exactly one year later to the day, the Focke-Achgelis Fw–61, designed by Professor Heinrich K. J. Focke, made its first flight. The Fw–61 also used counterrotating rotors— but on separate, side-by-side masts. Because the Germans gave the first public flight demonstration of a helicopter in February 1938, contemporaries credited Focke with developing the first successful helicopter. It was his machine that influenced Congress and the Army. American work on this type of craft was too rudimentary to be of much immediate use to the War Department.[41]

Instead, during the 1930s some officers of the ground arms turned to another solution, light fixed-wing aircraft. Light aircraft were small, lightweight, relatively inexpensive planes designed for individual rather than institutional owners. These aircraft represented the wedding of a light, strong airframe and a light, reliable engine. Normally during the 1930s, the fuselage consisted of doped canvas stretched over a welded steel-tube frame. Spruce spars and wooden ribs (aluminum ribs in Piper aircraft after 1940) maintained the longitudinal and cross-sectional shape of the canvas-covered wings. Two steel-tube struts, attached to the bottom of each wing, provided additional strength. The lightweight engines that made light aircraft feasible were classified as *opposed*. An opposed engine was a flat, internal-combustion engine with its cylinders opposite one another. Although long known in Europe, it became a popular design in American aviation circles only in the late 1920s. The U.S. light aircraft industry dated from its introduction. By the late 1930s the Piper Aircraft Corporation dominated the domestic market. Its popular two-place J–3 "Cub" owed its fuselage to the design of C. Gilbert Taylor, the original founder of the company, its wing to a National Advisory Committee for Aeronautics design that gave it exception-

---

[40] Peter W. Brooks, *Cierva Autogiros: The Development of Rotary-Wing Flight* (Washington, D.C.: Smithsonian Institution Press, 1988); Frank K. Smith, *Legacy of Wings: The Story of Harold F. Pitcairn* (New York: Jason Aronson, 1981), p. 42; Army Avn School, Department of Tactics and General Subjects, *History of the Helicopter* (Fort Sill, Okla.: Army Aviation School, 1953), p. 11; H. Franklin Gregory, *Anything a Horse Can Do: The Story of the Helicopter* (New York: Reynal and Hitchcock, 1944), pp. 50–67; Holley, *Evolution of the Liaison-Type Airplane*, pp. 45–49.

[41] On Bréguet and Dorland, see Brooks, *Cierva Autogiros*, pp. 292–302; Jay P. Spenser, *Whirlybirds: A History of U.S. Helicopter Pioneers* (Seattle: University of Washington Press and Museum of Flight, 1998), pp. 12–13. On the attribution of the first successful helicopter to Focke, see Gregory, *Anything a Horse Can Do*, pp. 82–83. Richard G. Hubler, *Straight Up: The Story of Vertical Flight* (New York: Duell, Sloan, and Pierce, 1961), pp. 50–52. Focke-Achgelis took over the development of the Fw–61 from Focke-Wulf, which had done the initial design, hence the designation. C. G. Grey and Leonard Bridgman, eds., *Jane's All the World's Aircraft, 1940* (London: Sampson, Low, Marston, and Co., 1940), p. 84c.

al low-speed handling characteristics, and its 65-horsepower, 4-cylinder engine to the Continental Engine Corporation (*Figure 1*).[42]

The J–3 was practically stall proof, but, if it did stall the pilot had ample and obvious warning so he could take corrective measures. The engine could even operate on automobile gasoline, if necessary. Instruments were very rudimentary: a tachometer to register the number of engine and propeller revolutions per minute; an air-speed indicator; a compass; an altimeter to measure the plane's height above its takeoff point; and oil temperature and pressure gauges (*Figure 2*). Both seats in a Cub with a tandem configuration had control sticks. The pilot usually flew from the front seat when he had a passenger; because of center-of-gravity considerations, he flew from the back seat when alone. In short, it was the perfect basic aircraft for an amateur flyer of limited skill. To William T. Piper, Sr., the marketing genius who headed the company, it was quite simply the "flivver" airplane, an appellation that appealed to a generation that had grown up driving Model T Fords.[43]

A 65-horsepower J–3 had a rated top speed of 85 miles per hour, a service ceiling of 9,300 feet, and a range of 190 miles, performance characteristics roughly equivalent, although somewhat inferior, to the most advanced World War I observation aircraft. The Cub burned three gallons of gasoline an hour, had a takeoff roll of 300 feet on sod, and landed at 35 miles per hour. Its small size—a wingspan of slightly more than 35 feet, a length of 22 feet, and a height of less than 7 feet—made it difficult to spot from the air and easy to hide on the ground. Its 730-pound empty weight allowed two or three men to manhandle it under tree limbs, a most convenient way to camouflage its presence from an aerial observer. The light weight also gave it good *flotation*, the ability to operate off soft and marshy ground, whereas a heavier aircraft would simply sink into the mud. However, on the basis of the characteristics by which the Air Corps normally judged aircraft, the J–3 was inferior even to the DH–4, except in reliability. But it had a number of features, which the Air Corps normally ignored, that made it feasible to operate out of forward areas and hence attractive to ground officers.[44]

Several of the private owners of light planes were Army officers in the ground combat arms, who were enthusiastic about the potential of this class of aircraft. At least two officers in the Texas National Guard, 1st Lt. Joseph M. Watson, Jr., and Capt. George K. Burr, began experiments with light aircraft directing artillery fire during their unit's summer camp in 1936. Most Air Corps officers were very cool to the idea, and in fact the autogiro drained off the available Air Corps funds and attention from light aircraft between 1934 and 1938. At the German Army maneuvers of 1937, and then at the Cleveland Air Races of September 1938, the Fieseler Storch, Fi–156, a slow plane developed for the *Luftwaffe* to transport German Army officers between headquarters in the combat zone, outperformed an American autogiro in length of takeoff (ninety-two feet on sod), carrying

---

[42] Interview (Interv), author with Col T. E. Haynes, 26 Feb 92, CMH files; Francis, *Mr. Piper and His Cubs*, pp. 16–25; Smith, *Aircraft Piston Engines*, pp. 191–214; Neil F. Rogers, "World War II Liaison Aviation in the United States Armed Forces" (Ph.D. diss., Northern Arizona University, 1992), pp. 33–36.

[43] Francis, *Mr. Piper and His Cubs*, pp. 22–68; Piper Aircraft Corporation, *How To Fly a Piper Cub* (Lock Haven, Pa.: Piper Aircraft Corp., 1946), p. 15.

[44] Swanborough and Bowers, *Military Aircraft Since 1909*, pp. 516–19; Interv, author with Haynes, 26 Feb 92; Holley, *Evolution of the Liaison-Type Airplane*, pp. 50–51.

FIGURE 1—CROSS-SECTIONAL DIAGRAM OF A PIPER CUB

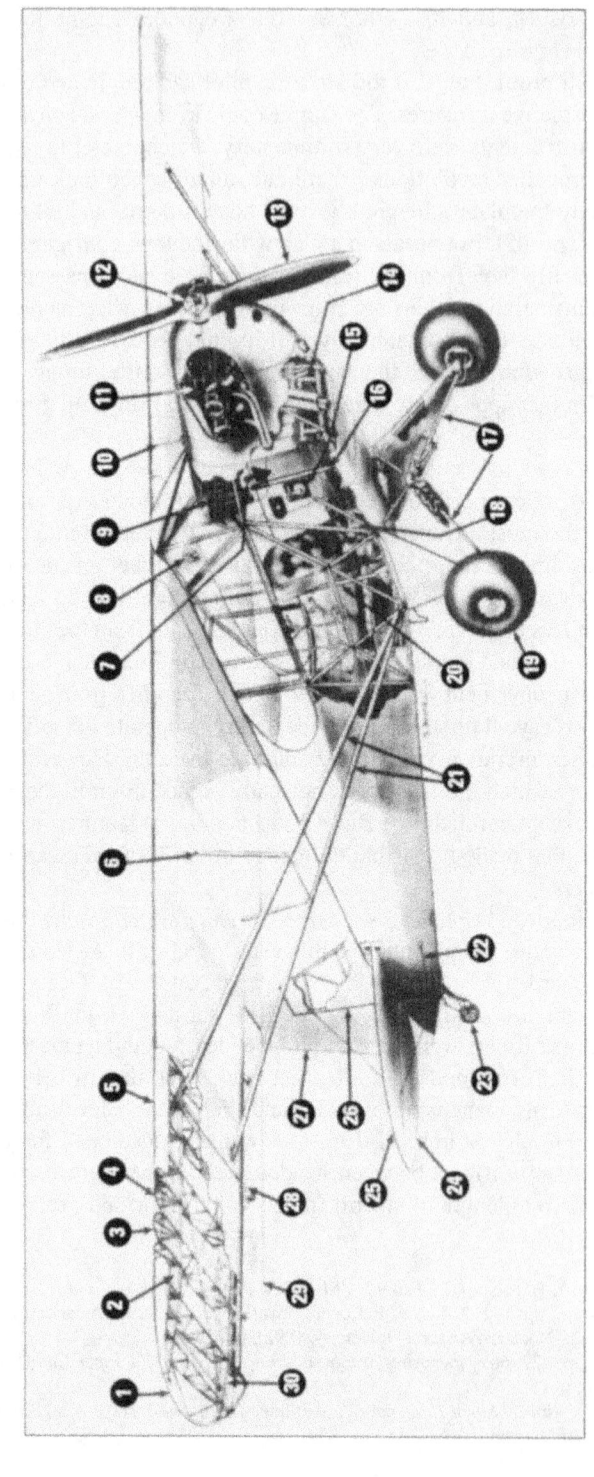

1. Wing Tip Bow
2. Front Wing Spar
3. Wing Rib
4. Wing Nose Rib
5. Leading Edge Cover
6. Jury Struts
7. Throttle
8. Ignition Switch
9. Fuel Tank
10. Fuel Gauge
11. Engine
12. Propeller Hub
13. Propeller
14. Front Rudder Pedal
15. Stabilizer Adjustment Crank
16. Front Control Stick
17. Landing Gear Shock Struts
18. Rear Rudder Pedal
19. Wheel and Tire
20. Rear Control Stick
21. Wing Lift Struts
22. Rudder Control Cable
23. Tail Wheel
24. Elevator
25. Stabilizer
26. Fin
27. Rudder
28. Aileron Control Cable
29. Aileron
30. Rear Wing Spar

Source: Piper Aircraft Corporation, *How To Fly a Piper Cub* (Lock Haven, Pa.: Piper Aircraft Corporation, 1946), p. 14.

FIGURE 2—INSTRUMENT PANEL OF A PIPER CUB

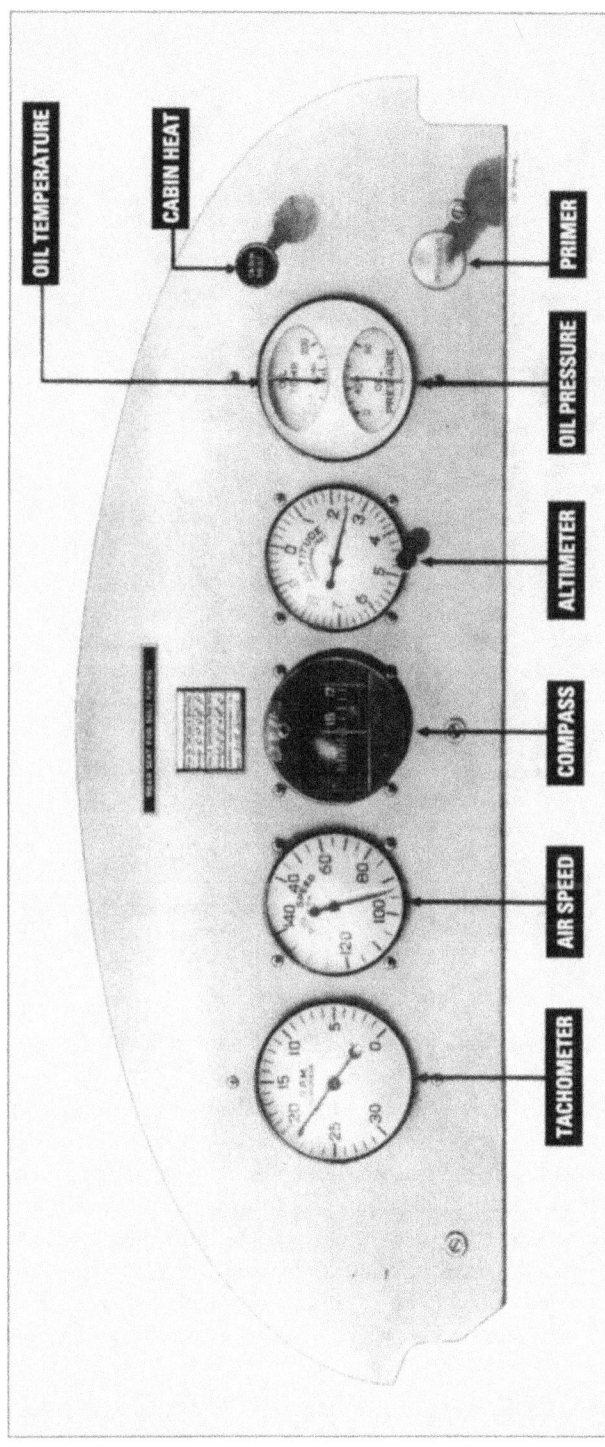

Oil Temperature: Registers in degrees Fahrenheit the temperature of the oil in the engine. High or low readings on this instrument are considered dangerous in flight operations.
Cabin Heat: By pushing or pulling this control, the flow of warm air from the heater is regulated to heat the cabin.
Tachometer: Registers the number of revolutions per minute of the engine and propeller. It is driven by a flexible shaft attached to the engine.
Air Speed: Registers the speed of the airplane through the air in miles per hour. Wind direction and velocity must be considered to determine the airplane's speed over the ground.
Compass: Shows the direction in which the airplane is traveling. Used to guide the pilot on the course he establishes before taking off.
Altimeter: Measures the height of the airplane above the takeoff point. Numbered dial may be turned to compensate for varying altitudes above sea level of different takeoff points.
Oil Pressure: Indicates pressure under which the oil is being circulated through the engine. High or low readings on this instrument are considered dangerous in flight operations.
Primer: For starting the engine only. A pumping motion of the handle pumps fuel into engine cylinders.

Source: Piper Aircraft Corporation, *How To Fly a Piper Cub* (Lock Haven, Pa.: Piper Aircraft Corporation, 1946), p. 15.

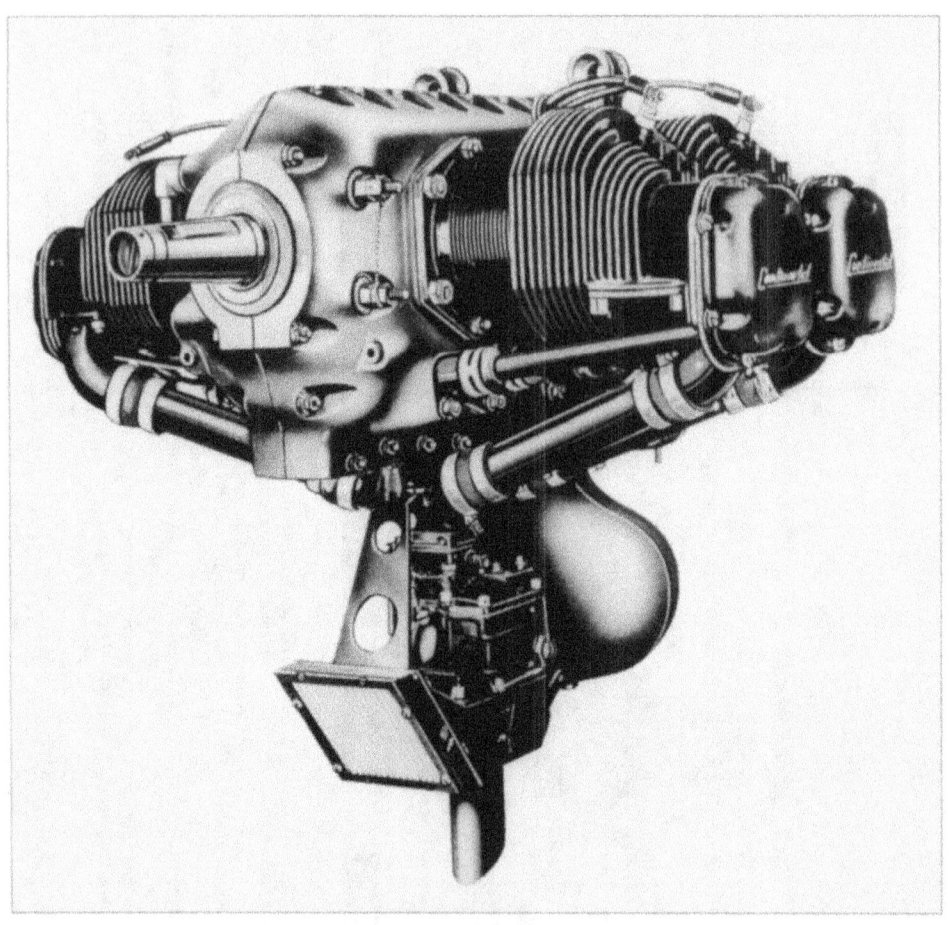

CONTINENTAL A–65 OPPOSED ENGINE

capacity, and endurance. These events immediately generated interest in producing an American equivalent.[45]

In 1939 the observation component, like the rest of the Air Corps, was undergoing the stresses inherent to the opening phases of mobilization and conversion to modern equipment. The Air Corps mobilization plan of 1936 called for an observation group in each of the nine corps areas of the United States. Each group was to consist of 4 squadrons, 3 drawn from the National Guard, with the Regular Army Air Corps providing 1 squadron and the group headquarters. In 1938 the Air Corps at last obtained 1 regular squadron for each corps area, which, combined with 1 observation squadron stationed in the Philippines, gave it a total of 10. The group headquarters, however, remained notional only.

---

[45] Interv, L. B. Epstein with Lt Col J. M. Watson, 14–15 Sep 76, U.S. Army Aviation and Troop Command History Office, St. Louis, Mo.; Holley, *Evolution of the Liaison-Type Airplane*, pp. 60, 62–67.

Fieseler Storch Fi–156

At full strength each squadron, as of 1939, consisted of 13 aircraft, 10 standard and 3 short-range observation, the latter term used synonymously with light aircraft.[46]

Because the Air Corps as yet had no short-range aircraft, all the planes were of the standard type. Such a categorization implies more uniformity than in fact existed. In 1938 the O–47 had only begun to join units in the continental United States. It existed side by side with a rich melange of earlier types, testimony to the Air Corps' interwar policy of purchasing only small production runs to facilitate advances in aeronautical design. The 2d Observation Squadron in the Philippines, for example, had no O–47s in 1939, but it had many fabric-covered biplanes dating from the 1920s. Its situation was indicative of the condition of many of the National Guard squadrons, if not the Regular squadrons, in the continental United States. Moreover, like the rest of the Regular Army, observation squadrons had survived the interwar period in a skeletonized status; only in 1939 did they begin to receive the men and equipment that allowed them to expand toward full strength. The small observation community within the Air Corps consequently had enough problems to distract it from concerns of ground officers about the state of observation.[47]

---

[46] WD, The Adjutant General's Office, *Army Station List and Directory, October 20, 1939* (Washington, D.C.: Government Printing Office, 1939), pp. 1–8; Futrell, *Command of Observation*, pp. 1–5.
[47] Maurer Maurer, *Aviation in the U.S. Army, 1919–1939*, USAF General Histories (Washington, D.C.: Office of Air Force History, 1987), pp. 427–48.

Ground officers took the lead in pressing for a more suitable observation aircraft. And among the ground arms, the Field Artillery had the most at stake. Two interrelated developments made this so. The Signal Corps had continued to seek a lightweight, static-free, air-to-ground voice radio after World War I. But the elimination of static had to wait until the discovery of frequency modulation. This breakthrough, along with crystal control, which allowed push-button tuning, was well in hand by 1938, although the Signal Corps did not exhibit the first service models of the new radios until the next year. The second development concerned Field Artillery doctrine. Beginning in 1929 a series of junior officers at the Field Artillery School revised American doctrine and organization for indirect fire. The battalion replaced the battery as the primary unit for the delivery of indirect fire, and a battalion fire-control center provided a method of massing that fire. These changes were incremental and not completed until 1941, but again the trend was well developed by the end of 1938. Experienced Field Artillery officers also knew, however, that effective indirect fire depended upon effective observation. World War I had demonstrated that ground observers could not provide adequate observation at all times and had to be supplemented by aerial observers in certain circumstances, especially when the enemy held the high ground.[48]

By the end of 1938 the evolving indirect-fire doctrine, improved radios, and light aircraft had created the possibility of a war-winning synthesis if someone could pull all the strands together. The Air Corps, distracted by mobilization and focused on the potential of strategic bombardment, was the least likely candidate to press for a radical change in the organization, equipment, and doctrine of aerial observation. Moreover, any attempt to shift institutional responsibility for the mission was certain to run up against the Air Corps axiom that the air was a separate element that only air officers understood. Habits of thought and questions of bureaucratic advantage predisposed the Air Corps to defend the status quo. It remained to be seen what the Infantry, Cavalry, and Field Artillery could do in these circumstances.

Conclusion

The U.S. Army's use of aerial observation between 1861 and 1938 depended on several interrelated factors. The type of aerial vehicle available as an observation platform and its flight characteristics obviously affected how the Army might employ it. This in turn depended on the state of technology in certain key areas, such as, depending on the period, balloon envelopes, gas generation, airframes, and lightweight piston engines. The status of communications technology acted as an independent variable, determining the degree to which aerial observers could coordinate their actions with units on the ground. The state of the art of war affected the degree of demand among ground officers for the services provided by aerial observers and hence the Army's receptiveness to the introduction of the function.

---

[48] Dastrup, *King of Battle*, pp. 197–200; Janice E. McKenney, "Field Artillery" (Unpubl Ms, CMH, 1992), pp. 249–57; Dulany Terrett, *The Signal Corps: The Emergency (To December 1941)*, U.S. Army in World War II (Washington, D.C.: Office of the Chief of Military History, 1956), pp. 178–85.

At one extreme, which the French rather than the American Army experienced, lay the eighteenth-century battlefield. Relatively small armies, maneuvering in the open and engaging at close range, provided only a minimal scope for aerial observers. Cavalry could and did perform all the necessary reconnaissance, and field army commanders could see all at a glance. At the other extreme lay the battlefields of World War I—mass armies, dispersed over a huge terrain, gone to ground. Senior officers and their staffs were far to the rear, isolated from the combatants. In many instances aerial observation was by necessity the primary means for collecting information about conditions in the battle zone, and the demand for it was correspondingly great.

Although technology was crucial, doctrine (how soldiers intended to use and integrate their tools of war) was no less so. The equipment that American field artillerymen possessed in 1917 and 1938 was remarkably similar, but their doctrine was radically different. Almost equally important was organization. Aerial observation lacked a stable institutional home in the nineteenth-century American Army and as a consequence had an episodic career in the service. In the twentieth century aerial observation secured an organizational niche, but consensus on its mission dissolved in the aftermath of World War I.

The divergence between the ground arms' continued emphasis on combined arms as the key to victory and the airmen's increasing reliance on strategic bombardment operating independently pulled the aerial observation mission in contradictory directions. The mix of technology, doctrine, the evolving nature of warfare, and institutional allegiances, combined with the political impact of changes on the international scene and the abilities and personalities of the individuals involved, determined the evolution of the aerial observation mission in the U.S. Army after 1938.

CHAPTER 1

The Ground Arms Seek Their Own Aircraft, 1939–1941

The question of organic aviation became a major source of contention between the ground arms and the Air Corps from 1939 to 1941. The outbreak of war in Europe in September 1939 gave the issue particular intensity. The Field Artillery first addressed the problem, both because of the potential advantage that effective aerial observation conferred on its own operations and because it enjoyed certain institutional advantages that the other ground combat arms lacked. The Cavalry, including the nascent Armored Force, and the Infantry nevertheless also joined the debate, although with varying degrees of enthusiasm and commitment. The disagreement between the Air Corps and the Field Artillery began with a polite exchange of views but then became increasingly contentious. Air and ground officers misunderstood and mistrusted the motives and intentions of the members of the other group. By the fall of 1941 the War Department appeared poised to render a judgment on the question. Political considerations internal to the organization seemed to weigh as heavily as military merit in determining the outcome.

The Field Artillery and the Aerial Observation Problem, 1939–1940

In 1939 and 1940 the Field Artillery took the lead among the ground arms in seeking a solution to the aerial observation problem. The chief of the branch, Maj. Gen. Robert M. Danford, was responsible for its organization, doctrine, and training. A 1904 graduate of the U.S. Military Academy, Danford had served as a key assistant to the chief of Field Artillery in World War I and as the executive officer to the chief of Field Artillery from 1931–1935. When he became chief of Field Artillery in March 1938, he brought with him considerable insight concerning the internal workings of the War Department. In January 1939 he laid out the Field Artillery position on aerial observation to the chief of the Air Corps, Maj. Gen. Henry H. Arnold, another Washington veteran and a close confidant of Brig. Gen. William Mitchell in the 1920s. Danford wanted the Air Corps to supply aircraft designed to meet the requirements of the Field Artillery, along with the necessary pilots and ground crew. The Field Artillery would determine how to organize and employ the aircraft. Danford thus favored assigning aircraft directly to field artillery

GENERAL DANFORD IN
FEBRUARY 1939

units rather than to corps headquarters as indicated by current Army doctrine. Arnold's response was negative.[1]

In general, like Mitchell and most other airmen of the period, Arnold believed in the centralized control of all aviation by an air force commander. Aircraft were too costly, and hence scarce, to parcel out to all ground force units. Only central control allowed their concentration on primary missions. An air force commander could shift his units during combat depending on the situation. Attaching aviation units to ground units destroyed this needed flexibility.[2]

Proponents of organic aviation countered with the argument that however wise centralization might be for some types of aircraft and missions, it was not optimal in all situations. A single-engine observation plane was very different from a four-engine bomber, just as directing artillery fire in the combat zone was very different from mounting a bombing raid hundreds of miles behind enemy lines. Aerial observers needed educated and discerning eyes to understand what was happening below them. They required a clear understanding of ground forces organization and doctrine, the nature of the terrain, the location of friendly positions, and the ground commander's scheme of maneuver. Aerial observers became useful only when they mastered a host of details, which they could best learn when part of a larger ground unit. In short, aerial observers needed to live close to the men they supported.[3]

---

[1] "Robert M. Danford," in George W. Cullum, et al., comps., *Biographical Register of the Officers and Graduates of the U.S. Military Academy at West Point, N.Y., Since Its Establishment in 1802*, 9 vols. (Boston: Houghton Mifflin and Co., 1891–1951), 6A:1092–93, 7:626, 8:155–56; Memo, Col F. C. Wallace, Executive Officer (XO), Office of the Chief of Field Artillery (OCFA), for The Adjutant General (TAG), 15 Jul 40, General Headquarters (GHQ), General Correspondence (Gen Corresp), 1940–1942, 665 (Fire Control Installations), Record Group (RG) 337, National Archives and Records Administration, Washington, D.C. (hereafter cited as NARA), summarizes Danford's January 1939 meeting. For Arnold, see Thomas M. Coffey, *Hap: The Story of the U.S. Air Force and the Man Who Built It, General Henry H. "Hap" Arnold* (New York: Viking Press, 1982).

[2] William Mitchell, *Winged Defense: The Development and Possibilities of Modern Air Power, Economic and Military* (New York: Dover, 1988), pp. 217–23; Henry H. Arnold and Ira C. Eaker, *This Flying Game*, 3d ed. (New York: Funk and Wagnalls, 1943), pp. 136–40, 152–58; Command and General Staff School (C&GSS), *Tactics and Technique of Air Corps (Tentative)* (Fort Leavenworth, Kans.: Command and General Staff School, 1936), ch. 4, pp. 1–14; War Department (WD), Field Manual (FM) 100–20, *Command and Employment of Air Power* (Washington, D.C.: The Adjutant General's Office, 1943), pp. 1–2.

[3] Memo Order, Office, Chief of Artillery (OCA), American Expeditionary Forces (AEF), 8 Dec 18; Brig Gen A. Hero, Jr., et al, "Report of Field Artillery Board, AEF, on Organization and Tactics" (Unpublished [Unpubl] Manuscript [Ms], hereafter cited as Hero Report [Rpt]), both in Morris Swett Technical Library, Field Artillery School (FAS), Fort Sill, Okla. (hereafter cited as Morris Swett Tech Lib).

January 1939 was hardly the best time for Danford to press Arnold to do something he did not want to do. The Air Corps, never the War Department's waif, possessed more power and prestige than ever before in the wake of the Munich settlement of October 1938. President Franklin D. Roosevelt concluded that German air superiority had allowed the German dictator, Adolph Hitler, to bully France and Great Britain into permitting the dismemberment of France's ally, Czechoslovakia. Roosevelt decided that the proper American response was to create a "shop front" air force of 10,000 aircraft, but without sufficient personnel to man or ground facilities to support them. While larger appropriations inevitably did increase the number of observation aircraft in the late 1930s, their percentage of the total force declined. With very substantial amounts of money flowing to the Air Corps—but not to the ground forces—for the first time since the end of World War I, Arnold was hardly in a mood to compromise with Danford over what he regarded as a matter of principle.[4]

Faced with Arnold's intransigence, Danford mounted a low-key campaign in the pages of the *Field Artillery Journal* published by his office. Dropping a long-standing policy against printing pieces that questioned existing aerial observation organization and doctrine, the journal solicited a critical article, which appeared in the May–June 1939 issue. It called for Field Artillery aerial observers who lived and worked with their compatriots on the ground, except when they were actually in the air observing fire. This was simply a restatement of one of the Hero Board's recommendations, based on World War I Field Artillery operations in France. In the same issue, the *Field Artillery Journal* reprinted an article from a French military journal calling for the French Army to own and operate its own observation aviation. Given the high esteem with which American field artillerymen had held their French counterparts since 1917, publication of the article suggested the direction of thought in the chief's office without overtly committing Danford. The muted discussion of the ensuing issues hardly influenced Arnold, but it did indicate to Field Artillery officers that the question was a matter of some professional concern and facilitated the development of a consensus within the branch over the next few years in favor of organic Field Artillery aircraft.[5]

This solution gained adherents only slowly. In August 1939 First Army staged the most ambitious American ground maneuvers since 1918 in the rugged terrain around Plattsburg, New York. Senior Field Artillery officers agreed unanimously that the Air Corps did not provide sufficient observation, although most blamed it on inadequate numbers of available aircraft. With the general scarcity of equipment, it was all too easy to overlook the design deficiencies of that available. As was to be the case in all the prewar maneuvers, standard corps and division aircraft such as the O–47 were chained by their weight and takeoff characteristics to fixed bases far to the rear. They were slow to arrive at

---

[4] On the Munich crisis, see Forrest C. Pogue, *George C. Marshall*, 4 vols. (New York: Viking, 1963–1987), 1:320–24; Irving B. Holley, Jr., *Evolution of the Liaison-Type Airplane, 1917–1944*, Army Air Forces (AAF) Historical Studies 44 [Washington, D.C.: Headquarters, Army Air Forces, 1945], p. 63.

[5] Anon, "This War Department Reorganization," *Field Artillery Journal* (*FAJ*) 32 (May 1942):376–77, discusses the *Journal*'s institutional affiliations. A. Verdurand, "Flying Observation Posts for Artillery," *FAJ* 29 (May–June 1939):197; H. W. Blakeley, "We Must See With Our Own Eyes," *FAJ* 29 (May–June 1939):215–18, reprinted in *Army* 10 (March 1961):62–63. General Blakeley's introduction to the latter comments on its initial publication. Hero Rpt, 29 Jan 19.

Stinson O–49

the front, and the aircrew most often did not understand the situation on the ground. One light-plane enthusiast commented that no standard observation aircraft could land within forty miles of any command post, while a light plane could land within a few hundred yards of one. Still, as of January 1940, when the War Department surveyed fifty-two senior Field Artillery officers, only three favored Field Artillery planes. On the other hand, most wanted the aerial observer to be a field artilleryman.[6]

If the organization of aerial observation posed problems, field artillerymen could take heart that the equipment problem appeared on the way to solution. In May 1939 a board of officers selected to determine the military characteristics of the short-range liaison plane settled on Storch-like characteristics: single-engine, two-place, unarmed, with a speed range of 40 to 125 miles per hour, and capable of clearing 50 feet after a 500-foot takeoff run on sod. By early September 1939 the Materiel Division of the Air Corps had negotiated contracts with three manufacturers for 106 aircraft. The Stinson YO–49 (the "Y" prefix indicated a limited production run for service testing) was the preferred model, with 100 on order. Over 50 feet in length, with a wingspan in excess of 34 feet and a height of more than 10 feet, the YO–49 was similar in size to the O–47, but less than half its weight. Even

---

[6] Ltr, Col L. B. Moody to Lt Gen Lesley J. McNair, 13 Jan 42, GHQ, Gen Corresp, 1940–1942, 452.1 (Binder 1), RG 337, NARA; Ltr, Maj Gen E. S. Adams, TAG, to Commanding Generals (CGs), 1st, 2d, 3d, 5th, and 6th Divisions (Divs), 25 Jan 40, sub: Questionnaire on Field Artillery (FA) Matters; Memo, OCFA, sub: Analysis of Questionnaire on FA Officers (Ofcrs); both in OCFA, Corresp, 1917–1942, 320.2/AA–65, RG 177, NARA; Jean R. Moenk, *A History of Large-Scale Army Maneuvers in the United States, 1935–1964* (Fort Monroe, Va.: U.S. Continental Army Command, 1969), pp. 23–26.

so, the YO–49 was half again the size of the Piper Cub, almost three times the weight, and powered by a Lycoming R–608–9, an engine over three times as powerful as the Continental A–65 in the Cub. The R–608–9 was a small radial engine, having a design in which the cylinders were arranged in a circle around the drive shaft. Big, muscular radials were a distinctive trademark of American military aviation during the interwar period, but they had to have at least seven cylinders to prevent excessive vibration. Seven cylinders exacted a substantial weight penalty. In fact, the YO–49 represented an intermediate step between standard observation types and true light aircraft. The YO–49's dimensions allowed enemy pursuits to find and shoot it more easily than light aircraft, while its weight made for poorer flotation on soft ground. Although the performance trade-offs were inherent in the design from its inception, not all were obvious. Air Corps and ground officers gained an appreciation for the YO–49's capabilities only as a result of rigorous field tests, as with any new aircraft, but in 1939 such tests lay in the future.[7]

Arnold quickly dissipated whatever goodwill he received for the Air Corps' purchase of the YO–49. Since 1937 the chiefs of Infantry, Cavalry, and Field Artillery had held the official position that the Air Corps should equip corps observation squadrons with a ratio of three slow-speed observation planes, the role envisioned for the YO–49, to each standard observation aircraft, such as the O–47. In establishing the requirement for slow-speed aircraft in 1939, the Air Corps reversed the ratio. Through the first half of 1940 Arnold continued to tout the virtues of standard observation aircraft in general and the O–47 in particular. Privately, he doubted whether a slow-speed aircraft could survive in the battle area. He procured YO–49s because of pressure from the ground combat arms, not because he agreed with the design assumptions.[8]

A series of actions in late 1939 indicated very clearly Arnold's low regard for the new class of observation planes. In November he attempted to reduce the required performance ratings for short-range observation aircraft, the official classification of the YO–49. That aircraft was proving more expensive than anticipated in both cost and plant space. Arnold hoped to substitute an off-the-shelf commercial plane, the Stinson Model 105 (subsequently given the military designation YO–54), and to liberate funds and equipment for other, more important, types of aircraft. Danford and the other affected branch chiefs succeeded in blocking this effort. When they sought to increase the number of slow-speed aircraft in production, however, the Air Corps refused to do so until the YO–49 had proved itself in the field. None could be ready for field tests in time for the 1940 maneuvers, which the branch chiefs considered key to developing correct techniques for employing slow-speed aircraft in conjunction with ground troops. Arnold's office refused to purchase any commercial light aircraft as a stopgap measure and doggedly maintained its higher priorities—the production of bombers, pursuits, and trainers. Although the 1938 mobilization

---

[7] Holley, *Evolution of the Liaison-Type Airplane*, pp. 60, 62–67; Frederick G. Swanborough and Peter M. Bowers, *United States Military Aircraft Since 1909* (Washington, D.C.: Smithsonian Institution Press, 1989), pp. 444–45.

[8] Ibid., p. 57; Memorandum for Record (MFR) on Memo, Col J. R. D. Matheson, Acting Assistant Chief of Staff (ACS), G–4, for TAG, 31 Jan 40, ACS, G–4, Numerical file, 1921–March 1942, 27277–12, RG 165, NARA; Memo, Chief of Air Corps (CAC) for Chief of Cavalry (CC), 5 Jan 40, sub: Air Unit for the Cavalry (Cav) Div, Microfilm A1409, U.S. Air Force Historical Research Agency, Maxwell Air Force Base (AFB), Ala. (hereafter cited as AFHRA).

plan had set aside 37 percent of all aircraft plant capacity for building observation aircraft, through the end of 1939 the Air Corps' plans had allocated less than 4 percent of the capacity for that purpose. Within the observation category, the Air Corps emphasized long-range reconnaissance craft that could accompany the independent bombing force.[9]

While Arnold backed away from a commitment to the YO–49, the decisive impetus for organizational and doctrinal change came, as it did so often in the interwar army, from a branch school. During the two decades between the world wars, both student officers at the Field Artillery School at Fort Sill, Oklahoma, and Air Corps observers trained at Brooks Field, Texas, more often than not failed their aerial firing problems. On the other hand, experienced Field Artillery officers with training as radio operators obtained "passable" results. Over the years, Field Artillery officers who had studied the role of aerial observation had blamed a host of factors for the inadequacies of the existing system: communications, firing techniques, the Fire Control Code (the shorthand Morse system for directing the fall of shells), training methods, and individuals. But no matter what adjustments the responsible authorities made, the results remained consistently unsatisfactory. In the late 1930s the commandant of the Field Artillery School, dismayed by the continuing inability to obtain satisfactory aerial observation during firing problems there, established the Air-Ground Procedures Board to monitor the situation and propose solutions.[10]

On 26 September 1939, Danford directed the commandant to have the board thoroughly test existing procedures and alternative solutions. The board completed its report in May 1940, the month the Germans invaded France and the Low Countries. The board recommended "as the only possible solution" that the Field Artillery have its own observation airplanes with pilots and mechanics who were artillerymen. The aircraft, in the board's view, should be equipped with the same radio equipment used for ground artillery communication. The following month, during which France succumbed to German *Blitzkrieg* and the British Army withdrew from the Continent, the board's recorder, Capt. Rex E. Chandler, reported to duty in Washington at the Office of the Chief of Field Artillery. He found the board's report on his desk as his first order of business.[11]

Chandler, though a nonflyer, had a passionate commitment to securing aerial observation for the Field Artillery. A 1923 graduate of West Point, he was one of the branch's most knowledgeable radio experts and a pioneer in the adaptation of frequency-modulated radio in the Field Artillery. He thus brought an awareness of the importance of control

---

[9] MFR on Memo, G–4 for TAG, 15 Dec 39, ACS, G–4, Numerical file, 1921–March 1942, 27277–12, RG 165, NARA; Memos, Brig Gen Carl Spaatz, Chief of Air Staff (CAS), for Chief of Staff, Army (CSA), 30 Oct 41, sub: Organization and Equipment for Observation (Obsn) Units in the Air Support (Spt) Command (Cmd), and Lt Col C. E. Duncan, Secretary (Sec) of the Air Staff (AS), 8 Dec 41, CSA, both in Numerical file, 1920–1942, 21276, RG 165, NARA, discuss the assumptions of Army Air Forces procurement policy. Irving B. Holley, Jr., *Buying Aircraft: Materiel Procurement for the Army Air Forces*, U.S. Army in World War II (Washington, D.C.: Office of the Chief of Military History, 1964), p. 156.

[10] Rpt, Col A. McIntyre, Commandant, FAS, to TAG, 20 Jul 39, sub: Rpt of Operations (Opns) of the FAS for the School Year 1938–1939, FAS Archives, Morris Swett Tech Lib; Speech, Brig Gen R. E. Chandler, 10 Nov 58, sub: Talk Delivered at the Grad Exercise, U.S. Army Aviation (Avn) Training Detachment (Fixed Wing), Gary Army Air Field, Camp Gary, San Marcos, Tex., in Rex E. Chandler Ms, U.S. Army Military History Institute, Carlisle Barracks, Pa. (hereafter cited as MHI).

[11] Rpt, Col A. McIntyre, Commandant, FAS, to TAG, 11 Jul 40, sub: Rpt of the Opns of the FAS for the School Year 1939–1940, FAS Archives, Morris Swett Tech Lib; Speech, Chandler, 10 Nov 58; WD, Special Orders (SO) 139, 13 Jun 40.

and communications to the successful integration of aircraft into field artillery units. He used the conclusions of the procedures board as the basis for drafting a proposal calling for a test of the concept of aviation organic to the Field Artillery, which Danford approved and forwarded to The Adjutant General for decision by the War Department.[12]

The general principles enunciated in what had become the Danford proposal served as the basis of Field Artillery policy over the next two years. The Field Artillery was interested in an airplane that could be used for observation, especially surveillance and the adjustment of fire. Reconnaissance and liaison missions were only secondary concerns. The primary mission of the Field Artillery was to mass fires in the enemy's rear areas upon reserves, upon counterattack forces moving up to their start lines, and upon enemy batteries that were "never seen except from the air." In 90 percent of these cases, noted Danford, terrestrial observation

CHANDLER IN OCTOBER 1942, FOLLOWING HIS PROMOTION TO COLONEL

was simply nonexistent. An elevated observation post was required, which under conditions of mobile warfare meant "some form of aircraft."[13]

The battalion was the crucial echelon at which to make aircraft available, because the Field Artillery had concentrated its principal means of fire control and fire direction at that level. During the 1939–1940 school year, the Air-Ground Procedures Board at Fort Sill had developed gunnery procedures and communications procedures that would permit one airplane to direct the fire of more than one battalion of field artillery. Chandler and his colleagues knew exactly what they wanted to do from the gunnery perspective. It only remained to secure an aircraft suitable for service with the battalion to accomplish their objectives.[14]

Danford envisioned a flight of at least seven aircraft organic to corps and division artillery. At least one aircraft would thus be "immediately available at all times" for each firing battalion. These light aircraft would be relatively simple to fly and maintain. The Field Artillery would require only pilots who had completed primary flight training but were unsuited for advanced instruction and hence not a drain on the pool of Air Corps

---

[12] [W. A. Harris], "Rex Eugene Chandler," *Assembly* 24 (Fall 1965):88–89; Rex E. Chandler, "The Adaptability of Ultra–Short Wave Radio to Field Artillery Communication," *FAJ* 23 (September–October 1933):450–51; Speech, Chandler, 10 Nov 58.

[13] Memo, Wallace for TAG, 15 Jul 40.

[14] Rpt, Maj W. D. Brown, et al., Air-Ground Procedures Board, to Commandant, FAS, 19 Aug 41, sub: Final Rpt of the Air-Ground Procedures Board, Tab F in "Field Artillery Observation" (Unpubl Ms, Morris Swett Tech Lib, 1941).

pilots. Likewise, Field Artillery mechanics, rather than highly specialized Air Corps mechanics, would provide normal maintenance in the division. The Air Corps would perform major overhaul at depots. Danford wanted "aggressive experimental and development work" on the air observation question by both the Field Artillery School at Fort Sill and the Field Artillery Board at Fort Bragg. In sum, Danford simply reiterated the position he had articulated in 1939 but substituted Field Artillery for Air Corps personnel.[15]

The Office of the Chief of the Air Corps, unimpressed by these arguments, regarded the concept of Field Artillery aircraft as a deviation from the War Department's policy of maintaining specialized arms combined at unit level under a common commander. Arnold's staff chose to rest its position solely on this narrow, if clever, organizational argument—the Field Artillery proposal was, after all, what members of the ground combat arms always had accused the Air Corps of doing. At the same time the thinking of many key Air Corps officers about observation as a class had undergone a veritable revolution because of the collapse of the Western Front in May and June 1940. The virtual massacre of British and French aircrews as they attempted to fly over the battle area in aircraft very similar to the O–47 caused the Air Corps to abandon all plans to employ O–47s in combat. In addition, Arnold argued that a light bomber adapted for visual and photographic reconnaissance could adequately handle "all kinds of tactical and minor strategic observation." By implication his assessment left short-range observation aircraft with no mission other than ferrying commanders and their staffs behind the lines—the liaison mission.[16]

The reaction of the General Staff was more muted. The acting assistant chief of staff, G–3, Col. Harry L. Twaddle, noted that the arguments made in favor of organic Field Artillery aerial observation could be made with equal force for the other branches. Before the War Department decided to shift to a decentralized system of aerial observation, he wanted to give the centralized system a further trial with modern equipment. Twaddle envisioned testing the concept during the 1941 summer maneuvers, when the first O–49s would be available in observation squadrons. (Because the O–49 was now classed as a standard type, the Air Corps had withdrawn the "Y" prefix.) At this point Danford concluded that his proposal faced almost certain rejection by the chief of staff, General George C. Marshall, Jr., and elected to try to withdraw his paper rather than endanger its future prospects for approval.[17]

Danford nevertheless received a formal response from the adjutant general disapproving an organic aviation component for the Field Artillery "at this time." In language even more restrictive than that of the acting G–3, the adjutant general justified existing

---

[15] Memo, Wallace for TAG, 15 Jul 40.

[16] Memo, Maj Gen George H. Brett, Assistant Chief of Air Corps (ACAC), for ACS, G–3, 10 Dec 40, sub: Air Obsn for FA, Headquarters (HQ), CAC, Security Classified (Class) Decimal file, 1939–1942, 322.172–A (Obsn Squadrons), RG 18, NARA, is the narrow rebuttal of the Field Artillery plan. For the wider context of Air Corps thinking, see Memo, sub: AC Technical Committee Meeting (Mtg) of 22 May 40, Office of the Chief of Cavalry (OCC), Gen Corresp, 1920–1942, 452.1, RG 177, NARA; Memo, Brig Gen R. C. Moore, G–4, for CSA, 29 Jun 40, ACS, G–4, Numerical file, 1921–March 1942, 27277–19, RG 165, NARA; Rpt, Lt Col Ira C. Eaker, XO, OCAC, to TAG, 11 Oct 40, sub: Obsn Airplanes, Obsn Balloons, Obsn Squadrons, Microfilm A1409, AFHRA; Henry H. Arnold, *Global Mission* (New York: Harper and Brothers, 1949), p. 224. Ltr, Col K. S. Bradford, XO, OCC, to Sec, AC Technical Committee, 4 Jun 40, sub: Non-Tactical Type of Airplane for Commanders (Comdrs), Their Staffs, Military Attachés, etc., OCC, Gen Corresp, 1920–1942, 452.1, RG 177, NARA.

[17] Memo, Col H. L. Twaddle, ACS, G–3, for CSA, 25 Nov 40, Microfilm A1409, AFHRA; Speech, Chandler, 10 Nov 58.

policy as "the most economical one in personnel, material, and operating facilities." Unless the chief of the Field Artillery could demonstrate "conclusively" that Air Corps observation squadrons could not meet the needs of the Field Artillery, the War Department would retain the existing organization. The adjutant general left only one small opening. He enjoined Danford to determine by 1 September the suitability of the O–49 for field artillery work and report on whether three O–49s sufficed for an observation squadron.[18]

While the Field Artillery's cause made little headway in the War Department, events and practical experience testified to its validity and won it new supporters in the field. The Field Artillery interpreted the lessons of 1940 somewhat differently than the Air Corps. Rather than focusing on the British and French experience, field artillerymen concentrated on the German example. The Fiesler Storch appeared to give the German Army excellent observed fire. "Appeared," however, is used advisedly. The *Luftwaffe* employed standard observation aircraft for this mission, while the Storch ferried commanders and staffs, the liaison mission that Arnold envisioned for the O–49. Wartime security and the increasing tension between Germany and the United States meant that in 1940 and 1941 the U.S. Army possessed only fragmentary information about certain German military techniques. Field Artillery officers took the known information and assumed that their German counterparts were thinking along the same lines as the Americans, but that the Germans had already implemented their ideas. Of course, the German example demonstrated that both standard observation and light aircraft could survive in combat if friendly pursuits achieved the degree of air superiority that the *Luftwaffe* attained in France and the Low Countries in 1940.[19]

The Field Artillery's misconstrued yet powerful argument resonated with the experience of Army ground units during the 1940 maneuver season. Air Corps observation squadrons equipped with O–47s experienced the same difficulties performing the aerial observation mission that they had the year before. At the same time firing battalions "seldom made any effort to get airplanes." Only the 61st Field Artillery Brigade in the 36th Division (Texas National Guard) enjoyed ample aerial observation and then only for two days. The brigade acquired this support by highly unusual means without the assistance or even knowledge of the Office of the Chief of Field Artillery.[20]

During the spring and early summer of 1940, the S–4 (supply and ammunition officer) of the brigade, 1st Lt. Joseph M. Watson, and the headquarters battery commander, Capt. George K. Burr, continued their experiments with light aircraft. At the IV Corps maneuvers at Camp Beauregard, Louisiana, using a Cub J–4 supplied by the Piper Aircraft

---

[18] Ltr, L. S. Ostrander, TAGO, to CFA, 7 Feb 41, Tab C in "Field Artillery Observation." Dr. Boyd Dastrup called this document to my attention.

[19] Photo, *FAJ* 30 (September–October 1940):355; Anon, "Employment of the Artillery Air Observer in the German Army," *FAJ* 32 (January 1942):16–20. In the first proposal to assign light aircraft to the Field Artillery, Danford stressed the German practice of making aviators an integral part of the units they supported and then jumped to the British experiments with light aircraft. Memo, Wallace for TAG, 15 Jul 40. See also WD, Technical Manual (TM)–Enemy (E) 30–451, *Handbook on German Armed Forces, 1 March 1945* (Baton Rouge: Louisiana State University Press, 1990), p. 606.

[20] Ltr, Col L. B. Moody to Lt Gen Lesley J. McNair, 13 Jan 42, GHQ, Gen Corresp, 1940–1942, 452.1 (Binder 1), RG 337, NARA. Memo, Anon for Chief of Staff (CS), GHQ, 3 Sep 40, sub: Notes on Recent Tour of Army Maneuvers, GHQ, Gen Corresp, 1940–1942, 354.2/1 (Maneuvers), RG 337, NARA. See also Memo, Lt Col Mark W. Clark for Maj Gen Lesley J. McNair, 31 Aug 40, from the same file. The War Department redesignated the 36th Division as the 36th Infantry Division in February 1942.

Corporation and piloted by Piper salesman Thomas A. Case, Watson successfully observed fire. He communicated by message drop to the ground and provided column control when the brigade made a 93-mile road march. The two days of practical experience convinced the brigade commander, Brig. Gen. Robert O. Whiteaker, of the utility of the light observation aircraft. Unaware of Danford's efforts along the same line, Whiteaker believed that he would need more comprehensive experience and a systematic collection of data before he could hope to convince higher authority of the wisdom of his conclusions, and thus he refrained from any immediate action.[21]

One of the umpires at the IV Corps maneuvers was an as-yet-obscure cavalryman, Col. George S. Patton, Jr. Like Whiteaker, he made no official recommendations. Four days before the Germans opened their offensive in France and the Low Countries, however, he concluded privately, "To be successful in rapid strokes the motorized div[ision] must have . . . first, organic aircraft for early information."[22]

While Whiteaker hesitated and Patton remained officially mute, another participant in the 1940 maneuver season acted. The commander of Battery I, 3d Battalion, 1st Field Artillery, Capt. William W. Ford, discovered that neither he nor anyone else he knew could obtain the services of an Air Corps observer. In the aftermath of the maneuvers, Ford, a 1920 West Point graduate and light-plane owner, submitted to the *Field Artillery Journal* an article, "Wings for Santa Barbara," in which he called for making light aircraft an integral part of field artillery battalions. Like Danford, he wanted both pilots and observers drawn from the Field Artillery. The article was important for several reasons. Ford defined the Field Artillery's observation problem with particular clarity and force. In the process he initiated a widespread discussion of his solution. Finally, he addressed the question of tactical employment and specifically the Air Corps' major critique—that light aviation could not survive in the modern battle area.[23]

Ford argued that the nature of modern war was such that victory depended on establishing air superiority, a necessary precondition for the landing of an American expeditionary force in Europe. Therefore, American war plans should assume that the Air Corps would establish air superiority or, at the minimum, air parity. Given either of these conditions, light airplanes could survive. As part of the field artillery battalion, the pilot and observer would already be familiar with the situation on the ground and would not require a lengthy period of orientation. Their flights would be short: They would simply hop to 500 feet to observe enemy positions and then land, all the while remaining behind friendly

---

[21] Ltr, Brig Gen R. O. Whiteaker, CG, 61st FA Brigade (Bde), to W. T. Piper, 15 Apr 41, J. E. P. Morgan Ms, MHI; Interview (Interv), R. J. Tierney with T. I. Case, Piper Aircraft Corporation, 21 Feb 62, *U.S. Army Aviation Digest (USAAD)* files, U.S. Army Aviation Museum Library, Fort Rucker, Ala. (hereafter cited as USAAML); Interv, L. B. Epstein with T. I. Case, c. 1975; Qualification Card, Lt Col J. M. Watson, 16 Feb 46, sub: Ofcr's and Warrant Ofcr's Qualification Card Copy; both in J. M. Watson Ms, U.S. Army Aviation and Troop Command History Office, St. Louis, Mo. (hereafter cited as USAA&TC).

[22] Patton did not make any recommendations concerning light aircraft in his report. Memo, Col G. S. Patton, Jr., Umpire, for Chief (Ch) Control Ofcr, 16 May 40, Personal and Official Corresp files, George S. Patton, Jr., Ms, Library of Congress, Washington, D.C. (hereafter cited as LC). He recorded his personal opinion in Notes, George S. Patton, Jr., 6 May [40], sub: March to Meridian, Military (Mil) Papers, in the same collection.

[23] W. W. Ford, "Wings for Santa Barbara," *FAJ* 31 (April 1941):232–34; Ltr, Brig Gen W. W. Ford to author, 20 Jun 82, Historian's files, U.S. Army Center of Military History, Washington, D.C. (hereafter cited as CMH); W. W. Ford, *Wagon Soldier* (North Adams, Mass.: Excelsior, 1980), pp. 105–14, 118.

Igor Sikorsky Hovers near a Tree in One of the Early Flights of the VS–300.

front lines. Enemy pursuits would find light aircraft, with upper surfaces painted to blend into the terrain, difficult to detect from altitude. If enemy pursuits descended to cruise at lower levels, they would become vulnerable to antiaircraft and small-arms fire. Ground observers, linked to the Field Artillery plane via radio, would often provide timely warning of the approach of enemy aircraft. Finally, if engaged by enemy pursuits, the artillery pilot would drop down to treetop level and throw his machine into a series of tight turns. A pursuit could not maneuver with a light aircraft and, if it made the attempt, ran a significant risk of crashing at such low altitudes.[24]

Danford, Ford, and Chandler (now a major) agreed that the Field Artillery needed its own aircraft under its own control. While Ford and Chandler were committed to light aircraft as the observer's platform, Danford remained more ambivalent. He regarded rotary-wing craft, either an improved autogiro or a helicopter, as the desirable solution. His expectations had some basis in recent developments. The Kellett Autogiro Company had developed a "jump start" version, a YG–1B, which could engage its motor to its rotor and rise

---

[24] Ford, "Wings for Santa Barbara," p. 233.

vertically 200 feet before disengaging and shifting power to its propeller. Like the helicopter, it was thus capable of vertical takeoff.

Danford was also hopeful about helicopters. Two American autogiro engineers, Harold Platt and W. Laurence LePage, had acquired the U.S. rights to the German helicopter and were building a prototype, eventually known as the Platt-LePage XR–1 ("R" stood for "rotary wing"), under an Air Corps contract. At the same time an emigré Russian engineer noted for his design of flying boats, Igor Sikorsky, and his design team at Stratford, Connecticut, had achieved a conceptual breakthrough in the development of a single-rotor helicopter. Sikorsky proposed a single main rotor that would provide direction, referred to as *cyclic control*, and lift, known as *collective control*. A small vertical rotor on a tail boom counteracted torque. Sikorsky flew his first prototype, the VS–300, on 14 September 1939 in a series of short hops, for a total flight time of about ten seconds. Although Sikorsky's success was revolutionary in its implications, the VS–300 clearly needed much more work before it could be considered anything other than highly experimental. In particular, the tail rotor presented many unsolved mysteries to the Sikorsky team. On 17 December 1940, an interagency meeting in Washington, with Chandler representing the Office of the Chief of Field Artillery, approved funding for further development of the Sikorsky design.[25]

The next day General Danford suggested that the War Department include at a minimum three light commercial aircraft—a Stinson 105/YO–54, a YG–1B autogiro, and a Platt-LePage helicopter, the XR–1—in the service tests for short-range observation aircraft from the 1939 design competition. Meanwhile, Chief of Staff Marshall had learned informally of the Field Artillery's problems with Air Corps equipment and asked the General Staff for a report on the status. "A smaller and possibly cheaper ship, maybe a purely commercial type, would serve the artillery purposes," observed Marshall. Danford's request, coming as it did on top of his proposal to create aviation organic to the Field Artillery, as well as Marshall's inquiry, injected the first notes of urgency into Air Corps deliberations on light aviation. Air Corps officers worked out an informal arrangement with their Field Artillery counterparts to transfer the first, and as yet only, O–49 to Fort Sill for comparative tests with the YO–54 and one other commercial aircraft. The Platt-LePage, even if the manufacturers met the delivery dates, was still a highly experimental craft, not ready for service tests. The autogiro would be ready for testing later in the spring.[26]

In a period of two years, Danford had thus publicly defined the aerial observation prob-

---

[25] Dorothy Cochran, et al., *The Aviation Careers of Igor Sikorsky* (Seattle: University of Washington Press, 1989), pp. 116–26; H. Franklin Gregory, *Anything a Horse Can Do: The Story of the Helicopter* (New York: Reynal and Hitchcock, 1944), p. 105; Frank K. Smith, *Legacy of Wings: The Story of Harold F. Pitcairn* (New York: Jason Aronson, 1981), pp. 255–56, 262–63; Butler, *Army Air Corps Airplanes and Observation*, pp. 145–49; Historical Division, Air Materiel Command, *AAF Helicopter Program*, 6 vols. (Wright Field, Ohio: Air Materiel Command, 1946), 1:11–13.

[26] Ltr, Brig Gen B. K. Yount, ACAC, to TAG, 6 Apr 40, sub: Service Test of Short-Range Liaison Aircraft; Ltr, A. P. Sullivan, TAGO, to Ch of Infantry (Inf), 13 Apr 40, sub: Service Test of Short-Range Aircraft; Ltr, Maj H. D. Clark, OCAC, to TAG, 15 Oct 40, sub: Service Test of Short-Range Liaison Aircraft; Ltr, Col H. C. Potter, XO, OCFA, to TAG, 18 Dec 40, sub: Service Test of Short-Range Liaison Aircraft, with Indorsement (Ind), Col G. E. Stratemeyer, XO, OCAC, to TAG, 7 Feb 41; Memo, Gen G. C. Marshall, Jr.; all located in TAGO Gen Document (Doc) file, 1940–1945, 452.1 (4–6–40), RG 407, NARA; MFR, 12 Feb 41, on Distribution Slip (DS), Col V. Meyer, Acting ACS, G–4, to TAG, 12 Feb 41, sub: Service Test of Short-Range Liaison Airplanes, ACS, G–4, Numerical file, 1921–March 1942, 27277–31, RG 165, NARA.

lem from the perspective of the Field Artillery and had advanced a solution that assigned an Air Corps light observation squadron organically to each division artillery headquarters. When Arnold had rejected this proposal, Danford, using the expertise accumulated at the Field Artillery School, had proposed Field Artillery aviation. With Ford's article in hand—the *Field Artillery Journal* did not publish it until April 1941—Danford even possessed the sketch of a tentative doctrine for employing organic aircraft. He also had, of course, Arnold's opposition, but the existing Air Corps observation squadrons had not yet demonstrated that they possessed the capacity to provide the desired results. While the War Department was not yet ready to abandon current doctrine and organization, Colonel Twaddle had implicitly recognized that the prevailing situation was unsatisfactory by alluding to the need to give observation squadrons a fair trial with "modern" equipment. It remained to be seen whether the War Department defined modern equipment as light aircraft, which was how Danford regarded the term, or light bombers, the Arnold solution. In the meantime, Danford had successfully maneuvered to avoid a definite refusal from the War Department.

Danford possessed three distinct advantages in this contest: his bureaucratic position, the professional reputation of his branch, and a clear idea of what he wanted. As a branch chief he had the opportunity by law, regulation, and custom to comment on a wide variety of issues and enjoyed a certain degree of access to the highest military and civilian leaders in the War Department. As the country edged closer to the possibility of war, the relative importance of the Field Artillery, based upon both its performance in the last war and the conflict then raging in Europe, could only increase in the counsels of the War Department. Finally, because Danford and his subordinates had an intellectual mastery of the subject, they could present their case convincingly to others—not the least important advantage when a question is inherently contentious.

None of these advantages, however, ensured the success of Danford's initiative. Arnold also had advantages of position, while the course of the war in Europe had certainly emphasized the importance of air (but not its ability to win the war unaided as some air power theorists had prophesied earlier). The Air Corps' prestige with the White House, Congress, and the public at large was all out of proportion to that of the Field Artillery. But at the same time Arnold lacked a sure grasp of the capabilities of the ground arms, a potentially fatal disadvantage since ground officers on the War Department General Staff would ultimately decide the question. To a certain extent Danford's prospects for success thus hinged on his ability to keep the decision-making process confined to the War Department and not let it become an issue of wide public debate.

Air Observation for the Cavalry, Armor, and Infantry, 1939–1940

The prospects of the Cavalry, armor, and Infantry obtaining their own organic aerial observation were not nearly as promising as those of the Field Artillery, because none of them enjoyed the same combination of advantages. Of the four, the Cavalry's outlook was probably the most dismal in December 1939. The U.S. Army Cavalry at that time was a profoundly schizophrenic institution, one segment in the process of dying, the other in the process of being born. Mounted units of course were nearing the end of a long and glorious history, though not without the stubborn resistance of certain horse soldiers. No one fought their demise more bitterly or effectively than the last chief of Cavalry, Maj. Gen.

John K. Herr (1938–1942). It was a measure of his success that at the end of 1939 the U.S. Army, despite the destruction of the Polish cavalry by German armor in the fall, still retained a mounted division while mustering only one mechanized brigade. In an organization undergoing such fundamental, even primal changes, all other questions were liable to receive less attention and energy than they deserved. Nevertheless, the Cavalry, both horse and mechanized, addressed the question of organic air observation.[27]

In December 1939 the Cavalry's position on aerial observation was very similar to that of the Field Artillery the previous year. The similarity was not entirely by chance, because Generals Danford and Herr kept one another informed about their initiatives on the subject. The Cavalry had its own distinct tactical concerns, primarily observation for screens in close contact with enemy forces and for advance guards during pursuits. Herr preferred making an observation squadron organic to each cavalry division. His preoccupation was of course with horse cavalry, but the commander of the army's proto-armored force, the 7th Cavalry Brigade (Mechanized) at Fort Knox, Kentucky, Brig. Gen. Adna R. Chaffee, Jr., shared Herr's interest in organic aviation. In 1938, during the brigade's first attempt to march cross-country, Chaffee's predecessor, Brig. Gen. Daniel Van Voorhis, had discovered that aircraft were essential to providing effective control of the multiple columns of the brigade when on the move. The brigade's subsequent experience had simply confirmed the importance of aviation in assisting the unit to perform a variety of missions. Chaffee favored assigning an observation squadron to each mechanized brigade. He envisioned that the squadron would perform route reconnaissance, column control, liaison, and artillery fire direction for the mechanized artillery battalion that supported the brigade. Arnold opposed such schemes, pointing out that the Air Corps had programmed observation squadrons on a one-to-one ratio with cavalry divisions, an explanation that at least momentarily satisfied Herr, if not Chaffee.[28]

General Herr still preferred the autogiro, based on its field tests with mounted units earlier in the decade. During the winter of 1939–1940, however, a board of officers at Fort Knox and the Cavalry Board at Fort Riley separately reported that the autogiro was "not fully satisfactory" and recommended concentrating on light aircraft, conclusions that Herr endorsed without enthusiasm. He preferred urging the Air Corps to fund research to perfect autogiros and helicopters. One man, Col. Byron Q. Jones, provided much of the intellectual force behind the conversion of this tepid assessment of light planes into a full-scale endorsement of both flivver aircraft and the use of cavalry pilots and mechanics.[29]

---

[27] Mildred H. Gillie, *Forging the Thunderbolt: A History of the Development of the Armored Force* (Harrisburg, Pa.: Military Service Publishing Co., 1947), pp. 136–61.

[28] Memo, Maj Gen J. K. Herr, CC, for CAC, 19 Dec 39, sub: Air Unit for the Cav Div, with Ind, Brig Gen A. R. Chaffee for CG, V Corps Area, 29 Dec 39; Memo, CAC for CC, sub: Air Unit for the Cav Div, 5 Jan 40, Microfilm A1409, AFHRA. For an account of the 700-mile motor march of the 7th Cavalry Brigade and the lessons derived, see Anon, "The Mechanized Cavalry Takes the Field," *The Cavalry Journal* 47 (July–August 1938):291–300. A. R. Chaffee, "The Seventh Cavalry Brigade in the First Army Maneuvers," *The Cavalry Journal* 48 (November–December 1939):450–61.

[29] Ind, Lt Col K. S. Bradford, XO, OCC, to Commandant, Cav School, 12 Mar 40, on Minutes, Board of Officers (B/O), 18 Oct 39, 23 Oct 39, 5 Jan 40, 20 Feb 40, sub: Autogiro, with Ind, Brig Gen R. C. Richardson, Commandant, Cav School, to CC, 22 Mar 40; Ltr, Maj J. H. Claybrook, OCC, to Maj F. P. Tompkins, 25 Jun 40, OCC, Gen Corresp, 1920–1942, 452.1, RG 177, NARA.

THE GROUND ARMS SEEK THEIR OWN AIRCRAFT, 1939–1941　　　　45

GENERALS HERR (*left*) AND CHAFFEE IN FRONT OF AN M3 SCOUT CAR, FORT KNOX, KENTUCKY, MAY 1939

Jones, a pre–World War I military aviator and one of General Mitchell's technical advisers, was one of the few proponents in the Air Corps during the interwar period for the idea that air was part of an air-ground team. Assigned to Fort Knox, he became involved in working on the problem of air-armor cooperation. He was an early and persistent advocate of light aviation, particularly of its value for contact missions, and was well placed to influence both Generals Chaffee and Herr; the latter was a personal friend. For them Jones became a one-man source of papers on organic air doctrine, force structure, and equipment. While he recognized the value of commercial models, his long-term goal was the development of an armed, single-seat light aircraft for direct fire support. In adopting this stance, he provided the intellectual bridge between the "cavalry reconnaissance" tactics of the 3d Observation Group in World War I and the experiments with armed light aircraft and helicopters during World War II and after that led ultimately to the armed helicopter.[30]

---

[30] Ltr, Col Byron Q. Jones to Maj Gen J. K. Herr, 12 Apr 40; Memo, [Col Byron Q. Jones] for Col M. Magruder, President, Board on Obsn Avn, 12 Mar 40, sub: Obsn Avn; Memo, Col Byron Q. Jones for Commandant, Army War College (AWC), 9 Dec 36, sub: Corps and Army Organization, Army Components; Lecture, [Col Byron Q. Jones], sub: Copy of Presentation, 2d part of Student Committee No. 6, G–3 Course, Class of 1938–1939; all in OCC, Gen Corresp, 1920–1942, 452.1, RG 177, NARA; "Byron Quinby Jones," in Cullum, *Biographical Register*, 8:249.

The success of the German *Blitzkrieg* against the Western Allies in May and June 1940 led the War Department to create the Armored Force Headquarters separate from the Cavalry. This ended the schism in the branch. But the decision left the Cavalry's reputation for relevance in modern war in free fall. Although promoted to major general, Chaffee, commanding general of the Armored Force, lacked entree into the War Department's internal decision making. He was a field commander, not a branch chief. He was also heavily involved in the expansion of armor in the Army. The 7th Cavalry Brigade (Mechanized) provided the nucleus for the 1st Armored Division, organized at Fort Knox on 15 July 1940, and the 2d Armored Division, activated at Fort Benning, Georgia, on the same day.[31]

The umpire from the 1940 IV Corps maneuvers, Colonel Patton, took command of the 2d Armored Brigade of the 2d Armored Division. Promoted to brigadier general in October 1940, he became the acting division commander the next month. He was intrigued to discover that the Infantry Board at Fort Benning was service-testing one of the competitors of the O–49, the Ryan YO–51 "Flying Motorcycle." Heavily flapped and with an unusually large wing area, the YO–51 could take off at speeds of approximately thirty miles per hour, making it exceptionally well suited for short-field operations. The Infantry Board permitted the division to use the aircraft in all its exercises and maneuvers. "It has proved . . . a valuable aid in transmitting orders to subordinate units and in locating and identifying such units," Patton reported. He and his staff also used it "to check the disposition of the command." On 8 January 1941, he recommended that Chaffee encourage "the rapid development and procurement" of aircraft similar to the YO–51. Until they became available, he urged that the Air Corps procure two Piper Cub–type aircraft from commercial manufacturers for each observation squadron assigned to an armored division. As long as the commander of an armored division had the light aircraft subject to his control, Patton was content for the Air Corps to man and maintain them. He remained committed to this proposition through mid-1942.[32]

The Infantry was seemingly well positioned to take the lead in the fight for organic air. It did not suffer from the disabilities that weakened the Cavalry and the Armored Force and possessed a professional reputation even greater than that of the Field Artillery. Moreover, there was interest in light aircraft within the branch. An infantry officer and light-plane enthusiast, Lt. Col. E. D. Cooke, in late 1940 called for light aircraft organic to the Infantry in an article in the *Infantry Journal*. Cooke, writing in a whimsical style but with a definite edge about the responsiveness of the Air Corps, became the first ground officer to make such a public declaration. Unfortunately for his idea, the incoming chief of Infantry, Maj. Gen. Courtney H. Hodges (1941–1942), was convinced that an infantry observer in a vertical-takeoff, rotary-wing aircraft piloted by an Air Corps offi-

---

[31] James E. Hewes, *From Root to MacNamara: Army Organization and Administration, 1900–1963*, Special Studies (Washington, D.C.: U.S. Army Center of Military History, 1975), pp. 65–66. Headquarters, and Headquarters Company, 1st Armored Division, perpetuates the lineage of Headquarters and Headquarters Troop, 7th Cavalry Brigade (Mechanized). John B. Wilson, comp., *Armies, Corps, Divisions, and Separate Brigades*, Army Lineage Series (Washington, D.C.: U.S. Army Center of Military History, 1987), pp. 119–20, 149–50.

[32] Ltr, Brig Gen George S. Patton, Jr., Acting CG, 2d Armored (Armd) Div, to CG, I Armd Corps, 8 Jan 41, sub: Courier Airplanes, Gen Corresp, Patton Ms, LC. See also Ltr, Maj Gen George S. Patton, Jr., CG, I Armd Corps, to Maj Gen Henry H. Arnold, Deputy Chief of Staff, Army (DCSA) for Air, WD, 11 Apr 41; Memo, Patton for CG, Armd Forces, 10 Jun 41, sub: Recommendations for the Organization of an Armd Div; both in Patton Ms, LC. Anon, "3 'Flying Motorcycles' on Order for Army," *Western Flying* 3 (1 March 1940):2.

cer was the correct solution for his branch and was prepared to await the Air Corps' development of a suitable craft. Hodges' attitude, given the unresolved engineering problems in rotary-wing technology, meant that infantry regiments would not receive their own aircraft for several years.[33]

Hodges thus effectively vetoed consideration of light planes for the Infantry and demonstrated the key role played by a branch chief in the development of new equipment, organization, and doctrine. While Herr and Chaffee continued to strive for the adoption of organic air, the constraints under which each man labored made their eventual success problematic at best. Their most hopeful prospect (and that of Infantry officers like Cooke) was that the Field Artillery might succeed and thereby open the way for their respective branches.

The Fight for Organic Air, January–September 1941

The first nine months of 1941 represented in some respects a replay of the preceding year. In the ground arms the same officers continued to favor the adoption of organic aircraft operated by ground forces officers, while the same Air Corps officers defended existing aerial observation organization and doctrine. There were, however, three major interrelated differences between the two years. The dispute over aerial observation in 1940 had a certain abstract quality absent in 1941. Service test quantities of O–49s at last began reaching the field in time to take part in the most extensive and largest-scale maneuvers in the history of the U.S. Army to that date. Practical experience added a depth and precision to the arguments, even if the basic doctrinal predispositions of the disputants remained unchanged. At the same time light-aircraft manufacturers made their appearance as a pressure group. Although innocent of any doctrinal proclivities, they did want to sell light planes. Because ground officers had few, if any, reservations about using light aircraft in combat, while Air Corps officers had many, the net effect of the intervention of the light-plane manufacturers was to favor the ground arms. Finally, the impact of the campaign of 1940 in France and the Low Countries continued to reverberate through the force structure of the Army. The failure of French and British observation squadrons in 1940 compelled the Air Corps to reorganize its own squadrons, if only in terms of equipment. Such a necessity weakened the position of the Air Corps at a time when it was trying to defend the status quo with respect to Generals Danford, Herr, and Chaffee.

Although General Chaffee was in the bureaucratically weakest position of all the senior ground officers seeking organic air, he inadvertently drew the light aircraft lobbyists into the situation, a necessary if not sufficient condition for the outcome he desired. Early in 1941 he "was pushing as much as he dared in Washington for the use of light aircraft organic to Army units." He believed "intensely" that all the combat branches needed organic aviation. He secured Stinson Model 105s—which under the designation YO–54 were General Arnold's choice to replace O–49s—for testing with armor units at Forts

---

[33] E. D. Cooke, "All God's Chillun Got Wings," *Infantry Journal* 47 (November–December 1940):603; Ind, Col Harry F. Hazlett, XO, Office (Ofc) of the Ch of Inf, to CC, 18 Dec 41, on Ltr, Lt Col R. W. Beasley, XO, OCFA, to CAC, 12 Dec 41, sub: Mil Characteristics for Light Liaison-Type Airplanes, OCFA, Gen Corresp, 1917–1943, 452.1/C–25, RG 177, NARA.

Knox and Benning, but the aircraft proved unsatisfactory. They could only take off from "smooth, prepared runways"—in fact, they required a 1,200-foot takeoff roll on turf and were so lightly constructed that they came apart when using rough, ungraded landing strips. Frustrated by his lack of success, Chaffee inquired directly to the Piper Aircraft Corporation about the possibility of obtaining Cubs for use during mechanized maneuvers to test their ability to direct armor columns from the air.[34]

Thomas Case, the Piper representative from the 1940 maneuvers, flew a Cub J–3 in conjunction with exercises at Fort Knox from 10 until 15 February 1941. On the last day the Armored Force Board inspected the aircraft and decided that it had "very definite possibilities for use on the command, liaison, and courier missions." The board recommended that the Air Corps purchase two Piper Cubs for further testing, a conclusion that Chaffee, but not the Air Corps, heartily endorsed. The Air Corps Materiel Division rejected the request, citing the comparative Civil Aeronautics Administration performance figures for the Cub and the YO–54, which indicated that the YO–54 was superior in all categories. In fact, the YO–54 was superior in speed, range, and endurance, the characteristics by which the Materiel Division normally judged aircraft. Chaffee took exception based on data the Armored Force Board had collected at Fort Knox. While the Air Corps did not purchase the Cubs, the War Department agreed to permit two armor officers to attend the Fort Sill service tests of the O–49 and several commercial models, including the YO–54, as official representatives of the Armored Force. The Piper Cub was not included in the test, but the Office of the Chief of Field Artillery arranged for the manufacturer to give an informal demonstration of a J–3 at Fort Sill at the same time, which Chaffee's representatives were also invited to observe.[35]

Chaffee's inquiry set off a complex reaction within the Piper Aircraft Corporation and ultimately within the light aircraft industry as a whole. Lieutenant Watson's request for a light plane the preceding summer had first drawn the attention of the president of the company, William T. Piper, to the market potential represented by the Army. During the intervening months, he had discussed the possibility of the Field Artillery's use of light aircraft with one of his employees, Michael J. Strok, a second lieutenant in the Field Artillery Reserve. Strok was enthusiastic about the prospect. Chaffee's request for a Cub consequently arrived after Piper had an opportunity to carefully weigh the commercial prospects. If there was a hard-headed business sense behind much of what followed, there was also a large measure of old-fashioned patriotism. Piper believed implicitly both in his product and in his country; he drew great satisfaction from the thought that the one might help the other. His emotional response was as important as his realism, because it allowed him to connect on a purely nonrational level with some equally hard-headed soldiers who cared nothing at all about the profitability of the Piper Aircraft Corporation but deeply about the success of the U.S. Army. The fact that Piper had served as an infantryman in the War with Spain and an engineer in World War I did not harm his case at all. Moreover, it ensured that he knew the difference between expressions of interest by, on one hand, a sec-

---

[34] Ltr, Maj W. H. Barnes, Assistant Adjutant General (AAG), HQ, Armd Force, to CAC, 20 Feb 41, sub: Cmd and Liaison Airplanes, with Ind, Maj B. E. Meyers, XO, Materiel Div, OCAC, to TAG, 27 Feb 41, TAGO Gen Doc file, 1940–1945, 452.1 (2–20–41), RG 407, NARA; Interv, Tierney with Case, 6 Feb 62.
[35] Interv, Tierney with Case, 21 Feb 61; Ind, Meyers to TAG, 27 Feb 41.

ond lieutenant in the Officer's Reserve Corps or a first lieutenant in the National Guard and on the other a general officer in the Regular Army. Chaffee's request thus precipitated much more than the dispatch of Case and a J–3 to Forts Knox and Sill.[36]

Piper and one of his directors, John E. P. Morgan, who was also president of a light-aviation trade association, immediately composed a letter to the Secretary of War, Henry L. Stimson, on the military potential of light aircraft. They set off for Washington and an interview with Stimson, who was encouraging but noncommittal. From the very beginning, Morgan lobbied the War Department in his role as president of the trade association, which meant that he also represented the interests of two other light aircraft companies: the Aeronca Aircraft Corporation of Middletown, Ohio, and the Taylorcraft Aviation Corporation of Alliance, Ohio. Morgan also visited his friend and fellow Wall Street investment banker, Robert A. Lovett, newly appointed assistant secretary of war for air. Lovett wanted to shift productive capacity from O–49s to combat aircraft, and was receptive to the idea of an off-the-shelf commercial airplane replacing it. But the attitude of officers in the Office of the Chief of the Air Corps was that the greatest contribution the light aircraft industry could make to mobilization was to cease production for the duration of the emergency. Morgan received more sympathetic treatment in the Office of the Chief of Field Artillery.[37]

While Morgan lobbied, Piper attempted to stimulate demand in the field. He instructed his district sales managers to meet with the commanders of local military installations and to demonstrate the Cub's potential. His manager for the West Coast and Intermountain Region, Henry S. Wann, approached several officers, including the chief of staff of the 3d Division at Fort Lewis, Washington, Lt. Col. Dwight D. Eisenhower. But Eisenhower, like most of Wann's contacts, was working under great pressure just to stay abreast of the administrative and training needs of a mobilizing force. Although he had no time to view a demonstration, he assured Wann that he was familiar with the military potential of light aircraft. Eisenhower had flown extensively in the Philippines during the late 1930s. This encounter took on significance only in retrospect. Of more immediate importance, Case also continued his work. On 17 March he and Piper flew to Camp Bowie, Texas, to allow the Texas National Guard to make an unofficial evaluation of a Cub J–3. The commander of the 61st Field Artillery Brigade, General Whiteaker, arranged for the Third Army commander, Lt. Gen. Walter C. Krueger, to attend. Krueger too became a supporter of light aircraft.[38]

In May 1941, after many delays, the Air Corps held service tests that appeared to affirm the superiority of the O–49. It possessed the best speed, climb, range, and service ceiling of the aircraft tested. The O–49 also had excellent short-field landing and takeoff characteristics, the product of manually operated flaps and slots, new technology in 1941.

---

[36] Intervs, author with Col Michael J. Strok, 30 Jun 82, CMH; Tierney with Case, 21 Feb 62; Epstein with Case, c. 1976; Francis, *Mr. Piper and His Cubs*, pp. 10–13, 79–88.

[37] Ltr, W. T. Piper to H. L. Stimson, Sec of War, 18 Feb 41; Memo, [J. E. P. Morgan], Sep 41, sub: History of the First Grasshopper Squadron; Memo, [Morgan], sub: Grasshopper Washington Story; all in Morgan Ms, MHI. Ind, Col W. C. Potter, XO, OCFA, to CAC, 17 Apr 41, TAGO Gen Doc file, 1940–1945, 452.1 (2–20–41), RG 407, NARA. Interv, author with Strok, 30 Jun 82.

[38] Intervs, author with Wann, 27 Aug 82; Tierney with Case, 21 Feb 62; Epstein with Case, c. 1976; author with Strok, 30 Jun 82.

MR. PIPER BRIEFS OTHER MEMBERS OF THE GRASSHOPPER SQUADRON DURING THE LOUISIANA MANEUVERS OF 1941. *Left to Right:* MR. MORGAN, J. M. HELBERT, MR. PIPER, T. H. MILLER (*with glasses*), DAVID KRESS (*below Miller*), MR. WANN, AND MR. CASE.

Of its competitors, only the Cub proved an acceptable substitute. The Air-Ground Procedures Board also observed the tests. The members reported to the commandant of the Field Artillery School that the Cub, because of its greater maneuverability and smaller size, was more likely to survive if attacked by opposing pursuits. Subsequent service tests by the Cavalry Board also found the light plane an acceptable substitute. Lovett was still interested in shifting the productive capacity used to build the O–49 to other types of aircraft. On the basis of these results, he arranged for twelve light aircraft, flown by factory pilots and led by Morgan, to participate in the summer and fall maneuvers. They were, in effect, in competition with the Air Corps O–49s. The manufacturers' contingent included 8 Cub J–3s, designated YO–59s (subsequently L–4s), 2 Taylorcraft planes, designated YO–57s (later L–2s), and 2 Aeronca planes, designated YO–58s (later L–3s). In appearance and standard performance measures they were very similar.[39]

During 1941 light aircraft participated in the Second Army maneuvers in Tennessee in June, the 1st Cavalry Division maneuvers at Fort Bliss, Texas, in July, the Second and

---

[39] Memo, Maj G. K. Gailey, General Staff, for Acting ACS, War Plans Division (WPD), 14 Mar 41, sub: Liaison-Type Airplanes, WPD, Gen Corresp, 1920–1942, 3807–84, RG 165, NARA; Ltr, TAGO to CS, GHQ, 19 Jun 41, sub: Test of Liaison Airplanes, GHQ, Gen Corresp, 1940–1942, 452.1 (Airplanes), RG 337, NARA. Rpt, Brown, et al., to Commandant, FAS, 19 Aug 41.

THE GROUND ARMS SEEK THEIR OWN AIRCRAFT, 1939–1941

"Gas Stop." A Light Aircraft of the Grasshopper Squadron Takes on Gas at a Country Filling Station During the Carolina Maneuvers.

Third Army maneuvers in Louisiana in August and September, and the First Army and IV Corps maneuvers in the Carolinas in October and November. Patton, promoted to major general in April 1941, was frustrated by the Air Corps' refusal to purchase off-the-shelf light aircraft as he had recommended. He bought his own light plane, a Stinson Voyager, and acquired his pilot's license. He flew it in both the Tennessee and Louisiana maneuvers. The success of the 2d Armored Division in those maneuvers heightened the impact made by a very senior officer controlling an armored division from the air. The tactical work by Morgan's flight for the 1st Cavalry Division and later Third Army proved even more arresting. Officers in light planes directing fire for field artillery battalions and conducting reconnaissance missions for higher headquarters proved so beneficial to Third Army that midway through the Louisiana maneuvers the umpires barred Morgan's pilots from flying such missions. Their presence, ruled the umpires, gave an unfair advantage to Third Army. In the process the light planes solidified the support of senior officers like Generals Krueger and Patton and Krueger's new chief of staff, the recently promoted Colonel Eisenhower, and gained new adherents such as the commander of the 1st Cavalry Division, Maj. Gen. Innis P. Swift, and his chief of staff, Col. Joseph M. Swing. Swift added the appellation "grasshopper" to light-plane lore when he saw a J–3 with Wann at the controls bouncing to a halt after landing on a stretch of unprepared desert near Fort Bliss. Thereafter the demonstration flight of light planes became the "Grasshopper Squadron," and grasshopper became a synonym for light aircraft during World War II.[40]

The service tests at Fort Sill had found the J–3 Cub an acceptable substitute for the O–49, meaning that the Cub provided adequate but inferior performance. But in the maneuvers light planes, particularly the J–3, actually proved superior to the O–49 in certain critical areas. Because the Cub weighed less, it could better operate out of wet and muddy fields. With less wing area, the Cub was more easily tied down when on the ground. (The only loss of a light aircraft during the maneuvers occurred when an O–49 broke its moorings in a wind storm and sailed into one of them.) Light planes could land and take off from ordinary two-lane roads, which O–49s, with their greater wingspan, could not do when there were obstacles close to the sides of the roads. In the air, the Cub was more nimble; it was able to turn and dive more quickly than the O–49. Pursuit pilots who made mock passes found it relatively easy to line up the O–49 in their gunsights and difficult to do so with the J–3. The O–49 excelled at flying commanders and staff officers behind friendly lines. Eisenhower later declared that for the liaison mission the O–49 was the best he saw during the entire war, which suggests that the engineers at Stinson succeeded in designing exactly the aircraft that Arnold and the Air Corps had wanted. It was not the type of aircraft, however, that Danford and the Field Artillery needed.[41]

At Fort Sill, officers of the Field Artillery School, taking as their basic assumption that the Field Artillery "must have aerial observation," prepared a series of reports that buttressed the chief of Field Artillery's call for organic aviation and in effect produced supporting documents for his case whenever he chose to reopen the issue. Twenty-two years of stagnation in Air Corps observation and that branch's current inability to settle on a standard type convinced two committees and one board that the existing War Department policy of assigning the artillery observation mission to the Air Corps would not work. All made the same general points but had different emphases.[42]

In May a committee of officers from the 1940–1941 advance course argued that the increase of the calibers of field artillery weapons since World War I and the greatly

---

[40] Rpt, Lt Col C. L. Hyssong, Adjutant General (AG), Third Army, to TAG, 5 Aug 41, sub: Test of Liaison Airplanes; Ltr, McNair to TAG, 8 Sep 41, sub: Light Obsn Airplanes, GHQ, Gen Corresp, 1940–1942, 452.1/33 (Airplanes) (Binder #1), RG 337, NARA; Interv, author with Wann, 27 Aug 82; Ltr, Lt Col H. S. Wann to author, 10 Apr 91, Historian's files, CMH; Ltr, Wann to Lt Col J. R. Riddle, 1 Feb 62, H. S. Wann Ms, Historian's files, CMH; L. Collins, "Grasshopper Haven," *Air Facts* (June 1943):7–18; Diary, J. E. P. Morgan, 15 and 17 Jul 41, Morgan Ms, MHI. For Patton's experiences, see Ltrs, Maj Gen George S. Patton, Jr., CG, 2d Armd Div, to Lt Col W. C. Crane, GHQ, 25 Apr 41; Patton to Air Assoc., Inc., 28 Oct 41; both in Gen Corresp, Patton Ms, LC; Briefing, [Patton], May 41, sub: Orientation on Maneuvers; Maj Gen G. S. Patton, Jr., CG, Desert Training Center (Ctr), "Notes on Tactics and Techniques of Desert Warfare (Provisional)," 30 Jul 42; both in Mil Papers, Patton Ms, LC. Edgar Snow, "Made in America Blitz: We Built a Mechanized Striking Force," *The Saturday Evening Post* (7 February 1942):37–38; Clipping, *Shreveport [La.] Times*, 7 Apr 42, mentions that Patton flew his own plane, in Patton Ms, LC. Konrad F. Schreier, Jr., considerably overstates Patton's influence in "How the Grasshopper Earned Its Wings," *Aviation History* (May 1996):30–36.

[41] Memo, Morgan, Sep 41, sub: History of the First Grasshopper Squadron; Ltr, Lt Col S. L. Ellis, Ch of Avn, Third Army, to Morgan, 12 Sep 41; Ltr, Lt Gen W. Krueger to Morgan, 4 Oct 41; Diary, Morgan, 21, 26 Aug, 10 Sep 41, all in Morgan Ms, MHI; Ltr, McNair to CG, First Army, 22 Dec 41, sub: Comments on First Army Versus IV Army Corps Maneuvers, 16–30 Nov 41, GHQ, Gen Corresp, 1940–1942, 354.2/26 (First Army), RG 337, NARA. For background, see Christopher R. Gabel, *The U.S. Army GHQ Maneuvers of 1941* (Washington, D.C.: U.S. Army Center of Military History, 1991).

[42] Quote from Rpt, Lt Col E. P. Tuttle, et al., chair, Advance Course (Special) No. 2, 1940–1941, 14 May 41, sub: Obsn Avn Required for Arty Missions, Tab D in "Field Artillery Observation."

enhanced mobility of all units meant escalating difficulties for traditional methods of ground survey and observation—functions that had to be performed accurately if the field artillery was to deliver indirect fire on target. In these changed circumstances only an aerial observation post could locate targets, adjust fire, and keep nearby hostile territory under constant scrutiny, the mission that the Field Artillery labeled surveillance. The Field Artillery needed its own aircraft, flown and maintained by its own personnel, to ensure even adequate performance of these missions. The second committee, drawn from the next advance course, evaluated the performance of the O–49 and the Piper J–3 and concluded that the latter was the more suitable Field Artillery aircraft. The Air-Ground Procedures Board, which continued meeting in August 1941, accepted these conclusions and argued that the War Department needed to organize a school for aerial fire direction at Fort Sill. The Air Corps school at Brooks Field treated fire direction as incidental to other observation training. It did not provide adequate preparation for observers who would spend most of their time directing fire from the air. The title of the second report succinctly summarized the conclusion of all three: "Artillery Should Carry Its Own OPs." Pressure for a Field Artillery aircraft was building, not only from light aircraft manufacturers but also now from the lower echelons of the Field Artillery.[43]

When Morgan returned to Washington to resume his lobbying, he brought with him some powerful evidence in favor of light aircraft. Morgan summarized the essence of his argument in a typically colorful phrase: "Why use a Rolls Royce when a Ford will do?" He also made a number of informal contacts. Along with Major Chandler, who was taking flying lessons, and the Armored Force liaison officer at the War Department, Col. George L. King, he organized the "Fuddy-Duddies Flying Club" for senior officers serving in Washington. It was a way of sharing enthusiasm for flying and discreetly selling the organic air concept. Soon its members included Assistant Secretary of War John J. McCloy. "Blitz" McCloy, Secretary Stimson's troubleshooter, had both interest and empathy. He had served as the operations officer of a field artillery brigade on the Western Front and had vivid recollections of "bitter disputes [about obtaining observed fire] with the air people . . . over a field telephone. . . . The planes never seemed to do the things we wanted them to do."[44]

However hopeful Morgan might have been about the future prospects of light aviation in the ground forces, aerial observation in the summer and fall of 1941 remained the province of the Air Corps. General Arnold had not changed his position on the issue. Paradoxically, his ability to impose his views had simultaneously waxed and waned. Institutionally he was in a much stronger position: He was almost autonomous. In July 1941 the War Department created the Army Air Forces to combine in one office both tech-

---

[43] Rpt, Brown, et al., 19 Aug 41. Rpt, Lt Col J. M. Jenkins, et al., 12 Aug 41, sub: Rpt of Committee 24: Artillery Should Carry Its Own Observation Posts (OPs), Tab E in "Field Artillery Observation."

[44] Diary, Morgan, Sep 41–18 Mar 42, 3 Jun 42, Morgan Ms, MHI. Only a summary is available for 25 September 1941 through 17 March 1942, a period in which Morgan says he did not keep a detailed diary. Internal evidence does not altogether support this contention. McCloy's recollections of his World War I experiences are in Ltr, John J. McCloy to Lt Gen Lesley J. McNair, 3 Mar 42, HQ, Army Ground Forces (AGF), Gen Corresp, 1942–1948, 353/2 (Restricted [R]) (FA Air Obsn), RG 337, NARA; Interv, Maurice Matloff with John J. McCloy, 24 Oct 83, Office of the Secretary of Defense (OSD), History Office, The Pentagon, Washington, D.C. For a recent study of McCloy, see Kai Bird, *The Chairman: John J. McCloy, The Making of the American Establishment* (New York: Simon and Schuster, 1992).

nical and operational control over aviation. Arnold became both the commanding general of the Army Air Forces and the deputy chief of staff for air, Marshall's chief adviser on air matters. The reorganization meant that Arnold was no longer even nominally equivalent to branch chiefs like Herr and Danford. (The name of the branch to which air officers and enlisted men belonged, however, remained the Army Air Corps.) The Office of the Chief of Air Corps remained a separate but subordinate organization responsible for training and materiel. It reported to Arnold as did the Air Force Combat Command, the headquarters responsible for all air units in the field. The reorganization also relieved Arnold's staff, now known as the Air Staff, from detailed General Staff supervision of its activities. The Air Staff's mobilization plans, approved by the War Department, reflected Arnold's opinions on the survivability of observation equipment. Despite the 1939 decision to include three short-range aircraft such as the O–49 in each observation squadron, the Air Staff now classified them as "obsolete," to be replaced by modified twin-engine bombers—Arnold's favorite observation type—as soon as possible.[45]

The airmen, however, were much less intellectually united than Arnold's consistency indicated. At least some air officers conceded both the survivability of light aircraft and their utility for liaison and possibly even Field Artillery observation missions. The commander of the Air Force Combat Command, Lt. Gen. Delos C. Emmons, even went so far as to formally propose creation of one light aircraft squadron organic to each division, manned by Air Corps personnel. After concurrence by Arnold's headquarters, the War Department approved the new organization. Arnold did not personally comment on the decision, but his subsequent actions demonstrated that approval of the Emmons proposal did not indicate any change in his view of the survivability of light aircraft. The new Army Air Forces light-plane squadron did, however, reflect an awareness of just how popular with ground commanders light aircraft had proved during the maneuvers. Left unclear was whether the Air Staff would actually program the light planes and if so, at what time.[46]

Late in the maneuver season the Army Air Forces fielded a demonstration flight of twelve commercial light aircraft manned by Air Corps personnel. Air Corps pilots were trained to fly aircraft that bored their way through the sky, pulled aloft by one or more powerful engines. Light aircraft floated with little more engine power than needed to keep them aloft. Arnold and the Air Staff regarded light aircraft as inferior to, rather than different from, service aircraft. The reigning view was that any pilot who flew a high-speed

---

[45] Memo, Arnold for CSA, 8 Oct 41, sub: Army Maneuvers; Memo, Col W. E. Lynd, Air Spt Section, GHQ, to CS, GHQ, 14 Oct 41, sub: Gen Arnold's Comments on Army Maneuvers, GHQ, Gen Corresp, 1940–1942, 354.2/1, RG 337, NARA; Chart, A–4, AS, 12 Jul 41, sub: 54 Groups (Grps), 1st Avn Strength with Suitable Equipment, Inclosure in Memo, Spaatz, 12 Jul 41, sub: Augmentation of the Various Army Avn Objectives; Chart, A–4, AS, 27 Jun 41, sub: 84 Grps All with Suitable Combat Equipment, WPD, Gen Corresp, 1920–1942, 3807/98, 3907/102, RG 165, NARA. For the very complex organization of the Army Air Forces from July 1941 until March 1942, see Wesley Frank Craven and James Lea Cate, eds., *The Army Air Forces in World War II*, 7 vols. (Chicago: University of Chicago Press, 1948–1958), 1:114–15. Robert F. Futrell, *Command of Observation Aviation: A Study in Control of Tactical Air Power* (Maxwell Air Force Base, Ala.: Historical Division, 1952), pp. 32–35, details the organization of observation aviation within this new structure.

[46] Ltr, Lt Gen Delos C. Emmons, AF Combat Cmd, to CG, AAF, 23 Oct 41, sub: Obsn Organization and Equipment, with Ind, Lt Col C. L. Hyssong, AG, GHQ, to CG, AAF, 24 Oct 41; Memo, Spaatz for CSA, 30 Oct 41, sub: Organization and Equipment for Obsn Units in the Air Spt Cmd, OCSA Numerical file, 1920–1942, 21276/8, RG 165, NARA.

service aircraft could fly a low-speed light aircraft. Consequently, the pilots assigned to the demonstration flight received no special transition training. They landed at speeds normal to the larger and heavier service planes they usually flew and frequently tore off the landing gear as a consequence. This performance did not inspire confidence among those ground forces officers who were veteran light-plane pilots or among ground commanders. Contrasted with the achievements of the Grasshopper Squadron, the first essay by the Army Air Forces into light aircraft raised questions about its professional mastery of the technology.[47]

Conclusion

In the fall of 1941 the contention over organic air had narrowed in practical terms to a dispute between the Field Artillery and the Army Air Forces. On one side stood the deeply held professional opinions of experienced officers in an arm essential to the success of the combined arms team in any future conflict with the Germans. Reinforcing the Field Artillery position was the presumed example of the German Army in the 1940 campaign, the U.S. Army's maneuver experience over the past two years, and the experiments with massed fire at Fort Sill. Among ground officers advocating organic air, only the chief of Field Artillery possessed the location in the military hierarchy, the sense that reform was critical for his branch to achieve its larger wartime mission, and the prestige needed to press a decision at the highest levels. The weakness of his case lay in his grasp, or lack of it, of air operations and whether the Royal Air Force and, if war came, the Army Air Forces could establish air superiority. Whether light planes could survive in disputed airspace remained a question of considerable practical importance for which there existed as yet only theoretical answers.

The commanding general of the Army Air Forces enjoyed equal if not greater strengths in this contest. Among the branches of the Army, only Air Corps officers possessed any considerable experience in flying and maintaining aircraft in all types of conditions. Only they had an in-depth understanding of some of the factors required to establish air superiority. Whatever else it had done, the *Luftwaffe*'s participation in the campaigns of 1939, 1940, and 1941 had emphasized the importance of the aerial weapon. Only a fool or a recluse (the chief of Field Artillery was neither) could have argued that military aviation's role in an overall national war effort had not changed dramatically between 1938 and 1941—and that transformation had redounded to the advantage of the senior American airman in the War Department. The metamorphosis of his power and responsibilities from chief of the Army Air Corps to commanding general of the Army Air Forces neatly illustrated in organizational terms the vast change in perceptions. As a consequence he enjoyed greater power and prestige, as well as closer proximity to the ultimate decision makers than did the chief of Field Artillery. Perhaps his strongest argument against organic aviation—extrapolated from the 1940 French and British experience—was that light aircraft could not survive in the battle area. The weakness of his position lay in his outdated conception of ground combat and doubts about his interest in supporting ground operations. Indeed, the history of air-ground relations over the previous twenty years meant that ground offi-

---

[47] Ltr, Moody to McNair, 13 Jan 42.

cers would adopt a certain skepticism toward claims by Air Corps officers to act as disinterested technical authorities on air-ground interactions.

Neither the Field Artillery nor the Army Air Forces had an indisputable technical case, given what was known about light aviation in the fall of 1941. Likewise, neither enjoyed an unassailable institutional power base. They were competitive. In the end much depended upon the intellectual acuity that Generals Danford and Arnold brought to their respective positions and the political skills with which they advanced them in the corridors of the War Department.

CHAPTER 2

The Field Artillery Acquires Its Own Aircraft, July 1941–June 1942

Field Artillery officers pressed the case for organic aviation to a succession of decision points between July 1941 and June 1942. The outcome depended upon actions on three interrelated but distinct levels. In the sphere of organizational politics, the chief of Field Artillery had to ensure that the senior decision makers had an opportunity to consider the case on its merits, in other words, negating the superior bureaucratic position of the commanding general of the Army Air Forces. On the technical level, officers with intimate familiarity with contemporary field artillery tactics and techniques and the capabilities of light aircraft had to design an organization to test the concept and develop in detail the doctrine that would guide such a unit. Finally, on the operational level, someone had to actually organize, man, equip, train, and lead a test element that would conclusively demonstrate the soundness of the concept. Success of the initiative depended upon achievements at each level. Failure at any point would doom the whole enterprise.

The War Department and Aerial Observation, July 1941–January 1942

The results of the 1941 maneuvers would have long-term consequences only if the chief of Field Artillery succeeded in changing the War Department's policy on aerial observation. During the summer both the commanding general of the Army Air Forces, Maj. Gen. Henry H. Arnold, and the chief of Field Artillery, Maj. Gen. Robert M. Danford, visited Great Britain to obtain firsthand information about modern war, and each returned even more firmly convinced of the soundness of his previous views on the proper organization and equipment of aerial observation. The explanation for their divergence of opinion was quite simple—they had talked to their opposite numbers in the Royal Air Force and the Royal Artillery. Since 1938 officers of the Royal Artillery had been agitating for their own light aircraft. In the wake of the very disappointing performance of the Royal Air Force's observation squadrons in France, the War Office formed air-observation-post squadrons, usually shortened to "air OP," with Field Artillery pilots and observers and Royal Air Force ground crew and administrative personnel. The Royal Air Force considered this at best a bad compromise, but necessary to head off complete independence for the Royal Artillery's aviation. None of the airmen expected that light aircraft would survive in modern battle conditions. The British airmen advocated using single-place unarmed pursuits equipped with high-speed cameras or light bombers for longer range observation missions.[1]

Danford witnessed a demonstration of an air observation post at Larkhill, the British artillery school. As soon as he returned to the United States, his office issued an intelligence bulletin encompassing his commentary on the British "Air OP." In this manner Danford first introduced into the American military lexicon the term *air observation post* as a synonym for Field Artillery light aircraft. Without explicitly adopting a position, the bulletin cited the results of recent exercises in the United Kingdom involving the Royal Air Force's Fighter Command, the interceptor command that won the Battle of Britain, and the British air observation posts. These cast doubt on the Royal Air Force's (and the Army Air Forces') contention about the extreme vulnerability of light aircraft to enemy air attack. Clearly, the Larkhill visit was important to Danford. It confirmed the utility and practicality of a light aircraft as a platform for an aerial observer and alleviated, at least in part, concern about its ability to survive in combat. On a more personal level, the British example validated everything that Capt. William W. Ford had argued in his article, "Wings for Santa Barbara," and thus indirectly called attention to Ford's value. That at least is the meaning of the visit suggested by Danford's actions in a month of hectic activity following his return.[2]

Danford paused only briefly in Washington. While he was overseas, the commander of the 13th Field Artillery Brigade at Fort Bragg, North Carolina, Brig. Gen. John A. Crane, had recommended that the Field Artillery fight to retain Army Air Forces observation balloons because they provided a superior aerial platform from which to direct fire. The action officer with the aerial observation portfolio in the Office of the Chief of Field Artillery, Maj. Rex E. Chandler, presented the case to Danford on his return and instead urged him to focus all his efforts on obtaining light aviation for the Field Artillery. Danford, who at times had appeared almost as skeptical of light aircraft as the chief of Cavalry, Maj. Gen. John K. Herr, adopted Chandler's solution as his own.[3]

Danford left for the Louisiana maneuvers, and his experience there only further confirmed his views about air observation posts. He then set off for Fort Sill and made a point of meeting the director of the Department of Communications at the Field Artillery School, the recently promoted Major Ford, who had joined the faculty in May 1941. Until

---

[1] Henry H. Arnold, *Global Mission* (New York: Harper and Brothers, 1949), pp. 224–25; Field Artillery (FA) Intelligence (Intel) Digest 18, 29 Sep 41, sub: The "Air OP" in the British Army, Office of the Chief of Cavalry (OCC), General Correspondence (Gen Corresp), 1920–1942, 452.1, Record Group (RG) 177, National Archives and Records Administration, Washington, D.C. (hereafter cited as NARA); H. J. Parham and E. M. G. Belfield, *Unarmed into Battle: The Story of the Air Observation Post* (Winchester, U.K.: Warren and Son, 1956), pp. 11–16. See also Shelford Bidwell, *Gunners at War: A Tactical Study of the Royal Artillery in the Twentieth Century* (London: Arms and Armour Press, 1970), pp. 67–117.

[2] FA Intel Digest 18, 29 Sep 41; Memo, British Army Staff for Chief of Field Artillery (CFA), 23 Feb 42, sub: Formation of Air Observation Post (AOP) Squadrons, OCC, Gen Corresp, 1917–1943, 320.2 (Secret [S]) (Binder 1), RG 177, NARA.

[3] Memos, Brig Gen J. A. Crane for CFA, 28 Aug 41, sub: Observation (Obsn) Balloons for Corps Artillery (Arty); Maj Rex E. Chandler for Brig Gen R. M. Danford, [Sep 41]; Brig Gen R. M. Danford for Maj Rex E. Chandler, [Sep 41]; all in Office of the Chief of Field Artillery (OCFA), Gen Corresp, 1917–1943, 452.3, RG 177, NARA. William W. Ford, *Wagon Soldier* (North Adams, Mass.: Excelsior, 1980), p. 120; Interview (Interv), author with Col J. W. Oswalt, 13–14 Jan 82, U.S. Army Center of Military History, Washington, D.C. (hereafter cited as CMH).

then Ford had had no idea how favorably disposed Danford was to his article. Danford assured Ford that the Office of the Chief of Artillery would take action soon on the air-observation-post concept. Ford owned his own aircraft and had given rides to senior officers to demonstrate his ideas, which in turn stimulated considerable interest among many of the junior officers at the post. Danford was encouraged by the number of young artillery officers who had learned to fly in anticipation, as he interpreted it, of the War Department's adoption of Field Artillery organic aviation. At least one officer in the 18th Field Artillery, 1st Lt. Robert R. Williams, rented a Taylorcraft that he used to observe for his battery, while his good friend, 2d Lt. Delbert L. Bristol, was taking private flying lessons.[4]

Even more important, Danford witnessed for the first time massed fire by division artillery using the new techniques developed at Sill. Within a few minutes all guns were firing on target, an operation, Danford noted, that had taken the Royal Artillery one hour and fifteen minutes during the recent invasion of Syria. The demonstration only heightened his awareness of the Field Artillery's need for its own aerial observation. In a speech to the faculty and students, Danford announced that he intended to set up an organic light aircraft program like the British. He introduced Ford to the assembled student officers as the "young man" who was going to organize this "grasshopper training." At the same time Danford did not minimize the difficulties he faced. In his trip report to the chief of staff of the Army, General George C. Marshall, Jr., he paraphrased Prime Minister Winston Churchill to express his frustration with the Army Air Forces: "Never have so few kept so much from so many."[5]

Shortly after Danford's visit, Ford submitted a proposal, favorably endorsed by the commandant of the Field Artillery School, Brig. Gen. G. R. Allin, to organize an air observation unit at Fort Sill. The plan called for procuring fourteen light aircraft "to determine the technique and procedure" of operating "slow-flying airplanes" as an organic part of the Field Artillery. Ford envisioned that the Army Air Forces would provide training for an initial detachment of Field Artillery pilots, observers, and mechanics who would in turn train whatever additional pilots, observers, and mechanics were needed. He also had a definite light aircraft in mind, the Stinson Model 76, a new plane that the Army Air Forces had service-tested at Fort Sill in September. It was a larger, more rugged version of the Model 105/YO–54. Powered by a 185-horsepower Lycoming engine, the Model 76 had a maximum speed of 130 miles per hour and a loiter time, the maximum time the aircraft could remain in the air, of almost four hours. It was the Field Artillery's introduction to the aircraft that would become the L–5.[6]

---

[4] Memo, Maj Gen R. M. Danford, CFA, for Gen George C. Marshall, Jr., Chief of Staff, Army (CSA), 6 Oct 41, sub: Brief of Visits of Inspection by CFA to Louisiana Maneuvers and to Fort Sill, General Headquarters (GHQ), Gen Corresp, 1940–1942, 354.2 (Reports [Rpts], 1941), RG 337, NARA; Ford, *Wagon Soldier*, p. 120; Intervs, Col R. J. Powell and Lt Col R. K. Andreson with Col D. L. Bristol, 1978, and Powell and Lt Col P. E. Counts with Lt Gen R. R. Williams, 1978, both at U.S. Army Military History Institute, Carlisle Barracks, Pa. (hereafter cited as MHI).

[5] Memo, Danford for Marshall, 6 Oct 41; Interv, author with Oswalt, 13–14 Jan 82, CMH. Oswalt was one of the student officers in the auditorium when Danford gave his speech.

[6] Ltr, Wright Field to Commanding Officer (CO), Air Corps (AC) Troops, Fort Riley, Kans., 30 Aug 41, sub: Accelerated Service Tests—Stinson Model 76 Airplane, OCC, Gen Corresp, 1920–1942, 452.1, RG 177, NARA; Plan, sub: Proposed General Plan for Establishment FA Air Obsn, Inclosure (Incl) in Indorsement (Ind), Brig Gen G. R. Allin, Commandant, Field Artillery School (FAS), to CFA, 11 Oct 41, on Ltr, Brig Gen C. W. Russell to CFA, 19 Sep 41, sub: Air Unit for FAS, OCFA, Gen Corresp, 1917–1942, 322.172/B–29, RG 177, NARA. Interv, author with Williams, 20 Feb 91, established that Ford was the author.

Once the proposal reached the Office of the Chief of Field Artillery, not much of it survived, other than those ideas General Danford had adopted earlier. Ford recommended forming a test detachment at Fort Sill, which Danford had already publicly announced he intended to do. Ford also wanted to assign mechanics directly to the detachment, which Danford had proposed in 1940. The interest in the Model 76 anticipated the quest by Ford and other field artillerymen during most of the war for an aircraft with standard performance characteristics superior to the Cub. The surviving record does not indicate why Danford's office rejected this part of the proposal, although the circumstances are suggestive. The Stinson Division of the Consolidated Aircraft Corporation had built the Model 76 on speculation in an attempt to meet criticisms of the O–49. Only a few models existed. To concentrate on the Model 76 would have meant a delay to the start-up of any organic air program if the War Department approved the aircraft.[7]

On 8 October 1941, Danford proposed directly to General Marshall that the War Department assign at least seven light aircraft with appropriate Field Artillery pilots and mechanics to each division artillery and separate field artillery brigade headquarters in the Army, essentially his proposal of the previous year. Danford wanted his office, in conjunction with the Office of the Chief of the Air Corps (the agency with primary responsibility for air materiel and training) and the General Staff, to work out detailed plans for organizing, training, and equipping the force. The other interested parties—G–3; General Headquarters, U.S. Army; and Headquarters, Army Air Forces—registered their objections. The most unexpected opposition came from General Headquarters, which, since its activation in 1940, had overseen the training and doctrine of the ground forces. While Marshall nominally remained its commander, his chief of staff, Lt. Gen. Lesley J. McNair, commanded in fact if not in name. Like Arnold, he doubted if light aircraft—he referred to them as puddle jumpers—could survive in the combat zone. Moreover, he was convinced that the Army Air Forces could do the job; in his view the Field Artillery should stop quibbling and let them get on with it.[8]

The exact chronology of what happened next is rather muddled—a compound of an incomplete official record and memories recorded long after the fact. Danford, blocked in staff channels, resorted to an unusual maneuver to break the logjam. He knew that the chief of staff's advisers were united in opposing Field Artillery control and that, while Marshall was favorably disposed, he would find it difficult to overrule their unanimous opinion. Concerned that Marshall would turn down the plan, Danford went directly to the secretary of war, Col. Henry L. Stimson. The military rank, now a courtesy title, referred to his World War I command of a field artillery regiment, the 31st Field Artillery, at the time Danford commanded the Field Artillery Replacement Depot at Camp Jackson, South Carolina. They knew one another from their World War I experience. Danford "poured out" his "needs for the flying 'O.P.'" to his sympathetic former associate. Stimson at once

---

[7] John Underwood, *The Stinsons: A Pictorial History* (Glendale, Calif.: Heritage Press, 1976), pp. 67–71.
[8] Memo, Lt Gen Lesley J. McNair for CSA, 21 Oct 41, sub: Rpt by the CFA, GHQ, Gen Corresp, 1940–1942, 354.2/2 (Rpts, 1941), RG 337, NARA; Rpt, Lt Col Lesley J. McNair, Assistant (Asst) Commandant, FAS, to Commandant, FAS, 15 Jun 32, sub: Annual Rpt, 30 Jun 32, FAS Archives, Morris Swett Technical Library, FAS, Fort Sill, Okla. (hereafter cited as Morris Swett Tech Lib). On the organization and mission of General Headquarters, see Kent R. Greenfield, Robert R. Palmer, and Bell I. Wiley, *The Organization of Ground Combat Troops*, U.S. Army in World War II (Washington, D.C.: Historical Division, U.S. Army, 1947), pp. 1–6.

THE FIELD ARTILLERY ACQUIRES ITS OWN AIRCRAFT

Measuring Takeoff and Landing Distances During the Stinson Model 76 Tests at Fort Sill

sent him to talk to Assistant Secretary of War John J. McCloy. McCloy conferred with Danford on 31 October 1941 about "the new field artillery." Years later Danford recalled the argument he used with McCloy: "'Two or three years ago the Army was struggling to carry on its work with a few millions of dollars—now it has suddenly been given billions—I believe that a few hundred thousand should be given to the Artillery with which to purchase a few of these planes—send them to Sill and give them a good try-out!'"⁹

---

⁹ Ltr, Maj Gen (Ret) R. M. Danford to Maj Gen E. A. Salet, 28 Apr 67, R. M. Danford Manuscripts (Ms), MHI; Speech, Brig Gen Rex E. Chandler, 10 Nov 58, sub: Talk Delivered at the Grad Exercise, U.S. Army Aviation (Avn) Training Detachment (Fixed Wing), Gary Army Air Field, Camp Gary, San Marcos, Tex., in Rex E. Chandler Ms, MHI; Diary, John J. McCloy, 31 Oct 41, John J. McCloy Ms, Special Collections, Amherst College Library, Amherst, Mass. Danford in his letter has confused this meeting with a second meeting on 14 January 1942 (see below). On Danford's World War I service, see William J. Snow, *Signposts of Experience: World War Memoirs* (Washington, D.C.: U.S. Field Artillery Assoc., 1941), pp. 70–80; for Stimson's, see Henry L. Stimson and McGeorge Bundy, *On Active Service in Peace and War* (New York: Harper and Bros., 1948), pp. 91–100.

The next morning McCloy met with Assistant Secretary of War for Air Robert A. Lovett. As soon as that meeting ended, Arnold telephoned McCloy about "planes for artillery observation," the first time such an explicit reference occurs in McCloy's desk diary. McCloy went immediately to Marshall, and when McCloy left the chief of staff's office he conferred once more with Lovett—in all, a very busy Saturday morning even for someone styled Blitz. Danford telephoned him on Monday about "planes for [the] Field Artillery." Two days later McCloy called Danford on the same subject. McCloy made only one further reference to light aircraft during the month—a demonstration of a puddle jumper to the commandant of the Field Artillery School.[10]

Mr. McCloy, April 1941

The diary and subsequent actions in the Office of the Chief of Field Artillery suggest that the McCloy-Danford telephone conversations of 3 and 5 November concerned strategy. The key date was 1 November. Nothing in the contemporary record suggests that McCloy dictated a decision. His own regard for the professional prerogatives of the military and his great esteem for Marshall mitigated against such blatant poaching of the chief of staff's responsibilities. Rather, McCloy's intervention and expression of concern had the effect of neutralizing the combined opposition of the staff. Marshall could weigh the issue on its own merits.[11]

As a result, an officer on Danford's staff, presumably Major Chandler, prepared a formal proposal to establish a test group. Even with McCloy's sympathetic interest, Danford and his officers were too experienced in the ways of the War Department not to use every bureaucratic advantage they could find. A young Field Artillery officer, Maj. Maxwell D. Taylor, had recently reported for duty with the Office of the Secretary of the General Staff. One of his personal friends at the Office of the Chief of Field Artillery telephoned him, impressed upon him the importance that General Danford placed on the issue, and asked him to take charge of the case personally. Marshall invariably asked action officers their opinion on cases they presented to him. Ensuring that Taylor was the action officer guaranteed the answer.[12]

---

[10] Diary, McCloy, 1, 3, 5, and 17 Nov 41.

[11] Danford says that McCloy made a decision at this point. This appears to be another instance in which Danford confused the 1 November 1941 and 14 January 1942 meetings. In the latter, McCloy did make a decision. Ltr, Danford to Salet, 28 Apr 67.

[12] Speech, Chandler; Interv, author with Gen M. D. Taylor, 24 Jan 83, CMH; Ltr, Lt Col R. W. Beasley to G–3, War Department General Staff (WDGS), 5 Dec 41, sub: Service Test of Air Obsn as an Organic Part of FA Units,

The issue fell under the province of the deputy chief of staff for air, General Arnold, acting in his staff rather than in his command capacity. Taylor first took the paper to Arnold and had no sooner started the briefing than Arnold interrupted him with a harangue. Arnold knew all about "the little tiny aircraft" that Danford wanted. The Army Air Forces was not interested in them, but they established a bad precedent. The ground arms would eventually want larger ones. Arnold preferred to squelch the idea in the beginning before organic aviation became a serious problem for the Army Air Forces. However, if Marshall wanted to give the Field Artillery its own planes, Arnold would not stand in the way. Taylor assured him that he would report his views to the chief of staff, which Taylor did, reporting some of Arnold's more colorful language verbatim. Marshall approved Taylor's paper for the test group on 3 December.[13]

On the same date McCloy provided a little added "cover" for the decision. At a conference in Secretary Stimson's office concerning the recent maneuvers, McCloy commented that all the commanders involved approved of the puddle jumpers and suggested that "greater use might be made of them, even going so far as to assign them organically to ground forces." The next day he talked to Danford's executive officer, Col. Rex W. Beasley, "re: puddle jumpers . . . and the Chief of Staff's decision."[14]

By this little drama, as stylized as a Victorian mating ritual with Major Taylor in the role of go-between, Arnold signaled that, while unhappy with the decision he knew was about to come, he would accept it and not carry dissent beyond the War Department. Marshall could make the decision that McCloy had all but dictated, knowing it would not endanger the fragile entente between the ground arms and the Army Air Forces upon which a relatively smooth mobilization depended. By cooperating, Arnold enhanced his own reputation and that of the Army Air Forces as responsible team players and made the eventual establishment of air as a separate service yet more likely. Besides, since he did not believe that light planes could survive in the combat zone, he was hardly mortgaging even a small part of the future of the Army Air Forces in allowing the Field Artillery to attempt the impossible.

On 5 December Major Chandler drafted recommendations on the conduct of the service test of organic air observation. These became the basis for a formal directive from The Adjutant General of the Army to the chief of Field Artillery five days later, remarkable speed considering that the Japanese attack on Pearl Harbor had intervened. The Field Artillery would organize, equip, and train two detachments at Fort Sill. One would test the concept with division artillery, the second with corps artillery. On 13 December Danford ordered Major Ford to report to Washington to prepare detailed plans for the project. Ford in turn brought along Maj. Gordon J. Wolf, an attorney from Cincinnati, Ohio,

---

Microfilm A1387, U.S. Air Force Historical Research Agency, Maxwell Air Force Base (AFB), Ala. (hereafter cited as AFHRA). Maxwell D. Taylor, *Swords and Plowshares: A Memoir* (New York: Da Capo, 1972), pp. 38–40, discusses in general Marshall's relations with his briefing officers. Diary, McCloy, 1, 3, 5, and 17 Nov 41. Interv, author with Taylor, 24 Jan 83.

[13] Interv, author with Taylor, 24 Jan 83; Memo, Col W. B. Smith, Secretary (Sec), WDGS, for ACS, G–3, 3 Dec 41, CSA Numerical file, 1920–1942, 21276, RG 165, NARA; Diary, McCloy, 4 Dec 41.

[14] Quote from Memo, E. L. H. for Sec of War, 4 Dec 41, sub: Notes on Conference, re: Maneuvers, OCSA, Minutes and Notes of Conferences Relating to the Emergency Planning Program, 1938–1945, RG 165, NARA; Diary, McCloy, 4 Dec 41.

with a commission in the Field Artillery Reserve, who had already expressed interest in the concept.[15]

Immediately after the publication of Ford's article extolling light aircraft organic to field artillery battalions, Wolf had written Ford and expressed his interest in the concept. Over the next several months they exchanged a series of letters on the aerial observation problem. Commissioned out of the Yale University Reserve Officers Training Corps in 1926, Wolf had practiced corporate law and since 1938 had represented the Aeronca Aircraft Corporation. After he became the company's counsel, he learned to fly and was immediately struck by the potential of light aircraft from a Field Artillery standpoint. He took his own aircraft to the 1940 maneuvers. The observation proved just as great as he had anticipated, but communication with the ground was awful. He had a citizens' band radio with him, and he could not net with the Signal Corps radios in the field artillery battalion to which he was assigned. After discussing these and related matters, Wolf closed the correspondence by asking Ford to remember him if anything ever came of Ford's proposal.[16]

As soon as Ford received his orders to report to Washington, he telegraphed Major Wolf to meet him in the railroad station in Cincinnati while Ford was between trains. Wolf, somewhat mystified about the purpose, agreed, and they spent a pleasant, if somewhat innocuous, forty-five minutes together. Later, Wolf realized that Ford had wanted to size him up. Almost immediately—the length of time it took Ford to travel from Cincinnati to Washington by rail—Wolf received orders calling him to active duty and directing him to report to the Office of the Chief of Field Artillery. There he discovered that he and Ford, with considerable assistance from Chandler and the executive officer, Colonel Beasley, constituted a planning cell on the aviation project. They prepared a detailed directive for the commandant of the Field Artillery School, which Danford dispatched on 23 December.[17]

The directive laid out the first phase of the test program, to be completed by 1 March 1942. It consisted of organizing the test detachments at Fort Sill for which the Army Air Forces would furnish twenty-eight Piper J–3 Cubs, now designated as YO–59s. Ford and Wolf intended to recruit licensed pilots, mainly from the enlisted ranks. Officers, aside from those supervising the program, would be below the grade of major. Instruction would consist of pilots developing their technique in operating from "small, unimproved fields." All the student pilots would train as pilot-mechanics, capable of performing day-to-day maintenance in the field, with only the occasional intervention of a more highly trained mechanic. The Office of the Chief of Field Artillery arranged for the Civil Aeronautics

---

[15] Ltr, R. G. Hersey, The Adjutant General's Office (TAGO), to CFA, 10 Dec 41, sub: Air Obsn; Ltr, Col R. W. Beasley, Executive Officer (XO), OCFA, to Commandant, FAS, 23 Dec 41, sub: Same; both in Gordon J. Wolf Ms, Historian's files, CMH. Ltr, Beasley to G–3, WDGS, 5 Dec 41, sub: Service Test of Air Obsn as Organic Part of FA Units; Memo, Brig Gen H. L. Twaddle for The Adjutant General (TAG), 8 Dec 41, sub: Air Obsn, with attached Memorandum for Record (MFR), Microfilm A1387, AFHRA; Interv, author with Col Gordon J. Wolf, 27 Sep 82, CMH; Ltr, Brig Gen William W. Ford to author, 20 Jun 82, Historian's files, CMH.

[16] Intervs, author with Wolf, 27 Sep 82; Maj Gen W. A. Harris with Col Gordon J. Wolf, c. 1983; Ltr, Ford to author, 11 Oct 82. General Harris interviewed Colonel Wolf for me using a questionnaire that I had prepared.

[17] Ltrs, Hersey to CFA, 10 Dec 41; Beasley to Commandant, FAS, 23 Dec 41; Beasley to G–3, 5 Dec 41; Memo, Twaddle for TAG, 8 Dec 41, with attached MFR; Interv, author with Wolf, 27 Sep 82; Ltr, Ford to author, 20 Jun 82.

THE FIELD ARTILLERY ACQUIRES ITS OWN AIRCRAFT

Ford (*left*) and Wolf, Following Promotions to Colonel and Lieutenant Colonel, Respectively, at Fort Sill in 1942

Administration to provide supervisors of flight and maintenance training and to select civilian flight instructors.[18]

The question of requiring radios for the aircraft sparked the one major disagreement in the planning cell. Ford was concerned about the weight of standard Signal Corps radios, which Chandler insisted the air observation posts needed rather than lighter commercial models. At issue was the strength of signal (and hence range) and the number of available channels by which to link the observers with the battalion fire-direction centers. Chandler argued for the optimum number to give maximum flexibility in the field even though, with a 170-pound pilot, a 170-pound observer, a full tank of gas, and a Signal Corps radio, the little Piper J–3/YO–59 was slightly overloaded. Chandler, who, Ford recalled, could be "very persistent when he thought he was right," prevailed in the end. Chandler had unrivaled contacts with the Signal Corps, through whom he secured prototypes of what became the standard wartime installation, the battery-powered SCR–609 (the SCR–509 in armored divisions), with little delay. Eventually, Ford came to consider Chandler's insis-

---

[18] Initial plans called for four officer and twenty-eight enlisted pilots. Ltr, Beasley to Commandant, FAS, 23 Dec 41, sub: Air Obsn, 23 Dec 41, Wolf Ms, CMH. Interv, author with Wolf, 27 Sep 82; Ltr, Brig Gen William W. Ford to author, 11 Oct 82, Historian's files, CMH.

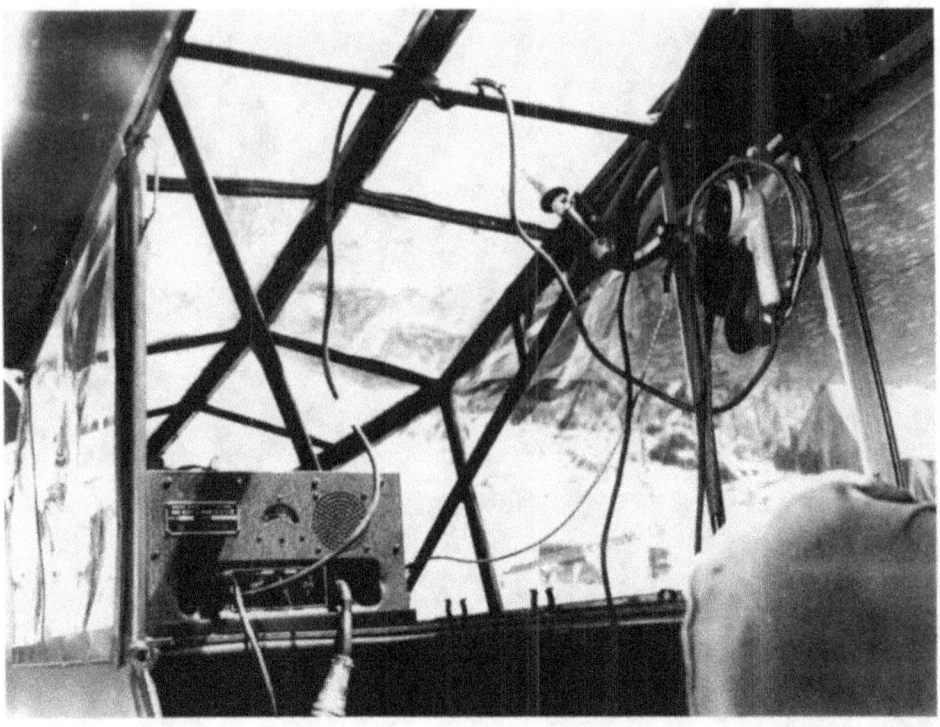

The SCR–610, a Vehicular Radio That Supplemented the SCR–609 During the Latter Stages of World War II, Showing the Typical Mounting in an L–4

tence on requiring standard radios as a very significant contribution to the ultimate success of the Air-Observation-Post Program.[19]

Testing the Concept

Newly promoted Lt. Col. William W. Ford returned to Fort Sill accompanied by Major Wolf. The success of the Field Artillery's initiative now depended in large measure upon Ford, a 43-year-old regular from Waverly, Virginia. He had been a student at the University of Virginia when the United States declared war on Germany in 1917. After serving on

---

[19] Ltrs, Beasley to Commandant, FAS, 23 Dec 41; Ford to author, 20 Jun 82. "SCR" originally meant "set complete radio," but in common usage it came to mean "Signal Corps Radio." Dulany Terrett, *The Signal Corps: The Emergency (To December 1941)*, U.S. Army in World War II (Washington, D.C., Office of the Chief of Military History, 1956), p. 28. Both the SCR–509 and the SCR–609 radios were hand-portable, frequency modulated, push-button-tuned sets. The 80 crystals of the former and 120 of the latter permitted them to scan all the channels allocated to the Armored Force and the Field Artillery, respectively. Each had two preset frequencies. The SCR–510 and SCR–610, sometimes used in their place in light aircraft, possessed similar technical characteristics but were designed for vehicles. George R. Thompson, et al., *The Signal Corps: The Test (December 1941 to July 1943)*, U.S. Army in World War II (Washington, D.C.: Office of the Chief of Military History, 1957), pp. 73, 233; George R. Thompson and Dixie R. Harris, *The Signal Corps: The Outcome*, U.S. Army in World War II (Washington, D.C.: Office of the Chief of Military History, 1966), p. 638.

active duty for over a year with the Virginia National Guard, he accepted an appointment to West Point. Because of the war, he graduated in two years and received a commission in the Field Artillery. Even then he was intensely interested in flying. He had seriously considered selecting the Air Service as his branch but rejected it because in his view its members lacked any sense of military tradition and esprit de corps. Ford had always wanted to be a soldier and had very definite ideas about what that involved. The Field Artillery fulfilled this emotional need. In 1932, however, while serving as the battalion reconnaissance officer of the 82d Field Artillery (Horse) at Fort Bliss, Texas, he went aloft as an observer as part of his official duties and reveled in the experience. He found that he could not resist flying any longer. After obtaining his private pilot's license the following year, he purchased and flew a succession of light planes for the remainder of the decade. Flying, however, did not change his concept of what constituted a good officer. He was meticulous, precise, and a stern disciplinarian.[20]

Ford immediately began organizing the flight detachment, officially designated the Air Training Detachment, Field Artillery School, on 2 January 1942. The commandant of the Field Artillery School made Ford director of air training. At the same time the Office of the Chief of Field Artillery solicited volunteers for the positions of pilot-mechanic and airplane mechanic. The two young officers at Fort Sill who were pilots, Lieutenants Williams and Bristol (Bristol had obtained his license since Danford's visit in the fall), immediately volunteered. Ford put them to work on his staff, giving Williams responsibility for operations and logistics while Bristol acted as the adjutant. Another student officer, Capt. Robert M. Leich, ultimately became the engineering officer. Some housekeeping details demanded immediate attention. The Army Air Forces provided twenty-four YO–59s, redesignated L–4s (for liaison) in February and hangar space at Post Field for the training detachment. Post Field already had an observation squadron at least technically in residence. To avoid overburdening the facility, Ford arranged to rent a nearby commercial field, Swain Field, which became the actual training site.[21]

With instruction scheduled to begin 15 January, Ford had to move very quickly to prepare a curriculum. While Ford's concept for the employment of light aircraft profoundly shaped the techniques taught, the chief flight instructor, Richard H. Alley; the superintendent of maintenance, Stanford J. Stelle; and three of the flight instructors, Theodore F. Schirmacher, Thomas F. Piper, and Henry S. Wann, worked out the details. They divided the pilot-mechanics' course into three phases. Stage A, varying from six to twelve hours, provided refamiliarization for the students, many of whom had not flown since their call to active duty over a year before, and gave them an opportunity to standardize their basic

---

[20] Memo, War Department (WD), 8 Feb 46, sub: William Wallace Ford, Biographical (Bio) files, Historical Reference Branch, CMH. Ford, *Wagon Soldier*, pp. 105–14, 118.

[21] Memo, Maj H. McK. Roper, XO, FAS, 2 Jan 42, Form Ltr, [Student Applicant] to CFA, sub: Application as Pilot-Mechanic of FA Air Obsn, Form Ltr, [Student Applicant] to CFA, sub: Application as Airplane Mechanic for FA Air Obsn, Wolf Ms, CMH. Ltr, Maj Gen E. S. Adams, TAG, to Commanding Generals (CGs) of all Armies, Departments (Depts), Corps Areas, etc., 23 Feb 42, sub: Change in Designation of Airplanes, GHQ, Gen Corresp, 1940–1942, 452.1 (Airplanes), RG 337, NARA. Massive confusion in the field characterized the shift from the "O" to the "L" series. From time to time the Cubs were referred to as O–59s, L–59s, and L–57s. To prevent utter confusion for the reader, I have consistently used the new designation, although its actual acceptance in general usage lagged the formal directive by several months. For comments on the relations with the Air Corps, see E-Mail, Lt Gen R. R. Williams to author, 16 Jul 96, Historian's files, CMH.

techniques of piloting. Recovery from stalls and rapid descents received particular emphasis. Stage B, a minimum of twenty hours and the heart of the program, emphasized developing "technique and accuracy" for short-field landings and takeoffs over barriers, minimum landing rolls, landing in crosswinds, and evasive maneuvers. Stage C, a minimum of ten hours, consisted of actual fire missions with observers from the 13th Field Artillery Brigade and the 2d Division Artillery, who were receiving their orientation for air observation. At the end of each phase students had to pass a "stage check" before proceeding to the next one. Students spent their mornings flying and their afternoons learning how to maintain their aircraft. Three nights a week they took ground courses on both piloting and maintenance. Ford's assumption that most of the pilots would be enlisted men proved to be invalid. Eventually, eleven officers and nine enlisted men passed the course. They were known thereafter as the Class Before One.[22]

The basic philosophy behind the pilot training program was quite simple: Show the student the extremes to which he could carry both the aircraft and himself and thereby "impress upon him the limitations of flight" of both plane and pilot. Alley and Schirmacher concentrated on Stage B. They had to devise extreme maneuvers and incorporate them into the curriculum. The power-on approach, designed to demonstrate to a student how slowly he could land a light plane, typified these maneuvers. One variant involved an aircraft making a low, slow flight across a field directly at an obstacle, pulling up and over it at the last moment. Barrier landings were but the first step; barrier takeoffs followed logically. Later they used bamboo fishing poles to set up an airplane version of the slalom. Students had to taxi around them in the ground-handling portion of the course. Students also had to become proficient at road landings, including landing around curves.[23]

Simultaneously with the pilot-mechanics course, six enlisted men, led by Sgt. James T. Kerr, Jr., reported to Lock Haven, Pennsylvania, to learn everything possible about repairing Piper aircraft. Kerr, a 21-year-old Mississippi National Guardsman from the 114th Field Artillery Regiment, had three years of civilian experience rebuilding Piper Cubs. He organized a training course that, beginning 15 January 1942, placed each of the student mechanics in one of the departments at the Piper plant—assembly, sheet metal, dope and fabric, woodworking, and engines—and then rotated them so that eventually each student had worked in each department. Major Chandler came up from Washington to inspect the training and left well satisfied with the results. Toward the end the enlisted men provided free maintenance for aircraft at the local airport, Cub Haven. Working under the supervision of a Civil Aeronautics Administration–certified mechanic provided by Piper, they gained valuable hands-on experience. (The aircraft owners had to supply the parts.) Instruction at Lock Haven ended on 15 February, and the men traveled to Fort Sill, where Stelle gave them fur-

---

[22] Memo, 15 Feb 42, sub: FA Air Training Course Flight Curriculum; Rpt, Lt Col William W. Ford, Director (Dir), Air Training, to Commandant, FAS, 30 Apr 42, sub: Rpt Test of Organic Air Obsn for FA: Training Phase, Fort Sill, Okla., 15 Jan–28 Feb 42; both in Wolf Ms, CMH. Interv, Col B. R. Kramer and Lt Col R. K. Andreson with Brig Gen O. G. Goodhand, 9 May 78, MHI; Ford, *Wagon Soldier*, pp. 121–22; Intervs, Harris with Wolf, c. 1983; author with Wann, 27 Aug 82. On 1 August 1942, the division was officially redesignated as the 2d Infantry Division. John B. Wilson, *Armies, Corps, Divisions, and Separate Brigades*, Army Lineage Series (Washington, D.C.: U.S. Army Center of Military History, 1987), pp. 160–61.

[23] Interv, R. J. Tierney with Lt Col T. F. Schirmacher, Mar 62, *U.S. Army Aviation Digest* (*USAAD*) files, U.S. Army Aviation Museum Library, Fort Rucker, Ala. (hereafter cited as USAAML).

ther training. Unlike the pilot-mechanics, all passed. Kerr, because of his "exceptional ability," was promoted to staff sergeant and the others to sergeant.[24]

After Ford and Wolf left Washington for Fort Sill, detailed planning for the actual service tests continued in the Office of the Chief of Field Artillery. Chandler probably wrote the instructions for the service tests that the Office of the Chief of Field Artillery issued on 1 February 1942, but the concepts represented a consensus of opinion among the principals, Ford, Wolf, Beasley, and Chandler. The instructions defined the primary and secondary missions of air observation posts—the former consisted of missions associated with the observation of artillery fires, the latter with the reconnaissance for firing positions and their occupation by field artillery battalions. The instructions also laid out a tentative doctrine for employing air observation posts, essentially a more detailed exposition of the ideas that Ford had first broached in his *Field Artillery Journal* article of the previous year. If the War Department approved the air-observation-post concept, Danford proposed to use the instructions as the basis for a technical manual on the subject of organic aviation for the Field Artillery.[25]

The author of the instructions also addressed all the major logistical and administrative problems posed by establishing a military aviation program outside the Army Air Forces. The service tests sought to demonstrate that light aircraft were of such simple design and rugged construction that field artillery units could maintain them easily by using field expedient measures. Unfortunately, the existing authority—a 6 January 1942 War Department directive that made the chief of Field Artillery responsible for all first-echelon maintenance of artillery light aircraft and the supervision of all associated technical instructions and inspections—was not quite broad enough to achieve the desired result. First-echelon maintenance referred to day-to-day upkeep of equipment, such as checking the oil level, which could be performed by operating personnel. Second-echelon maintenance, for which the chief of Field Artillery had no authority and that by default remained vested with the commanding general, Army Air Forces, encompassed repairs too difficult for the operators but simple enough for mechanics assigned to the using unit. The two categories combined constitute modern organizational maintenance, essentially the concept the advocates of organic air hoped to test. The anonymous author of the instructions sidestepped the issue by citing the authority for first-echelon maintenance and defining it broadly to include second-echelon maintenance. (This caused no end of confusion with the covering memoranda prepared by higher staff echelons but none at all with the test group where Field Artillery mechanics accompanied the pilots as intended.) The Army Air Forces would perform all higher-echelon maintenance, which required any specialized tools and equipment not assigned to the user units, and would provide repair parts necessary for the Field Artillery to perform first- and second-echelon maintenance.[26]

---

[24] Memo, sub: List of Mechanics, Incl in Rpt, Lt Col William W. Ford, Dir, Air Training, FAS, to Commandant, FAS, 30 Apr 42, sub: Rpt of Test of Organic Air Obsn for FA, Training Phase, Fort Sill, Okla., 15 Jan–28 Feb 42, Wolf Ms, CMH; Interv, author with Capt J. T. Kerr, Jr., 2 Mar 91, CMH.

[25] Ltr, Beasley, sub: Instructions for Test of Organic Short-Range Air Obsn for FA; Rpt, Lt Charles W. Lefever, Flight A, 3 Apr 42, sub: Rpt on Interceptions, Headquarters, Army Ground Forces (HQ, AGF), Gen Corresp, 1942–1948, 353/1 (R) (FA Air Obsn), RG 337, NARA.

[26] Ltr, Beasley, sub: Instructions for Test of Organic Short-Range Air Obsn for FA; Ltr, C. Grosse, Adjutant General (AG), to CG, Army Air Forces (AAF), 25 Feb 42, sub: Service Test of Organic Air Obsn for FA, HQ,

General Danford planned for the 2d Division Artillery stationed at Fort Sam Houston, Texas, and the 13th Field Artillery Brigade stationed at Fort Bragg, North Carolina, to test the air-observation-post concept for division and corps artillery. In accordance with existing regulations and procedures, these two organizations established local boards of officers to conduct the tests. On 28 February, even though Stage C, the training of the observers, remained incomplete, Ford divided the training detachment into two flights, A and B, to work with the 13th Field Artillery Brigade and the 2d Division Artillery, respectively. First Lt. Edwin F. Houser, "a quiet, modest, capable, soldierly fellow . . . [who] performed well," commanded Flight A; Major Wolf commanded Flight B.[27]

Ford initially accompanied Flight A to Fort Bragg and ultimately to Camp Blanding, Florida, where the 13th Field Artillery Brigade conducted the majority of its tests. The 2d Division Artillery carried out most of its tests near its home station. With the tests going on simultaneously, Ford shuttled back and forth between the two locations until the conclusion of the tests in mid-April. Although the test schedules devised by the two boards varied considerably, in general they followed the same formula: a period of training with the ground elements that the air observation posts would support; a phase of testing the aviators' ability to perform their primary and secondary missions when working with firing battalions; and a culminating stage, involving pursuits from the Army Air Forces, to determine the ability of the light planes to direct fire when under air attack. The 2d Division Artillery board added a significant variant: a head-to-head competition between Flight B and an Army Air Forces observation squadron to determine the relative effectiveness of the two concepts.[28]

Pilots in both detachments quickly demonstrated the light aircraft's value in the secondary missions of column control, reconnaissance of positions and routes for firing battalions, and aerial photography. To perform the last, an observer literally opened a door at 600 feet and held a 4x5 Speed Graphic camera out into the airstream, depending upon nothing other than a steady hand and a capable pilot for a good picture. The resulting

---

AGF, Gen Corresp, 1942–1948, 353/1 (FA Air Obsn) (R), RG 337, NARA; Ltr, Col L. P. Whitten, Dir, Base Services, AAF, to Lt Gen Lesley J. McNair, 26 Mar 42, HQ, AGF, Gen Corresp, 1942–1948, 452.1/1 (S), RG 337, NARA; WD, Technical Manual (TM) 20–205, *Dictionary of United States Army Terms* (Washington, D.C.: Government Printing Office, 1944), p. 97; Army Regulation (AR) 310–25, *Dictionary of United States Army Terms*, (Washington, D.C.: Department of the Army, 1975), p. 159. The question was made more complex in that while the ground arms recognized five echelons of maintenance, the Air Corps traditionally possessed only three and only in March 1942 shifted to a system of four echelons of repair. Robert W. Ackerman, *Maintenance of Army Aircraft in the United States, 1939–1945: General Development and Policies* (Washington, D.C.: Army Air Forces Historical Office, 1946), pp. 4–7, 29–55, 81–109.

[27] Questionnaire, [OCFA, Feb 42], sub: Service Test Questionnaire for Test of Organic Short-Range Air Obsn for FA, HQ, AGF, Gen Corresp, 1942–1948, 353/1 (R) (FA Air Obsn), RG 337, NARA. AR 850–25, *Miscellaneous: Development, Classification of, and Specifications for Types of Equipment* (Washington, D.C.: Department of the Army, 1936), laid out the Army's test and evaluation system. See Robert W. Coakley, Richard C. Kugler, and Vincent H. Demma, "Historical Summary of Evolution of U.S. Army Test and Evaluation System—World War II to the Present," (Unpublished Ms, CMH, 1966). The characterization of Houser is General Ford's. Ltr, Ford to Raines, 11 Oct 82.

[28] Ltr, Grosse to CG, AAF, 25 Feb 42. Training Memo 12, 13th FA Brigade (Bde), 9 Mar 42, sub: Test of Organic Short-Range Air Obsn; Order, 2d Div Arty, 14 Mar 42, sub: Service Test of Organic Air Obsn for FA; all in HQ, AGF, Gen Corresp, 1942–1948, 353/1 (R) (FA Air Obsn), RG 337, NARA. Originally, the Army Air Forces was scheduled to have a head-to-head observation contest with Flight A, but the Army Air Forces observation squadron never arrived. Interv, Laurence Epstein with Col D. L. Bristol, 1 Jul 75, U.S. Army Aviation and Troop Command History Office, St. Louis, Mo. (hereafter cited as USAA&TC).

THE FIELD ARTILLERY ACQUIRES ITS OWN AIRCRAFT

MEMBERS OF FLIGHT A REFUEL AN O–59 IN THE FIELD.

oblique photographs were of value for counterintelligence, checking the effectiveness of camouflage, and the designation of routes and firing positions for battalions. During the tests, light aircraft did not provide any of the vertical photographs that the Field Artillery required for map firing and damage assessment. These remained the province of high-speed Army Air Forces reconnaissance planes that could actually fly over the battle area.[29]

The primary function of corps artillery, in addition to reinforcing divisional fires, was counterbattery. The Office of the Chief of Field Artillery's instructions anticipated that a light aircraft flying at low altitude might have difficulty observing fire for long-range counterbattery missions. The tests in the 13th Field Artillery Brigade confirmed this limitation; air observation posts had difficulty picking out muzzle flashes beyond 10,000 yards. All the other tests of observed fire went entirely in their favor. Among these, the competition with the Army Air Forces observation squadron was critical. The failure to

---

[29] Memo, [Board of Officers (B/O), 13th FA Bde, Apr 42], sub: Other Missions, HQ, AGF, Gen Corresp, 1942–1948, 353/1 (R) (FA Air Obsn), RG 337, NARA. For a good discussion of aerial photography from a Field Artillery perspective, see C. C. Blanchard and E. L. Sibert, "The Use of Air Photographs by the Field Artillery," *FAJ* 20 (November–December 1930):650–62.

complete observer training at Fort Sill threatened to put Flight B at a disadvantage. The observation school at Brooks Field used the Leon Springs Military Reservation, where the 2d Division Artillery's firing ranges were located, to train rated observers, so the officers in Flight B could anticipate they would face observers very well acquainted with the terrain. The questionnaire from the Office of the Chief of Field Artillery, however, had asked the boards to consider whether Field Artillery officers required specialized training as aerial observers. The 2d Division Artillery board interpreted the question to mean that it should recruit observers from the artillery officers already in the 2d Division in addition to the ones partially trained at Sill.[30]

The operations officer of Flight B, Lieutenant Williams, consequently approached the S–3 of the 38th Field Artillery Battalion, 1st Lt. Robert F. Cassidy, who had graduated from West Point in 1939, a year ahead of Williams. Cassidy had washed out of primary flight training, but as battalion reconnaissance officer he often flew with the Army Air Forces observation squadrons. He knew every ripple of ground and every firing position at the Leon Springs Reservation. He had, moreover, a genuine flair for fire direction. In the comparative tests of observers before the arrival of the Army Air Forces squadron, Cassidy established the best record. He observed for Flight B in the competitive tests. Once airborne in an L–4 he took an average of two minutes to bring fire on target. In contrast, Army Air Forces observers first had to locate the firing battalion, which sometimes proved difficult. They also did not always find the target. When they did, they required an average of twenty-five minutes to adjust fire on the first target and an additional seven minutes on another. The contrast in performance led the members of Flight B to make Cassidy an honorary member of the Class Before One. His work constituted a resounding affirmation of the concepts that Danford, Chandler, and Ford had advocated over the previous two years.[31]

The last phase of the tests, potentially the most critical, involved the ability of the air observation posts to perform their mission when opposed by enemy air. In contrast to the J–3 Cubs that flew in the 1941 maneuvers, the L–4s had a "greenhouse," a large area covered with clear plastic panels, behind the wing. The greenhouse gave the observer good visibility overhead and to the rear. He could now spot enemy pursuits in time for the pilot to take evasive maneuvers. Ford, however, was particularly concerned when he learned that the Army Air Forces intended to mount gun cameras in their pursuits to provide irrefutable proof of the vulnerability of the light planes. The assumptions under which the local boards conducted the air-to-air tests became very important—and they diverged widely. The 2d Division Artillery board, which included Major Wolf, set aside two days for the air-to-air portion of the test and drew up rigorous criteria that worked to the benefit of the air observation posts. The 13th Field Artillery Brigade board at Camp Blanding, which consisted only of officers drawn from the brigade, set aside four hours to determine vulnerability

---

[30] Ltr, Beasley, sub: Instructions for Test of Organic Short-Range Air Obsn for FA, HQ, AGF, Gen Corresp, 1942–1948, 353/1 (R) (FA Air Obsn), RG 337, NARA; Interv, author with Col R. F. Cassidy, 29 Jan 91, Historian's files, CMH.

[31] Apps., sub: Tabulation of Results of Firing, and sub: Comparative Test, Air Force–FA, in Rpt, B/O, 2d Div Arty, 18 Apr 42, sub: Rpt of B/O Appointed to Test Organic Short-Range Air Obsn for FA, both in HQ, AGF, Gen Corresp, 1942–1948, 353/1 (R) (FA Air Obsn), RG 337, NARA; Interv, author with Cassidy, 29 Jan 91; Ltr, Cassidy to author, 10 Feb 91, Historian's files, CMH; Interv, author with Williams, 20 Feb 91.

THE FIELD ARTILLERY ACQUIRES ITS OWN AIRCRAFT

An Overhead Photograph of the YO–59A at the Piper Aircraft Corporation Plant in Lock Haven Shows the Improved Overhead Visibility Available in the Military Version of the Piper J–3 Cub, 12 February 1942.

with loosely drawn criteria that benefited the Army Air Forces. One of the members of Flight A, however, suggested an alternative: Station cameramen at light antiaircraft positions and photograph the pursuits. Although the pursuits generally massacred Flight A, pictures of P–39s doing turns at less than one hundred feet above gun positions served as a useful corrective. The Flight B results, more favorable to the L–4s, helped to sell the program and proved a better guide to actual combat conditions. The drubbing in Florida, however, may have been more useful in the long term. Lieutenant Bristol attended an informal conference with the pursuit pilots in which they frankly discussed vulnerabilities and tactics. He came away with a series of practical suggestions that Ford put to good use in improving light aircraft tactics and techniques.[32]

The questionnaire compiled at the Office of the Chief of Field Artillery had envisioned four different ways of organizing air observation posts: assigning 1 aircraft, 1 pilot-

---

[32] Rpt, Maj J. Hagood, Jr., S–3, 13th FA Bde, to CG, 13th FA Bde, 16 Apr 42, sub: Field Test on Vulnerability of L–59 Airplane When Attacked by Pursuit Avn; Rpts, 1st Lt J. H. Coune, Flight A, 3 Apr 42, sub: Rpt on Interception; Lt Charles W. Lefever, Flight A, 3 Apr 42, sub: Rpt on Interception; Lt L. M. Bornstein, Flight A, 3 Apr 42, sub: Same; Orders, 2d Div Arty, 9 Apr 42, sub: Field Exercise (Air Obsn Test), with App., sub: Vulnerability to Attack; all in Rpt, B/O, 2d Div Arty, 18 Apr 42; Ford, *Wagon Soldier*, pp. 125–26.

mechanic, and 1 mechanic to each firing battalion; allocating 3 aircraft, 3 pilot-mechanics, and 1 mechanic to each firing battalion; making all aircraft and personnel part of the headquarters battery of the field artillery brigade or the division artillery; or establishing a separate aviation battery containing all pilots, mechanics, and equipment that reported directly to the brigade or division artillery commander. Both boards found these options unacceptable. They agreed that the War Department should assign 2 aircraft, 2 pilot-mechanics, and 1 mechanic to each firing battalion, but disagreed about the aviation element in division artillery and field artillery brigade headquarters. The 13th Field Artillery Brigade board wanted 2 aircraft, 3 pilot-mechanics (1 of whom would serve as the brigade air officer), 1 mechanic, and 1 supply sergeant, while the 2d Division Artillery board requested 4 pilots (2 officers and 2 enlisted men) but only 3 aircraft. The senior officer would act as the division artillery air officer; the junior would become the engineering officer. One airplane mechanic, 2 truck drivers, and 3 enlisted men to act as ground crew rounded out the section.[33]

Maintenance in the field fully bore out the predictions of Ford and other advocates of light aircraft. The L–4 was quite literally "the Model T" of aviation—simple and rugged. When 1st Lt. John S. Sarko of Flight B tried to set down his aircraft a little too short while practicing short-field landings on a little dirt strip at Leon Springs, he broke his left landing gear, bent his left struts, and destroyed his propeller. It was a typical accident in this type of training. Sergeant Kerr and his mechanics had Sarko's craft ready to fly the next morning. At the end of the test phase all the aircraft and engines of the flight were "in superior condition, . . . despite the rigorous conditions under which they were flown." Flight A had to write off one aircraft, but the mechanics did succeed in rebuilding two damaged wings in the field and performed other, less serious, repairs equally well.[34]

The end of the field tests in mid-April brought a time of guarded anticipation to the test group. Both flights reassembled at Fort Sill. Colonel Ford prepared detailed plans to expand the test group to act as the training base for an approved program. He also prepared orders in case the War Department disapproved the concept and the members of the detachment had to return to their parent organizations. Continued evidence of high-level support kept morale from plummeting. Most dramatically, the commander of the 1st Division, Maj. Gen. Terry de la Mesa Allen, requested a demonstration before his unit, then under movement orders, shipped overseas. Ford hastily dispatched eight aircraft under Wolf to Fort Benning, Georgia. Success at Benning, however, could not compensate for the fact that what Ford and his men needed most was a triumph in Washington.[35]

---

[33] Questionnaire, [OCFA, Feb 42]. App., sub: Opns and Organization, in Rpt, B/O, 2d Div Arty, 18 Apr 42.

[34] Ltrs, Ford to author, 11 Oct 82, and Cassidy to author, 10 Feb 91. Intervs, author with Cassidy, 29 Jan 91; with Williams, 20 Feb 91; with Kerr, 2 Mar 91; Harris with Wolf, c. 1983. Ltr, Beasley, sub: Instructions for Test of Organic Short-Range Air Obsn for FA; Ltr, Grosse, AG, to CG, AAF, 25 Feb 42; Training Memo 12, 13th FA Bde, 9 Mar 42; Order, 2d Div Arty, 14 Mar 42. Memo, [B/O, 13th FA Bde, Apr 42], sub: Other Missions; Memo, [Flight A, Apr 42], sub: Maintenance; Rpt, B/O, 2d Div Arty, 18 Apr 42, with Apps., sub: Maintenance, sub: Tabulation of Results of Firing, and sub: Comparative Test, AF-FA; all in HQ, AGF, Gen Corresp, 1942–1948, 353/1 (FA Air Obsn) (R), RG 337, NARA. Interv, Epstein with Bristol, 1 Jul 75.

[35] Intervs, author with Kerr, 2 Mar 91; Harris with Wolf, c. 1983. The War Department reorganized and redesignated the 1st Division as the 1st Infantry Division on 1 August 1942. Wilson, *Armies, Corps, Divisions, and Separate Brigades*, p. 139.

THE FIELD ARTILLERY ACQUIRES ITS OWN AIRCRAFT 75

Approving the Concept

As the test of the air-observation-post concept went forward in the field, the debate over Field Artillery observation continued in Washington. Assistant Secretary of War McCloy became even more committed to the concept of light aircraft for the Field Artillery. Conversely, resumed opposition by the Army Air Forces and organizational changes in Washington threatened its adoption by the War Department.

Approval of the test group for the Field Artillery immediately stimulated comparable proposals from the other ground combat arms, which irritated Arnold no little amount. McCloy, on the other hand, came under pressure from the light-plane manufacturers. With their civilian market shut down for the duration of the war, they would have to shift to making parts for "big planes" unless the War Department soon placed an order for their craft. Between 6 and 13 January 1942, McCloy, in a series of telephone calls and meetings, attempted but failed to forge a consensus for a War Department response:

re: puddle jumpers. ASW [Assistant Secretary of War] felt ought to be used. General Arnold was against them because if in hands of the Infantry, Artillery, etc., they might encroach on jurisdictions of Air Corps. ASW felt this point was relatively unimportant as various branches ought to be made more conscious of air, by any method, regardless of jurisdiction.[36]

The process culminated in a meeting in the secretary of war's conference room on 14 January. All the principals attended: McCloy; one of the deputy chiefs of staff, Maj. Gen. Richard C. Moore; Arnold; Danford; the chief of Cavalry, General Herr; the chief of Coast Artillery, Maj. Gen. Joseph A. Green; the chief of Infantry, General Hodges; and the chief of the Armored Force, Lt. Gen. Jacob L. Devers. Danford recalled:

The conference in effect was a debate between Arnold and myself with no one else having very much to say. Arnold declared that if we were given the light plane it in effect would create a separate Air Force in the Army and that such a thing was unthinkable. He asked, "Who will buy your planes[?]" to which I responded, "You will, just the way the Q.M. [Quartermaster] buys my trucks and the Ordnance buys my guns." . . . I strongly argued that we had learned by experience that observing fire of the Field Artillery by Air Force officers was a job they thoroughly disliked—and that I did not blame them. I wanted "my work" to be done by "my own men" and not by officers whose chief concern was Air Force problems and not those of the Field Artillery.[37]

McCloy decided to purchase the aircraft.

The other participants at the conference were not quite as mute as Danford recollected. McCloy recorded: "General Arnold stated that he would take steps to procure the planes, but he doubted if they could be supplied to the extent indicated by the various Chiefs." Nor was this Arnold's last word on the subject. On 29 January 1942, in a meeting of General Staff principals, he publicly damned the entire concept. In response, Marshall declared "that armored and motorized divisions must have a few puddle jumper type of their own and that there should be a reservoir of a few squadrons from which puddle jumpers might from time to time be loaned to Infantry Divisions." It was one of the few instances in which Marshall openly intervened in the issue. By doing so, he set definite limits on the debate.[38]

---

[36] Diary, McCloy, 13 Jan 42. For earlier meetings and telephone calls, see entries on 6 and 8 January 1942.
[37] Diary, McCloy, 14 Jan 42, identifies the participants. Ltr, Danford to Salet, 28 Apr 67, describes the meeting.
[38] First quote from Diary, McCloy, 14 Jan 42. Second quote from Memo, L. S. K., 29 Jan 42, sub: Conference in Gen Marshall's Office, OCSA, Minutes and Notes on Conferences Relating to Emergency Planning Program, 1938–1945, RG 165, NARA.

Marshall's comment clearly indicates that he believed that ground force corps and division commanders would control the light aircraft that McCloy had decided to purchase. The surviving record, written in the bureaucratic passive voice, however, does not indicate which combat arm or arms ought to own, man, and support those planes. In October 1941 the War Department had approved the proposal by the commander of the Air Force Combat Command, Lt. Gen. Delos C. Emmons, to authorize one light Army Air Forces observation squadron per division, although the Office of the Chief of the Air Corps had not yet equipped them.

There were at least two interpretations of the McCloy decision. The positive one was that he had courageously acted to keep the light airplane manufacturers in business to preserve the option of puddle jumpers dedicated to the ground forces. The more negative one—the one more likely to appeal to Arnold—was that he had short-circuited the entire test program, which began the day after the 14 January meeting, and had prejudiced the results. In a practical sense, McCloy had probably ensured that the War Department would adopt Danford's proposal, unless the field tests produced overwhelmingly negative results.

General Danford, the last chief of his branch, retired for age on his sixty-fourth birthday, 28 February 1942. Since November 1941 various high-level War Department committees had considered a fundamental reorganization of the entire department to include General Headquarters and the Army Air Forces. Nine days after Danford retired the reorganization took effect. The War Department abolished the Offices of the Chief of Field Artillery, Chief of Infantry, Chief of Cavalry, and Chief of Coast Artillery and transferred their functions to General Headquarters, reorganized and renamed Headquarters, Army Ground Forces. The War Department also closed the Office of the Chief of the Air Corps. Overall responsibility for its functions was already lodged with Headquarters, Army Air Forces.[39]

General McNair became commanding general of the Army Ground Forces. While some officers in the Office of the Chief of Field Artillery transferred to Headquarters, Army Ground Forces, the two officers other than Danford most closely associated with the Air-Observation-Post Program, Colonel Beasley and Major Chandler, received assignments with troops. Two officers involved with Chandler in the Fuddy-Duddies Flying Club assigned to the G–3 section of Headquarters, Army Ground Forces, Cols. Thomas E. Lewis and John M. Lentz, provided some continuity of effort. They could not be as effective as Beasley and Chandler, however, because McNair was not committed to the project. In much the same manner, the reorganization ended most of the agitation for organic air in the other combat arms, at least temporarily.[40]

Danford's departure meant that Brig. Gen. Dwight D. Eisenhower, promoted in September 1941 and assigned to the War Plans Division of the General Staff on 14

---

[39] Anon, "Major General Robert Melville Danford," *FAJ* 32 (April 1942):258–59; Greenfield, et al., *Organization of Ground Combat Troops*, pp. 148–53, discusses the reorganization from the perspective of the Army Ground Forces. James E. Hewes, *From Root to McNamara: Army Organization and Administration, 1900–1963* (Washington, D.C.: U.S. Army Center of Military History, 1975), pp. 82–83, sketches the impact on the Army Air Forces.

[40] Diary, J. E. P. Morgan, 20, 23 Mar; 14 Apr; 8, 11, 12, and 22 May; 3 Jun 42, Morgan Ms, MHI. See Anon, "This War Department Reorganization," *FAJ* 32 (May 1942):376–77, for the impact on personnel in the Office of the Chief of Field Artillery.

December 1941, became the highest ranking officer in the War Department concerned about obtaining a positive decision regarding organic aviation for the Field Artillery. Even before Danford retired, Eisenhower vouched for the viability of the air-observation-post concept to Assistant Secretary of War for Air Lovett. Still later, Eisenhower volunteered to try to convert Arnold to the Field Artillery's view, surely more a testament to Eisenhower's confidence in his own persuasiveness than to his knowledge of the depth of Arnold's opposition. Given Eisenhower's responsibilities—he became chief of the War Plans Division (subsequently renamed the Operations Division) on 16 February 1942—he could hardly devote more than episodic attention to the issue.[41]

McCloy remained a highly visible supporter of organic aviation. When the commandant of the Field Artillery School, General Allin, first heard rumors of the War Department reorganization, he feared for the fate of the test program and contacted McCloy directly. McCloy in turn wrote to McNair, expressing the hope that McNair would keep his eye on the Air-Observation-Post Program "so that it does not die a-borning." At the same time McCloy, possibly hoping to persuade McNair to prejudge the results favorably, outlined the reasons why he thought the program should be approved, based upon his front-line experience in World War I. McNair, who had spent World War I in high-level training assignments and hence had an entirely different set of recollections about the conflict, remained noncommittal. He saw no danger to the proposal from oversight or neglect. He had, he admitted, always held to the view that the air arm should control observation aviation but noted that the introduction of light, commercial aircraft gave a whole new complexion to the issue. Further he would not go. The test results would be in his hands by 28 April 1942.[42]

While McNair remained skeptical, organic aviation by its performance in the field acquired important new supporters. They partially offset the loss of Danford and his position. On 18 April 1942, with the tests of Flight A just concluded, the chief of staff of the Army Ground Forces, Maj. Gen. Mark W. Clark, arrived at Camp Blanding. Colonel Ford took him on a short flight, using a road with pine trees on both sides very close to his wing tips for both takeoff and landing, a feat that impressed Clark immeasurably, and they talked about the air-observation-post concept. Clark was an infantryman and interested in nonartillery missions that light planes might perform. Afterward, Ford concluded that he had been rather "indefinite" in his reply to Clark's queries. In a very gritty move, Ford wrote Clark at length and emphasized that "by far the most important need for air observation in the division is in connection with the adjustment of artillery fire." It was just the sort of statement calculated to win Clark's respect.[43]

Both the 13th Field Artillery Brigade and 2d Division Artillery boards reported in favor of the air observation post. The commander of Third Army, Lt. Gen. Walter Krueger, in particular gave the 2d Division Artillery board report a ringing endorsement. He found the tests "well organized, comprehensive, and thorough." When the two reports arrived at

---

[41] Diary, Morgan, 8 Apr 42; Ltr, Morgan to R. A. Lovett, 4 Feb 42, Morgan Ms, MHI.

[42] Ltrs, Allin to McCloy, 27 Feb 42, and McCloy to McNair, 3 Mar 42; Memo, M[cNair] to G–5 (FA), 5 Mar 42; Ltr, McNair to McCloy, 7 Mar 42, HQ, AGF, Gen Corresp, 1942–1948, 353/2 (R) (FA Air Obsn), RG 337, NARA. On McNair, see Memo, WD, 7 Aug 44, sub: Lesley James McNair, Bio files, CMH.

[43] Memo, Ford for Clark, 22 Apr 42, HQ, AGF, Gen Corresp, 1942–1948, 452.1/312 (Airplanes), RG 337, NARA.

AIRCRAFT OF FLIGHT B PASS IN REVIEW WITH ELEMENTS OF THE 2D DIVISION AT FORT SAM HOUSTON, TEXAS, APRIL 1942.

Army Ground Forces Headquarters, McNair was away. Clark, who was never afraid of accepting responsibility, approved the reports and forwarded them to the War Department. McNair was not pleased when he returned. He noted on his retained copy of the report of the 13th Field Artillery Brigade board: "Proves little. Conclusions are opinions." McNair's opinion remained that the Army Air Forces should perform the mission, yet despite his displeasure with Clark's action he did nothing to reverse it. The War Department, lacking the benefit of McNair's personal view, established organic aviation in the Field Artillery on 6 June 1942.[44]

---

[44] Rpt, Lt Col H. J. D. Meyer, President, B/O, 13th FA Bde, to CG, 13th FA Bde, 20 Apr 42; Rpt, Maj T. J. Counihan, President, B/O, 2d Div Arty, 17 Apr 42; Ind, Brig Gen J. A. Crane, CG, 13th FA, to CG, II Corps, [2]4 Apr 42; Ind, Maj Gen L. R. Fredendall, CG, II Corps, to CG, AGF, 25 Apr 42; Ind, Brig Gen J. B. Anderson, CG, 2d Div Arty, 20 Apr 42; Ind, Maj Gen J. C. H. Lee, CG, 2d Div, to CG, VIII Corps, 24 Apr 42; Ind, Maj Gen D. I. Sultan, CG, VIII Corps, to CG, Third Army, 25 Apr 42; Ind, Lt Gen Walter Krueger to CG, AGF, 27 Apr 42, on Rpt, B/O, 2d Div Arty, 18 Apr 42; Note, McNair, 13 May [42], on Ind, Capt L. Duenweg, AAG, HQ, AGF, to CSA, 1 May 42; Memo Slip, Clark for Sec, HQ, AGF, 30 Apr 42, sub: Service Test of Organic Air Obsn for FA; all in HQ, AGF, Gen Corresp, 1942–1948, 353/1 (R) (FA Air Obsn), RG 337, NARA. Memo, Brig Gen I. H. Edwards, ACS, G–3, for CG, AGF, 6 Jun 42, sub: Organic Air Obsn for FA, Microfilm A1387, AFHRA. See also Ford, *Wagon Soldier*, p. 127.

Light Aircraft for the Other Combat Arms

The success of the Office of the Chief of Field Artillery in obtaining a test of the organic aviation concept did not encompass the other ground forces. Although the chief of Cavalry, General Herr, had decided in August 1941 that he wanted Cavalry airplanes flown and maintained by cavalrymen, the action officer assigned the project was at a loss as to how to proceed given the adamant opposition of the Army Air Forces. Shortly after Ford and Wolf completed their work in Washington, Herr forwarded a proposal to organize an air observation unit organic to the 1st Cavalry Division. Marshall, following the advice of the G–3, Brig. Gen. Harry L. Twaddle, turned Herr down. The War Department's approval of Emmons' proposal to establish one light aircraft squadron in each division meant that each mounted division now included, at least notionally, an Army Air Forces observation squadron of eighteen aircraft. If organized, such an observation squadron could, in the G–3's opinion, combine with the assigned air observation posts to provide ample observation support.[45]

In late December the new chief of the Armored Force, Maj. Gen. Jacob L. Devers, recommended creating an air-liaison test group at Fort Knox, Kentucky. Commanded by his air officer, an Air Corps officer, the group would consist of fifteen Stinson Model 76 aircraft flown and maintained by Armored Force officers and enlisted men. Devers envisioned the test group as the minimum aviation component for an armored division in addition to the observation squadron approved by the War Department. The light planes would perform "courier-liaison" work and artillery fire direction. The War Department used the same rationale to veto Devers' proposal as it had Herr's.[46]

The War Department's disapproval of Herr's and Devers' requests did not end the efforts of other branches to obtain their own organic air programs. Assistant Secretary McCloy tirelessly sought to proselytize others. The Armored Force continued to show interest in light aircraft, as did the Cavalry Board. During the spring and summer of 1942 other branches and specialties that had not demonstrated any desire previously, the Signal Corps, Corps of Engineers, tank destroyers, and airborne, sought or gave serious consideration to operating their own aircraft. The commander of the Tank Destroyer Center, Brig. Gen. Andrew D. Bruce, was both the highest ranking and most persistent of these supplicants. In March 1942 he ordered his staff to prepare a proposal, essentially a copy of the already-approved program for Field Artillery tests, with "Tank Destroyers" substituted for "Field Artillery." The Army Ground Forces staff considered this proposal "controversial" and buried it when it reached Headquarters, Army Ground Forces.[47]

---

[45] Ltr, Col H. M. Estes, XO, OCC, to TAG, 12 Aug 41, TAG Decimal file, 1940–1945, 452.1 (8–12–41), RG 407, NARA; Memo, Maj J. H. Claybrook for Chief of Cavalry (CC), 25 Aug 41, OCC, Gen Corresp, 1920–1942, 452.1, RG 337, NARA. The Army Air Forces observation squadron intended for the 1st Cavalry Division to remain a notional unit only. It consisted of 6 twin-engine bomber variants, 6 single-seat fighter variants, and 6 light aircraft. Memo, Brig Gen H. L. Twaddle, ACS, G–3, for CSA, 7 Jan 42, CSA Numerical file, 1920–1942, 212766, RG 165, NARA.

[46] Ltr, Maj Gen Jacob L. Devers, Chief, Armored Force, to CSA, 21 Dec 41, sub: Service Test of Air Obsn as an Organic Part of Armored Units, with Ind, Maj Gen E. S. Adams, TAG, to Chief, Armored Force, 14 Jan 42, sub: Same, TAG Decimal file, 1940–1945, 320.2 (12–18–41) (3), RG 407, NARA.

[47] Ltr, Maj C. M. Wells, AAG, Armored Center, to Chief, Materiel Div, OCAC, 31 Dec 41, sub: Rpt on Taylorcraft Airplane, TAG Decimal file, 1940–1945, 452.1 (12–31–41), RG 407, NARA. Ltrs, Morgan to W. T.

It was the political climate rather than the content of the tank destroyer proposal that the chief of the G–3 Training Branch, Colonel Lentz, found objectionable. Given the strenuous opposition of the Army Air Forces, Lentz decided to push first for the approval of the Field Artillery program, which he and Colonel Lewis considered the most important. Once it was established on a solid footing, Lentz proposed expanding organic air to the other branches.[48]

Conclusion

The Field Artillery acquired its own aircraft in June 1942, after three-and-a-half years of concentrated effort. Danford mounted his campaign because of three converging technical trends: the development of a system of indirect massed fire that placed a premium on accurate observation; the development of lightweight, static-free voice radio; and the development of light aircraft that could operate out of the forward battle area to provide reliable, on-call aerial observation. For the Field Artillery the control of aerial observation was a major issue because of how it affected its primary mission, the accurate delivery of fire on the enemy. Danford thus gave the issue almost continuous attention. He also had a superb action officer in Chandler to manage the issue on a day-to-day basis. (Cavalry efforts foundered, in part, on the lack of just such an officer.) Chandler built up a network of informal contacts reaching all the way up the War Department hierarchy to Assistant Secretary of War McCloy and used those contacts to predispose McCloy and others to favor organic air. And Danford was willing to take chances. When he approached the secretary of war directly, he in effect bypassed his superior, the chief of staff. Because Danford knew Stimson personally, the risk was a calculated one. But the fact that the chief of Field Artillery had a secretary and assistant secretary of war with Field Artillery experience from the last war was simply good fortune. Danford exploited the situation brilliantly.

Danford, like Generals Herr and Hodges, initially sought a rotary-wing rather than a fixed-wing solution to his observation problem. All three demonstrated a certain degree of perspicacity in this, because helicopters, if not autogiros, possessed greater potential for growth than light planes and, once fully developed, more battlefield uses. In so doing, however, all three men underestimated the engineering problems involved in helicopter development and the time required to find solutions. Such a misjudgment reflected not only their understandable lack of expertise in the area but also their position in the mili-

---

Piper, 21 Jan, 1 May, 8 May, 24 Sep, 15 Oct 42, Morgan Ms, MHI; Diary, Morgan, 26 Mar, 29 Apr 42. MFR, AGF, 16 Jul 42, sub: Liaison Airplanes; Ltr, Maj W. P. Ennis, Tank Destroyer Center (TDC), to CG, AGF, 25 Mar 42, sub: Small Plane Obsn; Ltr, Brig Gen A. D. Bruce, CG, TDC, to CG, AGF, 18 Jul 42, sub: Organic Tank Destroyer (TD) Air Obsn; Memo Slip, Walker, Special Training Branch, G–3, for Training Div, 6 May 42; Ltr, Maj Gen A. D. Bruce to CG, AGF, 9 Dec 42, sub: Rating of TD Liaison Pilots; all in HQ, AGF, Gen Corresp, 1942–1948, 452.1/364 (Airplanes), 353/1–5 (TD Air Obsn) (R), RG 337, NARA. Ltr, Morgan to McCloy, 14 Oct 42; Memo, Morgan for CG, AGF (Attn: Brig Gen J. M. Lentz), 29 Oct 42, sub: Light Planes, "Grasshoppers" or "1/4-Ton Jeeps with Wings"; Transcript (Trans), Telecon, Brig Gen J. M. Lentz, G–3, AGF, and Col W. P. Scobey, Executive Assistant to Assistant Secretary of War (ASW), 0900, 4 Nov 42; all in Office of the Assistant Secretary of War (OASW), Security Classified Corresp of John J. McCloy, 1941–1945, 452.1 (Grasshoppers), RG 107, NARA. The fullest discussion of McCloy's actions during this period is in Howard K. Butler, *Organic Aviation in the Ground Arms, 1941–1947* (St. Louis, Mo.: U.S. Army Aviation Systems Command, 1992), pp. 196–99.

[48] Trans, Telecon, Lentz and Scobey, 0900, 4 Nov 42.

tary hierarchy. As branch chiefs they had to be cognizant of their branches' long-range as well as immediate needs. The prewar mobilization constituted a cash windfall for combat arms starved of funds since World War I. If the United States remained out of World War II—the stated aim of the Roosevelt administration until Pearl Harbor—the availability of funds might be limited indeed. In such a circumstance, the branch chiefs were under a subtle pressure to opt for a long-term rather than a short-term solution. Danford was both realistic and open to advice from junior officers who were sufficiently informed technically to make a judgment about feasibility. Consequently, he could shift quickly from the long-term to the immediate solution. He threw himself behind light aircraft in September 1941 and never had cause to regret the decision.

The Field Artillery's acquisition of its own aircraft was facilitated by the existence of a light aviation community in the ground Army that provided an alternative to the Army Air Forces as a source of information about the tactical possibilities of light aircraft. Ford made two great contributions. He expounded the ideas common among that community about how to employ light aircraft, and he organized and commanded the test group. The experiments by 1st Lt. Joseph M. Watson and Capt. George K. Burr in the 36th Division were an interesting precursor, but they had less direct influence on policy formulation than they might otherwise have had because of the hesitation at a critical moment of their brigade commander, Brig. Gen. Robert O. Whiteaker. He at least partially redeemed himself by facilitating the conversion of the Third Army commander, General Krueger. Krueger was just the kind of tough, practical field soldier of long service whose opinion carried considerable weight with the War Department.[49]

The light-aircraft manufacturers' role was crucial throughout. They could and did lobby at all levels of the chain of command from the secretary of war down. This outside pressure sensitized the various command levels to the importance of the decision on light aircraft before it was made. Their presence made it less likely that any one opponent could quietly kill the idea of organic air, always a possibility in a hierarchial organization like the Army. William T. Piper and John E. P. Morgan were the key figures. Piper, because of his background and personality, was an effective salesman of the military potential of light aircraft, while Morgan became skilled in dealing with the military staffs in Washington. Existing evidence shows that Morgan was clearly involved in the establishment of the Fuddy Duddies, but whether he served as mother or midwife remains unclear.

At the same time the Army Air Forces, at the height of its influence, lost a mission that it did not want to lose, although whether it actually wanted to perform it is at least debatable. Arnold and most air officers believed that the trends of modern technology were gradually vindicating the theories of air power expounded by Arnold's one-time mentor, Brig. Gen. William Mitchell. They regarded visual observation over the battlefield of the early 1940s as an anachronism. The function would be superseded by high-speed photoreconnaissance aircraft. Here the Army Air Forces' argument broke down, although Arnold and his contemporaries may not have understood sufficiently the recent evolution of Field Artillery technology and doctrine to realize it. Visual observation implied the ability to adjust fire in real time. Photoreconnaissance meant the capacity to

---

[49] For a different view of Watson's influence, see L. B. Epstein, "Army Organic Light Aviation: The Founding Fathers," *USAAD* 23 (June 1977):2–17.

direct fire after elapsed time. Arnold was quite correct that map fire was the primary means of delivering indirect fire during World War I, but here he fell into a fallacy of which Mitchell has often been accused. Mitchell had projected the continued technical advance of the air forces but had assumed that the ground forces would remain static. Arnold lived through the technical advance of the ground forces but did not realize it. Still, conceding the idea that photoreconnaissance was an acceptable replacement for visual observation—a premise that no field artilleryman would allow—then fabric-covered light aircraft did appear to be vestigial remnants in an age of sleek aluminum pursuits and bombers. Arnold's predisposition and lack of knowledge about the Field Artillery was tied to the Air Corps' drive for institutional independence during the 1930s, which had led air officers to attempt to minimize connections with the ground arms. These factors contributed to the conventional Air Corps view that light aircraft were old-fashioned and inferior to standard service planes rather than, as the Field Artillery saw them, distinct types with different capabilities.

While previous events and the personalities of key individuals contributed to the Air Corps' and later the Army Air Forces' inability to recognize the possibilities of light aircraft, there was a larger institutional dimension involved. Like the members of any complex organization, the officers of the Army Air Forces had developed certain normal ways of analyzing problems and certain conventional approaches to solving them. Army Air Forces engineers had evolved certain orthodox methods of evaluating the performance of aircraft. Likewise, pilots over the years had acquired a set of common techniques for flying service aircraft. All these usual patterns of doing business—the formal and informal standard operating procedures of the institution—broke down and failed to cope with the challenge posed by light aircraft. Air and ground officers, throughout the controversy over organic air, communicated not so much with one another as past one another. They exchanged words but not meanings. And because of the history of chronic misunderstandings, they failed to communicate with candor. The most striking example of the latter occurred when the Army Air Forces service-tested the O–49 at the same time that its mobilization plan categorized all short-range observation aircraft as "obsolete," to be replaced with twin-engine bombers.

Large institutions develop their own world view, shaped by their mission. A shared perspective enables the individuals in any particular organization to effectively communicate with one another and work together to achieve the organization's goals. But occasionally a problem will develop that falls into a blind spot of the institutional world view. The common categories of thought do not work, but the members of the institution do not realize it. Light planes constituted such a case for the Army Air Forces. Preconceptions and intellectual rigidity made it less able than the Field Artillery to exploit the potential of light aircraft.

While Arnold considered the control of observation aircraft a major issue, it was one of a hundred he faced—for Danford, one of four or five. Danford may have enjoyed less power and prestige, but he was able to bring more of it to bear on the issue than was Arnold. Success in this bureaucratic engagement went to the officer who could concentrate his resources.

The complexity of the political machinations involved in securing War Department approval for organic aviation in the Field Artillery threatens to overshadow the significance of the technical competence Ford, Beasley, Chandler, and Wolf exhibited in designing the test group and laying out a proto-doctrine for air-observation-post operations. The speed and relative lack of rancor with which they worked testified to the excellence of the education they had received at Army schools during the interwar period. They knew tactics, techniques, organization, supply, and maintenance, and it showed in their product. In addition to this excellent theoretical foundation, the success of the Class Before One rested on both the superior training by the civilian instructors and high-quality leadership by Ford in molding a disparate group of soldiers into a cohesive unit intent on demonstrating the utility of light aviation in ground combat. The performance of the officers and enlisted men of Flights A and B at Camp Blanding and Fort Sam Houston demonstrated just how much he and the civilian instructors had accomplished.

CHAPTER 3

Creating the Air-Observation-Post Program, June–December 1942

The War Department decision of 6 June 1942 to establish the Air-Observation-Post Program constituted but the first step in the creation of organic aviation in the Field Artillery. Ground forces officers required some seventeen months to fully develop the program. Their first and most critical task was to create a training base. In the process of translating theory into practice they encountered many unanticipated problems. They also faced two additional pressures. American involvement in World War II made everything they did acutely time sensitive. With a late start on a formal program, compared to their counterparts in the Royal Artillery, the Americans had to play catch-up from the very beginning. Furthermore, the leaders of the Army Air Forces never accepted the legitimacy of the Air-Observation-Post Program and attempted to reverse the War Department's decision to initiate it. Because of this attitude, every problem had the potential of becoming a crisis that could end the program before it had fairly begun. These pressures proved especially intense and the corresponding dangers to the existence of the program particularly potent during the first seven months of its existence, June through December 1942.

Writing the Charter

Two War Department memorandums, one to the commanding general, Army Ground Forces, and the other to the commanding general, Army Air Forces, formally established the organic Air-Observation-Post Program for the Field Artillery and laid out the responsibilities of each command. The memorandums were the product of the collaboration of the War Department General Staff and Headquarters, Army Ground Forces. Two officers from the G–3 section, Col. Boniface Campbell and Col. Frank F. Everest, Field Artillery and Air Corps officers, respectively, represented the chief of staff, General George C. Marshall, Jr. The chief of the Training Branch in the G–3 section of the ground forces headquarters, Col. John M. Lentz, and the commander of the test detachment at the Field Artillery School, on temporary duty in Washington, Lt. Col. William W. Ford, stood in for the commander of the Army Ground Forces, Lt. Gen. Lesley J. McNair. The basic idea, Lentz later recalled, was to allow the ground forces to make their own plans, provided those plans did not interfere with the ongoing expansion of the Army Air Forces, then in high gear.[1]

Lentz and Ford initially disagreed about where to lodge responsibility for pilot training. Lentz accepted Ford's advice that the Field Artillery would draw pilots from licensed light-plane pilots who were already members of the ground forces and graduates of the Civilian Pilot Training Program. In late 1938 the Roosevelt administration had launched this program for college students to increase the country's pool of trained aviators in the event of war. The graduates automatically became privates in the Army Air Corps Enlisted Reserve despite their lack of military instruction. Lentz, however, balked at Ford's proposal to assign the Field Artillery the mission to provide primary training for its own pilots. In line with the Army Ground Forces policy to keep overhead as low as possible, Lentz preferred to draw directly upon the Civilian Pilot Training Program if he could do so without discomforting the Army Air Forces. Lentz coordinated the issue directly with the director of individual training in the Office of the Chief of Air Corps, Col. Luther S. Smith, who made suggestions that the conferees included in the final directives. Lentz's friend and fellow member of the Fuddy-Duddies Flying Club, Col. Thomas E. Lewis, did much of the actual drafting at Headquarters, Army Ground Forces. All the conferees regarded the directives as a starting point to be modified however experience might dictate.[2]

The 6 June 1942 directives, signed by the assistant chief of staff, G–3, Brig. Gen. Idwal H. Edwards, assigned 2 light aircraft, 2 pilots, and 1 mechanic to each light and medium field artillery battalion, division artillery headquarters and headquarters battery, and field artillery brigade headquarters. Edwards formally charged the commanding general, Army Air Forces, to serve as a source of supply and major repairs for "commercial low performance aircraft of the 'Piper Cub' type" and primary flight training for pilots. The commanding general, Army Ground Forces, became responsible for organizing at Fort Sill, or some other station, courses for the "operational training" of pilots, mechanics, and observers "in the tactical employment of organic air observation in Field Artillery units."[3]

---

[1] Memo, [Brig Gen J. M. Lentz, G–3, Army Ground Forces (AGF), for Assistant Secretary of War (ASW), 11 Nov 42], Office of the Assistant Secretary of War (OASW), Security Classified (Class) Correspondence (Corresp) of John J. McCloy, 1941–1945, 452.1 (Puddlejumpers) (11–11–42), Record Group (RG) 107, National Archives and Records Administration, Washington, D.C. (hereafter cited as NARA).

[2] Ibid.; Diary, J. E. P. Morgan, 3 Jun 42, J. E. P. Morgan Manuscripts (Ms), U.S. Army Military History Institute, Carlisle Barracks, Pa. (hereafter cited as MHI); Transcript (Trans), Telecon, Brig Gen J. M. Lentz, G–3, AGF, and Col W. P. Scobey, Executive Assistant (Exec Asst) to ASW, 0900, 4 Nov 42, OASW, Security Class Corresp of McCloy, 1941–1945, 452.1 (Puddlejumpers), RG 107, NARA; Memo, Lt Col J. W. Ramsey, Assistant Adjutant General (AAG), AGF, for Chief of Staff, Army (CSA) (Attn: Assistant Chief of Staff [ACS], G–3), 2 Jun 42, sub: Organic Air Observation (Obsn) for Field Artillery (FA), Headquarters (HQ), AGF, General (Gen) Corresp, 1942–1948, 353/3 (FA Air Obsn), RG 337, NARA; Interview (Interv), author with Col Michael J. Strok, 30 Jun 82, Historian's files, U.S. Army Center of Military History, Washington, D.C. (hereafter cited as CMH). Lentz was the action officer for the memorandum of 2 June, a line-by-line critique of the two memorandums. For the Civilian Pilot Training Program, see John R. M. Wilson, *Turbulence Aloft: The Civil Aeronautics Administration Amid Wars and Rumors of War, 1938–1953* (Washington, D.C.: Department of Transportation, 1979), pp. 97–106.

[3] Memo, Brig Gen I. H. Edwards, Assistant Chief of Staff (ACS), G–3, War Department General Staff (WDGS), for Commanding General (CG), AGF, 6 Jun 42, sub: Organic Air Obsn for FA; Memo, Edwards for CG, Army Air Forces (AAF), 6 Jun 42, sub: Organic Air Obsn for FA; both on Microfilm A1387, U.S. Air Force Historical Research Agency, Maxwell Air Force Base (AFB), Ala. (hereafter cited as AFHRA); Memo, Ramsey for CSA, 2 Jun 42.

Establishing the Training and Logistical Base, June–July 1942

To succeed, the Air-Observation-Post Program required the closest kind of cooperation between the G–3 Division of the War Department General Staff and Headquarters, Army Ground Forces. In a broad sense, the War Department General Staff established general policies for the program and the hundreds of other ventures related to the ground combat arms; Headquarters, Army Ground Forces, managed them on a day-to-day basis. The intermediate command between Headquarters, Army Ground Forces, and Fort Sill, the Replacement and School Command, exercised only slight influence on major issues involving Field Artillery aviation.

The G–3, General Edwards, and the commanding general of Army Ground Forces, General McNair, took diametrically opposed approaches to administering the program within their respective spheres. Edwards understood that managing an aviation program involved careful attention to hundreds of details, any one of which, if carelessly handled, might impact adversely on air operations. After coordinating the issue with his counterparts in G–1 and G–4, the personnel and logistics sections, he arranged for his section to temporarily handle all staff actions pertaining to air observation posts at the War Department level until the program became well established. In contrast, nothing in McNair's background caused him to think of aircraft as anything but another item of equipment. McNair, moreover, had an aversion to top-heavy, high-level headquarters. He resisted the idea of appointing an officer with an aviation background to provide close, technical supervision over the program, despite its extreme decentralization, the relative complexity of its maintenance and supply requirements, and the lack of familiarity of ground forces supply officers with the Army Air Forces supply system. The staff at Headquarters, Army Ground Forces, handled light aviation questions as they did other matters, with no single point of responsibility short of General McNair himself. Such an arrangement almost guaranteed a certain unevenness of results at the beginning of the program.[4]

Once the War Department decided to organize organic aviation in the Field Artillery, setting up a training base and devising at least the beginnings of a logistical support system became pressing priorities. The Field Artillery needed an instructional element to train its pilots and mechanics, a means for securing adequate numbers of students and aircraft, a training area, and a method of securing aviation supplies. These problems became the responsibility of the director of the test group, Colonel Ford.

Even before the formal approval of the program, Ford began selecting civilians for whom he hoped to obtain direct commissions. They, along with members of the Class Before One, would serve as the nucleus of a department of air training at the Field Artillery School. Instructors of the test group, such as Theodore F. Schirmacher, Thomas Piper, and Henry Wann, were obvious choices to be senior instructors for the program. Ford's assistant, Maj. Gordon J. Wolf, drew upon his contacts at the Aeronca Aircraft Corporation to attract several veteran light aircraft instructors from the Cincinnati area, most notably

---

[4] Disposition Form (DF), Edwards to ACS, G–1, 15 Sep 42, HQ, AGF, Gen Corresp, 1942–1948, 353/28 (FA Air Obsn), RG 337, NARA; Memo Slip, Walker, G–4 Section, AGF, for CG, 5 Jan 43, HQ, AGF, Personal Papers of the CG, Lt Gen Lesley J. McNair, Gen Corresp file, 1940–1944, "Ford, W. W.," RG 337, NARA.

Thomas S. Baker. Schirmacher, Piper, and Baker eventually received commissions as captains; Wann became a first lieutenant.[5]

Ford, while at Headquarters, Army Ground Forces, in Washington, D.C., in late May and early June, prepared a memorandum outlining what became the War Department procurement strategy through June 1943. He wanted 150 aircraft as of 1 July 1942, followed by 100 aircraft per month beginning 1 September. The total, 1,150, represented enough aircraft to outfit the training establishment at Fort Sill and the field artillery firing battalions and division artillery and artillery brigade headquarters in the 1942 troop list. When Headquarters, Army Air Forces, suggested additional aircraft to provide spares, Headquarters, Army Ground Forces, did not agree, presumably because the limiting factor on the size of the program was the number of available pilots, not the number of aircraft.[6]

Ford next addressed the pilot training program. The wartime expansion of the ground forces and the corresponding promotion of officers meant that few of the interwar lightplane enthusiasts were available. On the other hand, many junior Reserve and National Guard officers and enlisted men with experience in light planes had come on active duty in the mobilizing force. Ford calculated that he could find enough volunteers to fill the initial four pilot classes, the first of which he had scheduled to begin 3 August 1942. Thereafter he would have to depend on the Army Air Forces. A memorandum he wrote on 16 June, while still at Headquarters, Army Ground Forces, defined what became War Department policy: The Army Air Forces would provide 100 pilots per month, 25 per week, from 1 September 1942 through 30 June 1943. All would be graduates of the Civilian Pilot Training Program. After arrival at Fort Sill, they would automatically transfer from the Air Corps to the Field Artillery.[7]

Post Field at Fort Sill was the logical location for a department of air training. Unfortunately, it already had a permanent occupant, the 5th Observation Squadron. Relations between the Army Air Forces officers and the members of the test group had been strained since the inception of the test program. If the air-observation-post concept succeeded, the observation pilots would lose part or possibly all of their mission. Of even more immediate concern to Ford was the lack of sufficient space at the field to accommodate both the observation squadron and a training establishment of the size the Field Artillery needed, to say nothing of the airspace congestion. Not until late July, only two weeks before the first formal pilot course was scheduled to begin, did the 5th Observation Squadron receive orders to change station.[8]

---

[5] Intervs, author with Lt Col H. F. Wann, 27 Aug 82, 23 Mar 91; Maj Gen W. A. Harris with Lt Col Gordon J. Wolf, c. 1983, all at CMH. Ltrs, Morgan to W. T. Piper, 17 Jun 42, 23 Jun 43; Diary, Morgan, 17 Jun 42; all in Morgan Ms, MHI.

[6] Memo, Ramsey for CG, AAF (Attn: Materiel Division [Div]), 1 Jun 42, sub: Procurement of Liaison Planes [Action Officer (A/O) Lt Col William W. Ford]; Memo, Lt Col J. R. Dryden, AAG, AGF, for CG, AAF, 20 Jun 42, sub: Liaison Aircraft for FA, HQ, AGF, Gen Corresp, 1942–1948, 353/2 (FA Air Obsn), RG 337, NARA.

[7] Memo, Dryden for CG, AAF, 16 Jun 42, sub: Pilots for FA Duty [A/O Ford], HQ, AGF, Gen Corresp, 1942–1948, 353/1 (FA Air Obsn), RG 337, NARA; Ltr, Col C. L. Hyssong, Ground Adjutant General (GAG), AGF, to CG, Second Army, et al., 17 Jun 42, sub: Pilots and Mechanics for Organic FA Air Obsn, HQ, AGF, Gen Corresp, 1942–1948, 353/4 (FA Air Obsn), RG 337, NARA.

[8] Memo, Dryden for CG, AAF, 18 Jun 42, sub: Facilities at Post Field, Okla., HQ, AGF, Gen Corresp, 1942–1948, 353/4 (FA Air Obsn) (Restricted [R]), RG 337, NARA. Telegrams (Telgs), Maj Gen H. R. Bull, CG, Replacement and School Command (R&SC), to CG, AGF, 18 Jun 42, and McNair to CG, R&SC, 21 Jul 42, both in HQ, AGF, Gen Corresp, 1942–1948, 353/27 (FA Air Obsn), RG 337, NARA. Memo, Edwards for CG, AGF,

CREATING THE AIR-OBSERVATION-POST PROGRAM

WORLD WAR II AERIAL VIEW OF POST FIELD. THE BALLOON HANGAR IS AT LEFT.

With these necessary preliminaries on the way to completion, on 24 June Headquarters, Army Ground Forces, issued a directive establishing pilot, aircraft mechanic, and aerial observer classes at the Field Artillery School. The school could expect to receive thirty pilots each week—the extra five presumably available from the Army Ground Forces as a hedge against attrition. Pilot courses would continue from five to seven weeks, depending upon the skill and experience levels of the students upon entry. Ford expected the peak load to come at the end of the seventh week, when approximately two hundred student pilots would be at Fort Sill. Mechanic courses would begin every week,

---

10 Jul 42, sub: Redesignation and Reassignment of Obsn Squadrons; Indorsement (Ind), Hyssong to CSA (Attn: G–3 Div), 18 Jul 42; Memo, Col W. W. Dick, Adjutant General (AG), HQ, AAF, for CSA (Attn: G–3 Div), 7 Jul 42; all in HQ, AGF, Gen Corresp, 1942–1948, 320.2/4734 (Strength), RG 337, NARA; Interv, Harris with Wolf, c. 1983.

each with about fifteen students. The courses would last five weeks. Observer courses, starting every fifth week, would consist of twenty students and would run four weeks.⁹

The memorandums establishing the program provided that the War Department would rate Field Artillery pilots, that is, officially certify individuals as military pilots. Concomitant with the rating came flight pay. Left undecided was the question of the type of rating they would receive. On 27 June McNair's headquarters forwarded another memorandum written by Ford for the War Department General Staff's approval. He proposed the creation of the entirely new ratings, "Pilot (F.A.)" and "Mechanic (F.A.)." He further recommended the amendment of relevant Army Regulations to permit regular and frequent flights by participants in the program and to authorize flight pay. Headquarters, Services of Supply (later Army Service Forces), objected to giving a special rating to the aviation mechanics, while the Air Staff objected to a separate rating for Field Artillery pilots. Headquarters, Army Air Forces, wanted to rate them as liaison pilots. The War Department decided not to create special ratings but approved the remainder of Ford's recommendations.¹⁰

Ford continued to assume that only 20 percent of the pilots in the program would be officers; the rest would be enlisted men with staff sergeant as the highest possible grade. Headquarters, Army Ground Forces, anticipated that even with the relatively low number of officers required the pilot training program would not attract a sufficient number. This opened up the possibility of commissions for a sizable percentage of the enlisted volunteers. In late September the War Department granted the commandant of the Field Artillery School the authority to issue warrants of staff sergeant to enlisted men who successfully completed their training.¹¹

In July the Field Artillery School formally established the Department of Air Training with Ford as the director. (See *Chart 1*.) He organized it like the other departments at the school. The headquarters element included the director, an executive, Major Wolf (subsequently promoted to lieutenant colonel), and a departmental secretary, 1st Lt. Delbert L. Bristol, to perform the necessary administrative duties. Capt. (later Maj.) Robert R. Williams became chief of the Flight Division, in charge of the supervision of all flight instruction, with Captains Baker and Schirmacher as assistants. Capt. (later Maj.) Robert M. Leich became chief of the Maintenance Division, with two assistants, 1st Lt. Lloyd M.

---

⁹ Ltr, Dryden to CG, R&SC, 24 Jun 42, sub: Training of Pilots, Observers (Obsrs), and Mechanics for FA, HQ, AGF, Gen Corresp, 1942–1948, 353/5 (FA Air Obsn) (R), RG 337, NARA. Ind, Capt L. Duenweg, AAG, AGF, to CG, R&SC, 8 Jul 42, with Note, H., 7 Jul 42, on Ltr, Maj A. A. Altman, AG, R&SC, to CG, AGF, 29 Jun 42, HQ, AGF, Gen Corresp, 1942–1948, 353/18 (FA Air Obsn), RG 337, NARA. Recommendation and Routing (R&R) Sheet, G-3, WDGS, to CGs, AAF and AGF, 7 Aug 42, sub: Organic Obsn for FA, HQ, AGF, Gen Corresp, 1942–1948, 353/34 (FA Air Obsn), RG 337, NARA.

¹⁰ Memo, Dryden to CSA (Attn: ACS, G-1), 27 Jun 42, sub: Pilot and Mechanic Ratings, Authorization to Fly, and Flying Pay for FA Air Obsn [A/O Ford], HQ, AGF, Gen Corresp, 1942–1948, 353/8 (FA Air Obsn), RG 337, NARA; Memo, Col C. W. West, Acting Chief (Ch), Military (Mil) Affairs Div, Office of the Judge Advocate General, for Director (Dir), Mil Personnel, Services of Supply (SOS), 28 Jul 42; Memo, Col R. B. Reynolds, Deputy (Dep) Dir, Mil Personnel, SOS, for ACS, G-1, 30 Jul 42, sub: Pilot and Mechanic Ratings, Authorization to Fly, and Flying Pay for FA Air Obsn; Memo, Col J. H. McCormick, Acting Assistant Chief of Air Staff (ACAS), A-1, for ACS, G-1, 8 Aug 42; DF, Col H. J. Matchett, Acting ACS, G-3, to ACS, G-1 (Attn: Col Lynch, Officer's [Ofcr's] Section), 3 May 43; all in The Adjutant General's Office (TAGO), Decimal file, 1940–1945, 320.2 (Strength and Table of Organization [TO]) (2–5–42), RG 407, NARA.

¹¹ Ind, Maj H. L. Nelson, AGAG, to CG, SOS, 27 Aug 42, HQ, AGF, Gen Corresp, 1942–1948, 353/73 (FA Air Obsn), RG 337, NARA.

CHART 1—FIELD ARTILLERY SCHOOL, DEPARTMENT OF AIR TRAINING, OCTOBER 1942

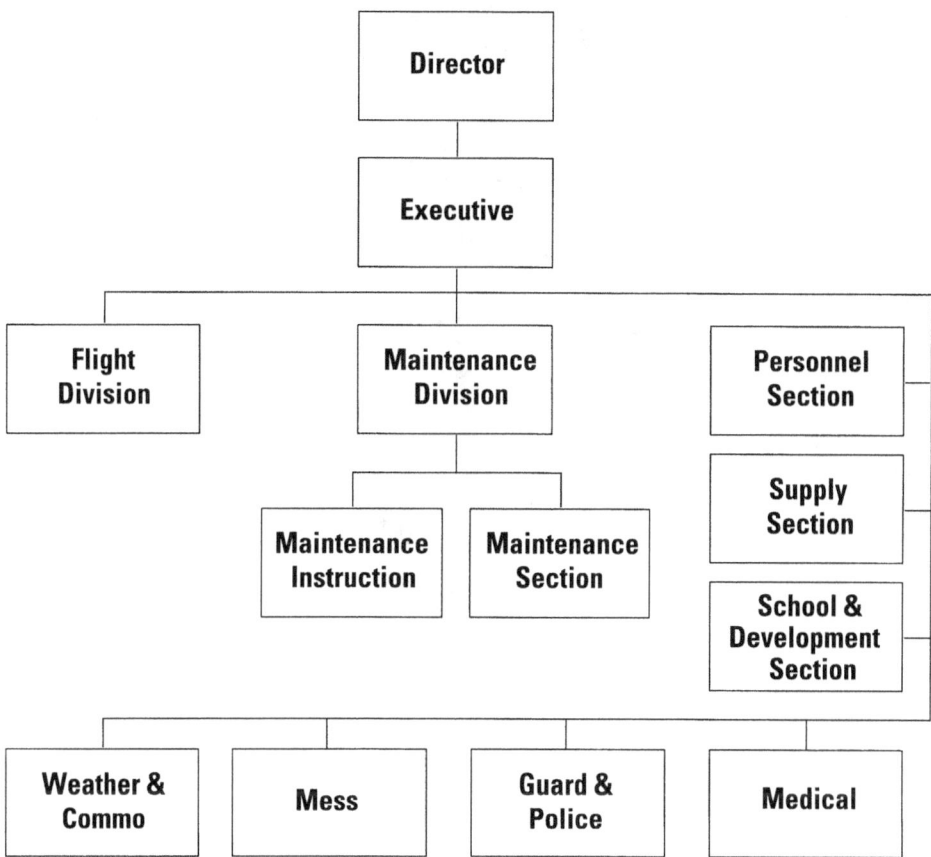

Bornstein in charge of maintenance instruction, and 1st Lt. Marion J. Fortner, the engineering officer, in charge of servicing the department's complement of aircraft. Separate personnel, supply, and school and development sections, the latter to demonstrate air-observation-post tactics to students in other departments at the school and to undertake special projects, plus four administrative elements reported to the department director without an intervening division chief.[12]

---

[12] Ltr, Brig Gen J. D. Balmer, Commandant, Field Artillery School (FAS), to CG, R&SC, 4 Jul 42, sub: Training of Pilots, Obsrs, and Mechanics for FA, HQ, AGF, Gen Corresp, 1942–1948, 353/35 (FA Air Obsn), RG 337, NARA; DF, Edwards to ACS, G–1, 15 Sep 42, sub: Increase in Allotment of Ofcrs to FAS, Fort Sill, Okla., for Training of Pilots, Obsrs, and Mechanics for FA, with Ind, R. A. O'Kelly, AG, to CG, AGF, 5 Oct 42, HQ, AGF, Gen Corresp, 1942–1948, 353/28 (FA Air Obsn), RG 337, NARA; Interv, R. J. Tierney with Lt Col T. J. Schirmacher, Mar 62, *U.S. Army Aviation Digest* (*USAAD*) files, U.S. Army Aviation Museum Library, Fort Rucker, Ala. (hereafter cited as USAAML).

CAPTAINS SCHIRMACHER *(left)* AND BAKER

The new men brought with them diverse experiences and differing training philosophies. As work progressed on the curriculum, Schirmacher and Baker engaged in a heated disagreement. Schirmacher argued for the approach used to good effect with the Class Before One, showing the students the limits of the equipment so they would know exactly what they could and could not do. Baker advocated what might be termed the Civil Aeronautics Administration method—instructing the students to fly in the safe center of the aircraft's capabilities. His views were not unique. They were shared by many of the instructors who had connections with him in civil life, with the Aeronca Aircraft Corporation, or with both. These men were known collectively as the Cincinnati Flying Club, a phrase that might convey either affection or derision depending on the attitude of the person using it. And they all owed their presence at Fort Sill to the influence of Major Wolf, the sometime corporate counsel for Aeronca.[13]

Of course, the disagreement over instructional strategy might simply have reflected the differing flight characteristics of the Piper L–4 and the Aeronca L–3. But that line of thought had some truly disturbing implications. The Department of Air Training was a military organization that contained former members of competing civilian companies. Most of them intended to return to their previous jobs at the end of the war. If they fell to dis-

---

[13] Intervs, author with Col T. F. Schirmacher, 13 Jun 92; with Lt Col R. R. Yates, 13 Jun 91; with Lt Col J. R. Forbes, 5 Jun 93; all at CMH.

MAJOR LEICH (*center*) AND LIEUTENANTS BORNSTEIN (*left*) AND FORTNER

puting training methods in which the alternatives would maximize the performance of one company's products but not the other's, the department faced the prospect of a disagreement so serious as to destroy all sense of cohesion and purpose. Piper and Aeronca might be united in trying to sell light planes to the War Department, but once that issue was settled they reverted to being commercial competitors.

Ford thus faced a decision that had both technical and political dimensions. He had two technical experts with approximately equal credentials arguing passionately for diametrically opposed solutions. He was too experienced a pilot not to have some views of his own on the relative merits of the Schirmacher and Baker positions, but what he needed for the health of the program was a consensual, not a dictated solution. And because the graduates were going to have to go into harm's way, he needed the best technical answer. His solution, urged by Schirmacher, was to divide each of the initial classes in half, giving one flight to Schirmacher and the other to Baker with the authority to instruct the students using their own philosophies. Then Ford appointed an impartial group of officers to give the graduates flight tests, colloquially known as check rides. These officers concluded that the students instructed in the techniques of the Class Before One were the best pilots. Thereafter, all student pilots trained in this manner.[14]

---

[14] Interv, author with Schirmacher, 13 Jun 92.

As the aircraft began arriving, Williams and other officers worked out a table of distribution and allowances for the school—everything from desks, chairs, and typewriters to spare engines, spare parts, and tool sets for maintenance training. Ford, promoted to temporary colonel in late June 1942, sent Williams to Washington to process the request through channels with Wann, not yet commissioned, accompanying him as a technical adviser. En route they acquired a chaperon, Lt. Col. Stewart L. Cowles, the G–4 at the Replacement and School Command. The long train ride gave the two pilots an opportunity to sell the program to the colonel. Wann, who had considerable experience with salesmen, was impressed by the cogency, enthusiasm, and good humor with which Williams argued his points. By the time the three arrived at Union Station in Washington, Cowles was a strong advocate of the air-observation-post concept.[15]

Of course, Cowles may not have had as much sales resistance as Williams and Wann imagined. A nineteen-year veteran of the Field Artillery, he had served in the Office of the Chief of Field Artillery until its disestablishment. Given the emphasis that Maj. Gen. Robert M. Danford had placed on the Air-Observation-Post Program during the last months of his tour as chief of Field Artillery, Cowles may not have been as innocent of information about organic aviation as he appeared. Whatever the case, his recent Washington tour and still-fresh contacts made him ideal to shepherd the Department of Air Training's request through channels. He began doing just that almost as soon as he stepped off the train.[16]

Cowles greatly facilitated the acquisition of certain specialized Army Air Forces equipment, especially trucks to refuel aircraft, which Williams and Wann thought they would never get. The sticking points unexpectedly became much more mundane items such as desks, chairs, typewriters, blackboards, and all the other sundries needed to equip an academic department. To draw such supplies they needed a revised table of distribution for the Field Artillery School that took into account the new department. Such an action took a minimum of six months to staff, but the department was supposed to open in two weeks. The Army Ground Forces officer in charge of tables of distribution refused to issue an interim table. Williams in desperation went to Wright Field, Ohio; he had flown private planes with the director of materiel there. The Army Air Forces officer laughed when he heard Williams' predicament and shipped the equipment to Fort Sill. Until aviation training moved to Fort Rucker, Alabama, in the 1950s, every desk and chair used by Army aviation instructors and student pilots was labeled "U.S. Army Air Corps."[17]

---

[15] Wann identified the officer who accompanied them as Cowles, while Williams identified the officer as "Colonel Sweet." The only officers with such a surname in the 1942 *Army Register* were Col. William H. Sweet, a coast artilleryman stationed in the Canal Zone, and Lt. Col. Joseph B. Sweet, an infantryman stationed in Washington in April but transferred to Birmingham by October. Interv, Col R. J. Powell and Lt Col P. E. Courts with Lt Gen R. R. Williams, 1978, MHI. Intervs, author with Wann, 27 Aug 82, 23 Mar 91, CMH; "William Wallace Ford" and "Stuart Lee Cowles," in George W. Cullum, et al., comps., *Biographical Register of the Officers and Graduates of the U.S. Military Academy at West Point, N.Y., Since Its Establishment in 1802*, 9 vols. (Boston: Houghton Mifflin and Co., 1891–1951), 9:345, 414–15; War Department (WD), TAGO, *Army Register, January 1, 1942* (Washington, D.C.: Government Printing Office, 1942), p. 846; WD, TAGO, *Army Directory, April 20, 1942* (Washington, D.C.: Government Printing Office, 1942), p. 335; WD, TAGO, *Army Directory, October 20, 1942* (Washington, D.C.: Government Printing Office, 1942), p. 354. For the approximate time of the trip, see Ltr, Lt Col H. S. Wann to author, 27 Mar 91, Historian's files, CMH.

[16] Interv, author with Wann, 27 Aug 82.

[17] Intervs, Powell and Courts with Williams, 1978; author with Wann, 27 Aug 82.

Concurrently, other officers attacked the problem of equipment resupply once air sections joined units in the field. Ford, while at Headquarters, Army Ground Forces, had opted for the Army Ground Forces' methods of resupply rather than those of the Army Air Forces. The latter utilized tables of supply, useful particularly when multiple types of widely differing aircraft were involved, but totally foreign to the ground forces supply officers who would have to use them. With only three similar models of aircraft in the program, all using the same engine, Ford did not regard tables of supply as a necessity. He intended that air-observation-post sections would go into the field with the supply packages included in their normal tables of organization and equipment.[18]

While Williams went to Wright Field in search of desks, Wann visited the three airframe manufacturers, Piper, Taylorcraft, and Aeronca, and the engine manufacturer, Continental. Working with the engineers at each company, he determined the number of spare parts, supplies, and hand tools needed for ninety days of operations in the field. Using this data, officers at the Department of Air Training designed two kits of maintenance parts to support ten aircraft, the normal complement for division artillery of an infantry division. One kit sustained the airframes, and the other maintained the engines. The officers also prepared two smaller kits to support two aircraft. Ford envisioned using these kits for corps artillery battalions and artillery group headquarters. The maintenance parts included one complete spare engine for each pair of aircraft. The spare engines would permit mechanics in the aircraft sections to perform complete overhauls. Late in August Williams revisited Wright Field, this time as an official representative of Army Ground Forces, and made the final arrangements with the Materiel Command for procurement of the logistical kits.[19]

By the end of July, less than two months after the approval of the Air-Observation-Post Program in the Field Artillery, Ford had set up the core of a training base, the Department of Air Training at Fort Sill. He had worked out and the War Department had approved policies governing the procurement of light aircraft and the matriculation of student pilots, mechanics, and aerial observers. In addition, by sending Williams and Wann to Washington and with Williams' subsequent visit to Wright Field, he had ensured the necessary logistical support for the Department of Air Training. Ford had even begun to address the question of equipping and supplying the first air sections that the early graduates of the department would form. Practical experience would require him to modify some parts of the program, but the speed with which he implemented his concepts reflected the degree of careful thought and planning he had already invested in making the program a success.

Pilot, Mechanic, and Observer Training, July–November 1942

While Ford included mechanic and observer training in the new Department of Air Training, pilot training constituted the central core of the program. Ford intended to use

---

[18] Interv, author with Wann, 27 Aug 82; Ltr, Dryden to CG, AAF (Attn: Materiel Command [Cmd]), 26 Aug 42, sub: Supply of Air Force Equipment to FA Air Obsn Sections, with Ind, Col W. W. Carr, AG, FAS, to CG, AGF, 16 Nov 43, HQ, AGF, Gen Corresp, 1942–1948, 353/40 (FA Air Obsn), 452.11 (Parts and Accessories), RG 337, NARA.

[19] Interv, author with Wann, 27 Aug 82; Ltr, Dryden to CG, AAF (Attn: Materiel Cmd), 26 Aug 42.

the flight instruction provided the Class Before One as a model for his department. He also assumed that there were enough experienced light-aircraft pilots to fill out the first pilot classes at Fort Sill and that graduates from the Civilian Pilot Training Program would thereafter meet the demand. Unexpectedly, the model and both assumptions landed Ford in trouble. The instructional model, solidly based on experience, propelled him into a controversy involving the War Department G–3, General Edwards, the new commandant of the Field Artillery School, Brig. Gen. Jesmond D. Balmer, and the commanding general of Army Ground Forces, General McNair. Ford's assumptions on the availability of experienced pilots in the ground forces and the state of training of graduates of the Civilian Pilot Training Program had proved wrong and signaled the beginning of a five-month crisis that threatened to kill the Air-Observation-Post Program almost before it began.

The pilot matriculation crisis came first. Ford was not the only officer who realized that the ground combat arms contained experienced light-plane pilots and desired their services. By the time Headquarters, Army Ground Forces, requested pilot volunteers for the Field Artillery, the Army Air Forces had already recruited most of them as service pilots to ferry aircraft to the overseas theaters. The first indication of trouble came from a special project at Headquarters, Army Ground Forces, under the direction of Col. Thomas E. Lewis. The General Staff had scheduled II Corps for early deployment as part of Operation BOLERO, the buildup in Great Britain preparatory to a cross-Channel attack. Lewis planned for the Department of Air Training to give accelerated training to pilot and mechanic applicants drawn from II Corps units in time for them to finish by 15 August. Only three pilots with sufficient experience volunteered. One of them, Capt. Ford E. Allcorn, was turned back for further instruction with one of the regular classes. He eventually graduated as a member of the second pilot class, P–2.[20]

By mid-July the returns from circular letters that Army Ground Forces had dispatched to invite volunteers for the regular courses indicated that the II Corps experience was not an anomaly. There simply were not enough available pilots in the ground forces. Although the staff at Headquarters, Army Ground Forces, attempted to alleviate the situation by enlarging the pool to include men in the Services of Supply with civilian pilots' licenses, Balmer was forced to consolidate the first six pilot classes into three. Only 47 pilots graduated. Ford had anticipated 150 graduates by this point.[21]

Student mechanics were a different case altogether. Not surprisingly, in a society in which "shade tree mechanics" abounded, the great citizen-army then mobilizing contained many more mechanics and would-be mechanics than pilots. Because of the small number of

---

[20] Memo, Lt Col T. E. Lewis, Training Div, AGF, for CS, AGF, 17 Jun 42, sub: School for FA Puddle Jumper Pilots; Memo, Moran, Training Div, AGF, 23 Jun 42, sub: Plan for Furnishing Pilots (FA) to II Army Corps; Ltr, Col C. H. Day, AAG, AGF, to CG, R&SC, 29 Jun 42; Ltr, Maj H. L. Whiteside, Secretary (Sec), FAS, to CG, AGF, sub: Detail of Student Pilots and Obsrs; all in HQ, AGF, Gen Corresp, 1942–1948, 353/1 (FA Air Obsn) (Confidential [C]), RG 337, NARA; Memo, McNair for ASW, 17 Aug 42, sub: Organic Airplanes for FA; HQ, AGF, Gen Corresp, 1942–1948, 353/69 (FA Air Obsn), RG 337, NARA.

[21] Ltr, Balmer to CG, AGF, 23 Jul 42, sub: Detail of Student Pilots and Obsrs; Memo, Hyssong for CSA (Attn: ACS, G–1), 14 Jul 42, sub: Organic Air Obsn for FA; Ltr, Balmer to CG, AGF, 30 Jul 42, sub: Detail of Student Pilots; all in HQ, AGF, Gen Corresp, 1942–1948, 353/4 (FA Air Obsn), RG 337, NARA; Ltr, Balmer to CG, R&SC, 5 Sep 42, sub: Mechanics for Organic FA Air Obsn, HQ, AGF, Gen Corresp, 1942–1948, 353/73 (FA Air Obsn), RG 337, NARA; Ind, Nelson to CG, SOS, 27 Aug 42; Thomas W. McCaw, "The Courses, Field Artillery School, World War II," 2 vols. (Bound Ms, FAS, 1946), 1:184.

CREATING THE AIR-OBSERVATION-POST PROGRAM

pilot volunteers from II Corps, staff officers at Headquarters, Army Ground Forces, arbitrarily closed the special air mechanic's course for the corps after sixteen acceptable enlisted men volunteered. Army Ground Forces could easily have accepted many more. This surfeit of air mechanic applications proved a harbinger. By 5 September the department had received 4,704 applications for the 390 positions it needed to fill in the regular courses through February 1943.[22]

During August the air observer's course, scheduled to begin on 7 September, became a casualty of a radical reevaluation of the whole issue of aerial observers in the Field Artillery. As planned, the course covered many of the subjects already taught in ground training at the Field Artillery School with two exceptions—photography and aerial adjustments of artillery fire. Because no one at Headquarters, Army Ground Forces, contemplated using cameras in L–4s, this topic, in the view of the staff at Washington Barracks, could be omitted altogether without loss to the students. Current thinking held that any officer capable of directing fire from the ground could direct fire from the air, if given a relatively short time to adjust and orient himself to the new environment. General McNair felt that all the officers in a field artillery battalion should learn how to direct fire from the air. To offer a course in aerial observation in the department would, he believed, inhibit this goal by creating a special class of officers in the firing battalions. Their commanders would assign to them all the aerial fire missions and thus would prevent a more universal diffusion of skills and knowledge. McNair canceled the air observer's course before it opened. Under the new arrangements, pilots, after graduation from the Department of Air Training, would instruct the other officers in their battalions in the aerial observation of fire.[23]

GENERAL EDWARDS IN 1943

At the same time that McNair killed observer training and Ford could not find enough light-plane pilots in the Army Ground Forces, a controversy erupted with General Edwards. An Infantry officer during World War I, Edwards had transferred to the Air Service in 1920 and had spent the remainder of his career in that branch. For sixteen months prior to joining the General Staff, he had commanded the Air Corps Basic Flying School at Randolph Field, Texas. He brought a different perspective to the question of

---

[22] Memo, McNair for ASW, 17 Aug 42; Ltr, Balmer to CG, R&SC, 5 Sep 42, sub: Mechanics for Organic FA Air Obsn, HQ, AGF, Gen Corresp, 1942–1948, 353/73 (FA Air Obsn), RG 337, NARA; Ind, Nelson to CG, SOS, 27 Aug 42.

[23] Ltr, Altman to CG, AGF, 18 Aug 42, sub: Detail of Ofcrs from Field Forces to FA Air Obsrs Course; Inds, Day to CG, R&SC, 22 Aug 42 [A/O Oakes], and 27 Sep 42 [A/O Oakes]; all in HQ, AGF, Gen Corresp, 1942–1948, 353/47 (FA Air Obsn), RG 337, NARA. McNair personally rewrote the sixth paragraph of the second indorsement.

basic flight training. In August 1942 an obviously angry Edwards came to Fort Sill and in a stormy interview with Balmer asserted that Ford's flight program was illegal. The Department of Air Training offered a remedial course, analogous to Stage A in the Class Before One training program. Edwards interpreted the word "qualified" in the 6 June directive establishing the program as equivalent to "rated." In his view the Department of Air Training should test all light-plane pilots arriving at Fort Sill. Those not qualified to receive ratings should be ordered to take primary training. Edwards assumed that the remedial course provided basic flight training to Army Ground Forces student pilots. From this premise, Edwards argued that the Department of Air Training had usurped the basic training mission given the Army Air Forces in the directives establishing the program.[24]

Ford had no idea that he was doing anything controversial. He simply wanted to replicate the program developed for the Class Before One. The preliminary course sought to ensure that all pilots met a minimum standard before they entered the advanced course, now Stages B and C combined. Edwards' supposition was false. Ford had rigorously enforced the 6 June directive that stipulated that pilots must be qualified—the reason why the initial classes were so small. Even before Edwards' visit to Fort Sill, Ford had rejected eleven out of twelve pilot applicants from the 2d Armored Division, largely on this basis. Ford argued that most of the ground forces pilots he accepted simply needed an opportunity to practice rusty flight skills and to strengthen weaknesses in technique rather than to begin their training all over again as Edwards desired.[25]

The disagreement far transcended, however, mere academic issues. At the very least the abruptness of Edwards' descent on Balmer suggested that someone influential in Washington, not necessarily someone in Balmer's chain of command, found the current flight training at Fort Sill unsettling. Whatever Balmer's and Ford's suspicions, however, Edwards was the G–3, speaking with the authority of the chief of staff and the secretary of war behind him. Balmer could not brush aside his concerns—in fact, they required resolution by a higher authority than that available at Fort Sill.

When Edwards descended on Fort Sill, he had skipped several links in the chain of command, most notably General McNair. The upshot was a meeting in Washington between Edwards and McNair's representatives. The conferees agreed to consider sixty hours of flight time as the absolute minimum for any candidate for advanced flight training in the Department of Air Training. Edwards regarded the decision as a vindication of his stand, but the results were far more ironic than that. The Department of Air Training had adhered to a sixty-hour minimum from the beginning. As a practical matter, Edwards' intervention produced only one slight alteration in the department's curriculum: The preliminary course became Stage A in the pilot's course. Because student pilots came from a variety of sources, the department found it necessary throughout the war to include a preliminary phase to make certain that everyone possessed certain basic piloting skills. This purely cosmetic change in nomenclature went hand in hand with a very real transforma-

---

[24] Ltr, Balmer to CG, AGF, 7 Aug 42, sub: Training Programs for Organic FA Air Obsn Courses at FAS, HQ, AGF, Gen Corresp, 1942–1948, 353/58 (FA Air Obsn), RG 337, NARA; Ltr, Bull to CG, AGF, 10 Sep 42, sub: Organic Air Obsn for FA, HQ, AGF, Gen Corresp, 1942–1948, 353/79 (FA Air Obsn), RG 337, NARA; "Idwal Hubert Edwards," in Anon, "Selected Air Force Case Histories," United States Air Force (USAF) Historical Study 91, 2 vols. (Bound Ms, Historical Div, Air University, Maxwell AFB, Ala., 1953), 1:n.p.

[25] Ltrs, Balmer to CG, AGF, 7 Aug 42, and Bull to CG, AGF, 10 Sep 42.

tion in the quality of the program's high-level support. McNair was incensed by Edwards' assertion, thinking that it called into question his willingness to loyally obey the dictates of his superiors. In reaction, he became a passionate partisan of the program at a time when the air-observation-post advocates needed all the prominent supporters they could find.[26]

McNair never explicitly stated why he changed his opinion on air observation posts. In August 1942 there was no body of practical experience to validate the concept other than the conclusions of the test group, which McNair had already indicated he considered less than persuasive. However, in May organic aviation was not yet the policy of the War Department; by August, it was. For a Regular officer of McNair's generation, that was a sufficient reason for him to support the policy enthusiastically—all the more so because he had opposed it in the first place. But there was more to McNair's behavior than his code of conduct, important as that was. McNair's rejection of the air observation post had never been absolute, always relative. He had never held that Field Artillery aircraft were incapable of providing observed fire, just that Army Air Forces observation squadrons could perform equally well. McNair's attitude toward organic air was always conditioned by his need to maintain good working relations with Headquarters, Army Air Forces. McNair recognized that the training of the Army's divisions would not be complete without realistic air-ground training. Occupying a coordinate rather than a superior position to the commander of the Army Air Forces, Lt. Gen. Henry H. Arnold, McNair could request but not command Army Air Forces units to participate.[27]

When Edwards attacked pilot training at Fort Sill, the 1942 maneuver season had just ended with the elaborate regime of air-ground training a shambles, due to the inability or unwillingness of the Army Air Forces to support it adequately. Staff officers at McNair's headquarters believed the latter. In their view Arnold and his senior subordinates were too preoccupied with mounting a combined bomber offensive against Germany to provide sufficient resources for the realistic training that both ground and tactical air units needed before entering modern combat. As a consequence, the divisions slated for the amphibious landing in North Africa had not received adequate air-ground training. The Army Air Forces might be capable of providing observation support, but the summer maneuvers suggested that they might not choose to do so. In this context, aerial observation under ground forces command meant that the mission would be executed to the extent the available equipment permitted. McNair's reversal of his position on air observation posts thus suggested the depths of his frustration with the Army Air Forces.[28]

---

[26] Message (Msg) (GNOAG 5606), Balmer to Maj Gen J. L. Devers, 8 Aug 42, retransmitted in Msg (45851), Devers to CG, AGF, 8 Aug 42, 1602Z, HQ, AGF, Gen Corresp, 1942–1948, 353/7 (FA Air Obsn) (R) (6–18–42), RG 337, NARA; Memo, Col J. H. Phillips, ACS, G–3, AGF, 2 Sep 42, sub: Report (Rpt) of Conference with WD G–3 on FA Air Obsn, HQ, AGF, Gen Corresp, 1942–1948, 353/81 (FA Air Obsn), RG 337, NARA; Trans, Telecon, Lentz and Scobey, 0900, 4 Nov 42.

[27] There is as yet no satisfactory study of McNair. The longest account is a pamphlet-length memorial volume, Ely J. Kahn, *McNair: Educator of an Army* (Washington, D.C.: Infantry Journal, 1945). The best succinct account setting forth the importance of McNair's career is Brooks E. Kleber, "Lesley James McNair," in *Dictionary of American Military Biography*, ed. Roger J. Spiller and Joseph G. Dawson III, 3 vols. (Westport, Conn.: Greenwood Press, 1984), 2:695–99. For insight into McNair's character, see Forrest C. Pogue, *George C. Marshall*, 4 vols. (New York: Viking, 1963–1987), 2:82–83.

[28] Kent R. Greenfield, *Army Ground Forces and the Air-Ground Battle Team, Including Organic Light Aviation* (Washington, D.C.: Historical Division, Army Ground Forces, 1945), pp. 17–20.

McNair's conversion coincided with the onset of the second phase of the matriculation crisis. In August 1942 Headquarters, Army Air Forces, perfected the administrative arrangements to allow graduates of the Civilian Pilot Training Program to transfer to the Field Artillery. General Arnold appointed a board of officers to meet at Fort Sill, beginning 19 September 1942, to test "the suitability of these candidates for Field Artillery Training." The board reported the men it deemed acceptable, and Arnold's headquarters transferred them to the Field Artillery. The first such classes, P–6 and P–6A, began instruction in the Department of Air Training on 26 September, three weeks later than the War Department had originally envisioned.[29]

If the first pilot program, based on volunteers from the ground forces, was a disappointment, the second, based on the graduates of the Civilian Pilot Training Program, was close to a disaster. The Army Air Forces rating board accepted only 41 of the first 104 Civilian Pilot Training Program graduates. The Department of Air Training tested a cross-section of 11 enlisted pilots approved by the board and found only 5 qualified to enter pilot training at Sill, and 2 of them were marginal at best. Using the same standards, the Department of Air Training had rejected only 15.3 percent of Army Ground Forces candidates. Moreover, an unrelated action by Headquarters, Army Ground Forces, had made the situation worse, at least temporarily. It introduced a change in field artillery battalion tables of organization and equipment that forced a fundamental reconsideration of the pilot problem. The new tables assigned one officer pilot to each air-observation-post section, dramatically changing the ratio of officer and enlisted pilots from 1:4 to 1:1. Faced with a choice of pilots who might possess the potential to become officers and officers who wanted to learn to fly, General Balmer favored the latter.[30]

The search for a permanent solution to the matriculation problem produced a major controversy between the Field Artillery School, supported by Headquarters, Army Ground Forces, and General Edwards, backed by Headquarters, Army Air Forces. As a stopgap, General Arnold agreed to supply thirty rated liaison pilots to the Field Artillery School each week. The Air Staff had programmed the pilots for Army Air Forces liaison squadrons (formerly observation squadrons), so the arrangement hampered the Army Air Forces' ability to field such units. This gesture generated little goodwill, however. Edwards' intervention over Stage A had already soured relations between the principals. Coupled with this, institutional relations reached an all-time low because of the lack of realistic air-ground training during the 1942 maneuvers. Ford had always thought that the logical solution to the training issue involved placing all flight training under the Field Artillery and giving the commanding general, Army Ground Forces, the authority to rate pilots. Balmer, McNair, and McNair's G–3 (since June), Lentz, recently promoted to brigadier general, now agreed. "We want undivided responsibility," argued Lentz. "We ought to make good and deliver, or we don't." Edwards, on the other hand, elaborated the position he adopted in the Stage A controversy. He proposed that Headquarters, Army Ground Forces, select

---

[29] Ltr, Duenweg to CG, R&SC, 12 Aug 42, sub: Training of Pilots for FA, HQ, AGF, Gen Corresp, 1942–1948, 353/6 (FA Air Obsn) (R), NARA; Ltr, Nelson to CG, R&SC, 14 Sep 42, sub: Students for FA School, Department of Air Training (DAT), HQ, AGF, Gen Corresp, 1942–1948, 353/62 (FA Air Obsn), RG 337, NARA; Memo, McNair for ASW, 17 Aug 42.

[30] Ind, Balmer to CG, R&SC, 17 Oct 42, HQ, AGF, Gen Corresp, 1942–1948, 353/47 (FA Air Obsn), RG 337, NARA; Ltr, Morgan to McCloy, 8 Oct 42, Morgan Ms, MHI.

CONTOUR FLYING AT FORT SILL

qualified personnel under their control and detail them to the Army Air Forces Flying Training Command for instruction as liaison pilots. Under this arrangement the candidate pilots would receive elementary training in the Civilian Pilot Training Program, primary training from a civilian flying school under contract with the Army Air Forces, and operational flight training at the Department of Air Training. The level of distrust was so high that neither side would accept the other's position.[31]

It took high-level official intervention to resolve the impasse. On 11 November 1942, the assistant secretary of war, John J. McCloy, held a conference with the affected agencies and decided in Edwards' favor. McCloy considered the problems at Sill simply "a false start," not indicative of "any real opposition" on the part of the Army Air Forces. Events bore him out. Six days later, Headquarters, Army Ground Forces, directed Balmer to send twenty-five Field Artillery officers every week to an Army Air Forces primary training school, beginning the week of 26 November. Balmer drew the initial class from volunteers from the faculty, staff, and school troops at the Field Artillery School. Subsequent classes came from the graduates of the Field Artillery officers candidate school and Field Artillery casuals on post. Later, any Field Artillery captain or lieutenant could apply. The Flying Training Command substituted liaison pilot graduates for any Field Artillery officers who "washed out." By August 1943 even Headquarters, Army Ground Forces, conceded that the program was "very satisfactory." Although the requirements to enter the program, the length of the advanced course, and its size varied according to the course of the war, the directive of 17 November set in place the broad outlines of the training system that would last until after the Korean War.[32]

---

[31] Ind, Balmer to CG, R&SC, 17 Oct 42, HQ, AGF, Gen Corresp, 1942–1948, 353/47 (FA Air Obsn), RG 337, NARA; Memo, Edwards for CG, AGF (Attn: Lt Gen McNair), 29 Oct 42; Memo, McNair for CSA (Attn: ACS, G–3), 20 Oct 42, sub: Organic Air Obsn for FA; both in OASW, Security Class Corresp of John J. McCloy, 1941–1945, 452.1 (Puddlejumpers), RG 107, NARA; Trans, Telecon, Lentz and Scobey, 0900, 4 Nov 42.

[32] Memo, McCloy for Maj Gen G. E. Stratemeyer, 11 Nov 42, OASW, Security Class Corresp of McCloy, 1941–1945, 452.1 (Puddlejumpers), RG 107, NARA; Ltr, Capt R. A. Meredith, AAG, AGF, to CG, R&SC, 17 Nov 42, sub: FA Ofcrs for Pilot Training, HQ, AGF, Gen Corresp, 1942–1948, 353/171 (FA Air Obsn), RG 337, NARA; Memo, Nelson for CSA (Attn: G–3 Div, Col Burwell), 19 Aug 43, sub: Liaison Pilots for FA, HQ, AGF, Gen Corresp, 1942–1948, 353/262 (FA Air Obsn), RG 337, NARA.

A Reexamination of Mission

The ongoing controversy from August through November 1942 over pilot training formed the backdrop for a renewed debate between the Army Air Forces and the Army Ground Forces over whether to continue the Air-Observation-Post Program. During the summer of 1942, many branches (Infantry alone excepted) and programs continued to demonstrate a desire for organic aviation. Much of the interest, paradoxically, derived from the actions of a single Infantry officer—one whose opinion on the subject was totally at variance with the views of his branch's official representative at Washington Barracks. Lt. Col. John C. L. Adams, a 42-year-old Texan, was a 1924 graduate of the U.S. Military Academy. Like Ford, Adams had learned to fly during the years between the world wars and had become enthusiastic about the military potential of light aircraft. In the spring of 1942, while serving as the executive officer of the 330th Infantry in the 83d Division, he made a memorable presentation on the subject to the command group of the newly formed Airborne Command at Fort Bragg, North Carolina, established to train airborne divisions and to develop doctrine and equipment for airborne operations. In July 1942 Adams became a force in Washington when the head of the Office of Strategic Services, Col. (later Maj. Gen.) William J. Donovan, appointed Adams as his adviser on "light airplane uses, sabotage, [and] guerrilla warfare."[33]

Adams was a man fertile in ideas and bursting with energy. Although he was especially interested in using light airplanes to deliver equipment and agents behind enemy lines, he outlined all their military applications in a series of lengthy memorandums—one was of book length—that he scattered about official Washington over the next nine months. An experienced infantry officer, he had a good feel for tactical possibilities. He anticipated virtually every use that the Army made of helicopters some twenty years later in Vietnam. The problem in 1942, of course, was that the Army had the light plane, not the helicopter. In his enthusiasm, Adams seriously overestimated the limits of what was technically feasible given existing equipment. His excitement was contagious, however, and one of those he influenced (either directly or simply though the ferment he generated) was a fellow member of the Fuddy-Duddies Flying Club, Assistant Secretary of War McCloy.[34]

While Adams attracted considerable attention and interest for light planes, the G–3 at Headquarters, Army Ground Forces, Colonel Lentz, continued to work behind the scenes to extend organic aviation to all the combat arms. By the summer of 1942, he considered

---

[33] Diary, Morgan, 29 Apr 42; "John Curtis Lafayette Adams," in Cullum, et al., *Biographical Register*, 9:455; Ltr, Brig Gen William W. Ford to author, 11 Oct 82, Historian's files, CMH; John T. Ellis, Jr., *The Airborne Command and Center*, AGF Study no. 25 (Washington, D.C.: Historical Section, Army Ground Forces, 1946), pp. 13–15. The War Department redesignated the 83d Division as the 83d Infantry Division in August 1942.

[34] Memo, Col E. W. Searby and Col R. F. Ennis, G–3, AGF, for ACS, G–3, 8 Oct 42, sub: Demonstration of Low-Performance Airplanes; Memo, A. M. D., Organization and Doctrine Branch, G–3, AGF, for Lt Col Dunne; both in HQ, AGF, Gen Corresp, 1942–1948, 353/101 (FA Air Obsn), RG 337, NARA. Memo, J[ohn] C. L. A[dams], sub: Points To Be Noted in Demonstration; Memo, Adams for McCloy, 26 Oct 42, sub: Future Uses of the Lightplane; Memo, Adams for Col M. P. Goodfellow, 27 Nov 42, sub: Rpt on Secret Tests Witnessed at Aberdeen, Md.; Memo, Adams, 17 Dec 42, sub: One Hundred and Fourteen Bombers or Twenty Thousand Lightplanes?; all in OASW, Security Class Corresp of McCloy, 1941–1945, 452.1 (Light Planes), RG 107, NARA; Ltr, Adams to Asst Commandant, Command and General Staff School (C&GSS), 16 Apr 43; John C. L. Adams, "America's Secret Weapon—The Lightplane: Military Uses of the Lightplane in Ground Forces" (Unpublished [Unpubl] Ms, Camp Wheeler, Ga., 1943); both at MHI.

the Field Artillery's program well established. He called a meeting of the representatives of all the combat arms in the Army Ground Forces G–3 section to plan for a further enlargement of the program. All the officers were enthusiastic except the Infantry representative, who to Lentz's dismay was decidedly uninterested. The Infantry was, of course, the largest and most prestigious branch in the ground forces. Without Infantry support, any attempt to expand the organic aviation program was bound to fail. Lentz conceded defeat—for the moment.[35]

In August 1942, just as Lentz contemplated how the Infantry's shortsightedness had made a shambles of his carefully thought-out strategy, McCloy called General McNair and without preamble inquired about the possibility of including the other combat arms in the organic aircraft program. McCloy also indicated that there was "some sort of movement on foot" in Headquarters, Army Air Forces, "to reopen the question of organic planes for the F.A." As a consequence, McNair talked to the secretary of the Air Staff, Maj. Gen. George E. Stratemeyer, who assured him that the Army Air Forces would make no effort to interfere in the Field Artillery program, "at least not for the present." McNair had by this time become a convert to the Air-Observation-Post Program and said so:

I informed General Stratemeyer that the Field Artillery had waited for many years for proper air observation, with disappointing results; that sheer necessity had forced the present procedure; that the proper outlet for the Air Forces in this connection lay in demonstrating with the regular observation units that the Air Forces could and would give the sort of observation that was so vitally necessary under modern conditions; that if and when they gave a convincing demonstration of this kind it would be time to discuss a change, not before.

At the same time, McNair believed it would be difficult to justify making aviation organic to the other arms until after the Field Artillery gained "more experience" with light airplanes.[36]

In mid-November, without any further discussion and no recorded explanation, McCloy directed McNair to submit to the chief of staff a proposal to expand organic aviation beyond the Field Artillery. McCloy's order came just five days after he had decided the pilot training controversy in favor of Headquarters, Army Air Forces. McNair's staff hastily prepared a directive that gave the commanding general, Army Ground Forces, the authority to establish parallel programs in other branches and specialties. Taking up only half a sheet of paper, the directive did not even identify or justify the changes but simply used the Field Artillery program as a model. It was, in short, totally dissimilar from the other staff papers generated at Headquarters, Army Ground Forces. Nevertheless, McNair dispatched it "by special messenger" to the War Department. Everything about it suggests that the paper was designed not to persuade, but to preempt.[37]

Three days later General Stratemeyer forwarded to the same destination the Army Air Forces' long-matured plan to disestablish the Field Artillery aviation program. The direc-

---

[35] Trans, Telecon, Lentz and Scobey, 0900, 4 Nov 42.
[36] Memo Slip, McNair for G–3, 11 Aug 42, sub: Organic Planes for FA; Memo, McNair for ASW, 17 Aug 42, sub: Organic Airplanes of FA [A/O McNair], both in HQ, AGF, Gen Corresp, 1942–1948, 353/69 (FA Air Obsn), RG 337, NARA. General McNair personally wrote to the assistant secretary of war the memo from which the quotation is drawn.
[37] Memo, McNair for CSA, 16 Nov 42, sub: Organic Air Obsn for AGF Units; Draft Memo, [CSA] for CG, AGF [Nov 42], sub: Same; both in HQ, AGF, Gen Corresp, 1942–1948, 353/150 (FA Air Obsn), RG 337, NARA.

tor of air support on the Air Staff, Col. David M. Schlatter, was the driving force behind the Army Air Forces' proposal. He had long distrusted light aircraft; he was convinced they could not survive in the battle zone. He viewed the Air-Observation-Post Program as nothing less than a profiteering boondoggle by politically well-connected light aircraft manufacturers taking advantage of naive and unsuspecting ground forces officers. At one point he directed one of his subordinates to prepare plans for the storage of all light aircraft for the duration—the only solution once the Cubs proved their unfitness in combat. Schlatter was not shy about sharing his views, and they provided the intellectual context in which the Army Ground Forces staff evaluated Schlatter's proposal—to retain liaison aircraft organic to the division, to centralize them in a flight at division headquarters, to man them with Army Air Forces pilots and mechanics, and to abolish the Department of Air Training.[38]

Something of McNair's attitude toward this turn of events can be deduced from the fact that McNair took his staff's proposed reply and rewrote it himself, strengthening it in the process. He totally rejected the idea of consolidating all organic aviation in a division into a single flight, an organization that would be "definitely objectionable, regardless of whether the unit is ground or air." His solution was to either maintain the status quo until the Field Artillery program had an opportunity to prove itself in battle or extend the new arrangements "at once" to "all interested elements of the Ground Forces." Moreover, he scrawled instructions in the margin about distribution: "Copy directly to Asst Secy War." For the moment the War Department did nothing. General Edwards simply held the papers. Not until February 1943, at Edwards' request, did McNair make the Army Ground Forces' position on expansion more precise. He wanted two organic aircraft for each tank destroyer battalion, mechanized cavalry regiment, and division, as opposed to division artillery, headquarters, in addition to the aircraft already allotted to the Field Artillery. In June 1943 Edwards' successor, Brig. Gen. Ray E. Porter, finally delivered a ruling. He denied both requests and continued the status quo.[39] Only the accumulation of combat experience could shift the evidence dramatically in favor of one or the other of these positions to break the deadlock. The immediate prospects for any change in the scope and mission of organic aviation were thus almost nonexistent.

McNair, Lentz, and the other ground forces officers never took at face value the claim by Schlatter and his deputy, Col. Otto P. Weyland, that they simply were seeking greater administrative and logistical simplicity. At the same time that Schlatter was mounting his effort to reverse the 6 June 1942 directives establishing the Air-Observation-Post Program, an Army Air Forces attempt to demonstrate the feasibility of the division flight concept at

---

[38] Diary, Morgan, 26 Mar 42, Morgan Ms, MHI; Memo, Maj Gen G. E. Stratemeyer, Chief of Air Staff (CAS), for CSA (Attn: G–3 Div), 19 Nov 42, sub: Organic Liaison Aviation (Avn) for Ground Units, HQ, AGF, Gen Corresp, 1942–1948, 353/150 (FA Air Obsn), RG 337, NARA. For a detailed discussion of the handling of the proposal by the Air Staff, see Robert F. Futrell, *Command of Observation Aviation: A Study in Control of Tactical Airpower*, U.S. Air Force Historical Studies 24 (Maxwell AFB, Ala.: U.S. Air Force Historical Division, 1956), pp. 16–17.

[39] Memo Slip, Brig Gen J. M. Lentz, G–3, AGF, for CS, AGF, 2 Dec 42, sub: Organic Liaison Avn for Ground Units; Memo Slip, McNair for CS, AGF, 9 Dec 42, sub: Same; Memo, McNair for CSA (Attn: ACS, G–3), 9 Dec 42, sub: Same; all in HQ, AGF, Gen Corresp, 1942–1948, 353/150 (FA Air Obsn), RG 337, NARA; Memo, Brig Gen R. E. Porter, ACS, G–3, for CG, AGF, 28 Jun 43, OASW, Security Class Corresp of McCloy, 1941–1945, 452.1 (5–15–43), RG 107, NARA.

An O–59 Loaded on a 2½-Ton 6x6 Army Truck for Cross-Country Movement

the Tank Destroyer Center proved unconvincing to the ground forces officers involved. The commander of the center, Maj. Gen. Andrew D. Bruce, was satisfied that only his desire to establish tank-destroyer organic air caused the Army Air Forces to send an observation squadron to the center in the first place, and he was dissatisfied with the support it provided once it arrived. Both he and his successor continued to call for light aircraft sections as an integral part of all tank destroyer battalions.[40]

Colonel Ford always projected optimism and radiated energy in dealing with his subordinates at Fort Sill. It was the West Point way. At the end of 1942, in the quiet of his own thoughts, however, he admitted that he found certain recent events "disturbing." During the years between the wars, he had served on the staff of the Reserve Officers Training Corps

---

[40] DF, Col D. M. Schlatter and Col O. P. Weyland to ACS, G–3, WDGS, 4 Jan 43, Microfilm A1387, AFHRA; Memo, G. B. V. Z., Sec General Staff, AGF, for Gen Parks, 14 Oct 42, with Ind by Brig Gen F. L. P[arks], HQ, AGF, Gen Corresp, 1942–1948, 452.1/676 (Airplanes), RG 337, NARA. Memo, Brig Gen A. D. Bruce, CG, Tank Destroyer Center (TDC), for CG, AGF, 18 Jul 42, sub: Organic Tank Destroyer (TD) Air Obsn, HQ, AGF, Gen Corresp, 1942–1948, 353/1 (TD Air Obsn), RG 337, NARA; Ltr, Bruce to CG, AGF, 9 Dec 42, sub: Rating of TD Liaison Pilots, HQ, AGF, Gen Corresp, 1942–1948, 353/5 (TD Air Obsn), RG 337, NARA; Ltr, Bruce to CG, AGF, 17 Dec 42, sub: Support Avn for Training Purposes, HQ, AGF, Gen Corresp, 1942–1948, 353/7 (TD Air Obsn), RG 337, NARA; Ltr, Maj Gen O. Ward, CG, TDC, to CG, AGF, 22 Sep 43, sub: Organic Liaison Planes for TDs, HQ, AGF, Gen Corresp, 1942–1948, 353/8 (TD Air Obsn), RG 337, NARA.

at Purdue University. He now wrote a private letter unburdening himself to the former professor of military science at the school, General McNair. McNair responded positively. He regarded the problems in the Air-Observation-Post Program as inherent in hastily improvising a new system. Many would work themselves out, once procedures became better established and the quality of personnel improved. McNair hoped to further the last objective by changing existing tables of organization to require all Field Artillery pilots to be officers. (This policy became official on 12 February 1943.) "More power to you in your able efforts to get going in spite of difficulties."[41]

Conclusion

The Department of Air Training at the Field Artillery School became the embodiment of the Air-Observation-Post Program between June and December 1942. Until a substantial number of pilots and mechanics actually reported to combat units, which did not start happening until late 1942, the department was, in truth, the program. In June 1942, despite the fact that the test group remained together at Fort Sill and provided a ready-made nucleus, the department remained more concept than reality. Colonel Ford had to simultaneously organize the department and assist in working out in greater detail the concept of the overall program.

Once the War Department General Staff and Headquarters, Army Ground Forces, agreed on the broad outlines, Ford enjoyed a relatively free hand in establishing policies, at least initially. Some of his solutions endured well beyond the war; others were intended only as interim answers; still others proved ephemeral either because their basic premises proved faulty or because the situation changed before they could be implemented. The pilot training crisis was without doubt the most serious of the problems Ford faced during this period, because it threatened to make the Air-Observation-Post Program stillborn. Its satisfactory resolution required intervention by higher authority.

Despite the difficulties involved in getting started, the benefits that air observation posts promised the Field Artillery in battle meant that the program retained its high- and mid-level sponsors—Assistant Secretary of War McCloy in the War Department and Colonels Lentz and Lewis at Headquarters, Army Ground Forces. It also gained supporters—Colonel Cowles at the Replacement and School Command, General Balmer at Fort Sill, and, most notably, General McNair. McNair's conversion reflected both frictions arising out of the joint training program with the Army Air Forces and General Edwards' maladroit intervention at Fort Sill. Edwards, an officer with a reputation for some tact, behaved in a manner almost calculated to harden support for organic aviation at Headquarters, Army Ground Forces. His uncharacteristic actions suggest just how sensitive an issue the pilot training program at Fort Sill was for some senior officers of the Army Air Forces.

The world views and ideologies of ground and air officers were still the salient reasons for either supporting or attacking organic aviation from June through December 1942.

---

[41] Ltrs, Ford to McNair, 29 Dec 42, and McNair to Ford, 7 Jan 43, both in HQ, AGF, CG, Lt Gen Lesley J. McNair, Gen Corresp file, 1940–1944 (Ford, W. W.), RG 337, NARA; Ltr, Col C. H. Day, AGAG, AGF, to CG, Second Army, et al., 12 Feb 43, sub: Officer Liaison Pilot-Obsrs for Organic FA Air Obsn, HQ, AGF, Gen Corresp, 1942–1948, 353/251 (FA Air Obsn), RG 337, NARA.

Colonel Lentz hardly waited for the first student pilot to arrive at Fort Sill before he was prepared to expand the program throughout the other combat arms. Opponents, led by Colonel Schlatter, waited only slightly longer before proposing to abolish it. In each case logical deductions from a series of preexisting beliefs sufficed to buttress their arguments—at least in their own minds and those of their supporters.

If, on the level of the program as a whole, the evidence as to success or failure was not yet available, it was much clearer on the level of the Department of Air Training. Ford, of course, had the other departments of the school on which to model his department. He also had the example of the Class Before One to draw upon, both for the structure of the training and the techniques that ought to be taught. When the dispute over pilot training occurred between Captains Schirmacher and Baker, Ford was conservative, empirical, and decidedly undogmatic. He gave each approach a fair test and chose the better one. He was greatly assisted in his labors by an intelligent and hard-working executive officer, Colonel Wolf; a number of young officers, notably Captain Williams, who possessed both energy and discretion; and several civilians not yet commissioned, such as Messrs. Piper and Wann, who provided invaluable technical expertise. Ford continued to demonstrate the high order of leadership that marked his performance during the test phase. He kept the test group together and focused on the problem of creating an air-observation-post program during the period of uncertainty while the War Department made its decision. Because of that, he had the core of his department at hand from the beginning. When problems surfaced, once the department began operations, he kept his worries to himself and his subordinates focused on completing the task at hand. The difficulties with pilot matriculation tended to mask the extent of this achievement. Between June and December 1942 he created a cohesive and technically proficient department that would serve as the heart of the program through the remainder of the war and beyond.

The complexities were immense in simultaneously creating an air-observation-post program that would extend throughout the Army, at least wherever field artillery battalions were stationed, and an air training department. The program rose from virtually nothing and then had to be integrated into an organization as complex as the U.S. Army, while that organization was both frantically expanding and attempting to fight a war. If the department sprang from a cohesive group, already formed, it likewise had to be fit into the Field Artillery School, also under wartime strains. Over all these difficulties lay the opposed perspectives of air and ground officers and a long history of mutual misunderstanding. The surprising circumstance was not that McCloy, McNair, Edwards, and Ford made some misjudgments, but that they got so many things right and that Ford and his staff accomplished so much in such a short time.

Ford's contribution to the ultimate success of the Air-Observation-Post Program can hardly be overstated. Between June and November 1942 the failure to secure a reliable source of pilots threatened the existence of the program. If Ford's miscalculations contributed to this difficulty, then his leadership and strength of personality helped keep the program going. Without denigrating the very real contributions of others, both in the Department of Air Training and at higher levels, he came close to being an indispensable man during this early period. In large measure, the ideas that became the program were his. At the same time, the fact that the program retained both high-level interest and support was clearly crucial. Assistant Secretary of War McCloy brokered the solution to the pilot matriculation problem. Once that difficulty was resolved, the administrative changes that followed simply represented necessary elaborations from a solid foundation.

CHAPTER 4

Developing the Air-Observation-Post Program, January–December 1943

The Department of Air Training at the Field Artillery School became a going concern between June and December 1942. During the next twelve months, ground forces officers arranged for light aircraft production sufficient to supply a fully mobilized U.S. Army, fleshed out a logistical system for air sections in the continental United States, and became involved in the development of new aircraft. Each of these stages involved unforeseen difficulties, the sort of problems attendant upon the start-up of any new program. Despite these complicating factors, by October 1943 the training establishment was graduating large numbers of pilots and mechanics. Upon joining units in the field, they had to sell the idea of organic aerial observation to ground officers who heretofore had little knowledge of Field Artillery aviation.

Aircraft Procurement for 1943

The annual cycle of congressional appropriations and the beginning of a new fiscal year on 1 July 1943 dictated the timing of the next major problem to confront the organic air program—light aircraft procurement for 1943. Aircraft procurement decisions for 1943, made in Washington between late November 1942 and January 1943, were some of the most important of the war for the Air-Observation-Post Program. Their significance stemmed from the impact of aircraft availability on training and unit readiness coupled with the War Department's mobilization planning. In the opinion of the director of the Department of Air Training at the Field Artillery School, Col. William W. Ford, air sections could not be rushed hurly-burly into combat. Air sections had to train with their units, so they would become as integral as the firing batteries to the operations of their battalions. Extended training before commitment to combat became possible only if the planes and pilots were available well before units deployed to the combat zone. Assistant Secretary of War John J. McCloy's November 1942 decision to send Field Artillery officers to primary flight training solved the problem of securing an adequate number of pilots. The issue of obtaining sufficient numbers of L–2s, L–3s, and L–4s remained. The definition of sufficiency depended in turn on the War Department's schedule for ground-unit activation. With the War Department committed to activating virtually all the Army's major formations by September 1943, the training requirements of the Air-Observation-Post Program dictated a procurement strategy consisting of an initial surge of production to equip these units, followed by a much lower level simply to replace losses. For the Army Ground Forces G–4 section, the agency with the responsibility for developing the production strategy and then securing War Department approval, the key was obtaining the necessary initial surge. It proved a very difficult assignment.[1]

The factor limiting light aircraft production in 1942 and 1943 was access to raw materials, rather than the overall productive capacity of the industry. Liaison planes had the lowest priority of any category of aircraft, just below trainers. Any trade-off between categories involved producing more light aircraft at the expense of trainers, which meant fewer pilots for bombers, fighters (the new term for pursuits), and transports. In effect, curtailing trainer production had the same impact on the availability of higher priority aircraft as directly diverting raw materials from these aircraft to light planes—a solution totally unacceptable to both the Navy Department and the Army Air Forces. The only viable possibility for the Army Ground Forces G–4 officer handling the problem, Lt. Col. Bjarne Furuholmen, was to secure all the aircraft that the Field Artillery required from the resources allotted—perhaps "left over" is a better description—for liaison planes.[2]

The forum for these decisions was the Joint Aircraft Committee, an interagency coordinating group that reported to the Army-Navy Munitions Assignment Board, the agency responsible for assigning military priorities for procurement projects. The committee, acting for the board, in effect allocated raw materials among aircraft manufacturers. At the 23 November 1942 meeting of its Subcommittee on Allocation of Deliveries, Colonel Furuholmen discovered that the interested agencies required 12,782 aircraft for 1943. The representative of the Office of Strategic Services, Lt. Col. John C. L. Adams, had been busily generating support for light aircraft. At the meeting, he not only presented the position of the Office of Strategic Services, but also served simultaneously as McCloy's personal observer. Adams wanted 4,370 light planes for his organization alone. The subcommittee adjourned, and the participants went back to their agencies to try to bargain for a compromise. The commanding general of the Army Air Forces, Lt. Gen. Henry H. Arnold, was concerned about the impact on the production of other types of aircraft. He decreed that whatever the needs, no more than 5,000 liaison aircraft would be produced in 1943—to include the Vultee (formerly Stinson) L–5 and the Interstate L–6, an aircraft of similar capabilities produced primarily because of a lack of plant capacity at Vultee. Neither had figured in the Subcommittee on Allocation of Deliveries' 23 November deliberations.

---

[1] Memo, [Col William W. Ford for Lt Gen Lesley J. McNair, 29 Dec 42], sub: Organic Field Artillery (FA) Air Observation (Obsn), Headquarters, Army Ground Forces (HQ, AGF), Personal Papers of the Commanding General (CG), Lt Gen Lesley J. McNair, General Correspondence (Gen Corresp) file, 1940–1944, "Ford, W. W.," Record Group (RG) 337, National Archives and Records Administration, Washington, D.C. (hereafter cited as NARA). For a background discussion of ground-force activation, see Robert R. Palmer, "Mobilization of the Ground Army," in Kent R. Greenfield, Robert R. Palmer, and Bell I. Wiley, *The Organization of Ground Combat Troops*, U.S. Army in World War II (Washington, D.C.: Historical Division, Department of the Army, 1947), pp. 189–259.

[2] Memo, Col W. F. Dean, Executive Officer (XO), Ground Requirements Section, AGF, for Col J. S. Burwell, War Department General Staff (WDGS), 26 Nov 42, sub: FA Organic Light Planes, HQ, AGF, Gen Corresp, 1942–1948, 353/169 (FA Air Obsn), RG 337, NARA; Memorandum for Record (MFR), 5 Dec 42, The Adjutant General's Office (TAGO) Decimal file, 1940–1945, 452.1 (12–4–42), RG 407, NARA.

The Piper Aircraft Corporation's Plant at Lock Haven, with a Row of L-4s in Front—A Wartime Photograph

Given the disparity between supply and demand, some organizations received no aircraft. The bulk of the available aircraft went to the Field Artillery and the Army Air Forces. The Field Artillery secured all the L-4 production and enough L-2s and L-3s to equip all units on the 1943 troop list and to form a reserve, 2,500 in all. In return the Army Ground Forces agreed to Arnold's terms—the Army Air Forces obtained all the L-5 and L-6 production, 1,354 aircraft, for 1943.[3]

This solution was probably the best possible from the perspective of the Army Ground Forces. Furuholmen and the rest of the Army Ground Forces staff worked under a very real time constraint. Production orders would run out at Taylorcraft, Aeronca, and Piper on 31 March 1943. Without new orders, the companies would have to shut down their produc-

---

[3] Memo, Capt R. W. Johnson for Recorder, Subcommittee on Allocation of Deliveries, Joint Aircraft Committee (JAC), 23 Nov 42, sub: Requirements in 1943 for Lightplanes of the L-2, L-3, and L-4 Class (Case 3182); Memo, Lt Col J. C. L. Adams, 16 Nov 42, sub: Estimated Lightplane Needs of Office of Strategic Services [OSS] for Year Beginning April 1, 1943; Memo, [Adams, 16 Nov 42], sub: Attendance at Conference to Determine Light Airplane, Engine, and Spares Requirements for JAC for Period 1 Apr 43 to 1 Apr 44; both in Headquarters, Army Air Forces (HQ, AAF), Central Decimal file (Security Classified [Class]), October 1942–May 1944, 452.01–A (Procurement and Requirements), RG 18, NARA; Memo, Brig Gen B. E. Meyers, Chief of Staff (CS), Materiel Command (Cmd), for Director (Dir), Individual Training, 27 Nov 42, sub: 1943 Puddlejumper Requirements, HQ, AAF, Central Decimal file (Security Class), October 1942–May 1944, 452.1–A (Obsn), RG 18, NARA; Memo, Brig Gen I. H. Edwards, Assistant Chief of Staff (ACS), G–3, for OSS, 10 Dec 42, sub: Light Plane Requirements of the Strategic Service (Svc) Cmd for 1943; MFR, 15 Dec 42, The Adjutant General (TAG), Class Decimal file, 1940–1942, 452.1 (2–10–42), RG 407, NARA; Memo, Edwards for CG, AGF, 30 Mar 43, sub: Liaison Airplanes, TAGO, Decimal file, 1940–1945, 452.1 (3–30–43), RG 407, NARA; Memo, Lt Col B. Furuholmen for Maj Gen R. C. Moore, CS, AGF, 4 Jan 43, sub: Distribution of Liaison-Type Airplanes for Year 1943; Memo, Lt Col B. F[uruholmen], 5 Jan 43; Memo Slip, Maj Gen R. C. M[oore] for Chief of Staff, Army (CSA), 5 Jan 43, HQ, AGF, Gen Corresp, 1942–1948, 452.1/94 (Airplanes), RG 337, NARA. On the Army-Navy Munitions Assignment Board, see John D. Millett, *The Organization and Role of the Army Service Forces*, United States Army in World War II (Washington, D.C.: Office of the Chief of Military History, 1954), pp. 19, 202–03. Based on Adams' calculations, production of all 12,782 light aircraft would have meant the production of 73 fewer four-engine bombers. John C. L. Adams, "America's Secret Weapon—The Lightplane" (Bound Manuscript [Ms], U.S. Army Military History Institute, Carlisle Barracks, Pa. [hereafter cited as MHI], 1943).

tion lines and lay off a substantial part of their work force. Given the booming wartime economy and the shortages of labor, skilled workers once laid off were skilled workers lost for the duration, whether or not the companies resumed production later. Although at least one member of the subcommittee wanted a fundamental reconsideration of production priorities, such an endeavor would have produced a major confrontation with the Army Air Forces. Even if resolved in favor of the Army Ground Forces, it would have taken time that the manufacturers simply did not have. On the other hand, this compromise introduced great rigidity, with unfortunate results, into the 1943 light aircraft production schedule.[4]

Creating an Air-Observation-Post Logistical System

The supply system for air sections became critical about the same time as the procurement issue. In the early winter of 1942–1943, graduates of the Department of Air Training began reaching the field in sizable numbers and forming actual air sections. For the first time resupply for air sections became a practical concern. Until then the supply system for Field Artillery aircraft had existed only in theory. As late as December 1942 it remained little more than the statement of mission in the 6 June 1942 directives, supplemented by informal coordination between the Materiel Command at Wright Field, Ohio, and the Department of Air Training, as well as more formal coordination between the Headquarters of the Army Ground Forces and of the Army Air Forces. Lt. Gen. Lesley J. McNair's headquarters had not disseminated any detailed instructions to units on how to obtain resupply. Initially, most equipment issued was intended for units deploying overseas and was shipped boxed and crated for overseas movement, not to be opened until the unit reached its destination. Units faced with imminent deployment received their liaison aircraft by rail express and never trained with them until they arrived overseas. The equipment of later-deploying units traveled more slowly as normal freight; thus, these units sometimes had a brief opportunity to train with their aircraft in the United States before departing for active theaters. Three staff officers at Washington Barracks—Lt. Col. V. A. St. Onge in the G–4 section, Lt. Col. John C. Oakes in G–3, and Lt. Col. R. H. Adams in G–1—were the Army Ground Forces officers most heavily involved in coordinating supply. Each of them had many other duties.[5]

On 30 December 1942, representatives of the Army Ground Forces, the Army Air Forces, and the Services of Supply met to work out the details of the supply system. The Services of Supply wanted one of the supply bureaus under its direction, such as the Ordnance or Transportation Corps, to store and distribute Army Air Forces equipment and supplies to ground forces units in the United States and overseas. All the bureaus, however, lacked sufficient depot space, which meant the Army Air Forces had to play a larger role

---

[4] Memos, Adams, 16 Nov 42; [Adams, 16 Nov 42]; Edwards for CG, AAF, 4 Dec 42, sub: Organic Air Obsn for FA, TAG, Decimal file, 1940–1945, 452.1 (12–4–42), RG 407, NARA.

[5] MFR, V. A. S., 28 Dec 42; Ltr, Col C. H. Day, Assistant Adjutant General (AAG), AGF, to CG, AAF, 27 Dec 42, sub: Assignment of Liaison Planes for FA Units; Ltr, Brig Gen F. W. Evans, Dir, War Organization and Movement, Air Staff (AS), to CG, AGF, 4 Jan 43, sub: Same, all in HQ, AGF, Gen Corresp, 1942–1948, 353/6 (FA Air Obsn) (Confidential [C]), RG 337, NARA; Ltr, Maj G. Seleno, AAG, AGF, to CG, 3 Feb 43, sub: Shipment of Tables of Basic Allowance (TBA) Equipment to AGF Units; MFR, V. A. S., 4 Feb 43, HQ, AGF, Gen Corresp, 1942–1948, 353/10 (FA Air Obsn) (C), RG 337, NARA.

DEVELOPING THE AIR-OBSERVATION-POST PROGRAM

Field Assembly of an L–4 on Oahu, Territory of Hawaii, 1943. Note the Overseas Crate in the Rear Containing the Wings.

in the supply system than originally envisioned. As an interim measure the conferees decided to establish air supply offices at all appropriate posts, camps, and stations to issue aviation equipment. A War Department directive of 18 January 1943 announced the plan, to take effect on 1 March.[6]

In the new system, the Army Air Forces became simply a source of supply in the United States while retaining supply, storage, and distribution responsibilities overseas. Its Air Service Command at Patterson Field, Ohio, furnished aircraft for both domestic assignment and overseas shipment. The Army Ground Forces indicated which units should receive aircraft and in what sequence. The Services of Supply coordinated the movement of aircraft, spare parts, tool sets, and supplies to units—arranging rail shipment or later, as flight delivery became more common for units in the United States, ensuring that a sufficient number of pilots picked up the aircraft at the appropriate times. The Services of Supply's responsibilities for the supply of units overseas was limited strictly to the ship-

---

[6] MFR, Distribution Division (Div), Services of Supply (SOS), 5 Mar 43; Memo W700–5–43, TAGO, 18 Jan 43, sub: Supply of AC Equipment to AGF Units Within the Continental Limits of the U.S., both in TAGO, Decimal file, 1940–1945, 400 (1–12–43), RG 407, NARA; Memo, Brig Gen F. A. Heileman, Dir of Supply, Army Service Forces (ASF), for ACS, G–4, WDGS (Attn: Lt Col F. R. Crom), 16 Feb 44, sub: Overseas Supply of Liaison-Type Airplanes for FA Units, HQ, AAF, Central Decimal file, October 1942–May 1944 (Security Class), 452.1–D (Aircraft), RG 18, NARA.

ment of aviation equipment and supply sets to the theaters in advance of the units for which they were intended.[7]

The conferees recognized that the success of the supply effort depended on detailed coordination—matching particular aircraft, spare parts, tools, or supplies with a specific unit. The War Department directive thus required the commanding general, Services of Supply, to establish a liaison office in his headquarters to "coordinate the distribution of Air Corps equipment to Army Ground Forces units." The engineering officer in the Department of Air Training, Maj. Robert M. Leich, transferred into the position, officially designated the chief of the Air Section, Miscellaneous Issue Branch, Stock Control Division, Services of Supply (Army Service Forces after 12 March 1943). He became the first artillery air officer to serve on a higher staff in Washington. Working full time on air-observation-post questions, Leich made the detailed administrative arrangements for supply and oversaw their execution. He also served as the staff officer responsible for preparing directives amplifying or modifying the air-observation-post logistical system.[8]

Within a short time Leich's influence extended far beyond this somewhat narrow range of issues. Because of his energy, enthusiasm, detailed knowledge, and personality, he became the one officer to whom junior officers handling air-observation-post issues turned for informal advice. In effect Leich became a one-man and highly unofficial coordinator of organic aviation problems at the highest levels, all but invisible to the senior officers heading the Army Service Forces, the Army Ground Forces, the Army Air Forces, and the various War Department General Staff sections involved. The number of action officers treating the subject was so small that they could congregate around one table in the Pentagon cafeteria, and Leich often gathered them there to settle problems over lunch.[9]

The air-observation-post logistical system did not allow such irregular shortcuts. In theory the air supply officer at each post, camp, or station served as a liaison between the ground forces units and Army Air Forces depots for supplies, replacement aircraft, and

---

[7] Ltr, Lt Col L. E. Bell, Acting Chief (Ch), Miscellaneous (Misc) Issue Branch (Br), Stock Control Div, ASF, to CG, Air Service (AS) Cmd, 10 Sep 43, sub: Transfer of TBA AAF Equipment in AGF Units; Memo, sub: Excess AAF Equipment To Be Redistributed; both in HQ, AGF, Gen Corresp, 1942–1948, 353/25 (FA Air Obsn) (Secret [S]), RG 337, NARA; Message (Msg), [Lt Gen Ben] Lear, CG, AGF, to CG, Second Army, 3 May 43, HQ, AGF, Gen Corresp, 1942–1948, 452.1/548, RG 337, NARA; Ltr, Day to CG, Armored (Armd) Cmd, 20 Jul 43, sub: Reassignment of FA Liaison Airplanes; MFR, E. F. O. to CG, ASF (Attn: Maj Leich, Stock Control Div); both in HQ, AGF, Gen Corresp, 1942–1948, 452.1/561 (Airplanes), RG 337, NARA; Ltr, Seleno to CG, Second Army, et al., 23 Aug 43, sub: Transfer of FA Liaison-Type Airplanes, HQ, AGF, Gen Corresp, 1942–1948, 452.1/16 (Airplanes) [Restricted (R)], RG 337, NARA.

[8] Memo W–700–5–43, TAGO, 18 Jan 43; MFR, ACS, G–4, 14 Apr 43; Memo W–700–19–43, TAGO, 13 Apr 43, sub: Procedure for Supply of AAF Equipment to Ground Units in U.S.; all in TAGO, Decimal file, 1940–1945, 400 (1–12–43), RG 407, NARA; Memo, Brig Gen H. A. Craig, Assistant Chief of Air Staff (ACAS) for Operations, Commitments, and Requirements (OC&R), for Lt Gen Barney M. Giles, Deputy (Dep) CG, AAF, 27 Dec 43, sub: Liaison Aviation (Avn) for AAF and Army Ground Units, HQ, AAF, Central Decimal file, October 1942–May 1944, 452.01–C (Procurement and Requirements), RG 18, NARA.

[9] "Energy, Inc.: Bob Leich," *Army Aviation* 32 (7 April 1983):18; Interview (Interv), author with Lt Gen (Ret) R. R. Williams, 20 Feb 91, U.S. Army Center of Military History, Washington, D.C. (hereafter cited as CMH); Ltr, Maj R. A. Meredith, AAG, AGF, to CG, Replacement and School Command (R&SC), 12 Nov 43, sub: Routing of Copy of Official Communication Outside Normal Channels, with Indorsement (Ind), Col W. W. Carr, Adjutant General (AG), Field Artillery School (FAS), to CG, R&SC, 24 Nov 43, [Action Officer (A/O) Lt Col Wolf]; Memo Slip, Lt Col J. C. Oakes, G–3, Training, HQ, AGF, for Brig Gen J. M. Lentz, G–3, AGF, 8 Nov 43, sub: Col. Ford's Proposal to Set Up a Corps Air Liaison Squadron, HQ, AGF, Gen Corresp, 1942–1948, 353/386 (FA Air Obsn), RG 337, NARA.

requests for third- and fourth-echelon maintenance. In practice the air supply officer was an overworked ordnance officer who assumed his air supply duties in addition to his regular ones. He received very little guidance from Washington. Initially, Leich made no effort to prepare a detailed statement of standard operating procedures for the air supply officers; he was quite overwhelmed by the problem of distributing aircraft. Most of the air supply officers had little or no experience in dealing with the Army Air Forces, and Leich wrongly assumed that they would maintain close contact by telephone with their air depot counterparts. The results, unfortunately, proved less than satisfactory.[10]

The executive officer of the Department of Air Training, Lt. Col. Gordon J. Wolf, and other observers from the Department of Air Training returned from Second and Third Army maneuvers in the spring of 1943 very disturbed about the supply situation in the field. While most units had received their organic aircraft, there was "an almost universal lack" of tool kits, spare parts, and spare engines. Aircraft production matched production goals very well, but production of ancillary equipment lagged badly. The situation was not peculiar to the liaison aircraft program; it reflected the widespread emphasis in Army Air Forces on "the numbers racket," the use of statistical measures to determine success without reference to actual conditions. Moreover, air sections in the field experienced considerable difficulty in obtaining proper fuels and lubricants in a timely fashion. Field-expedient use of whatever fuels and lubricants were available exacted a cost in engine life, particularly unfortunate in view of the scarcity of spare engines. Many pilots and mechanics sought assistance from their local air supply officers "with almost uniform lack of success." As a result the pilots and mechanics descended on the nearest Army Air Forces installation to borrow tools and supplies. Colonel Ford worried that they would "become such a pain in the neck to the Army Air Forces as to produce a reaction unfavorable to organic air observation for field artillery."[11]

The spare engine problem persisted into the fall of 1943. Once automatic issue to units in the United States began, Army Air Forces stocks of reserve engines, nowhere near prescribed levels, were depleted within one week. This failure produced the first serious high-level staff examination of the engine problem. Leich, in conjunction with his counterparts on the Air Staff, considered whether to adopt Army Air Forces supply procedures; they decided against that for the same reason Ford did originally—the ground supply officers' lack of familiarity with the system. In the process they discovered a flaw masked until then by the emphasis on numbers. When the Army Ground Forces staff had prepared the tables of organization and equipment for air-observation-post sections, someone had given the division artillery a battalion-size spare-parts kit and tool set rather than the large divisional set that Ford had intended. The Army Ground Forces staff now rectified the situation by prescribing one kit and tool set for each firing battalion and the division artillery head-

---

[10] Ltr, Brig Gen J. D. Balmer, Commandant, FAS, to Col J. F. Williams, 20 May 43, HQ, AGF, Gen Corresp, 1942–1948, 452.11/48 (Parts and Accessories), RG 337, NARA; Ind, Col R. A. Case, Dir, Stock Control Div, ASF, to CG, AGF (Attn: G–4), 24 May 43, HQ, AGF, Gen Corresp, 1942–1948, 353/26 (FA Air Obsn) (C), RG 337, NARA; Ltr, Lt Col R. M. Leich, ASF, to Col L. W. DeRosier, AAF Liaison Officer (Ofcr), ASF, 10 Apr 44, HQ, AAF, Central Decimal file, October 1942–May 1944, 452.1 (Liaison), Folder 3, RG 18, NARA.

[11] Ltr, Balmer to Williams, 20 May 43; Report (Rpt), Lt Col Gordon J. Wolf, 1 Apr 43, sub: Rpt of Observer (Obsr)—Third Army Maneuvers, 15–25 Mar 43, Gordon J. Wolf Ms, Historian's files, CMH; Memo, Gen Henry H. Arnold, CG, AAF, for CSA, 26 Jan 44, sub: FA Liaison Avn, HQ, AAF, Central Decimal file, October 1942–May 1944, 452.01–C (Procurement and Requirements), RG 18, NARA.

quarters, avoiding the possibility for confusion intrinsic to Ford's initial supply plan. Of course, there was an unavoidable delay while the increased numbers of engines went into production, but by October 1943, although real problems still remained, a functioning Field Artillery air logistical system existed in the continental United States in fact as well as on paper.[12]

Research and Development, Force Development, and Combat Development

The directives creating the Air-Observation-Post Program made no provision for research and development, in contrast to the explicit way in which they addressed procurement, supply, and maintenance issues. With one exception these issues gravitated to the Department of Air Training. No one thought much about research and development during the early months of the program. Colonel Ford was too busy with start-up problems to ponder long-term requirements. The difficulties of the moment prevented him from adopting the kind of perspective required to address research and development issues. Because the 6 June directives made the Army Air Forces responsible for procuring aircraft for the Field Artillery, logic appeared to dictate that General Arnold's organization would also assume responsibility for future research and development of follow-on aircraft. But this inference rested on the assumption that the program had a future beyond the immediate emergency. The Army Air Forces' attempt in late 1942 to regain control of organic air from the Field Artillery suggested that not everyone shared this assumption. Predictably, the Army Ground Forces took the view that in the absence of restrictions the Department of Air Training could engage in development; the Army Air Forces argued that without a written and specific charter Colonel Ford and his subordinates could do nothing.[13]

In addition to questions about the permanence of the program, the senior leaders of the Army Air Forces, Assistant Secretary of War for Air Robert A. Lovett and General Arnold, continued to distrust light aircraft and viewed them as a drain on scarce resources. They were much more enthusiastic about helicopters—and with some reason. The Sikorsky team continued to refine the VS–300, and on 20 April 1942, officers from the Air Staff and Wright Field attended a successful flight demonstration of the refined Sikorsky machine, which received the military designation XR–4. After the creation of the Field Artillery air program, Headquarters, Army Air Forces, shifted all development funds into helicopters. It still had several autogiros under contract, but these either crashed or were months, even years, behind their development schedules, a situation that ultimately led to their cancellation. In the Air Staff view there would be no follow-on to the L–4s and L–5s

---

[12] Ltr, Maj Gen L. Lutes, Dir of Operations (Opns), ASF, to CG, AGF (Attn: G–4 Section), 26 Jul 43, sub: Initial Issue of Spare Airplane Engines, O–170–3, to FA Units, with Ind, Day to CG, ASF (Attn: Maj Leich, Stock Control Div), 9 Aug 43, in HQ, AGF, Gen Corresp, 1942–1948, 452.11/54 (Parts and Accessories) (R), RG 337, NARA. Msg, [Maj Gen Walter H.] Frank, CG, AS Cmd, to HQ, AGF (Attn: Lt Col V. A. St. Onge), 18 Aug 43, 1816Z, HQ, AGF, Gen Corresp, 1942–1948, 452.11/56 (Parts and Accessories), RG 337, NARA. Ltr, Brig Gen F. A. Heileman, Dep Dir, Opns, ASF, to CG, AGF, 8 Sep 43, with Ind, Dryden to CG, ASF (Attn: Misc Issue Br, Stock Control Div), 24 Oct 44, sub: Kits, Maintenance Supplies (Aircraft), HQ, AGF, Gen Corresp, 1942–1948, 452.11/62 (Parts and Accessories), RG 337, NARA. Memo Slip, G–3, Requirements, AGF, for G–4, AGF, 25 Aug 43, sub: Spare Parts for FA Liaison Airplanes, with Ind, Col W. W. Carr, AG, FAS, to CG, AGF, 16 Oct 43, HQ, AGF, Gen Corresp, 1942–1948, 452.11/64 (Parts and Accessories), RG 337, NARA.

[13] Memo, Edwards for CG, AAF, 6 Jun 42.

DEVELOPING THE AIR-OBSERVATION-POST PROGRAM

Sikorsky XR–4 Helicopter at Stratford, Connecticut, 17 April 1942, Three Days Before Its Successful Flight Demonstration for the Army

of the current generation of fixed-wing liaison aircraft. Officers at McNair's headquarters and Fort Sill remained unaware of this shift in priorities and of helicopter developments generally during 1942. The disestablishment of the Office of the Chief of Field Artillery in March 1942 had severed many of the formal and informal links between the Field Artillery as a branch and the Army Air Forces. Given McNair's philosophy of a spare administrative overhead, they required years to restore.[14]

The faculty and staff at the Department of Air Training gradually became engaged in developmental issues, first because of dissatisfaction with two of the three standard fixed-wing liaison aircraft and second because of the need to develop air-observation-post sections for airborne artillery. Even casual observers realized there were performance differences between the L–2, L–3, and L–4. The Aeronca L–3 was a heavy aircraft with so much safety engineered in that, while it was by far the best of the three for cross-country flying, it was totally unsuited for short-field landings and takeoffs or low-altitude, slow-speed maneuvering of the type required in tactical flying. The Taylorcraft L–2 was the fastest of the three but also the most dangerous. While the undersides of the L–3 and L–4 wings were flat, the standard configuration among light aircraft, the underside of the L–2 wing was slightly convex. This cross-section accounted for both the extra speed and the extra danger. At slow speeds, L–2s stalled without warning. They could and did surprise even veteran pilots—with potentially fatal results at low altitudes. The L–4, in Ford's

---

[14] H. F. Gregory, *Anything a Horse Can Do: The Story of the Helicopter* (New York: Reynal and Hitchcock, 1944), pp. 110–11; Memo, Col D. M. Schlatter, Dir, Air-Ground Spt, HQ, AAF, for CG, AAF, 22 Apr 42, in "Helicopter Flight Demonstration, 20 Apr 42, VS–300, XR–4," (Unpublished [Unpubl] Ms, U.S. Army Avn Training Library, Fort Rucker, Ala., 1942).

view, was not perfect. It simply represented the best design compromise between short takeoff and landing capabilities, safety, and low-speed maneuverability. By its behavior it also provided ample warning of an impending stall. Unfortunately, it represented a mature design in 1942. The engineers at Piper seemingly had wrung all possible performance out of the airframe.[15]

At the time the War Department placed its initial light aircraft orders, Aeronca had no trainers available. Virtually all L–3s went to units in the field. The Department of Air Training had L–2 and L–4 trainers, with the latter the clearly preferable machine. The early problem of attracting suitable pilot candidates provided an unanticipated benefit: Ford had enough L–4s to ensure that all students in the early classes were instructed on them. The solution of the student pilot shortage forced him to use the dangerous L–2s as trainers. In November 1942 he requested that the Army Ground Forces secure sufficient additional L–4s to replace all L–2s at the school. To this request and subsequent appeals by the commandant of the Field Artillery School, Brig. Gen. Jesmond D. Balmer, the Army Ground Forces staff turned deaf ears for a variety of reasons. By the spring of 1943 the staff did not want to give the Army Air Forces any excuse to reopen the question of returning the aerial observation program to General Arnold's control. The division of the 1943 light-aircraft production program with the Army Air Forces also played a role. But the largest factor was simply the absence of anyone on the staff technically qualified to appreciate the import of Balmer's and Ford's requests. In July 1943, after the fifth fatal crash of an L–2, Balmer grounded all L–2s on his own authority. His action forced the Army Ground Forces and the Army Air Forces to replace all L–2s at the school with L–4s and led to the eventual substitution of L–4s for all L–2s and L–3s Army-wide.[16]

In November 1942, at the same time Ford began his campaign to replace L–2s and L–3s, he proposed a service test of L–5s to see if they might be usable for field artillery work. Rebuffed because the first L–5s were just coming off the production lines with many teething problems, he raised the issue the following month as part of a larger, but narrower, force structure issue: how to equip an airborne division. The first American airborne divisions were only formed in the fall of 1942. Their initial tables of organization and equipment did not provide for light aircraft. The Army Air Forces asserted that it could provide any organic aircraft elements that an airborne division needed. Ford argued that the division artillery needed air-observation-post sections just like a standard division, except that it needed a higher performance aircraft, one with sufficient speed to accompany standard troop carriers under its own power—the L–5. He succeeded in obtaining three L–5s in March 1943. A board of officers headed by the chief of the Flight Division in the Department of Air Training, Maj. Robert R. Williams, recommended that the Field Artillery adopt L–5s in addition to L–4s. The staff at Washington Barracks rejected the

---

[15] Rpt, Williams, et al., 2 Apr 43, sub: Rpt of a Board of Officers (B/O) Appointed to Compare Performance of Types L-2, L–3, L–4, and L–5 Airplanes, HQ, AGF, Gen Corresp, 1942–1948, 353/300 (FA Air Obsn), RG 337, NARA.

[16] Memo, Balmer for CG, R&SC, 29 Nov 42; Memo Slip, V. A. S., G–4, for G–3 Training (Attn: Col Oakes), 10 Dec 42, with Ind, Day to CG, R&SC, 29 Dec 42; MFR, S., 29 Dec 42, HQ, AGF, Gen Corresp, 1942–1948, 353/257 (FA Air Obsn), RG 337, NARA; Lt. Gen. R. R. Williams, ["Introduction"], *U.S. Army Aviation Digest* (*USAAD*) 20 (May 1974):1; Memo Slip, Lentz for CS, AGF, 15 Jul 43, sub: Type of Airplanes for FA Use; Ltr, Balmer to CG, R&SC, 23 Jun 43; Msg, Arnold to CG, AAF Training Cmd, 28 Jul 43; all in HQ, AGF, Gen Corresp, 1942–1948, 353/300 (FA Air Obsn), RG 337, NARA.

TAYLORCRAFT L–2

board's recommendation. Ford eventually had to accept defeat on the L–5 issue. Headquarters, Army Ground Forces, prepared tables of organization and equipment for airborne divisions that included L–4s in their air-observation-post sections. Transports would tow them to the drop area, just like gliders.[17]

It was only a short step from selecting the best available types of liaison aircraft in production to selecting an advanced design prototype superior to existing models. About the same time the Williams board evaluated the L–5, Ford learned about the Army Air Forces' helicopter developments and with Balmer's full backing sought to secure one to test at Fort Sill. Engineers understood little about the dynamic forces operating on rotating wings, and improvements on the Sikorsky and competing helicopter models were slow and hard won during most of 1943. Headquarters, Army Air Forces, could not ini-

---

[17] Memo, Balmer to CG, R&SC, 29 Nov 42; Memo Slip, V. A. S. for G–3 Training, 10 Dec 42; Rpt, Williams, et al., 2 Apr 43. Ltr, Lt Col D. G. McLennan, Secretary (Sec), FAS, to CG, R&SC, 17 Apr 43, sub: Issue of L–5 Aircraft, with Ind, Day to CG, R&SC, 10 May 43; MFR, Q. A. S., HQ, AGF, 10 May 43; Memo Slip, W. F. Dean, AGF, Requirements, for G–3, AGF, 1 May 43, sub: Issue of L–5 Aircraft; all in HQ, AGF, Gen Corresp, 1942–1948, 353/301 (FA Air Obsn), RG 337, NARA; Memo, Capt R. J. Delacroix, AAG, AGF, for CSA, 7 May 43, sub: Types of Airplanes for FA Use [A/O Oakes]; Memo, Brig Gen R. E. Porter, ACS, G–4, for CG, AGF, 5 Jun 43, sub: Same; both in HQ, AGF, Gen Corresp, 1942–1948, 353/300 (FA Air Obsn), RG 337, NARA; Memo, Balmer for CG, R&SC, 23 Dec 42, sub: Issue of L–5 Aircraft; Ind, Dryden to CSA (Attn: G–3), 31 Jan 43; Recommendation and Routing (R&R) Sheet, Col R. F. Stearley, Dir, Air Spt, to ACAS, 8 Feb 43, sub: Issue of L–5 Aircraft; all in HQ, AAF, Central Decimal file, October 1942–May 1944, 452.01 (Liaison Planes), RG 18, NARA.

tially provide a firm date, but progress toward the end of 1943 suggested the possibility of a mid-1944 delivery.[18]

Ford could not afford to wait for the helicopter. Reports from overseas of the L–4's anticipated poor performance in mountainous terrain made it necessary to find a fixed-wing aircraft with performance roughly comparable to the L–5 to supplement the L–4 in field artillery air sections. In April 1943 the manufacturer demonstrated the Rawdon T–1, which impressed senior officers in the Department of Air Training but not the engineers at the Air Materiel Command. The T–1 was not superior in performance to the L–5; the engineers argued that "the Helicopter would be more satisfactory." The Materiel Command report, which represented the Army Air Forces position, put Ford in a rather unhappy situation. On one hand, the Army Air Forces denied his request for L–5s because it needed all those available. On the other hand, it denied him an acceptable substitute based on the fact that the L–5 was already in production and readily available—except, that is, to the Field Artillery. Of course, even if the Materiel Command had been interested in the Rawdon, there was no money for development. All funds had been siphoned off into helicopter development—not necessarily a fact of which anyone at Headquarters, Army Ground Forces, was aware. To say the least, the Materiel Command's recommendation appeared self-serving.[19]

When a second manufacturer, Piper Aircraft Corporation, delivered its J–5D, subsequently designated the L–4X, to Post Field for consideration, Ford appointed a board, once more headed by Major Williams, to evaluate it. With the board's endorsement, the Field Artillery School sought a service-test quantity of J–5Ds. In Washington, at Major Leich's suggestion, McNair's staff bypassed Headquarters, Army Air Forces, entirely.

---

[18] MFRs, FA Section, HQ, AGF, [10 Jun 43], [19 Jun 43], sub: Sikorsky Helicopter for FAS; Ind, Delacroix to Commandant, FAS, 15 Dec 43; all in HQ, AGF, Gen Corresp, 1942–1948, 452.1/553 (Airplanes) (S), RG 337, NARA. Ltr, Brig Gen B. W. Chidlaw, ACAS for Engineering (Eng), to Lt Col J. C. L. Adams, OSS, 4 Dec 42; Memo Rpt, Maj L. B. Cooper, Eng Div, AAF Materiel Center (Ctr), 24 Mar 43, sub: XR–4 Helicopter—Final Rpt; Ltr, Maj Gen D. Johnson, Dir, Military (Mil) Requirements, AS, to CG, Materiel Cmd, 22 Jan 43, sub: Procurement of Helicopters, HQ, AAF, Central Decimal file (Security Class), October 1942–May 1944, 452.1–A (Helicopters), RG 18, NARA; Memo, Chidlaw for Lt Gen O. P. Echols, 14 Jul 43, sub: Status of Rotary-Wing Projects; Memo, Maj Gen B. W. Chidlaw for R. A. Lovett, Assistant Secretary of War (ASW) for Air, 31 Aug 43, sub: Ltr from Mr. J. F. Byrnes, dtd August 28, 1943, Regarding the Helicopter Program; Ltr, Maj C. D. Seftenberg, Asst Technical (Tech) Executive (Exec), Materiel Cmd, to CG, AAF, 25 Jun 43, sub: Contract W 535 AC–29005, Assignment of YR–4A Helicopters; Memo, Col H. F. Gregory, Eng Div, AAF Materiel Ctr, for CG, AAF, 11 Aug 43, sub: Tactical Use of Helicopters for French Army Special Missions; Msg, Eng Div, Air Materiel Ctr, to ACAS for Materiel, Maintenance, and Distribution (MM&D), Materiel Div (Attn: Lt Col A. P. Tappan), 7 Dec 43, HQ, AAF, Central Decimal file, October 1942–May 1944, 452.01 (Helicopters), 452.1 (Helicopters) (Folders 1&2); both in HQ, AAF, Central Decimal file, October 1942–May 1944, RG 18, NARA. Ralph H. Alex, "How Are You Fixed for Blades? The Saga of the Helicopter, Circa 1940–60," in *Vertical Flight: The Age of the Helicopter*, ed. Walter J. Boyne and Donald S. Lopez (Washington, D.C.: Smithsonian Institution, 1984), pp. 17–24. Alex was a member of the Sikorsky design team. His article is both history and memoir. Interv, author with Lt Col R. R. Yeats, 24 May 90, CMH.

[19] Ind, McLennan to CG, AGF, 15 Jan 43; Ltr, Brig Gen F. L. Parks, CS, AGF, to Senator M. F. Tydings, 19 Feb 43; Disposition Form (DF), Maj Gen O. P. Echols, CG, Materiel Cmd, for Arnold, 13 Jul 42, sub: Inspection of Plane at Baltimore, Md.; all in HQ, AGF, Gen Corresp, 1942–1948, 452.1/535, RG 337, NARA. Ltr, McLennan to CG, AGF, 24 Apr 43, sub: Rawdon T–1 Airplane; MFR, sub: Same, HQ, AGF, Gen Corresp, 1942–1948, 452.1/547, RG 337, NARA. Leonard Bridgman, ed., *Jane's All the World's Aircraft, 1949–1950* (New York: McGraw-Hill, 1949), pp. 269c–270c. The Rawdon T–1 had a maximum speed of 134 miles per hour, a cruising speed of 120 miles per hour, and a landing speed of 50 miles per hour with flaps. Its takeoff roll over obstacles was about two times longer than that of the L–4.

THE RAWDON T–1

Headquarters, Army Ground Forces, took the issue directly to the Joint Army-Navy Munitions Assignment Committee, where Under Secretary of War Robert P. Patterson sat as the War Department representative. The committee approved the procurement request. Only through this devious bureaucratic maneuver did Ford obtain J–5Ds for service tests.[20]

Ford was not the only ground forces officer with ideas about employing light aircraft in airborne divisions. The ubiquitous Colonel John Adams, reorganized out of his position as adviser to the head of the Office of Strategic Services, still retained the backing of Assistant Secretary of War McCloy and had captured the interest of senior officers at the Airborne Command at Fort Bragg, North Carolina. The result was a series of tests of the capabilities of light aircraft to deliver troops and supplies behind enemy lines. Adams, who served as the Army Ground Forces observer, was disappointed that it took over a month to train the Army Air Forces pilots assigned to the test so that only slightly more than one week could be devoted to tactical exercises. He conceded that his concept required a light aircraft with better performance than the L–5, but he remained optimistic about the results. The Army Air Forces reports, however, were decidedly negative. Standard-size transports were much more efficient, an industrial rather than a tactical criterion. The other senior ground observer perceived advantages in some if not all of Adams' proposals. They were

---

[20] Ltr, Col W. W. Carr, AG, FAS, to CG, R&SC, 9 Sep 43, sub: Improved Types of Liaison Aircraft for FA Use; Ind, Maj R. A. Meredith, AAG, AGF, to CG, ASF (Attn: Leich, Stock Control Div), 11 Oct 43; Rpt, Williams, et al., to Commandant, FAS, 6 Sep 43, sub: Rpt of Test on J–5D Piper Aircraft; Memo Slip, A. B. D., G–4, AGF, for Requirements, AGF, and G–3, AGF, 21 Sep 43; all in HQ, AGF, Gen Corresp, 1942–1948, 452.1/580 (Airplanes), RG 337, NARA.

not, however, pursued. Adams left, eventually to command a regiment at Anzio, where he won a Silver Star for gallantry in action. He bequeathed a descriptive phrase that encompassed many of his ideas, a phrase with which subsequent generations of ground officers venturing into the air would have to grapple: "air cavalry."[21]

The air cavalry tests at Fort Bragg constituted one of the few wartime exceptions to the tendency to center light aircraft combat development at Fort Sill. This inclination simply reflected the large number of highly skilled pilots and mechanics concentrated there to provide instruction and support for the aviation training programs. In October 1943, of course, there was no formal system to permit improvements in the organization, tactics, technique, or equipment of the liaison aircraft assigned to the Field Artillery. Members of the Army Air Forces had attempted to block Ford's efforts to obtain a follow-on aircraft for the L–4, but the Army Ground Forces staff, under Leich's influence, had succeeded in at least temporarily outmaneuvering the Air Staff. At best, however, this success constituted a one-time-only solution. A more comprehensive settlement of the research and development question remained for the future.

The Department of Air Training

The fact that the Department of Air Training played such a prominent role in the attempt to find a follow-on light plane to the L–4 was no accident. It reflected both the relative absence of Field Artillery pilots in administrative positions at higher headquarters—although Major Leich proved to be the first of many—and the large collection of experienced pilots on the instructional staff in the department. The department in fact represented the largest collection of such aviators at a single point anywhere in the world. Men of similar training, background, and interests could and did exchange ideas, identify problems, and explore solutions. When officers at higher headquarters had aviation concepts or equipment they wanted to test, they naturally turned to the department. But its primary mission remained training. The vast majority of Field Artillery pilots received their operational flight training in the department. That mutual experience gave graduates a sense of a larger, shared purpose that helped to hold the program together. In fact, what happened at Post Field was central to both the success of organic aviation in combat and the institutional future of the program.

The department designated each pilot class upon entry as a "flight" and placed it under the command of one of the senior instructors in the Flight Training Division. Under him instructors worked with usually 4, sometimes 5, students apiece—2 or 3 in the morning and 2 in the afternoon. Instructors also assisted in ground school. In general, instructors worked with the same students throughout both stages, until the students graduated or failed. Most flight instruction took place away from Post Field. Student pilots and instruc-

---

[21] Rpt, Adams, AGF Obsr, to CG, AGF, 13 Mar 43, sub: Rpt by Ground Force Ofcr Obsr on Air Corps Tests, Office of the Assistant Secretary of War (OASW), Security Class Corresp of J. J. McCloy, 1941–1945, 452.1 (Light Planes), RG 107, NARA; Memo, Maj L. Duenweg, AAG, AGF, for CG, AAF, 26 Sep 42, sub: Light Aircraft for Airborne (Abn) Opns, with Ind, Lt Col Rex F. Gilmartin to CG, AGF, 6 Oct 42, HQ, AGF, Gen Corresp, 1942–1948, 452.1/719 (Airplanes), RG 337, NARA. For a fair summing-up of Adams and his ideas, see Memo, Lt Gen Ben Lear, CG, AGF, for ASW, 14 May 43, sub: "America's Secret Weapon—The Light Plane," HQ, AGF, Gen Corresp, 1942–1948, 452.1/83 (Airplanes), RG 337, NARA.

tors flew to one of the numerous satellite fields, called stage fields, located on the Fort Sill reservation or on leased land nearby. There, the students practiced all the maneuvers they needed to qualify as Field Artillery pilots.[22]

Student pilots in the Department of Air Training spent half of their day flying and the other half learning to maintain their machines. The students were not officially called "pilot-mechanics." Col. (later Brig. Gen.) John M. Lentz at Headquarters, Army Ground Forces, had simplified their designation to "pilots," because he had deemed Ford's term undignified for officers. They were, however, expected to be able to repair and maintain their airplanes in the field. At night the student pilots attended ground school, where they took courses in meteorology, navigation, and so forth. Instruction in the tactical employment of aircraft followed the principles that Ford had laid down for the Class Before One, with one important exception. In accord with the difficulties that Flight B had experienced with Army Air Forces pursuits during the service tests with the 2d Division, instructors initially taught the student pilots that aerial observation was for emergency use only. Ground observation constituted the Field Artillery School's preferred method of directing artillery fire. The pilot courses also followed the same two-stage format used in instructing the Class Before One. A graduate knew the fundamentals of light-plane tactical operations. To achieve proficiency for combat operations, he had to continue to practice the Fort Sill techniques after he joined his unit.[23]

Sending Field Artillery officers to Army Air Forces primary schools did not alleviate the need for Stage A training, notwithstanding the contrary views of the War Department G–3, Brig. Gen. Idwal H. Edwards. The mobilization effort was so vast and the prewar cadre of Air Corps officers so small that by 1942 the Army Air Forces Flying Training Command contracted out all primary instruction to civilian aviation schools. Two schools were the primary suppliers for Field Artillery pilots in 1942 and 1943: the Harte Flying Service in Denton, Texas, and the Army Air Forces Primary Flying School in Pittsburg, Kansas. The quality of the graduates reflected the quality of instruction, which wartime pressures conspired to keep low. Stage A in the pilot course thus continued to perform an essential function by bringing all student pilots up to certain minimal levels of skill before they ventured into operational training.[24]

Check pilots, who judged the proficiency of the students at the end of each stage, stood apart from the flight organization. The chief of check pilots reported directly to the chief of the Flight Training Division. A check pilot might bump a student to a subsequent

---

[22] Intervs, author with Lt Col (Ret) H. S. Wann, 23 Mar 91, and with Maj C. M. Brown, Jun 82, both at CMH; Hughes Rudd, "When I Landed, The War Was Over," *American Heritage* 31 (October–November 1981):32–45.

[23] Intervs, author with Capt J. T. Kerr, 3 Mar 91, CMH; Col B. R. Kramer and Lt Col R. K. Andreson with Brig Gen O. G. Goodhand, 9 May 78, MHI; Memo, Lt Col J. W. Ramsey, AAG, HQ, AGF, for CSA, 2 Jun 42, sub: Organic Air Obsn for FA [A/O Lentz], HQ, AGF, Gen Corresp, 1942–1948, 353/3 (FA Air Obsn), RG 337, NARA.

[24] Interv, author with Yeats, 24 May 90, CMH; Anon, "History of Army Air Forces Flying Training Cmd, 7 July 1943 to 31 December 1944," 16 vols. (Bound Ms, AAF Training Cmd, 1945), 6:1353–60, Microfilm A2245, U.S. Air Force Historical Research Agency, Maxwell Air Force Base, Ala. (hereafter cited as AFHRA); A. R. Kooker, et al., "History of Army Air Forces Flying Training Command, 1 September 1939 to V-J Day," 8 vols. (Bound Ms, AAF Training Cmd, 1946), 6:1126–29, Microfilm A2246, AFHRA; Memo, Dryden for CG, AGF (Attn: Dir, Individual Training), 14 Mar 43, sub: Instructors for Obsn Post Course, Department of Air Training (DAT), FAS, HQ, AGF, Gen Corresp, 1942–1948, 353/276 (FA Air Obsn), RG 337, NARA.

class to sharpen his skills and techniques, but this was an exceptional occurrence. It was far more likely that the student would be washed out. When a student failed a major component of the course, his instructor handed him a "pink slip," actually a small piece of pink paper with the reason for the failure typed on it. When the student had received three pink slips, he failed the course. The precise nature of the flying and the new techniques—contour flying, which a later generation referred to as "nap of the earth" flying, landing on curved roads, and power stalls—caused problems for many students, even some of the veteran light-plane pilots.[25]

Check pilots performed one other important duty—they trained instructors. The expansion of the pilot training program, beginning with the increase in the normal class size to thirty-one with Pilot Class 10 in November 1942 and peaking at sixty beginning with Pilot Class 25 in March 1943, required a steady rise in the number of instructors until mid-1943. The original additions to the faculty came from graduates of the program. General McNair's headquarters gave the Department of Air Training priority over all field units for acquiring graduates. These men usually needed only additional practice. Once beyond the initial six classes, however, most graduates lacked the maturity and flying experience essential for good instructors, and Ford had to turn increasingly to civilians. In the spring of 1943 a certain number of instructors, mainly enlisted men, became available as the Army Air Forces began to scale back glider pilot training. All these men, even though many had been flight instructors before the war, needed training in the flying techniques peculiar to the Field Artillery program, which the check pilots provided.[26]

Early in 1943 Ford added the Tactics and Gunnery Division to his department. Maj. Robert F. Cassidy, the officer who had directed fire for Flight B during the test of the air-observation-post concept with the 2d Division, headed the new element. Cassidy took the Field Artillery pilot course and graduated on 6 March 1943 with Pilot Class 17. The reorganization represented a major shift in Ford's thinking (as well as that of Headquarters, Army Ground Forces) about the role of the pilot. Although there were two men in the aircraft, experience demonstrated that both had to participate in the conduct of the fire mission. The pilot as well as the observer had to identify the target, because the pilot had to hold the aircraft in position during the shoot. In combat the pilot often had to conduct the fire mission himself, while the observer scanned the sky for hostile pursuits. Ford proposed to train the pilot as an observer. The mechanic would thereby become the second man in the aircraft and would operate the radio. (This portion of his analysis did not become the norm in combat. Field artillery battalions usually used forward ground

---

[25] Intervs, author with Wann, 23 Mar 91; with Williams, 20 Feb 91; with Col M. J. Strok, 30 Jun 82; with Brown, Jun 82; all at CMH. Lt Col B. O. Ihlenfeldt, "Reminiscences from Thirty Years of Flying" (Unpubl Ms, Morris Swett Technical Library, FAS, Fort Sill, Okla. [hereafter cited as Morris Swett Tech Lib], 1986); Interv, L. B. Epstein with Lt Col J. M. Watson, Jr., 14–15 Sep 76, U.S. Army Aviation and Troop Command History Office, St. Louis, Mo. (hereafter cited as USAA&TC); Frank Perkins, "Army Aviation Pioneer," *National Guard Magazine* 33 (July 1979):22.

[26] The classes admitted on 28 September and 16 November 1942 were double in size, fifty and fifty-eight students, respectively, and were broken into two subclasses: 6A and 6B and 14A and 14B. In each instance, no class had begun the previous week. Thomas W. McCaw, "The Courses: Field Artillery School, World War II," 2 vols. (Bound Ms, FAS, 1946), 1:184. Intervs, author with Yeats, 24 May 90, and with Wann, 23 Mar 91. Interv, L. B. Epstein with Col D. L. Bristol, 1 Jul 75, USAA&TC. Ltr, Balmer to CG, R&SC, 7 Aug 43, sub: Civilian Flight Instructors, HQ, AGF, Gen Corresp, 1942–1948, 353/39 (FA Air Obsn) (C), RG 337, NARA.

observers as aerial observers.) Cassidy and four instructors taught students field artillery tactics and the conduct of fire from the air.[27]

Student pilots and mechanics received maintenance training at Post Field. A civilian, Forrest I. Nearing, an airframe specialist with Piper Aircraft before the war who had been one of the maintenance instructors for the Class Before One, headed the Maintenance Instruction Section of the Maintenance Division. Initially, M. Sgt. James T. Kerr, Jr., acted as both the senior enlisted maintenance instructor and the senior mechanic. Very early in the program Kerr identified a potential instructor from among his students, M. Sgt. Paul D. Lineberger, who soon took over Kerr's academic responsibilities. The student mechanics usually possessed considerable automotive experience before they arrived; the high ratio of applicants to authorized spaces meant that the Department of Air Training could be very selective in admissions to the course. While students had three airframes with which to become familiar in 1942 and 1943, all three aircraft used the same simple and reliable engine. Because the airframes were very similar, Lineberger gave virtually all maintenance instruction using L–4s. The experience of the students and the relative simplicity of the aircraft meant that the dropout rate in the mechanic course was very low, only 14 compared to 152 graduates in the first ten classes. (For pilots the comparable figures were 47 and 182 for the first ten classes.) The work of the graduates in the field was of uniformly high quality and gave the program an excellent reputation.[28]

Once Lineberger arrived, Kerr concentrated on keeping the school's fleet of aircraft airworthy—a never-ending task given their fabric construction. Despite Ford's strenuous efforts, the War Department consistently refused to build any more hangars at Post Field. Aside from ten or twelve machines undergoing repair in the existing hangars, the remainder had to remain outdoors at all times. As a consequence Kerr and his mechanics were constantly reapplying dope and replacing fabric. While weather caused a constant deterioration, the wind was another matter. Every spring lines of thunderstorms swept through southwestern Oklahoma, generating winds up seventy miles per hour, which often literally tore the planes apart, even though they remained securely tied down all the while. Although Ford had foreseen the damage high winds could cause unprotected light aircraft, he had no recourse but to cope as best he could without hangars.[29]

Fortunately, the Maintenance Division, under Major Leich and his successor, Maj. Marion J. Fortner, developed the capability to do all five echelons of repair. Working through the Supply Section, headed by Capt. Lloyd M. Bornstein, they obtained replacement aircraft and spare parts from the Army Air Forces Oklahoma Air Depot in Oklahoma City. Actual maintenance was performed by the mechanics in the Maintenance Division, supplemented by graduates from both the pilot and mechanic courses, who remained after graduation at the Field Artillery Replacement Center at Fort Sill until they received orders

---

[27] Memo, Maj J. D. Tanner, AAG, AGF, for CSA (Attn: ACS, G–3), 8 Jan 43, sub: Obsn Pilots for FA; Memo, Lt Col J. D. Tanner, AAG, AGF, for CSA (Attn: ACS, G–3), 16 Jan 43, sub: Same; both in HQ, AGF, Gen Corresp, 1942–1948, 353/216 (FA Air Obsn), RG 337, NARA; Interv, Powell and Courts with Williams, 1978; Ltrs, Col R. F. Cassidy to author, 10 Feb, 1 Mar 90, R. F. Cassidy Ms, Historian's files, CMH.

[28] Interv, author with Kerr, 3 Mar 91; McCaw, "The Courses," pp. 184, 198; Chart, FAS, DAT, 6 Nov 44, sub: Organization Chart, with Annotations by Col R. F. Cassidy, Mar 91, Cassidy Ms, CMH.

[29] Intervs, author with Kerr, 2 Mar 91; with Yeats, 24 May 90; Maj Gen (Ret) W. A. Harris with Col Gordon J. Wolf, c. 1983; all at CMH.

to join units. The Department of Air Training drew volunteers from the pools to work on the maintenance line. It was a good postgraduate education that readied the participants for conditions in the field. Fortner obtained use of the balloon hangar, left over from the days when Post Field was home station for one of the Air Corps balloon companies, and used it as the site for depot (fifth-echelon) repairs. Experienced mechanics could completely rebuild an L–4 in one-and-a-half days.[30]

During 1942 five student pilots and five student mechanics had experiences significantly different from their peers in the Department of Air Training. They were black. The U.S. Army, like much of American society, was still segregated during World War II. The Army's experience with large black units had not been altogether happy during World War I, and the War Department made certain that the two black infantry divisions were among the last large units mobilized. The War Department intended to allow blacks to enter the Field Artillery flight program once the divisions were further advanced in their mobilization. The *timing* of the arrival of the first black students at the Department of Air Training, when the state of training in the black units was still rudimentary, rather than the *fact* of their arrival, thus represented a surprise and something of an administrative oversight. There was never any question of setting up a segregated program in the Department of Air Training; the number of black pilots relative to the total program was simply too small to make such a solution economically feasible. One of the first black student pilots, 2d Lt. Charles M. Brown, noted that his instructors were both skilled and helpful. If race did not matter on duty—not every black student pilot would say this—it was certainly a factor off duty. Segregation was a constant psychological pressure and distraction, but to graduate Brown and the other black pilots who completed the course had to stay focused on flight training.[31]

Ford set high standards for himself and for the faculty and staff of his department. Even the first classes, which contained some of the most experienced pilots and men with the most extended Army service, consisted of little more than civilians in uniform. This tendency became more pronounced as the war progressed. Ford met this challenge by imposing strict discipline at Post Field. He sought to impress upon rather high-spirited young men that they were no longer civilians. They were in the Army and at Fort Sill for a serious purpose and had to comport themselves accordingly. In the words of one pilot graduate, Ford was "a tyrant," but a very effective one.[32]

---

[30] Intervs, author with Kerr, 3 Mar 91, and with Yeats, 24 May 90.

[31] Memo, Parks for ACS, G–1, WDGS, 26 Sep 42, sub: Assignment of Negroes to FA Air Obsn Units, HQ, AGF, Gen Corresp, 1942–1948, 353/92 (FA Air Obsn), RG 337, NARA; Telegram (Telg), Maj Gen E. M. Almond to Lt Col R. H. Adams, G–1 Sec, AGF, 18 Nov 42, HQ, AGF, Gen Corresp, 1942–1948, 353/166 (FA Air Obsn), RG 337, NARA; Telg, Lt Gen Lesley J. McNair, CG, AGF, to CG, AAF Flying Training Cmd, 30 Nov 42, HQ, AGF, Gen Corresp, 1942–1948, 353/182 (FA Air Obsn), RG 337, NARA; Ltr, 1st Lt S. J. Codner, AAG, AGF, to Commandant, FAS, 15 Dec 42, sub: Assignment of Liaison Pilots, HQ, AGF, Gen Corresp, 1942–1948, 353/14 (FA Air Obsn) (R), RG 337, NARA; Ltr, Codner to Commandant, FAS, 16 Dec 42, sub: Assignment of Airplane Mechanics, HQ, AGF, Gen Corresp, 1942–1948, 353/15 (FA Air Obsn) (R), RG 337, NARA; Ltr, Duenweg to Commandant, FAS, 29 Dec 42, sub: Assignment of Liaison Pilots and Mechanics, HQ, AGF, Gen Corresp, 1942–1948, 353/200 (FA Air Obsn), RG 337, NARA; Interv, author with Brown, Jun 82. Ulysses G. Lee, *The Employment of Negro Troops*, U.S. Army in World War II (Washington, D.C.: Office of the Chief of Military History, 1966), pp. 106, 128, 155, provides the most detailed account of blacks in the Army during World War II. John W. Kitchens, "They Also Flew: Pioneer Black Army Aviators," Part I, *USAAD* (September–October 1994):34–39, and Part II (November–December 1994):34–39, focuses on the training of black air-observation-post pilots during World War II.

[32] Interv, Kramer and Andreson with Goodhand, 9 May 78.

The Army Ground Forces had no formal air safety program until December 1943, but Ford gave the subject command attention and had Army Air Forces regulations to guide him. Throughout his tour, he insisted that instructors and students concentrate on perfecting details in both flying techniques and maintenance. After any major crash he convened an accident board with the department's flight surgeon in attendance. As was customary in the Army Air Forces at the time, the flight surgeon visited the scene of each crash. If he isolated a particular cause, he made a formal recommendation through Army Air Forces channels for changes in equipment or procedures or both. Ford also insisted that each crash scene be photographed from a variety of angles for a permanent record. The Department of Air Training also prepared a list of safe flying procedures that it sent to units upon request.[33]

The Medical element got off to an uncertain start. The first flight surgeon, Capt. Victor E. Frazier, did not report to the Department of Air Training until 26 August 1942, after the first two pilot classes had already begun. Decentralization and a lack of technically qualified staff supervision at Headquarters, Army Ground Forces, meant that there was no central repository for the health records of aviators. Frazier's attempt to establish such an office, which would also collect and evaluate liaison aircraft accident reports and statistics, ran afoul of the reluctance of Headquarters, Army Ground Forces, to risk a confrontation with Headquarters, Army Air Forces. McNair's staff, once again revealing a lack of familiarity with the technical issues, considered the matter to be of relatively little significance. Whether the Army Air Forces would oppose the request remained moot, because Headquarters, Army Ground Forces, disapproved it. Frazier did acquire a light ambulance plane, a Navy HE–1, a militarized version of the Piper J–5 Cub. It provided fast evacuation from the stage fields to a hospital, forestalling the additional trauma of a bone-jarring ride in a ground ambulance. His attempt to convince the Surgeon General's Office to make such craft organic to ground medical units suffered the same fate as his proposal to centralize records.[34]

In only one area did the Department of Air Training succeed in expanding the scope of its activities beyond "Cub-like" light aircraft, and this augmentation occurred only "off the books" and initially without reference to higher headquarters. A friend of Major Williams at Wright Field asked him if the department would like two UC–61s, the militarized version of the Fairchild 24, a single-engine, four-place airplane powered by a 165-horsepower Warner Scarab engine. Williams responded affirmatively. The department used them for cross-country flights when members of the staff had to visit other installations and schools. Although the UC–61s were larger and more powerful than the L–4s, the pilots

---

[33] Rpt, Maj V. E. Frazier, FAS, 7 Dec 43, sub: Flight Surgeon's Rpt of Aircraft Accident, HQ, AGF, Gen Corresp, 1942–1948, 452.1/588 (Airplanes), RG 337, NARA; Ltr, Ofc of Commandant, FAS, to CG, AGF, 26 Oct 43, sub: Weakness of Front Seat, L–2B Type Airplane, HQ, AGF, Gen Corresp, 1942–1948, 452.11/69 (Parts and Accessories), RG 337, NARA. War Department (WD), Training Circular 132, 14 Dec 43, sub: Organic Field Artillery Air Observation, laid out in very rudimentary fashion the first formal safety program for organic aviation.

[34] Memos, Tanner for CG, SOS, 22 Jun 42, sub: Flight Surgeons; Brig Gen D. N. W. Grant, Air Surgeon, for CG, AGF, 23 Jul 42; and Maj H. L. Nelson, AAG, AGF, for CG, AAF (Attn: Air Surgeon), 30 Jul 42, sub: Same; all in HQ, AGF, Gen Corresp, 1942–1948, 353/6 (FA Air Obsn), RG 337, NARA. Ind, McLennan to Commanding Officer (CO), 191st FA Group (Grp), 12 May 43, HQ, AGF, Gen Corresp, 1942–1948, 353/323 (FA Air Obsn), RG 337, NARA. Ltr, Frazier to CG, AGF, 14 Aug 43, sub: Avn Medicine in AGF, with Ind, Dryden to CG, R&SC, 10 Sep 43, HQ, AGF, Gen Corresp, 1942–1948, 353/364 (FA Air Obsn), RG 337, NARA. Rpt, Frazier to CG, ASF (Attn: Surgeon General's Ofc), [Sep 43], sub: Experience with Naval Airplane Ambulance, Type HE–1; MFR, [FA Section, Requirements Div, HQ, AGF], 20 Nov 43, sub: Same; both in HQ, AGF, Gen Corresp, 1942–1948, 452.1/575 (Airplanes), RG 337, NARA.

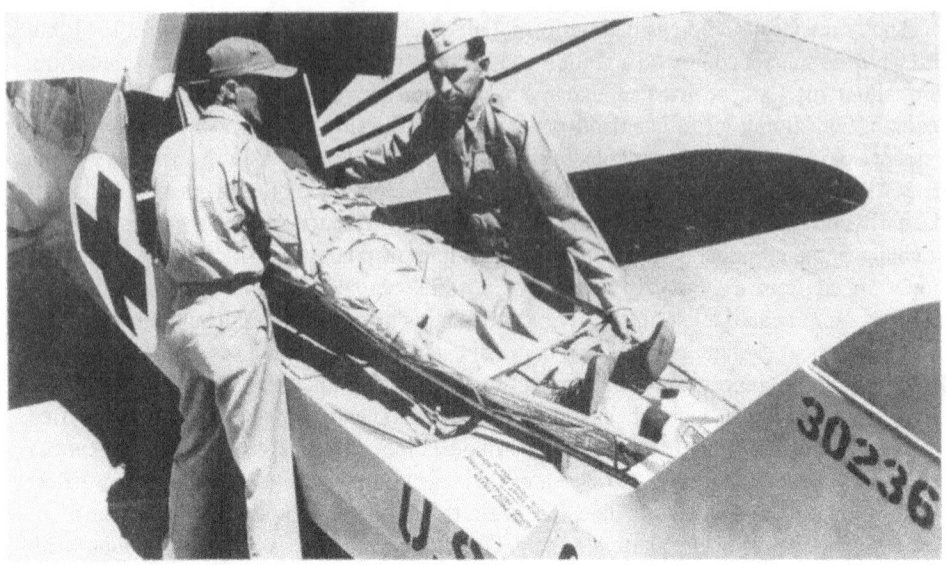

Major Frazier (*right*) Helps Load a Simulated Casualty Aboard a Navy NE–1, 1943.

had no difficulty flying them. One of the check pilots, Capt. Bryce Wilson, owned a Fairchild 24, which he had left in storage at home in California. Colonel Ford and Major Williams owned comparable aircraft, which they kept at the local civilian airport. "Any of the pilots we had could have become qualified with a couple of trips around the field." Likewise, the UC–61s posed no particular maintenance problems for Sergeant Kerr and his men. These aircraft were the first—and until after the war the only—multi-place aircraft capable of carrying more than simply a pilot and an observer in the Air-Observation-Post Program and in its successor Army Ground Forces light aviation program. After their arrival, Ford apparently took the precaution to obtain approval for their presence from Headquarters, Army Ground Forces. The informality of their acquisition—the fact that Headquarters, Army Air Forces, was not involved—prevented them from serving as a precedent. They were quite simply a successful wartime expedient.[35]

The Department of Air Training was well established by October 1943. Both pilot and mechanic training had assumed the forms they would have for the duration of the war. While a formal flight safety program did not exist, the command emphasis needed as a seedbed for such a program was already in place. The emphasis, of course, extended no further than the confines of the department other than by example. Captain Frazier's attempt to establish the centralized recordkeeping that would have made such a program possible on an Army-wide basis had failed, because the Army Ground Forces staff lacked a firm grasp of the issues involved.

---

[35] Ltrs, Williams to author, 14 Apr, 31 May 96, and 11 Aug 99, Historian's files, CMH; Journal, Chief of Staff, AGF, 20 May 43, HQ, AGF, Chief of Staff Journals, 30 Mar 42–13 Sep 43, RG 337, NARA. The quotation is from the letter of 31 May.

Unit Training

By the fall of 1942 the first graduates of the Department of Air Training began joining their units, where they eventually became organized into air sections. Initially, the Operations Division of the War Department General Staff claimed all graduates for assignment to units deploying to Great Britain or units in the United States designated to participate in the invasion of North Africa. In late September 1942, after Ford had culled potential instructors from Pilot Class 1, the nine remaining pilots, along with the nine graduates of the mechanic course, moved as casuals to the New York Port of Embarkation and sailed for Great Britain. Subsequently, the War Department placed the highest priority on assigning air sections to units about to deploy overseas, with units already overseas having second priority. Lowest priority went to units training in the continental United States with no immediate plans for departure. Not until October 1943 did such units receive all of their equipment.[36]

In practice two pilots, one mechanic, one driver (who after on-the-job training routinely acted as a mechanic's assistant), a ground-crew helper, and a radio operator made up the complement of an air section at full strength. Sections organic to division artillery and field artillery brigade headquarters also contained a mechanic's assistant and an additional driver, who could also function as a mechanic's assistant after training. Major equipment consisted of two light aircraft, usually L–4s, a jeep, and a 1/4-ton trailer, the latter intended to carry spare parts and tools. The slightly larger division and brigade air sections also had a 2 1/2-ton truck to transport the somewhat wider array of tools and spare parts available to them. This ground transport proved inadequate, and as the war progressed air sections acquired additional unauthorized trucks. Ground-crew helpers often doubled as truck drivers. Some firing battalions permanently assigned two observers to the air section; other battalions assigned all observers to duty with their air sections on a regular rotation. In still other instances, a few pilots preferred to substitute a jury-rigged auxiliary gasoline tank for their observer and to conduct fire missions on their own.[37]

In theory, at least as expounded by tables of organization and equipment, air sections did not exist. The Army Ground Forces G–3, General Lentz, had great difficulty obtaining an agreement with the War Department G–3, General Edwards, as to the composition of an air section. "It has been," Lentz reported to McNair in October 1942, "a dog fight."

---

[36] Intervs, Epstein with Bristol, 1 Jul 75, and with Watson, 14–15 Sep 76; Special Orders (SO) 231, FAS, 28 Sep 42 [Extract], Bristol Ms, Mrs D. L. Bristol, Florissant, Mo. Memo, Lt Col T. E. Lewis, Training Div, AGF, for CS, AGF, 17 Jun 42, sub: School for FA Puddle Jumper Pilots; Memo, Moran, Training Div, AGF, 23 Jun 42, sub: Plan for Furnishing Pilots (FA) to II Army Corps; Ltr, Day to CG, R&SC, 29 Jun 42; Ltr, Maj H. L. Whiteside, Sec, FAS, to CG, AGF, sub: Detail of Student Pilots and Obsrs; all in HQ, AGF, Gen Corresp, 1942–1948, 353/1 (FA Air Obsn) (C), RG 337, NARA. Memo, McNair for ASW, 17 Aug 42, sub: Organic Airplanes for FA, HQ, AGF, Gen Corresp, 1942–1948, 353/69 (FA Air Obsn), RG 337, NARA. Memo, Tanner for CSA (Attn: Operations Division [OPD]), 11 Mar 43, sub: Assignment of FA Liaison Airplanes, HQ, AGF, Gen Corresp, 1942–1948, 353/10 (FA Air Obsn) (S), RG 337, NARA. Memo, Porter for CGs, AGF and AAF, 27 Jul 43, sub: Liaison Pilots and Mechanics for FA; DF, Col A. D. Reed, Ch, European Section, OPD, to CG, AGF, 14 Sep 43, sub: Same; both in HQ, AGF, Gen Corresp, 1942–1948, 353/19 (FA Air Obsn) (S), RG 337, NARA.

[37] WD, Table of Organization (TO) 6–176, Change 1, 29 Oct 42, sub: HQ and HQ Svc Battery (Btry), FA Battalion (Bn), 75-mm. Pack Howitzer, Truck-Drawn; Memo, Day for TAG, 26 Sep 42, sub: Changes in FA TO with Incl MFR, [26 Sep 42], HQ, AGF, Gen Corresp, 1942–1948, 320.3 (FA)/60, RG 337, NARA; Capt. J. W. Oswalt, "The Air OP Is Here To Stay," *FAJ* 34 (August 1944):568–72; Intervs, author with Oswalt, 13–14 Jan 82, and with Lt Col Jack R. Forbes, Jr., 5 Jun 93; both at CMH.

An L–4 of the 29th Infantry Division Flies over a Battery of 105-mm. M2 Howitzers, March 1943.

Possibly for this reason, the Army Ground Forces staff did not redesign existing Field Artillery tables of organization and equipment; the staff provided for air sections simply by adding personnel spaces in existing categories on the tables. Air sections thus did not appear as such on the tables. At first, pilots were carried as members of the operations section of the headquarters battery; later, they were shifted to the headquarters element of these organizations. Two Army airplane and engine mechanics, with the ranks of technical sergeant and private, respectively, were officially members of the maintenance section, headquarters battery, as was a ground-crew helper, also a private. Drivers came out of the operations section. All these men constituted the official, if ambiguous, complement of the air sections. As a practical matter, air sections needed a radio at their airstrips to maintain contact with aircraft in flight and with the remainder of the headquarters element. Terrain and camouflage considerations often dictated the location of airstrips at some distance from the parent unit. (*Figure 3*) Battalion commanders invariably added a radioman and radio to the air section from the communications platoon of the headquarters battery. The observers came out of the firing batteries.[38]

---

[38] Memo, McNair for ACS, G–3, 19 Oct 42, sub: Changes in FA TO (Organic Air Sections); Memo Slip, Lentz for CS, AGF, 16 Oct 42, sub: Same, HQ, AGF, Gen Corresp, 1942–1948, 320.3 (FA)/60, RG 337, NARA; WD, Table of Organization and Equipment (TO&E) 6–10–1, 15 Jul 43, sub: HQ and HQ Btry, Motorized, Div Artillery (Arty), Infantry Div; WD, TO&E 6–12, 16 Jun 43, sub: HQ and HQ Btry, Motorized, FA Grp; WD, TO&E 6–36, 15 Jul 43, 27 Sep 44, sub: HQ and HQ Btry, Motorized, FA Bn, 155-mm. Howitzer, or 4.5-Inch Gun, Truck-Drawn or Tractor-Drawn.

DEVELOPING THE AIR-OBSERVATION-POST PROGRAM 131

FIGURE 3—ORGANIZATION OF A LANDING FIELD IN COMBAT

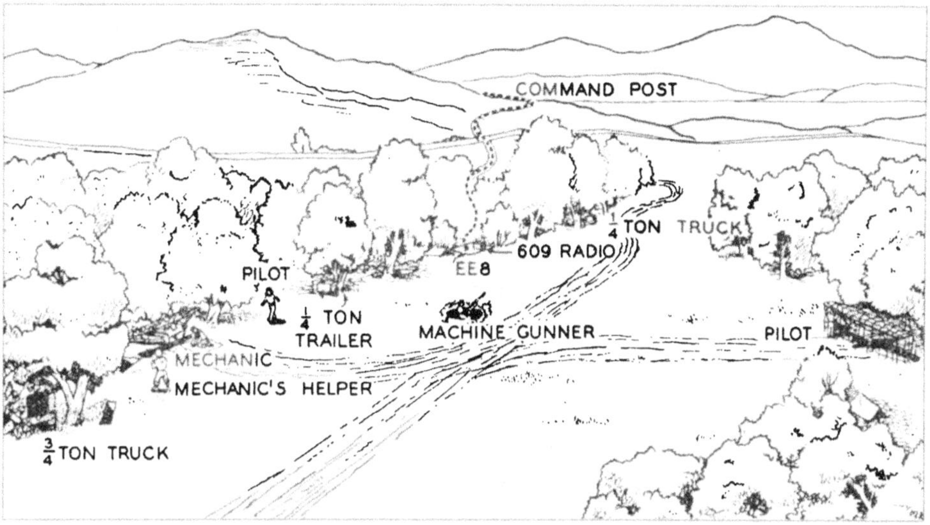

Source: U.S. War Department, *Organic Field Artillery Air Observation*, FM 6–150 (Washington, D.C.: War Department, 1944), p. 33.

Originally, headquarters batteries of each division artillery headquarters, field artillery brigade, field artillery group, and gun and howitzer battalion in the Army contained air sections. The only exceptions were airborne divisions. A controversy over the type of aircraft to assign to them delayed the creation of air sections, although the 82d Airborne Division established air sections with the approval of the theater commander soon after the division arrived in North Africa in May 1943. The number of air sections in a division depended on the number of firing battalions organic to it. A standard triangular infantry division (see *Chart 2*) had 5 sections, a total of 10 aircraft, 1 section in the division artillery headquarters, 1 in each of 3 105-mm. battalions operating in a direct support role, and 1 section in the 155-mm. battalion providing general support. Armored divisions, and later airborne divisions (until December 1944), had only 4 sections, 8 aircraft, because they lacked the general support battalion. In 1942 the armored division had only a division artillery section that was part of division headquarters rather than a separate division artillery headquarters (see *Charts 3–8*). The War Department consequently assigned the headquarters air section to the division headquarters company. When the War Department created a separate division artillery headquarters in the September 1943 reorganization of armored divisions, it temporarily left the aircraft with the division headquarters company. Not until February 1944 did it shift the aircraft to the division artillery headquarters battery. The 2d and 3d Armored Divisions, already in the European Theater of Operations, remained organized under the 1942 tables of organization and equipment until the end of the war. The 1st Armored Division in Italy delayed its reorganization until July 1944. Field artillery brigade and group headquarters had no organic firing battalions and consequently contained only the headquarters air sections. Groups were used to control separate battalions of corps artillery, each with its own section, under two circumstances: when several separate battalions reinforced the fires of a division or when more than four battalions were concentrated to support a corps. An artillery brigade headquarters controlled two or more groups. Not until March 1943 did the War Department authorize air sections at corps artillery headquarters. Formal authorization for air sections at higher echelons came only later.[39]

The senior pilots in the division artillery, field artillery brigade, and field artillery group air sections were known as division, brigade, or group artillery air officers, depending on the unit. At first, they were captains in the divisions and brigades, first lieutenants in the groups. They commanded their immediate sections, exercised technical control over all the aircraft assigned or attached to the division, brigade, or group, and acted as the staff adviser to the commander on the operational use of the assigned aircraft. The exercise of technical control involved inspecting aircraft and technical records, overseeing technical training and maintenance, and providing administrative and maintenance support. Given their complement of 4 mechanics, 2 by military occupational specialty and 2 by on-the-job training, division artillery and brigade air sections could provide battalion air sections slightly more sophisticated maintenance support than the battalion sections could with their own resources. Administratively, the division, brigade, and group artillery air officers ensured that adequate numbers of replacements, spare parts, and supplies reached the air sections in a timely fashion, once higher headquarters clearly delineated those resupply channels. Battalion air officers, the senior pilots in the battalion air sections, commanded the sections. General Edwards wanted to assign only sergeant pilots to these sections, but the demise of the enlisted pilot concept meant that lieutenants normally served as battalion air officers.[40]

The battalion commanders were responsible for the tactical training of the air sections in conjunction with the rest of the battalion, but they and the first graduates of the Department of Air Training faced a problem of mutual incongruity. Most of the pilots had only slight experience with active-duty field artillery battalions, while the battalion commanders had absolutely no experience with the air-observation-post sections. Whether graduates of the program first joined their units in the United States or overseas, they often discovered that one of their first responsibilities was to sell the program. Headquarters, Army Ground Forces, had announced the establishment of Field Artillery aviation, but this was but one item in a cascade of papers inundating commanders of mobilizing field artillery battal-

---

[39] Memo, sub: Proposed Addition to TO for FA Units; Ind, Balmer to CG, AGF, 11 Dec 42, on Ltr, McNair to Commandant, FAS, 12 Nov 42, sub: TOs, HQ; both in HQ, AGF, Gen Corresp, 1942–1948, 320.3/36 (FA), RG 337, NARA; Memo, Delacroix for CSA (Attn: G–3 Div), 16 Jul 43, sub: Organic Arty Air Obsn for Corps HQ, HQ, AGF, Gen Corresp, 1942–1948, 353/18 (FA Air Obsn) (S), RG 337, NARA; Memo, Meredith for CSA (Attn: ACS, OPD), 9 Aug 43, sub: Liaison Pilots and Mechanics for FA, HQ, AGF, Gen Corresp, 1942–1948, 353/19 (FA Air Obsn) (S), RG 337, NARA; WD, TO 17, 1 Mar 42, sub: Armd Div; WD, TO 17, Change 2, 29 Oct 42, sub: Armd Div; WD, TO&E 17, 15 Sep 43, sub: Armd Div; WD, TO&E 17, 12 Feb 44, sub: Armd Div; WD, TO&E 6–200, 1 Aug 44, sub: Div Arty, Abn Div; WD, TO 71, 15 Oct 42, sub: Abn Div; WD, TO 71, Change 2, 24 Feb 44, sub: Abn Div; WD, TO&E 6–200T, 16 Dec 44, sub: Div Arty, Abn Div; WD, TO 6–50–1, 20 Mar 43, sub: HQ and HQ Btry, Motorized, Corps Arty; Janice McKenney, "Field Artillery," (Unpubl Ms, CMH, 1993), pp. 273–79, 290–98.

[40] WD, Technical Circular (TC) 24, 1 Mar 43, sub: Organic FA Air Obsn. The Legislative Reference Center of the main National Archives building has a complete file of all War Department and Department of the Army technical circulars from 1941 through 1952.

ions. The deliberate vagueness of the amended tables of organization and equipment only compounded the problem. In the field, air observation posts were but an indistinct idea forced aside by more pressing issues until pilots, mechanics, and airplanes actually arrived. In a typical instance, the commander of the 5th Armored Artillery Regiment, Col. Newton D. Jones, noticed the wings sported by the first pilot to report to him. "I don't want any Goddamned Air Corps in my outfit," Jones growled. Second Lt. Michael J. Strok then had to explain the nature of the air observation program to this "chunky, stocky, . . . bald-headed gentleman" who was "smoking a big cigar and looking real tough." After Strok finished, Jones' attitude had softened: "Well, what the Hell, I can't lose anything. At least it's one more officer I can put to work."[41]

When the ranking artillery air officer in the regiment, 2d Lt. Robert Hutchins of Pilot Class 4, reported the next week, he immediately demonstrated a sophisticated appreciation of the need to sell the program to the regiment. Although all the aircraft for their section were in overseas crates, Hutchins and Strok discovered an L–4 at Bolling Field in Washington, D.C., and wrangled permission to fly it to maintain their proficiency. Hutchins made certain that Jones rode as a passenger on one of the first flights and that he received an aviator's jacket and glasses when the pilots did. The unit deployed too soon for Hutchins to do much more, but fortunately, it went into a cycle of intensive training once it arrived in North Africa. He and Strok gave rides to all the senior officers in the regiment as well as the ground observers and conducted fire missions during field exercises. Virtually everyone who graduated from the Department of Air Training during the first year of its existence went through a similar process of selling the program to somewhat skeptical ground officers.[42]

Even when battalion commanders conceded the necessity of an aerial observer and the utility of organic light aircraft in their units, their lack of technical knowledge about air sections and the pilots' lack of familiarity with field artillery battalions made integration of flight operations into unit training a matter of some difficulty. Pilots had their class notes (which the Department of Air Training enjoined them to retain after graduation), and graduates after 1942 had the Field Artillery School's instructional memorandum on "Organic Field Artillery Air Observation." But these documents lacked the directive force of doctrine. The obvious solution was a detailed compilation of standard procedures to guide the pilots and provide commanders a norm by which to judge their efforts. In December 1942 the Field Artillery School, presumably the Department of Air Training, completed a document that met at least part of this objective. This draft training circular, based on the earlier instructional memorandum, defined the duties and responsibilities of the battalion, group, brigade, and division air officers and laid out the doctrine for the tactical employment of the aircraft. The War Department published it as Training Circular No. 24 on 1 March 1943. If it was too late to assist the first graduates during their introduction to their units, it was timely and edifying for the vast majority.[43]

---

[41] Interv, author with Strok, 30 Jun 82. For similar experiences, see Intervs, author with Oswalt, 13–14 Jan 82; with Col Claude Shepard, 23 Sep 83; with Long, 23 Jul 82; with Lefever, 4 Sep 91; all at CMH.

[42] Interv, author with Strok, 30 Jun 82.

[43] Training Literature, sub: Notebooks: Pilots and Mechanics; Instruction Memorandum A–1, FAS, Nov 42, sub: Organic FA Air Obsn, in A. R. Hackbarth, [Pilot's Notebook], Michael J. Strok Ms, Mrs. Marcia Strok, Edgewater, Md. Ltr, Balmer to CG, AGF, 11 Dec 42, sub: TC on Organic FA Air Obsn, TAGO Decimal file, 1940–1945, 062.12 (12–11–42), RG 407, NARA. Headquarters, Army Ground Forces, disallowed an even more

Black officer pilots sometimes faced an additional problem—convincing white officers that black men could fly. When Lieutenant Brown reported to the 351st Field Artillery Group, a black unit with all-white senior officers, the headquarters battery commander refused to allow him to unpack his aircraft because "everyone" knew "you people" could not fly. Brown went to the group commander, a courtly Southerner, who heard him out and then ordered him to assemble his aircraft, which Brown did with the assistance of some of the battery's mechanics. He was very much aware that both he and the air-observation-post concept were on trial as he took off on his first flight with the group. When his motor quit at altitude, he thus greeted the event with more than ordinary consternation. Brown, however, made a perfect dead-stick landing, much to the amazement of the white officers of the group who were convinced he was a dead man. On examination, he discovered that he had failed to remove a bag of silica gel, used to protect the engine in storage, from the air intake. The engine had quit from lack of oxygen. Yet, in a strange sort of way, the emergency worked to Brown's advantage. He had demonstrated an ability to deal with a life-threatening situation with aplomb. Life in the group did not suddenly become easy, however. One black sergeant recalled: "He was harassed, and every attempt was made to keep him from flying a plane. Efforts were made to humiliate him before the enlisted men, and he was punished without cause, often given the assignment as Mess Officer." No one, however, could again question his basic competence in quite the same way. And he met the harassment with "confidence, courage, and dignity" and did the job he was rated to do.[44]

When serious training did occur, air-observation-post pilots spent much of their time familiarizing potential air observers with the conduct of fire from the air. Any ground observer who weighed 170 pounds or less when stripped was a potential air observer. Air observer training consisted of two stages: ground and air. Ground training involved a general orientation to the airplane—nomenclature, characteristics, and functions. Pilots discussed the ground handling of aircraft, cockpit procedures, and safety precautions. Air observer candidates practiced daily on a terrain board, that is, a contour model of the firing area, and reviewed ground procedures of fire control. Advanced training with maps and aerial photos followed, along with a review of friendly and enemy tactics to facilitate analysis of what the observer was seeing from the air. Finally, observers practiced the recognition of friendly and enemy equipment using aerial photographs, once more in preparation for what the observer would actually see in the air.[45]

The first portion of the air training phase involved giving the potential aerial observer frequent rides in an aircraft to acquaint him with how terrain looked from above while moving. One of the hardest skills for a novice to master was maintaining his sense of direction once an aircraft turned. He also needed practice estimating ground distances and alti-

---

detailed draft circular prepared in January. MFR, J. A. P., G–1, AGF, 20 Apr 43; Ltr, McLennan to CG, AGF, 19 Jan 43, sub: Proposed TC "Suggested Schedule for Training of Organic FA Air Observation"; FAS, Draft TC, Jan 42, sub: Training of Organic FA Air Obsn; all in HQ, AGF, Gen Corresp, 1942–1948, 353/19 (FA Air Obsn) (R), RG 337, NARA.

[44] Ltr to Editor, R. R. Nix, *Washington Post*, c. 1980, C. M. Brown Ms, Historian's files, CMH; Interv, author with Brown, Jun 82. All quotations are from the Nix letter. "Dead stick" refers to the fact that the propeller is no longer revolving.

[45] WD, Field Manual (FM) 6–150, *Organic Field Artillery Air Observation* (Washington, D.C.: Adjutant General's Office, 1944), p. 24.

tudes from the air. Simulated fire missions followed. By 1944 these had evolved into a "puff target range." The pilot flew the aircraft as he would in combat—four to six thousand yards from the target. There was an assumed gun position, also four to six thousand yards away. The target area consisted of a rectangle 800 yards wide and 900 yards deep. The base point, for orientation, consisted of a large white panel mounted on a 2 1/2–ton truck at one end of the rectangle. The target consisted of another large white panel similarly affixed to a second truck. Actual adjustments from the air involved the observer directing rounds, *sensing* in the field artillery lexicon, over an SCR–609 to a similar radio on the ground. Men in a simulated fire-direction center calculated where the round would fall given existing meteorological conditions. One of them contacted the nearest of four jeeps (located at the corners of the target area) to give the locale, to which the dri-

LIEUTENANT BROWN WAVES FROM THE COCKPIT OF AN L–4, 1943.

ver quickly drove. His assistant threw out a bag of lime with a detonator inside. The resulting explosion and "puff" of lime dust simulated the fall of a shell and gave the simulation its name. The observer adjusted fire until the puff was quite close to the target. Then the officer in charge shifted the assumed position of the guns, the base point, and the target, and the process started all over again.[46]

Following simulation training, aerial observers graduated to fire missions with the battalion. Often, they first monitored fire missions from the air, listening on their radio as another pilot-observer team delivered fire, and watched the fall of shell. Then they directed fire themselves. The usual method was to direct a single gun to the immediate vicinity of the target and then call for a battery concentration of 4 guns. (This proved to be the most common type of observed fire mission in combat as well.) Of course, battalion (12 guns), division (48 guns), and corps (96 guns or more) concentrations were also possible, but the aerial observer's technique remained the same no matter how many shells landed on the target.[47]

The training continually emphasized developing a sense of teamwork between the pilot and the observer. Engine noise made conversation in the cockpit difficult. Each had to understand and keep in mind the perspective of the other. The pilot, for example, needed to know how changes in the attitude of the plane affected the observer's view of the tar-

---

[46] Ibid., pp. 24–25, 103–05.
[47] Ibid., p. 25; MFR, author, 19 Sep 96, sub: Conversation with Col (Ret) Michael J. Strok, 16 Sep 96, Historian's files, CMH.

get. He did not want to inadvertently put a wing between the observer and the target just as a shell landed. Pilots and observers attained the desired level of proficiency by constant repetition. Training included more than directing fire, although this was the crucial mission for the Air-Observation-Post Program, both in terms of its importance and its complexity of execution. Observers also had to locate targets of opportunity, reconnoiter routes of march and possible firing positions, provide security patrols for ground elements, check the camouflage of friendly units, obtain information on nearby friendly and enemy units, and provide liaison for the control of multiple march columns. All these activities facilitated teamwork and made pilots and observers more comfortable in viewing the terrain from the air.[48]

The growing number of air sections organic to field artillery battalions in the United States—despite the early deployment of many such units overseas—created a problem of administrative and technical oversight for the field army staffs in the continental United States responsible for their training. On 21 May 1943, the commander of U.S. Second Army, with headquarters at Memphis, Tennessee, requested that Headquarters, Army Ground Forces, assign a Field Artillery air officer with the rank of captain or higher to supervise "the t[raini]ng in and use of the F[ield] A[rtillery] light observation airplane." The letter precipitated a decision at McNair's headquarters to send relatively senior Field Artillery air officers on temporary duty to all the major training commands in the United States to oversee the training of air-observation-post sections with their parent battalions. The Field Artillery School assigned two members of the Class Before One, Capts. Charles W. Lefever and Bryce Wilson, to Second and Third Armies, respectively, two of the army headquarters still in the United States.[49]

Second Army used Lefever as an inspector. He spent almost all his time on the road reporting on the condition of training and equipment of Second Army air sections. Wilson had much the same experience at Third Army headquarters, Fort Sam Houston, Texas, although he was perhaps slightly more involved with supply issues, particularly obtaining repair parts from Army Air Forces supply channels. Most of the battalion commanders he met had given little thought to the question of aerial observation. He found a vague awareness that the War Department had approved organic air, but little more. Approximately half the battalion commanders were open to the possibility that air observation posts might prove useful in the future. The remainder regarded the planes as simply obstacles and distractions from gunnery practice. In contrast, both senior staffs found Lefever's and Wilson's contributions indispensable. Their positions, at first only temporary expedients, became permanent.[50]

The Air-Observation-Post Program—like the Army as a whole—was fully mobilized by October 1943. The introduction of pilots and planes into units meant the formation of actual air sections. The graduates of the Department of Air Training knew from their training at Post Field how an air section should function. Now they had to make the one to which they were assigned work in the field. In addition to internal training in the section,

---

[48] WD, FM 6–150, pp. 1, 25.
[49] Ltr, Meredith to Commandant, FAS, 25 May 43, sub: Temporary Assignment of FA Liaison Pilots; MFR, [G–1, AGF], sub: 5/21/43 Basic Letter from HQ Second Army; both in HQ, AGF, Gen Corresp, 1942–1948, 353/309 (FA Air Obsn), RG 337, NARA.
[50] Intervs, author with Lefever, 4 Sep 91, and with Wilson, 3 Aug 91, both at CMH.

they also had to learn how to fit in and operate with the parent unit. This meant, particularly in 1942 but to some extent throughout the war, convincing the battalion commander and his staff of the capabilities of the air section. Only if the pilots succeeded in selling the concept of aerial observation could the battalion as a whole conduct realistic training. Most battalion air officers did accomplish this task, but a sizable minority could not, either because they lacked powers of persuasion or because their battalion commanders proved too resistant to new ideas. These battalions wasted much of their training time, and the infantry they supported lost men in combat as a result. Black pilots faced the additional handicap of racism—some senior white officers were disinclined to believe anything blacks told them.

No matter what the problems on the battalion level, however, the sheer number of air sections involved led to the establishment of Field Artillery air positions on field army staffs in the United States. The need to supervise unit training encouraged the beginnings of an administrative hierarchy just as the establishment of an air-observation-post logistical system led to the addition of a senior Field Artillery pilot to a headquarters staff in Washington.

Conclusion

In the seventeen months between June 1942 and October 1943, air observation posts evolved from an idea into a program. The test detachment at Fort Sill became the Department of Air Training of the Field Artillery School. In the continental United States, a logistical system took shape encompassing the Army Ground Forces, the Army Service Forces, and the Army Air Forces. Staff arrangements at General McNair's headquarters may have been inadequate, but at least Headquarters, Army Ground Forces, was able to secure sufficient numbers of light aircraft for the 1943 program. Unfortunately, the compromise with the Army Air Forces that made this possible introduced rigidities that, when coupled with inadequate technical supervision and the fear that the Army Air Forces might attempt to once more take over the program, made it difficult to concentrate production on one model of light aircraft when this became necessary. The same factors acted to retard the Field Artillery's attempts to obtain a higher-performance light plane to complement the L–4. As the Army Air Forces abandoned further light-aircraft development in favor of the helicopter, officers at the Department of Air Training exploited the ambiguities in the program's charter to begin the search for such an aircraft. Problems still existed in October 1943, but on the whole the first seventeen months represented solid achievement. The degree of that success could be seen in the numbers of pilots and mechanics graduating each month from the Department of Air Training and their integration into firing battalions in the field. Air observation posts were becoming organic in practice as well as in theory.

CHART 2—ORGANIZATION OF U.S. INFANTRY DIVISION, JULY 1943–MAY 1945

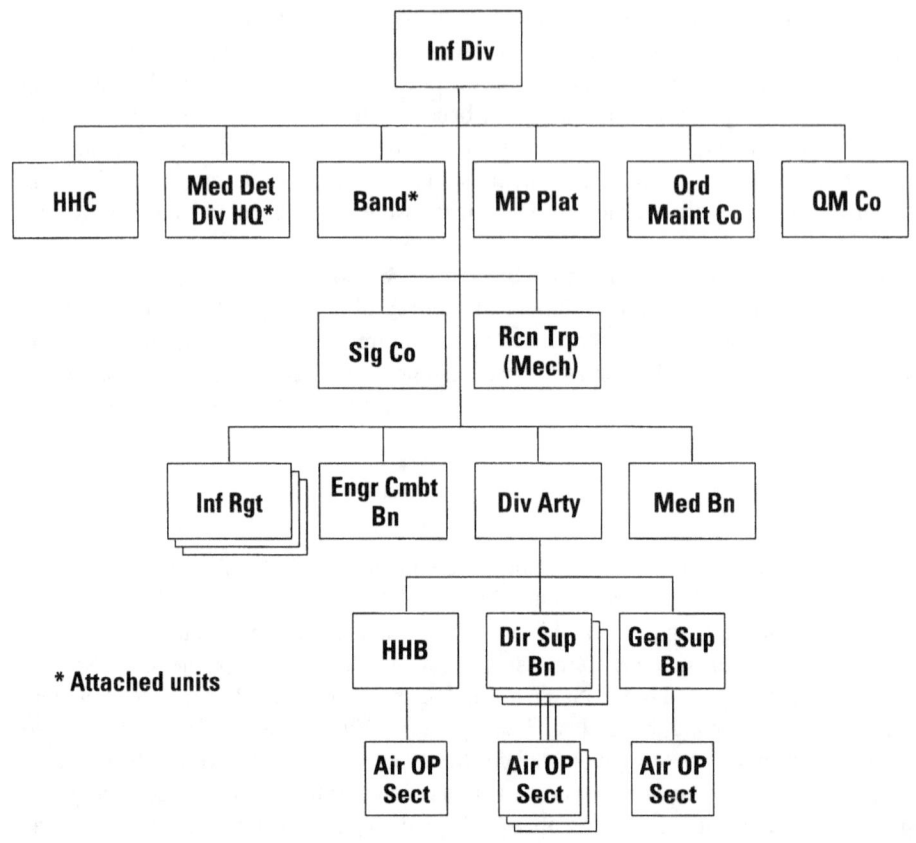

* Attached units

KEY TO CHARTS 2–8:

AA	Antiaircraft	Inf	Infantry
Abn	Airborne	Maint	Maintenance
Air OP	Air Observation Post	Med	Medical
Arty	Artillery	MP	Military Police
Bn	Battalion	Paracht	Parachute
Co	Company	Plat	Platoon
Dir	Direct	Rgt	Regiment
Div	Division	Sect	Section
Engr	Engineer	Sig	Signal
Gen	General	Sup	Support
HQ	Headquarters		

CHART 3—ORGANIZATION OF U.S. ARMORED DIVISION, OCTOBER 1942–SEPTEMBER 1943*

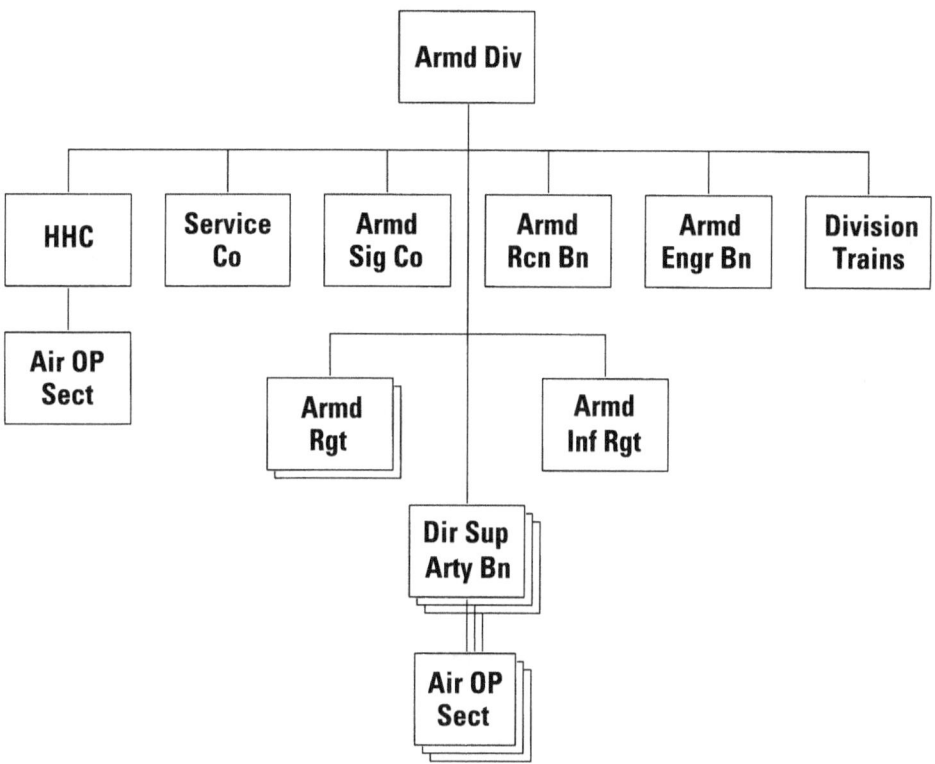

*The 1st Armored Division remained organized under this table until 20 July 1944. The 2d and 3d Armored Divisions retained the 1942 organization until January 1946 and November 1945 respectively.

CHART 4—ORGANIZATION OF U.S. ARMORED DIVISION, SEPTEMBER 1943–FEBRUARY 1944

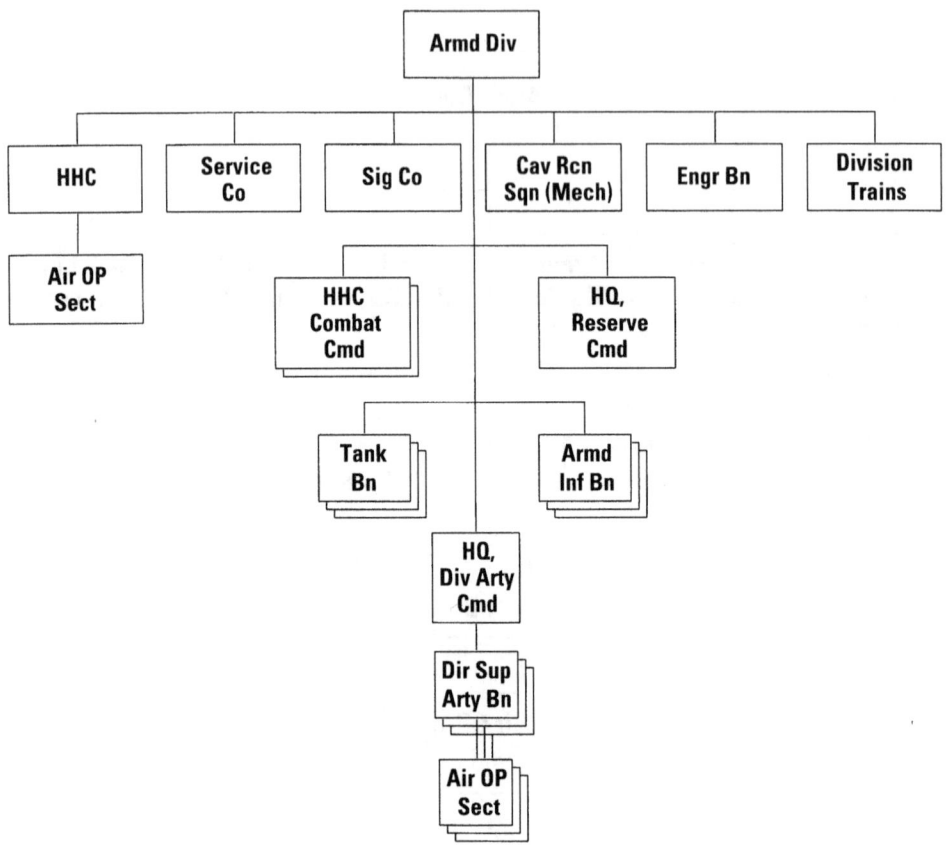

CHART 5—ORGANIZATION OF U.S. ARMORED DIVISION, FEBRUARY 1944–NOVEMBER 1945

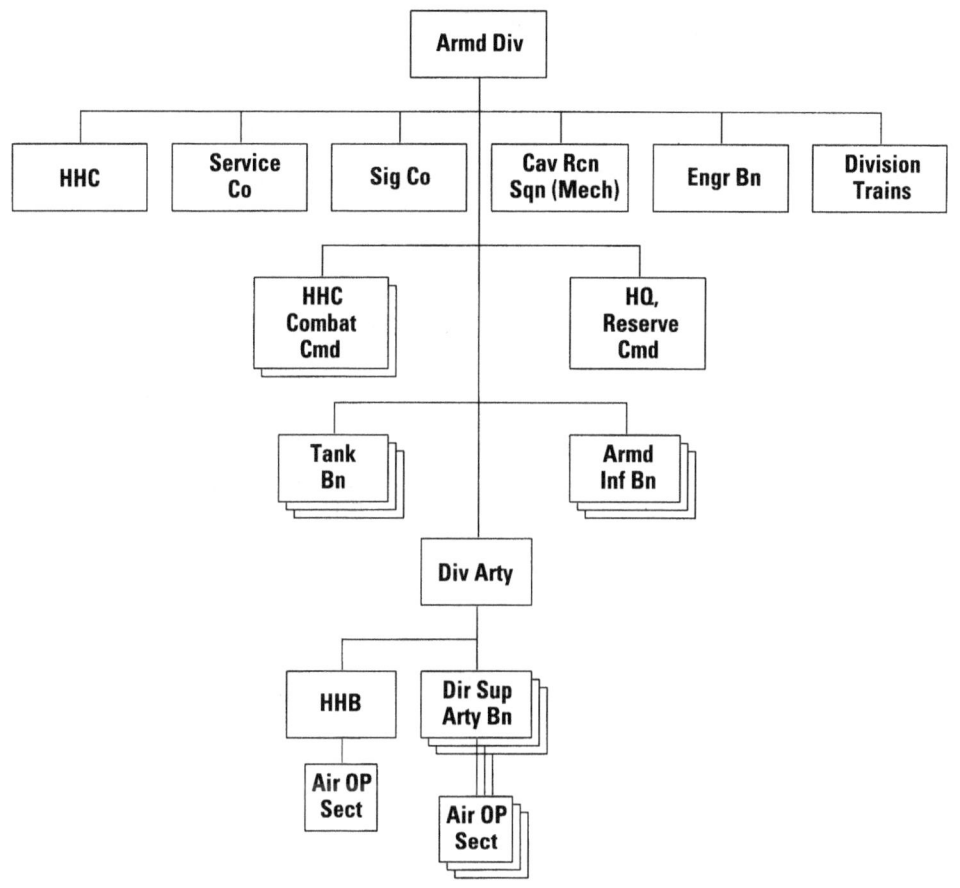

Chart 6—Organization of U.S. Airborne Division, February–August 1944

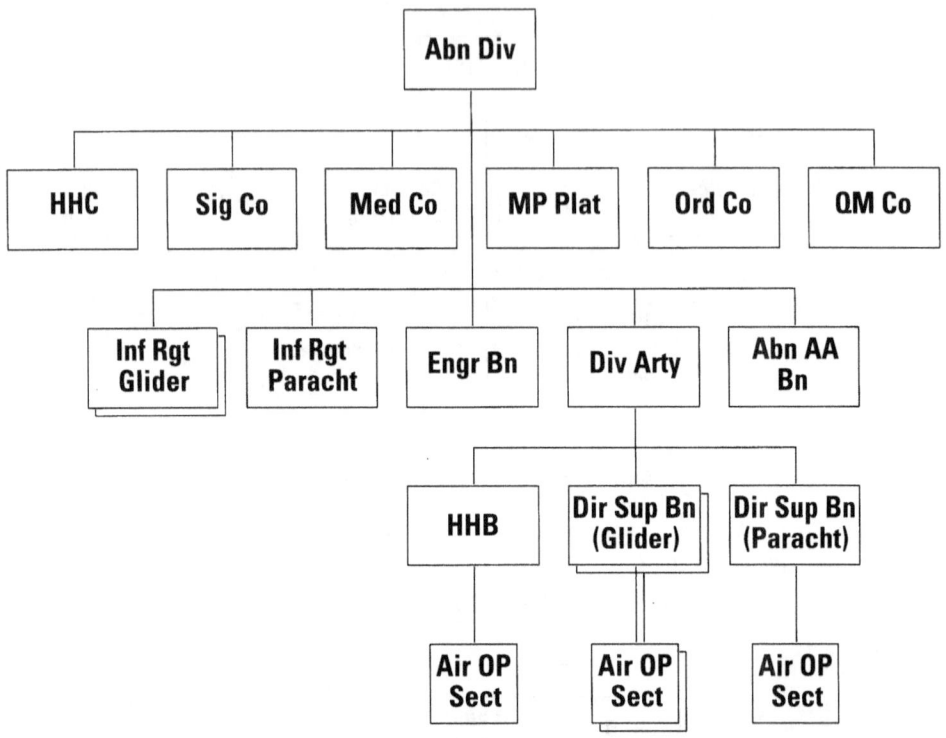

CHART 7—ORGANIZATION OF U.S. AIRBORNE DIVISION, AUGUST–DECEMBER 1944

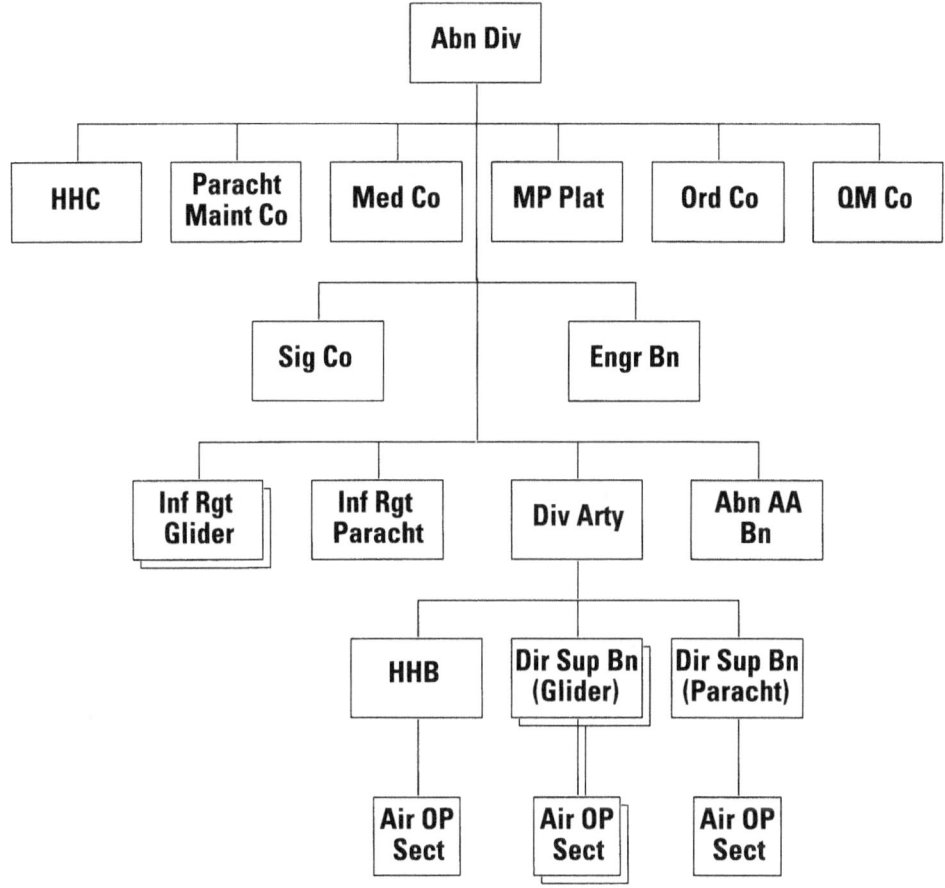

CHART 8—ORGANIZATION OF U.S. AIRBORNE DIVISION, DECEMBER 1944–DECEMBER 1945

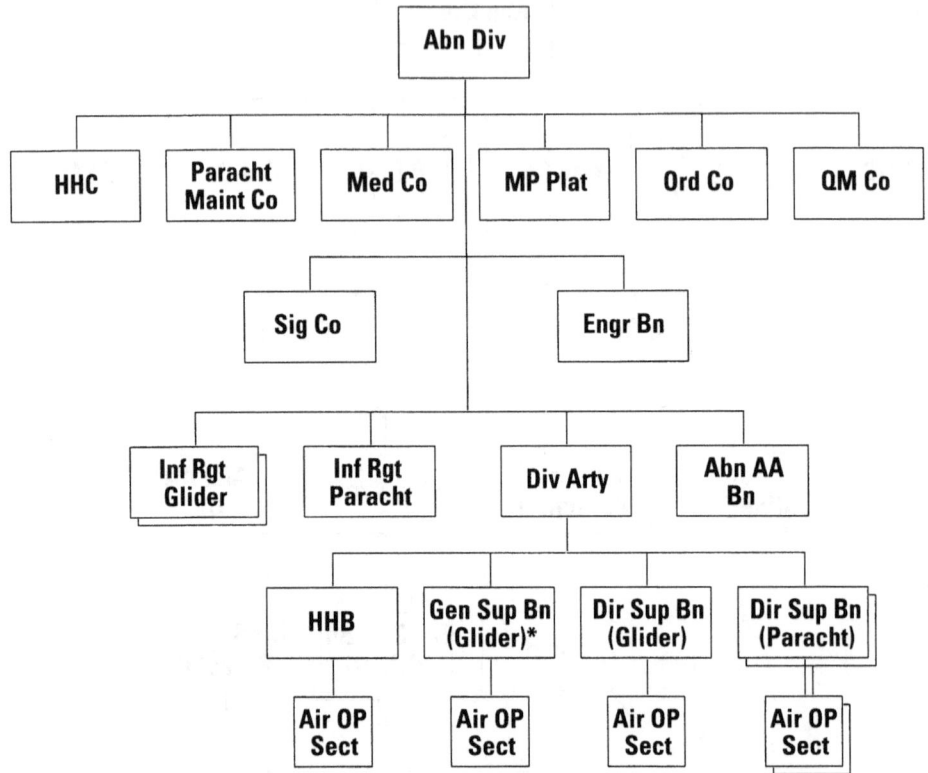

* When specifically authorized by the War Department, could be armed with 105-mm. howitzers rather than the standard issue 75-mm. pack howitzer.

CHAPTER 5

Initial Deployment and Combat in the North African and Mediterranean Theaters

The timing of the War Department's decision to create the Air-Observation-Post Program, six months after the attack on Pearl Harbor, meant that Army ground forces initially deployed overseas without organic air. When air sections did begin to move overseas and for many months thereafter, they did so in inadequate numbers and with insufficient supplies as a result of the difficulties in establishing a training base and an effective logistical system in the continental United States. The movement of artillery pilots and mechanics mirrored national priorities—first to England and North Africa, where the air sections became caught up in the subsequent campaigns in Sicily and Italy, and only secondarily to the Pacific. Whatever the destination, the aviators became involved in answering the question upon which the fate of the program depended: Could air observation posts effectively direct artillery fire in combat? But before the pilots and observers could even address this concern, they had to grapple with a series of problems not unlike those faced by their contemporaries in the United States.

The European Theater of Operations and North Africa

The deployment of air sections overseas exposed four major problem areas in the Air-Observation-Post Program: administrative support, supply, unit training, and appropriate doctrine. The absence of administrative support proved to be of the most immediate importance. The charter for the Air-Observation-Post Program made no provision for artillery air officers serving at any echelon of command higher than the division. The graduates of the first few pilot and mechanics classes at the Department of Air Training thus entered an administrative void: Almost no one at their new units expected them and few, if any, knew what to do with them. Officers at higher headquarters, with a few important exceptions, were either preoccupied with other duties or unaware of the existence of the program. Nothing better illustrated the prevailing state of affairs than the vicissitudes of the first serial of pilots and mechanics dispatched overseas in September 1942 to II Corps as part of BOLERO, the buildup of American troops in Great Britain.

The director of the Department of Air Training, Col. William W. Ford, anticipated difficulties and sent two members of the Class Before One—a pilot, 1st Lt. Delbert L. Bristol, and a mechanic, S. Sgt. William T. Roulson, Jr.—as part of the group. Ford told Bristol that if anything went wrong he should contact the chief of staff of II Corps, Brig. Gen. Alfred M. Gruenther, a personal friend of Ford. The nine pilots and nine mechanics comprising the first serial sailed for Great Britain in the charge of the senior officer in the group, Capt. Joseph M. Watson, Jr. When they arrived, administrative confusion at the reception depot resulted in their being sent as infantry replacements to the 34th Infantry Division stationed in Northern Ireland.[1]

The II Corps was the senior American tactical headquarters in the British Isles. Maj. Gen. Mark W. Clark, who had so greatly aided in the creation of the Air-Observation-Post Program the previous spring, commanded the corps with Col. (later Brig. Gen.) Thomas E. Lewis, one of the alumni of the Fuddy-Duddies Flying Club, serving as his chief of artillery. They not only knew of the program but had anticipated the arrival of the Fort Sill pilots. When the men did not appear, Clark and Lewis put the corps staff to work trying to locate them—without success. The II Corps was scheduled to participate in the upcoming invasion of North Africa. Clark knew that training at Fort Sill had fallen behind schedule and wanted to ensure that II Corps units had sufficient pilots and mechanics to organize air sections as quickly as possible. He decided to establish a local school using Watson's pilots and mechanics as the instructors. Their disappearance forced a postponement of this plan. Lieutenant Bristol broke the impasse. With little more than force of personality and sheer gall, he wrangled permission from the 34th Infantry Division to go to London, where he saw not only Gruenther but also Clark. Clark immediately transferred the Fort Sill pilots and mechanics to the 13th Field Artillery Brigade but then had to depart to take up his duties as deputy commander of the invasion force.[2]

His successor in II Corps, Maj. Gen. Lloyd R. Fredendall, activated the school on 21 November 1942 at Perlham Downs, Wiltshire. Lt. Col. John D. Salmon, a veteran Field Artillery officer and a rated aerial observer, became the commandant. Though not a pilot, he soon learned to fly. A graduate of Pilot Class 3 at Fort Sill, Capt. John T. Walker, served as his executive officer. Bristol took over as chief of flight training. His first task was to scour the United Kingdom for L–4s. They were available, because the rate of aircraft production exceeded the rate of pilot training. The former was in fact proceeding at a more rapid rate than Ford had initially proposed. And the Army Air Forces, at Army Ground Forces direction, was shipping the aircraft overseas in anticipation of the arrival of pilots. Watson and the other pilots and mechanics worked hard to produce the neces-

---

[1] Interviews (Intervs), L. B. Epstein with Col D. L. Bristol, 1 Jul 75, and with Lt Col J. M. Watson, 14–15 Sep 76, both at U.S. Army Aviation and Troop Command History Office, St. Louis, Mo. (hereafter cited as USAA&TC). Draft Paper, Lt Col D. L. Bristol, 6 May 57, sub: Insert for History of Army Aviation (Avn); Special Orders (SO) 231, Field Artillery School (FAS), 28 Sep 42 [Extract]; both in D. L. Bristol Manuscripts (Ms), Mrs. D. L. Bristol, Florissant, Mo.

[2] Questionnaire, Col T. E. Lewis, Artillery (Arty) Officer (Ofcr), Fifth Army, [Jul 43], sub: Air Observation Post (AOP) Planes, in Report (Rpt), Extracts from Army Ground Forces (AGF) Questionnaire, in AGF, "Report of Observer to North African Theater" (Bound Ms, Morris Swett Technical Library, FAS, Fort Sill, Okla. [hereafter cited as Morris Swett Tech Lib], 1943); SO 114, 13th Field Artillery (FA) Brigade (Bde), 29 Oct 42; Draft, Bristol, 6 May 57; Intervs, Epstein with Bristol, 1 Jul 75, and with Watson, 14–15 Sep 76.

sary instructional materials, and Salmon soon had a miniature version of the Department of Air Training operating in the United Kingdom. The student pilots, all volunteers, dubbed their new craft "Maytag Messerschmidts."[3]

"Maytag" constituted a back-handed reference to the size of the L–4's engine. To the would-be pilots, the aircraft's 65-horsepower Continental possessed just enough power to operate their mothers' washing machines. The under-powered washing-machine motors of the day were noisy and vibrated a great deal. "Messerschmidt" referred to the heavily armed, very fast, and very maneuverable German front-line pursuit plane, the Me–109, which had everything, except possibly maneuverability, that the L–4 did not. The Messerschmidt was also the aircraft with which Field Artillery pilots might find themselves playing a game of one-sided tag over the front. The nickname obviously contained a element of gallows humor.[4]

LIEUTENANT BRISTOL IN 1942

The Allied landings in North Africa took place on 8 November, some two weeks before II Corps was able to organize its air-observation-post school. Consequently, there were no pilots and mechanics available to support either the Central Task Force, which landed near Oran in western Algeria, or the Eastern Assault Force, part of the larger Eastern Task Force, which landed near Algiers in central Algeria. The American contingent in each instance came from II Corps with Fredendall commanding the Central Task Force and the commander of the 34th Infantry Division, Maj. Gen. Charles W. Ryder, commanding the Eastern Assault Force. In contrast, the Western Task Force, which staged from the continental United States and landed on the Atlantic coast of the French colony of Morocco, contained air-observation-post pilots and mechanics, recent graduates of the Department of Air Training at Fort Sill.[5] (*Map 1*)

---

[3] Chester G. Starr, et al., *Fifth Army History*, 8 vols. (Headquarters [HQ], Fifth Army, [1944–1945]), 1:11; Charles E. Hart, "Artillery Representation on High Level Before and During Combat," *Field Artillery Journal (FAJ)* 38 (September–October 1948):208–13. The earliest expression of Clark's concern about obtaining enough pilots for II Corps is in Indorsement (Ind), Maj Gen Mark W. Clark to Commanding General (CG), AGF, 17 Jun 42, HQ, AGF, General Correspondence (Gen Corresp), 1942–1948, 353/1 (FA Air Observation [Obsn]) (Confidential [C]), Record Group (RG) 337, National Archives and Records Administration, Washington, D.C. (hereafter cited as NARA). For the student pilots' view of their aircraft, see Andrew A. Rooney, "The Maytag Messerschmidts Are Here," *Stars and Stripes (European Edition)* (11 December 1942).

[4] Ibid.

[5] George F. Howe, *Northwest Africa: Seizing the Initiative in the West*, U.S. Army in World War II (Washington, D.C.: Office of the Chief of Military History, 1957), pp. 39–54.

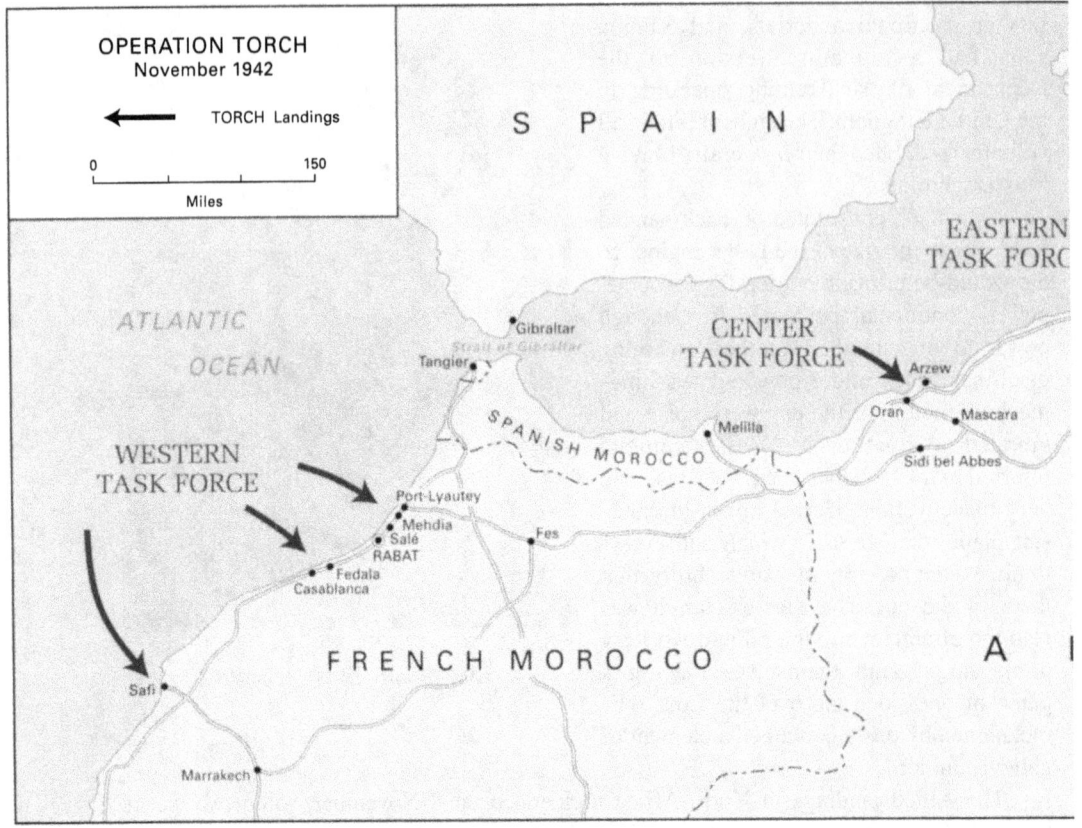

MAP 1

Lack of unit training, in which the absence of higher-level administration played a role, proved the major handicap for these men. The task force commander, Maj. Gen. George S. Patton, Jr., was familiar with the artillery air concept from the Louisiana maneuvers, but he had no one on his staff specifically detailed to handle this matter. Much needed coordination with the Navy was left undone in the haste to embark. Members of Pilot Class 2 joined their units aboard ship. Most had no opportunity to examine their aircraft, which were packed in overseas crates for shipping, let alone demonstrate their technique or become familiar with the ground officers with whom they would work. Four officers of the 3d Infantry Division, Capt. Ford E. Allcorn, Capt. Breton A. Devol, Jr., 1st Lt. John R. Shell, and 2d Lt. William H. Butler, joined the aircraft carrier USS *Ranger* at Bermuda and did see their planes. On her flight deck they found three weather-beaten early model L–4s. The four pilots had to spend virtually the entire voyage replacing and doping the fabric and tuning the engines of these craft.[6]

---

[6] An., Col J. B. B. Williams, Arty Ofcr, Western Task Force (TF), sub: Arty An. to Final Rpt of Operations (Opns) of Western TF, 8–11 Nov 42, Western TF—Ans. to Final Rpt—Opn TORCH, 95–TF3–0.3, An. 7, World War II Opns Rpts, 1940–1948, North African–Mediterranean Theater of Opns, RG 407, NARA; Interv, author

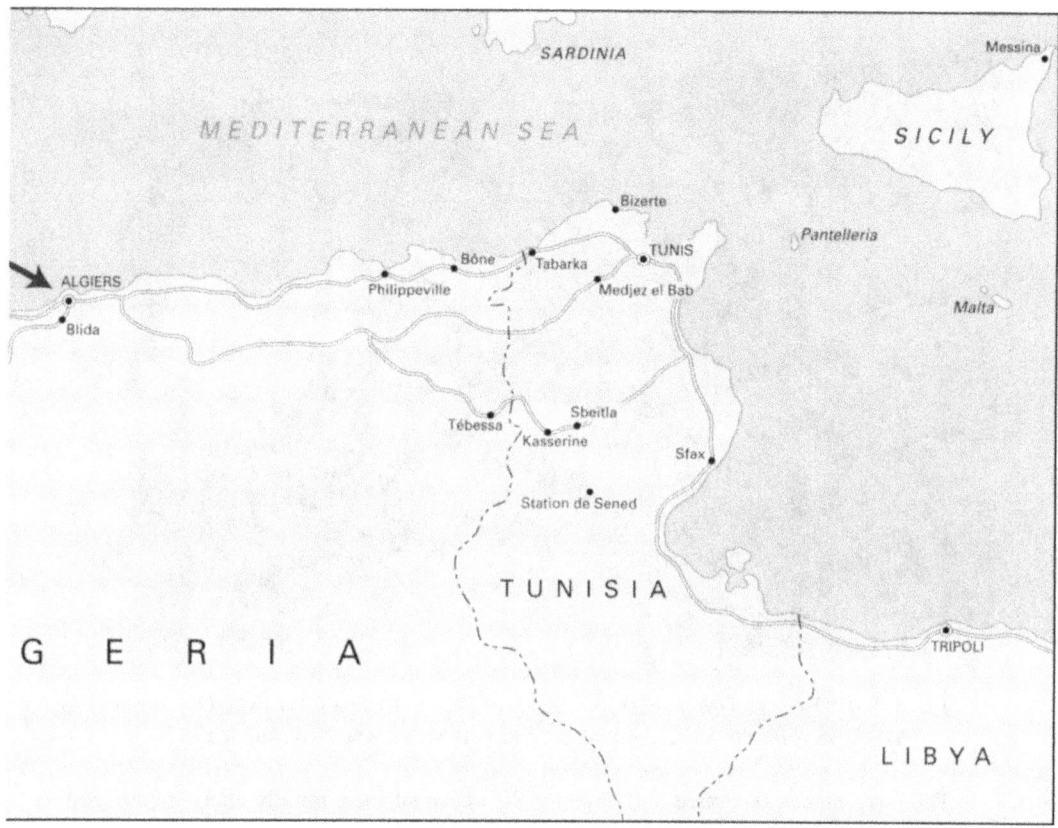

The mission of Allcorn and his fellow pilots was to provide aerial observation as the field artillery battalions landed in the initial stages of the assault. The landings, opposed by the French colonial garrisons loyal to the Vichy government, began on 8 November. The next day at approximately 1400 the off Casablanca *Ranger* headed into the wind and launched the three Field Artillery L–4s, festooned with invasion markings, into a 35-knot breeze. Allcorn, Butler, and Shell flew as pilots; Devol accompanied Butler as an observer. Minutes later, as they drew abreast of the cruiser USS *Brooklyn,* the ship's gunnery officer hastily consulted the book of Allied aircraft silhouettes and found nothing that resembled these aircraft. (Distribution of L–4 silhouettes was one of those matters that Patton's staff had overlooked during the planning.) The fleet had already suffered from several air attacks, so the gunnery officer took no chances. The *Brooklyn* opened fire. A 5-inch shell exploded directly behind Shell's aircraft.[7]

---

with Col J. W. Oswalt, 13 Jan 82, U.S. Army Center of Military History, Washington, D.C. (hereafter cited as CMH); Ltr, Lt Col F. E. Allcorn to W. E. Vance, 9 Apr 57, *U.S. Army Aviation Digest* (*USAAD*) files, U.S. Army Aviation Museum Library, Fort Rucker, Ala. (hereafter cited as USAAML); [Michael J. Strok], "WW II Army Aviators First Combat Mission," *L–4 Grasshopper Wing Newsletter* (December 1991/January 1992):1–3, 6.

[7] Ltr, Capt F. E. Allcorn to Col W. W. Ford, 11 Dec 42, Personal Corresp of Lt Gen Lesley J. McNair, 1940–1944, "Ford, W. W.," RG 337, NARA; Ltr, Allcorn to Vance, 9 Apr 57; Howe, *Northwest Africa*, p. 139.

LIEUTENANT BUTLER (*front seat*) AND CAPTAIN DEVOL PREPARE TO TAKE OFF FROM THE USS *RANGER* OFF CASABLANCA, FRENCH MORROCO, NOVEMBER 1942.

The three planes separated and dove for the ocean surface, rapidly altering course in a random pattern at an altitude of twenty feet to avoid a curtain of 20-mm. rounds as all the ships in the fleet opened fire. In short order Allcorn lost his windshield and door to machine-gun fire. Several rounds passed between his body and where his windshield had been. His engine was only "smoking slightly" when he passed over the shoreline, but then the ground forces, who had never trained with L–4s, opened fire. A tank machine-gunner put five slugs into one of Allcorn's legs. He lost control, and his plane crashed. Fortunately, he was able to crawl from the wreckage before it burned and then exploded. Butler and Devol succeeded in crash landing—behind the Vichy French lines. Captured, they rejoined their unit after the French surrendered. Shell landed on the race track at Fedala that was their objective, but when he attempted to take off again to try to direct artillery fire, he encountered such concentrated friendly small-arms fire that he had to land immediately. The first American attempt to use air observation posts in combat had ended in a bloody shambles, redeemed only by the heroism of the men who made the effort.[8]

To counterbalance the failure in Morocco came more heartening reports of air observations posts in action with the Eastern Task Force, commanded by British Lt. Gen. Kenneth A.N. Anderson. The Eastern Assault Force, the all-American component of the Eastern Task Force under General Ryder, secured Algiers early on 9 November through a

---

[8] Interv, author with Oswalt, 13 Jan 82; Ltr, Allcorn to Vance, 9 Apr 57.

combination of combat and diplomacy. General Anderson then came ashore and implemented plans to drive east toward Tunisia. In the unsuccessful race to forestall the Germans, Anderson pushed units east as soon as they became available, without regard for unit integrity or even national origin. The U.S. 175th Field Artillery Battalion, commanded by Lt. Col. Joseph E. Kelly, moved out to join the predominantly British force (subsequently designated British First Army) and quickly became engaged with a German column at the Tunisian town of Medjez el Bab. On 24 November 1942, during an attack to recapture the town, the battalion became the first American field artillery unit to use organic air observation in combat—but in this instance the planes and pilots were British.[9]

The Royal Artillery had continued to develop the air-observation-post concept after the last U.S. chief of Field Artillery, Maj. Gen. Robert M. Danford, visited the Royal Artillery School at Larkhill in August 1941. The British adopted a joint squadron organization in which the Royal Artillery supplied the pilots and observers and the Royal Air Force furnished administrative personnel and ground crew. Unlike their American counterparts, British air observation posts had trained intensively with ground units, largely because the British program was a year older. Consequently, they had achieved a high rate of operational readiness. By November 1942 the new organization had not yet spread beyond British Army units in the home isles. Because British Home Forces supplied the British Army units for the Eastern Task Force, it included the first British air observation posts to enter combat, the Royal Air Force/Royal Artillery 651st Squadron. It landed at Bone on 12 November. The squadron was equipped with standard British liaison aircraft, a modified Taylorcraft dubbed the Auster. Twelve days later a section from the squadron reported to Colonel Kelly for the shoot at Medjez el Bab. Accounts of the good performance of the British air observation posts thus became available through American as well as British channels, a circumstance of some consequence given the disappointing combat debut of the American light aircraft off Casablanca. A few American pilots even rotated through the unit to gain combat experience before their air sections joined U.S. field artillery battalions at the front. It was in these circumstances that 2d Lt. Paul A. DeWitt became the first American Field Artillery pilot to fly a combat mission on the Tunisian front—in a British Auster.[10]

The initial deployment overseas and the first operation in North Africa exposed both the administrative and the training weaknesses in the program, although the latter was by far the more obvious and consequently the first to draw attention. With most American units in the theater engaged in occupation duty, the U.S. commanders had time to address the problem. In Morocco, Patton instituted a rigorous training program for all units in which the air sections were necessarily involved. In Algeria, Fredenall ordered forward the

---

[9] Edward A. Raymond, "Some Battle Lessons," *FAJ* 34 (February 1944):104–05, recounts the experiences of the 175th Field Artillery Battalion in some detail. Howe, *Northwest Africa*, pp. 245–52, 277–98, provides invaluable background information on the seizure of Algiers and the attack into Tunisia.

[10] H. J. Parham and E. M. G. Belfield, *Unarmed Into Battle: The Story of the Air Observation Post* (Winchester, U.K.: Warren and Son, 1956), pp. 17–29. General Parham was one of the key figures in the Royal Artillery's adoption of the air observation post. Richard J. Tierney and Fred Montgomery, *The Army Aviation Story* (Northport, Ala.: Colonial Press, 1963), p. 126, recount the familiarization missions with the 561st Squadron. "Auster" is Middle English for "a southerly wind." Anthony Farrar-Hockley, *The Army in the Air: The History of the Army Air Corps* (Dover, N.H.: Alan Sutton Publishing, Inc., 1994), p. 138.

MARK III AUSTER WITH ROYAL AIR FORCE MARKINGS

advance echelon of the II Corps Air Observation Post School, commanded by Captain Watson. Watson set up at an abandoned French Air Force base near Sidi Bel Abbés, the location of the headquarters of French Foreign Legion. Shortly thereafter, Colonel Salmon and the remainder of the school arrived.[11]

A reorganization of the American command structure in North Africa had a major impact on the school. In January 1943 the theater commander, General Dwight D. Eisenhower, shifted II Corps to the Tunisian front to control American units under the British First Army. He also activated U.S. Fifth Army to handle training and planning for future operations. On 6 January 1943, Clark, now a lieutenant general, assumed command, with Colonel Lewis as the army artillery officer. Both remained as intensely interested in the success of organic aviation as before. Clark redesignated Colonel Salmon's school as the Fifth Army Air Observation Post School and gave it the mission of providing pilots and mechanics to all American field artillery battalions in the theater.[12]

One student pilot recalled meeting "a tough looking sergeant" after he reported to Sidi Bel Abbés. The sergeant inquired, "Do you see that big box? Well, in that box is an airplane, which you'll take out carefully. Assemble it by the book, and tomorrow you'll fly it. And that box will be your home as long as you're here in the school. Make yourself comfortable, and get to work." The pilot course at the school lasted about three months and gave graduates over seventy hours of flight time. The course emphasized road landings and

---

[11] Howe, *Northwest Africa*, pp. 192–228; Intervs, Epstein with Watson, 14–15 Sep 76, and with Bristol, 1 Jul 75.

[12] Starr, et al., *Fifth Army History*, 1:11; Questionnaire, Capt E. P. Gillespie, Fifth Army, 15 May 43, sub: AOP Planes, in AGF, "Report of the Observer to the North African Theater of Operations" (Bound Ms, Morris Swett Tech Lib, 1943).

contour flying. In practice, according to the same student, the latter consisted of "chasing sheep, goats, Arabs, etc." Operating first out of Sidi Bel Abbés and later out of Mascara, it immediately sent its first graduates to the Tunisian front. As of 15 May 1943, forty-five pilots and fifty-six mechanics had graduated. In addition, the school provided approximately two weeks of refresher training for replacement pilots before they were assigned to combat units. Clark attempted to regularize the school after the fact by securing War Department sanction and authority to rate the graduates, a proposal that both Army Ground Forces and Army Air Forces successfully opposed. As a consequence, graduates did not receive flight pay, unlike pilots from the Department of Air Training. Nevertheless, only the existence of the local school allowed U.S. forces to build up light aviation to authorized strength quickly.[13]

The first steps toward a solution of the administrative problem also occurred at this time as a result of the establishment of Fifth Army. (*Chart 9*) Lewis created a light aircraft subsection in the artillery section of the army staff. The Fifth Army artillery air officer, 1st Lt. Eugene P. Gillespie, organized the section by taking pilots and aircraft from the 13th Field Artillery Brigade. In the long term this diversion had no operational ramifications, because the War Department planned to maintain a 50 percent reserve of pilots and aircraft in overseas theaters. But there was an immediate cost. As of January 1943, ground forces in North Africa had only 34 of an authorized 134 organic aircraft. Gillespie's planes and pilots thus further reduced capabilities in operational units.[14]

As the Fifth Army artillery air officer, Gillespie had both operational and administrative responsibilities. He and his pilots ferried the army commander and his principal staff officers to planning conferences and to various installations scattered about the theater. Readily available aircraft allowed Clark and his staff to exercise close supervision of the training then in progress. Clark, who often used Gillespie as his personal pilot, had Gillespie's aircraft equipped with a loudspeaker, "primarily for shouting instructions to the ground when we flew low over troops engaged in training exercises." In fact, Clark acquired a habit of using air transportation that he retained for the remainder of his career.[15]

The artillery air subsection served as a collecting point for information about the number, destination, consignment, and markings on shipping cases of aircraft, repair kits, and tool sets en route to the theater from the continental United States. Gillespie also compiled data about the projected movement of trained Field Artillery pilots and mechanics into the theater. There was no point in assembling the aircraft until there was someone to fly and maintain them—which in turn implied that pilots and mechanics possessed the requisite skills. Gillespie thus exercised staff supervision over their training for Clark and Lewis. As a result of these diverse responsibilities, Gillespie not only interacted with his peers in

---

[13] Questionnaire, Gillespie, 15 May 43; Lt Col J. R. Dryden, Assistant Adjutant General (AAG), AGF, for Chief of Staff, Army (CSA), 20 Feb 43, HQ, AGF, Gen Corresp, 1942–1948, 353/8 (FA Air Obsn) (Secret [S]), RG 337, NARA; Ltr to Editor, Lt Col (Ret) Paynee O. Lysne, *L–4 Grasshopper Wing Newsletter* 60 (November/December 1996):2; quotes from Paynee O. Lysne, "In That Box Is an Airplane," *Army Aviation Magazine* 43 (January 1994):65–68.

[14] Interv, author with Col Claude Shepard, 23 Sep 83, CMH; Ltr, Col C. L. Bertholf, Adjutant General (AG), HQ, Fifth Army, to The Adjutant General (TAG), 24 Jan 43, The Adjutant General's Office (TAGO), Security Classified (Class) Decimal file, 1943–1945, 452 (24 Jan 43), RG 407, NARA.

[15] Mark W. Clark, *Calculated Risk* (New York: Harper and Brothers, 1950), pp. 151–52; Interv, author with Shepard.

CHART 9—ORGANIZATION OF A FIELD ARMY ARTILLERY SECTION, 1945

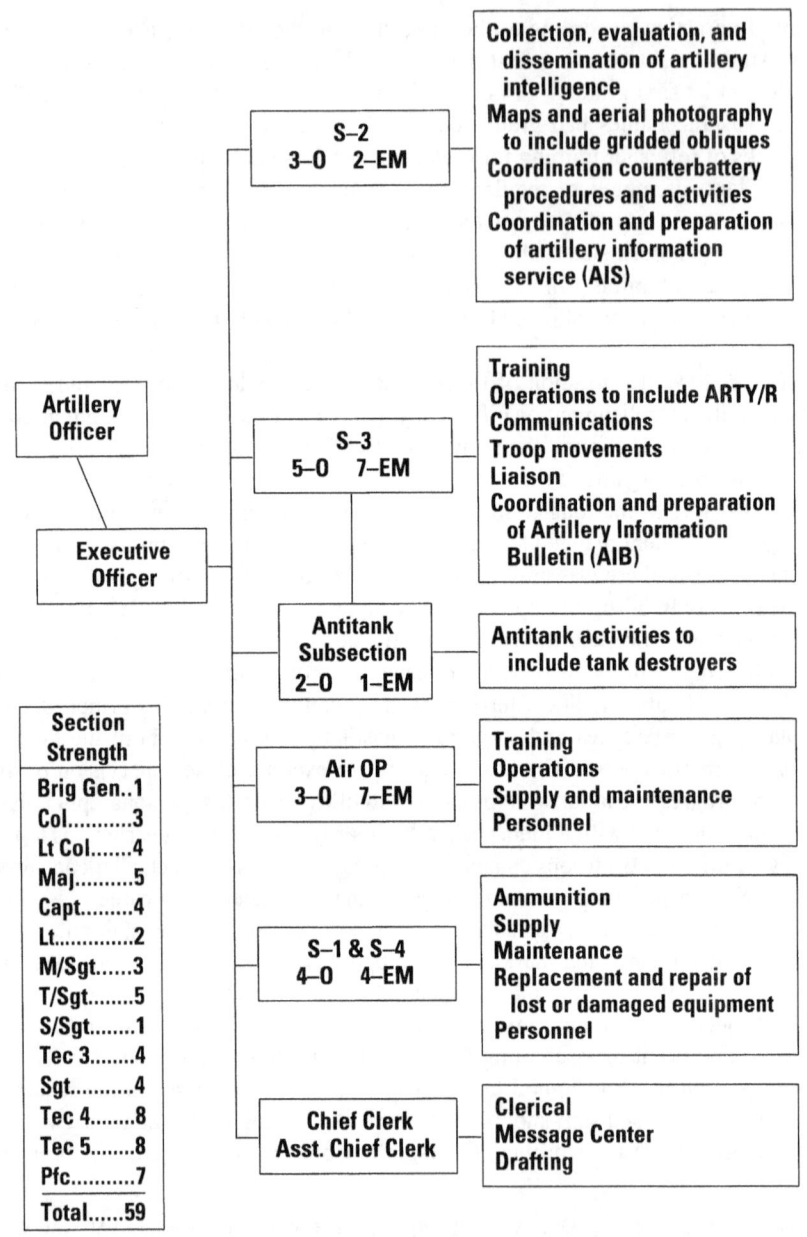

Section Strength	
Brig Gen	1
Col	3
Lt Col	4
Maj	5
Capt	4
Lt	2
M/Sgt	3
T/Sgt	5
S/Sgt	1
Tec 3	4
Sgt	4
Tec 4	8
Tec 5	8
Pfc	7
Total	59

KEY:			
Air OP	Air Observation Post	EM	Enlisted Men
Arty/R	Artillery Reconnaissance*	O	Officers

*The use of high-speed Army Air Forces reconnaissance aircraft to direct long-range fire.

Source: Brig. Gen. Charles E. Hart, "Artillery with an American Army in Europe," *FAJ* 37 (January–February 1947):55.

CHART 10—COORDINATION RESPONSIBILITIES OF A FIELD ARMY ARTILLERY AIR OFFICER, 1945

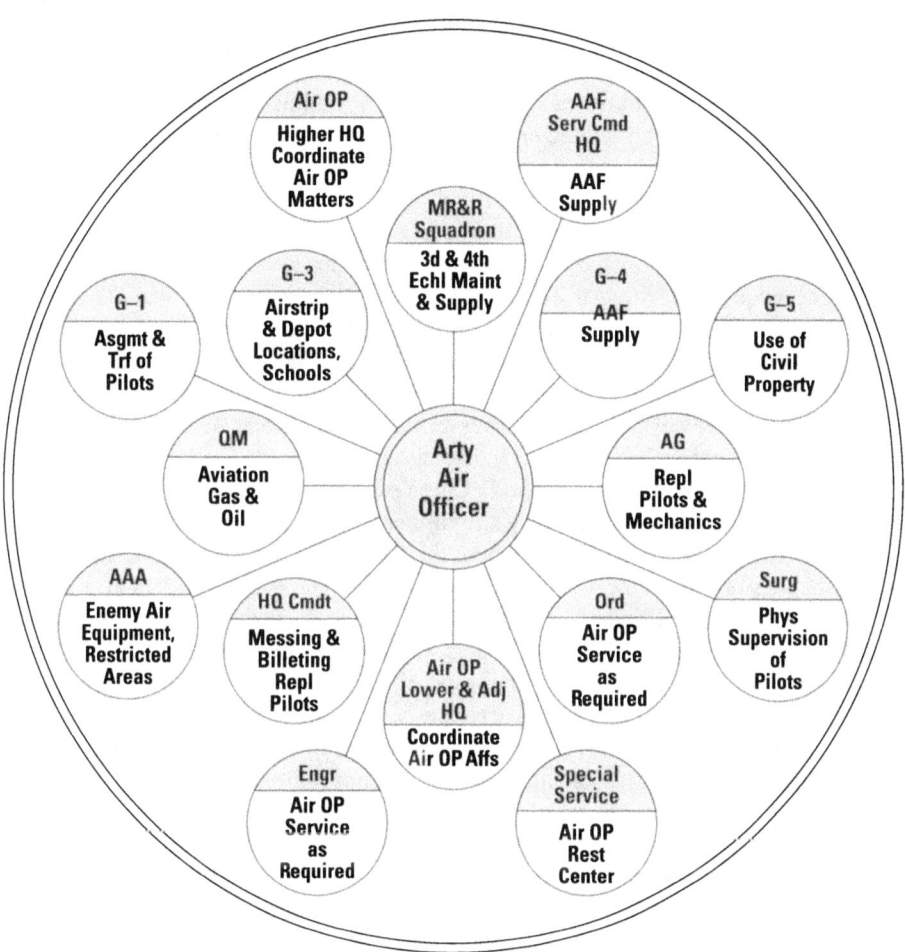

KEY:			
AAA	Antiaircraft Artillery	HQ	Headquarters
AAF	Army Air Forces	Maint	Maintenance
Adj	Adjacent	MR&R	Mobile Reconstruction & Repair
AG	Adjutant General	Ord	Ordnance
Air OP	Air Observation Post	Phys	Physician
Arty	Artillery	Repl	Replacement
Asgmt	Assignment	Serv	Service
Cmd	Command	Surg	Surgeon
Echl	Echelon	Trf	Transfer

Source: Brig. Gen. Charles E. Hart, "Artillery with an American Army in Europe," *FAJ* 37 (January–February 1947):57.

Colonel Lewis' section but also with members of the appropriate general staff sections at Fifth Army headquarters. (See *Chart 10.*) Gillespie's title was still strictly unofficial. Officially, he was just another assistant artillery officer—a staff officer. The section, and similar ones subsequently established at other field army headquarters, continued to evolve throughout the war. Through trial and error Gillespie, his contemporaries, and his successors identified what they needed to do and with whom they needed to work.[16]

Initially, the proper channels of resupply for the air-observation-post sections remained a mystery to all concerned. No one, least of all the staff of Twelfth Air Force, the major Army Air Forces command in Northwest Africa headed by Brig. Gen. James H. Doolittle, understood the Army Air Forces role. Despite the absence of a War Department directive, Doolittle's headquarters offered to furnish fourth-echelon maintenance, to perform major engine overhauls, and even to assemble aircraft when they arrived in theater. The attitude of helpful cooperation that animated Twelfth Air Force foreshadowed the relationship that would prevail in most instances in the field between Army Air Forces and Field Artillery pilots throughout the war. In this instance, however, Clark and Lewis opted to assemble aircraft at a single point, the II Corps Air Observation Post School, for purposes of both administrative convenience and further training for the students there.[17]

Fifth Army requests for information about the arrival of aircraft and associated equipment and supplies prompted the War Department to elaborate its air-observation-post supply policies. It directed all divisions stationed overseas to requisition aircraft, tools, and parts from the Army Air Forces overseas depots, which would make distribution directly to the units, and gave theater commanders the responsibility of reserving space for shipments of Field Artillery liaison aircraft aboard each convoy. This policy decision solved some but not all of Gillespie's problems. Likewise, simply assembling aircraft at the school as they arrived from overseas and forwarding them to units did not begin to address all the intratheater air-observation-post supply issues. This bitter reality soon became apparent to Captain Walker, who ranked Gillespie out of the position of Fifth Army artillery air officer. (Gillespie remained as Walker's assistant.) The confusion about divisional versus battalion repair kits affected units overseas just as it did in the continental United States; most aircraft arrived in theater without the requisite number of tool sets or repair parts kits. Ground officers in North Africa knew no more about Army Air Forces supply procedures than did their counterparts in the United States. At the same time Army Air Forces depot personnel in North Africa were too distracted by more immediate and pressing concerns to trouble themselves about crated light aircraft not assigned to specific units and spare parts that were shoved to the back of their depots. The result was that equipment for the Field Artillery air sections built up in Army Air Forces depots, and no one exercised stock control.[18]

---

[16] Interv, author with Shepard. The best description of the duties of a field artillery air subsection at a field army headquarters is found in War Department (WD), First Army, *First United States Army: Combat Operations Data, Europe, 1944–1945,* 4 vols. (New York: Headquarters, First Army, 1946), 3:161–63; Intervs, author with Col Michael J. Strok, 30 Jun 82, 13 Aug 91, CMH.

[17] Ltr, Bertholf to TAG (Attn: CG, AGF), 24 Jan 43, sub: Organic Air Obsn Sections for FA, HQ, AGF, Gen Corresp, 1942–1948, 353/7 (FA Air Obsn) (S), RG 337, NARA; Questionnaire, Lewis, [Jul 43].

[18] Memo, Col R. H. Ballard, Assistant Chief of Air Staff (ACAS), A–4, for Assistant Chief of Staff (ACS), Operations Division (OPD), 13 Mar 43, sub: Organic Air Obsn Sections for FA, HQ, Army Air Forces (AAF), Central Decimal file, October 1942–May 1944 (Security Class), 321 (Arty), RG 18, NARA; Interv, author with Strok, 30 Jun 82.

Air observation posts still flew, but only on the basis of rather desperate field-expedient measures. When Lieutenant Shell became artillery air officer of the 1st Armored Division early in 1943, one of his first acts was to establish a salvage replacement parts pool, even though at the time he had nothing to put into it. Creative cannibalism of all wrecked ground vehicles and aircraft, no matter what the type, kept the division's L–4s flying. Such efforts, while a testament to the ability of the pilots and mechanics to improvise, indicated the extent to which the intratheater supply system had broken down, a truth of which Walker was well aware. With the full backing of General Clark, he turned to a good friend, 2d Lt. (later Capt.) Michael J. Strok, to solve the problem. Strok, who had designed the shop-floor layout of Piper Aircraft that made mass production of the L–4 possible, became an assistant artillery air officer for Fifth Army with the official title of air engineering officer. He ferreted out the needed supplies and equipment and through barter and scrounging secured what was available.[19]

When Fifth Army closed down the air-observation-post school in the latter stages of the Tunisian campaign, Strok took the best mechanics and organized the Fifth Army Artillery Air Depot (Provisional). Although not recognized in formal Department of the Army unit lineages, it was the first in a long line of disparate organizations with similar missions, equipment, and even personnel designed to support organic aviation in the field. The provisional air depot gave way to Army Air Forces depot units (Army), followed after the war by Ordnance Corps light aviation companies and then Transportation Corps Army aviation maintenance companies during the 1950s.[20]

Air sections began joining units at the front in Tunisia as early as December 1942. First Lt. Jesse U. Overall III led the first three planes from Oran and joined the 1st Armored Division upon his arrival. Before the campaign ended, Overall became the artillery air officer of the 1st Infantry Division. Rain, mud, and the Germans produced a stable front that same month. In January II Corps became responsible for the central and southern sectors of the front, protecting the open flank of the Allied line. The small number of troops relative to the amount of ground they had to cover and the terrain on the southern end of the II Corps zone, level plain broken by hill masses, dictated the type of missions that air observations posts flew. Positions for ground observation posts were both excellent and numerous. The L–4s rarely directed fire in southern Tunisia. Instead, they flew flank guard patrols because II Corps elements occupied a series of strongpoints with open flanks rather than a continuous line.[21]

Lieutenant Shell in the 1st Armored Division established a weekly instructional memorandum for the division's air sections. Once the division entered combat, he appended lessons learned to it. By regularly circulating such information, Shell established standard procedures for the pilots, observers, and mechanics of disparate backgrounds arriving in

---

[19] 1st Lt. Paul A. DeWitt, "The Air OP of the Armored Artillery," *Military Review* 24 (September 1944):33; "A Grasshopper's Biography," *FAJ* 34 (February 1944):132; Intervs, author with Strok, 30 Jun 82, 13 Aug 91.

[20] Interv, author with Strok, 30 Jun 82; Questionnaires, Lewis, [Jul 43], and 1st Lt M. J. Strok, Fifth Army Air Engineering (Eng) Ofcr, 5 May 43, in AGF, Rpt of Obsr to North African Theater.

[21] DeWitt, "The Air OP of the Armored Artillery," pp. 33–39; Draft, Bristol, 6 May 57; Paul M. Robinett, *Armor Command: The Personal Story of a Commander of the 13th Armored Regiment, of CCB [Combat Command B], 1st Armored Division, and of the Armored School During World War II* (Washington, D.C.: McGregor and Werner, 1958), p. 123; Howe, *Northwest Africa*, pp. 297–362.

the division. This technique also helped both the aviators and the ground crew to focus on divisonwide concerns at a time when the army commander, General Anderson, had scattered units of the division over a wide area.[22]

The *Luftwaffe* was present and very active. In fact, the Germans enjoyed local air superiority over the front most of the time during the winter months. Unlike Allied airfields, which were unsurfaced and located several hundred miles behind the battle lines, the German airfields were close and hard surfaced. The flank protection missions dictated that the L-4s remain in the air for extended periods rather than use grasshopper tactics of the type Colonel Ford envisioned—a short bound into the air, quick observation from 500 feet, and then a landing before enemy fighters could react. Despite the deviation from doctrine, German fighters did not cause prohibitive losses. The light aircraft proved difficult to see and harder to hit. Air sentinels on the ground and cooperation between pilots when two or more L-4s were in the air made the difference between life and death. The Germans did not succeed in shooting down any artillery aircraft during the campaign, although one L-4, piloted by Lt. Robert Johnson, crashed and burned while attempting to escape German fighters. Like the pilots and ground crew, the ground troops, in an ironic commentary on their own lack of visible friendly air support, began calling the little artillery craft Maytag Messerschmidts, a term of endearment that the light planes carried for the remainder of the war against Germany.[23]

While air observation posts became a familiar presence at the front, they failed to perform their primary mission, which called the entire future of the program into question. On 1 February 1943, near Station de Sened, Lieutenant DeWitt directed fire from an L-4, the first and for a long time the only aerial fire mission of the campaign. In accord with doctrine as taught at the Department of Air Training, he was in the air only ten minutes. Thereafter, air observers deferred to ground observers. Grasshopper tactics for fire missions in this terrain ensured that ground observers provided superior observation to air observers. Even some backers of the program assumed that air observers did not perform the mission because they could not. Southern Tunisia convinced General Eisenhower that light aircraft could not survive at altitudes sufficient for directing fire. But Assistant Secretary of War McCloy, who made a brief tour of the front in southern Tunisia, was unwilling to concede the point. The Field Artillery in his view had not yet proven its case; he did not want the planes taken from the Field Artillery until the artillerymen had had a fair opportunity to demonstrate their usefulness. Army Air Forces observers believed that the results confirmed all their worst fears. Reports out of Southern Tunisia played a major role in the G-3 decision of June 1943 not to expand the organic air program beyond the Field Artillery.[24]

---

[22] DeWitt, "The Air OP of the Armored Artillery," p. 33.

[23] Ibid., p. 34; Interv, Epstein with Watson, 14-15 Sep 76; Rpt, Col C. E. Hart, II Corps Arty Ofcr, to HQ, First Army, 2 Mar 43, sub: Piper Cub Liaison Planes (L4B), TAGO, Class Decimal file, 1943-1945, 452.1 (3-11-43), RG 407, NARA; Ltr, Col J. W. Oswalt to R. J. Tierney, 27 May 74, *USAAD* 20 (May 1974):12-13.

[24] Ltr, Brig Gen T. J. Davis, AG, North African Theater of Operations (NATO), to TAG, 11 Mar 43, sub: Rpt on Liaison Aircraft; Rpt, Hart to HQ, First Army, 2 Mar 43; Memo, Brig Gen I. H. Edwards, ACS, G-3, for CG, AGF, 6 Feb 43; Memo, Dryden for CSA (Attn: ACS, G-3), 20 Feb 43, sub: Organic Liaison Avn for Ground Force Units; Rpt, Maj Gen J. P. Lucas, AGF Obsr, 28 Apr 43, sub: Excerpt from Rpt of Maj Gen J. P. Lucas . . . Regarding Avn in North African Theater; Memo, J. J. McCloy for Lt Gen Ben Lear, 15 May 43; Memo, Brig Gen R. E. Porter, ACS, G-3, for CG, AGF, 28 Jun 43; all in Office of the Assistant Secretary of War (OASW), Security Class Corresp of J. J. McCloy, 1941-1945, 452.1 (5-15-43), RG 107, NARA; DeWitt, "Air OP of the Armored Artillery," p. 34; Col. O. W. Martin, "Armored Artillery at Sened Station," *FAJ* 33 (August 1943):569-72.

INITIAL DEPLOYMENT AND COMBAT

LIFE IN THE FIELD: S. SGT. FRANK A. PERKINS, 1ST ARMORED DIVISION, WITH THE L–4 "SUPER SNOOPER" AT AN AIRSTRIP IN TUNISIA, 12 APRIL 1943.

In this crisis a further administrative innovation, one forceful individual, and a change of scene helped turn the situation around. In February, two days after General Patton assumed command of II Corps in the wake of the Kasserine Pass disaster, Lieutenant Bristol arrived at corps headquarters. The II Corps artillery officer, Col. Charles E. Hart, concerned about the state of his air-observation-post sections, had requested the temporary assignment of an artillery air officer to his staff. Bristol made certain that the air sections received supplies, bucked up morale, and fired two pilots who were not performing. Hart later commented that Bristol, more than any other individual, was responsible for the success of air observation posts in combat. The temporary appointment became permanent. Patton began using Bristol to fly him around the front, which stimulated other general officers in II Corps to do likewise with the light aircraft in their units. Bristol became the first corps artillery air officer in the U.S. Army, organized his own air section, and became a model for all subsequent corps artillery air officers.[25]

---

[25] Rpt, Hart to HQ, First Army, 11 Mar 43. Interv, Epstein with Bristol, 1 Jul 75. Ltr, Capt B. D. Morgan, AAG, Fifth Army, to Bristol, 8 Mar 43, sub: Travel Orders; SO 58, II Corps, 3 Apr 43; both in Bristol Ms, Florissant, Mo.; Memorandum for Record (MFR), HQ, AGF, n.d., sub: Organic Arty Air Obsn for Corps Headquarters, HQ, AGF, Gen Corresp, 1942–1948 (S), 353/18 (FA Air Obsn) (S), RG 337, NARA. The creation of the corps artillery air section in II Corps antedated the establishment of corps air sections Army-wide, but the War Department did not learn of Bristol's innovation until after instituting the reform.

The opportunity for redemption came relatively quickly. Following linkup with the British Eighth Army, the army group commander, General Sir Harold R. L. G. Alexander, reorganized the front, shifting II Corps to the far northern sector. In this rugged terrain, air observation posts were often the only available means of providing observed fire. Between 28 April and 1 May 1943, accurate artillery fire, delivered on target by aerial observers, enabled the U.S. 1st and 34th Infantry Divisions to break through the bitterly defended main German defensive position astride Hills 523, 531, 545, and 609 and to break up enemy attempts to concentrate for counterattacks. Because the *Luftwaffe* had retired from the skies over Tunisia, L–4s remained in the air for up to two hours, roaming behind the German lines to achieve superior observation. On 9 May Axis forces surrendered in northern Tunisia. But the victory was not without cost to the Field Artillery pilots. As German defenses crumbled, a German 88-mm. gun killed Lieutenant Shell while he was on the ground near the front.[26]

After the campaign ended, Bristol initiated night-flight training in II Corps. One day, while the fighting was still in progress, Bristol flew between Fifth Army headquarters and the II Corps Air Observation Post School. He failed to take into account the time zone changes, and by the time he reached his destination it was dark. Fortunately, a number of mechanics were working in a hangar. The main door was slightly ajar, emitting "a big long crack of light," while the remainder of the field was under blackout conditions. The crack of light told Bristol he was over the field, and he circled it, throttling back his engine to attract attention, until a pilot came out with a flashlight and guided him to earth. This incident and the experience of the campaign, where the guns needed to be reregistered each evening to ensure accurate support fires for the infantry during the night, convinced Bristol to establish a week-long night-flying course at Mascara as soon as the Germans surrendered. Bristol, assisted by a few mechanics, succeeded in training at least one pilot from each major unit in the corps in safe night-landing techniques.[27]

The Field Artillery pilots in North Africa derived two major lessons from the fighting; one concerned doctrine, the other equipment. They would never again consider air observation simply a supplement to ground observation. It was a primary means of observation. Tunisia also proved that it was very difficult for enemy fighters to shoot down light aircraft. At the same time, the L–4's often-sluggish performance in mountains raised the issue of obtaining a higher-performance replacement. The campaign ended, however, with the hopes of the partisans of organic aviation raised, even though opinions in some Washington circles were exactly the opposite.[28]

---

[26] Rpt, Col C. E. Hart, Atry Ofcr, II Corps, to CG, AGF, [1943], sub: Employment of Arty of the II Corps During the N[ORTH] TUNISIAN Campaign Ending in the Capture of BIZERTE and the Surrender of the German Forces in N[orth] Africa, in II Corps Arty, "Employment of Field Artillery of II Corps in Northern Tunisian Campaign" (Bound Ms, Morris Swett Tech Lib, [1943]); Interv, author with Strok, 30 Jun 82; Ltr, Oswalt to Tierney, 27 May 74.

[27] Interv, Epstein with Bristol, 1 Jul 75.

[28] Interv, Col B. R. Kramer and Lt Col R. K. Andreson with Brig Gen O. G. Goodhand, 9 May 78, U.S. Army Military History Institute, Carlisle Barracks, Pa. (hereafter cited as MHI); Ltr, Capt J. M. Watson, Jr., Arty Air Ofcr, 34th Infantry (Inf) Division (Div), to Col W. W. Ford, FAS, 10 Aug 43, sub: Experiences, Information, and Recommendations of the 34th Inf Div AOP Sections Secured During Combat in the Tunisian Campaign, in J. M. Watson Ms, USAA&TC.

Sicily

From their newly won North African base, the Allies launched successive campaigns against Sicily and Italy. In terms of grand strategy these two campaigns were closely related, but in terms of the institutional development of the Air-Observation-Post Program they were quite distinct. In Sicily the Seventh Army's air sections successfully addressed the final outstanding problem mitigating against their success in combat—air tactics. In Italy, the Fifth Army's air sections exploited the lessons of North Africa and Sicily so successfully that by the time Rome fell in June 1944 they collectively constituted a mature organization.

The U.S. I Armored Corps (Reinforced), under the command of Lt. Gen. George S. Patton, Jr., served as the American planning headquarters for the invasion of Sicily. The corps artillery officer, Col. John M. Willems, directed Capt. Claude L. Shepard, Jr., to organize an artillery air subsection. Shepard could only partially follow the Fifth Army model. He did not have the time to organize maintenance support along the lines of the Fifth Army Artillery Air Depot; in fact, Lieutenant Strok provided not only the L–4s to equip Shepard's section but also the third- and fourth-echelon support for Seventh Army throughout the campaign. Shepard found that many of the senior officers at Seventh Army headquarters, aside from Patton and Willems, were dismissive toward light aircraft—until they discovered the planes' value in ferrying them to the many planning conferences that preceded the invasion. Shepard thus had to practice the fine art of salesmanship on officers who did not have any previous personal experience with light aircraft.[29]

Planning for the invasion produced one significant air-observation-post innovation. The 3d Infantry Division was to land on the Allied left flank, and the division commander, Maj. Gen. Lucian K. Truscott, Jr., worried about how the enemy might counterattack. Consequently, he was very receptive to a proposal by the division artillery air officer, Captain Devol, to build a runway aboard a landing ship, tank (LST). Two ships, LSTs 525 and 906, were converted, although only the first actually supported the Sicily landing. A number of Field Artillery pilots assisted in the modifications. Lieutenant Strok served as a technical consultant. Each LST carried ten L–4s. The six aircraft stored along the sides of the flight deck had their rudders removed so the aircraft on the aft part of the deck could take off. The runways were too short to permit L–4s to return to the ships, so Devol planned for the aircraft to land behind friendly lines. Flying in relays from LST 525, they would keep the landing area under constant surveillance.[30]

The invasion of Sicily occurred on 10 July 1943 under the direction of Seventh Army, General Patton's headquarters under a new name. In the 3d Infantry Division, two pilots mistakenly took off at the same time but quickly proved their value as the division drove ashore around Licata. For more than two hours, 1st Lts. Oliver P. Board and Julian W. Cummings (the latter a graduate of the Fifth Army Air Observation Post School) flew back

---

[29] Intervs, author with Shepard, 22 Sep 83; with Strok, 30 Jun 82; with Col R. L. Long, 23 Jul 82. All at CMH.

[30] Rpt, HQ, 3d Inf Div Arty, 28 Aug 43, sub: Rpt of Arty During the Sicilian Campaign, [Extract], in AGF, "U.S. Field Artillery in World War II" (Bound Ms, Morris Swett Tech Lib, c. 1944); Intervs, author with Shepard, 23 Sep 83; Epstein with Bristol, 1 Jul 75; Lucian K. Truscott, Jr., *Command Missions: A Personal Story* (Novato, Calif.: Presidio Press, 1990), p. 213; "Ship Journeys To Fly-In," *Sixth Annual Sentimental Journey, August 22–25, 1991—Theme: Aviation Goes to War* (Lock Haven, Pa.: Sentimental Journey, Inc., 1991), pp. 17, 34.

A 3d Infantry Division L–4 Cub Takes Off from a One-Way Runway Built on an LST in the Mediterranean, July 1944.

and forth over the battle area reporting the location of friendly and enemy troops, guiding landing craft to the correct beaches, and directing naval gunfire on Italian artillery positions. This "Cub carrier" established a precedent emulated in virtually all subsequent landings in the Mediterranean.[31]

The other innovation—by far the more important—owed less to planning than to an ability to adapt to changing circumstances. Maj. Gen. Omar N. Bradley commanded the II Corps attack through the mountainous terrain of central Sicily (*Map 2*). Here, air observation posts proved their value by their ability to bring the far side of hill masses, hidden to ground observation posts, under observed fire. Initially, aircraft still used grasshopper tactics, but this changed as the campaign wore on. Limited resupply forced II Corps to ration artillery fire. The artillery air officer of the 45th Infantry Division, Capt. Samuel Freeman, noticed, however, that German artillery did not fire as long as one of the division's L–4s was in the air. In effect, the L–4 served as a counterbattery weapon without U.S. artillery firing a round. The division began flying its aircraft continuously during the day, and the practice soon spread throughout the corps and then Seventh Army. Artillery aircraft also

---

[31] Rpt, HQ, 3d Inf Div Arty, 28 Aug 43; Interv, author with Shepard, 22 Sep 83; Truscott, *Command Missions*, p. 213; Albert N. Garland and Howard M. Smyth, *Sicily and the Surrender of Italy*, U.S. Army in World War II (Washington, D.C.: Office of the Chief of Military History, 1965), p. 133. Technically, Headquarters, I Armored Corps, was inactivated at sea off Sicily on 10 July 1943, and Headquarters, Seventh Army, was activated on the same date. John B. Wilson, *Armies, Corps, Divisions, and Separate Brigades*, Army Lineage Series (Washington, D.C.: U.S. Army Center of Military History, 1987), pp. 30, 45.

provided route reconnaissance and close reconnaissance in advance of American infantry. As during the last days in Tunisia, pilots thought nothing of observing fire from the German side of the lines. While in Tunisia, the pilots had regarded such liberties possible because of the *Luftwaffe*'s withdrawal from the area of operations. In Sicily, they accepted them as standard operating procedures, even though German fighters attempted to intervene from time to time.[32]

The rugged Sicilian terrain forced some divisions to base all their aircraft at a single strip and thus inaugurated a controversy over centralization of control of organic air that persisted into the postwar period. Some division artillery commanders organized their air observation posts as provisional aerial companies, placing them under the command of the division artillery air officers and removing them completely from battalion control. Others, more in the spirit of Ford's original concept, provided centralized administrative and maintenance support at the division strip but left operational control strictly in the hands of the battalion commanders. Supporters of the former cited increased operational and administrative effectiveness, while advocates of the latter argued for operational flexibility and timeliness of response to requests for aerial observation. The issue was rarely judged strictly on its merits; there was a deeply emotional subtext. The supporters of decentralization had the specter of the Air Corps working in their favor. If aircrews did not live in the mud with the gun crews they supported, they would, so the argument went, fly off and become involved in their own concerns the way the Air Corps had done during the interwar period. The great emotion vested in the issue contributed to its persistence.[33]

The campaign in central Sicily featured rugged terrain and tenacious German resistance. Near the town of Troina, the 3d Battalion, 26th Infantry, of the 1st Infantry Division, was cut off for three days. The Army Air Forces attempted to drop supplies to the Americans but missed their dug-in-positions. Four Field Artillery officers, Lts. Donald Blair, William Cole, John Fuchs, and Oscar Rich, volunteered to make resupply runs in two L–4s. They dropped sandbags filled with K-rations and water purification tablets. "The flights," remembered one of the participants, "were a rather wild ride as we picked up a lot of ground fire from German rifles and machine guns both on the way in and the way out." Although the aircraft were hit many times, none of the Americans was wounded. And they delivered the supplies. The 1st Infantry Division Artillery commander, Brig. Gen. Clift Andrus, later awarded each man a Silver Star.[34]

The Sicilian campaign ended when the Seventh Army entered Messina on 17 August 1943. In its wake came one further administrative innovation of significance for air observation posts. At the urging of the artillery officer of II Corps, Colonel Hart, and the

---

[32] Intervs, author with Shepard, 23 Sep 83, and Epstein with Bristol, 1 Jul 75; James Edmonds, "Notes on Artillery Air Observation," *FAJ* 33 (December 1943):893–96; Rpt, Brig Gen Clift Andrus, CG, 1st Inf Div Arty, to TAGO, 13 Aug 43, sub: Unit Rpt of Battle from 9 May 43 to 9 Aug 43, Incl in 1st Inf Div Arty, "Reports" (Bound Ms, Morris Swett Tech Lib, 1943–1945). Intervs, Lt Col Arnote, S–3, Div Arty, 45th Inf Div; Capt Devol, Arty Air Ofcr, 3d Inf Div; Maj Boyett, S–3, 13th FA Bde; all in HQ, Allied Force, G–3 Training Section, *Training Notes from the Sicilian Campaign* (Allied Force Headquarters, 1943), pp. 50–56, copy at Morris Swett Tech Lib.

[33] Edmonds has the only available account of the inauguration of this debate, which had important doctrinal as well as force structure implications. Edmonds, "Notes on Artillery Air Observation," pp. 893–96.

[34] Oscar Rich, "Combat Report," *L–4 Grasshopper Wing Newsletter* 13 (February/March 1989):3; Garland and Smyth, *Sicily*, pp. 324–47.

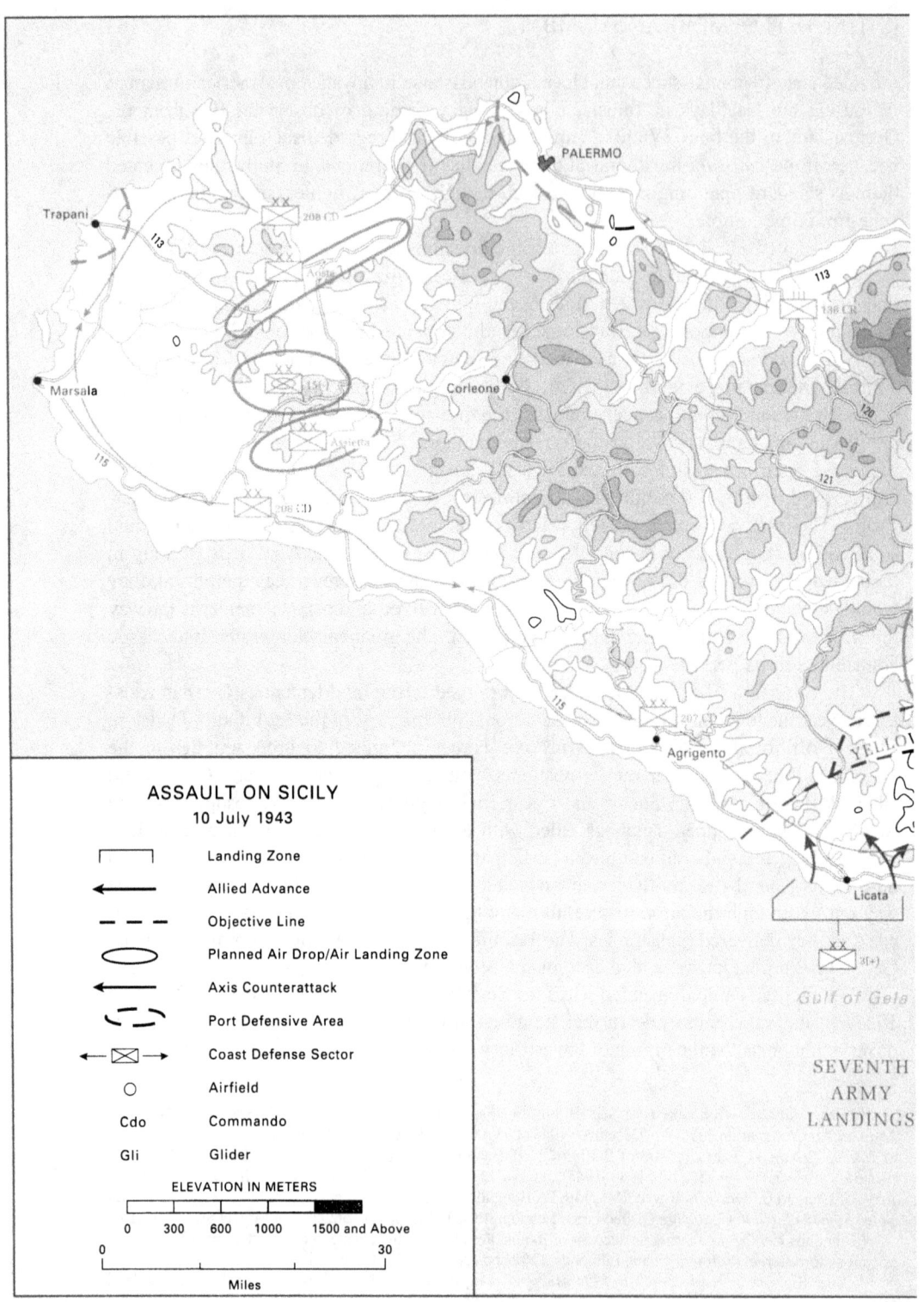

MAP 2

commander of the 13th Field Artillery Brigade, Maj. Gen. John A. Crane, General Eisenhower established a field artillery section at theater headquarters. This ultimately led to the creation of the position of theater artillery air officer. Crane praised Maj. Thomas L. Hendrix for being "able to accomplish important pioneering staff work" in this new post. The chief responsibility of the section became representing theater Field Artillery views to the War Department.[35]

Italy: Salerno to Rome

The U.S. Army's participation in the Italian campaign began with the Fifth Army's landing at Salerno on 15 September 1943 (*Map 3*). Pilots from the 36th Infantry Division flew L–4s off a decked-over LST in support of the invasion. While artillery pilots and ground crews subsequently continued to make innovations, they directed the vastly greater effort to elaborate and refine existing institutions and procedures. The Fifth Army artillery air officer, Maj. John T. Walker, organized the Fifth Army Air Observation Post Section into two subsections: one dealing with operations, initially under Captain Gillespie, and the second with maintenance and supply, under Lieutenant Strok. Operations conducted administrative flights, which gave replacement pilots reporting in theater an opportunity to practice their technique before joining their units. Administrative flights included a regular air courier service, carrying messages and staff officers between army headquarters and the various corps headquarters and to British Eighth Army headquarters. Walker usually flew the Fifth Army commander, General Clark, although Gillespie and Strok, both experienced pilots, also did so on occasion. After the landings at Anzio in January 1944, courier planes flew thirty miles out to sea and then parallel to the coast before making a 90-degree turn and flying directly for the beachhead. This circuitous route, totaling some ninety miles, allowed the Cubs to avoid interception. Walker outfitted some of his L–4s with pontoons so they could make water landings.[36]

Clark never hesitated to fly in light aircraft under circumstances that often involved a substantial amount of personal peril. He was unimpressed by the criticism that the commander of a field army had no business endangering his life in such fashion. In his view, the benefits far outweighed the risks:

I used light planes frequently in both training and combat situations in World War II because they permitted me to observe in a few minutes what it would have taken days to observe by any other means. I found invaluable the panorama of the terrain and the dispositions of forces that I could quickly fix in my mind when I could observe from the air. Then when I later studied the situation on a map, I could envision much more clearly the exact lay of the land. This was tremendously helpful in the overall direction of the Fifth Army, and it was of particular value in evaluating terrain and its influence on the courses of action I selected.[37]

---

[35] Maj. Gen. John A. Crane, "Must We Always Learn the Hard Way?" *FAJ* 36 (June 1946):329–31; Brig. Gen. C. E. Hart, "Artillery Representation on High Level Before and During Combat," *FAJ* 38 (September–October 1948):208–13.

[36] Arty Info Memo no. 7, Fifth Army, 11 Feb 44, in Fifth Army, "Artillery Information Bulletins" (Bound Ms, Morris Swett Tech Lib, 1943–1945); Clark, *Calculated Risk*, pp. 301–02; Interv, author with Strok, 30 Jun 82.

[37] Mark W. Clark, "Introduction," in Tierney and Montgomery, *Army Aviation Story*, p. v.

COLONEL WALKER, GENERAL CLARK, ROBERT P. PATTERSON, AND LT. GEN. BREHON B. SOMERVELL

Lieutenant Strok moved the Fifth Army Artillery Air Depot to the vicinity of Naples in November 1943. He edited an "Air OP Bulletin" that passed along information of interest to air sections—news of personnel changes, losses in combat, maintenance procedures, safety concerns, etc. He continued to provide the kinds of logistical support he had provided II Corps in North Africa and Seventh Army in Sicily and in addition fabricated various kinds of special equipment. When elements of the 509th Parachute Infantry Battalion were cut off in mountainous terrain above Venafro, Strok adapted a bomb shackle to drop rations, devised a release mechanism, and attached it to an L–4. The aircraft kept the soldiers resupplied for two weeks until ground forces could lift the siege. Proximity to the battle zone allowed Strok to return equipment to units much more quickly. Equally or possibly even more important, it allowed him to establish a close rapport with the commander of the large Army Air Forces depot in the Naples area, Lt. Col. K. W. Anderson, who became a strong supporter of the program. Anderson automatically shipped any liaison aircraft materiel that arrived in theater to Strok's rear echelon field near Naples.[38]

---

[38] Interv, author with Strok, 30 Jun 82; Margaret Bourke-White, *"Purple Heart Valley": A Combat Chronicle of the War in Italy* (New York: Simon and Schuster, 1944), p. 84. Fifth Army appears to have been the first to publish a separate air-observation-post bulletin. I have located only three issues, all reprints: AOP Bulletin no. 2, HQ, Fifth Army, Ofc of the Arty Ofcr, 7 Nov 43, and no. 5, HQ, Fifth Army, Ofc of the Arty Ofcr, 3 Dec 43, both in *L–4 Grasshopper Wing Newsletter* 39 (May/June 1993):3, 6–8; AOP Bulletin no. 6, HQ, Fifth Army, Ofc of the Arty Ofcr, 13 Dec 43, in *L–4 Grasshopper Wing Newsletter* 41 (September/October 1993):6–8.

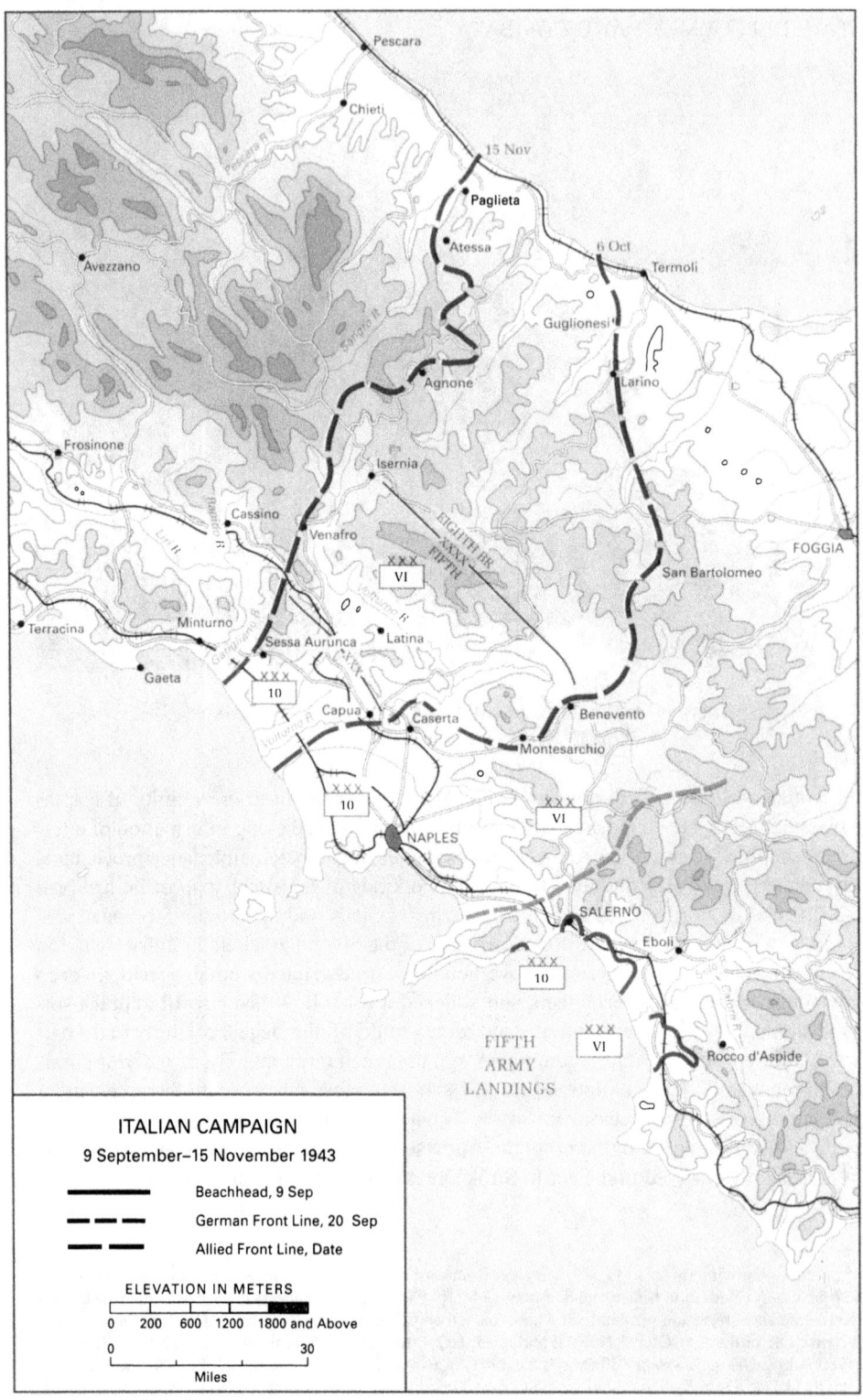

MAP 3

INITIAL DEPLOYMENT AND COMBAT

STROK, FOLLOWING HIS PROMOTION TO CAPTAIN, WITH FLAPS, THE UNIT MASCOT, DECEMBER 1944

Anderson played a key role in Fifth Army air sections acquiring a limited number of L–5s. When the first L–5s arrived in theater, Anderson asked Strok if Fifth Army wanted them. Strok responded in the affirmative; only later did he discover that the Army Air Forces had shipped them into theater in advance of the deployment of its 72d Liason Squadron. Walker told him to go ahead and assemble one. After Strok had test-flown the aircraft, neither officer wanted to give any of them back to the Army Air Forces. "It was," remembered Strok, "fantastic." With a 185-horsepower Lycoming engine, the L–5 had considerably more power than the L–4 with its 65-horsepower Continental. Walker arranged to fly Clark in one. Clark, with Eisenhower's backing, secured the War Department's approval to divert L–5s to Fifth Army Field Artillery air sections despite the opposition of the Army Air Forces. Walker, with Eisenhower's and Clark's support, had succeeded where Ford had failed. The diversion represented the first breach in the Army Air Forces' policy of restricting air observation posts to Cub-like aircraft. The exception involved only the Fifth Army, but it made subsequent exceptions easier.[39]

---

[39] Memo, [Jul 44], sub: Discussion of Advantages and Disadvantages of L–5 Airplane, HQ, AAF, Security Class Central Decimal file, 1942–1944, 452.1, RG 18, NARA; Ltr, Col H. V. Roberts, AG, NATO, to TAG, 14 Jul 44, sub: L–5 Liaison Airplanes in FA Air Obsn Sections; Ltr, Col J. R. Burrill, Acting Arty Ofcr, Fifth Army,

The rugged terrain affected operations in more ways than just the need for a more powerful light plane such as the L–5. As the Allied armies advanced north toward Rome, they encountered increasingly high mountains. Geography thus dictated that the German artillery's ground observation posts would always occupy the dominant terrain, looking down on the Allied forces advancing up the valleys from the south. Moreover, in German hands, the mountains shielded German rear areas from Allied ground observers. In these circumstances only liaison aircraft allowed the Allied artillery to conduct observed fires. During the increasingly bitter fighting north of the Volturno, the artillery air officer of the 18th Field Artillery Brigade, Lieutenant Cummings, reported that during the first three weeks of November, aerial observers conducted over 90 percent of the observed fires in his unit. Success in mountain warfare did not come easily, particularly in Italy where the mountains were higher and more numerous than in either Sicily or northern Tunisia. In this terrain, observed fire demanded the use of special techniques not required in the rolling countryside around Fort Sill. An air observer examined the washboard-like surface below him and then attempted to transfer what he saw to a plane surface, a gridded artillery map. The elevations of the mountains and ridges were usually not known. Consequently, a shell in flight often hit a peak before reaching its intended destination. Adjusting fire in mountains became challenging, because the forward slopes had the effect of diminishing perceived distances while the rear slopes magnified them. Unless the fire control center, the gunners, and the aerial observer were all aware of these influences, the pilot could become frustrated and suspend fire before reaching the target.[40]

The Americans' difficulty in perfecting their technique was not immediately apparent to the Germans. German artillery procedure, compared to American, was slow and methodical, if ultimately precise. Given equal observation, the American speed of adjustment allowed Fifth Army artillery units to smother German batteries with massed fire before the Germans could fire for effect. The most devastating American technique was known as *time on target*—massed fire in which batteries at different locations synchronized their fire so the shells arrived at one point simultaneously. No ranging was involved at the time; the technique required factoring in previously plotted locations of batteries, the position of the target relative to a known point, muzzle wear of each individual artillery piece, and current meteorological conditions. Soldiers in the target area had no inkling that they would be shelled until a mass of explosions killed or maimed everyone above ground.

---

4 Jul 44, [Extract]; Rpt, Lt Col C. V. Clifton, Commanding Officer (CO), 698th FA Battalion (Bn), to Arty Ofcr, Fifth Army, 27 Jun 44, sub: 240-mm. Howitzer Bn and the Gun in a Mobile Situation, [Extract]; all in HQ, AAF, Central Decimal file, October 1942–May 1944, 452.1–D (Obsn), RG 18, NARA. Disposition Form (DF), Maj Gen T. T. Handy, ACS, OPD, to TAG, sub: Same, TAGO, Class Decimal file, 1943–1945, 452.1 (14 Jul 44), RG 407, NARA. Interv, author with Strok, 30 Jun 82; Rpt, AGF Board, 5 Nov 43, [Extract], in AGF, "U.S. Field Artillery in World War II"; Rpt, Air Section, 697th FA Group (Grp), 21 May 45, sub: Most Interesting Opns, in XV Corps Arty, "Historical Examples Compiled Under the Direction of Brig. Gen. Edward S. Ott, Commanding XV Corps Artillery from the Campaigns of Normandy, Northern France, Rhineland, and Central Europe, During the Period July 1944 to May 1945" (Bound Ms, Morris Swett Tech Lib, 1945); Frederick G. Swanborough and Peter M. Bowers, *United States Military Aircraft Since 1909* (Washington, D.C.: Smithsonian Institution Press, 1989), pp. 574–75.

[40] Interv, 1st Lt J. W. Cummings, Arty Air Ofcr, 18th FA Bde, 26 Nov 43, in Rpt, AGF Board, 5 Dec 43, in AGF, "U.S. Field Artillery in World War II"; Interv, Epstein with Watson, 14–15 Sep 76; Arty Info Memo no. 8, Fifth Army, 4 Mar 44, in Fifth Army, "Artillery Information Memoranda" (Bound Ms, Morris Swett Tech Lib, 1944–1945).

There was simply no time to react and take cover. These shellings exerted a profound psychological impact on survivors.[41]

The ability of aerial observers to quickly and accurately call down such fire caused German artillery to routinely stop firing when a Cub was overhead. On at least one occasion during the advance to the Gustav Line, the main German defensive position south of Rome, American officers used this by-now-familiar German practice to good effect. By simply having an L–4 orbit in the general area, the Americans stopped German interdiction of a road long enough for a convoy to pass over it. No American artillery was in range to fire counterbattery.[42]

Interrogations of German prisoners supported the positive appraisal of the effectiveness of American aerial observation. One German prisoner, in a refrain repeated in endless variations, characterized light aircraft as simply "nerve wrecking." They circled over the German positions "and if we make the slightest move Hell breaks loose." Prisoner of war reports, however, were often suspect; a man slightly shocked and in fear of his life might well tell his captors what he thought they wanted to hear. Artillery pilots, however, soon received independent confirmation of the assessment of their value from a most unwelcome German source—the *Luftwaffe*.[43]

As in North Africa and Sicily, the Allies had theaterwide air superiority, but the Germans retained the ability to establish a fleeting local air superiority over any sector of the front virtually at any time. This circumstance accounted in part for the first artillery aircraft lost to enemy air action near Acerno, Italy, fifteen miles east of Salerno, in September 1943. The pilot, Capt. Edward B. Baetjer, was a graduate of the Fifth Army Air Observation Post School, assigned to the 13th Field Artillery Brigade. He had arrived at the front only four days earlier and was on a routine flight to observe fire for a field artillery battalion—routine, that is, except for the fact that he had the battalion commander aboard. Five German Fw–190s swept around the side of a mountain at low altitude on a strafing run. They were on Baetjer before he could react. Fortunately, the German pilots were just as surprised. Although all fired at him, they missed. He dove for the ground but, instead of landing, circled at about one hundred feet. "The next thing I knew a machine gun was barking again, and my engine sort of disintegrated." Two tailing fighters had seen him and attacked. He was able to nurse his crippled craft close to the ground, where it stalled and belly flopped into the top of a olive tree. Baetjer, who exited the aircraft through the windshield, had to be hospitalized and evacuated to North Africa. The colonel walked away with a scratched hand.[44]

As the German defenders realized the importance of light aircraft in the American artillery system, the *Luftwaffe* began to make L–4s a primary target. Over the next two

---

[41] Department of the Army (DA), Special Regulation 30–5–1, *Dictionary of U.S. Army Terms* (Washington, D.C.: Department of the Army, 1950), p. 239. Its predecessor, WD, Technical Manual (TM) 20–205, *Dictionary of United States Army Terms* (Washington, D.C.: Government Printing Office, 1944), does not include the term "time on target." Rpt, Lt Col J. C. Mott, AGF Obsr, 29 Dec 43, sub: Rpt on Italian Campaign, in AGF, "U.S. Field Artillery in World War II."

[42] Rpt, Mott, 29 Dec 43.

[43] Ltr, Maj Gen L. K. Truscott, CG, 3d Inf Div, to Capt B. E. Devol, Arty Air Ofcr, 3d Inf Div, [Extract], AOP Bulletin, Fifth Army, 7 Nov 43, in AGF, "U.S. Field Artillery in World War II."

[44] "All Good Things Must End," *FAJ* 35 (January 1944):41; E. A. R., "Last of a 'Grasshopper,'" *FAJ* 34 (December 1944):812. The latter consists of an interview with Baetjer. See also AOP Bulletin no. 6, HQ, Fifth Army, Ofc of the Arty Ofcr, 14 Dec 43, for Baetjer's return to duty.

months Cub losses mounted, although they "remained on an entirely acceptable scale." The standard L–4 evasive maneuver involved flying to the nearest ridgeline and then hugging one of the faces of the ridge.[45]

In the face of such pressure, Fifth Army coordinated air-observation-post operations much more closely with its organic antiaircraft defenses. By December 1943 the primary mission of the antiaircraft warning system was "protection of our Air OP." The aircraft warning system in the 13th Field Artillery Brigade supporting II Corps—the corps entered combat on the Italian mainland on 18 November 1943—included laying a land line from the brigade airfield to the closest heavy antiaircraft battery. Upon receiving warning of hostile aircraft over the antiaircraft artillery net, battery headquarters personnel telephoned the brigade airfield, which immediately broadcast a warning over the brigade air-observation-post net. The word "scramble" sufficed to warn of a *Luftwaffe* presence. In instances where aircraft were operating under battalion control from a battalion airstrip, the brigade commander required the battalion air officer to constantly monitor the Army channel, which the brigade officer would use to broadcast a general alert. Fifth Army artillery pilots did "limit somewhat" their penetrations over German lines but otherwise made no changes in their air operations. Ground units came to rely increasingly on high-speed fighters of the XII Air Support Command (later the XII Tactical Air Command) to observe fire for heavy and medium artillery at long ranges where penetration of German airspace was required. Between 6 October and 23 December, German fighters damaged at least five L–4s, but only two of these were actually shot down. In the process the *Luftwaffe* lost four fighters, victims of ground fire, of the pilots' failure to pull out of their attack runs in time to avoid crashing into mountainsides, or of some combination of the two. Such an unfavorable loss rate soon persuaded the *Luftwaffe* to seek more profitable targets, although a few chance meetings still occurred.[46]

The synchronization of air observation posts and antiaircraft defenses was typical of the sophisticated manner in which Fifth Army integrated air-observation-post operations with a broad range of activities. Liaison aircraft quickly became an important component of Fifth Army intelligence operations, valuable primarily for information on German troop movements and dispositions. The S–2 in the division artillery section or on the staff of an artillery group collected these reports and passed them on to the division or, where appropriate, corps G–2. When other means were not available, L–4s made special flights for G–2s to collect specific information. In addition, courier flights provided a quick and secure method of distributing time-sensitive documents and photographs.[47]

Despite the early concerns in the United States, enemy fighters did not prove to be the great nemesis of Field Artillery aircraft in the North African or later the Mediterranean

---

[45] "All Good Things Must End," p. 41; E. A. R., "Last of a 'Grasshopper,'" p. 812; Interv, Cummings, 26 Nov 43, in Rpt, AGF Board, 5 Dec 43, in AGF, "U.S. Field Artillery in World War II"; "Air OP Causes Trouble: Extract from History of the German Air Force in Italy," *FAJ* 36 (May 1946):271. Quote from Bourke-White, *"Purple Heart Valley,"* p. 11.

[46] Rpt, Lt Col L. A. Riggins, n.d., sub: Rpt on Italian Campaign; Notes, Maj Gen K. Truesdell and Lt Col G. W. R. Zethren, sub: Overseas Obsn Trip, Oct–Nov 43; Rpt, AGF Board, 4 Dec 43, [Extract]; Rpt, Lt Col P. L. Conant, 31 Dec 43, sub: Rpt on Italian Campaign During the Period 6 Oct to 22 Dec 43, [Extract]; Rpt, Lt Gen C. Hodges, CG, Third Army, 25 Dec 43, sub: Rpt of Visit to NATO, [Extract]; Interv, Cummings, 26 Nov 43; all in AGF, "U.S. Field Artillery in World War II"; "Air OP Causes Trouble," p. 271.

[47] Rpt, Mott, 29 Dec 43, sub: Rpt on Italian Campaign, in AGF, "U.S. Field Artillery in World War II."

Theater of Operations. Good airmanship, skillful use of terrain, flexible communications, and the integration of air-observation-post and antiaircraft artillery operations kept losses from enemy air action to manageable levels. Strok later estimated that 2 percent of all losses were due to German fighters. Flak and small-arms fire accounted for another 5 percent. The rest were due to accidents. "We certainly had a lot of accidents." Landings on rough fields accounted for most of these. Broken landing gears, the most common damage, "could be cobbled together" again, but broken propellers, also a common occurrence in such accidents, had to be replaced. Pilots could maneuver around enemy fighters and known flak locations, but they often could not avoid rough fields—and sometimes mountains.[48]

The onset of fall coupled with the rough terrain made even administrative flights very hazardous on occasion. On the morning of 26 October 1943, an assistant artillery air officer at Headquarters, Fifth Army, Capt. James Hall, took off with the Fifth Army artillery S–4, Maj. Thomas J. Webster, as a passenger. En route to a division airfield in the Volturno River Valley, they encountered a sudden fog. Disoriented, and without sufficient navigational aids, Hall flew into the side of a mountain near the village of Latina. Both men were killed instantly. Hall had graduated from Pilot Class 3 at Fort Sill and had served as a flight instructor at both the II Corps and Fifth Army Air Observation Post Schools. If such an experienced pilot could have such a crash, anyone could.[49]

Overall statistics on Fifth Army air-observation-post casualties are available for 1944. The first six months witnessed relatively heavy losses of aircraft—9 percent in January, 10 percent in February, 7 percent in May, and 6 percent in June. Not surprisingly, these were the months of heaviest ground combat. Fortunately, pilot casualties were not so severe. The two worst months, February and May, recorded loss rates of 4 and 7 percent, respectively. Pilot losses in other months remained at 2 percent or less.[50]

Air observation posts performed many missions in addition to observed fire, reconnaissance, and administrative flights. More often than not, these other missions were mundane rather than spectacular, but they facilitated Fifth Army operations in the rugged Italian terrain. With hills commonly interfering with line-of-sight radio transmissions from artillery observers accompanying advance elements of the infantry, it became standard procedure for liaison aircraft to act as radio relays. With somewhat less regularity, the planes relayed radio transmissions between adjacent line units. Where the tactical situation permitted, aircraft laid telephone wire to outposts. The limited carrying capacity of the L–4 initially restricted such missions to short stretches of the roughest terrain. Linemen could connect the ends of the air-laid wire to more conventionally built lines. On 28 May 1944, the 6th Field Artillery Group used this method to rapidly replace a telephone circuit that had taken over twenty-four hours to lay using traditional methods. Using Strok's modified bomb shackles, air observation posts frequently served as cargo carriers. An L–4 could drop two cases of rations and a five-gallon can of water to an iso-

---

[48] Incl, Dr. Jeffrey J. Clarke, Chief Historian, CMH, sub: Abbreviated Army Avn Panel Notes, in Memo, Clarke, 14 Jun 96, sub: Panel Rpt, Army Avn Ms, Historian's files, CMH. Strok collected statistics on losses of aircraft by cause during the war, but these documents have since been lost.

[49] AOP Bulletin no. 2, HQ, Fifth Army, Ofc of the Arty Ofcr, 7 Nov 43.

[50] Briefing Chart, sub: Fifth Army AOP Opns—1944, Strok Ms, Historian's files, CMH. The late Colonel Strok prepared this document after retirement to illustrate a talk he gave on air-observation-post operations during the war. He no longer had the original reports from which he extracted the statistics.

lated outpost and return to its field in thirty minutes. Many battalion commanders flew as passengers in air observation posts to select bivouac and command post locations. Once the II Corps secured the high ground south of the Rapido River in early December and ground observation became relatively more feasible, small strips sprouted near battalion command posts, and administrative and reconnaissance flights for the battalion command groups became more common.[51]

Operational control and air tactics represented in the main a continuation of techniques first developed in North Africa and Sicily. The dichotomy between centralized and decentralized control persisted. All corps artillery groups, at least through the winter of 1944, vested tactical control of the air sections with their respective battalion commanders. All administrative and logistical functions were centralized at the division artillery and group levels. This policy reflected the condition of the terrain. A scarcity of land suitable for airfields, as in Sicily, meant that division and group sections had to fly out of a central field. However, even in the decentralized groups, there was a measure of higher direction. The II Corps artillery air officer, 1st Lt. D. F. Dale, and later Capt. Jack L. Marinelli, assigned missions to groups, so the corps front was constantly covered by patrolling aircraft. Similar procedures developed in divisions. The artillery air officer assigned patrol sectors to each battalion section even where they remained under the operational control of the battalion commander. The 1st Armored Division artillery air officer, Capt. John W. Oswalt, recalled, "We were keeping almost a dawn to dusk patrol of the target area in order to locate gun flashes and [other things]." Air-observation-post operational tactics in practice thus closely approximated those of Air Service observation squadrons during World War I.[52]

Pilots in Fifth Army pioneered three tactical missions during the winter of 1943–1944. The importance of what became known as antiflak only increased as the war progressed. It involved sending light aircraft aloft just prior to scheduled close air support missions by XII Air Support Command light bombers and fighter-bombers. When German antiaircraft batteries opened fire on the American aircraft, they found battalion-size concentrations of artillery fire crashing down upon them. In this dilemma, German antiaircraft guns often remained silent, unless they were located beyond the range of American batteries or were

---

[51] Rpt, Col H. P. Storke, II Corps Arty Ofcr, to Arty Ofcr, Fifth Army, [Feb 44], in II Corps, "Employment of the Artillery of the II Corps During the Italian Campaign, 18 Nov 43 to 26 Feb 44" (Bound Ms, Morris Swett Tech Lib, 1944). Arty Bulletin no. 4, HQ, U.S. Army Forces Pacific Ocean Area (POA), 1 Nov 44, in U.S. Army POA, "Artillery Bulletins" (Bound Ms, Morris Swett Tech Lib, 1944–1945), describes wire laying in Italy. See also Memo, sub: Laying of Wire by Liaison Aircraft, Microfilm A1387, U.S. Air Force Historical Research Agency, Maxwell Air Force Base (AFB), Ala. (hereafter cited as AFHRA). For a discussion of aerial resupply in U.S. Third Army, see After Action Report (AAR), [Williams] to CG, Third Army, in Third Army, *After Action Report, U.S. Third Army, 1 August 1944–9 May 1945*, 2 vols. (Regensburg, Germany: 652d Engineer [Topographic] and 942d Aviation Engineer [Topographic] Battalions, 1945), 2:Arty–36.

[52] Arty Info Memo no. 2, Fifth Army, 20 Oct 43, in Fifth Army Arty, "Artillery Information Memoranda," lists the key personnel of the II Corps artillery section. Intervs, author with Strok, 30 Jun 82, and with Oswalt, 13–14 Jan 82; Memo, Lt Col R. D. Funk, 45th Inf Div, sub: Statement on FA, in Rpt, AGF Board, 2 Nov 43, [Extract], in AGF, "U.S. Field Artillery in World War II"; Interv, Lewis, in Rpt, AGF Board, 26 Nov 43, [Extract], in AGF, "AGF Board Reports" (Bound Ms, Morris Swett Tech Lib, 1943–1944); Arty Info Bulletin no. 1, U.S. Third Army, 28 Apr 44, in Third Army, "Third Army Artillery Information Bulletins" (Bound Ms, Morris Swett Tech Lib, 1944–1945). For the most extended (and poetic) account of "dawn patrols," see Maj. (Ret.) Alfred W. Schultz, "L–4 Dawn Patrol," *L–4 Grasshopper Wing Newsletter* 30 (December 1991/January 1992):1–3.

simultaneously attempting to repulse a major ground offensive. Without directing the fire of a single gun, one orbiting Cub could be as effective a counterbattery weapon for the Army Air Forces as for a truck convoy behind Allied lines.[53]

At the same time a number of pilots, including Capt. O. Glenn Goodhand, Jr., Captain Oswalt, and Lieutenant Strok, among others, began experimenting with directing artillery fire at night. The artillery air officer of the 35th Field Artillery Group, Captain Goodhand, recalled that because the group was highly decentralized at the moment, he had a great deal of time on his hands. His primary concern was providing observed fire at long ranges for the group's 155-mm. guns and howitzers. During daylight, the intervening hills obstructed an aerial observer's vision in a Cub, while the pilots in P–51s found they were moving too fast to identify the relatively small shell bursts. Goodhand conceived of night flights over the German lines as a means of solving this problem. Goodhand's first flight took him some twelve miles behind the German lines to make deep registrations on road junctions heretofore inviolate. Ground crews marked the edge of airstrips with homemade beacons—ration cans filled with dirt or sand, impregnated with gasoline, and set afire. If the field was too close to the German lines for such measures, ground crew members with handheld flashlights lined the landing area.[54]

While valuable—night flights were eventually used in virtually every theater—the procedure was possible, given the available technology, only in certain well-defined circumstances. It had to be a bright, moonlit night, with relatively little haze or fog, so terrain features were clearly visible. In some areas, particularly flat, low-lying coastal regions, meteorological conditions made night flights out of the question. Goodhand discovered this hard truth at Anzio when he attempted to replicate his Cassino successes. He simply could not see the ground well enough at night to observe fire. Even more common than true night flights, but usually referred to by that term, were twilight missions flown at first light and dusk, which required either a night takeoff or landing. German artillery, normally quiescent during daylight, became active in the hours of half light. Gun flashes, moreover, were much more visible at such times than in daylight. Consequently, it was a profitable time for spotter aircraft to be aloft and remained so because the Germans did not subsequently alter their artillery practices until the end of the war. No one had attempted or even contemplated an adjustment on a totally dark night.[55]

Artillery pilots and observers also began experimenting with aerial photography in the winter of 1943–1944. During the period of stalemate in front of the Gustav Line, counterbattery fire became the mission of primary importance for Allied artillery. The Germans skillfully concealed their battery positions, making them difficult to locate from the air unless caught in the act of firing. A skilled photographic interpreter, however, through close and often repetitious examination of aerial photographs, could often detect even well-cam-

---

[53] Rpt, Storke to Arty Ofcr, Fifth Army, [Feb 44]. For a discussion of subsequent employment of artillery aircraft on antiflak missions, see Rpts, Capt H. H. Reed, 975th FA Bn, to CO, 975th FA Bn, sub: Most Satisfactory Phase (Air Obsr); Pilot, 208th FA Grp, sub: Most Interesting Opn; Air Section, 208th FA Grp, sub: Most Interesting Opn; and Air Section, 250th FA Grp, sub: Most Interesting Opn or Phase; all in XV Corps Arty, "Historical Examples."

[54] Interv, Kramer and Andreson with Goodhand, 9 May 78.

[55] Rpts, Col N. P. Morrow, AGF Board Obsr, 5 Mar 44, sub: Special Rpt (NATO), [Extract], and Maj E. C. Townsend, G–2, 70th Inf Div, sub: Rpt on the Italian Campaign, [Extract], both in AGF, "U.S. Field Artillery in World War II." Interv, Kramer and Andreson with Goodhand, 9 May 78.

An L–4 with a Fairchild K–24 Aerial Camera Mounted for Oblique Photographs Takes Off from the Anzio Beachhead, 1944.

ouflaged gun positions, which created a great demand for such pictures. Aerial photography, however, was an Army Air Forces mission, and Army Air Forces units required photographic support just as ground units did. Unfortunately, from the ground forces perspective, the Army Air Forces units gave priority to the photographic requests of its own units. These circumstances stimulated L–4 observers to make oblique photographs of suspected battery positions using handheld aerial cameras. Such photographs supplemented the Army Air Forces' vertical photographs that when gridded could serve as a firing chart by allowing the photo interpreters at the Fifth Army Photographic Interpretation Center to distinguish real and dummy battery positions with much greater precision. On occasion, but relatively rarely in Italy, specially equipped L–4s could take vertical photographs as well.[56]

Air-observation-post sections also became some of the foremost consumers of aerial photographs. In its counterbattery program, Fifth Army artillery aimed not only to temporarily silence enemy batteries by driving gun crews under cover but also to physically destroy German guns. This required direct hits on individual German pieces. The procedure involved the Fifth Army Photographic Intelligence Center dispatching a grid photo-

---

[56] Ltr, Capt A. P. Colvocrisses, Fifth Army Photo Center (Ctr), to Eng, Fifth Army, 19 Oct 43, sub: Recommended Table of Organization (TO) for Eng Photo Intel Detachment and Duties of this Section; Ltr, Col F. O. Bowman, Eng, Fifth Army, to CS, Fifth Army, 25 Oct 43; Ltr, Col N. F. Grant, AG, Fifth Army, to CG, Allied Force HQ, Oct 43, sub: Activities and Assignment of Eng Photo Intel Section; all in HQ, AGF, Gen Corresp, 1942–1948 (C), 320.3/61, RG 337, NARA; Rpt, Lt Col P. P. Thoin, S–2, II Corps Arty, 20 May 45, II Corps Arty, "Aerial Photography and the Artillery Air OP" (Bound Ms, Morris Swett Tech Lib, 1945).

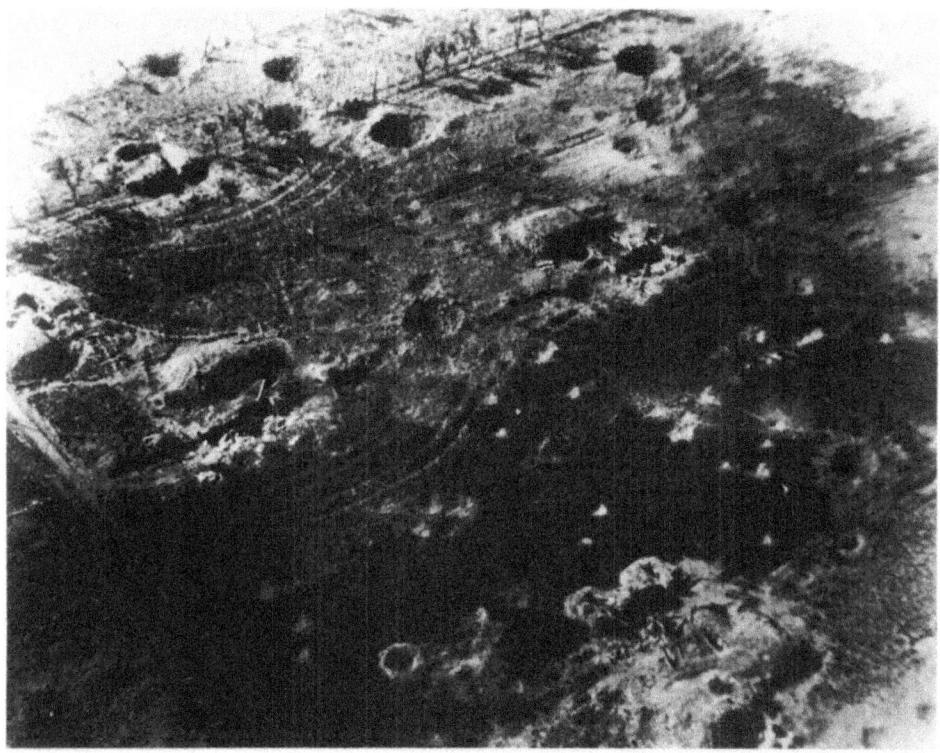

An Oblique-Angle Aerial Photograph Taken from an Air Observation Post Shows German Artillery Positions Destroyed by II Corps Artillery Counterbattery Fire. The Large Craters Were Caused by Aerial Bombs That Missed Their Targets.

graph with German battery positions indicated and a description of the batteries, including the number and caliber of the pieces, to the corps artillery S–2, who also functioned as the corps counterbattery officer. The assistant S–2 overlaid the batteries with concentric rings at 100-yard intervals and indicated the line of fire of the battery designated to engage the German guns. The S–2 forwarded copies to the relevant air sections through the corps artillery air officer. Every morning the S–2 and S–3 went over known German battery locations and selected some for deliberate counterbattery fire that day, and the corps artillery air officer notified the battalions involved. The pilots took the photographs during their normal patrols and, if no targets of opportunity developed, conducted the prearranged fires. Aerial photographs and the debris at captured German battery positions indicated the effectiveness of these procedures, which became standard American counterbattery practice in all theaters.[57]

The battle for the coastal town of Anzio behind the German lines became a kind of hothouse laboratory from which air observation posts benefited, along with American

---

[57] Rpt, Thoin, 20 May 45.

arms and services in general. The U.S. VI Corps landing at Anzio in January 1944 failed to force the Germans to abandon the defense of Italy south of Rome, but the German counterattacks designed to drive VI Corps back into the sea also failed. The result was stalemate with the Allies confined to a very shallow beachhead. The margin for Allied error was so small that the defenders of the beachhead were forced to refine their techniques and procedures to survive. The VI Corps artillery adopted special measures to ensure continuous observation and to reduce aircraft losses due to *Luftwaffe* attacks. Both corps and division air officers exercised a very tight centralized tactical control. The artillery air officer of the 35th Field Artillery Group, Captain Goodhand, operating under the guidance of the commander of VI Corps artillery, Brig. Gen. Carl A. Baer, prepared the standard operating procedure for air-observation-post operations over the beachhead. Goodhand divided the beachhead into four "air areas." Corps artillery allowed just one aircraft into an area at a time. Pilots were restricted to minimum time aloft. In contrast with operations on the main front, there were no air patrols initially. Each mission was carefully planned in advance. Air photos often were used to brief the pilots about their objectives.[58]

Given the air threat, the artillery pilots kept their altitudes to a minimum and avoided flying too far forward. Coordination of air-observation-post and antiaircraft operations became even closer than on the main front. The 3d Infantry Division Artillery first developed the "Islands of Safety" concept for artillery aircraft that spread to the rest of the corps and subsequently to the remainder of Fifth Army and other theaters. The division artillery commander, Brig. Gen. W. A. Campbell, emplaced concentrations of antiaircraft guns well forward and then notified the air-observation-post pilots of the location. If attacked in the air, the standard procedure in the division was for the pilot to fly to a position over one of these islands, so the antiaircraft artillery could ambush the intruder. In addition, corps arranged for air observation posts to receive warnings of incoming enemy aircraft from the antiaircraft artillery warning net. These arrangements sufficed to continue at Anzio the 2:1 ratio of *Luftwaffe* to liaison plane losses that prevailed on the main front and allowed the artillery observers to remain aloft, weather permitting, throughout the fighting around the beachhead (*Map 4*). By May 1944 air sections could mount standing patrols as on the main front. Although the *Luftwaffe* reacted aggressively, its actions only resulted in increased German losses. An officer in the 3d Infantry Division reported that in one two-day period German fighters made eleven separate attacks on division aircraft. The division lost no planes, while antiaircraft guns shot down three of the four enemy fighters making the last attacks.[59]

Air observation posts were a key element in the defense of the beachhead against two deadly weapons in German hands—tanks and mortars. Air observation posts and Army Air Forces reconnaissance squadrons provided the first warning of massed German armor, which

---

[58] Arty Info Bulletin no. 1, U.S. Third Army, 28 Apr 44, in Third Army, "Third Army Artillery Information Bulletins"; Interv, Kramer and Andreson with Goodhand, 9 May 78.

[59] Arty Info Memo no. 8, Fifth Army, 4 Mar 44, in Fifth Army, "Artillery Information Memoranda": Arty Info Bulletin no. 1, Eighth Army, Oct 44, in Eighth Army, "Artillery Information Bulletins" (Bound Ms, Morris Swett Tech Lib, 1944–1945); Interv, Kramer and Andreson with Goodhand, 9 May 78; Arty Info Bulletin no. 1, U.S. Third Army, 28 Apr 44, in Third Army, "Third Army Artillery Information Bulletins"; Ltr, Lt A. W. Schultz to Capt B. A. Devol, IX Corps Arty Air Ofcr, n.d., in Memo, Wolf, 15 Jun 44, sub: Informal Info, in FAS, Department of Air Training (DAT), "Training Memoranda" (Bound Ms, Morris Swett Tech Lib, 1944–1945).

INITIAL DEPLOYMENT AND COMBAT

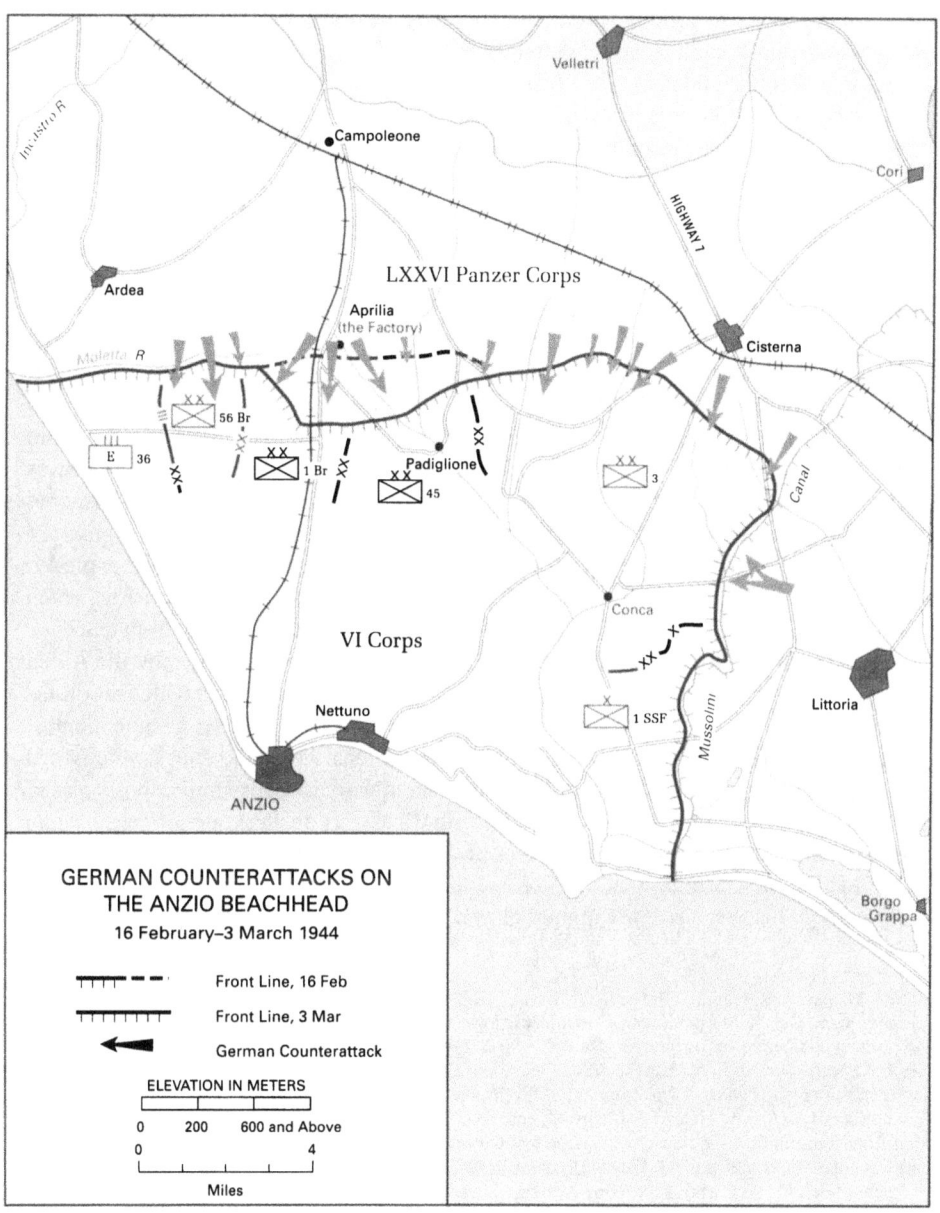

Map 4

tank destroyer battalions broadcast over an antitank warning net. This procedure allowed the defenders to mass their antitank guns in the threatened sector. Moreover, because the tank destroyers were tied into the division fire direction centers—a technique first experimented with in North Africa but only now brought to maturity—they could deliver indirect fire using artillery aircraft for observation. Mortars, in contrast, acted as a deadly weapon of harassment. The Germans became adept at determining the location of the Allied "no fire" line, within which artillery could not fire for fear of hitting friendly infantry, and then placing their mortars inside it. The 45th Infantry Division used its air observation posts to adjust the fires of its 4.2-inch chemical and 81-mm. mortars in a successful countermortar campaign.[60]

A shallow beachhead meant a very restricted airspace and brought two attendant hazards—that the German antiaircraft batteries would cover the entire area and prevent all aerial operations out of the beachhead and that friendly fire might shoot down air observation posts. Early in the operation some German gunners attempted to control the airspace. The artillery air officer of the 1st Armored Division, Captain Oswalt, won a Silver Star when a German 88-mm. shell struck his aircraft, breaking both of his spars but not exploding. Oswalt, who habitually flew without an observer, was able to keep his aircraft in the air for another ninety minutes adjusting fire on the German batteries, which were wiped out. Such retaliation eventually sufficed to deter the Germans from firing, but there was little that could be done about the second danger. When multiple calibers of friendly guns fired, there was little or no safe flight envelope over the beachhead. S. Sgt. Claude Allen of the 68th Armored Field Artillery Battalion, one of the members of Pilot Class 1 at Fort Sill, and his observer were killed over Anzio when an outgoing American tank round struck his L–4 and exploded just as Allen was taking off. It was the first of several such incidents during the war in which friendly fire directed at enemy ground targets struck a Field Artillery aircraft in midair.[61]

The planning and execution of Operation DIADEM, the spring offensive by the Allied armies in Italy against the Gustav and Hitler Lines, illustrated the degree to which air observation posts had become integrated into ground operations over the preceding nine months. To deceive the Germans as to the timing and the exact location of the attacks, the Allied armies in Italy engaged in an elaborate deception plan in which air observation posts played an important role. On Fifth Army's main front, the II Corps artillery air officer, Captain Marinelli, kept all corps artillery planes on one field, operating on a prescribed schedule, so as not to alert the Germans that a major operation was about to begin. In fact, the Allied artillery barrage that began on the night of 11–12 May caught the Germans by surprise.[62]

---

[60] Maj. Edward A. Raymond, "Brassing Off Kraut," *FAJ* 34 (October 1944):694–98; Arty Info Bulletin no. 1, U.S. Eighth Army, Oct 44, in Eighth Army, "Artillery Information Bulletins." For a further discussion of air observation posts in countermortar operations, see Rpt, Maj L. O. Rostenberg, Special Obsr, to CG, AGF, 21 Jan 45, sub: Rpt of Special Obsr in European Theater of Operations (ETO), 8 Sep–22 Dec 44, in AGF, "Report of Special Observer in European Theater of Operations (ETO)" (Bound Ms, Morris Swett Tech Lib, 1944–1945); Rpt, Col B. C. Anderson, FA Obsr, to HQ, AGF, 6 Nov 44, sub: AGF Rpt 372—Arty Rpt, HQ, AGF, G–4, Requirements Section, Development Div, FA Branch (Br), Decimal Corresp file, 1942–1945, 319.1 (ETO), RG 337, NARA; Robert C. Gildart, "Countermortar," *FAJ* 34 (December 1944):842–43, 847.

[61] Memo, [Gen M. W. Clark], sub: Army Avn Fact Sheet—1942–1949 Period, J. W. Oswalt, Col, U.S. Army (Ret), J. W. Oswalt Ms, Historian's files, CMH; Ltr, Maj H. L. Nelson, AAG, HQ, AGF, to CG, AAF, 19 Aug 42, sub: Orders, HQ, AGF, Gen Corresp, 1942–1948, 353/3 (FA Air Obsn) (Flying Status), RG 337, NARA; Michael Stern, "Up in a Maytag Messerschmidt," *True* (November 1944):17; Ltr, Oswalt to Tierney, 27 May 74; Interv, author with Oswalt, 13–14 Jan 82.

[62] Opns Memo no. 3, II Corps Arty, 8 May 44, sub: Arty Fire Plan for Corps Attack, App. A to Rpt 260, G–2, Fifth Army; Rpt, Fifth Army Interrogation Ctr, sub: Effects of Allied Arty Barrage; both in Fifth Army Arty, "The Artillery of the Fifth Army in the Initial Breakthrough Garigliano Offensive, May 11, 1944" (Bound Ms, Morris Swett Tech Lib, 1944). Rpt, Capt E. A. Gilleon, Air Obsr, 932d FA Bn, sub: Air Obsr—Most Interesting Opn, in XV Corps Arty, "Historical Examples." For background, see Ernest F. Fisher, Jr., *Cassino to the Alps*, U.S. Army in World War II (Washington, D.C.: U.S. Army Center of Military History, 1977), pp. 1–41.

INITIAL DEPLOYMENT AND COMBAT

Both U.S. Fifth and British Eighth Armies prepared elaborate artillery air plans for Operation DIADEM. Group pilots and observers were given the plan of attack of every corps in the two armies, and air sections collected all the intelligence needed by their respective corps. They knew the phase lines, points where the Germans might attempt to organize resistance, and current and possible locations of enemy batteries. An observer in an L–4 took oblique photographs of all known and suspected German battery positions, and photo interpreters at the Fifth Army Photographic Intelligence Center compared them with Army Air Forces overhead photographs. The juxtaposition allowed the photo interpreters to distinguish between real and dummy batteries. Consequently, the obliques played a key role in the developing Fifth Army's artillery fire plan.[63]

Once the operation began, directing counterbattery fire became the aerial

CAPTAIN OSWALT AT THE ANZIO BEACHHEAD, MARCH 1944

observer's first priority. Locating enemy movement, particularly counterattack forces, became his second. Army and corps headquarters, however, still needed immediate information about certain key areas, and pilots and observers from the six U.S. field artillery groups on the main front provided it. Because the operation involved crossing a major river and passing through a mountain barrier, group air sections played a crucial role in engineer operations. Planes from the 194th Field Artillery Group, for example, flew special sorties to keep informed in turn the engineers of the British XII Corps, Polish II Corps, and French Expeditionary Corps as to the presence of roadblocks and destroyed bridges. The pilot and observer in one aircraft witnessed the destruction of a bridge well in advance of friendly troops and radioed the information back to corps. The corps engineer staff studied photos of the site, determined the bridging materiel needed, and moved it forward, so when the infantry reached the river there was no delay in bridging the stream and passing wheeled and tracked vehicles to the other side.[64]

---

[63] An. 8 to Field Order (FO) 14, 13th FA Bde, 8 May 44, sub: Air Obsn Missions, in Fifth Army Arty, "Artillery of Fifth Army in the Initial Breakthrough"; Rpt, Air Section, 194th FA Grp, 29 May 45, sub: Most Interesting Opn, in XV Corps Arty, "Historical Examples"; II Corps Arty, "Aerial Photography and the Air OP"; Rpt, Col H. P. Storke, Arty Ofcr, II Corps, to Arty Ofcr, Fifth Army, [Feb 44], in II Corps, "Employment of Field Artillery with II Corps, Italian Campaign, 18 Nov 43–26 Feb 44" (Bound Ms, Morris Swett Tech Lib, 1944).

[64] An. 8 to FO 14, 13th FA Bde, 8 May 44, sub: Air Obsn Missions, in Fifth Army Arty, "Artillery of Fifth Army in the Initial Breakthrough"; Rpt, Air Section, 194th FA Grp, 29 May 45, sub: Most Interesting Opn, in XV Corps Arty, "Historical Examples"; Memo, sub: 194th FA Grp, Stroh Board files, Organizational History Br, CMH.

The 88th Infantry Division in the south, benefiting from the success of the French Expeditionary Corps on its flank, quickly broke through the German defenses and exploited enemy weakness. To keep the drive going, the division commander, Maj. Gen. John E. Sloan, used artillery pilots to drop food, ammunition, and maps to the leading infantry elements. Ration and supply trains, mule trains in the broken terrain, lagged far behind. These aerial resupply runs became so common, concluded the division historian, that "for a time at least, artillery could not be classed as rear echelon" as front-line riflemen had generally considered it.[65]

The VI Corps' simultaneous breakout from the Anzio beachhead unhinged the German defenses and inaugurated an all-too-brief period of mobile warfare in the Italian campaign. But it sufficed to carry the U.S. Fifth and British Eighth Armies well north of Rome. Once the Germans began to make deep daylight withdrawals, air-observation-post pilots and observers often experienced the frustration of discovering long columns of retreating Germans beyond the range of the nearest friendly artillery. Army Air Forces fighter-bombers constituted a possible solution, but there was no way for air-observation-post pilots to communicate directly with the fighter-bomber pilots. Going back through the division artillery S–3 was often too cumbersome a bureaucratic exercise to allow effective intervention on the battlefield. Moreover, in a rapidly changing situation, the pilot in a fast-moving aircraft like a P–40 or P–47, who had at best only a circumstantial familiarity with ground operations, had great difficulty distinguishing between friendly and enemy ground units. The 1st Armored Division in particular suffered numerous attacks by Army Air Forces fighter-bombers. One of the division's task forces, commanded by Col. Hamilton H. Howze—later the first director of Army Aviation and president of the 1962 Howze Board that led to the development of the first airmobile division—was strafed by P–47s coming back from a mission escorting bombers.[66]

This problem was temporarily overshadowed by the euphoria following the capture of the Italian capital. On 5 June 1944, General Clark entered Rome. The Italian campaign, which had until now represented the primary U.S. ground campaign against Germany, was about to be eclipsed by events to the north. Over the previous nine months air observation posts had developed into an integral part of ground operations in ways that their most ardent boosters of two years earlier had not even suspected. At the same time the Italian operations had become a model much studied by the rest of the U.S. Army as how best to use artillery aircraft in an active theater.

North of Rome

With the landings in Normandy, Italy became suddenly and irrevocably a secondary theater. While no one in authority completely ignored the Mediterranean Theater of Operations, it received much less attention in the War Department and Headquarters, Army Ground Forces, as a source for technique and doctrine. The Allied armies in the peninsula tied down thirty-one German divisions as of August 1944, and once the pursuit north of Rome ended,

---

[65] John P. Delany, *The Blue Devils in Italy: A History of the 88th Infantry Division in World War II* (Washington, D.C.: Infantry Journal Press, 1947), p. 79.

[66] Intervs, Kramer and Andreson with Goodhand, 9 May 78, and author with Oswalt, 13–14 Jan 82.

INITIAL DEPLOYMENT AND COMBAT   183

continued to advance, albeit slowly. One reason for the relative lack of movement was the terrain; the mountains north of Rome were even higher than south of the city. They created very demanding flying conditions, made the placement of airfields a skill that often required the wizardry of a sorcerer, and largely nullified Allied control of the air. Terrain plus the talent and tenacity of the German defenders created a powerful but unarticulated demand for some means to overcome this defensive combination other than by bloody frontal assaults. The demand remained unexpressed and unfulfilled, because in 1944 and 1945, given the available forces and shipping, there was no technical or tactical solution other than the one adopted.[67]

The pursuit north of Rome witnessed the development of a workable solution to the Army Air Forces friendly fire incidents that marred the Allied breakout from the Anzio beachhead. The commander of the 1st Armored Division, Maj. Gen. Ernest N. Harmon, was not the sort of soldier to suffer in silence. After the strafing of Task Force Howze, he threatened to shoot down any Army Air Forces aircraft that overflew the division in the future. In the end the XII Tactical Air Command and the 1st Armored Division worked out a compromise. The Army Air Forces supplied three high-frequency radios that permitted division pilots to communicate directly with the fighter-bombers. By this point Captain Oswalt had acquired three L–5s. He had the tops of their wings painted different colors to make them easily visible. Field Artillery pilots would call back to the fire direction center to report lucrative targets, and corps artillery would try to find out if any fighter-bombers were available. They system worked best if some were already airborne and in the general vicinity of the air observation posts. The 1st Armored Division Artillery pilots used the high-frequency radios to direct the fighter-bombers against German targets ahead of the division but out of artillery range. The procedure, code-named HORSEFLY and the antecedent of the modern forward air controller, proved quite effective but did not spread beyond the 1st Armored Division. Once the division reached the Arno River, it was pulled out of line and reorganized. The XII Tactical Air Command took back its radios at that time.[68]

The demise of the 1st Armored Division's HORSEFLY meant the elimination of Field Artillery aircraft and pilots from the emerging forward air control system, but not the end of the system itself. Over the first nine months of the Italian campaign, the XII Tactical Air Command had developed a system of ground-based controllers, fighter pilots equipped with high-powered radios and jeeps, called Rover Joe. Approximately the same time that Oswalt and other pilots from the 1st Armored Division Artillery flew HORSEFLY missions, XII Tactical Air Command, reputedly based on the suggestion of an anonymous pilot from the 1st Armored Division, developed a parallel system. Initially called Rover Joe's Cub and only later HORSEFLY, it used procedures similar to those in the 1st Armored Division. Fighter pilots acting as forward air controllers flew in L–5s from Army Air Forces liaison squadrons.[69]

---

[67] Fisher, *Cassino to the Alps*, pp. 302–03.

[68] Interv, author with Oswalt, 13–14 Jan 82; Hamilton H. Howze, "Thirty-five Years and Then Some: Memoirs of a Professional Soldier," (Unpublished Ms, MHI, c. 1992); John W. Oswalt, "L–4 Combat Operations: Operation HORSEFLY," *L–4 Grasshopper Wing Newsletter* 7 (February/March 1988):2–3. In 1983 the Air University honored Oswalt for his role in pioneering the forward air control system. MFR, author, 10 Jul 97, sub: Telephone Interv with Col John W. Oswalt, 10 Jul 97, Historian's files, CMH.

[69] "'Rover Joe' Control of Fighter Bombers," *OPD Information Bulletin* 4 (29 January 1945):6; AAF, *XII Tactical Air Command Tactical Operations: A Report on Phase 3 Operations of the XII Tactical Air Command for Army Air Forces Evaluation Board, European Theater of Operations* (n.p.: 64th Fighter Wing, 1945), pp. 11–12;

The administrative arrangements for air observation posts developed in Italy prior to the fall of Rome endured throughout the remainder of the war. There was one further elaboration. When the U.S. Fifth Army commander, General Clark, succeeded to the command of the 15th Army Group in December 1944, he created the post of artillery air officer on the army group staff and assigned the longtime Fifth Army artillery air officer, Colonel Walker, to fill the post. The II Corps artillery air officer, Major Marinelli, became the Fifth Army artillery air officer. When Walker was killed in February 1945, the 1st Armored Division artillery air officer, now Major Oswalt, advanced to the army group position.[70]

The Fifth Army Artillery Air Depot (Provisional), commanded by recently promoted Captain Strok, continued to provide logistical support for air sections in Italy but in a different guise. Headquarters, Army Air Forces, eventually discovered the existence of Strok's unit and developed a formal depot unit, army, modeled after it. The table of organization and equipment for the new unit, however, provided more personnel and equipment than Strok had available. The Air Staff decided to convert the provisional unit into a table of organization and equipment unit, the 3d Depot Unit (Army), which enabled Strok to provide better maintenance support. The only drawback from his perspective was that he and his men had to transfer from the Field Artillery to the Air Corps.[71]

Operational flying remained much as it had been during the first nine months of the campaign, except the mountains were higher. Pilots often had to fly through passes rather than over the mountains themselves. Weather conditions and wind currents could change quickly and cause trouble for even the best pilots. "You go out flying, real confident like, and a half hour later the field notifies you to return—weather is closing in." Near the mountaintops, "cold, turbulent winter wind[s]" buffeted aircraft; in the passes, sudden updrafts and downdrafts could fling aircraft around like toys. Two liaison pilots attempted to fly under cloud cover in one of the passes. They had approximately five hundred feet of clearance, but they did not make it. Turbulence flipped the aircraft onto their backs and slammed them into the side of a mountain. No one survived.[72]

The overall Fifth Army artillery statistics on air-observation-post losses for the last five months of 1944 bear out the weather-related dangers of light aircraft operations in the mountains. Beginning in August and extending through December, Fifth Army lost pilots and aircraft on a 1:1 ratio. In August the Allied armies arrived before the Gothic Line, the prepared position where the German theater commander, Field Marshal Albert Kesselring, hoped to hold them until spring. In so doing he protected the Po River Valley and the indus-

---

Richard P. Hallion, *Strike from the Sky: The History of Battlefield Air Attack, 1911–1945*, Smithsonian History of Aviation Series (Washington, D.C.: Smithsonian Institution Press, 1989), pp. 181–82. For development of the Rover Joe system, see Alan F. Wilt, "Allied Cooperation in Sicily and Italy, 1943–1945," in *Case Studies in the Development of Close Air Support*, ed. Benjamin F. Cooling (Washington, D.C.: Office of Air Force History, 1990), pp. 205–12.

[70] Memo 15, Fifth Army FA, 17 Sep 44, sub: Ofcr Personnel of Army and Corps Arty Sections, HQ, AGF, G–4, Requirements Section, Development Div, FA Br, Decimal Corresp file, 1942–1945, 319.1 (NATO), RG 337, NARA; Intervs, author with Strok, 30 Jun 82, and with Oswalt, 13–14 Jan 82; Forrest C. Pogue, *George C. Marshall: Organizer of Victory, 1943–1945* (New York: Viking Press, 1973), pp. 481–83; Fisher, *Cassino to the Alps*, p. 406; Truscott, *Command Missions*, p. 495. Clark was promoted to full general in March 1945.

[71] Interv, author with Strok, 30 Jun 82.

[72] Ltr, Oswalt to Capt J. W. Cummings, [Extract], in Memo, Maj D. V. Dale, 19 Mar 45, sub: Informal Info, Wolf Ms, Historian's files, CMH.

INITIAL DEPLOYMENT AND COMBAT

trial complex around Venice. British Eighth Army opened its offensive that same month, U.S. Fifth Army in September. The attacks continued until December, when the extreme fatigue of the ground troops and the increasingly bad weather led Kesselring's Allied counterpart, now Field Marshal Alexander, to postpone further major efforts until spring.[73]

Because air-observation-post losses were so low, only one aircraft and pilot per month for August, September, October, and December 1944—and five aircraft for November—it is impossible to draw any conclusions about individual months. The contrast between the last five months of the year and the first seven months is suggestive, however. Between January and July 1944, Fifth Army lost sixty-four aircraft and twenty-four pilots. Thus, 37.5 percent of the time that an aircraft either disappeared or was so badly damaged that it could not be rebuilt, the pilot was either killed or cap-

MAJOR MARINELLI, NOVEMBER 1944

tured or so severely injured that he had to be evacuated and consequently was lost to his unit for a considerable length of time. In contrast, between August and December, Fifth Army lost nine aircraft and nine pilots. Also striking about these figures is the small number of airplanes and pilots actually lost. This suggests that the Germans were considerably less capable of countering air-observation-post missions than earlier in the year.[74]

One of Major Oswalt's last flights for the 1st Armored Division illustrated the difficulties of flying in such demanding terrain. Early in December 1944 division artillery received a message from Combat Command A on the division's left flank that it was under artillery fire. The weather was awful—misting rain. Both passes through which a pilot would have to fly to complete the mission, Futa and Radicosa, were overcast. The cloud layer in the passes was "like a sliding lid on a cookie jar." Oswalt did not want to send up an airplane, but the need was urgent. At this point he was quite probably the most experienced combat aviator in the theater, so he elected to fly it himself. He thought a forced landing was very likely, and in such a circumstance a Cub was much more forgiving than an L–5. The breakaway landing gear on an L–4, a source of constant complaint from artillery commanders, absorbed much of the impact in a crash, snapping off but leaving the fuselage—and the pilot—intact.[75]

---

[73] Briefing Chart, sub: Fifth Army AOP Opns—1944, Strok Ms, Historian's files, CMH; Fisher, *Cassino to the Alps*, pp. 312–413.
[74] Ibid.
[75] Interv, author with Oswalt, 13–14 Jan 82.

Once over Combat Command A's position, Oswalt located the German artillery, a battery of 150-mm. guns, and adjusted fire on it. Then, a German antiaircraft battery took some P–47s under fire. He identified the battery's location and directed fire on it. At this point, some two hours and fifteen minutes into the mission, it was time to leave. A Cub normally had about two-and-a-half hours of endurance. Oswalt and the other veterans had learned to coax an extra hour out of the Continental A–65–8 engine by throttling back at altitude. The firing battalion, however, requested Oswalt to remain on station a little longer to observe the effectiveness of a time on target. He observed its success and then pointed the L–4 toward the division strip. Unfortunately, the passes had a venturi effect on the wind, greatly increasing its force. At full power the L–4 could make little progress against it. Reluctantly concluding that he indeed had to make a forced landing, Oswalt checked his bearings and descended into the overcast.[76]

Once in the clouds, Oswalt had to depend largely on his own instincts. The air speed indicator recorded only the velocity of the air passing the aircraft. To calculate the speed over the ground, the pilot had to know the force and direction of the wind. In a condition of no visibility, the standard compass could provide minimal information about heading. Unfortunately for Oswalt, the pass was not perfectly straight, and at the time he entered the cloud he was correcting for a crosswind. While without visual references, he flew into the shadow of a mountain that blocked out the crosswind. Unknowingly, he continued to correct for drift. In effect, he was flying into the side of the pass. He did not realize his error until he broke out of the overcast a few feet above ground. There was only time to gun his engine, which gave him enough power to bounce his wheels off the cab of an Army 2 1/2-ton truck and then "land" in about two feet of mud. The craft immediately stopped—there was no landing roll at all—and nosed over. Oswalt, still in radio contact with his division strip, gave the coordinates of his landing site. Someone in the air section thought for certain that he had made a mistake: "It's the side of a mountain." It was even worse than that: It was in the middle of an ammunition dump. The next day a truck fetched the plane and pilot. The former required a new landing gear and propeller, but both were soon flying again. A similar circumstance involving an L–5 with its shatterproof landing gear would have damaged the aircraft and possibly the pilot beyond repair. "But that was the beauty of a Cub."[77]

In December 1944 the new commander of U.S. Fifth Army, Lt. Gen. Lucian K. Truscott, Jr., established his advance headquarters at Futa Pass. Truscott made heavy use of liaison aircraft to facilitate command and control, just as he had as a division and corps commander earlier in the war. Consequently, the army artillery air officer, Major Marinelli, had to construct an airstrip for the army air section close to headquarters in totally unsuitable terrain. In fact, Marinelli eventually had to build the strip, known as the Ski Jump, on the side of a mountain. The name adequately conveys the contour of the landing area. It was shorter than a regular field, but takeoffs, all downhill, required only about one-third the usual takeoff roll.

---

[76] Ibid. "Venturi effect" refers to the changes in air or fluid forced from one chamber to another through a narrow, tapered opening—an increase in speed with a corresponding decrease in pressure.

[77] Interv, author with Oswalt, 13–14 Jan 82; Piper Aircraft Corp., *How To Fly a Piper Cub* (Lock Haven, Pa.: Piper Aircraft Corp., 1946), p. 15. Since the pilot was unharmed and the plane repairable, neither became a statistic in the Fifth Army air-observation-post losses for December 1944. These figures were maintained to request replacement aircraft and pilots, and researchers must bear this purpose in mind when utilizing them.

U.S. FIFTH ARMY'S "SKI JUMP" AIRSTRIP AT FUTA PASS, ITALY, 1944

This was fortunate, because the strip ended abruptly in a sheer drop. Landings, all uphill, also require less than the usual distance, another advantage in that the uphill end abutted a rock face. All who flew in or out of the Ski Jump remembered it vividly.[78]

The Allies opened what proved to be their final offensive in Italy on 9 April 1945. By 20 April Fifth Army had broken out of the mountains into the Po River Valley. A successful, if confused, pursuit followed as American armor columns sliced through and between elements of retreating Germans. This intermingling made it difficult for pilots and observers to sort out the situation on the ground. On 29 April Truscott attempted to fly over the 6th South African Armored Division, only to discover that a German flak battery held the ground. Only Marinelli's superb airmanship kept Truscott unscratched—if unsettled. Three days later the German armies in northern Italy surrendered.[79]

This brief, exhilarating mobile interlude did not, however, displace the months of grinding mountain warfare as the dominant memory among the veterans of the campaign.

---

[78] Intervs, Powell and Courts with Williams, 1978; Maj Gen W. A. Harris with Col Gordon J. Wolf, c. 1983; author with Oswalt, 13–14 Jan 82; Ltr, Lt Col R. R. Williams to Col R. C. Moffat, 17 Apr 45, Microfilm A1387, AFHRA.

[79] Rpt, [Maj Jack L. Marinelli], 26 May 45, sub: Fifth Army AOP Historical Data of Bologna–Po Valley Offensive, in Fifth Army Arty, "History of the Artillery of the Fifth Army: Po Valley Campaign, 14 April–2 May 1945" (Bound Ms, Morris Swett Tech Lib, c. 1945); Truscott, *Command Missions*, p. 495; Interv, author with Oswalt, 13–14 Jan 82.

Infantrymen and pilots together formed a ready-made constituency for a solution to the tactical conundrum posed by the terrain and the German Army. In the immediate postwar period some forward-looking veterans saw the troop-carrying helicopter as the answer. In fact, Marinelli and Oswalt became key players in the acceptance and early development of rotary-wing aircraft by the Army. Thus, in a real sense, while the Italian campaign became in its last eleven months a sideshow in the conduct of World War II, it remained a theater of central importance in the evolution of what would become Army Aviation.

Conclusion

By mid-1944 air observation posts had demonstrated their ability to perform the aerial fire-direction mission in combat in all the theaters in which they had been employed. Success came first in North Africa, but not without false starts and considerable local innovation. Field Artillery air officers joined the command staffs at army and corps levels and eventually, after the Sicilian campaign, at theater and army group levels. General Clark and Colonel Lewis created a school to provide pilots and mechanics to the North African Theater of Operations until Fort Sill could produce the necessary numbers. They also compelled the War Department to address the intertheater logistical problem, while they solved the worst of the intratheater supply and maintenance difficulties with the creation of Lieutenant Strok's Fifth Army Artillery Air Depot. The air section's relative failure in southern Tunisia called the existence of the program into question, but its senior backers, especially Assistant Secretary of War McCloy, remained firm in their support and granted the time needed to find a solution. The informal network of commanders and staffs assisting the program thus remained active behind the scenes and continued to have a major impact upon its success. The key was doctrine. Grasshopper tactics simply did not work in most combat situations, and over time pilots replaced them with more extended flights at higher altitudes that culminated in Italy with air sector patrols. In a real sense, Field Artillery pilots replaced tactics that mimicked balloon operations during World War I with observation squadron tactics from the same conflict. Of course, since officially their aircraft were unarmed, they lacked the ability to engage ground troops directly from the air. Their ability to influence the ground battle lay in the proficiency with which they could guide artillery fire to ground targets.

During Fifth Army's campaign south of Rome, air observation posts became a fully integrated component of ground warfare and a model for the rest of the Army. They performed such a wide variety of missions that L–4s became almost as ubiquitous as jeeps and just as much in demand. The Normandy invasion, however, reduced Italy to a secondary theater. After 6 June 1944, the expanded scale of air-observation-post operations in France and later in Germany meant that Fifth Army artillery aviators became much less important to the Army as a whole. Italy became something of a doctrinal backwater, at least superficially. The high mountains north of Rome simply reinforced a lesson already learned; Field Artillery pilots required aircraft more powerful than the L–4 in such terrain. But the tactical impasse posed by the terrain led in other altogether radical directions— toward vertical takeoffs and rotary wings.

CHAPTER 6

The European Theater of Operations, June 1944–September 1945

The Normandy invasion of 6 June 1944 opened the principal ground campaign of World War II for the U.S. Army against its primary enemy. The War Department concentrated more men and materiel in the European Theater of Operations than in any other overseas theater. Europe consequently obtained more air observation posts than any other theater because the light planes were organic to ground units. In western Europe, Field Artillery pilots demonstrated for the first time the ability of air sections to support ground units during extended mobile operations. Although Field Artillery pilots continued to perform invaluable services in both Italy and the Pacific, the number of aircraft involved and the sophistication of technique that developed during the last year of the war made western Europe the center of attention.

The European Theater of Operations: Administration and Logistics

Artillery air officers in the European Theater of Operations took over staff supervision of air observation posts at all echelons of command during late 1943 and early 1944, following standard practice in Italy. The Italian campaign model proved so influential in part because many of the senior American officers, beginning with the supreme commander, General Dwight D. Eisenhower, came out of the Mediterranean. The first of them to arrive in the United Kingdom (in October 1943), Lt. Gen. Omar N. Bradley, had a dual responsibility. He would command both U.S. First Army and the 1st Army Group during the initial stages of cross-Channel operations. First Army would actually control the American forces during the assault. The 1st Army Group, redesignated 12th Army Group before it deployed to France, would control multiple American armies once the Allies had secured a sufficient lodgment in Normandy to employ them. Eisenhower, who remained in the Mediterranean for the moment, allowed Bradley to bring selected staff officers with him, one of whom was the II Corps chief of artillery, Col. (later Brig. Gen.) Charles E. Hart. Hart in turn brought along two members of his artillery section, one of them his artillery air officer, Maj. Delbert L. Bristol. He became the First Army artillery air officer and the first aviator in the higher echelons of command. Maj. (later Lt. Col.) Charles W. Lefever arrived in January 1944 to become the artillery air officer of the 1st Army Group. By sum-

BRIG. GEN. H. B. LEWIS PRESENTS THE BRONZE STAR TO COLONEL LEFEVER, JUNE 1945.

mer Maj. Eugene P. Gillespie had taken up a similar post on the theater staff. Army headquarters deploying from the United States brought artillery air officers with them: Maj. (afterward Lt. Col.) Bryce Wilson in Third Army, commanded by Lt. Gen. George S. Patton, Jr.; Lt. Col. Robert M. Leich in Ninth Army, commanded by Lt. Gen. William H. Simpson; and Maj. Paget W. Thornton in the late-forming Fifteenth Army, commanded by Lt. Gen. Leonard T. Gerow. The higher headquarters that entered the theater out of the Mediterranean following the invasion of southern France contained similar positions. Maj. Ford E. Allcorn served as the 6th Army Group artillery air officer, while Maj. Claude L. Shepard, Jr., continued as the artillery air officer of Seventh Army, the post he had held in Sicily. Lt. Gen. Jacob L. Devers and Lt. Gen. Alexander M. Patch commanded these organizations.[1] (*Chart 11*)

The army group represented a new echelon of command for artillery air officers. The duties of Lefever and Allcorn mirrored the command philosophies of their respective commanders, Generals Bradley and Devers. Lefever's duties were primarily administrative and logistical. Bradley favored a large staff that prepared formal plans and detailed taskings for his army commanders. Like the other members of the army group artillery section, Lefever had three general functions: to anticipate air-observation-post operations and needs six months in advance; to troubleshoot; and to recommend the most advantageous deployment of air observation posts. Specifically, he maintained statistical data on the attrition rates of men, aircraft, and ancillary equipment and usage rates for all classes of supply so as to better forecast replacement and resupply needs. He also disseminated information on employing aircraft received from the United States and other theaters. He spent approximately one-quarter of his time coordinating with other headquarters—theater, Ninth Air Force, British, and the armies assigned to the army group. Allcorn, while not devoid of administrative and troubleshooting responsibilities, functioned much more as a personal pilot than did Lefever. Devers, unlike Bradley, favored an informal method of command and a much smaller headquarters. Devers gave his army commanders

---

[1] 12th Army Group (Grp), *Report of Operations (Final After Action Report)*, 14 vols. (n.p.: Headquarters, 12th Army Group, 1945), 1:5–7, 11:82–86, 99–100; Interviews (Intervs), author with Lt Col Charles W. Lefever, 4 Sep 91, U.S. Army Center of Military History, Washington, D.C. (hereafter cited as CMH); L. B. Epstein with Col Delbert L. Bristol, 1 Jul 75, U.S. Army Aviation and Troop Command History Office, St. Louis, Mo. (hereafter cited as USAA&TC); Charles E. Hart, "Artillery Representation on High Level Before and During Combat," *Field Artillery Journal* (*FAJ*) 38 (September–October 1948):208–13.

THE EUROPEAN THEATER

CHART 11—FIELD ARTILLERY AIR OFFICERS IN THE EUROPEAN THEATER OF OPERATIONS, 1944–1945*

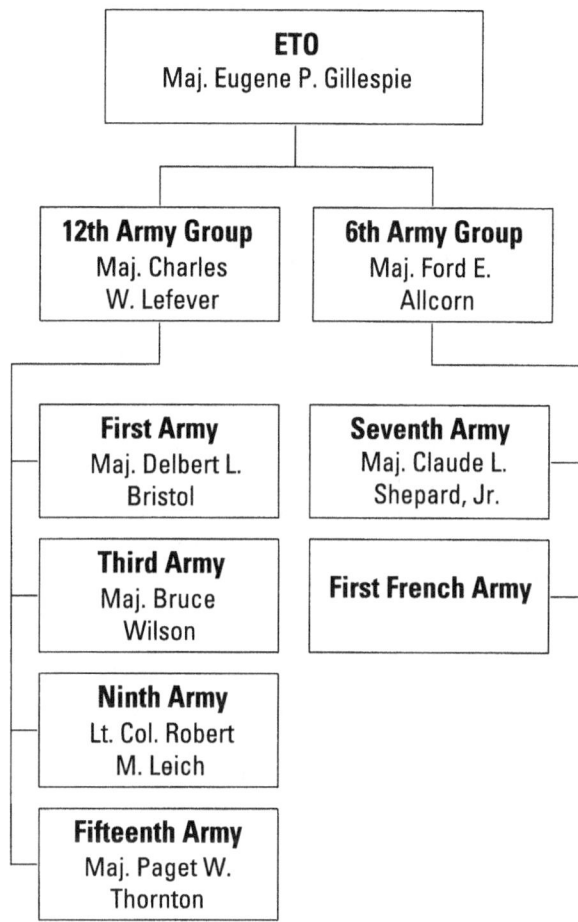

* This chart shows the command relations between the headquarters. The individuals named, however, were all staff officers.

general missions and expected them to perform the necessary detailed planning. Frequently using a light plane for transportation, he personally performed much of the necessary coordination with the army commanders at their headquarters.[2]

---

[2] 12th Army Grp, *Report of Operations*, 11:84–85, 99–100; Charles B. MacDonald, *The Mighty Endeavor: American Armed Forces in the European Theater in World War II* (New York: Oxford University Press, 1969), pp. 407–09; Interv, author with Col C. L. Shepard, 23 Sep 83, CMH; Seventh Army, *The Seventh United States Army Report of Operations: France and Germany, 1944–1945*, 3 vols. (Heidelberg, Germany: Aloys Graf, 1946), 1:1–149; Alan F. Wilt, *The French Riviera Campaign of August 1944* (Carbondale: Southern Illinois University Press, 1981); Jeffrey J. Clarke and Robert R. Smith, *Riviera to the Rhine*, U.S. Army in World War II (Washington, D.C.: U.S. Army Center of Military History, 1993).

Bristol became the key person in artillery air preparations for the invasion of France through a combination of factors—early arrival, prior experience, the First Army mission, and personality. He quickly acquired several assistants who enabled him to delegate questions of detail, allowing him to concentrate on the larger picture. His first and most important mission was to outfit the air sections organic to the four corps in First Army—involving some three hundred aircraft. Pilots and ground crew deployed from the continental United States with only their personal gear. They received their unit equipment, airplanes, spare parts, tools, and supplies upon arrival in theater. Bristol quickly discovered that logistical support for air observation posts in the theater was an administrative nightmare. Working closely with the staff of Headquarters, Ninth Air Force, he was able to establish administrative control over the issue of supplies and equipment. He also persuaded the Ninth Air Force to centralize artillery air supply and depot-level maintenance at the Third Tactical Air Depot located at Grove, England. During April and May 1944, the artillery air officer of XII Corps, Capt. (later Maj.) Thomas E. Haynes, working with a major from the Third Tactical Air Depot, coordinated the assembly and delivery of all Field Artillery aircraft.[3]

With the question of the initial issue of equipment on the way to solution, Bristol and Lefever, who had arrived in Great Britain by this time, turned their attention to setting up a system of supply that would sustain Field Artillery aircraft during combat. They conferred with Ninth Air Force representatives, who explicitly accepted responsibility for upper-echelon maintenance. Together they worked out in detail the channels for supply from Army Air Forces depots in the United Kingdom to air sections in the field. They also obtained an agreement on the levels of supply that organizations would maintain at each echelon in the supply chain. (See *Charts 12–14*.) During this period they met with one another almost daily and nearly as frequently with representatives from the Army Air Forces.[4]

Bristol also had to decide how to handle third-echelon maintenance in First Army. Third-echelon maintenance consisted of overhauls, repairs, and unit replacement beyond the capabilities of the air sections and was provided by mobile maintenance organizations. Establishing an artillery air depot as in Fifth Army was certainly one alternative—one that Bristol opposed. He thought the Fifth Army unit was too weak to provide adequate support. Moreover, it lacked organic vehicles and was thus essentially immobile, not the kind of unit needed to support armies engaged in the scale of mobile warfare

---

[3] Intervs, Epstein with Bristol, 1 May 75, and author with Col T. E. Haynes, 26 Feb 92, CMH.

[4] 12th Army Grp, *Report of Operations*, 11:84–85, 99–100; Interv, author with Lefever, 4 Sep 91. Charts 12 and 13 are composites drawn from the following sources: Wesley Frank Craven and James Lea Cate, *The Army Air Forces in World War II*, 7 vols. (Chicago: University of Chicago Press, 1945–1958), 3:107–21; Chart, 24 Nov 44, sub: Organizational Chart of the Ninth Air Force, and 8 May 1945, sub: Organizational Chart of the Ninth Air Force, both in William B. Reed, et al., eds., "The IX Service Command," vol. 8, part 1, of "The Ninth Air Force and Its Principal Commands in the European Theater of Operations" (Unpublished [Unpubl] Manuscript [Ms], U.S. Air Force Historical Research Agency, Maxwell Air Force Base, Ala. [hereafter cited as AFHRA]), charts following pp. 29, 41–42 (Reel B5587); Chart, sub: Organization of IX Air Force Service Command, "IX Air Force Service Command Headquarters History . . . September 1944" (Unpubl Ms, AFHRA), p. 9 (Reel B5598). Sources for Chart 14 include "[History of] Headquarters, First Tactical Air Force Service Command (Provisional)" (Unpubl Ms, Headquarters, U.S. First Tactical Air Force Service Command [Provisional], 1945) (AFHRA), Microfilm C5205; Organizational Charts, First Tactical Air Force (Provisional), Microfilm C5205; Interview, author with Col Richard L. Long, 23 Jul 82, CMH.

envisioned on the Continent. Using Colonel Hart's good offices, Bristol worked out an arrangement for Ninth Air Force to allot the responsibility for all third-echelon light aircraft repair to a single unit, the 23d Mobile Reclamation and Repair Squadron. It had over twice the manpower of the Fifth Army Artillery Air Depot as well as its own organic transportation. Acquiring additional officers and enlisted men for his staff subsection, Bristol used them to maintain liaison with the squadron to ensure that the squadron's repair priorities always coincided with First Army's, which would vary with the scheme of maneuver.[5]

The Ninth Air Force connection also proved valuable in two other respects. When the first Army Air Forces liaison squadron arrived in theater, Bristol arranged through Hart to exchange a limited number of L–4s for L–5s. Eventually, he provided two L–5s for each corps and division air section in First Army; like his counterparts in Italy, he was very impressed with the performance characteristics of the L–5. A second squadron, the 153d Liaison Squadron, was intended to support First Army. Bristol favored accepting it because the squadron promised to relieve artillery pilots of the secondary, but time-consuming, mission of communications flights. Because this would be the squadron's primary mission, he agreed that they should be assigned to the First Army signal officer, Col. Grant A. Williams. In practice, this decision proved unfortunate, because the squadron commander was uncooperative. Bristol could not coordinate the activities of the liaison squadron with artillery air operations because he was in a parallel chain of command. Only the army commander, first Bradley and then Lt. Gen. Courtney H. Hodges, could resolve disputes. Consequently, many problems were not settled.[6]

First Army's administrative and logistical arrangements became a model for the other armies that staged through the United Kingdom. Prior to commitment to combat, Third Army drew upon the Third Tactical Air Depot for aircraft equipment and higher-echelon maintenance. Once activated on the Continent, Third Army's air-observation-post sections obtained higher-echelon maintenance and technical supplies from the Army Air Forces' 43d Mobile Reclamation and Repair Squadron. The artillery air sections of the subsequently activated Ninth and Fifteenth Armies received support from the 50th and 27th Mobile Reclamation and Repair Squadrons, respectively. Seventh Army, coming out of the Mediterranean, followed the Fifth Army model for air-observation-post supply and maintenance. The 4th Depot Unit (Army), commanded by Capt. Richard L. Long, was activated in Italy during the spring of 1944 and attached to Seventh Army. In contrast to the mobile reclamation and repair squadrons, which remained in the Ninth Air Force chain of command, the 4th Depot Unit was under the operational control of Seventh Army.[7]

---

[5] Interv, Epstein with Bristol, 1 Jul 75; First Army, *First United States Army Combat Operations Data, Europe, 1944–1945*, 4 vols. (New York: Headquarters, First Army, 1946), 3:162; "Echelon Maintenance," in War Department (WD), Technical Manual (TM) 20–205, *Dictionary of United States Army Terms* (Washington, D.C.: Government Printing Office, 1944), p. 97.

[6] Interv, Epstein with Bristol, 1 Jul 75; First Army, *Combat Operations Data*, p. 247.

[7] Air Observation Post (AOP) Bulletin nos. 1, Third Army, 20 May 44, and 2, Third Army, 1 Sep 44, both in Third Army, *After Action Report, Third U.S. Army, 1 August 1944 to 9 May 1945*, 2 vols. (n.p.: [Third Army], 1945), 2:Arty-5, 8; First Army, *Combat Operations Data*, 3:162; WD, Table of Organization and Equipment (TO&E) 1–407, 4 May 44, sub: Depot Unit (Army); Interv, Epstein with Bristol, 1 Jul 75. Intervs, author with Lt Col B. Wilson, 3 Aug, 6 Nov 91; with Col William R. Mathews, 24 Feb 92; with Col Richard L. Long, 23 Jul 82; all at CMH.

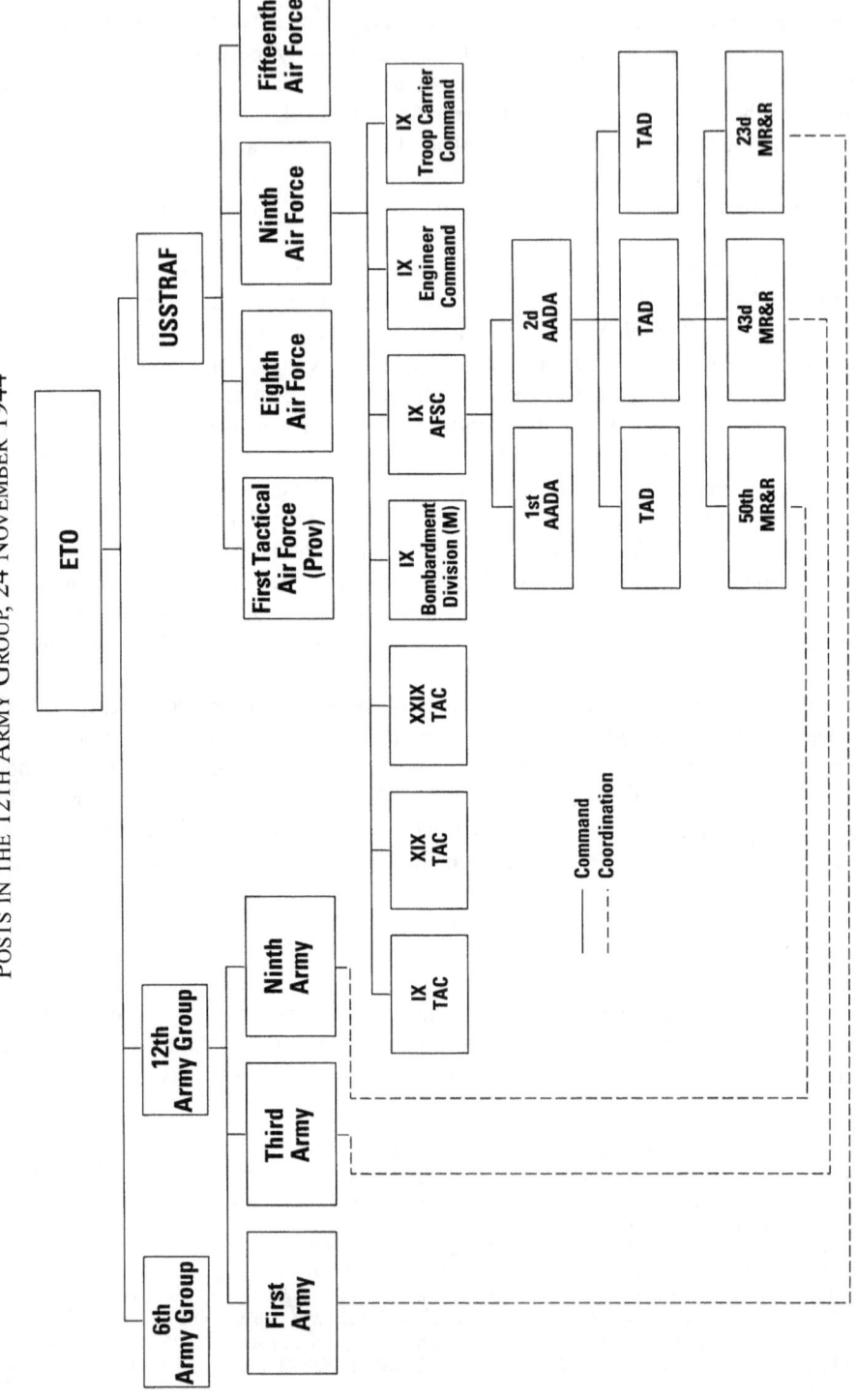

Chart 12—Organization of Army Air Forces Logistical Support for Field Artillery Air Observation Posts in the 12th Army Group, 24 November 1944

CHART 13—ORGANIZATION OF ARMY AIR FORCES LOGISTICAL SUPPORT FOR FIELD ARTILLERY AIR OBSERVATION POSTS IN THE 12TH ARMY GROUP, 8 MAY 1945

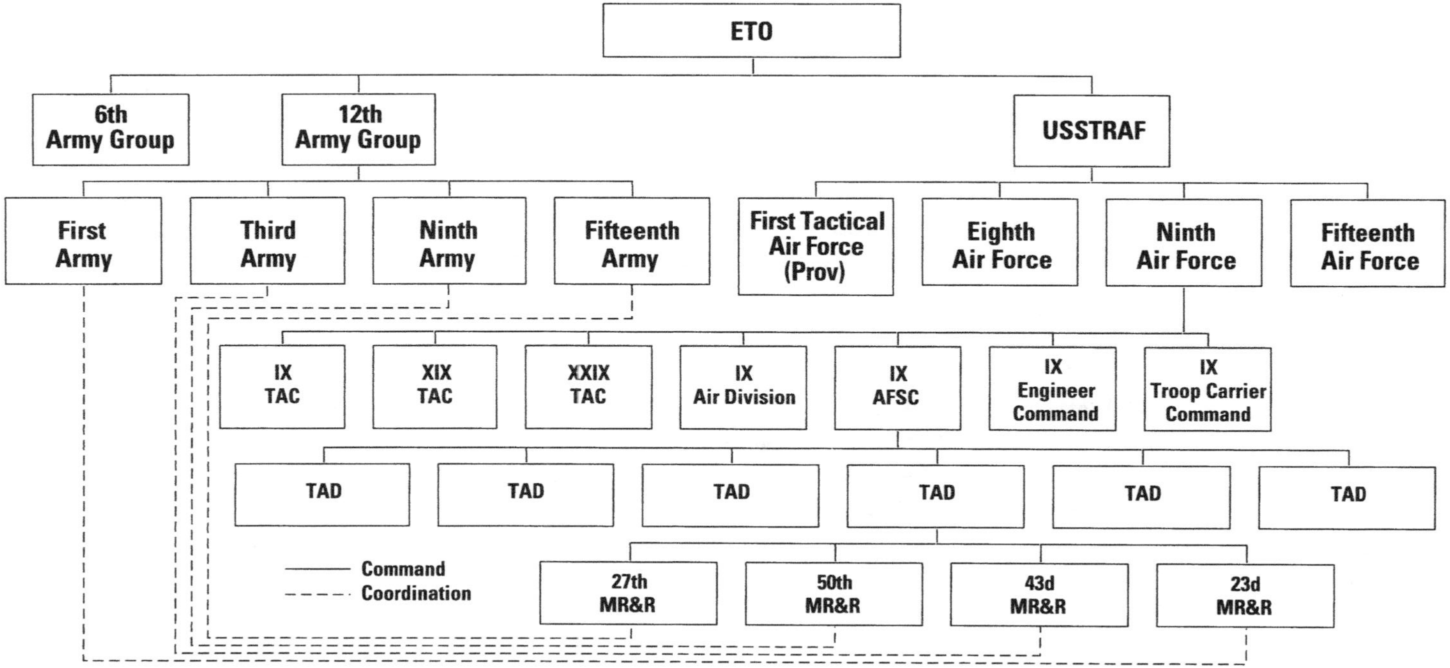

```
                                    ETO
                                     |
              ┌──────────────────────┼──────────────────────┐
              |                                             |
         12th Army Group                                USSTRAF
              |                                             |
   ┌──────────┼──────────┬──────────────┐      ┌────────────┼────────────┬─────────────┐
6th Army    Third      Ninth        Fifteenth  First      Eighth       Ninth       Fifteenth
 Group       Army       Army          Army    Tactical   Air Force    Air Force    Air Force
   |                                          Air Force
First                                          (Prov)
Army
```

```
    IX        XIX       XXIX       IX        IX        IX           IX
    TAC       TAC       TAC      Air Div    AFSC    Engineer    Troop Carrier
                                                    Command       Command

    TAD       TAD       TAD       TAD        TAD      TAD           TAD

    27th      50th      43d       23d
    MR&R      MR&R      MR&R      MR&R
```

——— Command
- - - Coordination

AADA	Advanced Air Depot Area
AFSC	Air Force Service Command
ETO	European Theater of Operations
M	Medium
MR&R	Mobile Reconstruction and Repair Squadrons
Prov	Provisional
TAC	Tactical Air Command
TAD	Tactical Air Depots
USSTRAF	U.S. Strategic Air Forces

Charts 12 and 13 are simplified to show only logistical support for air observation posts. All Ninth Air Force subordinate headquarters had a great many other responsibilities in addition to this one. Headquarters, U.S. Strategic Air Forces, was the senior Army Air Forces headquarters over the First Tactical Air Force (Provisional) and Ninth Air Force. The Allied Expeditionary Air Forces, however, exercised operational control over them, which meant that in practice Headquarters, U.S. Strategic Air Forces, performed only the administrative functions associated with command. In Ninth Air Force, the IX Air Force Service Command organized two intermediate headquarters, called Advanced Air Depot Areas, to control operations when the air force had units operating out of bases in the United Kingdom and the Continent. The service command closed the 2d Advanced Air Depot Area on 1 February and the 1st Advanced Air Depot Area on 1 March 1945. Chart 13 shows the organization as it had evolved by the end of the war.

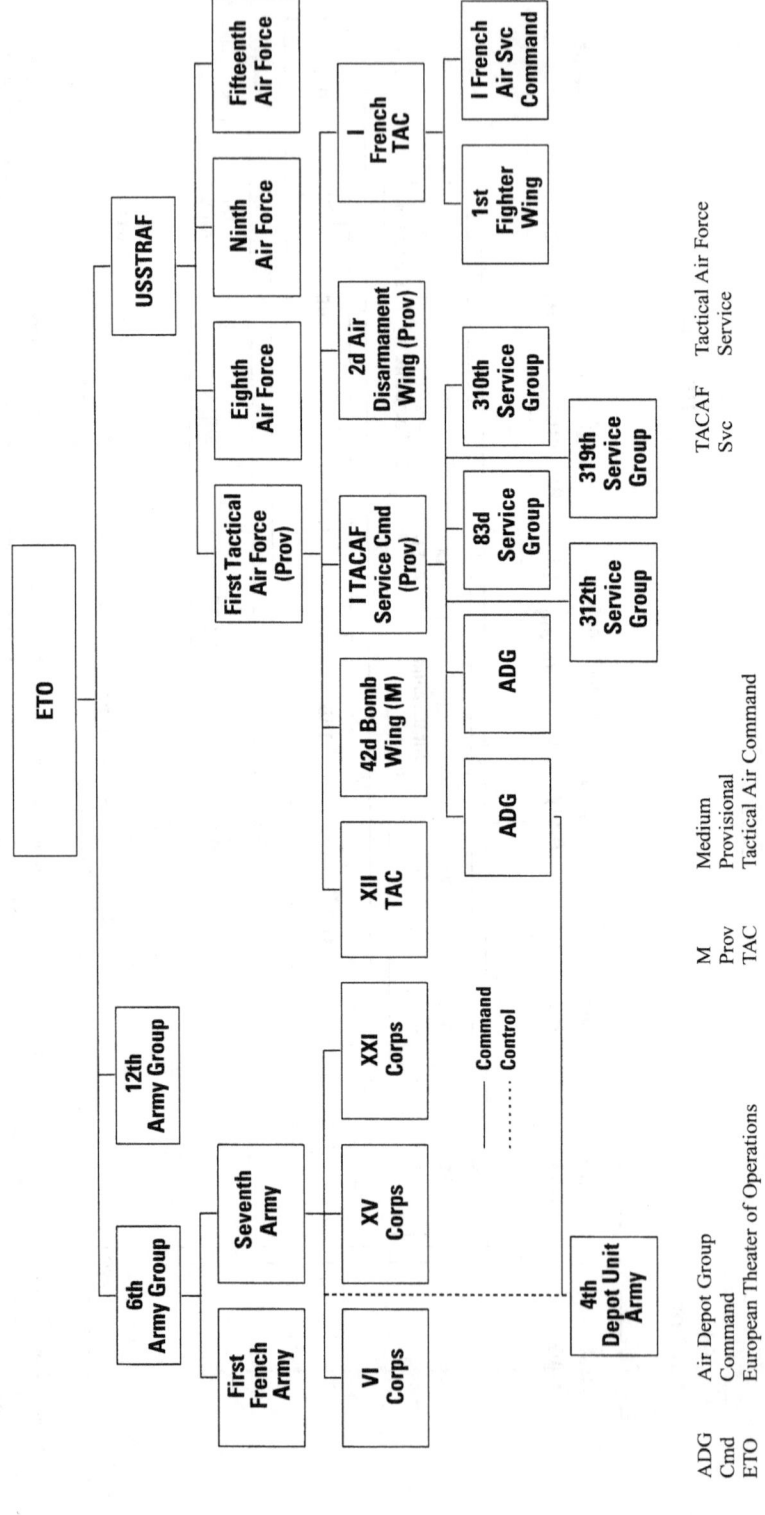

Chart 14—Organization of Army Air Forces Logistical Support for Field Artillery Air Observation Posts in the 6th Army Group, 11 March 1945

As the logistical system took shape, Captain Haynes and the major at the Grove depot became involved in an initially abortive development effort, but one that had some importance for the future—arming an L–4. Pilots in both Italy and New Guinea had already taken automatic weapons and hand grenades aloft. Senior artillery aviators attempted to discourage the practice, because a battalion of field artillery could do far more damage than whatever light weapons or explosives pilots could carry in an L–4. After Haynes and the major finished distributing L–4s to incoming units, they had one aircraft remaining. They decided to arm it with standard 2.3-inch antitank rockets, three on each wing, simply to see if it could be done. One of the few aeronautical engineers in the program, Haynes tested the result and discovered that it was possible to hit a target. The pilot had to get directly overhead and dive straight down, releasing the bazookas as he pulled out. Haynes concluded, however, that "it was a good way not to live through the war," given the large number of German automatic weapons and their high rate of fire. Consequently, he dropped any further thought of employing an armed Cub in combat.[8]

Once the logistics were sorted out, movement of about one thousand artillery aircraft to the Continent became Lefever's major concern. He left detailed operational planning to the field army artillery air officers, intervening mainly to troubleshoot major problems. Bristol considered flying the L–4s to the Continent during both the assault and reinforcement phases of the invasion. But this solution immediately raised questions: Could liaison pilots navigate well enough over water, and did the L–4 have sufficient range? In the spring Lefever and the artillery air officer of Third Army, Major Wilson, who had just arrived in theater, set out to investigate the first issue. They made several trial flights to Northern Ireland over approximately one hundred twenty-five miles of water and concluded that flights to France were indeed possible.[9]

Bristol, working closely with the personnel at the 23d Mobile Reclamation and Repair Squadron, dealt with the range issue. He judged that the L–4 could reach the French coast if conditions were favorable. The prevalence of head winds in the flight path, however, suggested the prudence of carrying reserve fuel. Technicians at the squadron fashioned a reserve tank using an oxygen bottle, designed for a B–17, which could hold eight gallons of aviation gasoline. Some copper tubing and a Y-clamp completed the reserve fuel system. The tank rode in the observer's seat. Bristol planned to send the tanks back to the United Kingdom and reuse them after each flight, so the number of reserve fuel kits required was far fewer than the total number of aircraft.[10]

Coordination of the movement of aircraft from Great Britain to the Continent rested initially with the First and Third Army artillery air officers, but after Bristol and Wilson deployed with their headquarters, Lefever assumed direct responsibility. Between July 1944 and January 1945 some six hundred replacement pilots made the flight in L–4s and L–5s, using the procedures Bristol had developed. Representatives of the various armies met them on landing and led them forward to join their units. All requests for replacement aircraft passed through the army group artillery air officer, who allocated replacements between the various armies. Army Air Forces pilots flew the replacement aircraft forward

---

[8] Interv, author with Haynes, 26 Feb 92.
[9] Intervs, Epstein with Bristol, 1 Jul 75; author with Lefever, 4 Sep 91, and with Wilson, 3 Aug 91.
[10] Interv, Epstein with Bristol, 1 Jul 75.

MAJOR WILSON AS A LIEUTENANT IN 1942

to the army areas where pilots from receiving units accepted transfer. Between July 1944 and May 1945 field artillery units in 12th Army Group received some three hundred fifty replacement aircraft.[11]

Lefever devoted much time and energy to wrestling with the pilot replacement issue. Initially, the War Department shipped replacement pilots based on the estimates of the staff at theater headquarters. Lefever convinced the theater staff to request a 10 percent overage to assure prompt replacement of losses and prevent pilot fatigue. As in Italy, the army artillery air officers discovered that pilots in the replacement pipeline had no opportunity to fly for periods ranging from one to three months before their arrival on the Continent. Wilson assigned excess replacement pilots in Third Army to units doing the most flying, so they could obtain both operational experience and flying time before they were assigned to fill vacancies.[12]

Bristol, Wilson, Leich, and Thornton required all air-observation-post sections to submit reports of major accidents within twenty-four hours of their occurrence. After the 12th Army Group became operational on the Continent on 14 July 1944, Lefever maintained a central file of reports from all the armies in the army group. This system permitted rapid replacement of losses in both aircraft and personnel. It also enabled the air sections at higher headquarters to develop statistics about accidents and to attempt to identify systemic problems and suggest solutions. Like Capt. Michael J. Strok in Fifth Army, Wilson in Third Army published an "Air OP Bulletin." It included a description of the circumstances of all accidents involving Third Army aircraft and Wilson's comments, when appropriate, on how the accidents could have been avoided. In December 1943 the War Department had established the first official flight safety program by outlining the division air officer's responsibilities for safety. The Third Army Air OP Bulletin, along with similar publications by other armies and Headquarters, Army Ground Forces, constituted in practice an extension of this program to include the echelons above division.[13]

Most crashes were the result of human, usually pilot, error. The assistant artillery air officer of the U.S. Ninth Army, Capt. William R. Mathews, formerly the artillery air officer of the 344th Field Artillery Battalion, noted in November 1944 that "cross-wind land-

---

[11] Report (Rpt), [12th Army Grp Artillery (Arty) Section], in 12th Army Grp, *Report of Operations*, 11:99, 101.
[12] Ibid., p. 100; After Action Report (AAR), [Williams] to Commanding General (CG), Third Army, in Third Army, *After Action Report*, 2:Arty–36; Interv, author with Lefever, 4 Sep 91.
[13] AOP Bulletin no. 1, Third U.S. Army, 20 May 44, in Third Army, *After Action Report*, 2:Arty–5, 6; 12th Army Grp, *Report of Operations*, 1:6; WD, Training Circular (TC) 132, 14 Dec 43, sub: Organic Field Artillery (FA) Air Observation (Obsn).

ings and poor judgment cause most of them." By mid-November 1944 there had been four midair collisions involving Third Army aircraft. Four pilots and three observers had been killed. A pilot with the air section of the 278th Field Artillery Battalion had a close encounter with another L–4 on 20 October 1944 and suggested a possible cause for these accidents. Pilots and observers became so focused on their fire missions that they became oblivious to the presence of any other aircraft in their immediate airspace.[14]

Pilot losses, and hence the number of replacements required, were intimately related to pilot fatigue. The headlong pursuit across France during August 1944 had strained both men and machines. Major Wilson noted that in Third Army some pilots had logged over one hundred flying hours for the month of August, instead of a preferred maximum of sixty hours. "Pilot fatigue must be given careful consideration in planning operations." The results of pilot fatigue did not necessarily show up in easily identifiable ways but in "an increasing accident rate, reduction in efficiency, and in a reduced ability to evaluate quickly a set of circumstances and react to the dictates of good judgment." Wilson well knew that few pilots would ever admit they were too tired. He wanted division and group artillery air officers to attack the problem by consolidating patrols and by carefully evaluating all missions and eliminating those that could be accomplished by some other means.[15]

Unfortunately, Wilson had identified a major problem without having the means at hand to solve it. Pilots had literally flown themselves into exhaustion. As the weather turned bad in the fall and winter and their flying time remained high, the strain became too much for many. The loss rate for artillery pilots in the European Theater of Operations escalated far beyond the War Department's projections. The resulting pilot shortage reflected a major institutional deficiency in the Air-Observation-Post Program. In 1943 Headquarters, Army Ground Forces, had rejected the idea of assigning flight surgeons to look after the medical needs of the pilots and observers in the program. The War Department opted instead to make the battalion surgeon responsible; he, of course, was also accountable for all the other members of the battalion. Consequently, there was no knowledgeable medical officer immediately at hand to make certain that the commander and the pilot exercised reason regarding maximum flight hours or even to perform a flight physical. In November 1944 Major Wilson surveyed the status of pilots' physical examinations in Third Army. Incomplete results (179 out of 224 pilots responded) indicated that 5 percent (9 pilots) had received their last examination in 1942, 53 percent (94 pilots) in 1943, and only 42 percent (76 pilots) in 1944.[16]

---

[14] Ltr, Capt W. R. Mathews, 23 Nov 44, in Memo, Maj D. V. Dale, Executive Officer (XO), Field Artillery School (FAS), Department of Air Training (DAT), 15 Dec 44, sub: Informal Info, in FAS, DAT, "Training Memoranda" (Bound Manuscript [Ms], Morris Swett Technical Library, FAS, Fort Sill, Okla. [hereafter cited as Morris Swett Tech Lib], 1944–1945). There are fleeting references to the air-observation-post bulletins produced by other armies. Aside from the scattered air-observation-post bulletins of Fifth Army mentioned in Chapter 5, I have located only those of Third Army. The army published the complete set in its final after-action report. AOP Bulletin no. 4, Third Army, 22 Nov 44, in Third Army, *After Action Report*, 2:Arty–12.

[15] AOP Bulletin no. 3, Third U.S. Army, 18 Oct 44, in Third Army, *After Action Report*, 2:Arty–10.

[16] Memo, Lt Col R. R. Williams for Col R. C. Moffat, 12 Jan 45, sub: Attached Study of Liaison Aircraft; Rpt, [Williams] to [Assistant Chief of Air Staff (ACAS) Plans, Post War Division (Div)], 5 Sep 45, sub: Liaison Aviation (Avn) in Post War Period, Microfilm A1387, U.S. Air Force Historical Research Agency, Maxwell Air Force Base, Ala. (hereafter cited as AFHRA). WD, Circular 250, 19 Jun 44, sub: Field Artillery (FA)—Supervision of Physical Condition of Liaison Pilots; Rpt, Brig Gen J. D. Balmer, et al., to European Theater of Operations (ETO) General Board, sub: Rpt on Study of Organic FA Air Obsn, in ETO, General Board, *Study of Organic Field Artillery Air Observation*, Rpt no. 66 (European Theater of Operations General Board, [1946]), pp. 29–30.

The Seventh Army artillery air officer, Major Shepard, partially alleviated the problem by arranging for the flight surgeon of the First Tactical Air Force (Provisional) to provide flight physical examinations for Seventh Army air-observation-post pilots. Through 22 December the flight surgeon had examined 118 pilots. He found that 54 percent (64 pilots) showed no fatigue, while 26 percent (32 pilots) showed slight fatigue, meaning they required only relatively short periods of regular rest for complete recovery. Some 12 percent (14 pilots) showed moderate fatigue. The affected pilots could resume combat flying after prolonged rest and rehabilitation. The remaining 8 pilots, 7 percent of the total, exhibited the symptoms of severe fatigue: extreme loss of confidence, fear of flying, hypochondria, and asocial tendencies. Only after hospitalization and prolonged rest could they, with luck, resume administrative flying. They could never again fly in combat.[17]

Seventh Army pilots of course had experienced less sustained combat than most of their counterparts in First and Third Armies and at least some in Ninth Army. Nevertheless, these results were so striking that Shepard convinced the Seventh Army staff to establish a rest camp at Grenoble, France, for Field Artillery pilots. The other armies followed this example. First Army established its camp at Liège, Belgium; Ninth Army at Maastricht, Holland; and Third Army at Esch, Luxembourg. Experience showed that the camps could retard but not prevent the onset of combat fatigue. Eventually, overstressed pilots had to be replaced.[18]

Logistical arrangements developed for air observation posts during the spring and summer of 1944 continued to function successfully during the remainder of the war. There was only one major change. Once American and British logisticians restored the port of Le Havre, France, to operation, essentially in mid-October, it replaced the United Kingdom as the destination for replacement aircraft shipped from the United States. Existing plans called for the Army Air Forces' 45th Air Depot Group to assemble these aircraft plus those organic to units deploying directly from the United States. The group's mission, however, also included the assembly of high-performance aircraft for Ninth Air Force. Understandably, the group commander placed higher priority on getting these aircraft forward than the L–4s and L–5s belonging to the ground forces. The group never assembled any of the aircraft arriving with units and fell behind in the assembly of replacement aircraft. A difficult situation became worse when the unit moved from Paris, which enjoyed relatively good rail connections with Le Havre, to Charleroi, Belgium, whose transportation links to the port were anything but good. Some forty crated aircraft accumulated at Le Havre as a result.[19]

At this point a detachment from the 27th Mobile Reclamation and Repair Squadron, the unit designated to support Fifteenth Army, assumed responsibility for assembling the aircraft at Airstrip B–81C near Rouen, France, seventy-five miles up the Seine from Le Havre. The artillery air officer of the 61st Field Artillery Brigade, Maj. Samuel Freeman, who had served as the artillery air officer for the 45th Infantry Division during the Sicilian campaign, supervised the work of the detachment. As the brigade's mission was to process all field artillery battalions arriving in theater, making certain that all equipment was ready

---

[17] Rpt, Balmer, et al., to ETO General Board, in ETO, General Board, *Organic Field Artillery Air Observation*, pp. 29–30.

[18] Ibid., p. 30.

[19] Ibid., pp. 26–28; 12th Army Grp, *Report of Operations*, 11:99; Roland G. Ruppenthal, *Logistical Support of the Armies*, 2 vols., U.S. Army in World War II (Washington, D.C.: Office of the Chief of Military History, 1953), 1:480, 2:60, 96–103.

for the field, and to provide higher-echelon maintenance on all field artillery ground vehicles, this arrangement possessed a certain logic and worked well in practice. It violated, however, the Army Air Forces policy of retaining mobile reclamation and repair squadrons in an exclusive Army Air Forces chain of command. Ultimately, the Aircraft Assembly Branch of the Army Air Forces' Central Air Depot assumed responsibility for putting liaison aircraft together.[20]

Supply, maintenance, and performance problems of the aircraft persisted throughout the campaign. Their solution required efforts by pilots and mechanics at all echelons of command to solve them or at least ameliorate their adverse consequences. At Headquarters, 12th Army Group, Lefever tackled a number of these logistical problems. To reduce weight in the already overloaded L–4, he had mechanics in his section develop a lightweight radio case to replace the standard-issue heavy steel case. The performance of the L–4s was so marginal in winter that even the bulky clothing worn by observers seriously detracted from the aircraft's performance. Lefever secured Army Air Forces cold-weather flying gear, already issued to the pilots, as a weight-reduction measure. Anticipating winter conditions, he obtained aircraft skis from the United States and made arrangements for the local manufacture of some two hundred sets. In practice the skis placed unanticipated stresses on the landing gears, leading to their frequent collapse during landings. Third Army aviators discovered that snow had to be firmly packed for the skis to work, but the L–4s with their low weight could land and take off from packed snow using their regular wheels. In the end, although a few pilots extolled them, most aviators made little use of skis. A more persistent problem involved the side windows in the L–4, which were made from a cheap grade of very thin plastic that "warped and wrinkled" over time. It distorted the vision of the pilot and observer "to a dangerous degree." Lefever made arrangements with Army Air Forces maintenance personnel to replace the plastic with Plexiglas, which solved the visibility problem. Unfortunately, Plexiglas was in very short supply, and the maintenance crews could never upgrade more than a few aircraft at a time. It took virtually until the end of the war to refit all 12th Army Group aircraft.[21]

The supply system Major Bristol had laid down prior to the invasion worked well for the armies deploying to the Continent from Great Britain. Because coordination rather than command relations were involved, the success rested on the willingness of Field Artillery and Army Air Forces officers to cooperate. Personalities played a major role, which meant there was some variation from army to army. In First Army the liaison system Bristol established between his staff subsection and the 23d Mobile Reclamation and Repair Squadron allowed him to anticipate problems before they arose. Wilson in Third Army was somewhat more dissatisfied with the 43d Mobile Reclamation and Repair Squadron. The officers and men provided excellent maintenance support, but having the unit in the Army Air Forces chain of command while serving in a field army meant that the squadron sometimes had difficulty obtaining rations, supplies, and services. Wilson believed that, if the War

---

[20] Rpt, Balmer, et al., in ETO, General Board, *Organic Field Artillery Air Observation*; Sgt. O. W. Hagan, *One Year of Operations, July 1944/July 1945: 61st Field Artillery Brigade* (n.p.: [61st Field Artillery Brigade], 1945), p. 9.

[21] Rpt, [Arty Section, 12th Army Grp], in 12th Army Grp, *Report of Operations*, 11:99–100. AAR, [Williams] to CG, Third Army, AOP Bulletin no. 4, Third Army, 22 Nov 44; both in Third Army, *After Action Report*, 2:Arty–11, 12, 36; Interv, author with Lefever, 4 Sep 91.

Department had assigned the squadron to Third Army under his supervision, he could have avoided these unnecessary difficulties. He also found that he had to visit all echelons of the Army Air Forces supply system and forcefully represent to the commanders that they had a responsibility to stock materiel and equipment to support Field Artillery aircraft. Once he realized he needed to do this, most supply problems evaporated. A persistent shortage of wooden propellers proved to be the only major supply problem resistant to such an approach. The difficulty lay not with the squadron but with the Third Tactical Air Depot, which provided the squadron with supplies and equipment. Wilson solved this particular complication by judiciously placing a case of Scotch with a supply sergeant at the depot.[22]

In Seventh Army Major Shepard enjoyed exceptionally able support from the commander of the 4th Depot Unit (Army), Captain Long. Long had been his assistant artillery air officer in Sicily and General Patton's personal pilot. The War Department might have transferred Long to the Army Air Forces, but his perspective and loyalties remained those of a Field Artillery officer. Long also benefited from a close professional and personal relationship with his Fifth Army counterpart, Captain Strok, that also dated back to the Sicilian campaign. They swapped supplies back and forth between Italy and the south of France to cover shortages. The Army Air Forces supply system also proved helpful. Initially, Long's major problem lay in securing fabric and dope to repair the fabric-covered L–4s. Then he made an amazing discovery. Although the Air Corps had converted to all-metal fighters in the 1930s, Army Air Forces fighter squadrons still received large automatic issues of fabric, dope, thinner, and varnish. Actually, the all-metal fighters might be characterized better as "almost all-metal fighters." Their control surfaces (ailerons, flaps, stablizers, and vertical fins), where weight was a prime consideration, remained fabric. But the automatic issues of fabric and other materials far exceeded the limited demand. Fighter pilots used the excess fabric for tablecloths and curtains in their messes. Long bartered to obtain all the fabric, dope, thinner, and varnish that he required.[23]

The limited number of L–5s assigned to air sections proved popular with the pilots who flew them and the commanders and staff officers who were their passengers. In fact, they became so popular they caused some dissension within the artillery air community. In the fall of 1944 the First Army artillery air officer, Major Bristol, controlled virtually all L–5s in the 12th Army Group not under Army Air Forces control. He regarded the aircraft as belonging to First Army rather than the corps or division artillery to which they were assigned. When the 12th Army Group shifted the 30th Infantry Division to Ninth Army, Bristol insisted that the division artillery air officer, Maj. Jack Blohm, return the aircraft. With the complete backing of his division commander, Blohm returned the L–5—disassembled to the bolt and bracket level—in the back of a 2 1/2-ton truck. Thereafter, the 12th Army Group took over distribution of L–5s, and all armies received a fair share of the available aircraft.[24]

---

[22] AOP Bulletin nos. 1, Third Army, 20 May 44, and 2, Third Army, 1 Sep 44, both in Third Army, *After Action Report*, 2:Arty–5, 8, 36; First Army, *Combat Operations Data*, 3:162; Intervs, Epstein with Bristol, 1 Jul 75, and author with Wilson, 3 Aug 91.

[23] Intervs, author with Shepard, 23 Sep 83, and with Long, 23 Jul 82. I obtained the information about the composition of the control surfaces from Dr. Daniel R. Mortensen of the Air Staff History Office. See Notes, D. R. Mortensen on Draft, 25 Jan 95, Historian's files, CMH.

[24] Interv, author with Mathews, 24 Feb 92.

Most of the burden of keeping the aircraft flying fell to the pilots, mechanics, and assistant mechanics in the air sections. Throughout the campaign, despite Lefever's efforts to the contrary, 73-octane aviation gasoline remained in short supply, although there was some improvement in 1945. The fuel situation made mounting continuous air patrols, the standard tactic in France and Germany as in Italy, a difficult feat. Sections resorted to 80-octane truck fuel with deleterious results on engine life. Mechanics had to remove the piston cylinders from the engines every twenty to thirty hours, grind the valves to remove excess carbon, and reseat them. The truck fuel often arrived in rusty cans and had a high water content. Mechanics had to strain the gas by hand through a chamois skin before refueling the aircraft.[25]

Cold weather introduced its own set of problems. Ground crews had to perform most maintenance outdoors exposed to the wind and snow. Ice often formed between the spark plug point and the engine post, forcing mechanics to remove the plugs and clean out the ice before every flight. Otherwise, the engine would not start. Carburetor icing was a constant threat on takeoff and landing. In Ninth Army, XIII Corps mechanics found a novel way of removing ice and snow from aircraft wings and tail surfaces. Mechanics detached an inspection plate in the wing or tail and inserted a flexible pipe attached to a truck's exhaust pipe. The warm air circulated, melted the ice and snow, and, equally important, left the surfaces dry.[26]

The logistical and administrative effort required to support air-observation-post operations in Northwest Europe was the greatest of the war in any theater in terms of both scale and complexity. The success of the artillery air officers assigned to field army, army group, and theater headquarters in performing these support functions meant that pilots in the air sections could conduct sustained operations throughout the campaigns in the theater. It was, however, the actions of the pilots and ground crews in combat that ultimately provided the justification for this level of support and ultimately laid the basis for the continuation of the organic air program into the postwar period. The North African, Sicilian, and Italian campaigns in effect had constituted preliminary matches for the Air-Observation-Post Program and in a sense the U.S. Army as a whole. The campaigns in Northwest Europe were the main event.

Normandy: Planning and Invasion

Air-observation-post operations in the European Theater went through six distinct phases as a result of changes in terrain, weather, and the posture of friendly and enemy forces. The landing in Normandy on 6 June 1944 and the initial movement of Field Artillery aircraft to the Continent represented the culmination of months of planning and preparation. Two months of close combat in the hedgerows of Normandy gave way to more than a month of pursuit across France. At the same time Allied forces landed in southern France. On the Franco-German border, stiffening German resistance and Allied logistical problems combined to produce a period of positional warfare, as fall gave way to winter and ushered in a period of very poor flying weather. The defeat of the great German coun-

---

[25] 12th Army Grp, *Report of Operations*, 11:99–100; Intervs, author with Lefever, 4 Sep 91 and 26 Feb 92.
[26] AOP Bulletin no. 6, Third Army, 27 Jan 45, in Third Army, *After Action Report*, 2:Arty–14.

teroffensive, known as the Battle of the Bulge, led to a resumption of the attack and the defeat of the German Army west of the Rhine River. The crossing of the Rhine and the exploitation to the east, ending with the linkup with the Soviets and the surrender of Germany, constituted the final phase.

Major Bristol at First Army took charge of air-observation-post operational planning for the Normandy invasion. He considered and rejected the use of a decked-over landing ship, tank (LST), as employed in the Mediterranean. He wanted the ability to sustain operations and requested an escort carrier. Major Lefever negotiated with the Navy to no avail. Once he and Major Wilson had determined that overwater flights were possible, Bristol arranged for the fabrication of reserve tanks and gave unit air officers the option of flying into the beachhead or carrying the aircraft ashore in the back of 2 1/2-ton trucks with other vehicles and supplies from their units. Air officers in VII Corps, scheduled to assault lightly defended UTAH Beach, opted for aerial deployment. As a security measure Bristol concentrated VII Corps air sections on the Isle of Wight. Their counterparts in V Corps, facing heavily fortified OMAHA Beach, chose to use trucks to have aircraft immediately available once they had airstrips ashore. At the last moment, the Navy offered the use of a carrier berthed in Ireland for air-observation-post operations. Bristol, after consulting with General Hart, concluded that the risk of confusion outweighed the benefits of continuous observation during the landing and declined the offer.[27]

The Normandy invasion of 6 June, Operation OVERLORD, went largely as anticipated. (See *Map 5*.) The VII Corps rapidly advanced inland. Once units had secured landing areas, they called for their aircraft, which flew en masse at predetermined altitudes along a reinforcement air corridor that Major Bristol had specified. The artillery air officer of the 4th Infantry Division, Capt. James Gregorie, for example, accompanied the ground forces and landed on D-day. He discovered that German artillery fire had rendered the field he had preselected from aerial photographs unusable as an airstrip. Not until the next morning did he find a suitable location. About 0700 on 7 June he wired the assistant division artillery air officer, 1st Lt. David E. Condon, to bring over the division artillery aircraft. Condon led the flight in one of First Army's few L–5s. When Condon reached the beachhead area, Gregorie set off smoke grenades to mark the new strip and via radio directed Condon's landing.[28]

The division's batteries had not been registered. Once everyone landed, the L–5's greater range permitted Condon to take off to register the guns at 1115 without refueling. The division artillery commander, Brig. Gen. Harold W. Blakeley, monitored the radio net. Halfway through his first adjustment, Condon broke off to announce that he had observed a German battery firing. He changed the coordinates. Midway through that adjustment he announced that he could see another battery firing and gave its location. Blakeley ordered one of the staff officers in the Fire Direction Center to lay another bat-

---

[27] Operations (Opns) Memo 17, Headquarters (HQ), First Army, 3 May 44, sub: Use of AOPs in Amphibious Opns, J. E. Swenson Ms, U.S. Army Aviation Museum Library, Fort Rucker, Ala. (hereafter cited as USAAML); Intervs, Epstein with Bristol, 1 Jul 75; author with Col W. R. Mathews, 3 Dec 91, CMH; with Lefever, 4 Sep 91; with Wilson, 3 Aug 91; Carl I. Hutton, "An Armored Artillery Commander in the European Theater," (Unpublished [Unpubl] Ms, Morris Swett Tech Lib, n.d.), p. 80.

[28] Interv, Epstein with Bristol, 1 Jul 75; Richard J. Tierney and Fred Montgomery, *The Army Aviation Story* (Northport, Ala.: Colonial Press, 1963), pp. 153–54.

tery on the second German position. As soon as Condon directed concentrated fire on the first battery (the Field Artillery term was "fired for effect"), Blakeley came on the net, identified himself, and told Condon another battery was ready. Within minutes it also fired for effect. Within thirty minutes of the beginning of the division's first air observation mission, Condon had neutralized two German batteries. As one veteran artillery pilot commented, once battalions entered combat all the skepticism about the effectiveness of organic light aircraft disappeared.[29]

The V Corps had a much more difficult time at OMAHA Beach. The artillery air officer of the 29th Infantry Division, Maj. J. Elmore Swenson, went ashore with the infantry to find a landing field for his aircraft. He was struck in the helmet, but he made it across the beach unharmed. On 7 June the 29th Infantry Division was still clearing the German coastal defenses in its zone. The following day Lt. Clarence F. Lange flew the division commander, Maj. Gen. Charles H. Gerhardt, in the first air mission by division aircraft. Gerhardt wanted to personally inspect the terrain before the division attacked toward the lower reaches of the Aure River. On 8 June Major Swenson flew his first mission, a brief reconnaissance of the front lines, again with Gerhardt aboard. The division commander soon earned the reputation of having more flight time than any man in the division other than the pilots.[30]

The assistant artillery air officer of the 1st Infantry Division, Lt. Oscar Rich, with half the personnel of the headquarters section, an L–5, and three jeeps, was in the fourth wave on OMAHA Beach. The wave was unable to land until 1200 on 6 June because of German fire. Even then, Rich's landing craft, tank (LCT), took a German mortar round just as it beached. Rich was wounded in the hand, his mechanic caught fragments in his face and had to be evacuated, and all three jeeps were put out of action. The plane suffered only minor damage to its fabric. Rich flagged down a passing bulldozer, which pulled the disabled jeeps and then the L–5 off the craft. Before loading the plane aboard ship, he had removed the wings and elevators and attached them along the fuselage. The aircraft could still roll on its own landing gear. He found an unattended jeep, put a tow line on the plane, and pulled it to his designated assembly area. By dusk, when the division artillery air officer, Capt. Kenneth Bryant, arrived with the headquarters section's L–4 and the remainder of the personnel, Rich had the L–5 about half-assembled. By early the next morning, the men had it fully assembled and the fabric patched. Meanwhile, the engineers had bulldozed a strip. Rich adjusted the fires of the 5th Field Artillery Battalion that morning.[31]

Normandy included the first division-size or larger airborne operation ever conducted by the U.S. Army. Neither the 82d nor the 101st Airborne Division towed L–4s to the airheads with transport aircraft as the director of the Department of Air Training, Col. William W. Ford, had envisioned in 1943. Instead, foreshadowing the procedures of all subsequent airborne operations in the theater, their aircraft flew in after the airborne infantry had secured airheads and the division artillery had landed. The change resulted

---

[29] Maj. Gen. H. W. Blakeley, "Artillery in Normandy," *FAJ* 39 (March–April 1949):53; Interv, author with Mathews, 3 Dec 91.

[30] "Division Air OP Running Taxi Service for a Change," *29[th Infantry Division] Let's Go!* (25 June 1944), (31 May 1945); Clipping, R. F. Karobvitz, "How Swenson Grew Wings," *The Salt Lake Tribune*, c. 1953; Capt J. E. Swenson, Pilot's Log, 14 Jun 40–19 Jun 45; all in Swenson Ms, USAAML.

[31] Oscar Rich, [Combat Narrative], *L–4 Grasshopper Wing Newsletter* 16 (August/September 1989):3, 6–7.

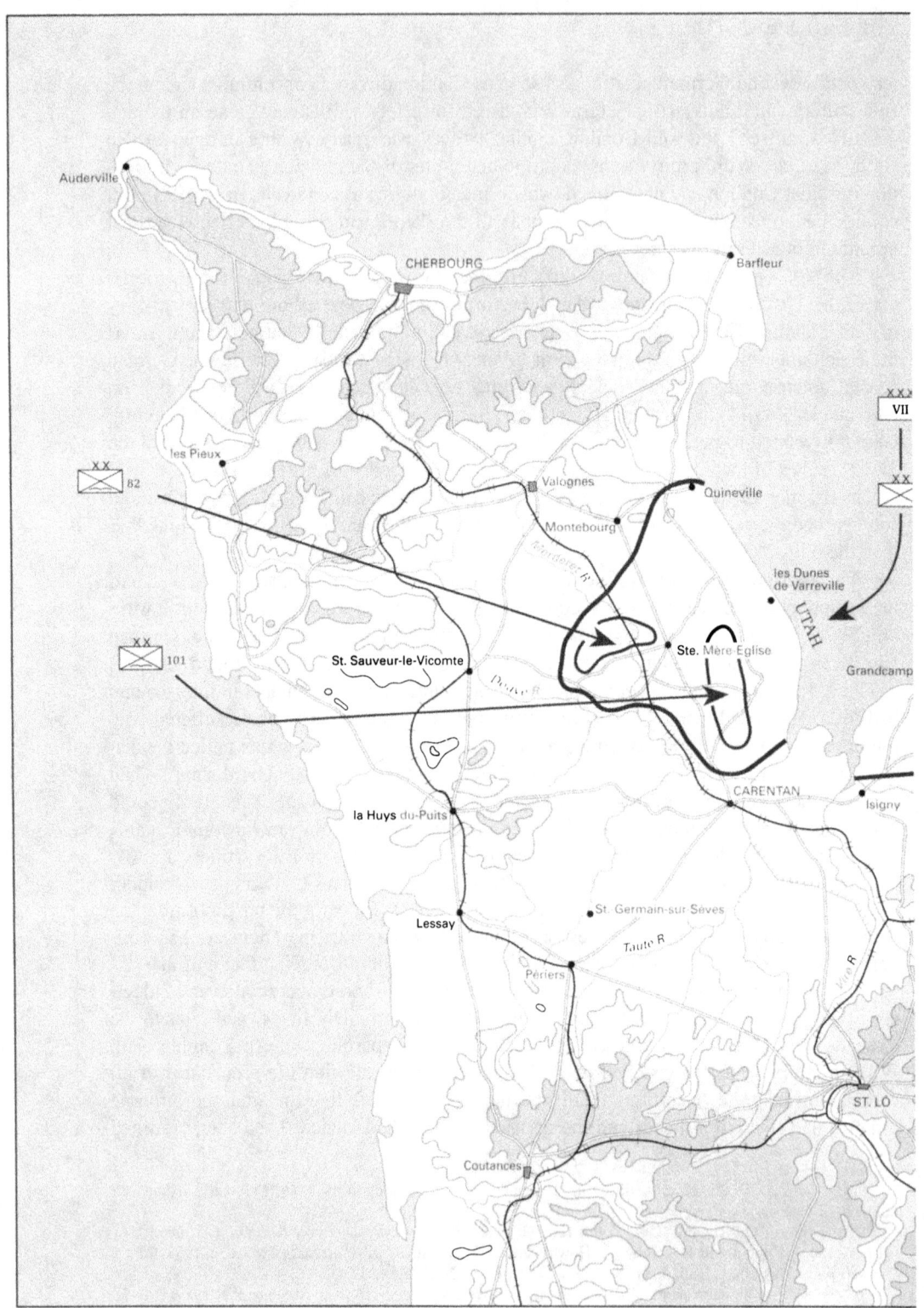

MAP 5

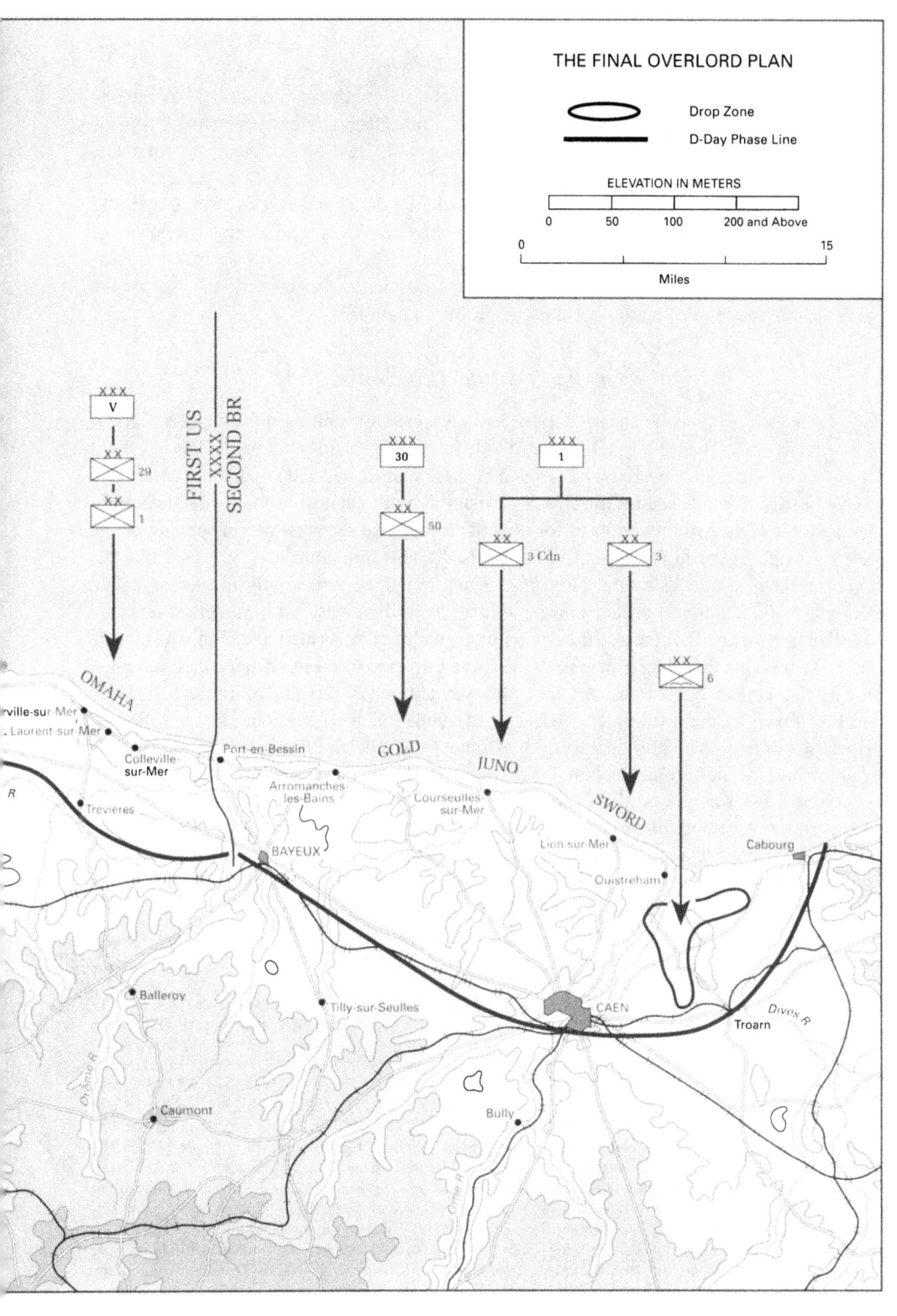

from a radical shift in the American theory of airborne operations. In early 1943 the airborne pioneers believed that airborne operations were deep strategic maneuvers (operational-level maneuvers in the current terminology). In reality American commanders employed airborne divisions in Europe in 1944 and 1945 to secure shallow, tactical objectives. The basis for the transformation was the airborne division's lack of ground mobility and relatively low firepower contrasted to the high mobility and heavy firepower of German armored divisions. Airborne divisions lacked the capacity to operate independently for extended periods of time. In these changed circumstances, flying L–4s into the airhead subsequent to the drop became the preferred option.[32]

The Battle for the Hedgerows

Once ashore the Americans experienced unexpected difficulties in the hedgerow country of Normandy. The rolling terrain was divided into small fields by "earth dikes . . . about four feet in height and covered with tangled bushes, hedges, and even trees," the latter from thirty to fifty feet tall. The resulting lack of visibility posed almost as many practical problems for the Field Artillery pilots as for the infantrymen. To see what was happening on the reverse slope of the high hedges, pilots had to fly at a minimum of 1,500 feet, but this exposed them to attacks by the *Luftwaffe*, which remained active early in the campaign. German light antiaircraft artillery posed a threat as well, at least until it received repeated antiflak treatments. To minimize the danger of ground fire, pilots attempted to fly just inside friendly lines, but this placed them in the airspace traversed by corps artillery shells en route to German targets. No one realized this, however, until an American 155-mm. shell struck an L–4 flown by the artillery air officer of the 90th Infantry Division, 1st Lt. Alfred R. Howard, killing him and his observer, Lt. William G. Windeler. Pilots ultimately concluded that the best location from which to direct fire was at altitude immediately over the target.[33]

June 1944 was the costliest month of the war for the air observation posts of First Army in terms of both planes and pilots. First Army lost thirty-six planes, either missing or damaged beyond repair. Twenty pilots were lost. Major Bristol included three categories in the "pilots lost" total: killed in action, evacuated for extended hospitalization,

---

[32] Intervs, author with Mathews, 24 Feb 92; with Brig Gen F. A. March, CG, 82d Airborne (Abn) Div Arty, 18 Dec 44, Microfilm A1387, AFHRA; Rpt, Balmer, et al., to ETO General Board, in ETO, General Board, *Organic Field Artillery Air Observation*, p. 25.

[33] Table, Maj D. L. Bristol, sub: AOP Opns, in Rpt, Maj L. O. Rostenberg, Special Observer (Obsr), to CG, AGF, 21 Jan 45, sub: Rpt of Special Obsr in ETO, 8 Sep–22 Dec 44, in AGF, "Report of Special Observer in European Theater of Operations" (Bound Ms, Morris Swett Tech Lib, 1944–1945); Ltr, Lt Col J. W. Mayo to Col W. W. Ford, in Memo, Lt Col G. J. Wolf, 15 Aug 44, sub: Informal Info, in FAS, DAT, "Training Memoranda"; Artillery Battalion (Bn) Commanders (Comdrs), 29th Infantry (Inf) Div, "After the Landing," *FAJ* 35 (March 1945):135–37; Lt. Col. Lewis R. Soffer, "An M12 Battalion in Combat," *FAJ* 35 (March 1945):29–31; Lt. Col. Frank W. Norris, "In France . . . with Mediums," *FAJ* 35 (March 1945):171–76; Hutton, "An Armored Artillery Commander," pp. 74–80. See also Carl I. Hutton, "Cubs in Combat," *U.S. Army Aviation Digest* (*USAAD*) 1 (March 1955):3–11. The hedgerow description comes from Martin Blumenson, *Breakout and Pursuit*, U.S. Army in World War II (Washington, D.C.: Office of the Chief of Military History, 1961), p. 11; Rpt, HQ, 90th Inf Div Arty, sub: 90th Div Arty Historical Account for Aug 44, in 90th Inf Div Arty, "90th Infantry Division Artillery Historical Account" (Bound Ms, Morris Swett Tech Lib, 1944–1945); Interv, author with Mathews, 3 Dec 91. For a study of combined arms in the European Theater of Operations, see Michael D. Doubler, *Closing with the Enemy: How GIs Fought the War in Europe, 1944–1945*, ed. Theodore A. Wilson, Modern War Studies (Lawrence: University Press of Kansas, 1994), especially pp. 94–95 for a discussion of air observation posts.

and missing. July 1944 was the second costliest month in terms of pilots—fourteen. First Army lost only thirteen aircraft that month. Bristol later stated that for the period June–September 1944, 10 percent of aircraft losses were due to attacks by *Luftwaffe* fighters; 20 percent due to German ground fire; 37 percent due to flying accidents; and 33 percent to rough fields, shelling of airstrips, and ground accidents. Superficially, Bristol's figures suggest that less than half the losses were due to enemy action. Aside from an irreducible minimum of accidents due to pilot inexperience, weather, and simple bad luck, however, the majority of these noncombat losses reflect the effects, albeit indirectly, of the German resistance.[34]

Noncombat accidents occurred in a variety of ways. Pilots damaged some aircraft while attempting to land on rough, unimproved fields; others lost their aircraft because they attempted to fly while excessively fatigued and made critical errors of judgment. Some accidents were undoubtedly due to lack of combat experience. Many American divisions on the beachhead had deployed from the United States, staged briefly in Great Britain, and then entered combat in France. Pilots assigned to these divisions had not flown a great deal for several months—an ample interlude for their piloting skills to become rusty. During June 1944 in particular, the beachhead was congested. This put a premium on what a later generation would label airspace management. Keeping planes from colliding in midair or from striking outgoing artillery rounds required levels of experience, skill, and luck not always present.

All these factors, while technically noncombat, were also a function of the determined defense that the German Army mounted in Normandy. Air observation posts flew from rough fields because of a lack of better ones and because the aircraft were needed over the front. If pilots became fatigued from long hours and stress, this was also a tribute to the tenacity of the defenders. The many inexperienced Allied divisions in the beachhead simply reflected the fact that the Allies did not possess a sufficient number of experienced divisions to carry out the invasion. Likewise, the congestion in the beachhead attested to the skill of the defenders in retarding the Allied advance and the need for the Allies to mass even greater forces to break through.

Early in the campaign fire missions predominated, particularly for pilots in battalion air sections. The 1st Infantry Division, on the left of the 29th Infantry Division, attacked south on 7 June toward the Aure River and the high ground around the village of Trévières, its D-day objectives. Four of the first five missions flown by Lt. R. S. Harper, a pilot with the 1st Infantry Division Artillery, were fire missions. He flew his first mission on 7 June, came under intense German ground fire, and consequently had to land more quickly than he had intended with a somewhat ventilated Cub. The assistant division artillery air officer, Lieutenant Rich, also noted that there was no enemy air activity "but lots of small arms and ack-ack," that is, antiaircraft fire.[35]

---

[34] Table, Bristol, sub: AOP Opns, in Rpt, Rostenberg to CG, AGF, 21 Jan 45. [Maj D. L. Bristol], "Statistical Analysis of Air OP Activities" in First Army, *Combat Operations Data*, 2:21. The latter provides the official statement of losses compiled after the war. The Rostenberg report, however, includes a note as to the causes of the losses based on a conversation with Bristol.

[35] First Army, *Combat Operations Data*, 2:21; Rich, Combat Narrative, pp. 6–7; Ltr, Lt R. S. Harper to Maj J. U. Overall, 2 Jul 44, in Memo, Wolf, 15 Aug 44, sub: Informal Info, in FAS, DAT, "Training Memoranda"; Tierney and Montgomery, *Army Aviation Story*, pp. 153–54.

Contention continued in Normandy over centralized versus decentralized control of air-observation-post operations. An attack by the 2d Armored Division on 13 June 1944, minor given the scope of the total operations in France, held important implications for the future development of organic aviation. On a day marked by low clouds and threatening weather, the division jumped off toward Carentan without support from its air observation posts. The division's liaison aircraft were concentrated at a division field, and someone there decided that conditions did not permit the airplanes to fly. This incensed the commander of the division's 14th Armored Field Artillery Battalion, Lt. Col. Carl I. Hutton. A graduate of West Point, Class of 1930, and a prewar light-plane enthusiast, Hutton thought his L–4s should have been in the air. He was convinced that aerial observation on that day would have converted the division's limited success into a German rout. Instead, the division's Cubs entered combat for the first time on 14 June. Twenty days later Hutton celebrated Independence Day by riding as an observer in one of the battalion's L–4s, an experience that only confirmed his views. "After seeing the enemy side of the lines from the air, I tended to put more faith than ever in the air OPs. They were really looking down the enemy's throat." These incidents left Hutton passionately convinced of the necessity of decentralized control, a position that he espoused for most of the next decade, when he became one of the most senior and influential officers in Army Aviation.[36]

At the beginning of the campaign, a noticeable gap existed between veteran and neophyte U.S. divisions in the sophistication of their air-observation-post operations. Divisions recently arrived from the continental United States and new to combat had to struggle to learn the basics others had learned in North Africa, Sicily, and Italy. No American division was more inept and unlucky than the 90th Infantry Division. Senior officers imbued with World War I concepts of artillery support proved impervious to the potential of light aircraft in both training and the early stages of combat. Infantry officers in the battalions and companies, unaware of the potential for accurate massed artillery fire, consequently saw no advantage in laying out their panels indicating friendly lines. The division's infantry-artillery coordination, as a result, was particularly poor. These unfortunate tendencies culminated on 23 July 1944, near St. Germain-sur-sèves, in the destruction of an isolated battalion from the division, even though an L–4 from the 344th Field Artillery Battalion, piloted by then–1st Lt. William R. Mathews, circled overhead. He could not make out the front lines because of dense foliage. The battle of "the island," as the action became known, also proved a turning point in the history of the division. A new division commander familiar with artillery technique in Italy, Brig. Gen. Raymond S. McLain, soon brought marked improvement in the infantry's willingness to cooperate with the division artillery.[37]

---

[36] Hutton, "An Armored Artillery Commander," pp. 74–80, 95–96.

[37] Panels were large cotton strips, lightweight and hence readily portable, usually colored orange on one side and red on the other, and used by ground troops for visual signaling with airplanes. They were issued in sets of ten and carried rolled in a canvas case. Army Service Forces (ASF), *Army Service Forces Signal Supply Catalogue: List of Items for Troop Use*, Signal 3 (Washington, D.C.: Army Service Forces, 1944), p. 73. Rpt, 90th Inf Div Arty, Jul 44, sub: 90th Inf Div Arty Historical Account for Jul 44, in 90th Inf Div Arty, "Historical Account"; Interv, author with Mathews, 3 Dec 91; Blumenson, *Breakout and Pursuit*, pp. 201–04. For further discussion of the problems engulfing the 90th Infantry Division, see William E. DePuy, *Changing an Army: An Oral History of General William E. DePuy, U.S. Army, Retired*, interviewed by Romie L. Brownlee and William J. Mullen (Carlisle Barracks, Pa.: U.S. Army Military History Institute, 1988), pp. 24–39. Paul H. Herbert, *Deciding*

Experienced divisions, on the other hand, soon reached and even surpassed the standards of the Italian campaign. The 29th Infantry Division had not seen combat before, but it had benefited from extended unit training in England. The division artillery air officer, Major Swenson, had already started the practice of briefing each pilot before a mission while the division was still training in Great Britain. In France, he and the other two pilots assigned to the division artillery air section acted as briefing and interrogating officers. Working in shifts, they briefed and debriefed each aircrew member before and after every mission and transmitted the information they collected to the division artillery S–2 and the division G–2. When the situation demanded, the S–2 or G–2 personally conducted the debriefings. As the campaign progressed, some variant of this system became standard practice in the most experienced combat divisions and groups. The artillery air officer maintained a continuously updated situation map that included such information as the location of the front lines, plan of operations of friendly troops, all field artillery battalion position areas, known enemy installations, and areas from which antiaircraft had fired on friendly aircraft. Green divisions did not make these arrangements and paid the price.[38]

The terrain in this hedgerow country compartmentalized the fighting. First Army advanced by squads, platoons, and companies. Individual victories were small-scale, but victories nevertheless. Air-observation-post operations contributed without spectacle to these successes. The front advanced only a few hundred yards at a time and at great cost. In the process, and in conjunction with the advance of the British Second Army holding the eastern end of the beachhead line, the German armies in the West suffered terrible, virtually irreplaceable losses. Cherbourg fell on 1 July, and by 19 July U.S. First Army had captured St. Lô, a key road junction, and stood poised on the edge of open, rolling country.

The XIX Corps, commanded by Maj. Gen. Charles H. Corlett, assigned an L–4 to guide the first American armor to pass through a thoroughly wrecked St. Lô. Even though the tanks came from the 113th Cavalry Group, the assistant artillery air officer of the 1st Infantry Division, Lieutenant Rich, drew the assignment of flying top cover. "It was scary. Lots of ground fire." Rich's mission ended once the armor cleared the built-up area, and he gratefully returned to his unit, resolving "no more tank guiding for me." In fact, he had just seen the future for many air-observation-post pilots. The armor column he left at the edge of the city, however, bumped into a new German defensive position some five hundred yards to the south. Before Rich's future became reality, First Army had to deal with those Germans.[39]

The British Second Army's repeated efforts to gain a breakthrough at Caen meant that the Germans had concentrated the bulk of their armor reserves on the British front. The commander of the 21st Army Group, Field Marshal Sir Bernard L. Montgomery, was

---

What Has To Be Done: General William E. DePuy and the 1976 Edition of FM 100–5, Operations, Leavenworth Papers, 16 (Fort Leavenworth, Kans.: Combat Studies Institute, 1988), pp. 12–16, provides a judicious commentary. John Colby, *War from the Ground Up: The 90th Division in World War II* (Austin, Tex.: Nortex Press, 1991), is both detailed and frank.

[38] Artillery Bn Comdrs, 29th Inf Div, "After the Landing," pp. 135–37; Rpt, Brig Gen W. B. Palmer, VII Corps Arty Officer (Ofcr), 12 Jun 45, sub: Battle Experience Conferences on VII Corps Arty Opns in Europe, in VII Corps Arty, "Battle Experience Conferences" (Bound Ms, Morris Swett Tech Lib, c. 1946); Lt. Col. Frederick C. L. Shepard, 30th Inf Div, "Coordination of Air OPs," *FAJ* 35 (July 1945):402–04, describes the same situation in the 30th Infantry Division. Tierney and Montgomery, *Army Aviation Story*, p. 154.

[39] Rich, Combat Narrative, p. 6; Blumenson, *Breakout and Pursuit*, p. 174.

ready to launch the American breakthrough offensive. On 25 July, after an abortive attack the previous day, the offensive began with a bombing accident by American heavy bombers that killed 111 American ground troops, among them Lt. Gen. Lesley J. McNair. Although the attack started slowly as a consequence, by the following day General Bradley felt confident enough to commit his armor.[40]

Pursuit and the Landing in Southern France

Normandy had been preeminently a tactical fight distinguished by small-scale, centrally controlled, often deliberate actions. The mobile phase that followed was characterized by great breadth and depth of maneuver, rapid improvisation, and considerable decentralization of control. The change in the nature of operations required officers and men at all echelons of command, including air sections, to make radical mental and sometimes physical adjustments, in some cases literally overnight. During the month and a half following the breakthrough, pilots set out on numerous early-morning missions not knowing where their strips would be located when they returned. Ground sections frequently discovered that they needed to know their exact location and that of their parent units—and often could find the correct answers only after some considerable delay and danger. Because air sections easily became separated from their parent battalions during moves, the battalion commanders commonly had to attach additional personnel to the air sections to provide security. During high-tempo pursuit operations, German and American units repeatedly became intermingled. Air sections had to be prepared to defend themselves from bypassed enemy units trying to regain their own lines—a concept that a later generation labeled *rear area security*. That term, however, implies a neatness belied by the messy reality that prevailed in France and Belgium from late July to early September 1944. Although fire control missions retained their importance, those integral to successful mobile operations—column control, close-in reconnaissance, and liaison—vied with it for pride of place.

The progressive collapse of the German front lines south of St. Lô between 25 and 27 July forced the Germans to make a rapid, deep withdrawal while collecting an armor force to strike back. Between 28 and 30 July, the 2d Armored Division and the 30th Infantry Division of the U.S. XIX Corps on the eastern flank of the American penetration became involved in a brawl with the counterattacking *2d Panzer Division*. In these circumstances fire direction became the overriding concern for the division pilots. A forward observer from the 14th Armored Field Artillery Battalion serving with the 66th Armored Regiment, 2d Armored Division, extemporized the technique of talking with the air observer to bring effective fire on his front. It proved so successful that it became a divisionwide policy in somewhat modified form. The division artillery S–3 monitored the air-observation-post net to give all the ground observers equal access and to prevent one ground observer from focusing the attention of the aerial observer on one narrow sector to the exclusion of all others.[41]

---

[40] Gordon A. Harrison, *Cross-Channel Attack*, U.S. Army in World War II (Washington, D.C.: Office of the Chief of Military History, 1951), pp. 336–449; Blumenson, *Breakout and Pursuit*, pp. 1–246.

[41] Hutton, "An Armored Artillery Commander," pp. 114–15.

No division played a greater role in exploiting the German defeat than the U.S. 4th Armored Division, commanded by Maj. Gen. John S. Wood. From the beginning of mobile operations in the newly activated Third Army, Wood used L–4s to reconnoiter ahead of the division's columns. The pilots used a common radio channel with the ground elements, allowing instantaneous communication. The division artillery air officer, Capt. Charles C. Carpenter, reported that scouting for armor and cavalry was "one of our most useful jobs." At times an aircraft would land in a field beside a column and would then take up the column commander so he could orient himself to the terrain. Having an aircraft at the head of a column markedly increased the rate of advance by lessening the degree of uncertainty involved in what was in the road around the next bend or over the next hill. If there was dug-in German infantry, an antitank gun, or a tank waiting in ambush, the column would deploy for combat and advance accordingly. If not, the Americans could barrel ahead at full speed. Carpenter's major difficulty was keeping the division airstrip close to the advance elements of the division each day. The Germans usually closed in behind the Americans once the tail of a column passed.[42]

The L–4 also served as a major element in Wood's system of command and control. Until shortly before the division's commitment to combat, one air section had been part of his headquarters company. That was how the division had trained. Now the section was part of the headquarters battery of the division artillery, but Wood continued to use it as if there had been no organizational change. He sought instantaneous action. Eschewing ground transportation, he flew to corps headquarters in a liaison aircraft, "listened to Third Army and corps plans, spoke briefly to corps and other division commanders about their parts in the plan, scratched a few boundaries, objectives, and notes on a map he pulled out of his shirt, and took off again in his Cub plane with a red streamer flying from the tip of each wing." The streamers indicated that Wood was aboard. The commanders of the combat commands displayed distinctive panels on their tanks so Wood could identify them from the air. Wood would then land, indicate the objective on the map, and issue verbal orders. He used the same procedure with division artillery and the division staff. Only after Wood had personally visited each element involved did he return to division headquarters to prepare concise written orders. Often the combat commands had already secured their objectives by the time the written orders arrived.[43]

Some elements of Wood's system existed in virtually all the divisions of First and Third Armies, although no other division commander used them in quite the way that Wood did. The 5th Infantry Division used its artillery aircraft to deliver maps to infantry and artillery command posts, "speeding delivery by several hours." The division artillery officer also used them to take oblique photographs of areas into which the division planned to attack. Although the system of using Field Artillery aircraft to vector fighter-bombers to ground targets never developed in Third Army, the Army Air Forces Air Support Party attached to the 5th Infantry Division monitored air-observation-post radio channels as part of its standard operating procedure. This allowed artillery pilots to transmit corrections for fighter-bombers attacking German ground units.[44]

---

[42] AOP Bulletin no. 3, Third Army, 18 Oct 44, in Third Army, *After Action Report*, 2:Arty–10.
[43] Hanson Baldwin, *Tiger Jack* (Fort Collins, Colo.: Old Army Press, 1979), pp. 40–41.
[44] AOP Bulletin no. 3, Third Army, 18 Oct 44, in Third Army, *After Action Report*, 2:Arty–10.

AN AIR OBSERVATION POST FLIES OVER AN M3A1 STUART LIGHT TANK, PARTIALLY OBSCURED BY SMOKE, SUPPORTED BY INFANTRY.

Battalion as well as division commanders found good uses for liaison aircraft in command and control. The commander of the 71st Armored Field Artillery Battalion, Lt. Col. Israel B. Washburn, found that planning for reconnaissance was impossible during the pursuit, because the commanders in the combat commands to which his battalion was attached never knew their exact route in advance. Reconnaissance elements at the head of the column always selected the route based on the tactical circumstances of the moment. Such tactical opportunism shredded German efforts to improvise a defense but also posed major control problems for American units not in immediate support of the lead elements. In these circumstances Washburn and his fellow field artillery battalion commanders kept air observation posts constantly in the air. At least one always flew in advance of any ground elements for route reconnaissance. Aerial observation made it much easier for the combat commands to operate in a coordinated fashion.[45]

Perhaps the most difficult problem facing the air-observation-post sections during the exploitation phase of the battle of France was simply keeping up with their battalions. In many instances, remarked the air officer of the 202d Field Artillery Battalion, 1st Lt.

---

[45] I. B. Washburn, "Armored FA Across France," *FAJ* 35 (April 1945):204.

Charles L. Kureth, this meant getting up before dawn, preparing the aircraft for flight, and packing and dispatching the ground vehicles before the airplanes took off. The ground crew was particularly overburdened. Acting in support of the 5th Armored Division following the breakout at St. Lô, the air section had to move over one hundred miles on some days. Kureth had to squeeze maintenance on the vehicles and airplanes between jumps. As the war progressed, technique improved. The movement of the air sections during a pursuit became much more a product of planning and less of hurried improvisation.[46]

Members of the air section of the 250th Field Artillery Battalion shared all these problems and more. Assigned to support the French 2d Armored Division, they faced a language barrier and the command group's total lack of comprehension as to the air-observation-post mission. The French had no ground panel markers, standard in American units, so from the air it was often very difficult to distinguish them from the Germans. One of the battalion pilots saved one of the division's armor columns from an attack by Army Air Forces fighter-bombers by interposing his L–4 between them and the tanks and waggling its wings. Lack of intelligence through command channels meant that the battalion had to use one of its planes to locate French forward positions so it could fire in their support. Over time the Americans and the French developed mutual respect if not mutual comprehension.[47]

Mobile warfare brought certain unique problems. As ordered, members of the air section of the 208th Field Artillery Battalion, reinforced by artillerymen from the parent battalion for ground security, were setting up their strip near Livet, France, a small town northeast of Laval, after a rapid overland move. "Suddenly a panting, French mademoiselle" ran across the road to warn them that a German column was approaching. The battalion air officer immediately set up a roadblock along the most likely approach route. When a German vehicle, later ascertained to be part of the reconnaissance element of a Panzer division, drew near, the Americans stopped it with small-arms fire. With the Germans at least temporarily halted, the air officer went in search of some higher headquarters to determine the location of the rest of the battalion. He eventually found the command group of the 30th Infantry Division, who informed him that his airstrip was the forward point of the American advance by some considerable margin. "We all cleared out, but fast."[48]

As early as 3 August General Bradley had decided to exploit the German disorganization by immediately attacking to the east in the hope of crossing the Seine River before the Germans could organize a defensive position behind it (*Map 6*). The need to widen the corridor around Avranches coupled with traffic congestion delayed the attack by U.S. Third Army's XV and XX Corps for two days. The XV Corps commander, Maj.

---

[46] Rpt, Air Section, 208th FA Bn, 19 May 45, sub: Most Satisfactory Opn; Rpt, 1st Lt C. L. Kureth, Air Ofcr, 202d FA Bn, to Commanding Officer (CO), 202d FA Bn, 29 May 45, sub: Opns of Air Section: Most Difficult Opn; both in XV Corps Arty, "Historical Examples Compiled Under the Direction of Brigadier General Edward S. Ott, Commanding XV Corps Artillery from the Campaigns of Normandy, Northern France, Rhineland, and Central Europe, During the Period July 1944 to May 1945" (Bound Ms, Morris Swett Tech Lib, 1945).

[47] Rpt, Air Section, 250th FA Bn, sub: Air Section: The Most Difficult Task, in XV Corps Arty, "Historical Examples."

[48] Rpt, Air Section, 208th FA Bn, 19 May 45, sub: The Most Interesting Opn, in XV Corps Arty, "Historical Examples."

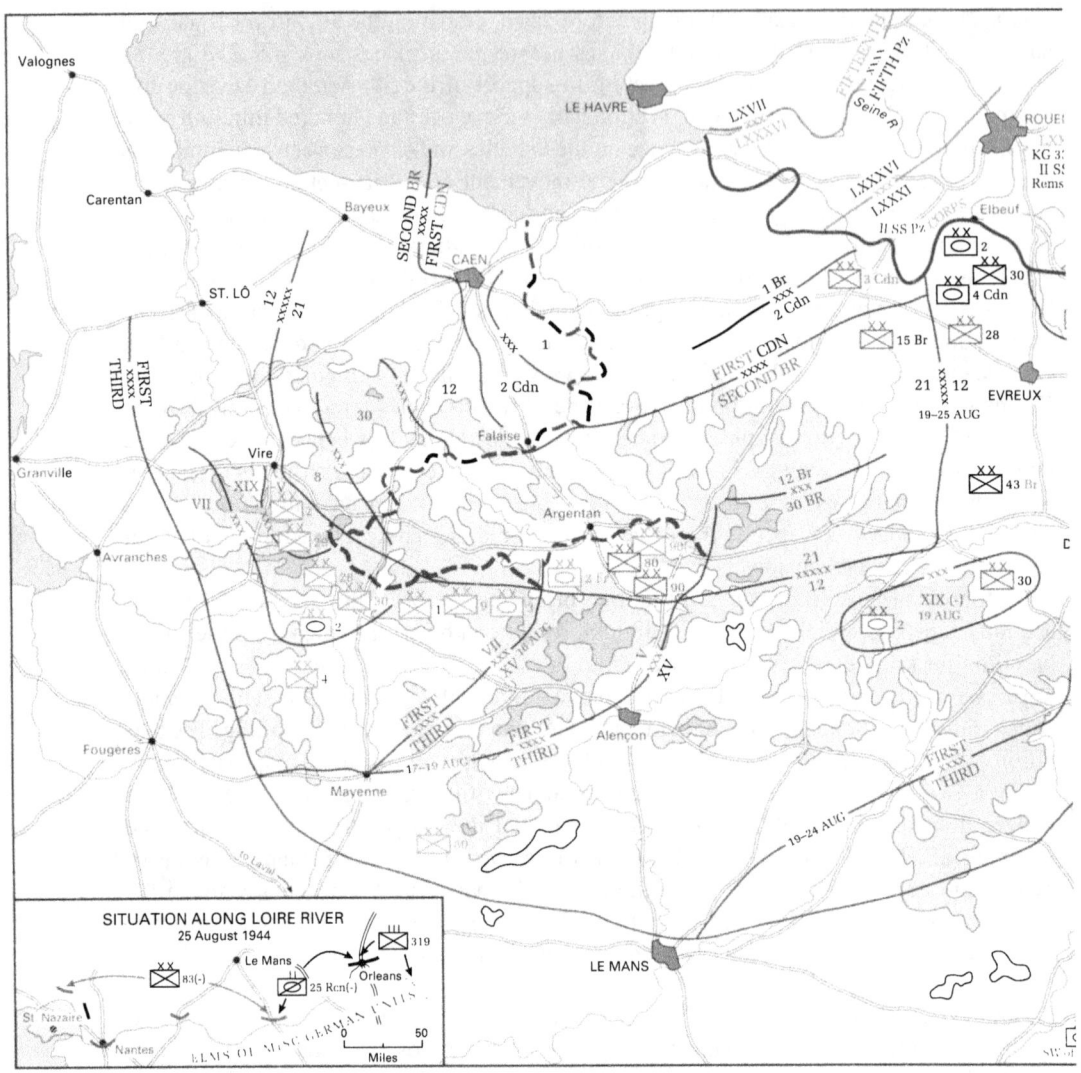

Map 6

Gen. Wade H. Haislip, with no clear idea of what enemy units lay to his front—there were very few—and with Army Air Forces photoreconnaissance responding too slowly to meet his needs, essentially attacked into an intelligence void. Once the attack began toward the city of Le Mans, he also had difficulty maintaining control over his rapidly advancing divisions. In this circumstance he used the corps artillery aircraft to keep him informed of the location of his front-line elements. The armor was advancing so rapidly that the corps artillery air officer had to maintain three airfields and leapfrog aircraft forward to keep abreast of the corps' leading elements. Although not a primary function of artillery aircraft, such contact missions were "a vital necessity for the corps com-

THE EUROPEAN THEATER

mander" and worked so well that Haislip repeatedly employed them in this role in the future.[49]

Two days after the Third Army attack began, the German *Seventh Army* counterattacked in an attempt to restore its lines around Avranches and cut off Third Army from the main Allied position in Normandy. The attack fell with particular force on VII Corps elements: The 30th Infantry Division had just taken up positions around the town of Mortain,

---

[49] Rpt, XV Corps Arty Air Ofcr to CG, XV Corps Arty, 1 Jun 45, sub: Historical Examples of FA Opns, in XV Corps Arty, "Historical Examples."

and the 4th Infantry Division lay just north of the town. The greatest concentration of German armor passed north of the town to a point where the 4th Infantry Division Artillery could bring it under a flanking fire. The division commander, Maj. Gen. Raymond O. Barton, regarded the division artillery "as my strongest tool" and habitually deployed it so he could shift its fire "in lieu of (or as) a maneuverable reserve." Ground observation became impossible; the forward observers had to withdraw or be overrun. The division's assistant artillery air officer, Lieutenant Condon, however, was airborne and directed the fire of the 20th Field Artillery Battalion, later reinforced by the 29th and 42d Field Artillery Battalions, on the numerous targets moving across the division front. Without the concentrated artillery fire, the massive counterattack in Barton's estimate "would have set us on our heels." Instead, the 4th Infantry Division Artillery "smeared" the Germans.[50]

The situation was somewhat different in the 30th Infantry Division sector. The 2d Battalion, 120th Infantry, with an attached forward observer, occupied a high hill near Mortain. Although isolated from the rest of the division by the first German onrush, the battalion was able to defend the hill for five-and-a-half days until relieved, while the observer called murderous fire on German armor below. On 9 August division artillery planes made a gallant but futile effort to drop supplies to the besieged unit but were driven off by concentrated German machine-gun fire. Subsequent attempts by Army Air Forces C–47s proved only marginally more effective; the altitude required to avoid enemy automatic weapons did not permit the needed accuracy. Thereafter, the division's air observation posts concentrated on their primary mission.[51]

From the perspective of the 30th Infantry Division Artillery, the crisis of the battle came on the evening of 9 August. A large number of German batteries suddenly opened, bringing the division under the most sustained artillery fire to date. Air observation posts directed thirty counterbattery missions in one hour.

> The radio channels were jammed with observers trying to adjust on three and four batteries at once. Active enemy batteries appeared so rapidly that the Air O[bservation] P[ost]s were forced to adjust on an enemy battery and pass on to the next one without really working over the first one thoroughly. Later on, when darkness prevented further adjustments, each battery that had been previously located was given a good going over.[52]

At the same time the 4th Infantry Division Artillery delivered its murderous fire against the German armor spearhead and the 30th Infantry Division Artillery silenced its German counterparts, fighter-bombers from IX Tactical Air Command worked over German armor columns in the immediate vicinity of the attack elements but not actually engaged with American ground troops. Once the 4th and 30th Infantry Divisions checked the lead elements of the counterattack force, the Germans lacked the follow-on forces to continue the drive. Through sheer happenstance but with great effectiveness, the liaison pilots and the fighter-bomber pilots divided the airspace over the combat area. The artillery pilots directed fire support against German units in direct contact with American infantry,

---

[50] Ltr, Maj Gen R. O. Barton to Maj Gen H. W. Blakeley, [1949], [Extract], in Blakeley, "Artillery in Normandy," p. 54. For background, see Blumenson, *Breakout and Pursuit*, pp. 457–75.

[51] Capt Norman F. Fay and 1st Lt Charles M. Kincaid, "History of the Thirtieth Division Artillery" (Bound Ms, U.S. Army Military History Institute, Carlisle Barracks, Pa. [hereafter cited as MHI], 1945), pp. 27–37.

[52] Ibid., p. 37.

while Army Air Forces pilots practiced battlefield air interdiction thirty years before anyone invented the concept. The result was the complete discomfiture of the Germans. By the time the attack completely fell apart on 8 August, the VII Corps commander, Maj. Gen. J. Lawton Collins, had concentrated seven divisions at the critical point. Worse, from the German perspective, U.S. Third Army was slicing into *Seventh Army*'s lines of communications, threatening to completely encircle that force by linking up with First Canadian Army of the 21st Army Group, attacking south from Caen in the vicinity of the town of Falaise. The question for the Germans became not whether they could establish a defensive position east of the Seine but simply whether they could survive.[53]

While the period of mobile warfare allowed the refinement of air observation posts in command and control and reconnaissance, one of the greatest successes of the period lay in air observation posts effectively performing their primary mission. As the Germans attempted to extract their *Seventh Army* from Normandy, American and British Commonwealth forces almost, but not quite, surrounded it. An escape route remained near Falaise. Moreover, U.S. forces remained very thin on the ground. The easternmost blocking force from Third Army's XV Corps, the 90th Infantry Division, covered a frontage of almost twenty miles with both flanks open. However, the division artillery commander could call upon two reinforcing battalions of corps artillery, a concentration of firepower that possibly suggested to the Germans that the infantry was thicker on the ground than it was in reality. Once again, Allied fighter-bombers worked over German columns deep within the pocket, preventing *Seventh Army* from massing its armor or coordinating its breakout efforts, but left the direct fire support of Allied infantry to the artillery.[54]

One aerial observer noted, in classic understatement, that "there were many targets of opportunity." Many of these targets during the early phases of the operation, however, consisted of flak batteries, which could be deadly against an aircraft flying low, slow, and unaware. Pilots and observers had to remain alert at all times. The *Luftwaffe* also dispatched what few fighters it had to try to protect the battered *Seventh Army*. The air section of the 208th Field Artillery Group countered by assigning two L–4s to each patrol. The second aircraft flew cover just below the observing aircraft. The cover craft's sole mission was to spot enemy flak and aircraft. Planes from many air sections were aloft over the German escape route and vied with one another to complete the most successful fire missions. When Allied fighter-bombers appeared overhead, aerial observers called down concentrations of fire on any German antiaircraft batteries that opened fire. The pilots and observers flew long hours every day, but morale remained high despite the strain and fatigue. It was evident that "one of the great victories of modern warfare was being won."[55]

---

[53] Blumenson, *Breakout and Pursuit*, pp. 457–75.

[54] Rpt, Capt H. H. Reed, Air Obsr, to CO, 975th FA Bn, sub: Most Interesting Phase (Air Obsr); Rpt, [Pilot], 989th FA Bn, sub: Most Satisfactory Phase, both in XV Corps Arty, "Historical Examples." For a more standard use of indirect fire to engage armor, see Rpt, 1st Lt N. N. Nielsen, Air Obsr, 961st FA Bn, sub: Most Interesting Opn, AOP; Rpt, Air Obsr, 144th FA Grp, sub: Least Satisfactory Opn; both in XV Corps Arty, "Historical Examples." Ltr, Capt W. R. Mathews, reprinted in Memo, Maj D. V. Dale, XO, FAS, DAT, 15 Dec 44, sub: Informal Info, in FAS, DAT, "Training Memoranda."

[55] Rpt, Reed to CO, 975th FA Bn, sub: Most Satisfactory Phase (Air Obsr); Rpt, Pilot, 208th FA Grp, sub: Most Interesting Opn; Rpt, Air Section, 250th FA Grp, sub: Most Interesting Opn or Phase; all in XV Corps Arty, "Historical Examples."

The streams of armored vehicles pouring out of the Falaise pocket, particularly the heavily armored Tiger tanks, obviously presented a different problem for the American defenders. Normal procedure in attempting to knock out a tank was to adjust a single gun on it. Usually, German armored vehicles did not move during the day, so once located they were fairly easy to destroy. After considerable experimentation, the commander of the 975th Field Artillery Battalion concluded that the best method at Falaise was to "start fire with a battery salvo" and then continue to adjust with the gun closest to the target.[56]

Motor convoys were a much easier proposition. German escape routes were obvious, based on a casual examination of a map. Air observers plotted sectors along these routes and adjusted guns on them. When leading elements reached a designated point, the battalion would fire a time-on-target salvo. The mass of shells, arriving simultaneously and without warning, destroyed the lead vehicles, jamming the road. Then the aerial observers would walk fire up and down the column until all vehicles were destroyed and all their occupants were either dead, wounded, or dispersed. A pilot with the 989th Field Artillery Battalion recalled the end of one such German column: "They were in all kinds of disorder and it was impossible and also useless to pick out any certain target. . . . We always hit something. We could see trucks loaded with gasoline and ammunition exploding, also horses and men flying in the air."[57]

Horse-drawn vehicles were even more vulnerable. Artillerymen used a mixture of white phosphorous and high explosives against them. The air officer of the 344th Field Artillery Battalion, Lieutenant Mathews, reported horses scattered all over the landscape after one such concentration. Field artillery dominated the killing ground; organized *Seventh Army* units could move only at night.[58]

The last remnants of *Seventh Army* escaped the pocket on 21 August, leaving behind some 50,000 prisoners of war and 10,000 dead. Its casualties in men and equipment were such that the Germans could establish no firm defensive positions short of the German frontier. They could only attempt a series of delaying actions and hope to build up along their prewar fortified position, the Siegfried Line. For the soldiers actually conducting the pursuit, the situation was much more fluid, and dangerous, than such a synopsis suggests.

On 15 August Patton sent part of XV Corps attacking to the east to gain a bridgehead over the Seine with the 5th Armored Division in the lead. Once again General Haislip used artillery aircraft to control his corps' columns. The corps artillery air officer dispatched a plane from the 208th Field Artillery Battalion to locate the forward elements of the 5th Armored Division, a mission that illustrated the difficulties pilots and observers faced on contact missions. Flying in a light rain with poor visibility, the pilot circled the city of Dreux. He and his observer could see ground troops. The Americans could not definitely identify them but thought they were friendly. Approaching cautiously, the flyers abruptly realized they were directly over German vehicles loaded with troops. The aircraft was so low at this point that the Americans "could see the expressions on their faces." The Germans opened fire with everything from rifles to 88-mm. antiaircraft guns. After violent

---

[56] Rpt, Reed to CO, 975th FA Bn, sub: Most Interesting Phase (Air Obsr).

[57] Ltr, Col W. R. Mathews to Col Munson, 28 Feb 91, William R. Mathews Ms, Historian's files, CMH; Interv, author with Mathews, 3 Dec 91. Rpt, Pilot, 989th FA Bn, sub: Historical Examples of FA Opn; Air Section, Most Satisfactory Phase, both in XV Corps Arty, "Historical Examples."

[58] Ltr, Mathews, Incl in Memo, Dale, 15 Dec 44.

evasive maneuvers, the pilot nursed his badly damaged aircraft back to the American lines and reported what he had seen.[59]

Flying was particularly difficult when a great deal of artillery was concentrated into a small area. U.S. Third Army established a bridgehead over the Seine River at Mantes, France, on the night of 19 August. The XV Corps concentrated so much artillery of so many different calibers (and hence of such varying trajectories) to support the bridgehead that the corps artillery staff could not give the corps artillery air officer a safe bracket of airspace for his aircraft. Many times he had to order all aircraft to land so the corps artillery could execute a time-on-target fire mission. Such a procedure hampered observation because of the time lost in landing and then gaining altitude again. At the same time this concentration of guns and organic air sections provided a tempting target for the *Luftwaffe*, continuing its strenuous efforts to assist the retreat of the German Army. The German Air Force bombed and strafed the 693d Field Artillery Battalion's airstrip, damaging both of the battalion's aircraft and wounding one man. Despite this attack, the air section was able to keep its aircraft flying the standard three missions daily.[60]

As the Normandy front collapsed, the German high command had to contend with new dangers to the south. During the spring and summer of 1944, no operation caused more controversy between the governments of the United States and Great Britain than the plan to invade southern France. Initially scheduled to coincide with the landings in Normandy, it was postponed until August 1944 due to a shortage of landing craft. The War Department, and particularly General Marshall, saw it as a means to bring pressure on the German rear, draw troops away from the strategically dubious Italian campaign (which the British considered far more promising), and secure additional ports to more quickly deploy Army divisions remaining in the United States without overloading the congested port facilities of northern France.[61]

Responsibility for the conduct of operations fell to the 6th Army Group, commanded by General Devers, activated on Corsica on 1 August. While preparing the overall plans for the invasion, Devers' headquarters, like Bradley's 12th Army Group, remained offshore until the buildup permitted the formation of two armies—U.S. Seventh and French First Armies. The commander of U.S. Seventh Army, General Patch, used VI Corps, led by Maj. Gen. Lucian K. Truscott, Jr., to make the amphibious assault. Patch's artillery air officer, Major Shepard, consulted with the division artillery air officers of the units involved—the 3d, 36th, and 45th Infantry Divisions—and discovered that each wanted to use decked-over LSTs to launch liaison aircraft. Shepard made arrangements with the Navy to construct the "Cub carriers," using design drawings prepared in the air section of the 3d Infantry Division. On 15 August artillery aircraft from the three divisions supported the successful assault against light resistance from the German *Nineteenth Army*.[62]

---

[59] Rpt, Liaison Pilot, 208th FA Bn, sub: The Most Interesting Opns, in XV Corps Arty, "Historical Examples."

[60] Rpt, Reed to CO, 975th FA Bn; Rpt, Air Section, 693d [FA Bn], sub: The Most Interesting Opn; both in XV Corps Arty, "Historical Examples."

[61] Forrest C. Pogue, *The Supreme Command: The European Theater of Operations*, U.S. Army in World War II (Washington, D.C.: Office of the Chief of Military History, 1954), pp. 108–17, 218–27.

[62] Interv, author with Shepard, 23 Sep 83; Seventh Army, *The Seventh United States Army Report of Operations: France and Germany, 1944–1945*, 3 vols. (Heidelberg, Germany: Aloys Graf, 1946), 1:1–149;

Truscott planned a battle of annihilation against *Nineteenth Army*, using fighter-bombers from the XII Tactical Air Command to cut key bridges in the German rear while the 36th Infantry Division maneuvered on the flank to block *Nineteenth Army's* retreat. Command and control of such a wide-ranging maneuver became possible because Truscott possessed as sophisticated an understanding of the potential of long-range voice radio, the ubiquitous jeep, and light aircraft as any American commander of his generation, including General Wood. Truscott used all three to maintain personal contact with the maneuver elements, delivering his orders orally and in person. Only later did his headquarters provide written confirmation. If the encirclement at Montélimar proved less successful than Truscott anticipated—5,000 prisoners, 4,000 destroyed German vehicles, and 2 German divisions eliminated—the fault derived from factors other than his method of exercising command. Moving "by Cub," he had fashioned a very considerable victory.[63]

A flight from the 72d Liaison Squadron supported VI Corps and, by General Truscott's express direction, reported directly to the corps artillery air officer, Capt. O. Glenn Goodhand, Jr. The Army Air Forces pilots "lived in the mud" with the artillery aviators and generally flew more tactical missions than similar organizations attached to other armies. They flew route reconnaissances for ground units, collected intelligence for corps G–2, and eventually, after some initial disagreements with the commander of the XII Tactical Air Command, Brig. Gen. Gordon P. Saville, directed air strikes by Army Air Forces fighter-bombers. "We would tape . . . [rifle] grenades together in clusters of five and drop them over the side and then use the smoke burst to orient the [P]–47s." An artillery observer normally flew with the pilots and directed the aircraft. Although this system was different from the kind of forward air control practiced by the 1st Armored Division in Italy, VI Corps referred to it as HORSEFLY.[64] Procedures by which Field Artillery pilots could call for fighter-bomber support in Seventh Army remained cumbersome until the end of the war.[65]

Collaboration with the Army Air Forces reached the point that Goodhand arranged to rotate P–47 pilots through the squadron "to assure cooperation and mutual respect." They arrived with the attitude that anyone could fly an L–5. Accustomed as they were to high-performance aircraft, short-field takeoffs and landings proved difficult at first. "We damn near had to shoot some of them down to get them on the ground when they would come in." It also took the P–47 pilots some little time to become accustomed to flying low and

---

MacDonald, *Mighty Endeavor*, pp. 407–08. For background, see Wilt, *The French Riviera Campaign*, and Clarke and Smith, *Riviera to the Rhine*.

[63] Lucian K. Truscott, Jr., *Command Missions: A Personal Story*, Presidio Classics Library (Novato, Calif.: Presidio Press, 1990), p. 433. This is a reprint of the 1954 edition. Clarke and Smith, *Riviera to the Rhine*, pp. 144–70, provides a very thoughtful analysis of this action.

[64] In fact, the image conjured up by the term of the large, pestiferous, persistent insect with a stinging bite that harassed any man or beast within its range proved so evocative of the role of forward air controllers in liaison aircraft that outside of Italy, everyone, even the Air Staff, used the term to include all such operations, no matter who owned or flew the aircraft.

[65] Interv, Kramer and Anderson with Goodhand, 9 May 78; Rpt, Maj Gen T. B. Larkin, DCS, ETO, 9 May 45, sub: Adjusting Close Air Support (Spt); Comments of Lt Braden Vanderventer, Jr., Acting Air-Ground Liaison Ofcr, 100th Inf Div, HQ, AGF, G–4, Requirements Section, Developments Div, FA Branch (Br), Decimal Corresp file, 1942–1945, 319.1 (Misc), RG 337, NARA.

slow over German territory. Practice and experience allowed them to do a fine job, and, once they rotated back to their units, cooperation with the fighter-bombers, already good, became even better. Goodhand's integration of Army Air Forces liaison pilots into light aviation tactical operations freed artillery aircraft to perform their primary mission—fire direction—and set the standard for good relations between Field Artillery and Army Air Forces liaison aviators in Europe.[66]

The question of centralized versus decentralized control remained a matter of some contention during mobile operations. Most corps removed the corps artillery battalions—and with them their aircraft—from centralized group control and distributed them among the corps' divisions in a direct support mission. In XX Corps, however, the corps artillery air officer, Maj. Richard A. Johnson, coordinated all air-observation-post operations, assigning patrol areas just as during positional warfare. Even during periods when the front was static, only a few divisions attempted to maintain centralized control, although, as in Italy, many used one division airstrip at such times. At least one division artillery commander, Brig. Gen. Reese M. Howell of the 9th Infantry Division Artillery, placed all the aircraft assigned or attached to the division under the command of the division air officer. Howell maintained centralized control at all times, much to the dismay of his battalion commanders. As the commander of the attached 957th Field Artillery Battalion, Lt. Col. James L. Collins, noted, on several occasions he had been unable even to obtain a plane to register his battalion.[67]

Most air sections reverted to battalion basing during mobile operations. In such situations, group and division aircraft that had enjoyed a high level of administrative and logistical support, possible when operating from one field, quickly found that such services had vanished and that they had to depend largely on their own resources. Pilots in VII Corps found lack of messing facilities to be the most serious organizational deficiency of the independent air section—possibly as much a comment on the effect of the K-ration on the gastrointestinal tract of pilots and observers at altitude as anything.[68]

The large numbers of bypassed Germans in American rear areas seeking to regain their own lines constituted a more immediate danger in a fluid situation when units had their flanks in the air. Constant vigilance and all-round security were necessary. This was possible only if the air section remained with its parent battalion, locating the landing strip within or immediately adjacent to the battalion perimeter. Topography did not always permit such an arrangement. Moreover, it had the disadvantage of calling the battalion position to the attention of enemy aircraft, which could follow a liaison plane home and shoot

---

[66] Interv, Kramer and Andreson with Goodhand, 9 May 78.

[67] Rpt, Brig Gen J. E. Slack, XX Corps Arty Ofcr, 20 Mar 45, sub: Notes and Obsns on Arty Opns—XX Corps Arty Battles of France and Germany, 1944–1945; Memo, sub: Roster of Ofcrs Serving with HQ and HQ Battery (Btry), XX Corps Arty, Between the Date of Activation, 210401Z Oct 43 and the Cessation of Hostilities, 090001Z May 45; both in XX Corps, "Battles of France and Germany" (Bound Ms, Morris Swett Tech Lib, 1943–1945); An., XII Corps Arty, 1 Nov 44, as revised 10 Apr 45, sub: Standing Operating Procedure, in XII Corps Arty, *XII Corps Artillery in Combat* (Regensburg, Germany: XII Corps, 1945); Intervs, Lt Col E. Hartshorn, AGF Obsr, with Lt Col W. C. Westmoreland, XO, 9th Inf Div Arty; Lt Col J. L. Collins, CO, 957th FA Bn (155H); both in Rpt, Lt Col E. Hartshorn, 6 Jun–22 Jul 44, sub: Obsrs Rpt on Opns of VII Corps in Normandy, Microfilm A1987, AFHRA.

[68] Rpt, Palmer, 12 Jun 45, sub: Battle Experience Conferences on VII Corps Arty Opns in Northern Europe, in VII Corps Arty, "Battle Experience Conferences."

up the battalion area. (The aircraft warning system often failed to perform adequately when the sections were dispersed with their battalions.)[69]

Consequently, air sections often found themselves in semi-isolated positions behind American lines. This meant that the battalions had to augment their air sections with additional men, machine guns, and half-tracks (or in the case of armored divisions a platoon of light tanks) to provide even a semblance of security. Such detachments only weakened the parent battalions' abilities to defend themselves against a sudden ground attack. The air section also had to maintain wire communication between the airstrip and the battalion fire direction center. Coordinating these arrangements with the battalion became a time-consuming task for the battalion air officer. Most pilots and observers who expressed an opinion favored centralized control and administration. Field Artillery battalion commanders often took the opposite point of view.[70]

Some division air sections became adept at centralized operations and gained a particularly strong reputation. The 100th Infantry Division Artillery air section, for example, always maintained one aircraft aloft searching for targets of opportunity and two on strip alert for special missions and registrations. Using this system, the pilot always contacted the S–3 of the battalion desiring the registration so they could agree on the target or targets. Such a procedure eliminated long, drawn-out radio transmissions and the possibility that the observer adjusted fire on one point while the fire direction center "computed corrections for another point."[71]

The 961st Field Artillery Battalion practiced a variant that tried to combine the best features of centralization and decentralization similar to the procedure followed in Italy. The battalion commander did not care what basing policy was used as long as he always had an airplane available when he needed one. The battalion air officer consequently kept his section at the 172d Artillery Group strip but maintained a forward field with the battalion. One pilot flew out of the battalion strip for half a day, while the other ran the air section. Then they reversed roles. This procedure worked even during mobile operations. "By contacting each other each half day, even with the battalion moving from one to three times a day, we had no trouble serving the battalion at all times and both knowing where the base strip was located, when it came night."[72]

---

[69] Ibid.; Rpt, HQ, 975th FA Bn, sub: The Air Section in Combat (Most Interesting Phase); Rpt, 1st Lt E. W. Shirley, AOP, 352d Armored (Armd) FA Bn, sub: Historical Examples of FA Opns—Air Section: The Most Difficult Task; Rpt, Pilot, 961st FA Bn, sub: Historical Examples of FA Opns; all in XV Corps Arty, "Historical Examples"; Hutton, "An Armored Artillery Commander," pp. 135–36.

[70] Rpts, Shirley, 6 May 45, sub: Historical Examples of FA Opns—Air Section: The Most Difficult Task; Pilot, 975th [FA Bn], sub: Most Satisfactory Method of Opn; 989th FA Bn, sub: Historical Examples of FA Opn—Air Section: Most Satisfactory Phase; 693d FA Bn, sub: Air Section: The Most Satisfactory Phase; 1st Lt L. Julian, Air Ofcr, 932d FA Bn, sub: Air Section: The Most Satisfactory Opns; all in XV Corps Arty, "Historical Examples." Hutton, "An Armored Artillery Commander," pp. 135–36; Rpt, Palmer, 12 Jun 45. For a contrary view, see Rpt, Air Section, 772d FA Bn, sub: The most Satisfactory Opn or Phase, in XV Corps Arty, "Historical Examples."

[71] Rpts, Shirley to CG, XV Corps Arty, 16 May 45; T3g James A. Willig, Ground Crew Chief, 342d Armd FA Bn, to CG, XV Corps Arty, 16 May 45, sub: Historical Examples of FA Opns—Air Section: The Most Satisfactory Opn; Air Obsr, 250th FA Bn, sub: Most Satisfactory Opn or Phase; 693d FA Bn; all in XV Corps Arty, "Historical Examples."

[72] Rpt, Air Ofcr, 961st FA Bn, sub: Historical Examples of FA Opn (Air Section), in XV Corps Arty, "Historical Examples."

During the pursuit beyond the Seine River, the air section of the 961st Field Artillery Battalion drew a particularly difficult assignment, flying reconnaissance patrols to protect the right flank of the southernmost division of U.S. Third Army. The pilots and observers had an extensive area to patrol, so extensive that one air section could not cover it adequately. The XIX Tactical Air Command also flew armed reconnaissance along this flank, but otherwise it was open. The Germans, however, were so disorganized by the rapid U.S. advance and distracted by U.S. Seventh Army's landing in the south of France that an organized counterattack never became a problem. German columns seeking to regain their own lines did present a more common difficulty. However, they were often out of range of the battalion's guns, either because the patrol radius took the air observation posts beyond their range or because the battalion had displaced forward. During the entire period of mobile warfare, an aerial observer fired only one registration.[73]

Pursuit operations opened up many opportunities as well as difficulties, even for the lightly armed ground elements of an air section. For example, on 3 September 1944, the 1st Infantry Division attacked north toward Mons, Belgium, approximately seven miles beyond the French border. "A confused and bewildered enemy" tried with only partial success to extricate himself from the path of the division. The division took many captives, including fifty-one Germans who surrendered to the air section of the attached 18th Field Artillery Group.[74]

The first weeks of September constituted the last phase of the great Allied pursuit from Normandy. General Eisenhower's command had outrun its logistical support. Gasoline had become so scarce that the First Army quartermaster started scouting the rear areas in an L–4 to search for advancing gasoline trucks. The armies needed time to refit and resupply, even as some of the most gifted combat commanders realized that the Germans still had not succeeded in cobbling together any kind of a firm defensive front. On 7 September the main force of the U.S. 2d Armored Division was immobilized around Tournai, Belgium, for lack of fuel. The division commander, Maj. Gen. Edward H. Brooks, however, had pushed reconnaissance elements as much as twenty miles in advance of the main body. The division artillery aircraft accompanied them.[75]

The pilot and observer in one air observation post working with an armored car section saw German infantry heading for some woods. After the observer alerted the armored cars, which had to negotiate a ditch to intervene, the pilot made several strafing runs to slow the enemy withdrawal. The observer fired a submachine gun out the window and even dropped hand grenades. During each pass, the Germans either took cover or stopped to return fire. On the last pass either the Germans or the observer, in his excitement, shot off the Cub's propeller. The pilot made a perfect dead-stick landing in the only open space—squarely in the midst of the Germans. They were clearly inclined to settle scores, but at that moment the armored cars drove into view and put an

---

[73] Rpt, Nielsen, sub: Most Unsatisfactory Task, AOP, in XV Corps Arty, "Historical Examples."

[74] AAR, Brig Gen Clift Andrus, 1st Inf Div Arty, to TAG, 5 Oct 44, sub: Unit Rpt of Action, 1 September to 30 September 1944, in 1st Inf Div Arty, "Unit Report of Action, 1942–1945" (Bound Ms, Morris Swett Tech Lib, 1942–1945).

[75] Blumenson, *Breakout and Pursuit*, pp. 676–702, provides an overview of the situation in early September 1942, as does Charles B. MacDonald, *The Siegfried Line Campaign*, U.S. Army in World War II (Washington, D.C.: Office of the Chief of Military History, 1963), p. 13. Hutton, "An Armored Artillery Commander," p. 150.

end to what had started as fun and ended as farce. There was nothing farcical, however, about the wreckage of the German armies in the west that stretched from the Channel coast to the French frontier.[76]

The Border Battles

The border battles in the fall of 1944 brought a new set of problems: the attack on permanent fortifications. In the north, U.S. First and Ninth Armies bumped up against the belts of pillboxes with interlocking fields of fire, known collectively as the Siegfried Line. To the south, Third Army had to attack towns at Metz, Thionville, and Nancy, which were protected by nineteenth-century ring fortresses. The XIX Corps worked out two techniques for dealing with the pillboxes of the Siegfried Line. Air observation posts played a major role in one of them. Light artillery, often directed from an L–4, forced the Germans to take cover. Then an aerial observer directed precision fire by a single heavy gun until a direct hit destroyed the pillbox or bunker. From the infantry's perspective, this clearly was preferable to the second technique, which required infantrymen to shoot at the embrasures and suppress the defender's fire until some of the attackers could fire a bazooka or push a pole charge into the bunker. In the south, the massive steel, concrete, and masonry forts proved impervious to the heaviest American ordnance. Third Army had to depend upon a variant of the second technique used against the Siegfried Line. Companies or even battalions had to gain the roofs of the forts by assault so combat engineers could blow a hole in the armored roof. Units engaged in this task often found themselves isolated. Light aircraft kept them supplied until reinforcements could break through or the attackers withdrew.[77]

In the 90th Infantry Division's assault on Fort Koenigsmacker outside Thionville, three companies gained the roof, but German machine guns firing from emplacements effectively isolated them from all reinforcement and resupply. In this crisis an artillery pilot, 1st Lt. Lloyd A. Watland, sought to find the best approach by air to the isolated companies on top of the fort—an approach that put aircraft at least risk to the numerous German light flak batteries in the area. Watland discovered that if he flew at treetop level and below (sometimes at an altitude of ten feet), the Germans could not depress their 20-mm. guns sufficiently to bring him under fire. This limitation, unfortunately, did not hold true for small-arms fire, but Watland located a "reasonably safe" approach. Division artillery L–4s dropped 5,000 pounds of supplies to the companies, including 1,500 pounds of explosives with detonator caps. Food, blankets, batteries, medical supplies, and a map of the fort constituted the remainder of the resupply effort. No aircraft were lost. "This was a hazardous operation," concluded the Third Army artillery air officer, Colonel Wilson, "and should be attempted only when all other means fail."[78]

---

[76] Hutton, "An Armored Artillery Commander," pp. 150–51.

[77] Rpts, sub: Narrative of the Attack: Arty and Air Spt; Lt Col B. Butler, Jr., CO, 258th FA Bn, to CG, XIX Corps, sub: Destruction of Concrete Pillboxes by Short-Range Fire from M–12, 155mm. Gun, [Self Propelled]; sub: Pillbox Reduction; all in XIX Corps, "Breaching the Siegfried Line: XIX Corps, U.S. Army, 2 October 1944" (Bound Ms, CMH Lib, c. 1946).

[78] AOP Bulletin no. 5, Third Army, 8 Jan 45, in Third Army, *After Action Reports*, 2:Arty–14; Hugh M. Cole, *The Lorraine Campaign*, U.S. Army in World War II (Washington, D.C.: Office of the Chief of Military History, 1950), pp. 390–92.

Some L–4s Temporarily Grounded by a Flood near the German Frontier, Rambervillers, France, 1944

The 95th Infantry Division, assaulting the city of Metz proper, twice resupplied isolated battalions by air. The division pilots called the operation the Red Ball Air Express, a reference to the 24-hour motor convoys keeping the field armies supplied from the beaches. In bitter fighting near Fort Jeanne d' Arc on 19 November, the regimental surgeon of the 379th Infantry rode in an L–4 into a pocket to care for wounded who could not be taken out overland. L–4s evacuated the most critically wounded, strapped in the observer's seat, and brought in medical supplies for the surgeon, who remained in the pocket until the reestablishment of a ground line of communications.[79]

---

[79] Rpt, G–4, 95th Inf Div, sub: Summary of G–4, 95th Inf Div, Actions from 1 Nov 44 to 30 Nov 44, in HQ, AGF, G–4, Requirements Section, Development Div, FA Br, Decimal Corresp file, 1942–1945, 319.1 (Misc), RG 337, NARA. "Red Ball Express" was used on U.S. railways to refer to fast, through freight trains. Headquarters, Services of Supply, U.S. European Command, used the phrase immediately following the Normandy invasion to designate a special delivery service for the speedy movement of critical supplies to the far shore. During the transportation crisis following the breakout from the Normandy bridgehead, Services of Supply organized a one-way, circular truck route from the beachhead to the field armies and back, which operated continuously. The transportation companies that hauled supplies and equipment thereupon were known as the Red Ball Express. Ruppenthal, *Logistical Support of the Armies*, 1:309–10, 559–60.

By then the 4th Armored Division had already demonstrated a new technique that held the most promise for the future of organic aviation. On 19 September during a fog-shrouded counterattack by *XLVII Panzer Corps* against the 4th Armored Division at Arracourt, France, the division artillery air officer, now Major Carpenter, reputedly knocked out two tanks from an L–4. No pilot was more enthusiastic about arming liaison aircraft than Carpenter, whose advocacy of his weapon of choice earned him the nickname Bazooka Charley. A civilian in uniform, he had been a high school history teacher in Moline, Illinois. During the breakout from Normandy, two lieutenants in the division put a bazooka under each wing of their L–4. They claimed to have knocked out two German trucks, which piqued Carpenter's interest. About the same time, Carpenter also learned of now Major Haynes' experiments with a rocket-firing Cub at Grove and secured permission to bring it to the Continent.[80]

Although all other aircraft were grounded because of fog on 19 September, Carpenter somehow took off successfully. Through a break in the mist he saw a company of German armor attacking toward the division's water supply point. He radioed a warning to the supply point crew, then regained altitude and went into a steep dive. He fired two rockets. Both missed. On a second pass his aim, or perhaps his luck, was better, and he knocked out one tank. His third pass added yet another victim. At that point he had expended all his antitank rockets, but the German commander, disconcerted by this totally unexpected intervention from the air, hastily broke contact and withdrew. In miniature this episode foreshadowed the fate that befell *XLVII Panzer Corps* later in the day when the fog cleared sufficiently for Army Air Forces fighter-bombers to take off. The only disconcerting element lay in higher headquarters' inability to find any physical evidence to support Carpenter's report, which might testify to the efficacy of German armor retrieval and repair efforts. While Carpenter and the 4th Armored Division had no doubts as to what had happened, considerable skepticism remained at higher levels.[81]

The German Counteroffensive

The German counteroffensive against First Army in the Ardennes—the Battle of the Bulge—opened on 16 December 1944. The initial German success, the deep penetration by German armor columns, and adverse weather conditions combined to make air-observation-post operations difficult. The first day of the attack in the lightly held VIII Corps sector was marked by haze and ground fog. Not even L–4s flew in the northern portion of the corps front, but farther south the two aircraft of the 42d Field Artillery Battalion were

---

[80] Intervs, author with Haynes, 26 Feb 92; with Wilson, 3 Aug 91; "Fighting Fronts: Puddle Jumped Panzers," *Newsweek* 24 (2 October 1944):31; Clipping, Earl Mazzo, "Rocket-Firing Cubs Kill Tanks," *Stars and Stripes*, Charles W. Lefever Ms, Historian's files, CMH.

[81] William D. Ellis and Thomas J. Cunningham, Jr., *Clarke of St. Vith: The Sergeant's General* (Cleveland, Ohio: Dillon/Liederbach, 1974), pp. 69–70, give the most detailed account of this incident. Rpt, Brig Gen A. Franklin Kibler, et al., sub: Liaison Aircraft with Ground Force Units, in ETO, General Board, *Liaison Aircraft with Ground Force Units*, Rpt 20 [General Board, European Theater of Operations, 1946]; Interv, author with Haynes, 26 Feb 92, and with Wilson, 3 Aug 91; *Newsweek* 24 (2 October 1944):31. See also Ken Wakefield, *The Fighting Grasshoppers: U.S. Liaison Aircraft Operations in Europe, 1942–1945* (Stillwater, Minn.: Specialty Press, 1990), p. 72. Carpenter claimed to have destroyed at least five tanks during the war. Mazzo, "Rocket-Firing Cubs Kill Tanks."

able to take off and bring fire down on German armor columns. The ability of artillery to deliver observed fire on this and subsequent days permitted VIII Corps to maintain a continuous front in this sector despite heavy pressure. In the north, German armor penetrated the front so rapidly that it overran the division airfields of the 99th and 2d Infantry Divisions on 17 December. The pilots of the 99th Infantry Division succeeded in flying their aircraft out at the last minute; the 2d Infantry Division pilots had to abandon their planes and seek friendly lines overland. The rapidity and depth of the German penetrations completely upset artillery command and control in the northern sector. Beginning on 18 December pilots from the First Army air section, led by Major Bristol, began directing Army Air Forces fighter-bombers onto the German armor columns, imposing an important check on one of them at Trois Ponts. Weather permitting, the artillery aircraft continued in this role through the remainder of the battle. Conditions were so confused for a time that four P–51s shot down a liaison plane from the First Army air section piloted by 1st Lt. Hugh K. Stephenson.[82]

Despite often appalling weather conditions, Field Artillery pilots played a role in the defense and relief of the garrison at Bastogne. When medical supplies ran low inside the perimeter, a pilot from the 28th Infantry Division, 1st Lt. Kenneth B. Schelly, flew a supply of penicillin into the city on the night of 24–25 December, landing at a strip hastily improvised for the occasion. Pilots supporting Third Army's efforts to break the siege found that low-lying clouds forced them to fly at altitudes of two to three hundred feet. Icing was a problem; XII Corps lost two aircraft to this condition. When Third Army hastily shifted its front to attack to the north, Third Army artillery pilots had to prepare their own strips. Pilots landed in snow-covered clearings and taxied back and forth until the snow was compact enough for takeoffs. Rain, freezing rain, snow, and high winds, however, kept air-observation-post operations on the southern shoulder much more restricted than in the north.[83]

Similar conditions made the winter months unsafe for light aircraft operations on other sectors of the front that were static or semistatic. A stable front meant that targets of opportunity for aerial observers appeared only at first light, before dawn, and at twilight. Only then did the Germans begin to move about. Otherwise, they remained well dug-in and camouflaged and thus for all practical purposes were invisible to aerial observers. Most division commanders insisted that air observation posts fly routine patrols over their front during all hours of daylight, if only to provide security against surprise attack. Poor visibility meant that pilots had to fly at abnormally low altitudes—one thousand feet or less—over German lines to observe the fall of shells, which in turn exposed the aircraft to small-arms fire. Pilots and observers carried out these missions with at best minimal returns.

---

[82] Lt. Col. Joseph R. Reeves, "Artillery in the Ardennes," *FAJ* 36 (May 1946):138–42, 173–84; Interv, Epstein with Bristol, 1 Jul 75; Ltr, J. C. Chislie to Col D. L. Bristol, 14 Jun 79, Bristol Ms, Florissant, Mo.; Hugh M. Cole, *The Ardennes: Battle of the Bulge*, U.S. Army in World War II (Washington, D.C.: Office of the Chief of Military History, 1965), pp. 242–43. See also Charles B. MacDonald, *A Time for Trumpets: The Untold Story of the Battle of the Bulge* (New York: William Morrow, 1985).

[83] Lt. Col. William R. Jesse, "Bastogne—An Artillery Classic," *FAJ* 35 (December 1945):718–20; Interv, Col. G. J. Wolf with Maj P. Thornton, 31 Mar 45, Incl in Rpt, Wolf to CG, AGF, 28 May 45, sub: Rpt of Special Obsr European and Mediterranean Theaters of Opns, 15 Mar–30 Apr 45, Wolf Ms, CMH; Intervs, author with Wilson, 3 Aug 91, and with Haynes, 26 Feb 92; Andrew Ten Eyck, *Jeeps in the Sky: The Story of the Light Plane* (New York: Commonwealth Books, 1946), pp. 49–50.

An L–4 Lands on Skis in France, January 1945; *below*, Tech. 5 William E. Huddleston Tunes the Engine of an L–4 of the 84th Infantry Division in Belgium.

The Final Battles

The fighting west of the Rhine ended with a pursuit that demonstrated how much artillery air sections had benefited from their experiences in France the previous year. Air observation posts in XV Corps of Seventh Army, for example, flew almost exclusively what in World War I had been known as infantry contact missions but now resided under the general rubric of reconnaissance. Aircraft covered the front, keeping division headquarters apprised of the location of their advance elements and occasionally flying route reconnaissance for those elements. The divisions maintained centralized control during the pursuit, which simplified keeping all sectors of the front covered while at the same time ensuring that pilots were always available. An aerial observer with the 693d Field Artillery Battalion, attached to the 3d Infantry Division for this operation, recalled flying three to four patrols daily. On one of these he succeeded in locating a German 88-mm. dual-purpose gun in ambush, warned off the advancing American armor column, and called fire down on the enemy position to destroy the gun. Cut-off Germans surrendered to following elements, in some instances to air sections making road marches.[84]

The advantages that organic aerial observation conferred in the fluid and confused conditions that characterized pursuits received stunning confirmation in the first Allied crossing of the Rhine River. The 9th Armored Division's seizure of the intact Ludendorff Bridge at Remagen, Germany, was a coup de main that depended on accurate intelligence, rapid movement, and superiority of force at the critical point. Delayed by soggy ground and rubble-filled roads, the commander of the division's Combat Command B, Brig. Gen. William M. Hoge, dispatched a task force toward Remagen at 1000 on 7 March 1945. Under heavy, low clouds that kept the planes of the Army Air Forces grounded, a L–4 flown by Lt. Harold E. Larson of the 16th Armored Field Artillery Battalion, with Lt. Frank L. Vaughn as an observer, reconnoitered the task force's route. At 1030 they became the first Americans to see the undamaged bridge, and their radio report convinced Hoge to try to capture it before the defenders could destroy it. By thus setting in motion the sequence of events that led to the successful dash of Company A, 27th Armored Infantry Battalion, across the span, aerial observation played a crucial role in one of the most dramatic and successful feats of arms by the U.S. Army during the war.[85]

In contrast to the relative simplicity and routine nature of the Field Artillery aviation role at Remagen, the other two major crossings of the Rhine highlighted both the complexity that air-observation-post operations had achieved during the final phase of the war and the future potential of organic air in ground operations. In the north, the 21st Army Group under Field Marshal Montgomery, including U.S. Ninth Army, prepared a carefully planned, deliberate attack. In preparation for the offensive, the XVI Corps artillery air officer, Maj. David Hallstein, assembled some one hundred-fifty aircraft in a normal divi-

---

[84] Rpt, 2d Lt K. L. Kirby, 202d FA Bn, to CO, 202d FA Bn, 29 May 45, sub: Opns of Aerial Obsn Pilot; Most Interesting Opn; Rpt, Air Obsr, [693d FA Bn]; Rpt, 1st Lt C. L. Kureth, 202d FA Bn, to CO, 202d FA Bn, 29 May 45, sub: Opns of Air Section: Most Satisfactory; all in XV Corps Arty, "Historical Examples."

[85] Maj. Elridge L. Brubaker, et al., *Armor in River Crossings: A Research Report Prepared by Committee 22, Officers Advanced Course, The Armored School, 1949–1950* (Fort Knox, Ky.: Armored School, 1950), pp. 8–14; Walter E. Reichelt, *Phantom Nine: The 9th Armored (Remagen) Division, 1942–1945* (Austin, Tex., Presidial Press, 1987), pp. 194–204. Doubler, *Closing with the Enemy*, pp. 159–168, provides an excellent analysis. Ken Hechler, *The Bridge at Remagen*, (New York: Ballantine Books, 1957) remains the classic account.

sional airspace. Such a concentration posed two related issues—how to prevent midair collisions in a congested airspace and how to keep the Germans from discovering the concentration and discerning the location of the impending American attack.[86]

The XVI Corps commander, Maj. Gen. John B. Anderson, ordered Hallstein to assume control over all the aircraft in the corps zone. Hallstein prohibited the new divisions from flying their aircraft at the front and restricted the 75th Infantry Division to having three aircraft in the air at any one time. They performed all the necessary aerial reconnaissance for the other divisions. The 34th Field Artillery Brigade, the assigned corps artillery element for XVI Corps, could fly two aircraft simultaneously. They performed the same function for the reinforcing corps artillery battalions. Occasionally, a new unit's plane would be allowed to fly at the front, but only if it was repainted with the 75th Infantry Division's or 34th Field Artillery Brigade's markings, operated under the division's or brigade's control, and conformed to the limits on the numbers of aircraft in the air.[87]

Use of the proximity fuze both contributed to the effectiveness of the XVI Corps Artillery's fire and complicated Hallstein's problems immeasurably. First introduced in ground combat during the Ardennes campaign, it consisted of a tiny transmitting and receiving radio set placed in the nose of a shell. In theory, the radio transmitted a beam that bounced off the target and back to the receiver. At a preset distance from the target, reception of the returning radio wave triggered the fuze, causing the shell to explode. Air bursts could be deadly against dug-in infantry unless they had overhead cover. Reality matched theory as long as the shell did not come close to any other solid object, such as an air observation post, while en route to its target. To prevent such an occurrence, the XVI Corps artillery staff devised an elaborate grid section, arbitrarily identified by certain code names. Any battalion commander desiring to fire proximity fuzes first had to obtain permission from the corps artillery officer. Hallstein then cleared all aircraft out of any affected grids. The system worked well. The XVI Corps lost no aircraft to proximity fuzes.[88]

In the Third Army area of operations to the south, the artillery air officer of XII Corps, Major Haynes, made plans almost equally elaborate. The Third Army artillery officer, Col. Edward T. Williams, suggested the possibility of landing an infantry battalion by light plane to seize a bridgehead east of the Rhine. General Patton approved the concept. Haynes and the corps air section, reinforced by the army air section and by Lt. Col. Robert R. Williams, then on a fact-finding mission for the War Department, prepared detailed loading plans to carry 300 infantrymen and their personal weapons to the far bank of the Rhine. Moving these men in a single lift meant using virtually every light aircraft under Third Army's control, so the planning had to be both intricate and precise. Haynes' plans con-

---

[86] Rpt, Brig Gen C. C. Brown, CG, XVI Corps Arty, [10 Aug 45], sub: FLASHPOINT: The Rhine Crossing, 24 Mar 45; Memo, sub: Organization of XVI Corps Arty During "FLASHPOINT"; both in XVI Corps Arty, "FLASHPOINT: The Rhine Crossing, 1945" (Bound Ms, Morris Swett Tech Lib, 1945).

[87] Ibid.

[88] Memo, Col J. P. Daley, XO, Arty Ofcr, Twelfth Army Grp, for Arty Ofcr, Twelfth Army Grp, 16 Feb 45, sub: Operational Experience with Pozit Fuze; Opns Memo 3, XVI Corps, 8 Feb 43; both in HQ, AGF, G–4, Requirements Section, Development Div, FA Br, Decimal Corresp file, 1942–1945, 319.1 (Misc), RG 337, NARA; Rpt, Brown, [10 Aug 45]. For the nontechnical description of the proximity fuze, see Roy E. Appleman, et al., *Okinawa: The Last Battle*, U.S. Army in World War II (Washington: Historical Division, 1948), p. 257.

THE EUROPEAN THEATER 233

A SECTION OF GERMAN AUTOBAHN SERVES AS AN AIRSTRIP FOR ARMY L–4S, MARCH 1945.

templated the rapid reinforcement of a preexisting bridgehead, a concept more in line with the capabilities of light aircraft.[89]

Events soon overtook the planners. The 5th Infantry Division secured a lodgment on the east bank during the night of 22–23 March, which produced a rare appearance by the *Luftwaffe* the next day. The German planes could not prevent the 5th Infantry Division's buildup in the bridgehead, but their presence did dissuade XII Corps from attempting what a later generation would style an airmobile assault. Despite the aborted outcome, Patton pronounced it a "good idea," although, with hindsight and visions of the airspace congestion involved, the army artillery air officer, Colonel Wilson, was just as happy that he had not had to execute it.[90]

The campaign east of the Rhine was, for Field Artillery pilots, essentially a repetition in its tactical detail of the pursuit across France. There were a few oddities. In April 1945

---

[89] Intervs, Col R. J. Powell and Lt Col P. E. Courts with Lt Gen R. R. Williams, 1978, MHI; author with Wilson, 3 Aug, 6 Nov 91, and with Haynes, 26 Feb 92; Diary, G. S. Patton, 21 Mar 45, George S. Patton Ms, Library of Congress, Washington, D.C. (hereafter cited as LC). Edward T. Williams was promoted to brigadier general on 21 March 1945, but since Patton still referred to him as "Colonel Williams" in his diary, presumably neither man yet knew of the promotion. Memo, Department of Defense, Public Affairs Office, Sep 59, sub: Lt Gen Edward T. Williams, Biographical files, Historical Resources Br, CMH.

[90] George S. Patton, *War As I Knew It* (Boston: Houghton Mifflin and Co., 1947), p. 267; Charles B. McDonald, *The Last Offensive*, U.S. Army in World War II (Washington, D.C.: Office of the Chief of Military History, 1973), pp. 266–73; Interv, author with Wilson, 3 Aug 91.

the air section of the 208th Field Artillery Group, temporarily located near Bamberg, Germany, was successfully strafed by a jet fighter, an Me–262, operating out of Augsburg, Germany. All but two of the ten aircraft of the group were flying missions at the time, but those craft, as well as much of the section's gear, were damaged, and their pilots injured. The next day an Me–262 attempted a return engagement, but four P–47s jumped the German craft. The jet left the piston fighters as if they were standing still. Later the artillery air officer for the 208th Field Artillery Group, Capt. John Gall, located a wrecked Me–262 near Salzburg, Austria. He always liked to think it was the same one that had given his unit such problems.[91]

One of the few air-to-air engagements involving L–4s during this period also added a new twist. An L–4 from the 71st Armored Field Artillery Battalion of the 5th Armored Division intercepted a German Fieseler Storch flying toward Berlin. The artillery pilot, Lt. Duane Francies, and his observer, Lt. William S. Martin, hit the Storch with pistol fire and forced it to crash-land. Francies then landed in a beet field. He and Martin captured the German pilot and a passenger, whom they turned over to a passing American tank column. Then Francies took off and resumed his patrol. He and Martin thus recorded one of the last aerial victories in the European Theater of Operations.[92]

The major difference between the campaign in France and the campaign in Germany was at the operational level—in the spring of 1945 the Germans had to fall back toward an on-rushing Red Army rather than a fortified sanctuary. The German surrender on 8 May 1945 meant that the U.S. Army had passed its greatest test. The aura of victory also validated the concept of organic aviation.

Conclusion

While air observation posts had attained a high level of sophistication in the early stages of the Italian campaign, they reached their greatest development during the campaigns in France and Germany in 1944 and 1945. Air sections demonstrated their ability to participate in mobile warfare on a sustained basis. Pilots and observers proved once more their ability to execute their artillery missions of observed fire, reconnaissance of position areas for batteries and routes for marches, security patrols on both the flanks and to the front of positions, camouflage checks of troop positions from the air, and the collection of information about nearby friendly and enemy forces. As in Italy, they performed many of the missions originally intended for Army Air Forces liaison squadrons in the combat zone from corps headquarters forward, to include messenger and courier service, transport and ferry service for ground forces personnel and equipment, visual reconnaissance, light photographic reconnaissance, and limited air evacuation. At the same time the Field Artillery aircraft vindicated the vision of Maj. Gen. Adna R. Chaffee, Jr., and the other American participants in the light aircraft experiments at Fort Knox in 1940 and 1941. The L–4 provided commanders an ideal means of maintaining control over far-flung, rapidly moving, mechanized and motorized columns as well as allowing those comman-

---

[91] Gall, Combat Narrative, p. 2.
[92] Wayne C. Dunlap, "The Last Fighter Pilot of World War II," *L–4 Grasshopper Wing Newsletter* 47 (September/October 1994):7–8.

ders to orient themselves to the ground over which they would pass. Field Artillery pilots performed distant reconnaissance on a regular basis for mobile columns. Like their counterparts in Italy, they carried out certain missions not anticipated before their commitment to combat, such as radio relay, limited aerial resupply, and emergency vectoring of fighter-bombers onto targets of opportunity. The utility of these missions and the ease with which ground commanders could direct them contributed to the sense among both pilots and the ground personnel they supported that air observation posts ought to be a permanent part of the Army, rather than just a temporary wartime expedient.[93]

During the postwar years, the campaign in Europe served as a model for what might be called the orthodox approach to organic aviation. Proponents emphasized the use of fixed-wing aircraft operating under decentralized control to provide observed fire for the Field Artillery and aerial transportation for commanders and senior staff officers in the battle area, the missions and equipment which contributed so much to the success of that campaign. Advocates of both new missions and new equipment had to accommodate themselves to the great appeal of this wartime success. Innovations had to enhance, not detract from, organic aviation's ability to carry out these "traditional" missions, validated in combat.

If the very degree of the air-observation-post success in France and Germany held conservative implications for the postwar force, two other functions, not yet formally codified as missions, suggested future directions of change. Both brought Field Artillery pilots to the very performance limits of their aircraft. The XII Corps' planned, but not executed, airlanding using light aircraft suggested the possibility of transporting ground troops by air within the battle area and inserting them at some decisive point for the ground battle, the concept that Lt. Col. John C. L. Adams had proposed at Fort Bragg in 1942. A subsequent generation termed the XII Corps concept *airmobility*. Major Carpenter's use of an L–4 in an antiarmor role in the 4th Armored Division hinted at a revival of the direct fire support of closely engaged ground troops from the air. (This had been performed on a limited basis by III Corps observation squadrons during World War I and championed by Col. Byron Q. Jones in the interwar period.) It is doubtful if a majority of Field Artillery pilots, let alone ground officers or Army Air Forces officers, would have agreed on the utility of organic aviation performing these functions. Yet, for the pilots as well as for the ground officers, the question was not one of doctrine but of technology: Could light aircraft accomplish these missions? By squeezing all potential performance out of L–4s and L–5s, Field Artillery pilots not only demonstrated what was possible but also what might become possible with improved equipment. Without realizing it, they created a demand among both themselves and the men they supported for a machine that most of them would not hear about until after the end of the war—the helicopter.

---

[93] Kibler, et al., *Liaison Aircraft with Ground Force Units*, pp. 2–4; Maj. Delbert L. Bristol, "Air OP Is Here To Stay," *FAJ* 36 (October 1946):586–87.

CHAPTER 7

The Pacific, June 1943–September 1945

The experiences of air-observation-post pilots and mechanics in the Pacific in many respects paralleled those in Europe and North Africa. Administrative, logistical, and doctrinal problems all demanded answers, and many evoked similar, if independently arrived at, solutions. At the same time, there were significant differences. Strong-minded individuals in positions of authority, disparate command structures, novel terrain, and vast amounts of water played their parts in making some elements of the air sections' Pacific operations unique.

Personalities, Command Arrangements, Terrain, and Water

Theoretically, the Pacific Ocean and all the lands that bordered it constituted a single theater (*Map 7*). Practical considerations led the Joint Chiefs of Staff to propose and the president to approve the division of the region into two major commands: the Southwest Pacific Area, commanded by General Douglas MacArthur, and the Pacific Ocean Areas, commanded by Admiral Chester L. Nimitz. The latter was further subdivided into three parts: the North Pacific Area (where Field Artillery aircraft flew no combat missions during the war), the Central Pacific Area, and the South Pacific Area. Nimitz also personally commanded the Central Pacific Area. After 18 October 1942, Admiral William F. Halsey commanded the South Pacific Area. The personalities and backgrounds of these men and the kinds of headquarters they established had a major impact on the employment of Field Artillery aircraft in their areas.[1]

General MacArthur, unlike General Dwight D. Eisenhower in Europe, remained detached from and uninterested in the Air-Observation-Post Program. MacArthur had left the United States after stepping down as Army chief of staff on 1 October 1935. As the commander of the Philippine Army, he had remained isolated from the main currents of military thought in the United States during the next six years. Recalled to active duty with

---

[1] Louis Morton, *Strategy and Command: The First Two Years*, U.S. Army in World War II (Washington, D.C.: Office of the Chief of Military History, 1962), pp. 240–63, 343–44.

MAP 7

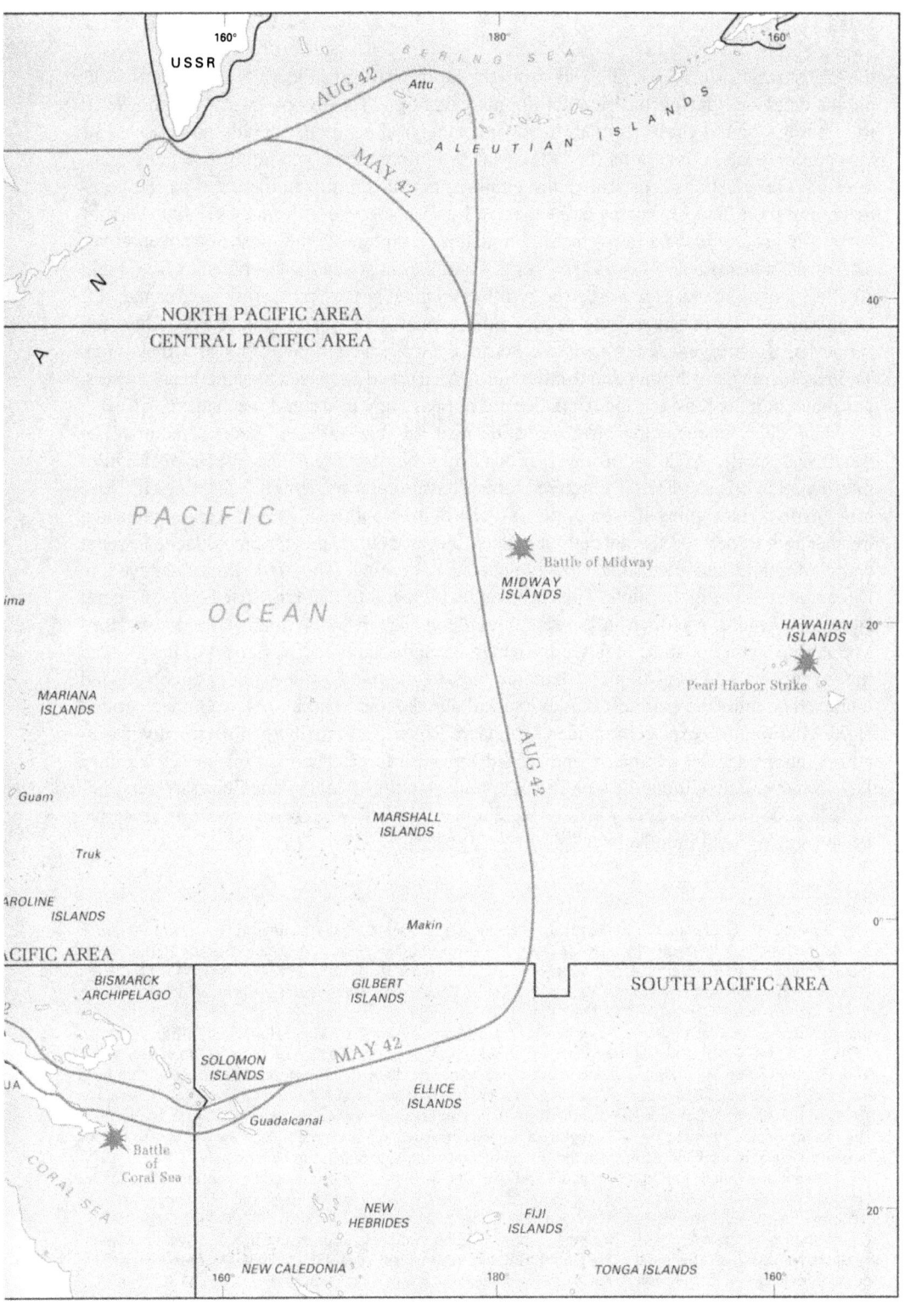

the U.S. Army in July 1941, he was properly appreciative of modern field artillery techniques employed during the first Philippine campaign. The troops on Bataan, however, fought too soon to benefit from all the refinements of the system, including the use of air observation posts. Concerning the latter, MacArthur remained both uninformed and uninterested. On questions concerning the employment of aircraft, he deferred to the commander of the Allied Air Forces in the theater, Lt. Gen. George C. Kenney. Of all the senior Army Air Forces officers in overseas commands, Kenney was the most outspoken advocate of the advantages of centralized control and the most adamant opponent of the Field Artillery's organic aviation. Some senior officers, notably the Sixth Army commander, Lt. Gen. Walter C. Krueger, and the deputy chief of staff of I Corps, Col. Rex E. Chandler, supported the program. But they were not, like Lt. Gen. Mark W. Clark and Brig. Gen. Thomas E. Lewis in England and later North Africa and Italy, at the same headquarters. For many months Krueger and Chandler did not have any pilots and mechanics.[2]

This delay in receiving air-observation-post sections reflected several factors. The Southwest Pacific Area had a lower priority than North Africa. The effects of the pilot matriculation crisis at Fort Sill lingered long after the solution, simply because of the lead time involved in training liaison pilots. No one in the Southwest Pacific Area organized a local school to provide the needed personnel, but, of course, the command lacked even a cadre of pilots and mechanics to conduct such training. The first aircraft arrived in December 1942 without pilots. The commanding general of the Army Air Forces, General Henry H. Arnold, was then in the region conferring with MacArthur. Arnold convinced MacArthur's chief of staff, Maj. Gen. Richard K. Sutherland, to divert most of the L–4s to the Army Air Forces. Colonel Chandler knew something of the issues involved and launched an immediate protest, but to no avail. On the north shore of New Guinea, around Buna Mission, the corps commander, Maj. Gen. Robert L. Eichelberger, personally directed operations against a strongly entrenched Japanese force. The men of the 32d Infantry Division operated without the benefits of organic aviation. "One of our Cubs (artillery liaison planes) would have been worth its weight in gold there. We received no Cubs," recalled Eichelberger, "until months later."[3]

---

[2] Ltrs, Col R. E. Chandler to Lt Gen R. L. Eichelberger, 21 Dec 42, and Chandler to Brig Gen C. Byers, 8 Jan 43; both in R. E. Chandler Manuscript (Ms), U.S. Army Military History Institute, Carlisle Barracks, Pa. (hereafter cited as MHI); Henry H. Arnold, *Global Mission* (New York: Harper, 1949), pp. 331, 343–47. George C. Kenney, *General Kenney Reports* (Washington, D.C.: Office of Air Force History, 1987), pp. 29–30, 47–48, 51–53, 75–76, 88–89, 99, 101–04, 111, 114, 117, 133, 140–41, 144–46, 151–52, 163–64, 178–79. On MacArthur, see D. Clayton James, *The Years of MacArthur*, 3 vols. (Boston: Houghton Mifflin and Co., 1970–1985), 1:479–619, and Geoffrey Perret, *Old Soldiers Never Die: The Life of Douglas MacArthur* (New York: Random House, 1996), the best one-volume biography. For MacArthur's reaction to the new Field Artillery doctrine, see [Douglas MacArthur], "General MacArthur's Tribute," *Field Artillery Journal* (*FAJ*) 32 (June 1942):418. John W. Whitman's discussion of artillery employment in *Bataan: Our Last Ditch* (New York: Hippocrene Books, 1990), pp. 69–87, provides a needed corrective to MacArthur's "over the top" optimism. An in-depth account of the Field Artillery in the first Philippine campaign remains to be written.

[3] Memo, Brig Gen R. E. Porter, Assistant Chief of Staff (ACS), G–3, for Commanding Generals (CGs), Army Ground Forces (AGF) and Army Air Forces (AAF), 27 Jul 43, sub: Liaison Pilots and Mechanics for Field Artillery (FA), Headquarters (HQ), AGF, General Correspondence (Gen Corresp), 1942–1948, 353/19 (FA Air Observation [Obsn]) (Secret [S]), Record Group (RG) 337, National Archives and Records Administration, Washington, D.C. (hereafter cited as NARA); Ltr, Chandler to Byers, 8 Jan 43; Arnold, *Global Mission*, p. 331; quote from Robert L. Eichelberger, *Our Jungle Road to Tokyo* (New York: Viking Press, 1950), p. 39.

In the neighboring South Pacific Area, the same situation prevailed, although for somewhat different reasons. Admiral Halsey organized his headquarters on naval lines and did not create a single land force headquarters. The largest Army formation was XIV Corps; consequently, the XIV Corps artillery air officer was the senior technical officer in the area. Field Artillery pilots in the South Pacific Area did not enter combat until December 1943 on Bougainville. The date reflected War Department priorities for shipping air sections, even lower than for the Southwest Pacific Area, but also certain operational constraints. Until Bougainville, the Americans had lacked bases close enough for L–4s to fly into the area of operations. The Navy, at this stage of the Pacific war, had no carriers to spare for ferrying light aircraft to a landing as the USS *Ranger* had done off Casablanca. Some pilots flew aircraft to the island after the ground troops established a defensive perimeter. Other aircraft arrived in shipping crates; pilots and ground crew had to assemble them.[4]

Through May 1944 the Field Artillery's liaison aircraft found no combat role in the simultaneous offensive in the Central Pacific Area under the personal direction of Admiral Nimitz. As in the South Pacific, Nimitz maintained a naval headquarters. The Navy in the Central Pacific also lacked carrier deck space to ferry light aircraft. But these were primarily contributing factors. The major reasons involved the composition of Nimitz's ground forces and the nature of the area of operations. Marine Corps divisions did much of the ground fighting, and, where Army units were involved, the small size of the objectives in the Gilbert and the Marshall island groups led most commanders to depend for fire support upon naval guns afloat and mortars organic to the Infantry.[5]

Doctrinal developments in the Pacific also differed from those in North Africa. The late entry into combat meant that from the beginning Field Artillery pilots had the advantage of at least some of the lessons derived from North Africa. Already in decline, the Japanese Army and Navy air arms never posed the same degree of threat as did the *Luftwaffe*. Pilots in the Pacific consequently did not go through an extended phase of grasshopper tactics as did their counterparts in North Africa and Sicily. At the same time, air-observation-post operations were very terrain sensitive, and the peculiarities of the atolls of the south and central Pacific and the triple-canopy jungle of New Guinea were very different from the arid rolling uplands of southern Tunisia or the mountains of northern Tunisia, Sicily, and southern Italy.[6]

Southwest Pacific Area: New Guinea, June 1943–June 1944

The first air observation posts entered combat in New Guinea in June 1943 (*Map 8*). Capt. Edwin H. Leer and six sergeants comprised the entire complement of Field Artillery pilots in the Southwest Pacific Area. Leer became the I Corps artillery air officer. He and the sergeant-pilots discovered that the jungle growth did make a difference for air operations during their first commitment to combat, the Nassau Bay–Salamaua offensive, begin-

---

[4] Robert C. Gildart, "Artillery on New Georgia," *FAJ* 34 (February 1944):86–87, discusses the deficiencies of aerial observation in the Solomons before the Bougainville operations.
[5] Philip A. Crowl, *Campaign in the Marianas*, U.S. Army in World War II (Washington, D.C.: Office of the Chief of Military History, 1960), pp. 1–52.
[6] Capt. Robert M. White II, "Air OPs in New Guinea," *FAJ* 34 (May 1944):278–80.

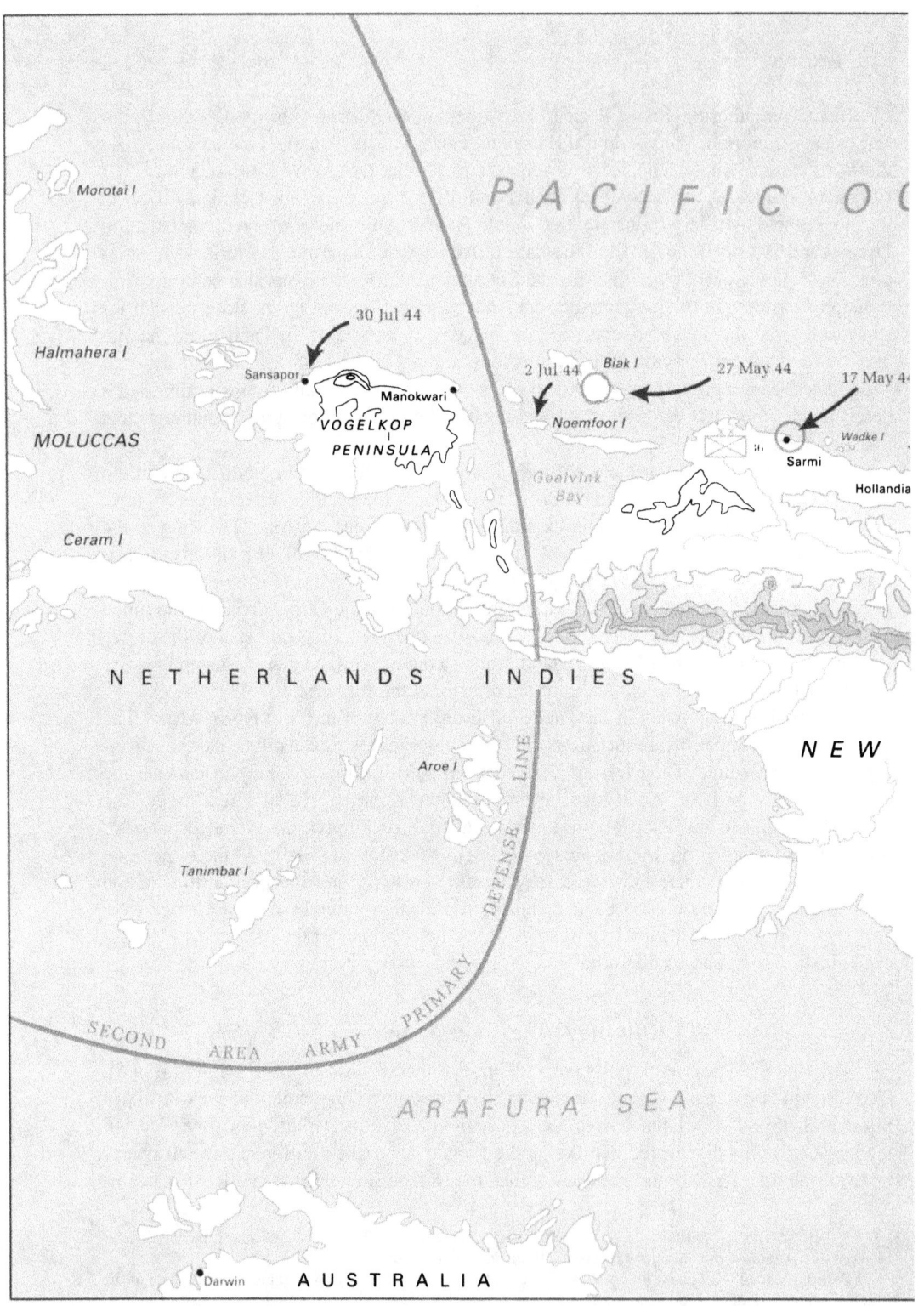

Map 8

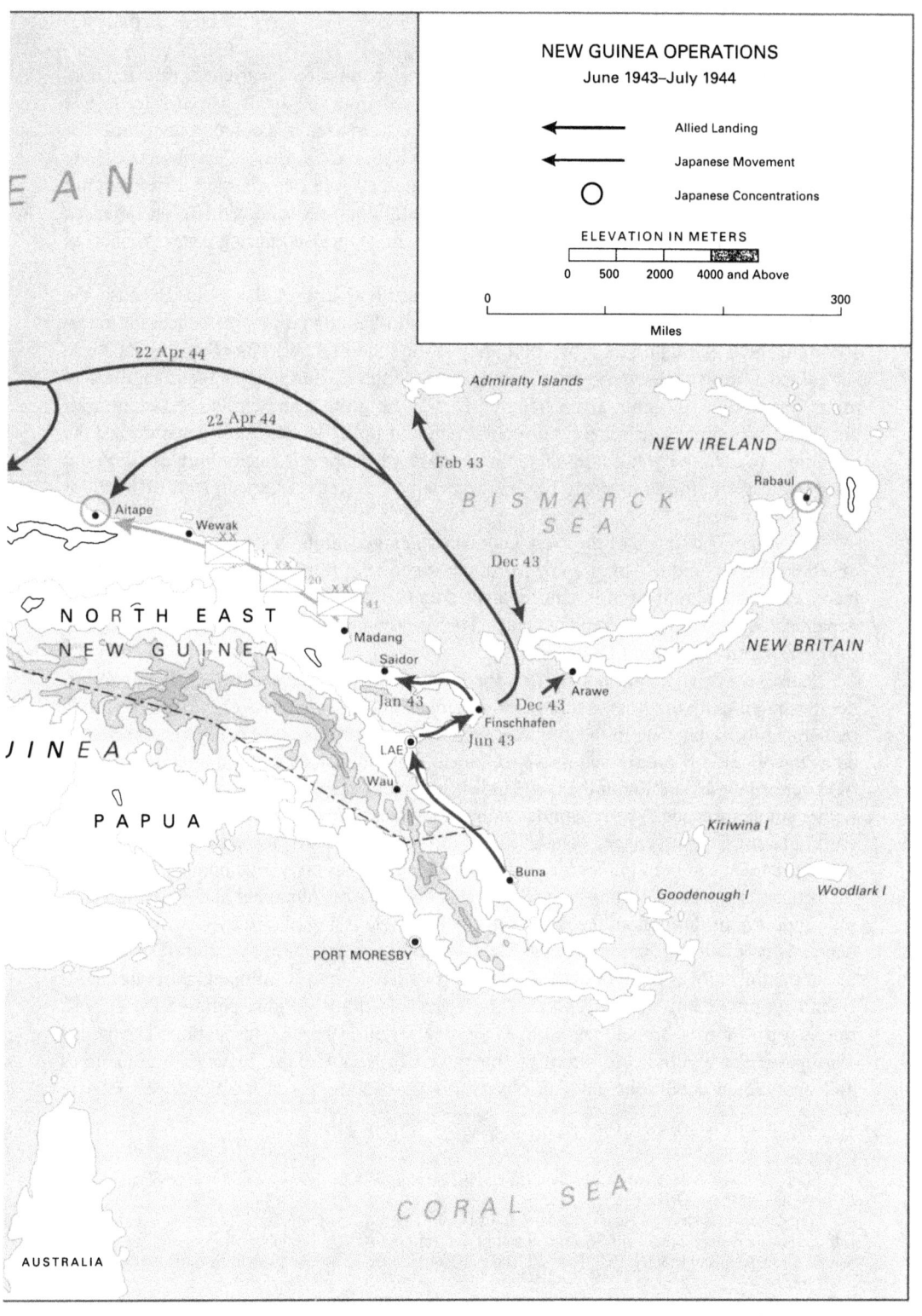

ning 30 June 1943. They directed only one fire support mission for friendly infantry during the entire battle. Because visibility was restricted from the air, it proved safer to use ground observers for such shoots. The L–4s initially were used in a counterbattery role. S. Sgt. Glenn E. Case flew the inaugural mission with S. Sgt. C. N. Guy as his observer. They succeeded in silencing a Japanese gun that had harassed American barge traffic bringing up supplies to the American beachhead. Later the light aircraft directed fire on Japanese antiaircraft positions around Salamaua, keeping them suppressed during Army Air Forces bombing raids.[7]

At first the Japanese used light antiaircraft artillery against the L–4s. Because the penalty for missing with the opening shots proved to be a battalion-size concentration of 105-mm. shells falling on their position, they shifted their tactics. The efforts of Japanese fighters to destroy the L–4s, however, also proved fruitless. The approved tactic for the L–4 pilots was to dive to within a few hundred feet of the ground and circle U.S. antiaircraft positions. This proved sufficiently discouraging, and no L–4s were shot down during the operation. In fact, the greatest threat to the air observation posts' successfully carrying out their artillery fire missions proved to be the desire of various American staff officers for an aerial taxi service.[8]

In subsequent stages of the New Guinea campaign, pilots in I Corps perfected their observed fire technique. An infantry patrol advanced until it made contact; then the patrol leader called for a light aircraft. Once it arrived and circled overhead, the patrol set off "the dependable smoke pot" and broke contact. The aerial observer then adjusted fire using the smoke as a reference point.[9]

Patrols were an important part of the war in the Pacific, and the artillery aircraft demonstrated early that they could greatly increase the effectiveness of American patrols by helping them navigate in the jungle. Resupply of patrols also became more sophisticated as the operations progressed in New Guinea. Some divisions used "mass" drops by all the aircraft in a division with the lead aircraft in a pathfinder role, marking the drop point with a smoke grenade. The remainder came in at treetop level. On such missions the aircraft did not carry passengers. "Believe me," reported one pilot, "it's quite a feat to fly just above the trees and boot out a case of ammo, which weighs sixty-five pounds."[10]

Logistical responsibilities in the Southwest Pacific Area remained ill defined and supply support poor throughout the war. Conversely, jungle flying placed special maintenance demands on pilots and ground crews. Metal structural members of the aircraft would rust in the humid, salty air. The pilots and ground crew had to inspect all metal parts frequently and refinish them when necessary. The spars and other wooden parts of the aircraft might warp or rot—sometimes both. They also required regular inspection. The wings were particularly vulnerable. From the beginning in New Guinea, logistical deficiencies and operational conditions gave air-observation-post activities in the Southwest Pacific

---

[7] Ibid.

[8] Ibid.; William F. McCartney, *The Jungleers: A History of the 41st Infantry Division* (Washington, D.C.: Infantry Journal Press, 1948), p. 55.

[9] Ltr, Officer in Southwest Pacific (SWP) to Lt Col G. J. Wolf, n.d., in Memo, Wolf, 29 May 44, sub: Informal Info, in Field Artillery School (FAS), Department of Air Training (DAT), "Training Memoranda" (Bound Ms, Morris Swett Technical Library, FAS, Fort Sill, Okla. [hereafter cited as Morris Swett Tech Lib], 1944–1945).

[10] Ibid.

AN L–4 ON PATROL ALONG THE BEACH AT AITAPE, DUTCH NEW GUINEA, JULY 1944

Area a hand-to-mouth quality they never lost for the remainder of the war. The same drama, with local variations, played out in the South Pacific Area.[11]

South Pacific Area: Bougainville

When the first pilots arrived on Bougainville in December 1943, they found higher authority skeptical of their value in the jungle. The senior pilot assigned to the 37th Infantry Division, 1st Lt. Don B. Thompson, received a searching interrogation from the division artillery commander, Brig. Gen. Leo M. Kreber, who only grudgingly gave Thompson thirty days to prove the concept. Thompson thought Kreber would be happy to press all the pilots into service as ground forward observers, a specialty that did not promise long life in the jungle. Checking with the S–4, the supply officer, on Kreber's staff, Thompson learned that there "should be" some boxes on the beach marked "airplane." These might belong to the air sections. From the S–1, the personnel officer, Thompson learned that the division had no aircraft mechanics. Thompson convinced him to allow the pilots to interview the automotive mechanics to see if any were interested in becoming airplane mechanics. With these volunteers and the pilots, he located the crates "half hidden already in the jungle on the Torokino Beachhead." Using notes that the pilots

---

[11] War Department (WD), Field Manual (FM) 20–100, *Army Ground Forces Light Aviation* (Washington, D.C.: Government Printing Office, 1947), pp. 72–73.

had saved from their classes in the Department of Air Training and "appropriated" tools, they assembled the first airplane "by the numbers," complete with installation of a tactical radio. They flew their first mission the next day. "The Division Artillery people were quite impressed." Using "Get it done or we all become Forward Observers out there in that damn jungle" as a rallying cry, Thompson and his pilots kept division artillery impressed until the end of the war.[12]

As in New Guinea, work with patrols quickly became a high priority mission for Field Artillery aircraft. On 6 December 1943, two days after L–4s arrived on Bougainville, they resupplied a long-range patrol from the 37th Reconnaissance Troop that had penetrated to the vicinity of the village of Ibu, twenty miles from U.S. lines (*Map 9*). Their intervention permitted the patrol to complete its mission. Before the Bougainville operation ended, the Cubs airdropped over a ton of supplies. They also performed area reconnaissance and acted as radio relays. The aircraft quickly showed their ability to aid the navigation of patrols in deep jungle. The procedure involved the ground patrol setting off a smoke pot and the air observer giving the soldiers a compass bearing and estimated distance to a designated objective.[13]

The Americal Division participated in the final phases of the Bougainville battle. The division artillery had difficulty surveying its position accurately in the "flat, tree-covered country" that constituted its sector of the American defense perimeter. Survey, the process of accurately determining the location of field artillery batteries relative to potential targets, was essential to delivering fire effectively in support of the infantry. During IV Corps maneuvers in the eastern Oregon desert in 1943, the 104th Infantry Division Artillery, commanded by Brig. Gen. William C. Dunckel, had used "plane survey and terrain oblique photographs" to produce very accurate trace maps of previously unmapped areas. Given this previous experience, Dunckel, who assumed command of the Americal Division Artillery in December 1943, turned to his air sections for a solution at Bougainville. A group of officers under the leadership of Dunckel's executive officer, Col. Paul A. Gavan, worked out an answer using the L–4s to perform both target- and position-area surveys. Both involved a ground station easily identified from the air and an aircraft flying along a straight line oriented on a terrain feature: one in the general area of potential targets, the other inside friendly lines. In target-area survey, the pilot dipped his wings or said "Mark" on the radio when he was on course, allowing the ground station and another a measured distance away to read the angle from their locations to the Cub. In position-area survey, the pilot flew over a known point and indicated when he was directly overhead. Then the two ground stations took readings on the angles to the aircraft. Aerial survey was much less time-consuming than conventional ground survey, which meant that the artillery was pre-

---

[12] Don B. Thompson, "Combat Operations: L–4 Tactics in the South Pacific Command," *L–4 Grasshopper Wing Newsletter* 11 (October/November 1988):4–5.

[13] Lessons Learned (LL), XIV Corps, 37th Infantry (Inf) Division (Div), Americal Div, Detachment 93d Inf Div, sub: Use of Artillery (Arty) Plane, in XIV Corps, "Report on Lessons Learned in the Bougainville Operation Prepared by the Commanding General, XIV Corps" (Bound Ms, U.S. Army Center of Military History, Washington, D.C. [hereafter cited as CMH] Lib, 1944). This report is a compilation under various subject headings of the lessons learned submitted by XIV Corps staff and all subordinate units. Capt. John C. Guenther, "Artillery in the Bougainville Campaign," *FAJ* 35 (June 1945):330–34. For a description of artillery-infantry cooperation on Bougainville, see Robert F. Cocklin, "Bougainville—1944," *FAJ* 34 (July 1944):451.

A K–20 Aerial Camera in a Special Mount on an L–4H, Allowing the Camera To Take Vertical Photographs

pared to deliver effective indirect fire much sooner after displacing to a new location. One of the participants, Col. J. C. McCole, reported on the technique in an article he published in the *Field Artillery Journal* in February 1944. Further refinement using an aerial camera to take vertical photographs permitted even greater accuracy and became the subject of a report in the *Information Bulletin* of the Operations Division of the War Department General Staff.[14]

Pilots in the 37th Infantry Division pioneered the technique (later used extensively in Vietnam) of employing light aircraft to mark targets to improve the accuracy of Army Air Forces' bombing of enemy positions. Pilots flew out beyond artillery range of the perimeter "to search for supply trails, intersections, troop concentrations, or other suspicious movements." They carried the hand-held K–20 aerial camera, which allowed the photographic intelligence experts to examine the overflown area carefully. If anything looked suspicious, XIV Corps arranged for a Navy dive bomber to rendezvous with an L–4 in the general area. The Field Artillery pilot then marked the target with a smoke

---

[14] Report (Rpt), Brig Gen W. C. Dunckel, CG, Americal Div Arty, to CG, Americal Div, 26 Mar 44, in HQ, AGF, Gen Corresp, 1942–1948, 353/134 (FA Air Obsn), RG 337, NARA; Memo, WD, 23 Jun 45, sub: William Caldwell Dunckel, Biographical (Bio) files, Historical Resources Branch (Br), CMH; Col. J. C. McCole, "'Grasshopper' Survey," *FAJ* 34 (February 1944):115–16; *Operations Division Information Bulletin* 2 (26 May 1944):3–5.

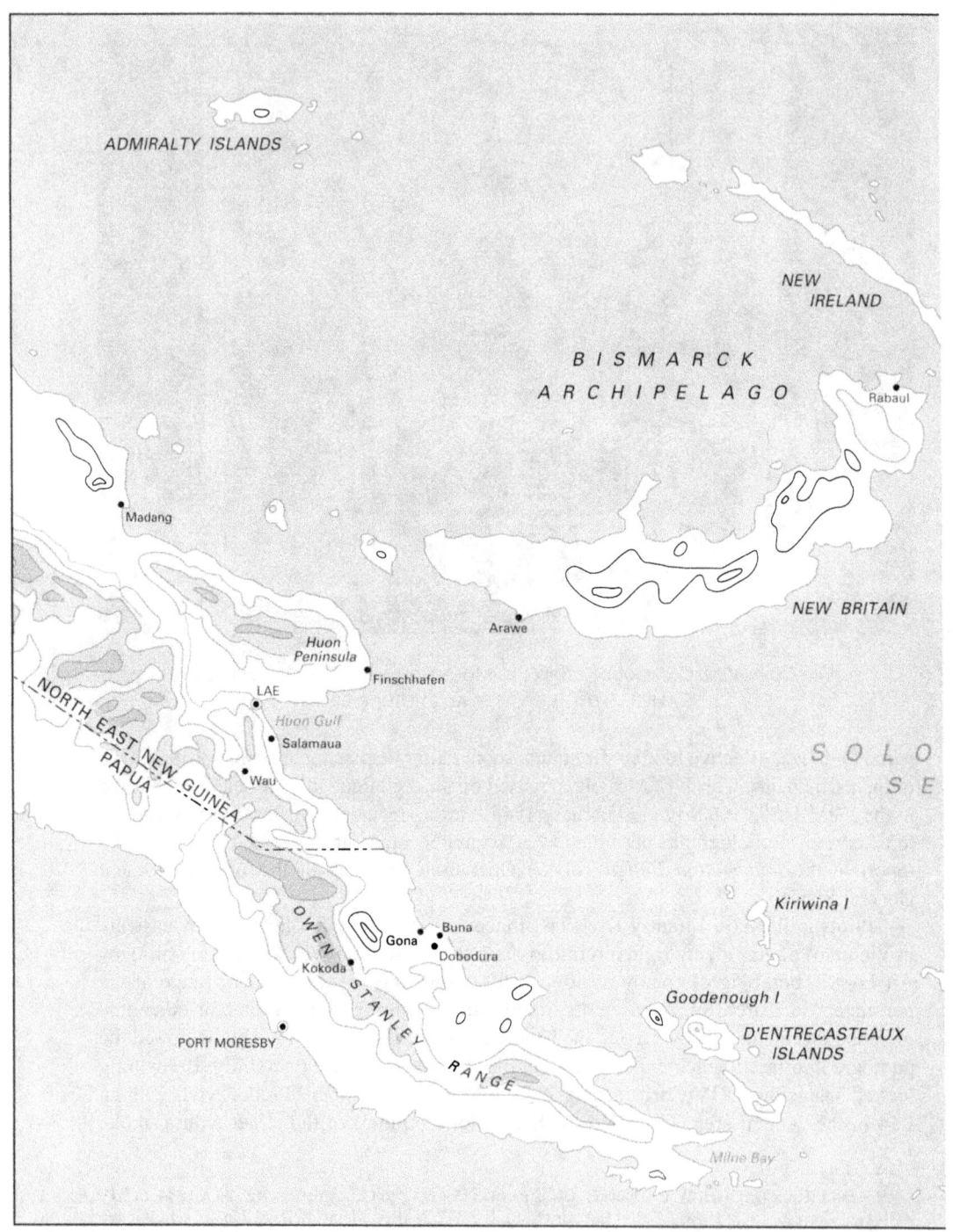

MAP 9

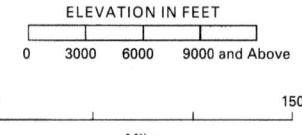

bomb, and the Navy aircraft attacked it with two 500-pound bombs. The 37th Infantry Division Artillery also used this technique when the Japanese took up positions in narrow valleys where they assumed they were safe from American artillery fire. Given the benefits that air observation posts conferred during the latter stages of the operation, not surprisingly one of the lessons that the XIV Corps Artillery staff drew from Bougainville was that invasion plans should include the construction of "a landing field for Cub planes at the earliest possible time after D-Day." This conclusion influenced all future planning in the Pacific.[15]

The same supply situation prevailed in the South Pacific Area as in the Southwest Pacific Area. The advance Army Air Forces depot on Guadalcanal, an element of the 13th Air Depot Group that supported Thirteenth Air Force operations in the Solomons, was supposed to provide aviation supplies and spare parts for all Field Artillery aircraft on Bougainville. After about six months of operational flying, the air officer of the 37th Infantry Division, Lieutenant Thompson, went back to Guadalcanal to see what support the depot could provide. A master sergeant took him to "about ten boxes" of L–4 supplies on pallets in the middle of the swamp. They were all filled with water-soaked, "delaminated" wooden propellers, which were "absolutely no good." The air sections had to accomplish all repairs using the materials at hand. The most difficult—and pressing—came from the use of beach sand, actually highly abrasive volcanic ash, to hold down moisture on the runways. After the sun had dried up the sand, the engines of taxiing L–4s sucked the particles into the engine manifold, where they quickly destroyed the oil seal. The pilots realized they had a problem when they discovered a fine sheen of oil across their windshields, often at altitude. Visibility quickly became almost impossible. Thompson, who had owned a Piper Cub as a civilian, could identify the difficulty but could not fashion a solution. He approached the master machinist of the 737th Ordnance Battalion, an old master sergeant. After thinking it over, the sergeant fabricated new seals using a jeep seal as a pattern and the brass base plate of a spent artillery round for material. These lasted through the end of the war.[16]

Compared to North Africa and Europe, air-observation-post operations in the Pacific—both the Southwest Pacific Area and the South Pacific Area—were fairly small-scale until June 1944. This condition simply mirrored ground operations where campaigns involving multiple corps were the exception rather than the rule. At the same time, the late arrival of Field Artillery aircraft into combat in the Pacific meant that the air sections matured as an integral part of the combined arms team at a somewhat later date than in North Africa and Europe. Much of the pilots' and mechanics' efforts up to mid-1944 focused on perfecting technique. Of course, the jungle presented Field Artillery air sections in the Pacific an operational and logistical environment with unique challenges that their counterparts did not face on the other side of the globe. Nevertheless, the performance of air observation posts in the Pacific won them high-level backers, just as in North Africa and Europe. The I Corps commander, General Eichelberger, became a strong sup-

---

[15] Don B. Thompson, "Combat Operations: L–4 Tactics in the South Pacific Command [Part II], *L–4 Grasshopper Wing Newsletter* 12 (December 1988/January 1989):2–3; LL, XIV Corps, sub: Use of Arty Plane, in XIV Corps, "Report on Lessons Learned in the Bougainville Operation."

[16] Donald B. Thompson, "Only an L–4 Could Survive," *L–4 Grasshopper Wing Newsletter* 16 (August/September 1988):7–8.

porter. His artillery officer, Brig. Gen. Horace Harding, was even more enthusiastic; he personally accompanied some missions as an observer, learned to fly, and flew over one hundred hours solo. He became one of the few corps artillery officers to win the Air Medal during the war. As the 37th Infantry Division reported after Bougainville, air observation posts were "indispensable to jungle warfare."[17]

Central Pacific Area, 1944

By mid-1944 the American offensive in the Pacific focused on two axes of advance, mirroring existing command arrangements in the theater. The northernmost drive consisted of a Navy and Marine Corps–heavy force in the Pacific Ocean Areas. Commanded by Admiral Nimitz, it attacked through the Marianas toward Formosa and the China coast. Air observation posts participated in this campaign. Like Halsey earlier in the South Pacific, Nimitz did not place an artillery air officer on his staff. The relatively small scale of Field Artillery air operations prevented this organizational defect from exerting large operational consequences. The real achievement for the members of the Field Artillery air sections was that they were there at all.

In the Central Pacific Area, the operational conditions that had prevented the use of air observation posts before June 1944 disappeared. The Japanese fleet, while still dangerous, no longer posed the same degree of threat that it had earlier for the now rapidly expanding U.S. Navy. Carrier deck space, once at a premium, became accessible for Field Artillery aircraft, and the planes in turn became available to support landings on islands in the mid-Pacific. In June 1944 American forces attacked the Marianas, large islands surrounded by coral reefs and covered by jungle, swamps, and mountains. In this environment, light aircraft became not only available but also necessary for aerial fire direction during the fighting on Saipan, Tinian, and Guam.[18]

The landings on Saipan, beginning 15 June 1944, soon resulted in the commitment of one Army and two Marine divisions. Although better remembered for command controversy, Saipan also marked the first employment of Field Artillery aviation in combat in the central Pacific and was representative of the fighting in the island group. The XXIV Corps Artillery, acting independently of its corps headquarters, supported the Marine V Amphibious Corps. The corps artillery commander, Brig. Gen. Arthur M. Harper, placed all six L–4s under the control of the corps artillery air officer. All aircraft were based on Aslito Field, which was captured on 18 June. The corps artillery had the mission of deep support, so all observation was over enemy lines. When feasible, pilots flew along the island's shore to minimize ground fire. The corps artillery air officer established a regular patrol schedule to keep the Japanese-held portion of the island under continuous surveillance. The assistant S–2 on the corps artillery staff remained constantly at the airfield. He maintained a complete set of vertical and oblique photographs and thoroughly debriefed pilots and observers when they returned from missions. The air activity caused the

---

[17] Ltr, J. M. Harding to author, 14 Nov 91, Historian's files, CMH; "Horace Harding," in George W. Cullum, et al., comps., *Biographical Register of the Officers and Graduates of the U.S. Military Academy at West Point, N.Y., Since Its Establishment in 1802*, 9 vols. (Boston: Houghton Mifflin and Co., 1891–1951), 9:254–55; LL, 37th Inf Div, sub: Use of Arty Plane, in XIV Corps, "Report on Lessons Learned in the Bougainville Operation."

[18] Crowl, *Campaign in the Marianas*, pp. 1–52.

Japanese to cease all daylight movement. Consequently, the smallest changes in terrain—a new set of tire tracks—might indicate some modification of enemy intentions.[19]

A reporter noted that Cubs were very popular with the infantry. "The flying artillerymen lived like everyone else—in foxholes, unwashed, unshaved, and fed on K-rations. They flew from dawn to dusk, piddling around over Jap guns all day long and calling shots for the big guns emplaced miles away." Numerous targets and relative shortages of pilots and planes combined to produce long hours. One pilot on Saipan flew forty combat hours in nine days, possibly "some sort of a record." Darkness brought little rest or relaxation. Japanese aircraft dropped bombs "nearly every night" on the airfield occupied by the artillery planes, and one night a raiding party of Japanese infantry attacked the air sections. The artillerymen beat back the attackers with no loss of aircraft. Only the relatively short duration of the campaign made the strain endurable.[20]

Southwest Pacific Area, June 1944–September 1945

The other major Pacific axes of advance in 1944 involved an Army-heavy force, including the Army Air Forces, in the Southwest Pacific Area. Commanded by General MacArthur, it attacked along the northern coast of New Guinea with the Philippine Islands as a distant objective. As before, MacArthur did not place an artillery air officer on his staff. During the last fifteen months of the war, however, he acquired two field army headquarters that exercised operational control over ground units. Each of these contained an artillery air officer—Maj. James McCord in Sixth Army and Lt. Col. Robert F. Cassidy in Eighth Army.[21]

In contrast to their counterparts in the Marianas, for more than a year commanders and pilots in the Southwest Pacific Area had enjoyed the opportunity to perfect techniques of light aircraft operations in combat and to develop an understanding of the advantages they conferred. Even so, the way in which MacArthur conducted his offensive in 1944, amphibious assaults in lightly defended Japanese rear areas, posed a difficult problem for air-observation-post pilots. Like their counterparts on Bougainville, artillery air officers in the Southwest Pacific wanted to provide aerial observation for fire support from the earliest possible moment after the landing force established a beachhead and the guns came ashore. The 24th Infantry Division Artillery, supporting the division's landing at Tanahmerah Bay, New Guinea, in April 1944, during the Hollandia operation, used two L–4s equipped with plywood floats to assist the invasion force from the beginning of the assault. The float planes proved a makeshift expedient at best. The aircraft could stagger into the air on a calm day, but only if the pilot flew alone. However, the floats were neces-

---

[19] Rpt, [XXIV] Corps Arty, sub: Rpt on Saipan and Tinian Operations (Opns), in Arty Bulletin no. 3, HQ, U.S. Army Forces Pacific Ocean Areas (POA), 4 Oct 44, in U.S. Army Forces POA, "Artillery Bulletins" (Bound Ms, Morris Swett Tech Lib, 1945). Crowl, *Campaign in the Marianas*, p. 135.

[20] Keith Wheeler, "Tiny Cub Spotter Planes Unsung Heroes of Saipan," 17 July [1944], reprinted in Memo, Lt Col G. J. Wolf, Director (Dir), DAT, 25 Jul 44, sub: Informal Info, in FAS, DAT, "Training Memoranda."

[21] Rpt, [Col H. W. Kiefer], Sixth Army Arty Officer (Ofcr), in Sixth Army, *Report of the Leyte Operation, 20 October 1944–25 December 1944*, (n.p.: Sixth Army, c. 1945), p. 226; Memo, Lt. Col. R. F. Cassidy, Eighth Army Air Ofcr, for CG, AGF, 21 Jun 45; Rpt, sub: FA Rpt, in Eighth Army, *Report of the Commanding General Eighth U.S. Army on the Leyte-Samar Operation (Including Clearance of the Visayan Passages)* (n.p.: [Eighth Army], c. 1945), pp. 43–44.

sary. Only these planes succeeded in directing any fire missions. By the time strips were prepared—in some instances it simply meant clearing supplies from the beaches so the L–4s could land there—the surviving Japanese had fled. Most flights consisted of messenger service, flying staff officers up to the front lines, hauling medical supplies to aid stations, and evacuating ambulatory wounded to the rear.[22]

During the latter stages of the Hollandia operation, L–4s belonging to the 32d Infantry Division Artillery made a contribution to Allied success that went beyond the tactical advantages normally conferred to encompass the operational level of war. In response to the landings at Hollandia, the Japanese *Eighteenth Army*, commanded by Lt. Gen. Hatazo Adachi, fell back from its forward positions at Madang, New Guinea. Along the Driniumor River, Adachi's forces bumped into elements of the 32d Infantry Division and the 112th Cavalry Regimental Combat Team. Commanded during most of the engagement by Maj. Gen. William H. Gill, the covering force blocked *Eighteenth Army's* line of retreat at the same time that it protected airfields at Aitape. *Eighteenth Army* attacked on 18 July, and the battle continued for two weeks. After frontal assaults proved futile, Adachi attempted to turn the American right flank. Gill countered by sending a force across the Driniumor. Cubs from the division artillery directed its movement across the Japanese line of retreat. The American ability to maneuver in dense terrain significantly contributed to turning a Japanese defeat into something approaching a disaster.[23]

Even before the operations around Aitape reached a climax, Sixth Army, under the code name ALAMO FORCE and commanded by General Krueger, conducted landings in the Wakde Island area of northern New Guinea and then on Biak Island off northwestern New Guinea. On 27 May elements of the 41st Infantry Division landed on Biak in the face of only scattered resistance. The Japanese chose to heavily defend the amphitheater-like terrain that dominated the three large airfields on the island, the immediate objective of the campaign. Formed by an upheaval that sent part of the ocean's bottom to the surface, Biak was honeycombed with caves that the Japanese incorporated into their defensive scheme. The 41st Infantry Division captured the first of the airfields, the Mokmer Airdrome, but Japanese defensive fires covered the runways and prevented the Army Air Forces from using them. The field was needed to support operations in the Marianas, and General Krueger reacted to the delay by placing General Eichelberger in direct command of the operation on 14 June. Three days later Eichelberger arrived in an L–4 to survey the situation: "As we came in (I believe we were the first to set down at Mokmer) the Japanese opened fire from a distance of two thousand yards. There were no hits then, and there were no hits later when a salvo celebrated our departure."[24]

---

[22] Ltr, E. S. Marman to Col G. J. Wolf, 22 May 44, in FAS, DAT, "Training Memoranda"; An. 1 to G–3 Lessons, sub: Arty Lessons—Hollandia Campaign, in Reckless Task Force (TF), "History of the Hollandia Operation" (Bound Ms, CMH Lib, 1944).

[23] Eichelberger, *Our Jungle Road*, pp. 161–63; Douglas MacArthur, *Reminiscences* (New York: McGraw-Hill, 1964); Robert R. Smith, *The Approach to the Philippines*, U.S. Army in World War II (Washington, D.C.: Office of the Chief of Military History, 1953), pp. 191–205. See, in particular, Edward J. Drea, *Defending the Driniumor: Covering Force Operations in New Guinea, 1944* (Fort Leavenworth, Kans.: Combat Studies Institute, 1984), especially pages 126–32, for an account of the 112th Regimental Combat Team's contribution and Stephen R. Taaffe, *MacArthur's Jungle War: The 1944 New Guinea Campaign* (Lawrence: University Press of Kansas, 1998), pp. 205–09. Taaffe is particularly good on command relations.

[24] Eichelberger, *Our Jungle Road*, p. 144.

AN L–4 LANDS AT MOROTAI ISLAND, DUTCH EAST INDIES,
AFTER OBSERVING JAPANESE POSITIONS.

Reinforcements and pinpointing the cave mouths solved the tactical impasse. Existing maps ignored the caves, while high-level photographic missions by the Fifth Air Force failed to find them. Eichelberger, who was as supportive of organic aviation as were Generals Eisenhower or Clark, initiated a systematic mapping program using L–4s. The corps G–3, Col. William Bowen, and his assistants made repeated low-level flights as observers, locating all the cave entrances. Once I Corps had identified them, the operation became one of systematically isolating and destroying the Japanese strongpoints. On 22 June, when the American offensive unwittingly approached the Japanese command center, the garrison commander ordered a banzai charge by the survivors and then committed suicide. Mopping-up operations continued well into July. Cave warfare on Biak constituted a harbinger of the tactical realities that Allied soldiers would face during the last fifteen months of the war in the Pacific—stubborn Japanese defenders taking advantage of every terrain feature, including caves, and willing to fight to the death.[25]

The Southwest Pacific offensive reached the Philippine Islands in October 1944 with the landings on Leyte (*Map 10*). Terrain, climate, lack of suitable fields, and Japanese air and ground operations compounded by continuing logistical problems made Leyte one of the most difficult campaigns of the Pacific war for the Field Artillery air sections. Air-observation-post losses were heavy. Leyte also involved large numbers of air observation posts, because for the first time Sixth Army fought as a coordinated whole.

---

[25] Ibid., pp. 150–51; Smith, *Approach to the Philippines*, pp. 281–390.

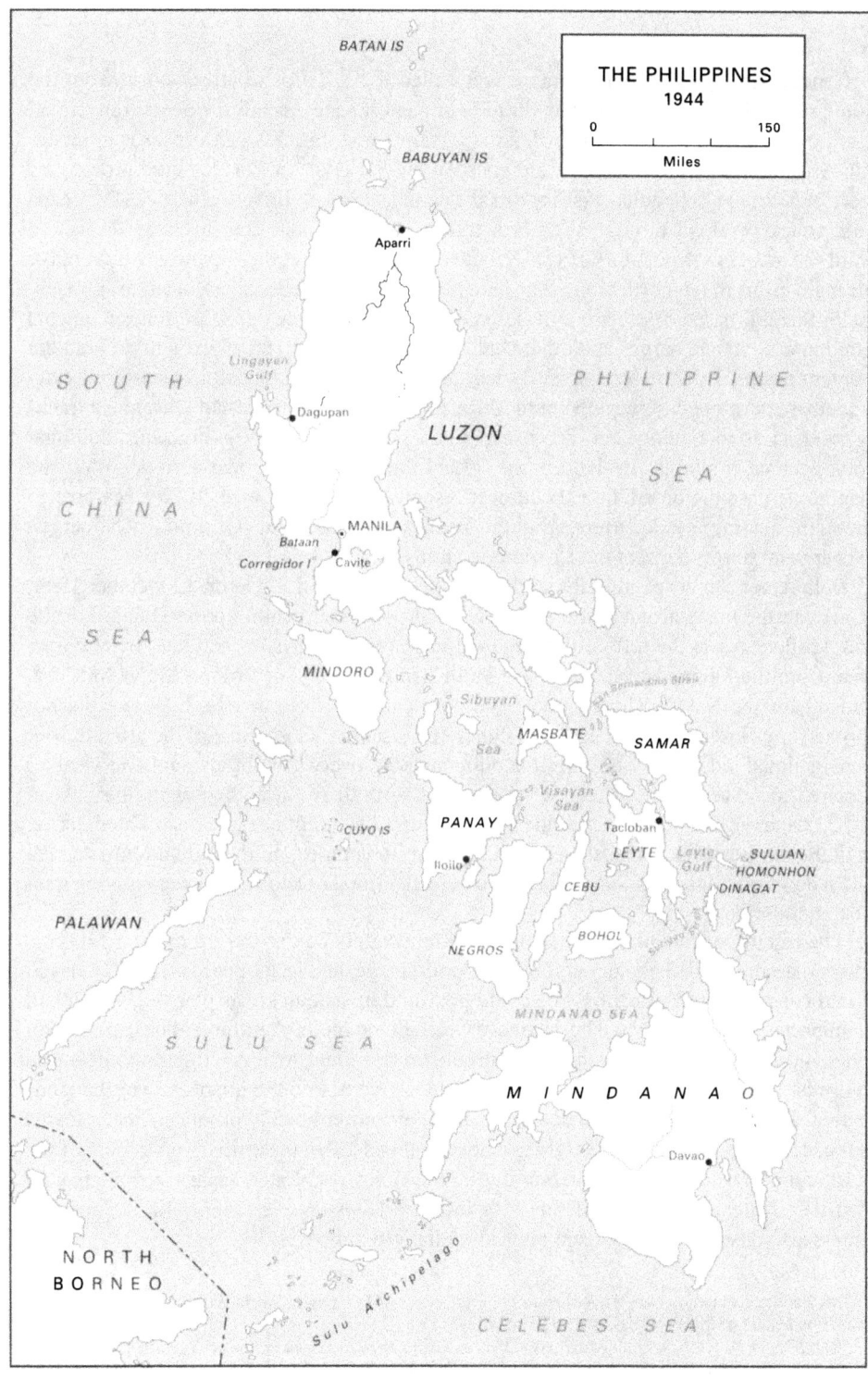

MAP 10

General Krueger's scheme of maneuver called for X Corps to attack north from the landing site and seal off the San Juan Strait to prevent Japanese reinforcements from crossing to Leyte from the nearby island of Samar. At the same time XXIV Corps was to secure Sixth Army's major objectives, airfield sites, so the Far East Air Forces could provide air cover for the next scheduled landing on the main island of Luzon. Then XXIV Corps would attack overland through the north-south mountain range that bisected the island toward the west coast port of Ormoc. Krueger anticipated that the Japanese would make their main effort in the north along San Juan Strait. Instead, the local commander, Lt. Gen. Sosaku Suzuki, based his scheme of defense on Ormoc, where Japanese reinforcements poured into Leyte via barges and other shallow-draft watercraft. Suzuki sought to hold the mountain passes while he built up sufficient forces for a counterattack into eastern Leyte. A stalemate developed. Krueger sent the 11th Airborne Division overland through a trackless wilderness to unhinge the defenses. When this proved slow going and additional troops became available, he landed the 77th Infantry Division near Ormoc. With the Japanese defense disrupted, he handed over responsibilities for Leyte on 26 December to a new field army headquarters, Eighth Army, commanded by General Eichelberger. Krueger went north to direct the Luzon operations.[26]

Both American corps initially landed on the east coast of Leyte on 17 October 1944, X Corps in the north around Palo and XXIV Corps farther south around Dulag. For the Field Artillery pilots the difficulties began almost immediately. To facilitate aerial observation from the moment of landing, the Sixth Army artillery air officer, Major McCord, arranged for the Navy to load some L–4s onto carriers. The carriers, however, did not approach any closer than fifty miles offshore. The distance, short range of the aircraft, lack of navigational aids or any training for pilots making overwater flights, and bad weather conspired to prevent the first carrier-transported aircraft from landing at the beachhead until 22 October. The remainder landed the next day. One pilot became disoriented during the flight and landed on Japanese-occupied Samar. In contrast, all the light aircraft carried broken down on transports were unloaded on either 21 or 22 October and began flying missions on those days.[27]

The capture of the airfield sites did not immediately confer the anticipated benefits. "Torrential rains, unsatisfactory soil base, poor drainage, and lack of access roads" delayed airfield construction. Fifth Air Force could not build up as quickly as planned, which had two important consequences: The Japanese were able to rapidly reinforce their garrison on Leyte, and, for the first time since the introduction of Field Artillery light aircraft in the Southwest Pacific Area, Japanese aviation seriously contested the airspace over the landing area. The unanticipated presence of Japanese air power quickly produced heavy losses among artillery pilots. Japanese fighters shot down and killed the artillery air officer of the 7th Infantry Division and his observer during the first week. Later, Japanese fighters shot down the artillery air officer of the 24th Infantry Division over enemy lines. Japanese fighters also destroyed four liaison aircraft on the ground.[28]

---

[26] M. Hamlin Cannon, *Leyte: The Return to the Philippines*, U.S. Army in World War II (Washington, D.C.: Office of the Chief of Military History, 1954), pp. 103–45.

[27] Rpt, [Col H. W. Kiefer], Sixth Army Arty Ofcr, in Sixth Army, *Report of the Leyte Operation*, p. 226.

[28] Ibid.; Rpt, Lt Gen Walter Krueger, sub: Rpt of Leyte Opn, in Sixth Army, *Report of the Leyte Operation*, p. 83.

Amid these difficulties, commanders and pilots continued to find innovative ways of carrying out their missions. During the 1st Cavalry Division's relatively rapid advance toward San Juan Strait, the commander of the division artillery, Brig. Gen. Rex E. Chandler, developed the procedure of sending a pilot forward with every artillery reconnaissance party. The pilot quickly selected the site for the battalion airstrip and ensured an immediate start on its preparation. An engineer bulldozer followed close behind to begin grading the site chosen. This system allowed the battalions to bring their aircraft within the battalion perimeter every night, a necessary precaution against Japanese infiltrators, and to have the planes available for use throughout the day.[29]

One major innovation in the operational technique of air observation posts—mass aerial resupply—came out of Leyte. The 11th Airborne Division, commanded by Maj. Gen. Joseph M. Swing, attacked toward Ormoc through mountainous, jungle-covered terrain so difficult that carabaos (Philippine water buffalos) and porters could not keep the forward units adequately supplied. Swing used aerial resupply on a scale never before attained, while at the same time developing many other minor refinements. He had planned to depend on airdropped supplies, but the Fifth Air Force's C–47s proved inadequate for the task. Their relatively high speed made accurate drops problematic in the washboard-like terrain and dangerous for the air crews—one C–47 flew straight into a hillside after completing its run. Weather often grounded them. In addition, they required fighter cover, often not available, before they could fly a mission. Most important of all, other units clamored for their support, so their availability for the division was sporadic. In these circumstances, Swing turned to the division artillery air officer, Capt. Felix A. Coune, a member of the Class Before One, who with nine L–4s and seven L–5s organized aerial resupply missions that averaged twenty-one tons a day and kept the advance moving. The L–5s were particularly valuable because they had greater power and carrying capacity than the L–4s. In the process the division's aircraft earned the sobriquet "biscuit bombers" from the pilots' practice of kicking ration boxes without parachutes out of their planes at low altitude when directly over American columns.[30]

Resupply became the main, but not the only, mission of the division's aircraft during the campaign. The division surgeon organized two portable surgical hospitals (parachute), the 5246th and 5247th, which the L–4s dropped into Manarawat, a small village where Swing located his headquarters, and another jungle clearing before airstrips were ready. There, doctors stabilized the division's wounded; then liaison pilots, many of them returning to the coast for more supplies, flew the patients to the rear for long-term care. The division's remaining L–4, dubbed "Milk Run" by its pilot, flew courier and contact missions continuously, keeping division headquarters informed of the infantry's progress and acting as a radio relay. On one occasion, during a tactical emergency, the artillery aircraft airdropped a rifle company into a threatened sector. Even with all the divisional aircraft participating, pilots had to fly multiple missions to deliver the soldiers.[31]

---

[29] Pacific Warfare Board, Rpt 45, 7 Aug 45, sub: Battle Experiences Against the Japanese, in Pacific Warfare Board, "Pacific Warfare Board Reports" (Bound Ms, Morris Swett Tech Lib, c. 1945).

[30] Ltr, Maj Gen J. M. Swing, CG, 11th Airborne (Abn) Div, to Lt Gen T. T. Handy, 25 Dec 44, Microfilm A1387, Air Force Historical Research Agency, Maxwell Air Force Base (AFB), Ala. (hereafter cited as AFHRA); Maj. Edward M. Flanagan, Jr., "Biscuit Bombers (Leyte Style)," *FAJ* 38 (March–April 1948):73–75.

[31] Ltr, Swing to Handy, 25 Dec 45; Flanagan, "Biscuit Bombers," pp. 74–75.

Eleventh Airborne Division L–4s Transport Christmas Dinners for the Troops at Manawaret, Leyte Island, the Philippines, 1944.

In a desperate attempt to prevent the Americans from gaining air superiority, General Suzuki planned a coordinated attack on the airfield complex by two divisions coupled with an airdrop by two Japanese airborne regiments. The difficult terrain, an almost impossible supply situation, and opposition by the 11th Airborne Division caused the overland attacks to miscarry. The Japanese airborne regiments nevertheless struck with some force. On the evening of 6 December 1944, the paratroopers attacked a number of fields, including San Pablo Field Number 2, where the 11th Airborne Division based its aircraft. The Japanese overran part of the strip. In the confused fighting they damaged or destroyed seven division aircraft and booby-trapped the rest. Captain Coune died at the field. Another pilot, cut off in the Japanese airhead, survived by hiding under a log for twelve hours. On 7 December the 127th Airborne Engineer Battalion and the 674th Glider Field Artillery Battalion, fighting as infantry, cleared the strip in a "Civil War–style" frontal attack. Although the elements of the 11th Airborne Division in the mountains had to go on short rations, within days the air sections resumed their supply efforts using all new aircraft.[32]

Suzuki's counterattack was both too little and too late. As the Japanese paratroopers assembled for their assault, members of the 77th Infantry Division, commanded by Maj. Gen. Andrew D. Bruce, staged on the southern shore of Leyte. That night some eight thou-

---

[32] Flanagan, "Biscuit Bombers," p. 75; Memo, [Cassidy], [Feb 91], sub: Early WWII FA Liaison Pilots (Original Test Group [Grp]), Historian's files, CMH.

sand members of the division boarded small landing craft and sailed for an 0700 landing the following day at the village of Deposito on the eastern shore of Leyte, some ten miles south of Ormoc. The division artillery air officer, Maj. John C. Kriegsman, had L–4s in the air to cover the landing. Once the division had a secure lodgment, Bruce sent a message by L–4 to the commander of XXIV Corps, Maj. Gen. John R. Hodge: "Have rolled two sevens in Ormoc. Come 7 and 11." And so they did. As Bruce's men successfully attacked through Ormoc on 10 December, the 7th Infantry Division drove up the coast for a linkup, while the 11th Airborne Division continued its overland offensive. When all three units joined hands, a Japanese defeat turned into a bloody disaster. The Ormoc landing essentially meant the end of a coherent scheme of Japanese defense, although dangerous pockets of resistance remained.[33]

The guns and Cubs of the 902d Field Artillery Battalion supported the first wave of the assault at Deposito. The pilots conducted their initial flights from a dangerous stretch of beach at the landing site; not until the fall of Ormoc did division engineers construct a strip. Mud closed the first strip before the division's air sections had completed even a single day of operations. The second field proved better situated and lasted as a forward field throughout the duration of the campaign. Because of the availability of maintenance facilities, Major Kriegsman kept all the division aircraft under centralized control at Baybay in the 7th Infantry Division area. Although the Baybay basing scheme required pilots to fly over extensive enemy territory to reach the 77th Infantry Division's zone of operations, Kriegsman rightly judged the risk minimal because of the Japanese reluctance to fire on liaison aircraft.[34]

The 77th Infantry Division drove north from Ormoc, up the Ormoc Valley, to link up with X Corps. Once the division secured the all-weather airfield at Valencia, midway up the valley, the division surgeon began using Cubs to evacuate casualties with serious stomach wounds. These men could be strapped in an upright position in the observer's seat. Only Army Air Forces liaison squadrons were equipped with L–5s modified to take stretcher cases. Using L–4s as air ambulances sometimes created a shortage of aircraft for artillery missions. During this campaign air sections used flat fields and sections of road for airstrips. On occasion, pilots and observers dropped rifle grenades to flush Japanese out of buildings. The aircraft hauled white stove gas, used for cooking and heating, "to infantry units stalled in the mud." They also evacuated the dead. Kriegsman was prepared to do anything to assist the infantry: "I always figured we were morale boosters. I felt so sorry for the doughfeet slogging it out in the mud that we tried anything and everything we could to keep their spirits up."[35]

---

[33] Cannon, *Leyte*, pp. 331–46; John C. Kriegsman, "The L–4 Piper Cub and LST 776 Aircraft Carrier (A WW II Poorman's Carrier)," *L–4 Grasshopper Wing Newsletter* 20 (April/May 1990):2–3, 6–8. James M. Burns and Paul R. Leach, *Ours To Hold It High: The History of the 77th Infantry Division in World War II* (Washington, D.C.: 77th Infantry Division Assoc., 1947), p. 159, gives the text of General Bruce's message.

[34] Maj. Eugene R. Smyth, "Fighting the Nips—With 105s," *FAJ* 35 (September 1945):529–34; Rpt, Maj John C. Kriegsman, Arty Air Ofcr, 77th Inf Div, sub: Rpt of Air Liaison Section, Leyte Opn, in 77th Inf Div, G–3, "Operation Summary: Liberation of Leyte, 23 Nov–25 Dec 44" (Bound Ms, Morris Swett Tech Lib, 1944).

[35] Rpt, G–3, 77th Inf Div, sub: Liberation of Leyte, Operational Summary (Op Sum), 23 Nov–25 Dec 44, [Extract], HQ, AGF, G–4, Requirements Section, Development Div, FA Br, Decimal file, 1942–1945, 319.1 (South West Pacific Area [SWPA]), RG 337, NARA. Kriegsman, "L–4 Piper Cub and LST 776," p. 2, is the source of the short quote, while Ltr, John C. Kriegsman to Michael J. Strok, n.d., *L–4 Grasshopper Wing Newsletter* 20 (April/May 1990):1, provides the extended quote.

The 11th Airborne and the 77th Infantry Divisions were not alone in basing all their aircraft on a hard-surface runway in the rear and using forward strips, such as the one at Manarawat, only during the daytime. Leyte's clouds and rain had a marked effect on liaison aircraft operations, as it did on the larger craft of the Army Air Forces, even though the L–4s flew under conditions that kept all other planes grounded. Cubs supporting Sixth Army operations initially used the beaches for airstrips, but the soft sand made flights with observers, essential as lookouts for hostile fighters, very hazardous. While some air sections could shift their operations to captured hard-surface Japanese airfields, other air sections, especially in X Corps, had to make do with landing and taking off on roads. Heavy traffic and rain soon left the roads so rutted that no aircraft could take off or land with any degree of safety. The air sections then turned to the only flat, cleared areas for strips—dry rice paddies. Rain and heavy use soon turned these strips into bogs of gelatinous mud. Attempts to stabilize the strips by laying steel mesh borrowed from the Fifth Air Force only resulted in the mud seeping between the links, making the surface extraordinarily slick and leading to numerous skids on takeoffs and landings. Sixth Army found no good solutions for these problems during the rainy season, but pilots continued to fly despite the dangers and the marginal fields. Sixth Army eventually lost thirty-two aircraft during the campaign.[36]

Theoretically, the Army Air Forces depot units designed to support light aircraft operations should have alleviated Sixth Army's repair and replacement problems, but theory and reality diverged. Equipment resupply through Army Air Forces channels proved entirely unsatisfactory during the Leyte campaign. When the War Department ordered the Far East Air Forces to organize depot units, General Kenney's headquarters claimed that it lacked sufficient officers and men to do so. Instead, the Sixth Army Artillery officer, Col. Homer W. Kiefer, and his Eighth Army counterpart, Col. Myron E. McGinley, combed the necessary officers and men out of the Field Artillery air sections in the Southwest Pacific Area. The soldiers were then transferred to the Army Air Forces as members of either the 5th or 6th Depot Units (Army). The 5th Depot Unit arrived in the midst of the Leyte campaign with almost no equipment or supplies. The unit, consequently, was unable to perform much higher-echelon maintenance. Moreover, the Far East Air Forces used it "to the limit of its capabilities" to maintain the Fifth Air Force's liaison aircraft. Although Sixth Army air sections had begun the operation with the authorized amount of spare parts, the incidents of the campaign—damage due to enemy fire and accidents—rapidly depleted these reserves. No spare parts were forthcoming from either the 5th Depot Unit or any other Army Air Forces' entity. Under these circumstances McCord directed the pooling of all "wrecked and unserviceable planes" in one central location where mechanics cannibalized them under his supervision.[37]

The Far East Air Force Service Command, a subordinate command of the Far East Air Forces, provided all aviation gasoline for both Army Air Forces and ground forces units in

---

[36] Flanagan, "Biscuit Bombers," pp. 74–75; Rpt, Kiefer, in Sixth Army, *Report of the Leyte Operation*, p. 226.

[37] Rpt, Kiefer, in Sixth Army, *Report of the Leyte Operation*, p. 227; Memo, Lt Col R. F. Cassidy for CG, AGF, 15 Jun 45, sub: Replacement of Depot Units, Army, in SWPA; Memo, Col J. N. Bell, Chief (Ch), Abn and Liaison Section, Requirements Div, Assistant Chief of Air Staff (ACAS) for Operations, Commitments, and Requirements (OC&R), [Jun 45], sub: Notes from Colonel Bell's Visit to SWPA; both in Microfilm A1387, AFHRA.

the theater. Ever since these craft arrived in theater, the Far East Air Force Service Command had had difficulty supplying the 73-octane unleaded aviation gasoline used by both L–4s and L–5s. (Normal 100-octane aviation gasoline burned out the engines.) Late in 1944, during the Leyte campaign, the Far East Air Force Service Command announced that extensive service tests at Wright Field had proven that 80-octane, leaded, all-purpose motor fuel was a perfectly satisfactory substitute. Consequently, it would no longer supply 73-octane aviation gasoline to either ground or air units. Field Artillery pilots had an entirely different view of the matter. The higher-octane gasoline burned more slowly, generated less power, and left a gummy residue on the engine valves, causing them to stick. The 80-octane fuel required air sections to perform complete engine overhauls after very short periods of operation, between forty and sixty hours. Despite the precautions, stuck valves caused several forced landings. Pilots also argued that the loss of power made them much more vulnerable in combat.[38]

Both McCord and his counterpart, Colonel Cassidy, initiated separate letters through theater headquarters. They requested that the Far East Air Forces direct the commanding general, Far East Air Force Service Command, to procure 73-octane aviation gasoline. The Far East Air Forces headquarters staff responded to the effect that "if the Ground Force units performed proper maintenance on their airplanes, no operating difficulties would result." MacArthur's headquarters concurred. McCord and Cassidy collected extensive evidence and resubmitted their requests. This time the Far East Air Forces accepted their arguments. Representatives of Sixth and Eighth Armies and the Far East Air Force Service Command met and agreed that the latter would supply 550 gallons of 73-octane aviation gasoline per Field Artillery airplane per month.[39]

This agreement came well after Sixth Army concluded its portion of the campaign on Leyte, and even then there were difficulties. The Far East Air Force Service Command insisted on continuing to supply only 80-octane gasoline to Army Air Forces L–5s. Pilots of these aircraft, whose primary mission was the evacuation of the wounded, were usually based on the same fields as the air sections. The Army Air Forces pilots begged 73-octane aviation gasoline from their Field Artillery counterparts, and because of their mission, no one was inclined to deny it to them. The upshot, of course, was that air sections once again found themselves forced to depend at least part of the time on 80-octane fuel with all the attendant side effects. The problem persisted until the end of the war in the Pacific.[40]

The destruction of the Japanese strategic reserves on Leyte greatly facilitated Sixth Army (and later Eighth Army) operations on Luzon. MacArthur, recently promoted to general of the Army, mandated a headlong dash down the Lingayen Plain to Manila. Much as in Europe, the commander of the leading element, Brig. Gen. William C. Chase of the 2d Brigade, 1st Cavalry Division, used the liaison aircraft of the attached field artillery battalion to conduct route reconnaissance and column control. By these means Chase avoided Japanese roadblocks and ambushes and enabled his division to claim honors as "First

---

[38] Memo, Cassidy for CG, AGF, 21 Jun 45, Microfilm A1387, AFHRA; Rpt, Kiefer, in Sixth Army, *Report of the Leyte Operation*, p. 226.

[39] Memo, Cassidy for CG, AGF, 21 Jun 45; Rpt, sub: FA Rpt, in Eighth Army, *Leyte-Samar Operation*, pp. 43–44.

[40] Memo, Cassidy for CG, AGF, 21 Jun 45; Rpt, G–3, 77th Inf Div, sub: Liberation of Leyte, Op Sum, 23 Nov–25 Dec 44, [Extract], HQ, AGF, G–4, Requirements Section, Development Div, FA Br, Decimal file, 1942–1945, 319.1 (SWPA), RG 337, NARA.

in Manila" on 3 February 1945. During the bloody month-long battle for the capital city, American artillery often fought in a direct-fire role. Because Field Artillery pilots had little occasion to perform their primary mission, reconnaissance and liaison flights predominated. Flights in L–4s were a good means of orienting infantry commanders—and the press—to conditions on the ground.[41]

The Japanese commander in the Philippines, General Tomoyuki Yamashita, sought to tie down as many American divisions as long as possible by fighting a delaying action in the mountains east and west of the Lingayen Plain. Most Japanese Army units reached these areas in good order. The scale of post-Manila operations on Luzon thus remained large enough to be similar to the campaigns in Europe, but the terrain and the nature of the enemy produced subtle differences. The number of troops available and the extent of the area of operations meant that division frontages were very extended. Japanese defenders were also widely dispersed and well dug in. The strength of these field fortifications led infantry battalion commanders to request precision adjustments very close to their own front lines—often too close, thought the Sixth Army artillery officer, Colonel Kiefer, for the safety of friendly troops.[42]

Whereas American doctrine—and the American artillery's practice in Europe—emphasized the battalion as the basic unit of fire, the extended frontages plus the infantry's heavy dependence on artillery meant that in Sixth Army most fire was done by individual batteries. In the largely open Lingayen Plain, this had not made a great deal of difference, because terrestrial observation was possible in the Southwest Pacific Area on a large scale for the first time. But once in the mountains, whether east or west of the plain, the troops found themselves in jungle reminiscent of the New Guinea wilderness. Observed missions became once more almost the exclusive prerogative of air observation posts.[43]

The extended frontages meant that air observation posts had much larger areas to patrol. Japanese artillery continued to cease firing when L–4s passed overhead, but the liaison pilots' expanded "beats" meant that the planes, while almost continuously in the air, were often not long over any particular point. Moreover, Major McCord possessed a wasting asset. Although Luzon was proportionately less costly than Leyte for Sixth Army air sections, the Army Air Forces supply system was unable to recoup their losses. Sixth Army lost thirty-seven artillery planes from all causes and received twenty-eight replacements. The 6th Depot Unit (Army) supported Sixth Army, although it remained under Army Air Forces control throughout the campaign. The unit did not arrive on Luzon until early April and then without any equipment. As late as 31 May 1945, it still had not received any. Only "hard work and ingenuity" in the air sections kept the planes in the air.[44]

---

[41] William C. Chase, *Front Line General: The Commands of William C. Chase, An Autobiography* (Houston, Tex.: Pacesetter Press, 1975), pp. 77–100; Capt. J. Richard Hearn, "Early Luzon Experience," *FAJ* 35 (June 1945):328–29; Maj. Nelson H. Randall, "The Battle of Manila," *FAJ* 35 (August 1945):450–56; Robert R. Smith, *Triumph in the Philippines*, U.S. Army in World War II (Washington, D.C.: Office of the Chief of Military History, 1963), pp. 237–70.

[42] Memo, Sixth Army Arty, sub: An Analysis of Fires by Div Arty in the Luzon Campaign, Sixth Army, *Report of the Luzon Campaign, 9 January 1945–30 June 1945*, 4 vols. (n.p.: [Sixth Army], n.d.), 3:84–85.

[43] Ibid.

[44] Quote from Rpt, [Brig Gen H. W. Kiefer], sub: Rpt of the Arty Ofcr, Sixth Army, *Report of the Luzon Campaign*, 3:69. Rpt 37, Pacific Warfare Board, 3 Aug 45, sub: Battle Experiences Against the Japanese, "Pacific Warfare Board Reports"; Capt. J. Richard Hearn, "Early Luzon Experience," *FAJ* 35 (June 1945):328–29; Col. Frank J. Sackton, "Battle Notes of Division Artillery on Luzon," *FAJ* 35 (September 1945):539.

As the Japanese became aware of the importance of liaison planes in American ground operations, Japanese night infiltration raids often set out to destroy artillery aircraft. (Sixth Army lost twelve aircraft in the Luzon campaign due to direct enemy action, eight of them to infiltrators.) As one survivor noted, there were "few experiences more nerve-shattering than a Jap[anese] 'Banzai' attack or attempted infiltration of a demolition squad." Initially, the 32d Infantry Division assigned its aircraft to battalions, but then one of its units put its strip too far forward. The Japanese infiltrated and destroyed the aircraft. Afterward, the division artillery officer retained all aircraft under central control, based on one airstrip in the rear. As in Leyte, but for tactical rather than terrain considerations, each battalion maintained a forward strip where a pilot could land and be oriented before flying a mission. Such a procedure also minimized the amount of engineering support the artillery aircraft needed. In Eighth Army, fighting in the southern Philippines, this became standard procedure for all air sections. The forward strips required the same kind of perimeter defense as a field artillery battalion. If the strip was not within the battalion perimeter, the battalion would have to find enough soldiers to defend it.[45]

Sixth Army lost twenty-one aircraft to operational accidents on Luzon. (In addition, friendly fire downed one plane.) Inadequacies of logistical support and pilot fatigue undoubtedly played a role, although it is impossible to determine to what degree. Kiefer noted that, because of excessive demands placed on pilots, some flew as many as eight hours each day for weeks on end. Some corps and division commanders required their air-observation-post sections to have one light aircraft available at all times at headquarters to convey key commanders and their staffs to high priority meetings. This only followed General Krueger's example. Major McCord maintained a flight of four airplanes at Sixth Army headquarters, ready to act as a taxi service for Krueger, who was promoted to full general in March, and his staff. While McCord had no requirement to fly combat missions, pilots at lower echelons did. They had to superimpose these command liaison flights on top of their observed fire missions.[46]

Within these logistical and tactical confines, Sixth Army Field Artillery pilots and observers continued to develop their technique. Sometimes they further refined procedures already developed in the Pacific; at other times they introduced methods first employed in Europe. In addition to using L–4s to make emergency resupply drops to isolated patrols, the 33d Infantry Division, operating in northern Luzon around the former summer capital of Baguio, used L–4s to guide C–47s to drop zones to resupply its advance elements of infantry. Without the Cubs, the transports could not locate the troops. The 38th Infantry Division Artillery, also operating in northern Luzon, reported that on moonlit nights it "effectively employed" L–4s to spot artillery fire. Other units attempting such missions reported somewhat less success.[47]

Individual ground forces units also took the initiative to improve the accuracy of Fifth Air Force close air support missions. The separate 112th Cavalry Regimental Combat

---

[45] Col. C. de W. W. Lang, "Perimeter Defense," *FAJ* 35 (November 1945):647; Rpts 11 and 37, Pacific Warfare Board, 3 Jul, 3 Aug 45, subs: Battle Experiences Against the Japanese, both in "Pacific Warfare Board Reports."

[46] Rpt, [Kiefer], in Sixth Army, *Report of the Luzon Campaign*, 3:69.

[47] Rpt 13, Pacific Warfare Board, 4 Jul 45, sub: Battle Experiences Against the Japanese, "Pacific Warfare Board Reports"; Col. Ralph MacDonald, Executive Officer (XO), 33d Inf Div Arty, "Artillery Cubs in Mountain Operations: 33d Infantry Division in Northern Luzon," *FAJ* 35 (October 1945):616.

Team used artillery liaison aircraft to drop 81-mm. phosphorous shells to mark targets out of artillery range for air support aircraft. Communication went through artillery radio channels back to the air support party at division headquarters. It worked satisfactorily except for a one- to ten-minute delay "resulting from the indirect route." The 33d Infantry Division developed a much more sophisticated system, very similar to HORSEFLY as practiced in Italy. As the division penetrated the northern mountains, it had an increasing number of friendly-fire incidents involving Army Air Forces fighter-bombers. Division artillery developed the expedient of using a liaison pilot to lead the attacking aircraft. The artillery pilot, who knew the ground well, marked the target with smoke grenades. Then his passenger, an Army Air Forces controller, directed the fighter-bombers to the target. The new procedure, reported the division artillery S–3, had greatly increased the effectiveness of the close air support. Equally important, in the more than forty missions flown under this system, no American ground troops were hit.[48]

General MacArthur had formed Eighth Army in September 1944. After the capture of Manila, it directed operations south of the city. Although the army commander, General Eichelberger, came from the Southwest Pacific Area, most of the staff, including Colonel Cassidy, consisted of members of the staff of Second Army from the United States. Most of these officers had worked together for several years and had a good idea of their responsibilities. Cassidy, fresh from the Department of Air Training at Fort Sill, was still uncertain about the duties of an artillery air officer when he arrived in theater. He soon found out. His job "consisted primarily of coordinating and facilitating the supply of aircraft and A[rmy] A[ir] F[orces] equipment to F[ield] A[rtillery] units." The primary problem was that the Army Air Forces shipped the air-observation-post equipment from the United States to several scattered air depots in the Southwest Pacific Theater. No one at the depots knew who should get the equipment or how it was to be used. They stored it in warehouses "and promptly proceed[ed] to forget all about it." Only through considerable "not so amateur detective work" and much flying in Army Air Forces C–47s up and down the coast of New Guinea did Cassidy locate the equipment.[49]

Eighth Army, unlike Sixth Army, did not employ two corps in the same operation. Consequently, Cassidy's responsibilities remained largely administrative. He developed and put into effect "the first planned program of distribution and stockage of liaison airplanes, equipment, and supplies" in the theater and began rotating artillery pilots suffering from combat fatigue. Most important, he became the representative for both Sixth and Eighth Armies in negotiations with the Far East Air Forces concerning the unsatisfactory state of higher-echelon maintenance in theater. Largely on his representations, the Far East Air Forces moved the 6th Depot Unit (Army) to Luzon but then refused to transfer operational control to Sixth Army. The Far East Air Forces affirmed the same policy regarding the 5th Depot Unit (Army), which remained on Leyte to support Eighth Army. While lack of equipment and supplies prevented the 6th Depot Unit from performing its mission adequately, operational control proved the crucial variable for the

---

[48] MacDonald, "Artillery Cubs in Mountain Operations," pp. 613–14; Rpt 29, Pacific Warfare Board, 30 Jul 45, sub: Battle Experience Against the Japanese, in "Pacific Warfare Board Reports."

[49] Ltr, Lt Col R. F. Cassidy, Eighth Army Arty Air Ofcr, 24 Nov 44, in Memo, Wolf, 15 Jan 45, sub: Informal Info, in FAS, DAT, "Training Memoranda."

5th Depot Unit. The XIII Air Force Service Command diverted the men to serve as stevedores unloading Army Air Forces equipment. Field Artillery officers found this situation doubly frustrating, because they had provided the personnel to man these units. The Sixth Army artillery officer, General Kiefer, reported one Army Air Forces officer, was "a little hot" about the subject after they failed to support his aircraft on either Leyte or Luzon. Even though Cassidy carried the issue all the way to the War Department, the problem remained until the end of the war. Denied adequate support, air observation posts were a wasting asset in both armies.[50]

Eighth Army's campaign in eastern Mindanao between 17 April and 30 June 1945 was the largest of its operations in the southern Philippine Islands, and the air-observation-post missions were correspondingly the most complex. The X Corps, commanded by Maj. Gen. Franklin C. Sibert, directed the maneuver.

CASSIDY AFTER HIS PROMOTION TO FULL COLONEL IN 1955

Prior to the assault, the X Corps artillery air officer, Maj. Frederick W. Sinon, overflew the landing area as a passenger in an Army Air Forces B–24 to report on the condition of the beaches and roads to the corps artillery commander. The 24th Infantry Division made a successful amphibious landing at Parang on 17 April against light opposition. Division pilots initially used a stretch of road for a runway. The next day the corps artillery and attached battalion air sections landed and joined the division pilots. Sinon had already selected a location for an airstrip, but the engineers assigned to build it were still aboard ship on 21 April. Sinon simply flagged down passing road graders and bulldozers and convinced the operators to clear and level an area for him. Eventually, this impromptu field served as a base for X Corps and 24th and 31st Infantry Division air sections—twenty-eight aircraft in all.[51]

Air rescue, the retrieval of aircrews shot down behind enemy lines, was, like medical evacuation, a primary mission for Army Air Forces liaison squadrons. On occasion, air-observation-post pilots also performed this task. One of the most spectacular of such missions occurred during the Mindanao campaign and involved the rescue of two Marine Corps aviators from the 24th Marine Air Group. Their aircraft went down on the side of a volcano near Lake Lanao. The artillery air officer from the 983d Field Artillery Battalion

---

[50] Rpt, [Col M. E. McGinley], sub: FA Rpt, in Eighth Army, *Leyte-Samar Operation*, pp. 43–44; Memo, Cassidy for CG, AGF, 15 Jun 45; Memo, Bell, sub: Notes from Colonel Bell's Visit to SWPA.

[51] Rpt, [Maj F. W. Sinon], sub: Opn of Air Section—Mindanao Opn, in X Corps Arty, "Historical Account of Mindanao Operation, 30 Apr 45–30 Jun 45" (Bound Ms, Morris Swett Tech Lib, c. 1945).

volunteered to fly a Navy corpsman to the scene. The pilot attempted to land on a nearby volcano ash wash, a clear and relatively smooth surface, but crashed due to the high altitude (in excess of 6,000 feet) and rough terrain. Both men, however, walked away unhurt. They kept the injured marines alive for the next week as Sinon and the other pilot from the 983d Field Artillery Battalion kept them supplied through continuous airdrops of food, medical supplies, and spare parts. After some rough improvements to the landing area, the pilot from the 983d attempted to land, but he also crashed. Sinon loaded his plane with the necessary spare parts and landed successfully. The three pilots then repaired the two planes and flew the injured marines and the aid man to safety.[52]

The period after May 1944 represented both the expansion and maturation of air observation posts in the Southwest Pacific Area. The introduction of two field army headquarters with artillery air officers on their staffs and the unofficial coordination between them gave the program a measure of high-level staff oversight and technical supervision heretofore lacking in the command. The doctrine and techniques for jungle flying developed by I Corps pilots at and immediately after Nassau Bay and Salamaua continued to form the basis for the expanded air-observation-post operations. Ground commanders, Field Artillery pilots, and ground crews continued to innovate, but more in the performance of additional missions, such as medical evacuation, airdrop of infantry at key points in the ground battle, and air rescue, than in the development of new air tactics. Weather and terrain, especially in Leyte, kept ground crews improvising. On the other hand, some aspects of air-observation-post operations remained drearily familiar, namely General MacArthur's indifference, General Kenney's opposition, and the resulting lack of logistical support. Fortunately, Japanese countermeasures remained generally ineffective. The Japanese Army lacked the strength to sustain its one spectacularly effective countermove, the parachute landing on the 11th Airborne Division's airstrips on Leyte.

Central Pacific Area: Okinawa, 1945

Following the successful landings in the Philippines, the thrust of the central Pacific drive shifted north, away from Formosa and toward the Japanese home islands. The Marine Corps landed on Iwo Jima in February 1945. Substantial ground combat continued into April. Okinawa became the objective of the next attack. It was the last of the offshore islands scheduled for assault before the invasion of Japan proper. (Administratively, if not quite culturally and geographically, it was part of the home islands.) Both the size of the island and the strength of the Japanese defenses dictated a multicorps operation. This in turn required the use of a field army headquarters to control the ground battle. Tenth Army, commanded by Lt. Gen. Simon B. Buckner, Jr., had a conventional field army staff. The artillery section, headed by Col. Edmund B. Edwards, included an artillery air officer, Maj. Norman E. McKnight. While Nimitz, like MacArthur, continued to exclude an artillery air officer from his staff, McKnight, like Colonels McCord and Cassidy in Sixth and Eighth Armies, handled the necessary administrative and technical problems. The relative brevity of the campaign, the restricted area in which it was fought compared to New Guinea or the

---

[52] Ibid.

Philippines, and the absence of General Kenney from the command structure made his assignment considerably easier.[53]

At the very opening of the ground campaign, Tenth Army introduced a major innovation in air-observation-post operations, at least as far as the U.S. Army was concerned. Selected pilots used the Brodie device to provide observed fire during the landings. The Brodie device was a Rube Goldberg–like contraption consisting of wires, poles, a hook, a trolley, a trapeze—actually a rectangle of nylon line—and a cable (*Figure 4*). The trapeze hung from the trolley that ran along the cable, which was stretched between poles. The hook was attached to the top of an L–4 and allowed a pilot to catch the trapeze. A line ran from the trolley to a winch that helped slow the plane on landing and boost it when taking off. Mounted on a landing ship, tank (LST), with the cable stretched over the water on the port side between the forward and aft cargo booms, the Brodie device permitted Field Artillery planes to observe fire continuously during a landing. It eliminated the dependence on aircraft carriers to transport light aircraft to the landing area, while the ship equipped with the rig could maneuver much closer to the shore than could a carrier. Assault troops could have observed fire even before they secured a strip ashore.[54]

The Tenth Army artillery air officer, Major McKnight, made arrangements for an LST, the USS *Brodie*, named for the device it carried, to support XXIV Corps during the Okinawa invasion. The XXIV Corps artillery air officer, Maj. Charles Ernest, had learned to fly off a land-based Brodie rig in Hawaii and took it with him to Leyte. Once relieved of operational responsibilities on Leyte, he began training selected pilots in its use. A team arrived from Fort Sill to take up the instructional burden, as did the *Brodie* herself, fresh from action off Iwo Jima. There, Marine Corps and Navy pilots, relatively untrained in the device's peculiarities, had attempted to use it and had suffered a series of operational accidents. Aircraft already "hooked" on the wire had fallen into the ocean. In contrast, Ernest and most of his men received the intensive training needed to operate such complex gear. When XXIV Corps landed on Okinawa on 1 April 1945, the Brodie device and the pilots using it functioned almost flawlessly, making twenty-five takeoffs and landings until engineers could prepare strips ashore. The only operational damage was two broken propellers.[55]

Okinawa was a three-month-long campaign, against a skillful, dug-in defense that resembled nothing so much as the Italian campaign south of Rome. The "cave tactics" of

---

[53] Roster, HQ, Tenth Army, 8 Sep 44, sub: Roster of Ofcrs, attached w/GO 20, HQ Tenth Army, 18 Nov 44, Directory, Tenth Army, 1 Jul 45, sub: Telephone Directory; Memo, [Tenth Army, Public Affairs Office (Ofc)], 1945, sub: Bio Data: Col Edmund B. Edwards; both in The Adjutant General's Office (TAGO), World War II Opns Rpts, 1940–1948, Tenth Army, 110–1.19, RG 407, NARA.

[54] WD, *Army Ground Forces Light Aviation*, pp. 135–39, contains an excellent description of the device. See also Memorandum for Record, author, 1 Aug 96, sub: Remarks by Col Michael J. Strok, U.S. Army (Ret), Concerning the Operation of the Brodie Device, 13 Jun 96, Historian's files, CMH.

[55] Rpt, Maj C. Ernest, Arty Air Ofcr, XXIV Corps, to CG, Tenth Army, 18 Apr 45, sub: Brodie Device, HQ, AGF, Gen Corresp, 1942–1948, 452.11 (Brodie Device), RG 337, NARA; Memo, Operations Division (OPD), *Information Bulletin* 4 (16 June 1945):2. The Morris Swett Technical Library has a bound set of these bulletins dating from 1944 and 1945. Ltr, Ernest to Wolf, [Extract], in Memo, Maj T. S. Baker, 13 Apr 45, sub: Informal Info, Wolf Ms, CMH. The latter is the source of the quote. For the experience of the marines off Iwo Jima, see Robert Sherrod, *History of Marine Corps Aviation in World War II* (Baltimore, Md.: Nautical and Aviation Publishing, 1987), p. 348. Pilots from the 77th Infantry Division did not receive specialized training for the Brodie device. They appear to be the sole exception among Army pilots. Kriegsman, "The L–4 Piper Cub and LST 776 Aircraft Carrier," pp. 2–3, 6–8.

FIGURE 4—LAND INSTALLATION OF THE BRODIE DEVICE

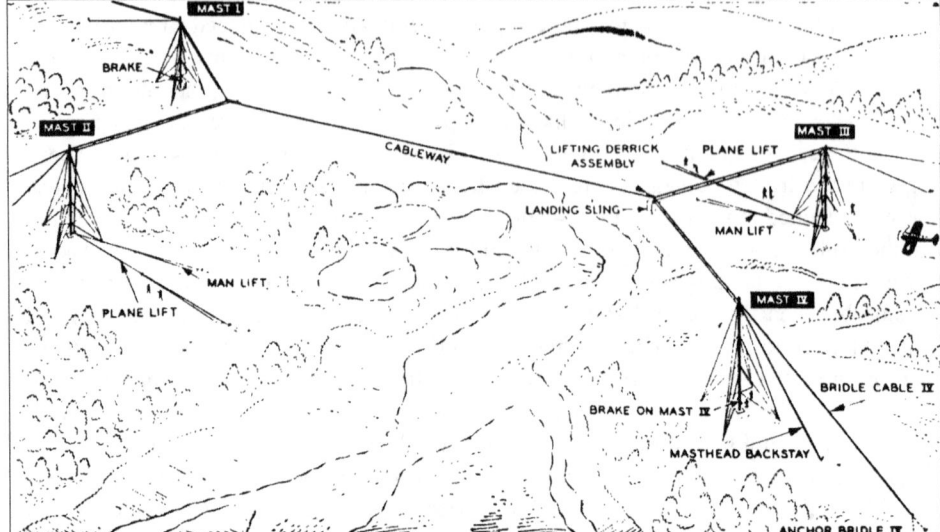

Source: U.S. War Department, *Organic Field Artillery Air Observation*, FM 20–100 (Washington, D.C.: War Department, 1947), p. 136.

the Japanese *Thirty-second Army* proved costly for American ground forces. Accurate artillery fire on cave mouths and bunkers proved a necessary prerequisite for the success of the ground attack, which in turn demanded good observation. Air observation posts once again confirmed their worth in such situations. The Tenth Army artillery officer, Colonel Edwards, initially planned that organic air observation posts would fly only on-call missions. The Japanese Imperial Army, however, occupied the high ground on the island. Ground observation proved impossible during much of the campaign. Normal procedure in Tenth Army became keeping one artillery aircraft in each division sector in the air continuously from dawn to dusk. This required coordination of flights and centralization of control within corps and divisions. As in Italy, pilots flew regular beats. The 7th Infantry Division, for example, required approximately fourteen 1-1/2-hour single-plane flights daily for complete coverage. There had to be overlap on each end of each flight. One plane had to be in the air while another was taking off or landing. By proper scheduling, the division artillery air officer could ensure that no pilot flew more than two such flights in any one day. Pilots and observers thus remained fresh and alert. Their "efficiency remained high" throughout the campaign.[56]

The concentration of U.S. air and naval strength was so great that artillery pilots could conduct missions without any concern about intervention by Japanese aviation. In fact, the

---

[56] Rpt 12, Pacific Warfare Board, 3 Jul 45, sub: Battle Experiences Against the Jap[anese]—Jap[anese] Combat Methods on Okinawa, in "Pacific Warfare Board Reports"; Rpt, [Col E. B. Edwards], sub: FA, in Tenth Army, "Action Report Ryukyus, 28 March–30 June 1945" (Bound Ms, CMH Lib, c. 1945), p. 11–VI–57; 7th Inf Div, Opn Rpt (Bound Ms, CMH Lib, c. 1945), p. 45. The Edwards report is the source of the first quote.

THE USS *BRODIE*, LST 776, IN THE PACIFIC IN 1944 WITH THE BRODIE DEVICE INSTALLED

main hindrance to observed fire from the air became "the promiscuous use of smoke [shells]" by U.S. artillery. Good landing strips, 900 feet long, 60 feet wide, and surfaced for all-weather use, cut operational losses. The 7th Infantry Division Artillery, for example, lost only one airplane during the entire campaign. Overall, Tenth Army lost thirteen Field Artillery aircraft, only four to direct enemy action. The engineering effort to surface the strips also paid dividends during bad weather. "Several days of observation which otherwise would have been lost," reported the 7th Infantry Division, "were obtained in periods of heavy rain."[57]

While logistical support remained unsatisfactory throughout the war in the Southwest Pacific Area, maintenance support in the Pacific Ocean Areas was fully equal to the best levels obtained in Europe. Command influence played a large role in the different results. The commander of the Far East Air Forces, General Kenney, remained adamantly opposed to Field Artillery aviation, while the commander of Army Air Forces, Pacific Ocean Areas, Maj. Gen. Millard F. Harmon, strove to ensure that Field Artillery aircraft received adequate maintenance and replacement parts. Major McKnight requested a depot unit to support the Tenth Army air observation posts during the invasion of Okinawa. The War

---

[57] Rpt 12, Pacific Warfare Board, 3 Jul 45; 7th Inf Div, "Operation Report," p. 45.

Maintenance Specialists of the 1st Depot Unit, Army, on Okinawa, Inspect the Engine of an L–4 and Remove a Battle-Damaged Wing for Immediate Repair.

Department assigned the 1st Depot Unit (Army), which arrived in Hawaii in January 1945 without equipment or supplies. McKnight worked with the commander to develop the supply level required for the operation. General Harmon's headquarters, particularly Maj. Harold F. Read and a civilian, Mr. G. P. Williams, expedited the action. The Hawaiian Air Depot could supply much of the required equipment, but other items could be obtained only from the continental United States. To speed their arrival, Harmon's staff ordered them for direct delivery to the 1st Depot Unit. Because the lines of communication to Hawaii were extended and dope needed to repair fabric was in short supply, Harmon's headquarters authorized McKnight to carry an extra twenty-one aircraft with him to make up operational losses.[58]

Harmon's staff took the same attitude about providing L–5s for selected air sections in the two corps assigned to the operation, XXIV Corps and the Marine III Amphibious Corps, a measure that McKnight considered absolutely essential given the frequent high winds on Okinawa. The Army Air Forces in the Pacific Ocean Areas succeeded in delivering the L–5s to units staging from such diverse areas as Leyte, Espiritu Santo, and New Caledonia in a timely fashion. Some ten L–5s thus became available for the campaign. Kenney, in contrast, had denied air sections the use of L–5s in the Philippines.[59]

The Brodie device was the major tactical innovation of the Okinawa campaign. The major thrust of its development was the attempt to relieve light aircraft of their dependence

---

[58] Rpt, [Edwards], sub: FA, in Tenth Army, "Action Report Ryukyus," pp. 11–VI–53–56.
[59] Ibid.

on landing strips. In a way, this converged with the emphasis on ground fighting earlier in the South, Southwest, and Central Pacific Areas, where rugged terrain and dense jungle put landing strips at a premium. In an unstated but very real way these experiences created a demand for a machine that could take off and land vertically.

Organizationally, the Okinawa campaign, like the ones in New Guinea and the Philippines, suggested the need for a greater centralization of control of air operations than the founders of the Air-Observation-Post Program originally envisioned. In the area of logistical support, the disparate experiences of Field Artillery aircraft of Sixth and Eighth Armies on one hand and Tenth Army on the other demonstrates once again the importance of command influence. There is no indication that General Harmon was any more enamored of organic aviation as an abstract principle than was General Kenney, but Harmon knew how to support the policies of his superiors even if he disagreed with them. Consequently, Tenth Army air sections received first-rate maintenance and supply support. On the other hand, the record in the Southwest Pacific Area suggests that in these regions Sixth and Eighth Army Field Artillery pilots and mechanics succeeded despite, rather than because of, General Kenney and his staff.

Conclusion

Prior to June 1944 the contrast between conditions in the Pacific and the situation in the Mediterranean in terms of the numbers of aircraft and the amount of administrative and logistical support could not be more striking. Many of the senior officers in North Africa and the Mediterranean—General Eisenhower, General Clark, Lt. Gen. George S. Patton, Jr., Maj. Gen. Lloyd R. Fredendall, and General Lewis—had been associated with getting the program started in the United States. The most senior area commanders in the Pacific where artillery aircraft operated—General MacArthur, Admiral Halsey, and later Admiral Nimitz—were uninterested and detached. Even after the number of air observation posts increased dramatically in the Southwest Pacific and Central Pacific Areas in 1944, they remained organizationally stunted in contrast to Europe and the Mediterranean. Nevertheless, the program was no less a success in the Pacific. Pilots began modifying their tactics from the moment they entered combat to adapt to war in the tropics. The primary constant in the combat experience of the program in the Pacific on the one hand and North Africa, Sicily, Italy, France, and Germany on the other was the quality of the participants. Ultimately, the success of the Air-Observation-Post Program depended upon the skill, bravery, dedication, and willingness to innovate of hundreds of mainly anonymous pilots, mechanics, and observers. Because of them, organic aviation had a future in the U.S. Army.

In the Pacific, different climatic conditions and a sizable number of air sections encouraged continued innovation, but the differences with operations in France and Germany were more of degree than kind. In France, the 90th Infantry Division used L–4s to resupply isolated companies; in the Philippines, the 11th Airborne Division used its air sections to resupply regiments. Field Artillery pilots in the Pacific evacuated casualties by air during combat emergencies in numbers never approached in Europe. The 11th Airborne Division's airdrop of a company into the battle zone using light aircraft suggested the possibility of placing ground troops very precisely on some key objective, but so did XII

Corps' proposed airlanding on the east bank of the Rhine River. The Brodie device was used only in the Pacific, but this simply reflected its late availability in the war. If otherwise pilots in Italy and the Pacific performed missions comparable to their counterparts in western Europe, then the similarity simply attested to the universal value of organic light aircraft. Their utility in all theaters also underlined the validity of Maj. Delbert L. Bristol's contention, based on experiences in North Africa, Sicily, France, and Germany, that air observation posts would become a permanent part of the ground forces after the war.[60]

If the differences between air-observation-post operations in the Pacific and western Europe were of degree rather than kind, they were nevertheless differences. Their existence was hardly surprising. The U.S. Army in World War II was optimized to fight the German Army in western Europe—the principal opponent in the primary theater. All combat required adaptation, but ground units assigned to other theaters had more adaptations with which to contend. In Italy, the mountains and the coordinated German resistance sustained over many months drove change for the air observation posts. In the Pacific, vast distances covered by water, jungle, and the tenacious, last-ditch defense by the Japanese Imperial Army patterned the air-observation-post response. Experience in neither theater contradicted the lessons of the war in Europe, but it threw into starker relief the potential and need for further change and adaptation. Even more than in Europe, the experience of air sections in the Pacific, as in Italy, helped prepare the way for the postwar demand for and acceptance of helicopters and a concomitant expansion of organic aviation missions.

---

[60] Maj. Delbert L. Bristol, "Air OP Is Here To Stay," *FAJ* 36 (October 1946):586–87.

CHAPTER 8

Creating Army Ground Forces Light Aviation

The combat successes of air observation posts eventually had a major impact upon the policy gridlock between the Army Ground Forces and the Army Air Forces over organic aviation. The Air Staff retreated only gradually from a position of total opposition and then only because of expediency, not because of any fundamental shift in its view of the soundness of the principle of organic aviation. With the end of the war approaching, the question of the postwar future of Field Artillery aircraft attracted increasing attention. The stakes in this contest were so high that a host of subsidiary issues—the role of the Department of Air Training after the completion of mobilization, the training of Field Artillery pilots to fly at night, the equipping of air observation posts with cameras, and the arming of light aircraft—became caught up in this larger problem.

*War Department Policy and the Air-Observation-Post Program,
September 1943–October 1944*

The existence of the Air-Observation-Post Program remained a matter of contention between the Army Ground Forces and the Army Air Forces. A series of attempts by both Headquarters, Army Ground Forces, and overseas theater commanders to strengthen the Field Artillery program precipitated an Air Staff attack on the program in early 1944. The arguments remained virtually unchanged from the disputes in 1942 and the spring of 1943. The Army Ground Forces staff, buoyed by very positive reports from the field about the performance of Field Artillery air sections, continued to staunchly support the organic air concept. The Air Staff remained just as adamantly opposed. In the Air Staff view the War Department ought to return control of all liaison aircraft to the Army Air Forces.

The first attempt to reorganize air observation posts came in September 1943. With the end of operations in Sicily, the Seventh Army commander, Lt. Gen. George S. Patton, Jr., initiated a major effort to identify the lessons learned from the campaign. The ensuing report was the most elaborate by any American field army headquarters prior to the cessation of hostilities in 1945. It had an immediate impact on training in the United States. In preparing the air-observation-post portion of the report, the Seventh Army artillery air

SHEPARD IN 1958, FOLLOWING HIS PROMOTION TO FULL COLONEL

officer, Capt. Claude L. Shepard, Jr., convened an air officers' conference on 3 September 1943 to discuss experiences. The conferees considered the courier and reconnaissance missions equally important and just as common as fire direction. They recommended reducing the number of aircraft to one in each field artillery battalion and assigning the excess generated to division headquarters to perform these other missions. The Seventh Army signal officer, Col. Elton F. Hammond, went even further. He advocated organizing a Signal Corps aerial messenger company for assignment to each field army to carry important messages and staff officers.[1]

The commander of the 13th Field Artillery Brigade, Maj. Gen. John A. Crane, was not allowed to send a representative to Shepard's conference and learned of the conclusions only informally. Crane, who had fought to retain the observation balloon in 1941, had become a complete convert to light aircraft. While he admitted the importance of the other missions, he would not concede their equality with observed fire. His solution was to add more aircraft to division tables of organization and equipment rather than to take them from the Field Artillery. As he conceived the issue, removing aircraft from the firing battalions would prevent the Field Artillery from performing its primary mission—the accurate delivery of fire. Despairing of blocking the proposal in Seventh Army, he protested directly to

---

[1] Ltr, Col R. E. Cummings, Deputy Chief of Staff (DCS), Seventh Army, to The Adjutant General (TAG), 1 Oct 43, sub: Report (Rpt) of Operations (Opns); General Order (GO) 1, Headquarters (HQ), Seventh Army, 10 Jul 43; Rpt, [Capt Claude L. Shepard], sub: Air An. to Artillery (Arty) Rpt; all in Seventh Army, *The Seventh Army in Italy* (n.p.: 62d Engineer Topographic Co., 1943), pp. G–3, G–4. Interview (Interv), author with Col C. L. Shepard, 23 Sep 83. Questionnaire, Col Charles E. Hart, Arty Officer (Ofcr), II Corps, to Commanding General (CG), 13th Field Artillery (FA) Brigade (Bde), et al., 19 Aug 43, sub: FA Rpt Covering Period 10 Jul to 17 Aug 43; both in II Corps Arty, "Employment of the Artillery of the II Corps during the Sicilian Operations, 10 Jul to 17 Aug 43" (Bound Manuscript [Ms], Morris Swett Technical Library, Field Artillery School [FAS], Fort Sill, Okla. [hereafter cited as Morris Swett Tech Lib], 1943). Memorandum for Record (MFR), HQ, Army Ground Forces (AGF), for TAG, 18 Dec 43, sub: Messenger Aircraft, HQ, AGF, General Correspondence (Gen Corresp), 1942–1948, 353/45 (FA Air Observation [Obsn]) (Confidential [C]), Record Group (RG) 337, National Archives and Records Administration, Washington, D.C. (hereafter cited as NARA). Memo, Col S. Beckley, AGF Representative (Rep), for CG, AGF, 6 Nov 43, sub: Messenger Aircraft, HQ, AGF, Gen Corresp, 1942–1948, 353/29 (FA Air Obsn) (Secret [S]), RG 337, NARA. Ltr, Lt Col W. G. Caldwell, Adjutant General (AG), Seventh Army, to TAG, 24 Aug 43, sub: Messenger Aircraft; Draft Table of Organization (TO), [Seventh Army], sub: Same; Memo, Col S. A. Beckley, AGF Rep, for Communications Coordinating Committee, 22 Oct 43, sub: Rpt of Conference; Memo, Maj Gen Ray E. Porter, Assistant Chief of Staff (ACS), G–3, for TAG, 18 Dec 43, sub: Messenger Aircraft, The Adjutant General's Office (TAGO), Secret Corresp, 1941–1945, 452.1 (24 Aug 43), RG 407, NARA.

Headquarters, Army Ground Forces. "General Crane," noted the G–3 at Army Ground Forces, Brig. Gen. John M. Lentz, "has jumped channels." In effect, Crane had risked his career to save air observation posts for the Field Artillery. He found a sympathetic audience in the Field Artillery–dominated staff at Washington Barracks. Lentz protected Crane's career by simply filing Crane's letter. He protected the Air-Observation-Post Program by also filing the revised tables proposed by Seventh Army. He could not, however, do the same when the director of the Department of Air Training, Col. William W. Ford, submitted a plan to reorganize the Air-Observation-Post Program along the lines recommended by Seventh Army.[2]

During World War II, Headquarters, Army Ground Forces, served as a conduit for doctrine rather than as a locus for the writers of doctrine. Officers at branch schools prepared doctrine based on reports of official Army Ground Forces observer teams, after-action reports and lessons learned reports prepared by units, and informal communications from branch officers serving overseas. Graduates of the Department of Air Training continually wrote to friends on the faculty and staff. There was thus no mystery about how Ford quickly learned of Seventh Army's conclusions. His reaction, in contrast to Crane's, was favorable, and he drafted a proposal, part of which he sent for comment to the officer at Headquarters, Army Service Forces, charged with air-observation-post matters, Maj. (later Lt. Col.) Robert M. Leich. Leich in turn talked about Ford's ideas with colleagues on the War Department General Staff. Staff officers at Army Ground Forces headquarters were disconcerted to discover that officers on the General Staff knew about Ford's proposal before they did. (They suspected, but could not prove, that Ford had attempted to circumvent them.) Perhaps equally disconcerting, the General Staff officers were impressed with Ford's ideas. Lentz took the position, which the commanding general of the Army Ground Forces, Lt. Gen. Lesley J. McNair, adopted as his own, that the organic air program should be expanded beyond the Field Artillery without diminishing the size of the air-observation-post sections. The War Department G–3, Maj. Gen. Ray E. Porter, waited until December 1943 and then turned down the Army Ground Forces plan.[3]

Porter did not deny the need for additional light aircraft in forward areas; he based his decision entirely on changes in Army Air Forces organization. The standard observation squadron with which the Army Air Forces entered the war, consisting of twin-engine bombers and single-seat fighters converted to photographic reconnaissance and light aircraft, had not proven battleworthy in North Africa, and the Army Air Forces had withdrawn it from combat. In its place, the Army Air Forces substituted photographic reconnaissance

---

[2] Ltr, Brig Gen John A. Crane, 13th FA Bde, to CG, AGF, 17 Sep 43; Memo Slip, Brig Gen John M. Lentz, G–3, AGF, to Chief of Staff (CS), AGF, 3 Oct 43; both in HQ, AGF, Gen Corresp, 1942–1948, 353/31 (FA Air Obsn), RG 337, NARA.

[3] Ltr, Col W. W. Carr, AG, FAS, to CG, AGF, 9 Oct 43, sub: Suggested Reorganization of Liaison Aviation (Avn) for Ground Force Units, with Indorsement (Ind), Maj R. A. Meredith, Assistant Adjutant General (AAG), AGF, to CG, Replacement and School Command (R&SC), 4 Nov 43; Memo, Porter for CG, AGF, 3 Dec 43, sub: FA Liaison Avn; Memo, Lt Gen Lesley J. McNair, CG, AGF, for Chief of Staff, Army (CSA) (Attn: G–3 Division [Div]), 28 Dec 43, sub: FA Liaison Avn; all in HQ, AGF, Gen Corresp, 1942–1948, 353/29 (FA Air Obsn) (S), RG 337, NARA. See Dennis J. Vetock, *Lessons Learned: A History of U.S. Army Lesson Learning* (Carlisle Barracks, Pa.: U.S. Army Military History Institute, 1988), for a discussion of battle experience as a basis for doctrine during World War II.

squadrons equipped exclusively with high-performance aircraft and liaison squadrons equipped with L–5s and L–6s and intended strictly to work behind friendly lines. Headquarters, Army Air Forces, planned to assign a liaison squadron to each field army. Normally, a flight of eight aircraft would be attached to each corps in a field army. Porter rejected the Signal Corps aerial messenger company, because the Army Air Forces squadron already existed. The first ones were ready for deployment overseas. As to other organic aircraft, he simply lectured that air observation posts had to perform multiple missions within combat divisions.[4]

Possibly stimulated by the controversy over the Ford proposal, officers in the War Department G–3 developed their own plan for organizing Field Artillery air observation posts. In late 1943 General Porter suggested reorganizing the air observation posts into division flights. General McNair opposed Porter's design. The Army Ground Forces staff regarded the Porter plan as the first step in returning light aircraft to the Army Air Forces. In successfully rebutting Porter, McNair drew heavily upon the reports of Army Ground Forces observers in the North African Theater of Operations (still the American designation for operations in the Mediterranean) and the testimony of the sometime assistant artillery air officer of Fifth Army, Capt. Eugene P. Gillespie, then in Washington between assignments. At the end of seventeen months, organic aviation was in terms of force structure at the same position it had occupied on 6 June 1942, notwithstanding the battle experience it had gained in the interim.[5]

On the other hand, McNair's staff regarded a portion of Porter's proposal favorably. Porter wanted to increase the rank of division artillery air officers to major. McNair's headquarters brought the acting director of the Department of Air Training, Lt. Col. (later Col.) Gordon J. Wolf, to Washington on temporary duty to comment on the idea. Wolf prepared a draft training circular that went far beyond Porter's initial premise. Wolf contemplated making theater, army group, army, corps, division, brigade, and group artillery air officers majors. For the first time he defined the duties and thus gave official sanction to the position of the corps artillery air officer. This officer, in Wolf's formulation, was the staff adviser on air matters for the corps artillery commander and exercised staff supervision over the operation, training, maintenance, and supply of all the organic aircraft in the command. The changes he recommended did not involve increasing the number of light aircraft assigned to ground units, the kind of reform almost guaranteed to elicit opposition from the Army Air Forces. Wolf also restated the responsibilities of the division artillery air officer with more precision than Training Circular 24 of 1 March 1943,

---

[4] Memo, McNair for CSA (Attn: G–3 Div), 28 Dec 43. Memos, Porter for CG, AGF, 3 Dec 43, sub: FA Liaison Avn, and Lentz for CS, AGF, 17 Dec 43, sub: Same, both in HQ, AGF, Gen Corresp, 1942–1948, 353/35 (FA Air Obsn) (S), RG 337, NARA; Memo, Col L. S. Partridge, Acting ACS, G–3, for CGs, Army Air Forces (AAF) and AGF, 31 Dec 43, sub: Liaison Avn for Ground Force Use, HQ, AGF, Gen Corresp, 1942–1948, 353/45 (FA Air Obsn) (C), RG 337, NARA. Robert F. Futrell, *The Command of Observation Aviation* (Maxwell Air Force Base [AFB], Ala.: Historical Division, 1956). The 154th Observation Squadron supported operations in Tunisia with a mixture of A–20s, P–39s, P–38/F–4s, and P–51s. Its O–47s and O–49s were withdrawn before it entered combat. Maurer Maurer, ed., *Combat Squadrons of the Air Force: World War II* (Maxwell AFB, Ala., and Washington, D.C.: Albert F. Simpson Historical Research Center and Office of Air Force History, 1982), p. 353.

[5] Memo, Porter for CG, AGF, 3 Dec 43. Memo Slip, Lentz for CS, AGF, 10 Dec 43, sub: FA Liaison Avn; Memo, McNair for CSA (Attn: G–3 Div), 28 Dec 43, sub: Same; Interv, Capt [Eugene P.] Gillespie, 18 Dec 43; all in HQ, AGF, Gen Corresp, 1942–1948, 353/35 (S), RG 337, NARA; Interv, Maj Gen William A. Harris with Col Gordon J. Wolf, c. 1983, U.S. Army Center of Military History, Washington, D.C. (hereafter cited as CMH).

which his draft was designed to supersede. In particular, Wolf devoted much attention to the officer's responsibilities for maintaining flight safety and outlined a training cycle for divisional air sections.[6]

These changes represented an initial bargaining position. Wolf was certain that Headquarters, Army Air Forces, would block at least some of these reforms. But through administrative error, the War Department published the circular, designated Training Circular No. 132, on 14 December 1943, before the Air Staff had an opportunity to comment on the scheme. Commands in the field immediately promoted their artillery air officers. Rescinding the training circular became in this circumstance a practical impossibility.[7]

This episode was but one of several during the fall and winter of 1943 that caused officers on the Air Staff to feel increasingly aggrieved about the Air-Observation-Post Program. They were very critical of the commander of the North African Theater of Operations, General Dwight D. Eisenhower, who obtained L–5s for Field Artillery air sections in Fifth Army. They regarded the L–5 as much more complex than the L–4 and in their view well beyond the competence of Field Artillery pilots and mechanics to fly and maintain. The Air Staff held that Field Artillery personnel would have to be retrained, which in fact proved not to be the case. Army Air Forces officers also complained that the diversion of L–5s required a complete review and revision of L–5 production schedules, an accurate assessment but also a common occurrence for other aircraft types during the war. Using the same rationale, they found fault with the Army Ground Forces decision to abandon L–2s and L–3s and to convert all air sections to L–4s, overlooking the performance deficiencies of the two aircraft that drove the decision.[8]

Members of the Air Staff were on firmer ground when they complained about their inability to obtain an official statement of ground forces requirements for L–4s during 1944, which they needed before letting production contracts. They did receive unofficial figures from a variety of sources, but their wide variance—3,245 L–4s according to the Operations Division of the War Department General Staff and 1,200 as stated by the Stock Control Division of the Army Service Forces—confused rather than clarified the situation. Officers on the Air Staff found it impossible to formulate a long-range program for liaison aviation because of the recommendation of "numerous spot requirements . . . without sufficient consideration" of their overall impact. These conditions were symptoms of the absence of officers with light aviation expertise in both the War Department and Headquarters, Army Ground Forces. Moreover, officers of the Air Staff at last had an organization to replace Field Artillery air sections: the Army Air Forces liaison squadron.[9]

---

[6] Memo, McNair for CSA, 28 Dec 43; Interv, Gillespie, 18 Dec 43; War Department (WD), Training Circular (TC) 132, 14 Dec 43, sub: Organic FA Air Obsn; Interv, Harris with Wolf, c. 1983.

[7] Memo, McNair for CSA, 28 Dec 43; WD, TC 132, 14 Dec 43; Interv, Harris with Wolf, c. 1983.

[8] Memo, Brig Gen Howard A. Craig for Lt Gen Barney M. Giles, 27 Dec 43, sub: Liaison Avn for AAF and Army Ground Units; Memo, Col N. D. Sillin, Chief (Ch), Requirements Div, Assistant Chief of Air Staff (ACAS), Operations, Commitments, and Requirements (OC&R), for Craig, 29 Dec 43, sub: L–4 and L–5 Requirements; both in HQ, AAF, Central Decimal file, October 1942–May 1944, 452.01–C (Procurement and Requirements), RG 18, NARA.

[9] Draft Memo, Unsigned for CSA, 26 Jan 44, sub: FA Liaison Avn, in HQ, AAF, Central Decimal file, October 1942–May 1944, 452.01–C (Procurement and Requirements), RG 18, NARA. For the progress of Army Air Forces liaison squadrons, see Kent R. Greenfield, *Army Ground Forces and the Air-Ground Battle Team, Including Organic Light Aviation* ([Washington, D.C.]: Historical Section, Army Ground Forces, 1948), p. 63.

These discontents might have remained simply that, but on 31 December 1943, the outgoing commander of the European Theater of Operations, Lt. Gen. Jacob L. Devers, dispatched a message to the War Department recommending the expansion of the organic aviation program beyond the Field Artillery to include two additional aircraft for each division headquarters and six additional aircraft for each corps, army, and army group headquarters. He wanted them to perform "messenger and liaison service," a primary mission of the Army Air Forces liaison squadrons just beginning to deploy overseas. In fact, Devers argued that with these additional organic aircraft he could dispense with the liaison squadrons altogether. He wanted to use both their personnel and their aircraft to create the desired organic air sections immediately.[10]

The senior member of the Air Staff most concerned by this proposal was the assistant chief of Air Staff for Operations, Commitments, and Requirements, Brig. Gen. Howard A. Craig, who had recently served as chief of staff of the Mediterranean Air Command when Field Artillery air sections had experienced so much difficulty in southern Tunisia. Apparently, he initiated a comprehensive review of the Field Artillery liaison aircraft program.[11]

The staff study, prepared by Col. William J. Bell, enumerated the points of friction between the Field Artillery and the Army Air Forces. In addition, Bell laid out his view of the deficiencies of the Air-Observation-Post Program. It was disorganized, duplicative, and possessed no mission that the Army Air Forces could not perform as well as or better than the Field Artillery. Specifically, the supply system was not well articulated; in addition, the air sections were much too decentralized to permit effective supply and maintenance. Bell regarded the Department of Air Training's test of the Piper J–5D in July 1943 as an attempt "to duplicate or short circuit AAF development and service test facilities."[12]

Bell saved his heaviest strictures, however, for Field Artillery air doctrine, which in his view had "deviated" from its original intent. Since everyone now admitted that observers needed to accompany pilots, he saw no reason why the pilot had to be a Field Artillery officer. Attempts by the Field Artillery to equip aircraft with cameras were a clear encroachment upon an Army Air Forces mission. He argued that the Field Artillery was attempting to establish "a Field Artillery Air Force." The obvious solution was to return control of all aviation to the Army Air Forces.[13]

In mid-December 1943 the commanding general of the Army Air Forces, General Henry H. Arnold, en route to Washington from the Cairo and Teheran Conferences, stopped in Sicily and Italy. He toured the front lines, at least part of the time in a light plane flown by the Fifth Army artillery air officer, Maj. John T. Walker. In Sicily, the Fifth and Seventh Army commanders, Lt. Gen. Mark W. Clark and General Patton, gave Arnold a

---

[10] Ltr, Lt Col R. P. Fisk, AAG, European Theater of Operations (ETO), to TAG, Dec 43, sub: Liaison Planes for Ground Units Other than Arty, TAGO, Classified (Class) file, 1943–1945, 452.1 (31 Dec 43), RG 407, NARA; Forrest C. Pogue, *The Supreme Command*, U.S. Army in World War II (Washington, D.C.: Office of the Chief of Military History, 1954), pp. 32–33, 58–59.

[11] "Howard Arnold Craig," in Robert P. Fogerty, comp., *Selected Air Force Case Histories*, 2 vols. (Maxwell AFB, Ala.: U.S. Air Force Historical Division, 1953), 1:n.p.

[12] Record and Routing Sheet (R&RS), Sillin to ACAS, OC&R, 27 Jan 44, sub: FA Liaison Aircraft, HQ, AAF, Central Decimal file, October 1942–May 1944, 452.01–C (Procurement and Requirements), RG 18, NARA; Draft Memo, Unsigned, for CSA, 26 Jan 44.

[13] Draft Memo, Unsigned, for CSA, 26 Jan 44.

CREATING ARMY GROUND FORCES LIGHT AVIATION

Left to Right: GENERALS CLARK, ARNOLD, AND PATTON IN SICILY, DECEMBER 1943

briefing on the progress of the campaign. In the process they emphasized the success of Field Artillery air observation posts in combat. After returning to Washington, Arnold read Bell's memorandum and decided it expressed his own views. Arnold had another staff officer redraft it in a less controversial—and emotional—style, retaining Bell's main points, for Arnold's own signature. The revision added one personal touch, apparently based on Arnold's Sicilian meetings. Arnold argued that night flying was yet another example of the way in which the Field Artillery had inappropriately developed organic aviation beyond "the original 'Aerial OP' concept." Three days after Bell completed the original memorandum, Arnold signed the revision and dispatched it by messenger—a full colonel—for hand delivery to the chief of staff, General George C. Marshall, Jr.[14]

When Generals Porter and McNair saw the proposal, they disagreed with Arnold's conclusion. On 7 February 1944, Porter observed that Arnold assumed that the War Department intended to expand the current "limited program" of artillery aviation. The War Department had no such intent. Most of Porter's extended memorandum, however,

---

[14] Memo, Gen Henry H. Arnold for CSA, 29 Jan 44, HQ, AAF, Central Decimal file, October 1942–May 1944, 452.1–C (Obsn), RG 18, NARA; Air Observation Post (AOP) Bulletin no. 6, HQ, Fifth Army, Office (Ofc) of the Arty Ofcr, 14 Dec 43, reprinted in *L–4 Grasshopper Wing Newsletter* 41 (September/October 1993):6–7.

consisted of an eloquent defense of air observation posts. McNair was briefer and very much to the point:

> The main issue is satisfactory air observation for field artillery. The present system is outstandingly successful—one of the remarkable developments in connection with the effective artillery support which is being given the infantry in all theaters. On the other hand, field artillery air observation by the Air Forces has been unsatisfactory since the advent of military aviation.

He saw no reason to expect any different results in the future, nor, for that matter, did General Marshall.[15]

By late February the Air Staff knew that Marshall had disapproved Arnold's recommendation. The official statement, signed by General Porter, did not appear until 28 March. While defending the existing program, it did not encourage expansion of the program beyond the Field Artillery. In fact, it explicitly permitted Arnold to resubmit his proposal any time the expanded program came under consideration. This statement, as intended, inhibited the Army Ground Forces staff from testing conclusions again with the Army Air Forces. The officer in the War Department G–3 Division charged with air-ground policy, Col. James B. Burwell, an Air Corps officer, reinforced this disinclination by repeatedly stating that if Army Ground Forces raised the issue of an expanded organic aviation program once more, the War Department would restore all aviation to the Army Air Forces.[16]

Air-Observation-Post Logistics

General Porter had long been dissatisfied with arrangements for the logistical support of Field Artillery aircraft. As early as June 1943 he had labeled the division of responsibility between the Army Service Forces and Army Air Forces "cumbersome and inefficient." Blocked at the time, he used Arnold's memorandum as a basis for successfully reopening the issue. War Department Circular No. 208 of 25 May 1944 gave the commanding general, Army Air Forces, direct responsibility "for the research, development, procurement, distribution, and maintenance (as prescribed) of liaison airplanes, spare parts, repair materials, auxiliary flying equipment, parachutes, radio controlled targets, and similar items for use by Army Ground Forces." The Army Service Forces no longer played any part in air-observation-post supply. The new system took effect on 15 June.[17]

---

[15] Memos, Porter for Deputy Chief of Staff, Army (DCSA), 7 Feb 44, and McNair for CSA (Attn: G–3 Div), 16 Feb 44, both in Microfilm A1387, U.S. Air Force Historical Research Agency, Maxwell AFB, Ala. (hereafter cited as AFHRA).

[16] Memo, Porter for CG, AAF, 28 Mar 44, sub: Liaison Aircraft in the AGF, HQ, AAF, Central Decimal file, October 1942–May 1944, 452.1 (Obsn), RG 18, NARA. Memo, Lt Col Earnest for Lt Col Laux, 26 Feb 44, HQ, AAF, Central Decimal file, October 1942–May 1944, 452.01–C (Procurement and Requirements), RG 18, NARA. For Burwell, see Greenfield, *Air-Ground Battle Team*, pp. 100–101.

[17] Memo, Porter for DCSA, 7 Feb 44. MFR, Col S. A. Blair, Ch, Planning Branch (Br), G–4, 1 Jun 44, sub: Liaison Aircraft in the AGF; Memo, Maj Gen Russell L. Maxwell, ACS, G–4, for CGs, AGF and AAF, 19 Apr 44, sub: Same; both in TAGO, Class Decimal file, 1943–1945, 452.1 (8 May 44), RG 407, NARA. WD, Circular 208, 25 May 44, sub: AAF. Ltr, Lt Col Robert M. Leich, Ch, Air Section, Misc Issue Br, Army Service Forces (ASF), to Col L. W. DeRosier, AAF Liaison Ofcr, ASF, 10 Apr 44, in HQ, AAF, Central Decimal file, October 1942–May 1944, RG 18, NARA.

The shift in logistical responsibilities from the Army Service Forces to the Army Air Forces suggested the desirability of creating a position on the Air Staff analogous to that which Major Leich had held in Headquarters, Army Service Forces. Capt. (subsequently Maj.) Lloyd M. Bornstein, formerly on the staff at the Department of Air Training, assumed this new post in August 1944 and soon convinced the Army Air Forces officers with whom he was in daily contact that he was a very able officer.[18]

During the staff review of the air-observation-post supply policy, the G–4 on the War Department General Staff, Maj. Gen. Russell L. Maxwell, noted the failure of the Army Air Forces to provide third-echelon maintenance as mandated in the Air-Observation-Post Program. During World War II, third-echelon maintenance consisted of care, repair, and component replacement beyond the capabilities of the troops using their own tools. Mobile maintenance organizations performed this level of upkeep. Maxwell called on the Army Air Forces and Army Ground Forces to collaborate in designing an "army air depot" to handle liaison aviation supplies and equipment and to provide third-echelon maintenance in the field. The initial efforts, however, produced little more than contention over command and control. Army Ground Forces staff officers, using the Fifth Army Artillery Air Depot (Provisional) as a starting point, wanted the artillery air officer of the field army to which the unit was assigned to command it. Another Field Artillery pilot, designated the depot engineering officer, would actually conduct its day-to-day maintenance and supply operations. The Air Staff countered that the Army Air Forces was a technical service as well as a combat arm. It followed that the depot should be an entirely Army Air Forces organization. All personnel should come from and be organized and trained by the Army Air Forces. The depot would be attached to a field army headquarters in the same manner as an ordnance company. Faced with an impasse and with the need to organize these units pressing as the spring campaign season approached in Europe, General Maxwell decided in favor of the Army Air Forces. Staff officers from the two headquarters worked out the details of the organization of depot units (army) in late March 1944, and shortly thereafter the Army Air Forces began activating them.[19]

The transfer of all logistical responsibilities to the Army Air Forces also entailed certain administrative changes at the highest levels. On 28 March 1944, the head of the Operations Division of the General Staff, Maj. Gen. Thomas T. Handy, like Maxwell anticipating the new policy, ruled that it was the function of the Army Air Forces to compute Field Artillery aircraft requirements for 1945. Handy's ruling, coupled with the virtual completion of mobilization and the deployment of most divisions overseas, greatly

---

[18] Ltr, Maj D. S. Blossom, Executive Officer (XO), ACAS for Plans, to ACAS for Personnel (Attn: Maj J. G. Keith), 26 Oct 44, Microfilm A1387, AFHRA; D. L. McCaskey, "The Role of Army Ground Forces in the Development of Equipment," Studies in the History of the AGF, no. 34 (Bound Ms, AGF History Ofc, 1945), ch. 4, p. 11n39. Copies may be found in the History Office files of Army Ground Forces records in Record Group 337, National Archives and Records Administration, the U.S. Army Center of Military History Library, and the U.S. Army Training and Doctrine Command History Office.

[19] Memo, Maxwell for CGs, AAF and AGF, 24 Feb 44, sub: Army Air Depot Squad; Memo Slip, Donovan, G–3, AGF, for G–4, AGF, 11 Mar 44, sub: Same; Memo, Lt Col R. A. Meredith, HQ, AGF, for CSA (Attn: ACS, G–4, Col Blair), 27 Mar 44, sub: Army Air Maintenance and Supply Depot; Memo Slip, Donovan for G–4, 11 Mar 44; all in HQ, AGF, Gen Corresp, 1942–1944 (S), 320.2/121 (S), RG 337, NARA; WD, *Telephone Directory, War Department, April 28, 1944* (Washington, D.C.: Telephone Division, 1944). The Center of Military History Library has a bound copy. "Third Echelon Maintenance," in WD, Technical Manual (TM) 20–205, *Dictionary of U.S. Army Terms* (Washington, D.C.: Government Printing Office, 1944), p. 97.

diminished the influence of Headquarters, Army Ground Forces, on the War Department's goal for annual aircraft production. McNair's headquarters, unlike Arnold's, had no technical responsibility for units deployed outside the continental United States. The end of mobilization meant that replacement aircraft were the sole reason for new production. Deployment and combat ensured that most losses would occur overseas—and that replacement issues became the concern of the individual theater commanders. As a practical matter the theater commanders were too far removed from Washington to become involved in projecting losses. They became involved only if the estimates of losses were wildly incorrect.[20]

The Air Staff thus enjoyed virtual autonomy in setting aircraft production goals. Pilot losses were a function of aircraft losses. In computing an estimated aircraft loss rate, the Air Staff in effect determined the number of student pilots who would matriculate at the Department of Air Training. The Air Staff based its estimates of the projected loss rates for Field Artillery air sections on the historical loss rates of Army Air Forces liaison squadrons. The latter flew a preponderance of their missions in the rear areas, while the former flew most commonly in the combat zone, with a corresponding difference in losses. On the eve of the initiation of large-scale ground combat in France, the Air Staff established much lower production and training goals than Headquarters, Army Ground Forces, considered wise under the circumstances.[21]

Training

Whether the department would continue to train pilots or even remain in existence became an issue for serious consideration in June 1944. Seven days after the landings in Normandy, the deputy assistant chief of staff, G–3, on the General Staff, Brig. Gen. Willard W. Irvine, raised the issue. He noted that the two pilot classes scheduled to enter the Army Air Forces liaison pilot schools in July 1944 completed their advanced training at the Field Artillery School on 18 November and 2 December. At that point the Field Artillery would have enough pilots to meet the requirements of all units and installations plus a 10 percent overstrength as well as all replacements until 1 January 1946. Given these circumstances, Irvine directed General Arnold to suspend training of Field Artillery liaison pilots for one year, maintaining the capability to resume training, if necessary, on two months' notice.[22]

McNair's successor as commanding general of the Army Ground Forces, Lt. Gen. Ben Lear (July 1944–January 1945), launched an immediate reclama. The completion of the current training schedule would force the closing of the Department of Air Training, with a concomitant distribution of instructors and staff to units in the field. Operational flight

---

[20] Memo, Maj Gen Thomas T. Handy, ACS, Operations Division (OPD), for CG, AAF, 28 Jan 44, sub: Reappraisal of Liaison Aircraft Requirements, HQ, AAF, Central Decimal file, October 1942–May 1944, 452.01–D (Procurement and Requirements), RG 18, NARA.

[21] Memo, Brig Gen William W. Welsh, ACAS for Training, for ACS, G–3, 3 Oct 44, sub: Liaison Pilots for FA, HQ, AAF, Security Class Central Decimal file, October 1942–May 1944, 211–G (Pilots), RG 18, NARA.

[22] Memo, Brig Gen Willard W. Irvine, Deputy Assistant Chief of Staff (DACS), G–3, for CG, AAF, 13 Jul 44, sub: Liaison Pilots for FA, HQ, AAF, Security Class Central Decimal file, October 1942–May 1944, 211–H (Pilots), RG 18, NARA.

training was "as important as any other type of training now being conducted at the school." Once disbanded, the department would be difficult to reconstitute, particularly at the level of efficiency it had currently attained. Lear wanted to continue flight training on a restricted basis to meet vacancies caused by wartime attrition, "possible augmentation" of the organic aviation program, and the needs of the peacetime establishment. Furthermore, the department was particularly valuable in disseminating techniques learned in combat theaters, developing new tactics and techniques, testing new equipment, and modifying old equipment.[23]

Lear's defense of the Department of Air Training evoked a mixed response. The director of training on the Air Staff, Maj. Gen. Robert W. Harper, commented that the objective could be attained. If the War Department deemed the issue sufficiently important, Harper could schedule three classes per year, each consisting of forty students, at an Army Air Forces flying school rather than at a contract school. The G–3, General Porter, was unwilling to schedule additional classes simply to keep the department open without a genuine requirement for additional pilots, but he promised a review of the replacement question at the end of 1944, once the current classes graduated. At the same time he accepted Lear's argument as to the necessity of keeping the department open, although he emphasized that he wanted the number of instructors reduced. He restated the additional functions enumerated by Lear into a formal mission statement to which he added participating in field artillery demonstrations and conducting problems at the Field Artillery School. Porter's memorandum thus gave the first formal recognition to the department's role in equipment and doctrine development and defined its functions into the postwar period.[24]

Only one aspect of the content of Field Artillery pilot training remained controversial: night flying. Army Ground Forces observers in Italy, impressed by the achievements of Fifth Army pilots, recommended that the Department of Air Training include night flying in its pilot training. In a conference at the Field Artillery School convened on 17 March 1944, representatives of the Department of Air Training and the Army Air Forces Training Command agreed that training in this specialty should conform to the policies developed for the rest of the curriculum. The Army Air Forces would teach the basic techniques of night flying, and the Field Artillery would train pilots under tactical conditions, including short-field takeoffs and landings. When Headquarters, Army Ground Forces, formally proposed this change in the program, Porter disapproved it. The G–3 Division held that true night flying was not possible without instruments and that the L–4 simply could not carry the additional weight. Rather than making night flying a strictly Army Air Forces mission, however, Porter directed the Army Ground Forces to prepare specifications for the development of an advanced liaison aircraft that would permit it.[25]

---

[23] Memo, Lt Col R. A. Meredith, AAG, AGF, for CSA (Attn: G–3 Div), 26 Jul 44, HQ, AAF, Security Class Central Decimal file, October 1942–May 1944, 211-H (Pilots), RG 18, NARA.

[24] Memo, Irvine for CG, AAF, 3 Aug 44, sub: Continuation of FA Liaison Pilot's Operational Flight Training at FAS; Memo, Porter for CGs, AAF and AGF, 2 Sep 44, sub: Liaison Pilots for FA, HQ, AAF, Security Class Central Decimal file, October 1942–May 1944, 211-H (Pilots), RG 18, NARA.

[25] Memo, Maj Gen Robert W. Harper, ACAS, Training, for ACS, G–3, 30 Mar 44, sub: Liaison Pilots for FA, HQ, AAF, Security Class Central Decimal file, October 1942–May 1944, 211-G (Pilots), RG 18, NARA; Rpt, Col N. P. Morrow, AGF Board Obsr, 5 Mar 44, sub: Special Rpt [North African Theater of Operations (NATO)], [Extract], in AGF, "U.S. Field Artillery in World War II" (Bound Ms, Morris Swett Tech Lib, c. 1944).

Porter's negative response affected only the Fort Sill portion of the program. The Army Air Forces Training Command added ten hours of night flying in May 1944 to the basic liaison pilot flight training course and three months later established a remedial course at Goodfellow Field, San Angelo, Texas, in night and instrument flying for Field Artillery pilots who had received their ratings before this curricular change. Students received fifteen hours' flying time in both instrument and night flying. The training fell far short of providing the skills needed for an instrument rating, but, as intended, it enabled Field Artillery pilots to carry out their missions under marginal weather conditions and at night. The more rigorous standards of the Goodfellow Field program, which closed in March 1945, became the norm for the basic course by the end of the war.[26]

Despite this progress, the frustrations over the Air-Observation-Post Program led the Army Ground Forces staff to treat Porter's decision as yet another setback. In fact, it was anything but that. Porter had given the War Department imprimatur for the first time to the idea that there should be a follow-on aircraft for the L–4, which in turn carried the implication that the Air-Observation-Post Program was something more than a temporary wartime expedient.[27]

Research and Development

General McNair's immediate reaction to the controversy in January 1944 over control of the artillery air program was defensive; he wanted to avoid giving the Army Air Forces an opening to raise the issue again. Such a stance had an inhibiting effect upon the ground forces' ability to explore developmental issues. Despite General Eisenhower's requests, McNair viewed the whole question of adopting L–5s as risky. Use of Army Air Forces equipment might lead General Arnold to claim that similarity of equipment dictated employment by only one organization. Attempts to improve existing equipment, however, did not appear to raise this issue. Headquarters, Army Ground Forces, consequently approved tests at Fort Sill of convertible pitch propellers on L–4s. When the tests revealed that the propellers gave the aircraft 15 percent more power, the Army Air Forces made them part of the standard equipment of production model L–4s.[28]

The Air Staff did not prove nearly so amenable on any other equipment issues during this period. The problems associated with procuring the Brodie device were much

---

[26] A. R. Kooker, et al., "History of Army Air Forces Training Command and Its Predecessor Commands, 1 Jan 39–V-J Day," 8 vols. (Barksdale Field, La.: Headquarters, Army Air Forces Training Command, 1946), 6:1133, in Microfilm A3349, AFHRA. Ind, Maj Gen Kenneth P. McNaughton, Director (Dir), Training and Requirements, Air Staff (AS), to Dir, Organization and Training, 5 Aug 49, Ofc of the Ch of Army Field Forces, Decimal file, 1949–1950, RG 337, NARA.

[27] Memos, Brig Gen Mervin E. Gross, Ch, Requirements Div, ACAS, OC&R, 23 Aug 44, sub: Development of AAF Liaison Aircraft, and John J. McCloy, Assistant Secretary of War (ASW), for CG, AAF, 23 Apr 44, sub: Future Development of Liaison Aircraft, both in HQ, AAF, Class Decimal file, 1944, 452.1–D (Obsn), RG 18, NARA; Memo, Col Sidney F. Giffin, Deputy (Dep) Ch, Requirements Div, ACAS, OC&R, AAF, for ACAS for Materiel and Services (M&S), 24 Nov 44, sub: Military (Mil) Characteristics of Aircraft, HQ, AAF, Class Decimal file, 1945, 452.02 (Mil Characteristics), RG 18, NARA. Greenfield, *Air-Ground Battle Team*, p. 103.

[28] Rpt, Capt W. E. Wynn, Materiel Command (Cmd), to CG, AAF (Attn: ACAS for Materiel, Maintenance, and Development [MM&D], Production Br), 31 Mar 44, HQ, AAF, Security Class Central Decimal file, October 1942–May 1944, 452.01 (Procurement and Requirements), RG 18, NARA; Greenfield, *Air-Ground Battle Team*, pp. 66–67, 104.

more typical. An officer in the Ordnance Corps, 1st Lt. James Brodie, working in his off-duty hours, developed the device to permit light aircraft to take off from and land aboard ship without the use of a carrier deck. He fabricated a test copy and persuaded an Army Air Forces pilot awaiting shipment overseas to demonstrate its feasibility. The Air Staff proved uninterested, but the Navy Department and the Office of Strategic Services were more encouraging. The latter ordered a limited quantity of the devices for test. General McNair saw a demonstration of the Brodie device in February 1944 and immediately grasped its possibilities, not only for supporting amphibious assaults but also as a substitute for landing strips in rough terrain. He wanted to procure a few for test at Fort Sill, but the Air Staff was so strongly negative that he dropped the approach. Instead his staff made arrangements with the Office of Strategic Services to borrow two of their rigs and, contingent upon their successful test, ordered the production of twenty-two additional devices for the ground forces. McNair's subsequent death in Normandy in July 1944 eliminated high-level interest for the moment, but by then events were well in train.[29]

Installation of cameras in L–4s also provoked controversy with the Air Staff. Seventh Army, on the basis of its experience in Sicily, recommended mounting cameras in L–4s to permit oblique photography. Headquarters, Army Air Forces, objected that such an installation infringed on the mission of its yet-to-be-deployed liaison squadrons. They would provide all the oblique photographs the ground forces required. In January 1944 General Porter decided this dispute in the favor of the Army Air Forces. (At Fort Sill, Colonel Wolf was forbidden to install cameras on liaison aircraft.) When the Americal Division reported from the Pacific in April 1944 that it had successfully used its L–4s to survey both its battery positions and targets, General McNair feared that any proposal to implement the Americal system, which involved fitting L–4s with aerial cameras, would lead Porter to accuse him of disloyalty. Only with great reluctance and under pressure from his staff did he forward a proposal to make a photographic outfit part of each set of division artillery air equipment deploying to the Pacific. Porter disapproved the request, although he did permit air sections on isolated Pacific islands to borrow photographic equipment from Army Air Forces units, provided the theater commander approved such arrangements. The Air Staff did not appreciate even this limited deviation from an absolute prohibition. In practice the necessities of combat compelled the ground forces in all overseas theaters to use artillery aircraft to obtain aerial photographs.[30]

---

[29] Memos, [1945], sub: [History of the Brodie System], and [1944], sub: Brodie System, both in FAS, Department of Air Training (DAT), "Brodie System—Information File" (Bound Ms, U.S. Army Aviation Technical Library, Fort Rucker, Ala. [hereafter cited as USAATL], 1944–1945). WD, *Operations Division Information Bulletin* 3 (10 June 1944):7–8. A bound set is located in the Morris Swett Technical Library at the Field Artillery School. Ltr, Lt Col R. S. Quinn, Air Ofcr, Ofc of Strategic Services, to Officially Interested Parties, 12 Apr 44, sub: Demonstration of Brodie Landing and Launching System, HQ, AGF, Gen Corresp, 1942–1948, 452.11 (Cable Landing Apparatus—Brodie Design), RG 337, NARA. Ltr, Maj R. J. Delacroix, AAG, AGF, to CG, ASF (Attn: Development Div), 6 Feb 44, sub: Suspension Landing Apparatus for Light Planes, with Ind, Col L. A. Denson, ASF, to CG, AAF, 8 Feb 44, both in TAGO, Decimal file, 1940–1945, 452.11 (6 Feb 44), RG 407, NARA. MFR, [24 Jun 44], TAGO, Decimal file, 1940–1945, 452.11 (24 Jun 44), RG 407, NARA.

[30] Ltr, A. E. O'Leary, AG, to CGs, Southwest Pacific Area (SWPA) and Pacific Ocean Area (POA), 31 Jul 44, Microfilm A1387, AFHRA; Interv, Harris with Wolf, c. 1983; MFR, OPD, 1 May 44, OPD, Decimal file, 1942–1945, 061/156 (Maps), RG 165, NARA. The records delineating the internal debate in AGF are missing. See Greenfield, *Air-Ground Battle Team*, pp. 102–03.

Porter's March 1944 directive on night flying mandated that Headquarters, Army Ground Forces, go beyond the development of ancillary equipment to address the question of a replacement for the L–4. McNair remained very cautious. At his personal direction, the staff at Headquarters, Army Ground Forces, developed requirements that could be met by a craft that performed better than the L–4 but not as well as the L–5. On 17–18 August 1944, almost a month after McNair's death, the Army Air Forces Materiel Command tested the available models and rated the L–5, 9–X (manufactured by Taylorcraft), and the L–4X the best in that order. A test board at the Field Artillery School headed by Colonel Wolf subsequently recommended procurement of a modified L–5, the L–5X, for Field Artillery use as a transition aircraft until the Army Air Forces could develop a new plane designed primarily for artillery observation. However, after Army Ground Forces staff officers laid out McNair's rationale for avoiding the L–5, conferees at Headquarters, Army Ground Forces, including the new commandant of the Field Artillery School, Maj. Gen. Ralph McT. Pennell, and Wolf, produced a unanimous recommendation that the Army Air Forces procure the L–4X, subsequently designated the L–14.[31]

A three-seater with a 135-horsepower Lycoming engine, the L–4X was in outward appearance very similar to the L–4 and had the traditional canvas-covered, steel-tube-frame fuselage. It was over twice as heavy as the L–4, with a gross weight of 1,800 pounds, which made suspect its ability to operate out of muddy, unimproved fields. It could, however, carry a litter patient, although it did not perform as well as the L–5 when fully loaded. (It had only two-thirds the horsepower of the L–5.) Moreover, it had side-by-side seats up front, rather than the traditional tandem seating favored for Field Artillery observers.[32]

The G–3 Division did not approve this selection. It insisted that the L–14 was inferior to the L–5X. The G–4 on the War Department General Staff, General Maxwell, first agreed with General Porter and then reversed his decision and accepted the Army Ground Forces position. In addition to the political reason of desiring to clearly differentiate the organic aviation program from the Army Air Forces' liaison squadrons, the Army Ground Forces staff could adduce three technical reasons for preferring the L–14. It was much cheaper to produce than the L–5; it clearly required no transition training; and it had better short-field landing and takeoff characteristics than the L–5X. However, the contention had not hastened production; in January 1945 the Army Air Forces Materiel Command was once again running comparative tests on the L–5X and the L–14 while the Air Staff prepared revised military characteristics for a "Ground Force[s] liaison aircraft." If the Army Ground Forces desired a higher performance aircraft than the L–4 for organic air reconnaissance sections, the L–5 constituted the only immediately available aircraft.[33]

Porter's night flying directive was one of two factors that forced the Army Air Forces to develop separate statements of military characteristics for liaison aircraft and heli-

---

[31] FAS, Special Orders (SO) 238, 5 Oct 44, Gordon J. Wolf Ms, Historian's files, CMH; Memo, Irvine for CG, AGF, 25 Aug 44, sub: FA Liaison Aircraft, TAGO, Class Decimal file, 1943–1945, 452 (25 Aug 44), RG 407, NARA; Memo, Requirements Section, AGF, sub: Remarks Reference Rpt of Special Board, in FAS, "Report of Special Board Appointed To Review Developments in Field Artillery" (Bound Ms, Morris Swett Tech Lib, c. 1945); Greenfield, *Air-Ground Battle Team*, pp. 104–05.

[32] Frederick G. Swanborough and Peter M. Bowers, *Military Aircraft Since 1909* (Washington, D.C.: Smithsonian Institution Press, 1989), p. 401.

[33] Memo, Giffin for ACAS, M&S, 8 Jan 45, sub: Mil Characteristics of Aircraft, Dir of Services, Supplies, and Procurement (SS&P), G–4, Decimal file, March 1942–June 1946, 452.1 (Aircraft), vol. III, 2431, RG 165, NARA.

PIPER L–14 AT LOCK HAVEN, 1945

copters. The other was continued technical difficulties in helicopter development. In the late summer and fall of 1943, the Sikorsky design team appeared to have solved the most pressing stability problems. The YR–4, intended to serve as a trainer because of its lack of lift, went into limited production (one per week), while two follow-on models, the XR–5, designed as a light transport, and the XR–6, a two-place light observation helicopter, successfully flew for the first time. In January 1944, amid the euphoria generated by these successful flights, the Air Staff queried the Army Ground Forces about its 1944 requirements for helicopters. The Army Ground Forces position was that it would substitute R–6s for L–4s on a one-for-one basis just as soon as the rotary-wing aircraft passed their service tests. In the summer of 1944 the First Air Commando, commanded by Col. Philip G. Cochran, deployed to Burma. Cochran took four YR–4s with him. The Air Staff considered them too underpowered for combat operations, but Cochran believed they would demonstrate the military utility of vertical flight in combat. They soon did, rescuing downed flyers from heavy jungle and resupplying light infantry raiding columns, the Chindits, behind Japanese lines.[34]

---

[34] Memos, Gross for OC&R, 23 Aug 44, sub: Development of AAF Liaison Aircraft, and McCloy for CG, AAF, 23 Apr 44, sub: Future Development of Liaison Aircraft, both in HQ, AAF, Security Class Central Decimal file, October 1942–May 1944, 452.1–D (Obsn), RG 18, NARA; Rpt, Capt Knute W. Flint, sub: Helicopter Opns in China, HQ, AAF, Security Class Central Decimal file, October 1942–May 1944, 452.1–B (Helicopters), RG 18, NARA; Memo, Giffin for OC&R, for ACAS for M&S, 24 Nov 44, sub: Mil Characteristics of Aircraft, HQ, AAF, Security Class Central Decimal file, 1945, 452.02 (Mil Characteristics), RG 18, NARA; Rpt, Capt A. C. Bostwick, Acting AAF Resident Rep, Sikorsky Aircraft Div, to Lt Col A. P. Tappan, 15 Nov 43, sub: Progress Rpts, HQ, AAF, Central Decimal file, October 1942–May 1944, 452.1 (Helicopters) (Folder 2), RG 18, NARA; R&RS, Col J. W. Sessums, Jr., XO, MM&D, to ACAS for OC&R, 7 Sep 43, sub: Helicopter Allocations, HQ, AAF, Security Class Central Decimal file, October 1942–May 1944, 452.1–A (Helicopters), RG 18, NARA. Greenfield, *Air-Ground Battle Team*, p. 103.

The operations in Burma marked the high point of the military helicopter during World War II. Because there were few ground forces units in the China-Burma-India Theater, the exploits of the YR–4s had little immediate impact on Headquarters, Army Ground Forces. The staff continued to wait for the service tests of the R–5 and R–6, but teething problems for those craft persisted. The Army Air Forces had to push the dates of the tests ever further into the future. Some members of the Air Staff began to wonder openly whether a failure of the program might not discredit the reputation of the Army Air Forces. Nevertheless, in November 1944 a special Army Ground Forces board, established to review current and pending developments in Field Artillery materiel, adopted the view that the helicopter was the ultimate solution for aerial observation, an opinion endorsed by the Requirements Section at Headquarters, Army Ground Forces.[35]

Department of Air Training

The Department of Air Training, in line with Army Ground Forces policies on lengths of tours in school assignments during wartime, underwent major personnel changes beginning in the fall of 1943. General McNair wanted to ensure that training in the United States mirrored combat realities as closely as possible; the Army Ground Forces therefore sought to rotate veterans of recent combat to faculty positions in the United States. On 23 October the director, Colonel Ford, departed on temporary duty. He did not return. Ultimately, he became commander of the 87th Infantry Division Artillery and saw combat in France and Germany. His executive, Colonel Wolf, succeeded him and remained as head of the department through the rest of the war.[36] (*Chart 15*)

Initially, the head of the Division of Flight Training, Maj. (later Lt. Col.) Robert R. Williams, became the acting executive, until someone realized that the chief of the Tactics and Gunnery Division, Maj. (later Lt. Col.) Robert F. Cassidy, was senior to Williams. Cassidy became the executive, a post he held until 6 May 1944, when he became the artillery air officer of U.S. Second Army with headquarters at Memphis, Tennessee. Maj. D. V. Dale succeeded him as executive and held the post for the remainder of the war. Williams left the department in June 1944 also for Second Army; Capt. (later Maj.) Thomas S. Baker succeeded him in the Division of Flight Training. Other long-time members of the faculty also departed during this period for assignments with tactical units. At Ford's request, Capt. Theodore F. Schirmacher became the artillery air officer of the 87th

---

[35] Draft Memo, Earnest for Laux, 26 Feb 44, sub: Aircraft Requirements for Last Six Months of 1944, HQ, AAF, Security Class Central Decimal file, October 1942–May 1944, 452.01–C (Procurement and Requirements), RG 18, NARA. Tab E, sub: FA Obsn Airplane, in Rpt, Maj Gen Ralph McT. Pennell, et al., to CG, AGF, 27 Nov 44, sub: Rpt of Special Board Appointed To Review Developments in FA; Memo, Requirements Section, AGF, n.d., sub: Remarks Reference Rpt of Special Board; both in FAS, "Report of Special Board." MFR, E. F. O., 20 Oct 43, sub: Meeting To Determine Possibilities of Messenger Aircraft, HQ, AGF, Gen Corresp, 1942–1948, 452.1/47 (Airplanes) (S), RG 337, NARA. For a different view of the Army Ground Forces' interest in helicopters, see John W. Kitchens, "Army Aviation and the Helicopter," *Army Aviation* 40 (31 May 1991):36–39. On Burma, see Interv, Maj J. Hanscow with Capt L. S. Durf, Jr., and Lt Col G. B. Van Zee, 3 May 44, Microfilm A1387, AFHRA.

[36] William W. Ford, *Wagon Soldier* (North Adams, Mass.: Excelsior Printing, 1980), pp. 128–29; "William W. Ford," in George W. Cullum, et al., comps., *Biographical Register of the Officers and Graduates of the U.S. Military Academy at West Point, N.Y, Since Its Establishment in 1802*, 9 vols. (Boston: Houghton Mifflin and Co., 1891–1951), 9:345.

CHART 15—FIELD ARTILLERY SCHOOL, DEPARTMENT OF AIR TRAINING, 6 NOVEMBER 1944

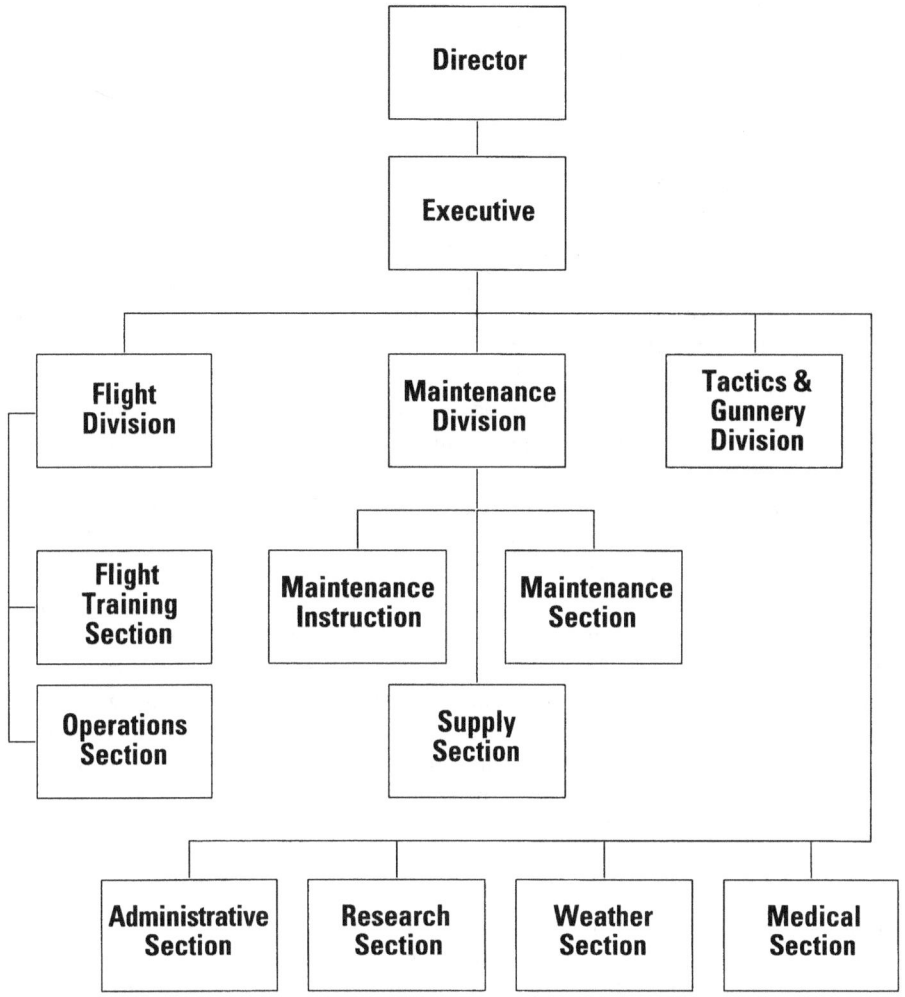

Infantry Division, while 1st Lt. Henry S. Wann went to the 418th Field Artillery Group, training in Texas. Capt. Joseph M. Watson and 1st Lt. Julian W. Cummings were among the returnees from North Africa and Italy assigned to the department.[37]

---

[37] "Robert R. Williams," in Cullum, et al., comps., *Biographical Register*, 9:1050; Interv, Harris with Wolf, c. 1983; Memo, Cassidy, [Feb 91], sub: [Career of] Robert F. Cassidy, Historian's files, CMH; Interv, author with Wann, 27 Aug 82; Officer's and Warrant Officer's Qualification Card Copy, sub: J. M. Watson, J. M. Watson Ms, U.S. Army Aviation and Troop Command History Office, St. Louis, Mo. (hereafter cited as USAA&TC); Interv, author with Lt Col Theodore F. Schirmacher, 13 Jun 92, CMH.

Wolf was a caretaker-director in many respects, administering policies already established by Ford. With the declining demand for pilots and mechanics, the training mission, while still primary, became less important in the department than it had been just a few months earlier. In two areas—training black pilots and training aerial observers for the U.S. Navy—Wolf set precedents. In part due to policies generated outside the school, he placed greater stress than Ford on writing formal doctrine, salvaging used aircraft, and developing ancillary equipment.

The department trained the vast majority of black pilots and mechanics after Wolf became director, simply because of the timing of the mobilization of the black divisions. Wolf was very sensitive to the local racial climate, and, before the first large consignment of black student pilots arrived from the Army Air Forces training center at Tuskeegee, Alabama, he called the staff and faculty together and announced his policies. He wanted barracks and the messes integrated, and none of the black students were to have southern flight instructors. Despite these precautions (and the Flight Division's definition of "north" was apparently sufficiently wide to include Texas), the washout rate at the end of Stage A was unacceptably high. Wolf called the instructors together and announced a new policy: All black students found deficient would be sent back to repeat the program until they passed.[38]

The instructors received this dictum with a good deal of consternation. Any sizable group of prospective pilots, no matter what their race, will include some individuals who will not take instruction and others who are "mechanical pilots." The latter fly by the numbers without any real instinct about their own limitations or those of their aircraft in the various phases of flight. They might master normal flight skills sufficiently to obtain a civilian pilot's license but will find involved maneuvers and the type of contour flying taught at Fort Sill beyond their abilities. Both types of pilots constitute a danger to themselves and to anyone flying with them. While the black students included many individuals who developed into fine pilots, as anticipated they also included some people who lacked such potential. Wolf, as an experienced pilot, knew this as well as the instructors, and once the attrition rate for black students approximated that of whites, he allowed blacks to wash out. He repeated the same process in Stage B, the short-field work, as well.[39]

Training a substantial number of black pilots at Fort Sill was a logical consequence of the War Department's mobilization plans, but instructing large numbers of naval observers about how to direct fire on land masses was something entirely different. In the spring of 1944 two naval aviators happened to stop at Fort Sill and discovered the Department of Air Training. This chance meeting led to an agreement with the Navy to train naval observers, already proficient in delivering fire against ships, to direct fire against the kind of land targets they would face when supporting amphibious assaults. Because of their previous training, the naval observers required only two weeks of additional work. The first class of the Special Naval Air Liaison Course (subsequently renamed the Spotting and Gunnery Training Course and later the Naval Air Spotter Course), forty-five students, reported on 6 April 1944. The students in this and the next three classes brought high-speed naval air-

---

[38] Intervs, Harris with Wolf, c. 1983, and author with Lt Col Robert R. Yeats, 24 May 90, CMH.
[39] Interv, Harris with Wolf, c. 1983; Lt Col Bruce O. Ihlenfeldt, "Reminiscences from Thirty Years of Flying" (Unpublished [Unpubl] Ms, Morris Swett Tech Lib, 1986); Interv, author with Yeats, 24 May 90.

craft with them. The remaining twenty-two classes (the last class graduated on 28 August 1945) trained in L–4s. All but 2 of 465 students graduated and received a certificate of attendance. Wolf assumed that the course was successful: "There weren't any complaints." He never received any authorization for it other than the verbal orders of the commandant of the Field Artillery School.[40]

There were some changes in the pilot's course based on experience in the overseas theaters—notably instruction in how to take off and land on water using L–4s with plywood pontoons. The impending completion of the wartime mobilization and consequent lessening of demand for new Field Artillery pilots led to a gradual lengthening of the pilot's course and a reduction of class size in both the primary and advanced phases of training. Representatives of the Department of Air Training and the Army Air Forces Training Command conferred to work on the details.[41]

Training black pilots and naval observers counted as successes, but night tactical training remained an unrealized ambition due to circumstances outside the school and hence beyond Wolf's control. In December 1944 General Porter authorized night-flying training at Fort Sill using L–5s borrowed from the Army Air Forces. Some twenty-five aircraft arrived, and Wolf began transition and night training for instructors. The European Theater of Operations' call for large numbers of replacement pilots, far exceeding the projections of Headquarters, Army Air Forces, produced a crisis. Although the Army Ground Forces and the Army Air Forces immediately increased pilot quotas, the lack of pilots in the replacement pipeline meant a six-month delay before new graduates would become available. Increasing the length of their course appeared injudicious under the circumstances. Moreover, the Army Ground Forces cannibalized the instructional staff in the Department of Air Training to obtain immediate replacements, including many of the instructors newly trained in night flying. Not until after the end of the war did Wolf inaugurate the training.[42]

Wolf placed great stress on the writing of formal doctrine. He told the members of every graduating class to write him a letter if they did anything that they thought would be of interest to the department. He had the departmental secretary compile comments on air-observation-post operational technique from a variety of sources including letters from graduates, newspaper clippings, articles in professional journals, and after-action reports. Beginning in May 1944 and continuing until the end of the war, Wolf published them as occasional memoranda addressed to the faculty and students. He also served as a member of a board, presided over by Col. Charles A. Pyle of the Field Artillery School, which prepared a manual for the technical and tactical training of Field Artillery air sections. In practice Wolf, Cassidy, and Williams (the latter two not members of the board) did much of the

---

[40] Interv, Harris with Wolf, c. 1983; Lt Col Thomas W. McCaw, "The Courses: Field Artillery School, World War II" (Bound Ms, Morris Swett Tech Lib, c. 1945); MFR, Col W. E. Shallene, ACS, G–3, R&SC, 31 Jan 45, sub: Training of Air Spotters, U.S. Army R&SC, Cmd Grp MFRs, 1943–1945, 1 Jan–10 Feb 45 file, in HQ, AGF, Special Staff, Historical Section, Chronological file, 1942–1945, RG 337, NARA.

[41] Ltr, Delacroix to CG, ASF (Attn: Dir, Requirements Div, Development Br), 17 Mar 44, sub: Seaplane Opns of FA Organic Aircraft, TAGO, Decimal file, 1940–1945, 452.1 (17 Mar 44), RG 407, NARA; Memo, Wolf, 15 Aug 44, sub: Informal Info, Wolf Ms, Historian's files, CMH.

[42] Interv, Harris with Wolf, c. 1983; Memo, Lt Col R. A. Meredith, AAG, AGF, for CSA (Attn: G–1 Div), 30 Dec 44, sub: Liaison Pilots for FA; Memo, Maj L. N. Chitwood for CSA (Attn: G–3 Div, Col Burwell), 7 Dec 44, sub: Same; Memo, Capt H. Hamilton, AAG, AGF, for CSA (Attn: G–3 Div, Col Arnett), 29 Dec 44, sub: Same; all in HQ, AGF, Gen Corresp, 1942–1948, 353/127–129 (FA Air Obsn), RG 337, NARA.

An L–4 Nears the End of Its Takeoff Run on a Lake in the Fort Sill Military Reservation During Seaplane Training in the Department of Air Training.

actual writing. They incorporated the most recent techniques developed in combat, including night operations and decking over a landing ship, tank, for flight operations. Their draft became Field Manual 6–150, issued by the War Department on 30 August 1944, the first published official statement of air-observation-post doctrine.[43]

Wolf's emphasis on rebuilding unserviceable L–4s represented an intensification of efforts to restore the department's own fleet of aircraft begun during Ford's tenure. Between 17 March and 16 July 1944, the Maintenance Division, under the direction of Maj. Marion J. Fortner, overhauled and recovered 126 aircraft, most of them victims of Oklahoma weather, using materials supplied by the Army Air Forces Oklahoma City Air Depot. The project represented a savings of over $230,000 to the government and became the subject of a statement of official appreciation by the commanding general, Army Ground Forces.[44]

The Department of Air Training's increased role in development reflected changing polices at higher headquarters as well as a continuation of policies begun under Ford. Shortly before departing to become artillery officer for XII Corps in February 1944, the

---

[43] Interv, Harris with Wolf, c. 1983; WD, Field Manual (FM) 6–150, *Organic Field Artillery Air Observation* (Washington, D.C.: Government Printing Office, 1944). On the authorship of the manual, see Ltr, Cassidy to Wolf, 29 Nov 44, Microfilm A1387, AFHRA; FAS, SO 89, 14 Apr 44, Wolf Ms, Historian's files, CMH.

[44] Ltr, Maj Gen Orlando Ward, Commandant, FAS, to CG, AGF, 26 Oct 44, sub: Overhaul of Liaison Airplane by the FAS; Ind, Pennell, CG, FA Replacement Center (Ctr), to Wolf, DAT, 5 Dec 44; Ind, Wolf to Maj Marion J. Fortner, DAT, 13 Dec 44; all in Wolf Ms, Historian's files, CMH.

AN L–4 ON THE LAND-RIG VERSION OF THE BRODIE DEVICE AT FORT SILL

G–3 of Army Ground Forces, General Lentz, gave the commandant of the Field Artillery School blanket authority to conduct tests: "The commandant of the field artillery school can test Navy beans if he wants to." An Air Corps officer in the G–3 section of Headquarters, Army Ground Forces, acting as a liaison officer to Headquarters, Army Air Forces, Lt. Col. H. Farley Vincent, became a primary source of requests for testing concepts and equipment. By November 1944 the work load was sufficiently large for Wolf to create a separate research section, reporting directly to him.[45]

During the fall of 1944 the Department of Air Training received two Brodie devices to test. The results were so promising and the interest in the overseas theaters so great that the department immediately began training demonstration teams. At the request of the

---

[45] Chart, FAS, DAT, 6 Nov 44, sub: Organizational Chart, Wolf Ms, Historian's files, CMH; Interv, Harris with Wolf, c. 1983.

Navy Department, one of these teams, consisting of 1st Lts. James K. Knox and Wilmot G. Rhodes and two enlisted mechanics, reported for temporary duty with the Training Command, Amphibious Forces, Pacific Fleet, on 29 September 1944. They successfully trained pilots in the use of the rig in San Diego and later Hawaii. The Field Artillery pilots they trained in Hawaii instructed more pilots in the Philippines preparatory to the Okinawa landings.[46]

Final Steps to a Permanent Program, September 1944–January 1945

The fall of 1944 marked the beginning of a major shift in the position of the Air Staff on organic aviation for the ground forces. The new commanding general of the Army Ground Forces, General Lear, did not take a personal interest in the question as McNair had. This removed any pressure for his counterpart at Headquarters, Army Air Forces, General Arnold, to become personally involved, and on the staff level Major Bornstein's presence as a liaison officer helped to defuse tensions. Moreover, in September 1944 Arnold told intimates that as far as he was concerned the war was won. The important question henceforth was the "future of air power" in the postwar world, and his highest priority was the creation of an independent air force. He directed his staff to prepare studies on the postwar period. He of course had expressed the opinion on several occasions that aviation under ground forces control was antithetical to the basic principles of air power. His view, however, was not the only one on the subject in the Air Staff. As early as 1940 one of the key figures in the development of strategic bombardment doctrine, Col. Robert L. Olds, had argued that observation and liaison missions for the ground forces, although necessary and legitimate, were a diversion from the primary mission of an air force. He had favored giving the ground commanders whatever light aircraft they desired. Olds had a shrewd suspicion that such a stance might facilitate the conversion of his branch into an independent and coequal service with the Army and the Navy. Now the requirement to study the future of liaison aircraft not assigned to the Army Air Forces arrived on the desk of an officer of the same intellectual persuasion as Olds.[47]

The deputy chief of the Operations, Commitments, and Requirements Division, Col. Sidney F. Giffin, a 1933 graduate of West Point, had served in the Coast Artillery Corps until transferring to the Army Air Forces in 1943. He faced the intellectually demanding task of squaring Arnold's strongly held beliefs with the War Department decision of March 1944 to retain the Field Artillery air program. At the same time he wanted to cast the Army Air Forces' position in such a way as to limit the Navy's claims on land-based

---

[46] Memo, Vice Adm Charles M. Cooke, Jr., DCS to Comdr in Ch, U.S. Fleet, for Vice Ch of Naval Opns, 23 May 44, sub: Brodie Shipboard System for Launching and Recovery of Cub Type Arty Liaison Aircraft—Installation in [a Landing Ship, Tank], OPD, Decimal file, 1942–1945, 560/329, RG 165, NARA. Ltr, Unsigned, FAS, to CG, AGF (Attn: Maj C. N. Adkisson, Air Support [Spt] Br, G–3 Section), 15 Dec 44, sub: Training of Brodie Teams; Memo, DAT for S–1, FAS, 6 Jan 45, sub: Brodie Personnel; all in FAS, DAT, "Brodie System—Information File." Ltr, Meredith to CG, 97th Inf Div, 26 Sep 44, sub: Operational Tests of the Brodie Landing Device, in FAS, DAT, "Brodie Device" (Bound Ms, USAATL, c. 1945). See Greenfield, *Air-Ground Battle Team*, pp. 101–02.

[47] For Arnold's agenda in September 1944, see Thomas M. Coffey, *Hap: The Story of the U.S. Air Force and the Man Who Built It* (New York: Viking Press, 1982), pp. 350–51.

aircraft, at that time a subject of considerable contention. Giffin proved equal to the task. General technological trends and increased understanding of aviation fostered by the war suggested, he argued, "a continually wider and more general use of aircraft" in the postwar period. In such circumstances "it might be as absurd to demand that all aircraft be organic only to an Air Force as that all boats, including crash boats and the like, be organic only to the Navy."[48]

Having established that general premise, Giffin went on to enumerate in general terms the principles he believed should govern military aviation. Of these the fundamental obstacle to his case was the concept of the inherent advantage in the centralized control of air operations. "Air power, in terms of aircraft, must be employed as a whole to exploit its inherent flexibility. It must not be so parcelled out as to confine to a single and limited use aircraft susceptible of repeated or multiple use." Light aircraft, argued Giffin, from the perspective of the Army Air Forces in October 1944, were not capable "of repeated or multiple use." Making them organic to the ground forces did not nullify the general principle. The deputy commander of the Army Air Forces, Lt. Gen. Barney M. Giles, approved Giffin's paper and sent it under his own signature to the chief of staff, General Marshall.[49]

By stating his argument in terms of general principles and avoiding specifics, Giffin at least implicitly suggested that organic aviation might well expand. Headquarters, Army Ground Forces, certainly accepted the statement of principles with alacrity. In fact, most opposition came from the Air Staff, where staff officers attempted to have the paper recalled without further action. General Lear, however, did not permit it. Speaking for General Marshall, General Porter also accepted Giffin's formulation. He could not forbear from adding that the principles concerning the assignment of liaison aircraft had been War Department policy for some time. In a sense, the Army Air Forces had finally and publicly acquiesced to that policy.[50]

However heartening the expression of principles, their practical implications remained to be spelled out. Using a series of pointed questions, Lear's staff solicited the view of the European and Mediterranean theaters on expanding the Air-Observation-Post Program outside the Field Artillery. Based on the responses, the Army Ground Forces staff concluded that the most pressing need was for additional aircraft to perform reconnaissance. In January 1945 Lear authorized another approach to the War Department. His staff recommended the inclusion of an air section, organized and equipped like a Field Artillery air section, in each cavalry reconnaissance squadron (mechanized)—they existed both as separate entities and as organic components of the 1st Cavalry Division and all armored divisions. The proposal assigned two liaison aircraft per section but left indefinite the specific type of aircraft. The action officer noted, however, that the officer who coordinated L–5 allocations on the Air Staff had indicated that the Army Air Forces could provide ten L–5s

---

[48] "Sidney Francis Giffin," in Cullum, et al., *Biographical Register,* 9:756; Disposition Form (DF), Lt Gen Barney M. Giles, Dep CG, AAF, to G–3, War Department General Staff (WDGS), and CSA, 10 Oct 44, [Action Officer (A/O) Col Giffin], Microfilm A1387, AFHRA.

[49] DF, Giles to G–3 and CSA, 10 Oct 44.

[50] Memo, Porter for CGs, AGF and AAF, 29 Oct 44, sub: Organic Assignment of Aircraft Other Than to the Air Forces, Microfilm A1387, AFHRA. On the attempt to recall the document, see DF, Welsh to ACAS, OC&R, 4 Jun 45, sub: Liaison-Type Aircraft, in Microfilm A1387, AFHRA.

per month to the Army Ground Forces beginning in April, suggesting the direction in which the staff preferred to go.[51]

The War Department G–3, General Porter, did not approve the expansion. No aircraft, reported Porter, were available to equip the proposed sections. In his view the ground forces were not fully utilizing existing aircraft in both Field Artillery air sections and Army Air Forces liaison squadrons for command and control. Likewise, the ground forces were not effectively employing high-level photoreconnaissance by tactical air. The former head of the Flight Division at the Department of Air Training, Colonel Williams, then conducting an extended study of the liaison aircraft situation for the Army Air Forces, believed that General Porter was misinformed as to the availability of liaison aircraft. No officer was better placed than Williams to make such a judgment, but the Army Ground Forces staff was content to bide its time, collecting additional information in an effort to make its case irrefutable. The fact that the Lear proposal had apparently included L–5s in mechanized cavalry air sections represented a major shift by Headquarters, Army Ground Forces. Earlier, it had sought to avoid adopting the L–5 during the contention over selecting a follow-on aircraft to the L–4. Moreover, the Army Ground Forces staff had regarded the plan as a minimalist proposal—it added only a total of ninety-eight pilots and planes to the ground forces. Porter's rather cavalier rejection of the expansion reinforced the perception among Lear's advisers that internal War Department politics required organic aviation to have its own distinct models of aircraft.[52]

The Creation of the Army Ground Forces Light Aviation Program, February–August 1945

The seven months from February through August 1945 produced a dizzying succession of policy decisions concerning the Air-Observation-Post Program. Some, such as aerial photography and a follow-on aircraft for the L–4, represented a culmination of efforts stretching back many months. Others, such as night bombing from light planes, represented old concerns moving in wholly new directions. At the same time Headquarters, Army Ground Forces, renewed its agitation for an expansion of the organic aviation program to include arms and services other than the Field Artillery. Infusing these efforts were the lessons of combat derived from all theaters and the recognition of additional requirements generated by changing battle conditions.

The development program at the Department of Air Training reached fruition in the spring and summer of 1945. Although some of the tests pertained exclusively to the modification of existing equipment, those with the most future significance revolved around night operations. Reports from Army Ground Forces observers overseas indicated that both

---

[51] Message (Msg), Gen George C. Marshall, Jr., to HQ, Communications Zone, ETO, and CG, Armed Forces Headquarters (AFHQ), Mediterranean Theater of Operations (MTO), 22 Sep 44; Msg, Gen Dwight D. Eisenhower, ETO, to WD, 9 Oct 44; Msg, Lt Gen Jacob L. Devers, AFHQ, to WD, 14 Oct 44; all in Microfilm A1387, AFHRA. Memo, Capt H. Hamilton, AAG, AGF, for CSA (Attn: G–3 Div), 5 Jan 45, sub: Liaison-Type Aircraft, HQ, AGF, Gen Corresp, 1942–1948, 353/130 (FA Air Obsn) (S), RG 337, NARA. This file has been heavily weeded. See "List of Papers [353/130]" in the same file for a calendar of the missing documents.

[52] Memo, Hamilton for CSA (Attn: G–3 Div), 5 Jan 45; Memo, Lt Col Robert R. Williams for Col Moffat, 5 Feb 45, sub: Liaison Aircraft for AGF, Microfilm A1387, AFHRA. Greenfield, *Air-Ground Battle Team*, p. 110.

AN L–5 AT THE DEPARTMENT OF AIR TRAINING OUTFITTED WITH
SIX ROCKET LAUNCHERS WITH ONE NAVY 5-INCH HIGH-VELOCITY
AERIAL ROCKET IN FIRING POSITION, 1945

the Germans and the Japanese were moving supplies and troops at night in truck convoys with their lights ablaze until they came within range of Allied artillery. These reports stimulated the Army Air Forces liaison officer at Headquarters, Army Ground Forces, Colonel Vincent, to search for a corrective. He argued that armed light aircraft, while they could not stop these convoys, could appreciably slow them down by forcing the trucks to travel without lights.[53]

His analysis raised a series of questions that required immediate answers before attempting such operations in a combat zone. Could Field Artillery pilots in L–5s navigate with sufficient accuracy to find a target forty or fifty miles behind enemy lines and then successfully return to their strips? Could L–5s accurately deliver sufficient ordnance to pose a threat to German and Japanese truck convoys? If so, what kinds of ordnance were most appropriate for light aircraft? Could light aircraft operate on totally dark nights and direct accurate fire on a target? These questions served as the basis for a series of concurrent Army Ground Forces–mandated tests at Fort Sill.[54]

Preliminary tests of night bombing and night navigation that members of the Department of Air Training conducted in early 1945 demonstrated considerable promise. Headquarters, Army Ground Forces, dispatched Colonel Wolf to the European and Mediterranean theaters. In addition to collecting information about current air-observa-

---

[53] Rpt, Lt Col H. F. Vincent, 3 Mar 45, sub: Rpt of Tests of Close-In Night Bombing by Liaison Aircraft, in HQ, AGF, Gen Corresp, 1942–1948, 353/134 (FA Air Obsn) (S), RG 337, NARA; Interv, Harris with Wolf, c. 1983.
[54] Rpt, Vincent, 3 Mar 45.

tion-post "operations, organization, maintenance, supply, materiel, [and] communications," he was to conduct a service test of night bombing from liaison aircraft under combat conditions. Unfortunately, someone stole his bombsights and bomb racks before he could conduct the tests, but the department concurrently conducted detailed operational tests in four areas: night navigation, rocket firing, night bombing, and night fire direction. The results confirmed Colonel Vincent's expectations. Pilots were able to navigate successfully to and from a designated point sixty miles from their home field. The L–5s could carry a load of 500 pounds of light bombs and, on dark nights, bomb by flares or serve as a pathfinder for fighter-bombers. The use of flares also permitted accurate direction of artillery fire in the battle area on dark nights. The L–5 proved a stable launch platform for newly developed slow-burning Navy rockets, the 5-inch aerial rocket and the 5-inch high-velocity aerial rocket. The 2.36-inch Army rockets used in the bazooka tended to be erratic in flight when fired from the air, while the 4.5-inch M9 Army rocket had the unfortunate side effect of blowing a hole in the aircraft's wing.[55]

Clearly, some of the capabilities explored at Fort Sill fell within missions normally performed by the Army Air Forces. The acting assistant chief of Air Staff for training, Col. Llewellyn O. Ryan, became alarmed by the Fort Sill experiments. He warned that the Army Air Forces could lose all control of liaison aircraft if the Air Staff used the same obstructionist tactics against arming light planes as it had against developing the Brodie device. The dominant reaction on the Air Staff, however, was a complete lack of concern—a tendency to file and forget.[56]

The temper at Headquarters, Army Ground Forces, was entirely different. Concern about Japanese cave warfare was at its height, and the Army Ground Forces staff saw rocket-firing light aircraft as the best possible countermeasure. The new commander of the Army Ground Forces, General Joseph W. Stilwell (January to June 1945), had a history of acrimonious disputes with the Army Air Forces while commanding the China-Burma-India Theater and a reputation for absolute fearlessness in bureaucratic conflict. Stilwell took a personal interest in the experiments. At least some of his officers thought armed light aircraft could "assist in disrupting sudden attacks by armored forces." Rocket-firing planes, based in the forward area, could react and mass quickly. The case for immediate action was buttressed by the success of similar tests the Navy conducted with rocket-firing light aircraft at Quantico, Virginia. Ground officers informally told their Army Air Forces counterparts that the Army Ground Forces had no designs on a ground attack mission for organic aviation. They simply wanted to be able to use light planes as target markers for artillery or fighter-bombers. They were willing to concede

---

[55] Rpts, Vincent, 3 Mar 45; Wolf, sub: Night Bombing Sub-Project, Fort Sill Experimental Project; Wolf, sub: Rpt of Test of Rocket Sub-Project, Fort Sill Experimental Project; Wolf, sub: Rpt of Test of Night Gunnery Sub-Project, Fort Sill Experimental Project; Wolf, sub: Rpt of Test of Night Navigation Sub-Project, Fort Sill Experimental Project; all in HQ, AGF, Gen Corresp, 1942–1948, 353/134 (FA Air Obsn) (S), RG 337, NARA. Rpt, Wolf to CG, AGF, 28 May 45, sub: Rpt of Special Obsr—European and Mediterranean Theaters of Opn, 15 Mar to 30 Apr 45, in Wolf Ms, Historian's files, CMH; Interv, Harris with Wolf, c. 1983.

[56] Memo, Col L. O. Ryan, Acting ACAS for Training, for ACAS for Plans, 21 Feb 45, sub: AAF Policy Regarding Liaison Avn, in Microfilm A1387, AFHRA; Ltrs, Col D. C. Doubleday, Ch, Engineering Br, Materiel Div, ACAS for M&S, to Dir, Air Technical Service (Svc) Cmd, 10 Mar 45 and 23 Mar 45, sub: Close-In Night Bombing by Liaison Aircraft, in HQ, AAF, Security Class Central Decimal file, 1945, 353.14 (Bombing), RG 18, NARA.

direct fire on enemy ground forces as part of the legitimate province of Army Air Forces liaison squadrons. As long as Stilwell remained head of the Army Ground Forces, however, no one put such a concession in writing. The pressure thus remained on the Army Air Forces to develop an attack capability in its light aircraft, because an Army Ground Forces L–5 configured to fire target markers could also launch rockets with the intent to kill enemy ground forces. Stilwell's interest and his bureaucratic tactics meant that the Air Staff could not maintain its indifference. In June the Army Air Forces Board began "thorough tests of the combat potentialities of light aviation" and soon obtained the same kind of results achieved at Fort Sill and Quantico.[57]

Even as Colonel Wolf and his subordinates in the Department of Air Training worked to develop fully the potential of existing Field Artillery aircraft, the question of an aircraft to succeed the L–4 continued to spark considerable debate. In January 1945 the War Department adopted a separate statement of military characteristics for Field Artillery aircraft. Then the G–4, General Maxwell, decided that the War Department would procure one aircraft for each set of military characteristics—the L–14 to meet the requirement for a standard Field Artillery aircraft and the L–5 as the standard Army Air Forces liaison plane. The Army Air Forces would, however, supply limited quantities of L–5s adapted for Field Artillery use until the L–14 became available.[58]

In settling the controversy between the Field Artillery and the Army Air Forces, Maxwell unwittingly stirred up yet another dispute, this time within the organic aviation community. However politically astute the L–14 selection, it meant the adoption of an aircraft that featured side-by-side rather than tandem seating for the pilot and observer— with all the limitations this configuration imposed on the observer's range of vision. When the artillery air officer of the 12th Army Group, Lt. Col. Charles W. Lefever, learned about the L–14, he called a conference attended by some of the most experienced Field Artillery pilots to discuss the desirable characteristics for the next generation of Field Artillery aircraft. They drew up a list of military characteristics. General Eisenhower, recently promoted to general of the Army, took a personal interest in the matter. He dispatched one of them, the First Army artillery air officer, Maj. Delbert L. Bristol, back to the War Department to represent the theater on this matter. At the War Department's invitation, the Southwest Pacific Area also sent a representative, the Eighth Army artillery air officer, Colonel Cassidy, to Washington. Cassidy also prepared a statement of military characteristics; it differed only slightly from Bristol's. Cassidy wanted

---

[57] Memo, Williams for Moffat, 20 Jun 45, sub: Developments in Liaison Avn; Memo, Giffin, 21 Apr 45, sub: Combat Employment of Liaison Avn, [Extract]; Memo, [Williams], sub: Developments in Liaison Avn; all in Microfilm A1387, AFHRA. Memo, Meredith for CSA (Attn: New Developments Div), 7 Jun 45, sub: Development of Rocket-Firing Avn for Close Spt of Ground Combat Troops, in OPD, Decimal file, 1942–1945, 471.61/194 (Grenades, Hand, Rifle, and Aerial Darts), RG 165, NARA. The Army Ground Forces files are missing. See Greenfield, *Air-Ground Battle Team*, pp. 111–12. Charles F. Romanus and Riley Sunderland, *Stilwell's Command Problems*, U.S. Army in World War II (Washington, D.C.: Office of the Chief of Military History, 1956), gives a complete account of the policy disputes between Stilwell and Maj. Gen. Claire L. Chennault, the commander of the Fourteenth Air Force. Barbara Tuchman's *Stilwell and the American Experience in China, 1911–1945* (New York: Macmillan Co., 1971), pp. 301–509, describes the personalities involved.

[58] DF, Maxwell for CGs, AAF and AGF, 2 Feb 45, sub: FA Liaison Airplanes, in Dir, SS&P, G–4, Decimal file, March 1942–June 1946, 452.1 (Aircraft), vol. 2, 8358, RG 165, NARA; DF, Roberts to ACS, G–4, 3 Jul 45, sub: Rpt Concerning Development of Aircraft for FA Use, in Dir, SS&P, G–4, Decimal file, March 1942–June 1946, 452.1 (Aircraft), vol. 3, 2131, RG 165, NARA.

an aircraft that could carry an additional passenger, haul a small amount of critical supplies, and evacuate battle casualties in an emergency—the sort of additional missions that artillery pilots in the Pacific performed on an almost daily basis.[59]

After considerable negotiation, the War Department in July 1945 adopted the European Theater of Operations characteristics; in the postwar period they led to the development of the L–15. The L–15 would have none of the special features for which Cassidy lobbied and would replace interim aircraft that did. The L–14 became that interim design; it was to be used until the L–15 became available sometime after the war. In a concession to the Southwest Pacific Area, the War Department decided to assign L–14s to all light and medium (105-mm. and 155-mm.) field artillery battalions and L–5s to all heavy (240-mm. and 8-inch) battalions and higher-echelon field artillery headquarters. Implicit in this settlement was the assumption that the campaigns in France and Germany represented the norm for future wars, while the Pacific was an exception. The lessons of ground combat in the European Theater of Operations would dominate the evolution of the Army's organic aviation in the postwar world.[60]

At virtually the same time, pressure from Eisenhower and the commanding general, U.S. Army Pacific Ocean Area, Lt. Gen. Robert C. Richardson, Jr., led the War Department to hold a conference to explore tactical reconnaissance issues. The ground forces representatives, who included Colonel Cassidy, insisted that there was "an urgent requirement to provide frontline visual and photographic reconnaissance for Corps and Divisions" using liaison aircraft. Despite Air Staff opposition, the War Department authorized the issue of aerial cameras to certain Field Artillery air sections and made photographic processing units organic to the ground forces. The department reiterated that aerial photography remained a "primary function of the Army Air Forces" and that artillery aircraft would perform this function "only when the Army Air Forces is unable to provide adequate coverage."[61]

As the War Department revised the Air-Observation-Post Program in detail, the Air Staff continued to wrestle with planning for liaison aircraft in the postwar Army Air Forces.

---

[59] Intervs, author with Lefever, 4 Sep 91, CMH, and Epstein with Bristol, 1 Jul 75, USAA&TC. Ltr, Lt Col H. L. Allen, AAG, Supreme Headquarters, Allied Expeditionary Forces (SHAEF), to Bristol, 17 Mar 45, sub: Orders; Ltr, Maj Gen Harold R. Bull, ACS, G–3, SHAEF, to Maj Gen J. E. Hull, ACS, OPD, 16 Mar 45; Memo, sub: Record of Trip of Maj Bristol; all in Dir, SS&P, G–4, Decimal file, March 1942–June 1946, 452.1 (Aircraft), vol. 3, 2131, RG 165, NARA. Msgs, Hull to CG, SWPA, 20 Apr 45, and CG, U.S. Army Forces Far East (USAFFE), to WD, 13 May 45, both in OPD Decimal file, 1942–1945, 210.482/1194, RG 165, NARA; Ltr, Bristol to Bull, 2 Jun 45, in OPD Decimal file, 1942–1945, 312.12/135. Memo Slip, Shallene, Misc Div, AGF, for G–3, AGF, 29 Jun 45, sub: Rpt of Lt Col R. F. Cassidy's Temporary Duty at this HQ, Microfilm A1387, AFHRA.

[60] Draft Memo, Bristol, sub: Proposed Mil Characteristics of FA Obsn Aircraft; Memo, sub: Mil Characteristics of FA Obsn Aircraft; Memo, Bristol for ACS, OPD, 31 May 45, sub: Rpt Concerning Development of Aircraft for FA Use; Ltr, Meredith to CG, AAF, 22 Jun 45, sub: Aircraft for FA Use; DF, Roberts to ACS, G–4, 3 Jul 45, sub: Same; DF, Maxwell to ACS, G–3, and CG, AAF, 21 Jul 45, sub: Rpt Concerning Development of Aircraft for FA Use; all in Dir, SS&P, G–4, Decimal file, March 1942–June 1946, 452.1 (Aircraft), vol. 3, 2131, RG 165, NARA.

[61] Ind, A. J. Bahr, AG, to CG, U.S. Army Forces, Middle Pacific, 5 Jul 45, sub: Aerial Photographic Equipment for FA Air Sections; Ltr, Lt Col L. Duenweg, AAG, U.S. Army POA, to TAG, 2 Apr 45, sub: Same; Memo, Col L. O. Peterson for ACAS for OC&R, 27 Jun 45, sub: Diary of Requirements Div; Minutes, AAF General Council, 7 Jun 45, sub: Employment of Photographs from Liaison-Type Airplanes in Aerial Survey; Memo, sub: Extracts from Recommendations of WD Tactical Reconnaissance Conference Held 15–27 Jun 45; Ltr, Lt Gen Ira C. Eaker, Dep CG, AAF, to Gen George C. Kenney, 26 Jul 45; Memo Slip, Shallene for G–3, AGF, 29 Jun 45; all in Microfilm A1387, AFHRA.

Colonel Williams, assigned to the Air Staff to assist in this project, proposed expanding organic aviation to the other combat arms, while the Liaison and Airborne Branch of the Operations, Commitments, and Requirements Directorate favored restricting such aircraft to the Field Artillery. Faced with this impasse, the Air Staff dispatched Williams and the executive officer of the Liaison and Airborne Branch, Col. John C. Bennett, Jr., on a fact-finding mission to the overseas theaters. As Williams anticipated, combat realities in the theaters converted Bennett. Williams did not complete his final report until after the war ended, but he and Bennett prepared a series of interim reports on conditions in each of the theaters while they were overseas. Stilwell's headquarters used their reports to buttress the case for expanding organic aviation.[62]

COLONEL WILLIAMS

Despite the pressure, Colonel Bell, the author of the January 1944 Air Staff plan to abolish Field Artillery aviation, calculated that the Army Air Forces would succeed in blocking expansion. As long as any one of the major theater commanders opposed it, the War Department would not authorize it. General Douglas MacArthur in the Southwest Pacific Area had always followed the lead of his Army Air Forces commander, General George C. Kenney, Jr., on all matters pertaining to aviation. Bell counted on Kenney maintaining his ascendancy, but then MacArthur changed his mind.[63]

Only the circumstances of, not the rationale for, this reversal have survived. In February 1945 the U.S. Army Forces in the Far East Board, following an extensive investigation of air-observation-post operations in the Southwest Pacific Area, recommended doubling the size of existing Field Artillery air sections and formally authorizing one in all field army headquarters. Four days later the commanding general of XIV Corps Artillery, Brig. Gen. James A. Lester, recommended establishing air sections at corps and division headquarters in addition to the artillery air sections that already existed at those echelons. At Sixth Army, the chief of staff, Brig. Gen. George H. Decker, signed a long and thoughtful endorsement, more detailed than the original proposal. In addition to approving the

---

[62] DF, Maj D. S. Blossom, XO, ACAS for Plans, to ACAS for Personnel (Attn: Maj J. C. Keith), 26 Oct 44, sub: Request for One Ofcr to Develop an AAF Liaison Avn Post-War Program; Memo, Moffat for Williams, 20 Dec 44, sub: Liaison Avn; Rpt, Col J. C. Bennett and Williams to CG, AAF (Attn: ACAS for OC&R, Requirements Div, and ACAS for Plans, Post-War Div), 1 Apr 45, sub: Liaison-Type Aircraft in Air Forces and Ground Forces; all in Microfilm A1387, AFHRA; Interv, author with Lt Gen Robert R. Williams, 20 Feb 91, CMH.

[63] MFR, [Col J. N. Bell], sub: Notes from Col Bell's Visit to SWPA, Microfilm A1387, AFHRA.

original concept, Decker recommended equipping these new sections with L–5s, or L–14s when the latter became available.[64]

Officers at MacArthur's headquarters regarded Decker's views as the mirror image of the opinions of the Sixth Army commander, General Walter Krueger. Krueger had demonstrated an interest in light aircraft even before the Louisiana maneuvers of 1941. Given the importance that Decker, and by inference Krueger, attached to the recommendation, this proposal could not be disposed of in a routine way. MacArthur had great respect for Krueger's judgment. During the 1930s, when MacArthur was chief of staff of the Army and Krueger was the chief Army planner for a war with Japan, Krueger had revealed the most sophisticated understanding of any senior officer in the War Department on the role of air power in a future Pacific campaign. To the surprise of Army Air Forces officers, MacArthur adopted the Sixth Army position as his own. On 24 May General Stilwell's chief of staff at Army Ground Forces, Maj. Gen. J. G. Christiansen, made a formal application to expand the organic aviation program along the lines suggested by General Decker.[65]

The following month the Army Ground Forces Equipment Board, more familiarly known as the Cook Board after its president, Maj. Gen. Gilbert R. Cook, reported and gave expansive support to the new initiative. Created as part of the War Department's effort to determine the shape of the postwar Army, the board emphasized that success in infantry close combat required the support of an aviation component. In the view of the board members, all veterans of the ground fighting, the Army Air Forces emphasized strategic and tactical missions independent of the ground battle. Consequently, the board recommended giving the close air support, photographic and tactical reconnaissance, troop transport, aerial supply, and aeromedical evacuation missions to an expanded organic aviation program equipped with light and medium fixed- or rotary-wing aircraft.[66]

Stilwell's staff pressed the Air Staff for an early decision on the expansion of the organic aviation program in the ground forces, but this proved impossible. The Air Staff was bitterly divided. Some officers argued for a literal interpretation of War Department Field Manual 100–20, *Command and Employment of Air Power*, which would overturn the Army Air Forces policy on light aircraft enunciated the previous November. Others urged practical compromise. The commanding general of the Army Air Forces, General of the Army Henry H. Arnold, clearly favored the latter but was much enfeebled by the four heart attacks

---

[64] Rpt, Lt Col L. S. Carroll, AAG, USAFFE, to TAG, 14 Feb 45, sub: USAFFE Board Rpt 113, Arty Liaison Airplane Units; Ltr, Brig Gen James A. Lester, CG, XIV Corps Arty, to CG, XIV Corps, 18 Feb 45, sub: Air Sections for Div and Corps HQ, with Ind, Col J. T. Walsh, HQ, XIV Corps, to CG, Sixth Army, 20 Feb 45, and Ind, Brig Gen George C. Decker, CS, Sixth Army, to CG, USAFFE, 26 Feb 45; all in Microfilm A1387, AFHRA.

[65] Memo, Maj Gen James G. Christiansen, CS, AGF, for CSA (Attn: G–3 Div), 24 May 45, sub: Liaison-Type Aircraft; all in HQ, AAF, Security Class Central Decimal file, 1945, 452.1 (Obsn), RG 18, NARA. Paul P. Rogers, *The Bitter Years: MacArthur and Sutherland* (New York: Praeger, 1990), pp. 58–59, gives the view of MacArthur's headquarters on the Krueger-Decker relationship. On Krueger's role in prewar planning and for an evaluation of his impact, see Edward S. Miller, *War Plan Orange: The U.S. Strategy To Defeat Japan, 1897–1945* (Annapolis, Md.: Naval Institute Press, 1991), pp. 184–85, 344.

[66] An. I, sub: Air Spt Equipment, to Rpt, Maj Gen Gilbert R. Cook, et al., 20 Jun 45, sub: B/O Convened to Study the Equipment of the Post-War Army, HQ, AGF, Gen Corresp, 1942–1948, 334/2 (Equipment Review Board) (S), RG 337, NARA. For an overview, see Michael S. Sherry, *Preparing for the Next War: America Plans for Postwar Defense, 1941–1945* (New Haven, Conn.: Yale University Press, 1977).

CREATING ARMY GROUND FORCES LIGHT AVIATION

he had suffered during the course of the war. He created an ad hoc committee, chaired by the wartime commander of the Ninth Air Force, Lt. Gen. Hoyt S. Vandenberg, which dutifully recommended retaining organic aviation in the Field Artillery, but without expansion. At this point the new deputy commanding general of the Army Air Forces, Lt. Gen. Ira C. Eaker, arrived from Europe with the news that General Eisenhower, who everyone anticipated would be the next chief of staff of the Army, had made expansion of organic air a quid pro quo for his support of an independent air force in the postwar period. The G–3 (since January 1945), Maj. Gen. Idwal H. Edwards, presumed by contemporaries to be speaking for Marshall, now general of the Army, suggested that the War Department would approve expansion no matter what the Air Staff response. Resistance by the Air Staff crumbled.[67]

GENERAL COOK

During July 1945 Eaker and General Jacob L. Devers, Stilwell's successor as commanding general, Army Ground Forces, negotiated the terms of the expansion. They agreed to a substantial increase in the number of liaison aircraft organic to ground units over those requested by General Christiansen in May: 6 in infantry, airborne, and mountain divisions; 9 in armored divisions; 7 in cavalry divisions; 2 in separate tank battalions, cavalry squadrons, cavalry groups, and separate tank destroyer battalions; and 1 in separate engineer battalions. Nine days later Eaker officially recommended the expansion to the War Department. At the same time he reiterated the Army Air Forces doctrine assigning liaison squadrons to tactical air commands. On 9 August 1945, the same day as the atomic bombing of Nagasaki, the acting assistant chief of staff, G–3, Brig. Gen. J. S. Bradley, promulgated the new policy. The Air-Observation-Post Program became Army Ground Forces light aviation.[68]

---

[67] Memo, Meredith for CSA (Attn: G–3 Div), 7 Jun 45, sub: Liaison-Type Aircraft; Memo, Maj Gen Donald Wilson, ACAS, OC&R, for Chief of Air Staff (CAS), 23 May 45, sub: Employment of Liaison-Type Aircraft by the AGF; both in HQ, AAF, Security Class Central Decimal file, 1945, 452.1 (Obsn), RG 18, NARA; Memo, Brig Gen Patrick W. Timberlake, Dep CAS, for Lt Gen Hoyt S. Vandenberg, Maj Gen Frederick L. Anderson, Jr., Brig Gen Lauris Norstad, 2 Jun 45, sub: Organic Assignment of Aircraft Other Than to the Air Forces, in Security Class Central Decimal file, 1945, 452.01 (Assignment). Memo, Brig Gen William F. McKee, Acting ACAS for OC&R, for Col Proctor, 30 May 45, sub: Ground Force Employment of Aircraft, Microfilm A1387, AFHRA.

[68] R&RS, Eaker to ACS, G–3, 3 Aug 45, sub: Liaison-Type Aircraft; Ltr, Brig Gen Joseph S. Bradley, Acting ACS, G–3, to ACS, G–4, and CG, AGF, 9 Aug 45, sub: Same; both in HQ, AAF, Security Class Central Decimal file, 1945, 452.1 (Obsn), RG 18, NARA.

Conclusion

The U.S. Army Field Artillery's Air-Observation-Post Program from its inception in June 1942 both benefited and suffered from a certain ambiguity in its charter. Were light planes to become a permanent part of the Field Artillery or were they simply a wartime expedient? The War Department, by not answering that question (and as a corollary by not setting up an elaborate administrative organization to manage the program), encouraged innovation. It provided only the overhead and support that experience demonstrated was necessary. On the other hand, lack of clarity encouraged opposition from the Army Air Forces. General Arnold opposed organic air in the ground forces both because he accepted the tenets of the air power ideology that developed during the interwar period and because he wanted to avoid competitors, no matter how small. Principle and bureaucratic self-interest combined.

In 1942 the Army Ground Forces wagered certain minimal resources (the cost of the equipment and supplies; the buildings, airstrips, and instructional materials required to sustain the Department of Air Training; and the personnel diverted into the program) that light aircraft could survive on the battlefield and could make a contribution to the combined arms team that was commensurate with these costs. The Army Air Forces acquiesced in the program for expediency but with the firm belief that it would fail. By the end of 1943 the senior ground commanders in Italy, at the time the most important overseas theater in terms of the number of American divisions engaged, were unanimous in evaluating the air observation post an outstanding success. The combat experience, however, could not change Arnold's deeply ingrained world view or his calculation of bureaucratic advantage. If anything, it impelled him to make an even stronger plea for eradicating organic air. The combat realities did affect the War Department; General Porter's decisions in the spring of 1944 for the first time clearly indicated that organic aviation would remain in the ground forces after the war ended. It took the Air Staff another six months to acknowledge that fact.

That the admission was made at all reflected a larger political dynamic within the War Department. Since 1919 one of the major questions confronting the ground forces was the degree of autonomy that aviation should enjoy. As long as the War Department insisted on retaining the Air Corps as a component of the Army, secretaries of war and chiefs of staff made concessions at the margin to keep internal dissension within reasonable bounds, thus forestalling congressional intervention. Once the War Department yielded independence for a postwar air force, the position of advantage in institutional politics shifted. The ground arms could extract concessions at the margin from the leaders of the Army Air Forces who thereby sought to ensure an orderly transition without controversy. The permanence of organic aviation and its expansion to the other combat arms in terms of this larger issue were peripheral considerations. Between January 1944 and September 1945, Arnold and like-minded members of the Air Staff did not change their ideology or their perception of narrow bureaucratic self-interest. But once they perceived the relationship between an independent air force and organic air, the logic of events forced them, not without protest and internal division, to accept Army Ground Forces Light Aviation as an integral part of the postwar settlement.

To say that organic aviation was peripheral in relation to the question of an independent air force is to state a relative, not an absolute, judgment. No one thought organic aviation was unimportant, otherwise the issue would not have been the subject of such long and contentious dispute between very senior ground and air officers. The importance that Army Air Forces officers attached to the organic air question is attested to by what it required to wrest the concession from them: advocacy of change by General Krueger, aggressive and intelligent bureaucratic infighting on the part of General Stilwell and his staff, unanimity of all the major theater commanders in favor of expansion, General Eisenhower's suggestion of a quid pro quo, and hard bargaining by General Devers. At the same time the reports of Colonels Williams and Bennett on conditions in the overseas theaters supplied the Army Ground Forces staff with ammunition to support an expansion of organic air and at the same time contributed to division of opinion in the Air Staff.

Army Ground Forces Light Aviation, redesignated Army Aviation in 1949, owed its existence to the wartime exploits of thousands of air-observation-post pilots, mechanics, and observers. These men had an opportunity to contribute to the war effort because of the actions of field grade aviators such as Bristol, Cassidy, Ford, Lefever, Leich, Shepard, Walker, Williams, and Wolf, who created the administrative and logistical structures needed to effectively employ Field Artillery aircraft in both training and combat. On decisions that fell within the purview of the War Department—as opposed to questions that Headquarters, Army Ground Forces, could resolve—the Field Artillery aviators were generally too low-ranking and without sufficient prestige to affect the formation of policy. Through happenstance Williams had an opportunity to influence the outcome of the expansion controversy in 1945, and he did so brilliantly. But his role was clearly less important than any one of the four general officers, Krueger, Stilwell, Eisenhower, or Devers. Three of these men had supported the idea of organic light aircraft in 1941, even before the establishment of the program. Their efforts in 1945 only underlined the importance of the informal network of high-ranking supporters who had sustained the program throughout the war. In 1941 they had surmised that such aircraft might assist the Army in performing its primary mission—closing with and destroying enemy land forces. Three years of combat had validated that conjecture.

A number of disputes—aerial cameras, night flying, and the selection of a follow-on aircraft to the L–4—were simply attempts to increase the combat effectiveness of the air observation posts. They stalled at the War Department level because of two unresolved central issues: Would the program continue into the postwar Army, and would it expand beyond the Field Artillery to the other ground combat arms? Once the War Department answered these questions in the affirmative, it could settle the ancillary issues. But by then the war was virtually over. Fortunately, units in combat had been able to use field expedient means to obtain workable solutions, ignoring the policy gridlock in Washington.

EPILOGUE

Air Observation Posts, World War II, and Army Aviation

The Air-Observation-Post Program, 1945

The exact size and disposition of the Air-Observation-Post Program during World War II must remain somewhat uncertain. The War Department did not maintain centralized records for Field Artillery aircraft. Headquarters, Army Ground Forces, did not begin collecting statistics about organic aircraft until 1946, and these figures apply to the continental United States only. No agency collected Army-wide figures until several years later. Every retrospective statement about the size of the program is an estimate and must be accepted with great care. The organic aviation program was quite controversial at various times after the war. Often the authors of the estimates had agendas related to these contemporary issues not connected to the war. Such considerations may have influenced the numbers they used.

The secretary of the Field Artillery School, Lt. Col. Thomas W. McCaw, compiled descriptions of all courses taught there during the war and the number of students matriculating and graduating. During the conflict, 2,939 students successfully completed the field artillery pilot's course. With the 21 graduates from the test group, the Fort Sill total is 2,960. Such a figure does not include light aircraft instructors at Fort Sill who received direct commissions from civil life or graduates from the Fifth Army, II Corps, and the 29th Infantry Division Air Observation Post Schools. At least one other division established its own pilot training school in the continental United States, and there may have been others. No figures are available as to the number of graduates from each of these schools, but some of the pilots also later completed the course at the Field Artillery School. Further complicating the picture, at least some nonrated officers with valid Civil Aeronautics Administration pilot licenses flew Field Artillery aircraft in the rear areas of the overseas theaters. Obviously, the total number of ground forces pilots during the war exceeded 3,000, but by how much is questionable.[1]

The maximum size of the program at full mobilization is even more problematic. The table of organization and equipment strength of division artillery remained constant

---

[1] Thomas W. McCaw, *The Courses: The Field Artillery School, World War II* (Fort Sill, Okla.: Field Artillery School, 1946), pp. 182–86, 194.

throughout the war: ten pilots for infantry divisions and eight for armored divisions. Separate corps artillery groups and battalions each contained a standard air section of two pilots as did the corps artillery air section, authorized in 1943. Air sections at echelons above corps were not sanctioned by the War Department; they ranged from one to five pilots in size, depending on local circumstances. Fixed installations, both overseas and in the continental United States, were also authorized pilots. Little information remains about the size of these establishments, only the fact that they existed. The War Department attempted to maintain an overstrength in the overseas theaters, and there was always a certain number of pilots en route to the theaters or in the Field Artillery Replacement Center at Fort Sill. At full mobilization, the ground forces in all theaters contained approximately fifteen hundred pilots, with roughly the same number of mechanics and mechanics' assistants.

Although the creation of Army Ground Forces aviation eventually led to a reorganization of aviation in the field forces, at war's end air observation posts retained the same organization they had had since the inception of the program in June 1942. An air section of two pilots and planes was organic to each firing battalion of field artillery (whether a part of division or corps artillery) and each division artillery, artillery group, and corps artillery headquarters. The December 1943 reorganization simply made explicit what heretofore had been only implicit: The corps artillery air officer also functioned as the corps artillery commander's staff adviser for all matters affecting air observation posts. The great bulk of the aircraft committed to combat in the spring of 1945 were L–4s. Virtually all the L–2s and L–3s had already disappeared from the inventory, and as yet only a relatively small number of L–5s had joined selected air sections. Air sections existed in effect at all field army and army group headquarters and at most theater headquarters, but these arrangements still lacked War Department sanction.

Wartime Casualties

The absence of a central agency to collect air-observation-post statistics in either the War Department or at Headquarters, Army Ground Forces, meant that no consolidated figures existed at these levels for the war. Although Maj. Charles W. Lefever at the 12th Army Group collected statistical information, including both pilot and aircraft losses, he did not prepare a comprehensive statistical report on Field Artillery air operations in the army group at the end of the war. He redeployed to the United States relatively early and received another assignment almost immediately. The Fifth Army artillery air officer, Lt. Col. Jack L. Marinelli, prepared a detailed narrative of air-observation-post operations in the final campaign of the war, but he also left early for an important assignment in the continental United States. The commander of the 3d Depot Unit (Army), Capt. Michael J. Strok, also departed to another assignment. His statistical compilation of losses remained unpublished, and many of the documents from which he had derived those statistics have since been lost. Of all the artillery air officers at the field army level, only one stayed with his wartime organization for any appreciable period after the end of hostilities. Maj. Delbert L. Bristol remained with Headquarters, First Army, and in 1946 helped write the fifteen-volume First Army report. His discussion of artillery air operations is consequently the most comprehensive, detailed, and sophisticated in any of the field army reports prepared at the end of the war. He included a statistical table detailing air-observation-post activities in First Army during combat. No other army published a similar compilation.[2]

The figures for both aircraft and pilot losses are very revealing. (*Table 1*) June 1944 was the most dangerous month of the campaign for First Army aircraft and pilots. The incidence of aircraft missing or salvaged during that month, 13.8 percent, meant that if this rate continued First Army would have suffered total elimination of its initial complement sometime in early January 1945. Losses of pilots were considerably less, 6.9 percent, but still the worst of the war by a considerable margin. But perhaps the most revealing figure was the "hours lost pilot" line: First Army pilots averaged only 235 flying hours for every one of their number killed, captured, or otherwise incapacitated. Two hundred thirty-five flying hours represented almost 67 percent fewer hours than the figure for the next lowest month, 704 hours in July 1944. A combination of factors—the restricted size of the Allied lodgment, the rate of buildup within the beachhead, the absence of recent battle experience among some American artillery commanders and their staffs and their concomitant reliance on World War I procedures, and the pilots' own lack of exposure to combat—contributed to this outcome. Of course, the number of operational accidents was also related to the effectiveness of the German defense.

Bristol did not provide a further breakdown of the losses by cause—combat-related or noncombat accident. Consequently, it is not possible to assign an exact weight to these various factors for individual months. But total aircraft losses approached the June figures only during December, and the thirty aircraft lost then primarily represent planes destroyed on the ground when their airstrips were overrun during the German counteroffensive in the Ardennes. First Army lost only four pilots in that month. July 1944, with the battle of Normandy still in progress but with greater success for First Army—the breakout at St. Lô came on 25 July—was second only to June in terms of pilots lost, followed by August 1944 and April 1945, months given over to pursuit. A nonexistent or ill-defined enemy front line could be almost as deadly for air-observation-post pilots as a well-defended one. During

---

[2] Information on the Fifth Army statistics is based on Telecon, author with Mrs. M. J. Strok, 9 Aug 96; Memorandum for the Record (MFR), author, 19 Sep 96, sub: Conversation with Col (Ret) Michael J. Strok, 16 Sep 96; both in author's files. "Statistical Analysis of Air OP Activities" in First Army, *First United States Army, Combat Operations Data, Europe, 1944–1945*, 4 vols. (New York: Headquarters, First Army, 1946), p. 21. In checking the table, I discovered a number of computational errors in the original "Aircraft Hours, Average," "Average Hours, Pilot," "Hours Lost, Pilot," "Percentage Aircraft Lost," and "Percentage Pilots Lost" lines, which have been corrected. I had no breakdown as to the number of infantry division, armored division, corps artillery, or army artillery pilots and so could not recompute average hours in these categories. Report (Rpt), [Maj Jack L. Marinelli], 26 May 45, sub: Fifth Army Air Observation Post (AOP) Historical Data of Bologna–Po Valley Offensive, App. to Rpt, Brig Gen Guy O. Kurtz, Artillery (Arty) Officer (Ofcr), Fifth Army, 16 Jul 45, sub: History of the Arty of the Fifth Army: Po Valley Campaign, 14 Apr–2 May 45, in "Fifth Army Artillery: Po Valley Campaign" (Bound Manuscript [Ms], Morris Swett Technical Library, Field Artillery School [FAS], Fort Sill, Okla. [hereafter cited as Morris Swett Tech Lib]); Interview (Interv), author with Lt Col Charles W. Lefever, 4 Sep 91, U.S. Army Center of Military History, Washington, D.C. (hereafter cited as CMH). Colonel Strok also had a table dating from World War II that showed pilot losses in First, Third, Seventh, and Ninth Armies, June through November 1944: Table, sub: Field Artillery (FA) Liaison Pilot Losses, 1944, in Michael J. Strok Ms, author's files, CMH. The figures in the table for First Army vary widely from both the 1946 First Army report and the figures in Rpt, Maj L. O. Rostenberger, 21 Jan 45, sub: Rpt of Special Observer (Obsr) in European Theater of Operations (ETO), in Ms, Rpt of Special Obsr in ETO, 8 Sep–22 Dec 44 (Bound Ms, Morris Swett Tech Lib, [1945]), which do agree with one another. Consequently, I have been unwilling to use the figures for Third, Seventh, and Ninth Armies.

TABLE 1—STATISTICAL ANALYSIS OF AIR-OBSERVATION-POST ACTIVITIES IN U.S. FIRST ARMY, JUNE 1944–APRIL 1945

Aircraft	Jun	Jul	Aug	Sep	Oct	Nov	Dec	Jan	Feb	Mar	Apr
Aircraft Operational	261	243	191	216	203	240	237	213	248	252	253
Pilots Operational	289	264	214	247	246	276	281	264	299	301	289
Aircraft Lost	36	13	10	9	24	14	30	9	4	7	20
Pilots Lost	20	14	8	6	5	2	4	2	2	7	11
Total Flying Hours	4,690	9,851	7,982	9,189	4,677	4,610	6,303	3,598	6,160	10,332	11,023
Average Hours, Aircraft	18.0	40.5	41.8	42.5	23.0	19.2	26.6	16.9	24.8	41.0	43.6
Average Hours, Pilot	16.2	37.3	37.3	37.2	19.0	16.7	22.4	13.6	20.6	34.3	38.1
Average Hours, Infantry Division Artillery Pilot	24.4	40.0	42.8	39.2	19.2	17.9	20.3	13.6	24.0	38.8	45.3
Average Hours, Armored Division Artillery Pilot	23.6	37.0	59.8	49.0	19.8	19.7	33.9	19.6	20.9	44.3	44.0
Average Hours, Corps Artillery Pilot	17.8	36.8	29.8	24.7	19.0	15.8	21.8	14.5	15.5	30.1	38.5
Average Hours, Army Artillery Pilot	15.8	21.5	34.6	32.6	18.0	12.4	18.1	8.9	17.8	26.4	30.9
Hours Lost, Pilot	235.0	704.0	998.0	1,532.0	935.0	2,305.0	1,576.0	1,799.0	3,080.0	1,476.0	1,002.0
Percent Aircraft Lost	13.8	5.3	5.2	4.2	11.8	5.8	12.66	4.2	1.6	2.8	7.9
Percent Pilots Lost	6.9	5.3	3.7	2.4	2.0	0.7	1.42	0.76	0.67	2.3	3.8

Note: The "Aircraft Lost" line refers to aircraft missing or actually salvaged, that is, officially declared nonflyable. The "Pilots Lost" line alludes to pilots missing in action, killed, or seriously injured and withdrawn from flight duty. The "Hours Lost, Pilot" line indicates the average number of hours flown per pilot lost for First Army as a whole.

exploitation, pilots could easily fly over German columns and not realize their mistake until the Germans took them under fire.

Total flying hours dipped appreciably (average hours per aircraft even more so) with the onset of the autumn rains and associated fogs in October and did not increase markedly until the weather improved in March 1945. Such a reduced tempo of operations could only be expected given the technical limitations of Field Artillery aircraft. The L–4 and the L–5 were designed and equipped to operate only under visual flight rules. The slight increase in December 1944 reflected the tactical emergency that forced pilots to fly in extremely marginal conditions rather than any improvement in weather conditions. That First Army lost only four pilots during the month is one indication of how experienced the pilots and ground crews had become by this stage of the war.

This growing experience was one of the reasons why the German Army was not able to sustain the rate of casualties they inflicted on First Army in June 1944, although this possibly was not the most important factor. The Germans of course were able to reconstitute most of the divisions that the Allies had decimated in Normandy, but it is at least questionable whether these formations ever again attained the degree of military effectiveness they had exhibited early in the Normandy campaign. Finally, short of winning total command of the air, the Germans simply did not have an effective response to the problem posed by the air observation post. That solution was so beyond the capacity of Germany from early 1944 on that it does not warrant serious consideration. The Germans mounted a supreme effort in June 1944, as the casualty rates attest, but they could not sustain it. With some justification American light-aircraft pilots feared the *Luftwaffe* more than any other threat, but they rarely had to face German pursuits in the European Theater of Operations, including Normandy. Even if the Germans had mounted a sustained aerial threat, there was no reason why First Army could not have launched the kind of counterair program devised by VI Corps in the Anzio beachhead. Assuming for the sake of argument that the Germans had a credible opportunity to achieve at least limited command of the air, they could not have devised a better scheme for losing it than exchanging Me–109s on a one-to-one basis for L–4s.

The surviving Fifth Army air-observation-post figures reinforce this argument. (*Table 2*) Most Fifth Army aircraft losses occurred during the months of intense ground combat—January and February 1944 during the severe fighting at Anzio and May and June 1944 during the breaching of the Gustav Line and the breakout from Anzio. The range of losses, expressed as a percentage of the total operational aircraft and pilots available to each field army, is also very similar, although First Army generally sustained slightly higher aircraft (but not pilot) losses. First Army suffered aircraft losses fluctuating from 13.8 percent in June 1944 to 1.6 percent in February 1945. Fifth Army losses peaked at 9.9 percent in February 1944 and fell to a low of 1 percent for the months of August through October 1944. Pilot losses in First Army ranged from 6.9 percent, also in June 1944, to .67 percent in February 1945. Fifth Army pilot losses hit a high of 6.7 percent in May 1944 and a low of 0 percent in January 1944.[3]

---

[3] Briefing Chart, [Col M. J. Strok], sub: Fifth Army AOP Operations—1944, Strok Ms, author's files, CMH. This chart was compiled from reports no longer extant and has remained unpublished until now. I checked the computations of the "Average Hours, Aircraft," "Average Hours, Pilot," "% Aircraft Lost," and "% Pilots Lost" lines and rounded the results to the nearest tenth of a percent to make the results compatible with First Army figures.

TABLE 2—AIR-OBSERVATION-POST OPERATIONS IN U.S. FIFTH ARMY, 1944

	Jan	Feb	Mar	Apr	May	Jun	Jul	Aug	Sep	Oct	Nov	Dec
Operational Aircraft	139	142	132	155	145	156	109	90	88	91	85	98
Operational Pilots	136	135	127	144	136	151	103	87	88	88	87	139
Aircraft Lost	12	14	7	6	10	10	5	1	1	1	5	1
Pilots Lost	0	6	1	3	9	3	2	1	1	1	5	1
Total Flying Hours	2,878	2,727	4,353	4,936	7,572	7,427	6,923	4,814	4,263	3,049	2,280	1,722
Average Hours, Aircraft	20.7	19.2	33.0	31.8	52.2	47.6	63.5	53.5	48.4	33.5	26.8	17.6
Average Hours, Pilot	21.2	20.2	34.3	34.3	55.7	49.2	67.2	55.3	48.4	34.6	26.2	12.4
Percent Aircraft Lost	8.6	9.9	5.3	3.9	6.9	6.4	4.6	1.1	1.1	1.1	5.9	1.0
Percent Pilots Lost	0.0	4.4	0.8	2.1	6.6	2.0	1.9	1.1	1.1	1.1	5.7	0.7

Average Type of Mission Per Airplane

	Artillery Adjustment	Reconnaissance	Patrol	Courier	Other	Total
Number	8.0	2.0	10.0	2.0	4.0	26
Percent	30.8	7.7	38.5	7.7	15.4	100

A IV Corps L–4 Rests in a Large, Water-Filled Shell Hole on Lucca Air Strip, Italy, 1944. Sun in the Pilot's Eyes Caused the Accident.

Even at their apogees the loss rates for aircraft and pilots in First and Fifth Armies were low enough to be sustained by the Americans. The unused capacity at the Piper Aircraft plant ensured that the aircraft losses could be endured so long as the Air Staff programmed sufficient numbers. In low-technology missions, which the air-observation-post operations represented in the context of the rest of World War II, the equipment losses were never crucial, provided there was an ample supply of replacements. The most expensive part of an air observation post in terms of time of production and capital invested was not the light airplane but the light-airplane pilot and his observer, both of whom were trained Field Artillery officers. The pilot represented the additional investment of time and money required for flight training. *Table 3* gives the ratio of pilot to aircraft losses for each month of the First Army campaign in western and central Europe and for Fifth Army in Italy during 1944. Only once, in First Army in July 1944, did pilot losses exceed aircraft losses. In seven of the eleven months, pilot losses in First Army were 56 percent or less of aircraft losses. Even excluding the anomalous month of December 1944, in which so many First Army aircraft had to be destroyed on the ground, this is an impressive result.

These figures suggest that the L–4, despite its genuine operational limitations, was a perfect aircraft for a low-technology niche in a high-technology war. The verb "suggest" is used advisedly. These aggregate figures include pilots severely wounded, killed, or captured on the ground as well as in the air. They also encompass situations in which the pilot was killed and the observer was able to land the aircraft safely. Taking these factors into

TABLE 3—RATIO OF AIR-OBSERVATION-POST PILOT LOSSES TO AIRCRAFT LOSSES IN U.S. FIRST AND FIFTH ARMIES, JANUARY 1944–APRIL 1945

	First Army Percentage	Fifth Army Percentage
January 1944	—	0
February	—	43
March	—	14
April	—	50
May	—	90
June	56	30
July	108	40
August	80	100
September	67	100
October	21	100
November	14	100
December	13	100
January 1945	22	—
February	50	—
March	100	—
April	55	—
Total	46	45

consideration, the numbers still imply that even when an L–4 was wrecked beyond repair, the pilot often walked away.[4]

Anecdotal evidence supports the same conclusion. Maj. John W. Oswalt's crash at Futa Pass is only the most spectacular example. In early 1945 the director of the Department of Air Training, Lt. Col. Gordon J. Wolf, queried the artillery air officer of the 83d Infantry Division, Maj. Jerome W. Byrd, one of the graduates of Pilot Class No. 1, as to the comparative advantages of the L–4 and L–5. The tenor of his letter indicates that Wolf assumed a clear superiority for the L–5. If so, the results surprised him. Byrd convened a meeting of all the pilots in the division. They emphatically agreed that the L–4 was the superior aircraft. "One pilot stated that 30% of those present would not be at our meeting if we had had L–5s."[5]

The information on the causes of air-observation-post losses for the war as a whole is much more fragmentary than Major Bristol's figures on the timing of losses in First Army. Four snapshots of losses by cause exist. Colonel Strok's estimate for Fifth Army losses— 2 percent due to German aircraft; 5 percent due to enemy antiaircraft and small-arms fire; and the rest due to accidents—must be somewhat suspect because it was made so long after the fact. Still, the trend—more losses due to operational accidents than direct enemy action—is borne out by First Army figures from June through September 1944, Sixth Army losses during the Luzon campaign, and Tenth Army operations on Okinawa. Enough detail has survived about each individual aircraft loss on Okinawa to construct *Table 4*. Direct enemy action accounted for four aircraft, or 30.8 percent of the losses; operational

---

[4] MFR, author, 19 Sep 96; Interv, author with Col W. R. Mathews, 3 Dec 91, CMH.
[5] Ltr, Maj J. W. Byrd to Lt Col G. J. Wolf, 3 Feb 45, J. Elmore Swenson Ms, U.S. Army Aviation Museum Library, Fort Rucker, Ala.

TABLE 4—AIR-OBSERVATION-POST LOSSES IN U.S. TENTH ARMY DURING THE OKINAWA CAMPAIGN, 1 APRIL–30 JUNE 1945

Period To	Total	Enemy Action			Operational Accidents				
		Air	AAA	Ground	Friendly Fire	Landing	Takeoff	In-Flight	Ground
L+9	5			1	1	1	1		1
L+30	5		2					1	2
L+60	2		1				1		
L+90	1							1	
Total	13	0	3	1	1	1	2	2	3
Percent	100	0	23.1	7.6	7.6	7.6	15.4	15.4	23.1

Note: L = Landing. The original report begins at L - 6. Apparently, the artillery air officer for Tenth Army, Maj. Norman E. McKnight, had a requirement to begin reporting losses at L - 6. However, other evidence in the Tenth Army report makes it clear that no light aircraft were lost before the landing. Consequently, to keep the periodization relatively even, the table begins with L-day.

accidents accounted for nine aircraft, or 69.2 percent of the losses. Seventy-five percent of the losses due to direct enemy action occurred during the first thirty days of the operation, while 77.7 percent of the operational accidents occurred in the first thirty days, a pattern that supports the indirect influence of enemy actions on operational accidents. Not one of these planes was lost to air action. Japanese aircraft—the *kamikazes*—participated in the defense of Okinawa, but they were too busy attempting to crash into the invasion fleet to pay any attention to the light aircraft flying over Tenth Army's front. The limited evidence available thus bears out Strok's point that prewar fears about the dangers posed by enemy air proved to be overdrawn once the air observation posts entered combat. This outcome, of course, was attributable to four factors: the success of the Allied air forces in wresting command of the air away from the Germans, Italians, and Japanese; the way in which the U.S. Army integrated light aviation with the ground combat arms; the flight characteristics of the L–4s and L–5s; and the training and skills of individual pilots.

Conclusion

In the simplest possible terms, the U.S. Army gained its own organic aircraft during World War II because of supply and demand. The evolution of the art of war created a demand for an aerial observer intimately connected to the ground forces. At the same time several parallel technical developments supplied the equipment needed to put him in the air over the battlefield.

The potential to use an aerial observer in combat had existed ever since the invention of the balloon in the late eighteenth century, but only during World War I did such a position become a necessity for armies. Then a combination of the lethality of modern weaponry and a lack of tactical mobility in the killing zone made aircraft and balloons important as a means of preventing surprise at the strategic and operational levels. Aerial observers also directed artillery fire because the guns had to hide behind folds in the land in order to survive on such a battlefield, and ground observers were often unable to provide the necessary information to the gunners. However, the state of radio technology greatly hampered the observers' ability to effectively direct fire in a timely manner, while American field artillery organization and doctrine made it impossible for artillerymen to quickly mass fire on a single point. Only during the interwar years did a number of young field artillery officers develop the doctrine and organization that made feasible such a concentration of fire. This capability in turn made the demand for an on-call aerial observer critical to the U.S. Field Artillery for the first time.

The development of a lightweight opposed engine and its marriage to a steel-tube, canvas-covered airframe provided rugged, easily maintained aircraft with performance characteristics equivalent to World War I observation planes. The light planes of the 1930s also enjoyed enhanced reliability and durability that made them capable of operating out of forward areas. The parallel development of frequency-modulated voice radio made flexible and reliable air-ground communication possible, also for the first time. The technologies thus existed to meet the Field Artillery's need; it remained only for someone to recognize it.

Supply and *demand* suggest the existence of a market. The market in which armies contend is war, but war, at least in the twentieth century, has been discontinuous. Armed forces thus enter a conflict with certain predispositions based upon their understanding of the "lessons" of the last war and the institutional momentum built up during peacetime to address certain aspects of those lessons. In short, no technical, doctrinal, or tactical result is predetermined; all are contingent. Consequently, the U.S. Army Air Corps in the years between the world wars, but particularly in the 1930s, focused largely on the doctrine of strategic bombardment and the aircraft needed to implement it. Most Air Corps officers dismissed both the potential of and the need for light aircraft in combat. Ground officers who were light aircraft pilots outside of their official duties had a much better grasp of this technology's potential than did most of their rated counterparts in the Air Corps. Ground officers who were private pilots better understood the capacities of light aircraft. At the same time these officers also had a much better sense of how war on the ground was changing. The thinking of their Air Corps contemporaries often remained frozen in the regime of 1918 as far as ground battle was concerned. Consequently, ground officers were more likely to see the possibilities provided by light aircraft and how best to mesh these aircraft into the evolving combined arms doctrine.

In initially rejecting light aircraft, Air Corps officers also made a professional judgment about their potential airworthiness in combat and found them wanting. During the war that followed, this miscalculation proved to be of sufficient magnitude to warrant some discussion. The officers involved based their conclusions on World War I experience in which the speed, rate of climb, turning radius, armament, and range of aircraft were all important, depending on the mission assigned, in determining their survivability. Of these, speed was by far the most important. Piper Cubs and their counterparts were profoundly slow (all the better to observe ground targets). Since they were not going any great distance, loiter time was more important than range. An efficient engine was more important than a powerful one. Rate of climb was not so important because the preferred altitudes (except of course in high mountains) were relatively low. In fact, given their lightweight construction, "soared" is probably preferable to "climbed" as a description of how they achieved operational altitudes. They were, of course, unarmed. Only in turning radius and maneuverability did Cubs possess characteristics that Air Corps officers recognized as contributing to their ability to survive in combat. In the Air Corps view, however, these characteristics did not offset the already enumerated deficiencies.

Light planes suffered an added disability—at least from the perspective of Air Corps officers. Light aircraft were constructed out of "old-fashioned" materials. Steel tubes, fabric, wood, and varnish harkened back to the previous generation of aircraft, which the Air Corps was in the process of replacing during the 1930s. Sleek aluminum monoplanes represented the future. In an image-conscious organization that prided itself on being at the cutting edge of modernity, the wrong sort of appearance was no little disadvantage.

Air Corps officers believed that their expertise encompassed everything that flew. In fact, by training and experience they were authorities in the design and operation of aircraft optimized to perform certain key missions—bombardment, pursuit, etc. Light aircraft by their normal standards of measurement were inferior, "low-technology" planes. Thus, the very expertise that gave Air Corps officers the intellectual authority to comment on the characteristics of light aircraft distorted their views of what was and was not important. The narrowing of vision that is almost synonymous with becoming specialists denied them the breadth of view that might have allowed them to arrive at different conclusions.

The phrase *low technology* needs some qualification when applied to light aircraft because of this association with culture-bound Air Corps standards of evaluation. In their own sphere, light aircraft were just as modern as the most up-to-date Air Corps bomber or pursuit. They possessed the performance characteristics of World War I service planes but had the ruggedness, simplicity, and reliability of a mature technology. Their airframes represented state-of-the-art lightweight construction. Their lightweight, opposed, four-cylinder engines provided adequate horsepower in a fuel-efficient manner. They were cheap to build, economical to operate, and easy to maintain. Due to Maj. Rex E. Chandler's insistence, each one carried a standard, multichannel Signal Corps radio into combat. Although the ability to maneuver proved just as beneficial as the Air Corps officers surmised, the ability to carry a pilot, observer, and Signal Corps radio was probably the attribute that most facilitated the survival of Cub-like planes in forward areas. On one hand, two-way, frequency-modulated voice radio provided the flexible medium that linked the observer to the artillery fire direction center and allowed him to quickly shift massed fire on targets of opportunity. On the other, it allowed the development of ground warning nets prepared to alert light aircraft of the approach of hostile aircraft and the close integration of air-observation-post and antiaircraft artillery operations. Light aircraft were "low technology" only in the sense that they were different, not second-rate, technology.

Three combat arms—Infantry, Cavalry, and Field Artillery—and two combat elements not yet recognized as separate arms—armor and tank destroyers—had potential uses for light aircraft. Yet only the Field Artillery possessed the necessary combination of advantages to achieve organizational success. First, Field Artillery officers recognized the importance of the light aircraft issue. They also possessed a mission widely recognized as essential outside their branch. Finally, the chief of Field Artillery had the bureaucratic advantage of proximity to the decision makers. The other strengths became operative only after the chief of Field Artillery, Maj. Gen. Robert M. Danford, accepted the premise that a problem existed. The second advantage meant that the Field Artillery could attract non–Field Artillery allies, such as Generals Walter Krueger, Dwight D. Eisenhower, and

Some L–4s at the Aolito Airport on Saipan, 1944. Note the Revetments To Protect Against Japanese Artillery Fire.

Mark Clark. The third, the location of the Office of the Chief of Field Artillery in the War Department, offered proximity to the secretary of war and the chief of staff. Even with these benefits, successful innovation required men with the bureaucratic acumen and moral courage to exploit them. The Field Artillery had such officers in Danford, Lt. Col. William W. Ford, and Major Chandler. Danford also possessed a large measure of luck in the shape of a secretary and assistant secretary of war who were Field Artillery veterans, Henry L. Stimson and John J. McCloy, and the fact that at a critical moment General Clark was the senior officer present at Headquarters, Army Ground Forces.

The fact that the chief of staff, General George C. Marshall, Jr., was favorably disposed to an organic air program was of incalculable benefit to its advocates. He was, after all, the formal authority for approving both the testing of the concept and its implementation once the test board reported favorable results. More to the point, he was the one person with the prestige and authority to kill the program at its inception. Instead, he encouraged it.

Marshall's approval and initiation of the Air-Observation-Post Program did not ensure its speedy implementation. In addition to the difficulties inherent in creating a new program from nothing in the midst of a global war, Field Artillery aviation faced concerted opposition from Army Air Forces officers. To them, light aircraft flown by ground officers represented an inappropriate and wasteful use of scarce aerial resources. The War Department's insistence on implementing the program despite their reservations indicated in their view a lack of faith in their professional expertise. At the same time at least some

Troops Inspect an L–5 Damaged by Japanese Raiders.

of the senior officers, such as the commander of the Army Air Forces, Lt. Gen. Henry H. Arnold, viewed Field Artillery aviation as a possible future competitor with his own organization. Thus, a combination of their perception of principle and self-interest led senior Army Air Forces staff officers and some field commanders to oppose organic aviation and work to limit the impact of the wartime program. They consequently took on many of the attributes of an organized pressure group operating within the government, rather than outside of it. During the first eighteen months of the program, they could confidently expect that combat would prove the soundness of their views. Some, generalizing from the early difficulties in North Africa and selectively reading the evidence reported by the other overseas theaters, thought that it was so.

General Marshall's support of the Air-Observation-Post Program put some limits on what opponents could do, but only in a very general sense. Field Artillery aviation represented an issue of mid-level importance in the universe of problems with which the War Department had to contend. Whether to adopt organic air was an issue important enough for Marshall to decide personally, but it was not salient enough for him to monitor its implementation on a day-by-day basis. That task fell to the War Department General Staff, and it was in the staff arena that the Air-Observation-Post Program became a shuttlecock between those Army Air Forces officers who wanted to abolish it and those Army Ground Forces officers who wanted to expand it. Neither group could muster enough support to defeat the other. Consequently, at the War Department level, organic aviation policy remained largely static for most of the war despite the thrust and counterthrust of the opposing camps.

By 1944 members of the Air Staff thought they had discovered a solution to the organic aviation conundrum, Army Air Forces liaison squadrons that would be attached, but not assigned, to field armies. Thus, the ground army commander exercised operational control over them, but they remained in the Army Air Forces chain of command for supply and administration. Such an arrangement promised economies through enhanced procedural efficiencies. In addition, there was little distinction between the two programs in terms of the skill and courage of the young men who flew Army Air Forces light aircraft and those who flew Field Artillery aircraft. When given the opportunity, as in Burma, Army Air Forces enlisted pilots in L–5s gave every evidence of possessing as much panache as the junior officers flying Field Artillery L–4s. Moreover, the Air Staff thought that the liaison squadrons were equipped with superior aircraft. Many ground officers would have agreed. Certainly, the L–5 appeared so by all the conventional measures—speed, range, rate of climb, and carrying capacity. Only that handful of pilots who had flown both aircraft in combat might have contested that assumption in early 1944, and definitive evidence was not available until much later. The L–4 had, as argued earlier, possessed the supreme characteristic of any low-technology weapon in a high-technology war—the ability to bring its operators home alive. But this was not realized at the time, and on the basis of the information available the Air Staff had a very plausible and reasonable argument.

The officers on the Air Staff were also profoundly wrong, because of six factors—mission, doctrine, training, organization, culture, and timing. Many years ago, Elting E. Morison defined military organizations as societies organized around weapons systems. Weapons systems are more than the weapons involved; in this case, air sections and liaison squadrons were more than simple reflections of two apparently very similar light aircraft, the L–4 and the L–5. Weapons systems are a combination of equipment; what the equipment is intended to do, or mission; how the equipment is expected to be used to fulfill the mission, or doctrine; the operators and their training; the particular organization designed to optimize these factors and integrate them with other military institutions; and the social networks and patterns of behavior, or organizational cultures, that develop among the human beings assigned to the organization and who ultimately make these things possible. Consequently, air sections (even when consolidated as provisional companies) and liaison squadrons were profoundly different kinds of weapons systems.

Air sections were optimized to direct artillery fire and to provide close-in battlefield reconnaissance; liaison squadrons were intended to provide courier service in the rear areas. Mission, doctrine, training, organization, and the informal relationships developed by serving in field artillery battalions prepared Field Artillery pilots to live, fly, and survive in the battle area. For their more limited role, Army Air Forces liaison pilots did not receive the same preparation. Given the quality of the men in the liaison squadrons, the pilots could have learned to fly the missions performed by the Field Artillery pilots, but it is unlikely that they could have performed them as effectively. Even with the advantages of mission, doctrine, training, organization, and culture, it took about six months after entering combat for the first air-observation-post pilots to become very proficient. Given the internal resistance in the Army Air Forces to any pilots performing these missions, the length of time for Army Air Forces liaison pilots to adapt successfully would in all probability have been considerably longer.[6]

---

[6] Elting E. Morison, *Men, Machines, and Modern Times* (Cambridge: Massachusetts Institute of Technology Press, 1966), pp. 67–87.

Time, of course, was an all-important factor. The first air observation posts appeared in combat in November 1942. In March 1944 the first Army Air Forces liaison squadron deployed to an overseas theater containing large numbers of ground forces units actively engaged in combat. Assuming the absence of any organic air program, it could have become reasonably effective performing combat missions perhaps as early as October or November 1944. Such an estimate is predicated on the fact that the existence of Field Artillery aviation did not delay the deployment of the liaison squadrons. The timing of their movement overseas was contingent upon when L–5s became available to equip the units. This in turn was a consequence of the internal debate over the light-aircraft production program of 1943 and a result of the priority that the Army Air Forces assigned to light aircraft as a type. Because liaison aircraft had the lowest priority, liaison squadrons were the last to be organized.[7]

Victory for the Air Staff position in 1942 would have meant no light aircraft for the ground forces in Tunisia and Sicily, at Salerno, along the Winter Line in Italy, at Anzio, during the drive north from Rome, in Normandy and southern France, during the pursuit across France and the opening battles along the German frontier, or on New Guinea, Bougainville, and Saipan. It is at least reasonable to question whether the war would have progressed in quite the way that it did without flexible aerial observation readily available to American ground commanders. Could the Allies have remained in the Anzio beachhead without artillery dominance in the area of contact—a dominance permitted by the superior observation provided by Field Artillery aircraft? Could the 32d Infantry Division and the 112th Regimental Combat Team have achieved the overwhelming victory that they did on the Driniumor River without the capability to maneuver forces through dense jungle, a competence that existed because L–4s were available to guide those forces? These and similar questions must remain moot because history is a linear process, not a laboratory experiment. But one conclusion is inescapable—the delay would have been paid for with the lives of American soldiers.

This is exactly the frame of reference that gripped Lt. Gen. Lesley J. McNair and his senior staff at Headquarters, Army Ground Forces, beginning in 1942 in their debates with the Air Staff. The stakes in the debate were very small given the conventional way in which such things are measured in bureaucratic fights—only at most some six thousand officers and men in a ground Army that numbered almost six million at full mobilization. Clearly, numbers had little to do with the issue. McNair and his staff invested so much of their own energy, passion, and continuous attention to this issue because they understood its implications. They recognized that this small increment of men and aircraft could significantly increase the combat power of the existing combined arms team. Moreover, McNair and his advisers had a profound appreciation of the correspondence in war between time and lives. The concept of bureaucratic politics can explain how the Air Staff and the Army Ground Forces staff interacted, but it does not explain why.[8]

In the debate over light aircraft weapons systems, the Air Staff placed its emphasis on the *weapon*; the Army Ground Forces staff stressed the *system*. At first glance this diver-

---

[7] See deployment statistics for liaison squadrons in E. F. Raines, Jr., "Activation and Deployment of Army Air Forces Liaison Squadrons in World War II" (Unpublished Ms, Historical Services Branch, CMH, 1996).

[8] At full mobilization on 31 May 1945, the ground army consisted of 5,983,330 officers and men. Department of the Army, *Pocket Data Book Supplement, 1966* (Washington, D.C.: Office of the Comptroller, Office of the Chief of Staff, Army, 1966), p. 4.

gence is surprising. A reverence for hardware and an engineering approach to problem solving was a common inheritance of both air and ground officers. In the American context the approach dated back at least to the establishment of the U.S. Military Academy and the introduction of an engineering-based curriculum for officer education early in the nineteenth century. The difference in approach, one of degree rather than kind, was rooted in the dissimilar experiences of air and ground officers during the interwar years. Aviators always feel a special affinity for airplanes; their lives and the successful completion of their missions, and hence their careers, depend on their aircraft and all their ancillary equipment performing as designed. Even in peacetime, the hazards of military flight help to create a tight psychological bond between men and machines. The revolution in airframe design and the increase in engine power beginning in the late 1920s placed Air Corps officers under added pressure to focus on equipment and the operational consequences of the design changes.

At the same time the widespread desire for organizational independence from the ground army attuned air officers to the reasons for cutting rather than strengthening ties to the ground combat arms. The same could not be said of the members of the observation aviation community, but, within the internal status order of the Air Corps, observation pilots stood at the bottom in terms of both prestige and budget. Moreover, it was difficult for them to stay abreast of the latest thinking about ground combat and their role in it because so much of that innovation was going on in the schools of the various ground arms. Observation pilots flew antiquated aircraft and until the mid-1930s had no opportunity to work on a regular basis with large ground formations, themselves saddled with transport, weapons, and gear of the same vintage. In contrast, pilots in bombardment units garnered both status and modern aircraft. The officers at the center of the doctrinal revolution at the Air Corps Tactical School, those developing the theory of precision bombardment, focused not on the tactics of air warfare but on an analysis of the national economies of potential enemies to locate possible choke points and to develop appropriate target lists. In a sense Air Corps officers concentrated on the development of equipment and its purposes with rather less consideration of the techniques of its use.[9]

Ground officers, on the other hand, received a thorough training in technique. Such an approach was almost implicit in a combined arms philosophy, except that prior to World War I only a small percentage of officers had received such training. The reform in officer education following World War I represented not so much a change in content as in comprehensiveness. The War Department instituted and the Congress funded an interlocking system of branch schools that culminated in the Command and General Staff School, a true combined arms school. Both philosophy and education predisposed ground officers to concentrate on the system, while air officers focused on the weapons for the same reasons.

To use the term *weapons system* to characterize their debate is to introduce something of an anachronism. Neither ground nor air officers used the expression at the time; it was a concept that gained currency in the services immediately after rather than during World

---

[9] Curtis E. LeMay and McKinlay Kantor, *Mission with LeMay* (New York: Doubleday, 1965), pp. 129–93, discusses this issue at some length; LeMay, et al., *Strategic Air Warfare: An Interview with Generals Curtis E. LeMay, Leon W. Johnson, David A. Burchinal, and Jack J. Catton*, ed. Richard H. Kohn and Joseph P. Harahan, (Washington, D.C.: Office of Air Force History, 1988), pp. 19–31.

War II. Still, the reality preceded the abstraction, and it was the World War II experience of ground and air officers that made the idea meaningful in the postwar period. The lack of such terminology, however, probably embittered the debate by allowing both sides to misinterpret the motives of the other. To air officers, the ground forces position was based on a parochial lack of understanding of the principles of air power and possibly suggested an intent to derail the independent air force of the future. To ground officers, air officers exhibited a mulish obstinacy and blind indifference to the basic principles of the profession—principles so basic that ground officers saw no need to articulate them. The controversy over organic air thus featured principled opponents talking past one another, scoring debaters' points rather than communicating.

While the Air Staff and the Army Ground Forces staff grappled over policy, the informal alliance between senior officers who favored organic air; midlevel field grade officers, usually in the Field Artillery, who fostered its development; members of the light aircraft industry who wanted to sell their planes; and participants in the Air-Observation-Post Program continued throughout the war and into the postwar period. Active high-level support by Assistant Secretary of War McCloy, Generals Danford, McNair, Clark, and Eisenhower, and others gave the Air-Observation-Post Program time to develop. Given the range of issues that demanded their attention, however, they could give this particular problem only episodic attention. Day-to-day oversight fell upon staff officers such as Major Chandler and later Cols. John M. Lentz and Thomas E. Lewis. Much of the success of the program depended upon their insights on the workings of the bureaucracy and their skills in managing the program throughout the process. In the early stages such men also played key roles in identifying potential allies, both inside and outside the Army, and in building an informal support network that complemented, and sometimes bypassed, the formal chain of command. The light aircraft industry and its representatives, especially Mr. William T. Piper and Mr. John E. P. Morgan, were important not only as suppliers of equipment but also as participants in the network. As civilians, completely uninhibited by the chain of command, they would ensure that no idea would be stifled because an opponent occupied a position of advantage in the bureaucracy. Such support gave Colonel Ford and his subordinates in the Department of Air Training the opportunity to develop an effective training base and for pilots overseas to work out the administrative and logistical arrangements and the tactics required to perform effectively in combat. Ultimately, it was the success of air observation posts in combat that permitted the continuation of the program into the postwar period and its expansion to encompass the other branches.

The impact of air observation posts on the U.S. Army's conduct of World War II is difficult to assess with precision because of their thorough integration, as intended, into ground combat operations. Clearly, light aircraft were an important component of the American field artillery system, permitting observed fire when terrain or the circumstances of combat prevented or limited ground observation. Air observation posts also played a valuable role in close-in reconnaissance for armor columns during exploitation, just as Brig. Gen. Adna R. Chaffee had foreseen in 1940. Moreover, by providing speedy conveyance for senior officers and their staffs, light aircraft contributed to a face-to-face, oral style of command. Avoiding the possibilities for misunderstanding inherent in total reliance upon cryptic radio messages or the time-consuming resort to detailed written orders, American leaders could develop a command style appropriate for fast-moving mobile operations.

In the Pacific, aerial evacuation, aerial resupply, and guidance of maneuver units and patrols in dense jungle took on greater importance for air observation posts than in Europe or North Africa. Only occasionally could it be said with certainty that light aircraft were a necessary—but not a sufficient—condition for victory. Anzio, the 11th Airborne Division's operations on Leyte, and possibly the 32d Infantry Division and the 112th Cavalry Regimental Combat Team at the Driniumor fall within this category. In other instances the presence of air observation posts significantly increased the magnitude of the victory, most notably in the Falaise Gap. Usually, air observation posts were one of the factors that weighted the tactical battle in favor of the Americans. Their presence meant that on an average day a few more young Americans lived and that a few more young Germans, Italians, and Japanese died. Air observation posts added to the lethality, tempo, and flexibility of the U.S. Army in the terrible attrition of modern combat.

The United States and its Allies waged a successful war of materiel against the Axis between 1941 and 1945. To the troops on the receiving end, it may well have seemed a war of "brute force." The internal debate in the U.S. Army over the Air-Observation-Post Program suggests that, however massive the force, it was not mindless. Beyond the details of bureaucratic infighting, the disagreement shows ground and air officers engaged in an effort to make that force as powerful and discriminating as the technical means of the day would allow. The history of organic air thus suggests another reason for Allied victory— the rational and measured application of force implicit in a series of decisions made before units ever entered combat. It is a line of inquiry that deserves further development.[10]

While the impact of air observation posts on the conduct of the war was modest though real, the impact of World War II on air observation posts was overwhelming. The war generated the need for and served as the occasion of the establishment of modern organic aviation in the U.S. Army. A few years earlier the War Department had sufficient confidence in its control over the Air Corps that a separate organic aviation program appeared at best superfluous. Later, the Air Force as a separate service was simply too powerful to permit the initiation of an entirely new program. As the War Department's hold on its air arm weakened but before the Air Corps gained its complete independence, a relatively brief moment of opportunity existed. In that interval, responding to a set of imperatives divorced from the institutional evolution of the Air Corps, Danford and Ford pressed forward. Because of their efforts the Army possessed the institutional capacity to exploit the potential of the helicopter in the years after the war. At the same time the wartime experience with light aircraft imbued a large number of field artillery pilots and nonflying officers alike with the idea that helicopters constituted the next logical step in the evolution of organic aviation.

The success of the Field Artillery aviators in combat thus allowed the War Department to transform the Air-Observation-Post Program into Army Ground Forces Light Aviation in the summer of 1945. Light aircraft became available for the other combat arms. In 1949, with the Air Force a separate service, the Department of the Army renamed the program simply Army Aviation. The war also bequeathed certain administrative arrangements that persisted into the postwar period. The Air Force remained responsible for supply and

---

[10] See John Ellis, *Brute Force: Allied Strategy and Tactics in the Second World War* (New York: Viking, 1990), especially pages 525–41, which summarize his argument.

AN L-4 OF THE 1ST CAVALRY DIVISION TAKES OFF FROM ITIBASHI-KU AIRFIELD, TOKYO, JAPAN, OCTOBER 1945. WRECKED JAPANESE WARPLANES LINE THE SIDES OF THE FIELD.

upper-echelon maintenance of organic Army aircraft until 1949 and the elementary phase of Army Aviation pilot training and aircraft procurement until 1955. The Air Force transferred research and development to the Army as well, beginning in 1955 but in stages that took a decade to complete.

As the policies endured, so did the men. Wartime pilots largely dominated the organic aviation program in the first decade after the war and continued to exercise considerable influence in subsequent years. Col. Delbert L. Bristol commanded a brigade in the 11th Air Assault Division (Test) in 1963–1965; Col. J. Elmore Swenson remained on active duty into the early 1970s. Lt. Gen. Robert R. Williams retired in 1974. His high rank, however, was an exception. Most who remained on active duty after World War II did not become general officers. Nevertheless, they set a standard of excellence against which subsequent generations of Army aviators measured themselves. Air-observation-post pilots and ground crews also developed an innovative and can-do attitude, the "Cub spirit," that the very best aviation units exhibit to this day.

World War II also foreshadowed the future of relations between the Army and the Air Force over the existence of Army Aviation. Organic aviation in the ground forces proved controversial from its very inception. In this dispute each of two large, complex organizations claimed that the aerial observation mission fell under its own jurisdiction. Each had a view about how to carry it out congruent with how it performed its other missions—the Army Ground Forces from a combined arms perspective, the Army Air Forces from a centralized air power perspective. Unfortunately for peace and amity between the services, their views on this issue were diametrically opposed, particularly over command and control. Their positions were, however, logically compatible with their larger world views. In essence the controversy over air observation posts represented a clash between two competing ideologies. Acceptance of the premises of one ideology led logically to the conclusion that the premises of the other were completely in error.

In such a situation the only practical test outside the ideologies is the test of reality. "What works?" If that test is applied, then despite the implications of air power theory air observation posts were an essential part of the combined arms team during World War II. They met the demands of their marketplace—combat. In a very real sense the subsequent history of Army Aviation rests upon the record established by the men who served in the field artillery air sections during World War II—some 3,000 air-observation-post pilots, a similar number of aviation mechanics and mechanics' assistants, 1,500 radio operators, and over 1,000 aerial observers who, although not formally a part of the program, were essential to its success. They made what followed possible.

APPENDIX A

Selected U.S. Army Field Artillery and U.S. Army Air Forces Liaison Aircraft and Helicopters, 1942–1945

Fixed-Wing Aircraft[1]

L–1 Vigilant—Vultee-Stinson, two-place (pilot and observer). Observation, reconnaissance, and medical evacuation. Models ranging through F were obtained by the Army Air Forces. This aircraft was formerly designated O–49. All models were powered by a 295-horsepower Lycoming engine (R–680–9).

Model	Total Obtained	FY First Obtained	Notes
L–1	142	1942	
L–1A	182	1942	
L–1B	3	1942	Ambulance aircraft.
L–1C	1	1943	L–1A converted for use as an ambulance with one litter.
L–1D	21	1943	L–1A converted for familiarization in glider training.
L–1E	2	1943	L–1 converted for use as an amphibious ambulance.
L–1F	1	1943	L–1A converted for use as an amphibious ambulance.

---

[1] Excerpt from M. Sgt. Thomas M. Lang, "The Army Aviation Story, Part III: Fixed Wing Aircraft," *U.S. Army Aviation Digest* (*USAAD*) 8 (August 1962):13–17.

L-2 Grasshopper—Taylorcraft, two-place (pilot and observer). Observation and reconnaissance. Models range through M (except I). The Army Ground Forces and the Army Air Forces both used the L-2. The aircraft was formerly designated O-57. All models had a 65-horsepower engine except the L, which had a 50-horsepower Franklin.

Model	Total Obtained	FY First Obtained	Notes
L-2	74	1942	Tandem seating; Continental engine (O-170-3).
L-2A	476	1942	Tandem seating; Continental engine (O-170-3).
L-2B	490	1943	Tandem seating; Continental engine (O-170-3).
L-2C	1	1942	Tandem seating; commercially designated DC-65; Continental engine (A-65-8).
L-2D	1	1942	Tandem seating; commercially designated DL-65; Lycoming engine (O-145-B2).
L-2E	1	1942	Tandem seating; commercially designated DF-65; Franklin engine (4AC-150).
L-2F	1	1942	Side-by-side seating; commercially designated BL-65, formerly UC-95; Lycoming engine (O-145-B1).
L-2G	1	1942	Tandem seating; commercially designated BFT-65; Franklin engine (4AC-150).
L-2H	1	1942	Side-by-side seating; commercially designated BC-12-65; Continental engine (A-65-7).
L-2J	1	1942	Side-by-side seating; commercially designated BL-12-65; Lycoming engine (O-145-B1).
L-2K	1	1942	Side-by-side seating; commercially designated BF-12-65; Franklin engine (4AC-150).
L-2L	1	1942	Side-by-side seating; commercially designated BF-50; Franklin engine (4AC-150).
L-2M	900	1943	Tandem seating; Continental engine (O-170-3). Modified L-2A with the addition of spin strips.

L-3 Grasshopper—Aeronca, two-place (pilot and observer). Observation and reconnaissance. Military version of commercial Aeronca "Challenger." Models range through J (excluding I). The Army Ground Forces and the Army Air Forces both used the L-3. This aircraft was formerly designated O-58. All engines were 65-horsepower.

APPENDIX A

Model	Total Obtained	FY First Obtained	Notes
L–3	54	1942	Tandem seating; Continental engine (O–170–3).
L–3A	20	1942	Tandem seating; Continental engine (O–170–3); fuselage four inches wider than on the L–3.
L–3B	875	1942	Tandem seating; Continental engine (O–170–3).
L–3C	490	1943	Same as the L–3B, except that radio equipment was omitted; Continental engine (O–170–3).
L–3D	10	1942	Tandem seating; commercially designated 65–TF; Franklin engine (4AC–176).
L–3E	10	1942	Tandem seating; commercially designated 65–TC; Continental engine (A–65–8).
L–3F	1	1942	Side-by-side seating; commercially designated 65–CA; Continental engine (A–65–8).
L–3G	2	1942	Side-by-side seating; commercially designated 65–LB; Lycoming engine (O–145–B1).
L–3H	1	1942	Tandem seating; commercially designated 65–TL; Lycoming engine (O–145–B1).
L–3J	2	1942	Tandem seating; commercially designated 65–TC; Continental engine (A–65–7).

L–4 Grasshopper—Piper, two-place (pilot and observer, except F and G models). Observation and reconnaissance. Models range through J (excluding I). All have tandem seating except those indicated below. The Army obtained 5,671 of the L–4 series. Records at the Piper Aircraft Corporation indicate that between 1942 and 1945, there were 5,424 L–4s produced for the Army. However, Piper did not consider some models of its J series as L–4s, while the Army did. The L–4 was formerly designated O–59. The civilian nickname was "Cub."

Model	Total Obtained	FY First Obtained	Notes
L–4	144	1942	Commercially designated J3; 65-horsepower Continental engine (O–170–3).
L–4A	948	1942	Commercially designated J3C–65; 65-horsepower Continental engine (O–170–3).
L–4B	981	1943	Same as the L–4, but without radio.
L–4C	10	1942	Commercially designated J3L–65; 65-horsepower Lycoming engine (O–145–B1).

Model	Total Obtained	FY First Obtained	Notes
L–4D	5	1942	Commercially designated J3F–65; 65-horsepower Franklin engine (4AC–176).
L–4E	16	1942	Two-place, side-by-side seating; commercially designated J4E; used for pre-glider training; 75-horsepower Continental engine (A–75–9).
L–4F	45	1942	Three-place, one in front and two in back. Commercially designated J5A; used for pre-glider training; 75-horsepower Continental engine (A–75–9).
L–4G	41	1942	Same seating as L–4F; commercially designated J5B; used for pre-glider training; 100-horsepower Lycoming engine (GO–145–C2).
L–4H	1,801	1943	Improved L–4B with a fixed-pitch propeller; 65-horsepower Lycoming engine (O–170–3).
L–4J	1,680	1943	Same as L–4H, but with a controllable-pitch propeller.

L–5 Sentinel—Vultee-Stinson, two-place (pilot and observer). Observation, reconnaissance, and medical evacuation. Models range through G (excluding D, which was designed but cancelled prior to production). All have tandem seating. This aircraft was formerly designated O–62. The Army Ground Forces began using L–5s in 1943. All were powered with the 185-horsepower Lycoming engine except the G model, which was 190-horsepower. Models A through F had engine O–435–1; model F had O–435–2, and model G had O–435–11.

Model	Total Obtained	FY First Obtained	Notes
L–5	1,731	1942	Used by Army Air Forces and U.S. Navy.
L–5A	688	1942	Remodeled L–5 with 24-volt electrical system.
L–5B	679	1943	Modified to incorporate litter or cargo-carrying capability.
L–5C	200	1944	Modified for K–20 camera and litter.
L–5E	558	1944	Same as L–5C, except for drooping ailerons.
XL–5F	1	1944	Altered L–5B with a reworked engine.
L–5G	115	1945	Improved L–5E.

L–6—Interstate, two-place (pilot and observer). Observation and reconnaissance. Procured for use by the Army Air Forces, this tandem-seated aircraft was formerly designated O–63.

APPENDIX A 331

Model	Total Obtained	FY First Obtained	Notes
XL–6	1	1942	Commercially designated S–1B Cadet; 100-horsepower Franklin engine (XO–200–5).
L–6	250	1942	Commercially designated S–1B1 Cadet; 102-horsepower Franklin engine (O–200–5).

L–14—Piper, four-place (pilot, observer, and two passengers). Utility. A large Piper with long landing gear. The Army Ground Forces obtained five of these aircraft in fiscal years 1945–1946. Each had a 130-horsepower Lycoming engine (O–290–3). A production order for an additional 845 was cancelled on V-J Day.

L–15 Scout—Boeing, two-place (pilot and observer). Observation and reconnaissance. The Army obtained ten of these tandem-seated aircraft in 1949 for service tests only. Eventually, they were transferred to the Alaskan Forestry Service. Each had a 125-horsepower Lycoming engine (O–290–7).

Rotary-Wing Aircraft[2]

R–1—Platt-LePage, two-place (pilot and one passenger). Observation. The Army Air Forces obtained only one R–1 in FY 1944 and one R–1A in FY 1945. The R–1 had a 440-horsepower Pratt and Whitney engine (R–985–21), and the R–1A had a 450-horsepower Pratt and Whitney engine (R–985–AN–1).

R–4—Sikorsky, two-place (pilot and one passenger). Observation, reconnaissance, and medical evacuation. Models ranged through XR–4C and were used by the Army Air Forces. All models had side-by-side seating.

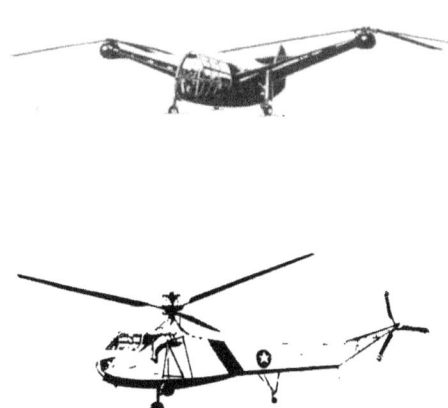

---

[2] Excerpt from M. Sgt. Thomas M. Lang, "The Army Aviation Story, Part IV: Rotary Wing Aircraft," *USAAD* 8 (September 1962):30–32.

Model	Total Obtained	FY First Obtained	Notes
XR–4	1	1942	This model featured an antitorque tail rotor. It had a 165-horsepower Warner engine (R–500–3).
YR–4A	3	1942	This model had a 180-horsepower Warner engine (R–550–1).
YR–4B	27	1943	This model was equipped with racks for litters or bombs. It had a 180-horsepower Warner engine (R–550–1). Three were transferred to the Navy.
R–4B	100	1944	This model had a range of 130 miles. It had a 200-horsepower Warner engine (R–550–3). Twenty were transferred to the Navy.
XR–4C	1	1943	This was a modified XR–4. It had a 180-horsepower Warner engine (R–550–1).

R–5—Sikorsky, two-place (pilot and one passenger). Observation. Models range through YR–5D. These aircraft were used by the Army Air Forces. All models except the YR–5D had a 450-horsepower Pratt and Whitney engine (R–985–AN–5). The D model had a 600-horsepower Pratt and Whitney engine (R–1340).

Model	Total Obtained	FY First Obtained	Notes
XR–5	5	1944	Tandem-rotor model; two were later converted to XR–5A. Other models all had a single rotor.
YR–5	0		This model was redesignated and completed as the YR–5A.
XR–5A	2	1944	Modified XR–5.
YR–5A	26	1944	Each aircraft equipped with two litters. Two were transferred to the Navy.
R–5A	34	1945	All were transferred to the Navy and the Coast Guard. Sixty-six had been ordered, but the contract was cancelled.
R–5B	0		Contract cancelled.
YR–5C	0		Contract cancelled.
YR–5D	20	1946	YR–5A with a more powerful engine.

R–6—Sikorsky, two-place (pilot and one passenger). Observation. Models range through R–6B. These aircraft were used by the Army Air Forces.

APPENDIX A

Model	Total Obtained	FY First Obtained	Notes
XR–6	1	1944	Side-by-side seating; 225-horsepower Lycoming engine (O–435–7).
XR–6A	5	1944	Same as XR–6, except for 240-horsepower Franklin engine (O–405–9). Three were transferred to the Navy.
XR–6A–NK	26	1944	Same as XR–6A, except it was manufactured by Nash-Kelvinator.
R–6A–NK	193	1945	Nash production model. Thirty-six transferred to the Navy.
R–6B–NK	0		Cancelled.

APPENDIX B

Letter from the Chief of Field Artillery Proposing Organic Air Observation for the Field Artillery, 15 July 1940[1]

COPY   COPY

334
T–1/B   (O5)

July 15, 1940.

Subject   :   Air Observation for Field Artillery.

To   :   The Adjutant General.

    1. This letter presents a brief discussion of the problem of air observation for Field Artillery and recommendations as to the proper organization of observation aviation considered essential for Field Artillery and for changes in the Air Board Report of September 15, 1939 (AG 320.2, (6–26–39), M–F M) which will be necessary if the preceding recommendations are put into effect.

    2. The Field Artillery is primarily interested in an airplane that can be used for observation (surveillance and adjustment) of artillery fire. Reconnaissance and liaison missions are considered of secondary importance in so far as the employment of field artillery observation aviation is concerned and will not be discussed herein.

        a. Suitable observation posts in average terrain for the surveillance and adjustment of artillery fires can seldom be found from which targets of importance to the Infantry or Cavalry can be located. Artillery observers who push forward with front line units have but limited perspective and are invariably concerned with the problems of their

---

[1] General Headquarters, U.S. Army, General Correspondence, 1940–1942, 665/1 (Fire Control Installations), Record Group 337, National Archives and Records Administration, Washington, D.C.

immediate fronts. In the defiladed areas in rear of the hostile lines targets (hostile troop concentrations, counterattacks forming, artillery batteries, and the like) which present a definite menace to the contact troops, are never seen except from the air. The primary mission of Field Artillery is to concentrate its fire on these targets, yet in 90% of the cases, terrestrial observation is non-existent for these types of targets. Therefore, if the Field Artillery is to perform its mission effectively, an elevated observation post which will allow surveillance of defiladed areas within hostile front lines to the limit of observation is absolutely necessary.

b. The solution is in some form of aircraft. As pointed out by the Chief of Field Artillery, in conference with the Chief of the Air Corps and the Chief Signal Officer in February, 1939, the problem concerns the three arms. The Air Corps to develop a suitable type of observation aircraft, the Signal Corps to furnish satisfactory communication equipment, and the Field Artillery to effect a suitable procedure in its employment and use. In the accomplishment of its part in this triangular responsibility, the Field Artillery has, for the past three years, given concentrated thought and study to the subject. Very definite ideas have been formulated as to needs (number and assignment of aircraft for artillery observation purposes), training of observers, and essential military characteristics of the type of airplane selected. A discussion and statement of each of these ideas follow:

(1) Needs: The artillery has concentrated its principal means for fire control and fire direction into the battalion. The sources of calls for fire of the battalion will be from supported units, higher units, adjacent units, and from its own observers. The most effective fire which the battalion can deliver will be observed fire irrespective of the source of call. Whenever practicable, terrestrial observers will be used; but, as stated earlier, effective terrestrial observation is seldom available. An aerial observation post is needed. Therefore, each b[a]ttalion should have at least one aircraft ready for use or immediately available at all times. One flight of not less than seven aircraft with pilots and maintenance crews should be an organic part of the equipment and personnel of each artillery brigade headquarters (square division and corps artillery) or regimental headquarters (triangular or armored division). This conclusion raises at once the questions of pilots, and personnel for and extent of maintenance. These may be answered, from an artillery viewpoint, as follows: It is expected that the operation of the relatively simple and inexpensive type of aircraft which will satisfy the requirements of division artillery, will not require as extensive training of the pilot as is required by combat aviation. Therefore, the division artillery can use those pilots who have received primary flying training but who cannot qualify for combat flying. As a result of the present flying training program, and the widespread influence it is likely to have on increasing flying throughout the nation, there should soon be a considerable number of suitable pilots. They could be enlisted in the Field Artillery, given basic field artillery training, and provided with a grade in the higher enlisted bracket commensurate with their work and training. The maintenance personnel, given initial training at Air Corps training centers, could be organized to form a section of the unit headquarters battery to which they pertain. It is contemplated that the maintenance of the aircraft will be similar to maintenance now performed by each field artillery unit on automotive and ordnance equipment. It is contemplated that the respective functions of the Air Corps and the Field Artillery in the development, procurement, operation, and maintenance of

APPENDIX B

aircraft for Field Artillery be the same as those of the Quartermaster Corps, the Ordnance Department, and the Field Artillery as regards motor transportation and weapons. Thus the Air Corps, in cooperation with the Field Artillery, would develop and procure aircraft suitable for field artillery observation and surveillance of fire and perform major repairs on, and overhaul of, these airplanes (corresponding to third and fourth echelon maintenance of motor vehicles by the Quartermaster Corps, see Section III, AR 850–15); the Field Artillery would operate the airplanes and perform servicing, preventive maintenance, and minor repair and unit replacement of parts (corresponding to first and second echelon maintenance of motor vehicles).

(2) <u>Training of observers</u>: Any officer of Field Artillery who has been trained in the observation of artillery fires from terrestrial observation posts and who has a knowledge of the reading of air photos and maps is an officer on whom should devolve the responsibility of satisfactorily performing artillery adjustments or the surveillance of artillery fires from the air. He should basically be so trained. Furthermore, in maneuvers or battle the artilleryman is familiar with the disposition of the artillery installations, the location of the batteries, location of the front lines and the situation in the front of his battalion. It has been the experience at the Field Artillery School and of recent maneuvers that the air observer must have a knowledge of artillery technique beyond that which it is practicable to give general observers in the time available at air corps training centers.

(3) <u>Essential military characteristics of artillery observation aircraft</u>: In order that an observation aircraft be immediately available to the artillery, it should be able to land and take off from small unprepared landing fields in the vicinity of the artillery command posts or along its route of march. Low cruising speed to permit of continued spotting of artillery fire is desirable but the primary consideration is low landing and takeoff speeds. For the past two years, the Field Artillery has insisted upon this characteristic in setting up military characteristics for the courier type airplane, short range liaison (light) now represented by the O–49, O–50, and O–51 airplanes. None of these airplanes have been tested to date by the Field Artillery. Additionally, the development of rotary wing aircraft, as a possibility in meeting full artillery needs, should be energetically pushed.

3. Extracts from recent military attache reports indicate that the idea of making an observation unit a part of the unit for which it observes is not revolutionary. For example, "In Germany x x x air units are attached to certain ground units; division observation squadrons, for example, wear the same uniform and insignia as the unit to which they are attached. <u>They are an integral part of the combat team to which they are assigned</u>." In England: "Small aircraft able to observe from inside our own lines over our own battery positions are strongly recommended. x x x x <u>They would be attached to land units and be extra eyes fro [sic] the army, quite apart from the general air arm</u>."

4. It is granted that the plan herein proposed by the Chief of Field Artillery for attaining efficiency in the air observation of artillery fire is not workable on the battle front if the enemy dominates the air. However, it is the confident expectation that our army is now embarked upon a preparedness program that will insure our dominance of the air on our next battlefield.

5. Accordingly, in order to insure the most effective employment of the division field artillery, it is strongly recommended:

<u>a.</u> That one flight of not less than seven aircraft with pilots and maintenance crews be assigned as an organic part of each artillery component of each infantry, motorized armored and cavalry division and of each corps artillery brigade.

<u>b.</u> That Tables of Organization and Tables of Basic Allowances of these units be changed accordingly, and

<u>c.</u> That the following changes be made in the Air Board Report of September 15, 1939:

Tab A; add a paragraph after paragraph <u>b</u> as follows:

<u>Field Artillery Observation Aviation</u>.

This consists of that aviation <u>organically</u> assigned as a part of field artillery brigades or regiments of division artillery units.

Tab B; add a paragraph as follows under the heading Observation and Liaison Aviation:

<u>Field Artillery Observation Aviation</u>.

To provide observation (adjustment and surveillance) of fires and reconnaissance for division field artillery units, and those corps units armed with the 155-mm howitzer.

Tab E; change subparagraph <u>b</u> to read:

"<u>b.</u> Detailed observation of the forward area of our own and the enemy's combat zone to include the location of objectives and the adjustment of <u>long range</u> artillery fires x x x x".

<u>d.</u> That aggressive experimental and development work be carried on at Fort Sill, Oklahoma, by the Field Artillery School, and at Fort Bragg, N. C. by the Field Artillery Board, with, at both places, the energetic cooperation of the Air Corps and the Signal Corps, to improve and perfect planes, communication equipment, and field artillery methods, in solving the problem of air observation of artillery fire with the highest attainable degree of efficiency.

For the Chief of Field Artillery:

/S/   Fred C. Wallace,
Colonel, Field Artillery,
Executive.

Bibliographical Note

Manuscript records available in the Washington, D.C., area form the essential foundation for this monograph. After I completed my research, the National Archives and Records Administration moved most post-1940 military records to the Archives II Building in College Park, Maryland. Historians need to check in advance as to the exact location of each file discussed below.

Only a portion of the records of the Office of the Chief of Field Artillery has survived in Record Group 177, Records of the Chiefs of Arms, at the National Archives. The records were divided shortly after the disestablishment of the office in 1942. Most of the files went to the Replacement and School Command, headquartered at Birmingham, Alabama. They do not appear to have found their way into the National Archives system. The most important of the surviving records are in the General Correspondence File, 1917–1942, organized by War Department decimal number. They should be supplemented by the General Correspondence, 1917–1942, Index File, which consists of the still-intact index cards to the whole file. Most cards have a one-sentence summary of the contents of the documents to which they refer. The Photographic File, 1917–1943, is a collection of photographs of Field Artillery equipment. The file is located with the textual records. Perhaps because the horse cavalry was soon to disappear from the Army, the records of the Office of the Chief of Cavalry were not broken up when the office was abolished, and they have made their way into the Archives relatively intact. The General Correspondence File, 1923–1942, also in Record Group 177, holds many documents pertaining to the Field Artillery's as well as the Cavalry's efforts to obtain organic aviation. The Office of the Chief of Infantry, General Correspondence File, 1920–1942, in the same record group, suffered the same fate as the records of the Office of the Chief of Field Artillery. No records pertaining to aviation remain in this file, although correspondence by the chief of Infantry on this subject appears in the files of the other offices.

Record Group 337, Records of the Army Ground Forces, is the single most important collection for the study of air observation posts during World War II. The very valuable General Headquarters, Decimal Correspondence File, 1940–1942, is less useful than it once was. It shows evidence of systematic weeding. The Headquarters, Army Ground Forces, General Correspondence File, 1942–1948, is very rich for the years 1942–1943 and 1946–1948. While the records were on loan to the Office of the Chief of Army Field Forces, the successor headquarters, a colonel on the Army Field Forces staff, in what can only be characterized as a disastrous decision, destroyed approximately 95 percent of the headquarters records covering the last two years of the war. Apparently, he acted on the assumption that they were "waste paper." The Archives further compounded the confusion when, sometime after accession, they combined several distinct files into one "general correspondence file." At the time I did my research, this file was extraordinarily difficult to use, but the richness of the contents amply repaid the labor. Since then, Ms. Jo Anna Williamson of the National Archives staff has compiled a magnificent finding aid, "Record Group 337, Headquarters, Army Ground Forces, List of Folder Titles," which is available in draft form to researchers at the National Archives. Its publication and wide dissemination would be a boon for World War II scholars. The General Correspondence File provides the best extant contemporary record of developments at the Department of Air Training.

The reports of Army Ground Forces observers from the overseas theaters are also excellent contemporary sources for the evolution of air-observation-post tactics and techniques in combat. The records of one small staff subsection, the Decimal Correspondence File, 1942–1945, of the Field Artillery Branch in the Developments Division of the Requirements Section, G–4, have survived and fill in some of the gaps in the General Correspondence File. Most of these records, however, relate to developments overseas rather than to the evolution of policy in the continental United States. Also useful are the Historical Reports and Background Papers of Army Field Forces, 1942–1945, consisting of the monographs prepared by the command historians with the comments of the various staff sections. Some files contain extended memorandums for record based on interviews conducted with members of the headquarters staff during the war. A separate portion of the file consists of memorandums for record prepared by the command group of the Replacement and School Command covering the period 1944–1945. These appear to be the only extant records of this headquarters. A small file, Personal Correspondence of the Commanding General, Army Ground Forces, 1942–1945, contains items found in Lt. Gen. Lesley J. McNair's office after his death, in addition to some correspondence relating to the first few months of General Jacob L. Devers' tenure. Included in this collection are the Seventh Army report on Sicily with staff comments and the Ford-McNair correspondence. A few World War II documents are also available in the records of the successor Office of the Chief of Army Field Forces, in particular the Secret Decimal Correspondence File, 1949–1950, which contains a copy of the Robert R. Williams report.

Record Group 18, Records of the Army Air Forces, is something of a misnomer, because it encompasses documents dated as early as 1912. The following files proved particularly useful: Office of the Chief of the Air Corps, Central Decimal File, 1939–1942, and Security Classified Central Decimal File, 1939–1942; and Headquarters, Army Air Forces, Central Decimal File, 1942–1944, Security Classified Central Decimal File, 1942–1944, Central Decimal File, 1945, and Security Classified Central Decimal File, 1945. Army Air Corps and Army Air Forces records include not only documents providing the views of the Office of the Chief of the Air Corps and later the Air Staff but of the ground arms as well. They are particularly valuable in bridging the gaps in the Office of the Chief of Field Artillery and General Headquarters records prior to March 1942 and the 1944–1945 gap in Army Ground Forces records.

The General Correspondence File, 1941–1945, and the Security Classified Correspondence File, 1941–1945, of the Assistant Secretary of War (John J. McCloy), in Record Group 107, Office of the Secretary of War, are particularly useful for McCloy's role in establishing the program and his attempts to protect it from what he considered unfair criticism during its startup phase. The Secretary of War, Special Reports File, 1940–1945, contains material on the evolution of mobilization policies and their effect on the Field Artillery.

Unfortunately, to save space the National Archives destroyed most of the Chief of Staff, Army, Correspondence, 1921–1942, in Record Group 165, War Department General and Special Staffs. Among those records lost are many of the documents pertaining to the establishment of the initial test group. The Chief of Staff, Army, Correspondence, 1942–1945, is valuable, but most air-observation-post questions were handled by lower echelons of the General Staff during this period. The Office of the Chief of Staff, Army, Minutes and Notes of Conferences Relating to Emergency Planning Program, 1938–1945, is a small but exceedingly useful collection. At the time of my research the Archives staff believed that the Army had destroyed the Assistant Chief of Staff, G–3, Numerical File, 1941–1945. I was able to piece together G–3 policies and activities, particularly important for the year in which the G–3 Division handled all staff actions pertaining to air observation posts, by consulting the records of several other staff agencies. Fortunately, the report of the records' destruction proved premature. They resurfaced during the movement of records from Archives I to Archives II. The G–4 records, Numerical Correspondence, 1921–1942, Decimal Correspondence, 1942–1946, and Decimal Correspondence, 1946, have survived and are most useful, particularly for matters relating to equipment. The G–4 usually retained only internally generated documents. Its records can be misleading if they are the only ones available on an issue. The records of the War Plans Division, Numerical Correspondence, 1921–1942, hold several documents pertaining to War Department policy toward organic aviation. The successor Operations Division, Decimal Correspondence File, 1942–1946, contains considerable information concerning air observation posts in the overseas theaters. The New Developments Division, Decimal File, 1944–1946, and the Research and Development Division, Decimal File, 1943–1947, are invaluable on certain aspects of arming light aircraft.

Record Group 407, Records of the Adjutant General, 1917–1988, contains information on the action taken by the War Department on any subject, something that is not always available in other files. In many instances, however, these files contain only the decision paper for any particular issue rather than the staff backup papers that give the rationale for the action taken. A few include extensive backup documents that permit reconstruction of the internal staff debate. The following files proved particularly useful: Decimal Correspondence, 1926–1939; Decimal Correspondence, 1940–1945; Security Classified Decimal Correspondence, 1940–1942; and Security Classified Decimal Correspondence, 1943–1945. The Adjutant General World War II Operational Records, 1940–1948, are also part of Record Group 407. They contain detailed accounts of specific operations, but usually the Army Ground Forces records proved more useful for the doctrinal implications of those operations.

The Still Picture Branch of the National Archives, now located in College Park, Maryland, contains the following photographic collections valuable to the student of Field Artillery aviation: Record Group 80, Department of the Navy, World War II (80–G); and Record Group 111, Office of the Chief Signal Officer, World War II Personalities File (111–P), World War II Color Photographs (111–C), and World War II Signal Corps Central Photographic File (111–SC). These files are valuable primarily for the pictures of senior and midlevel supporters of the Air-Observation-Post Program, as well as a few operational photographs. Photographs of pilots and ground crew are less numerous, and the individuals are often not identified by name.

The U.S. Army Center of Military History maintains a number of useful manuscript collections in its permanent holdings. The Unit History Files of the Organizational History Branch provide authoritative information as to the designation and campaign credits of all active (and many inactive) units in the Army. The Historical Resources Branch, besides having an incomparable collection of manuscript histories, including a complete set of the Army Ground Forces Historical Monographs produced during and immediately after the war, maintains a collection of public affairs biographies of general officers dating back to World War II. The Center of Military History Library has several bound manuscript reports of wartime operations. In addition, while preparing this study, I had access to the backup files collected by Maj. Donald F. Harrison in his work on a history of Army Aviation for the Center of Military History. Unfortunately, most of the materials pertaining to World War II had disappeared from the Harrison files.

The U.S. Air Force Historical Research Agency, formerly the Albert F. Simpson Historical Center, at Maxwell Air Force Base, Alabama, has a rich collection of World War II documents. These include papers gathered by the historians writing the official history of the Army Air Forces in that conflict, as well as the quarterly historical reports prepared in the field during the war by Army Air Forces commands and subordinate units, copies of which were forwarded to the Army Air Forces historical office. All these records have been microfilmed and are available at the Air Force History Support Office (formerly the Center for Air Force History), Anacostia Naval Air Station, Washington, D.C. They contain some information about liaison aircraft found nowhere else.

The Historical Division of the Office of the Secretary of Defense holds the transcript of an interview by Dr. Maurice Matloff with John J. McCloy that, while not referring to McCloy's efforts in behalf of light aircraft, is very instructive as to both his personality and his duties in the War Department.

The Manuscripts Division of the Library of Congress in Washington, D.C., contains the papers of a number of senior Army Air Forces officers, including General Henry H. Arnold. This collection was a disappointment. All the air-observation-post materials in the Arnold papers only duplicate holdings in the National Archives. While the George S. Patton, Jr., Papers, also at the Library of Congress, include only a few documents and clippings pertaining to light aviation, they were very instructive. The Library of Congress also has a microfilm copy of the Henry L. Stimson diaries; the originals are located at Yale University. This is a magnificent source for the highest-level political and military decisions of World War II. Given the magnitude and variety of issues with which Stimson dealt as secretary of war, it is not surprising that he did not record anything in his diary about air observation posts.

The National Air and Space Museum Library, Smithsonian Institution, contains a priceless collection of photographs. At the time I did my research, these included the official photographs of the Army Air Forces during World War II. Subsequently the Smithsonian transferred the Army Air Forces photographs to the Still Picture Branch of the National Archives. The staff at the National Air and Space Museum Library maintains an Aircraft Reference File arranged by aircraft model number and a General Reference File that includes information about aircraft engines and other components. Both these files repay close study.

The John J. McCloy Papers, Special Collections, Amherst College Library, Amherst, Massachusetts, contain particularly rich holdings for the period during which McCloy served as assistant secretary of war. For the purposes of this study, his diary, which began as a simple daily list of appointments and evolved into something much more, proved particularly useful.

The George C. Marshall, Jr., Papers at the George C. Marshall Library on the campus of the Virginia Military Institute, Lexington, Virginia, provide abundant information to students of World War II and the institutional development of the U.S. Army in the first half of the twentieth century. Only a few scattered items, however, pertain to air observation posts.

The U.S. Army Military History Institute at Carlisle Barracks, Pennsylvania, proved a very useful source of Field Artillery air-observation-post documents. The Robert M. Danford, John E. P. Morgan, Rex E. Chandler, Edward M. Almond, and Hamilton H. Howze Papers deserve careful examination. In the 1970s Army War College students conducted a series of interviews pertaining to the history of Army Aviation. The most pertinent to the history of air observation posts during World War II are the Delbert L. Bristol, O. Glenn Goodhand, and Robert R. Williams transcripts, although the Edwin Powell and the two Hamilton H. Howze interviews, one part of the Senior Officers' Oral History Collection, make some references to Field Artillery aviation during the war.

The Morris Swett Technical Library at the Field Artillery School, Fort Sill, Oklahoma, contains a stupendous amount of manuscripts, virtually all bound, pertaining to the history of the U.S. Army Field Artillery during the twentieth century. These collections are absolutely indispensable to the student of air-observation-post operations during World War II, because the overwhelming majority of all reports about Field Artillery aircraft are sections or annexes to larger reports dealing with all phases of Field Artillery operations. The Field Artillery School and Fort Sill Museum also has a small library and photographic and manuscript holdings that deserve careful scrutiny.

The U.S. Army Aviation Museum Library at Fort Rucker, Alabama, has a sizable collection of World War II materials. The library's holdings include the extensive J. Elmore Swenson Papers. The files of the *U.S. Army Aviation Digest*, located at the library, contain the surviving backup materials (primarily notes of interviews) for Richard J. Tierney's and Fred Montgomery's *The Army Aviation Story* (Northport, Ala.: Colonial Press, 1963). The library also maintains a substantial photographic collection, which contains many Signal Corps photographs that were never forwarded to the Central Photographic File of the Office of the Chief Signal Officer in Washington. The core of this collection came to the library from the *Aviation Digest*, but donations from aviators and their families have enlarged it further.

The real strength of the collections of the Army Aviation Technical Library of the Army Aviation School at Fort Rucker begins with the 1950s. Still, the library contains a few documents, almost always bound, dating from World War II. Some of the materials on the Brodie device are available nowhere else.

The holdings of the Historical Office, U.S. Army Aviation and Troop Command (formerly the U.S. Army Aviation Systems Command), St. Louis, Missouri, were likewise devoted to the 1950s and subsequent years. They did include, however, the very important interviews that Laurence Epstein conducted with Delbert L. Bristol, Thomas I. Case, and Joseph M. Watson, as well as small collections of the personal papers of Watson and Wesley Brisben. After I completed my research there, the Department of the Army closed this headquarters as a separate command and shifted the aviation functions to the newly designated U.S. Army Aviation and Missile Command at Redstone Arsenal, Alabama. The holdings of the Historical Office were scheduled for transfer there.

The Army Aviation Association of America in Westport, Connecticut, maintains an important collection of biographical information and photographs pertaining to significant participants in the program. I was able to borrow these materials thanks to the kindness of Mr. Arthur Kesten.

Three memoirs deserve special mention. Shortly before his death, Brig. Gen. William W. Ford arranged for the private publication of his recollections, *Wagon Soldier* (North Adams, Mass.: Excelsior Printing Co., 1980). They are very valuable for the test phase of the program but skip the period when he was director of Air Training at Fort Sill. Brig. Gen. Carl I. Hutton did not enter the aviation program until after the war, but his wartime memoir, "An Armored Artillery Commander in the European Theater," available in manuscript at the Morris Swett Technical Library, is packed with commentary about air observation posts. General Hamilton H. Howze's memoir, "35 Years and Then Some: Memoirs of a Professional Soldier," was available only in manuscript form at the Military History Institute when I conducted my research. The Smithsonian Institution published it as *A Cavalryman's Story: Memoirs of a Twentieth Century Army General* (Washington, D.C.: Smithsonian Institution Press, 1996). Less focused on World War II than Hutton's work, it nevertheless contains valuable insights and is delightful to read.

I had access to the personal papers, still in private hands, of the following participants in the Field Artillery aviation program: Delbert L. Bristol, Charles M. Brown, Robert F. Cassidy, Charles W. Lefever, William R. Mathews, John W. Oswalt, Theodore J. Schirmacher, Claude Shepard, Michael J. Strok, Henry L. Wann, Bryce Wilson, Gordon J. Wolf, and Robert R. Yeats. Most consist of only a few documents and clippings, but the Bristol, Strok, Wolf, and Yeats collections are quite extensive. Mrs. Marcia Strok plans to donate the Strok papers, which include the A. R. Hackbarth class notes and training literature from the Department of Air Training, reminiscences of veterans, and extensive photographs from North Africa and Italy, to the Army Aviation Museum Library. The Lefever materials consist of a large photographic collection and some clippings—all very valuable. I interviewed all these men—although in Colonel Wolf's case the primary interview was by proxy—except Colonel Bristol, who died before this project began. His wife, Mrs. Vivian Bristol, very kindly consented to an interview. I also interviewed Chauncey Eskridge, Jack R. Forbes, Thomas E. Haynes, James T. Kerr, Richard L. Long, Delk Oden, Maxwell D. Taylor, Richard K. Tierney, and Robert R. Williams. I did not have an opportunity to interview Brig. Gen. William W. Ford, although General Ford sent some very informative letters before his death.

A number of professional and business journals provide valuable firsthand accounts of the war. *The Field Artillery Journal* was an indispensable source on developments in the Field Artillery before, during, and after the war. *Military Review*, the publication of the U.S. Army Command and General Staff College, also contained several important articles on air observation posts in the war and postwar periods. Articles in *The Cavalry Journal* helped put the 1941–1942 Fort Knox and Fort Benning experiments with light aviation in perspective. *Western Flying* and *American Aviation* gave the industry perspective during this period. A perusal of the first volumes of *American Helicopter* provided a good introduction to the state of helicopter technology at the end of the war. Over the years, the *U.S. Army Aviation Digest*, the official publication of the Army Aviation School, and *Army Aviation*, the unofficial publication of the Army Aviation Association of America, have included scattered firsthand accounts of the wartime experience. Both journals began publication in the 1950s, however, and have given greater space to more contemporary conflicts. A more recent publication, the *L–4 Grasshopper Wing Newsletter*, initially edited by Col. (Ret.) Michael J. Strok, has placed considerable emphasis on publishing World War II–era memoirs. Its back files will be indispensable for any future student of the subject.

The historical literature on air observation posts is relatively small but includes several first-rate works. Two of the best are two of the earliest. Irving B. Holley, Jr., first prepared *Evolution of the Liaison-Type Airplane, 1917–1944,* Army Air Forces Historical Studies 44 (Washington, D.C.: Headquarters, Army Air Forces, 1945) in 1944 while a captain with the Army Air Forces Air Technical Service Command Historical Office. While his treatment of liaison aircraft occurs in something of a doctrinal vacuum and mirrors many of the limitations of contemporary Air Staff views, his monograph remains the best discussion of the evolution of the standard observation-type aircraft in the 1920s and 1930s. As the first historian to treat military technology in a subtle and sophisticated fashion, he has placed all his successors in his debt. Kent Roberts Greenfield was a colonel and chief historian of Army Ground Forces when he completed his monograph, *Army Ground Forces and the Air-Ground Battle Team, Including Organic Light Aviation,* in 1945, but it was not published in offset form until later as AGF Historical Study 35 (Washington, D.C.: Historical Section, Army Ground Forces, 1948). He devoted three chapters to air observation posts. Writing from a Headquarters, Army Ground Forces, perspective, Greenfield overemphasizes the personal role of the commanding general while undervaluing the work at Fort Sill and largely ignoring the overseas theaters except as they impinged upon policy formulation at Army Ground Forces. This skewed perspective stemmed from Greenfield's larger purpose, to write a backup monograph for a comprehensive narrative history of the Army Ground Forces, which was never completed. Greenfield depended entirely upon Army Ground Forces records, which means that his account of the origin of the Air-Observation-Post Program is seriously flawed. Likewise, his narrative trails off in the summer of 1945, undoubtedly reflecting when he prepared it. The monograph's great strength is Greenfield's concision and analytical skill. He packs a great deal of information into a very limited space. Like Holley's work, it did not receive the wide circulation it deserved.

Two other official histories, Richard P. Weinert, Jr., *A History of Army Aviation, 1950–1962*, TRADOC Historical Monograph Series (Fort Monroe, Va.: Office of the Command Historian, 1991), a one-volume reprint of two monographs prepared in 1971 and 1976, and Donald F. Harrison, "A History of Army Aviation" (Unpublished Manuscript, Office of the Chief of Military History, 1971) do not represent an advance on Greenfield in their treatment of 1942–1945 and are primarily valuable for their account of the subsequent history of Army Aviation and the perspective it provides on the World War II experience. Howard K. Butler's *Army Air Corps Airplanes and Observation, 1935–1941* (St. Louis, Mo.: U.S. Army Aviation Systems Command, 1990) and *Organic Aviation in the Ground Arms, 1941–1947* (St. Louis, Mo.: U.S. Army Aviation Systems Command, 1992) are solidly but narrowly based on the official records. Dr. Butler has done a tremendous amount of research in the National Archives, but his footnoting technique makes it difficult to locate the individual documents he cites. At the same time, he has been most gracious in helping me locate documents at the Archives. His "Command, Control, and Operation of Army Liaison Airplanes in the Pacific in World War II," a paper presented at the Conference of Army Historians in June 1994, while my manuscript was undergoing revision, helped me avoid several mistakes. Throughout his work his focus is on policy formulation with particular emphasis on the logistical component.

Like all veterans, air-observation-post pilots did not want the record of their exploits to fade from the collective memory of the war. This helped produce several memorial volumes resting primarily on interviews, two of which are of sufficiently high quality to deserve mention. Lt. Col. Andrew Ten Eyck, an Army Air Forces officer, wrote *Jeeps in the Sky: The Story of the Light Plane* (New York: Commonwealth Books, 1946). Lt. Col. Robert M. Leich worked very closely with Ten Eyck and made Army Ground Forces records available to him. Although Ten Eyck did not use footnotes, I located some of the documents he used and found that he gave very accurate summaries. For some of the 1944 and 1945 documents that were destroyed by the Army, he and Greenfield constitute the best sources for the information they contained. Ken Wakefield in *The Fighting Grasshoppers: U.S. Liaison Aircraft Operations in Europe, 1942–1945* (Stillwater, Minn.: Specialty Press, 1990) relied heavily on interviews, but he also examined Army Air Forces records in some detail. Where an opportunity existed to check his account against the official records, it proved very reliable.

Three articles by John W. Kitchens, until recently the command historian at the Army Aviation Center, provide the best summary of the existing literature: "Organic Aviation in World War II, 1940–1943," *U.S. Army Aviation Digest* (May–June 1992):10–17; "Organic Aviation in World War II, 1944–1945," *U.S. Army Aviation Digest* (July–August 1992):14–25, and "Army Aviation and the Helicopter," *Army Aviation* 40 (31 May 1991):36–39. His two-part article, "They Also Flew: Pioneer Black Army Aviators," *U.S. Army Aviation Digest* (September–October 1994):34–39 and (November–December 1994):34–39, goes well beyond the existing literature and is the best available account on the subject. Kitchens buttressed his work with extensive research at the Air Force Historical Research Agency.

Herbert P. LePore, Kitchen's predecessor at Fort Rucker, wrote "Army Aviation in the North African Campaign," *Military Review* 72 (November 1992):80–83. It is both more and less than the title implies. Lepore provides a summary of the evolution of observation aviation up to the North African campaign but as a consequence devotes less attention than might be expected to the conduct of air observation posts in the campaign.

Two semiofficial publications, prepared during the Vietnam War by civilians close to the program, are worthy of note. The earlier-mentioned *Army Aviation Story* is by Tierney and Montgomery, the editors of the *U.S. Army Aviation Digest*. Unfortunately, particularly for World War II, they did not have on hand the documents that would have corrected some of their misconceptions about the organization of the Army at that time. Still, the authors succeeded in what they intended—they captured in print the recollections of a generation of officers who were rapidly passing from the active list. W. E. Butterworth, a staff writer for the U.S. Army Aviation Safety Board, prepared *Flying Army: The Modern Air Arm of the U.S. Army* (Garden City, N.Y.: Doubleday, 1971), which is particularly strong on aviation technology. A fine writer, Butterworth went on to produce a series of novels under the pen name W. E. B. Griffin.

Army Aviation has attracted only slight attention from academics. By far the most important study to date is Frederic A. Bergerson, *The Army Gets an Air Force: Tactics of Insurgent Bureaucratic Politics* (Baltimore: Johns Hopkins University Press, 1980), the work of a political scientist who was also an Army helicopter pilot in Vietnam. He relied largely on interviews, and, as his subtitle indicates, the volume carries a heavy weight of theory, arguing that lower-ranking members of a bureaucracy can initiate and carry into effect far-reaching change. His thesis was recently attacked strongly by Christopher Chien-San Cheng, a young historian also interested in theory, in "United States Army Aviation and the Air Mobility Innovation, 1942–1965" (Ph.D. dissertation, University of London, 1992). Cheng's study is solidly grounded in the published record and is strongest for the 1950s. A revised version has recently been published as *Air Mobility: The Development of a Doctrine* (Westport, Conn.: Greenwood Press, 1994). Nevertheless, Bergerson, in part because he based his account on his own experience, has the better of the argument. He certainly has a better feel for the ethos of the U.S. Army. Neil F. Rogers' 1992 Northern Arizona University dissertation, "World War II Liaison Aviation in the United States Armed Forces," is strongest on equipment. The author's archival research appears to have been restricted to the records at the Air Force Historical Research Agency.

Accounts of the virtually simultaneous effort by officers of the Royal Artillery to obtain their own air observation posts proved very useful in understanding some of the problems their American counterparts faced. H. J. Parham and E. M. G. Belfield, *Unarmed into Battle: The Story of the Air Observation Post* (Winchester, U.K.: Warren and Son, 1956), combines both history and memoir. General Parham was the key figure in starting the British program. Peter Mead, *The Eye in the Air: History of Air Observation and Reconnaissance for the Army, 1785–1945* (London: Her Majesty's Stationery Office, 1983), provides a thoughtful discussion of the evolution of the mission. Shelford Bidwell, *Gunners at War: A Tactical Study of the Royal Artillery in the Twentieth Century* (London: Arms and Armour Press, 1970), places air observation posts within the context of the development of British artillery. Sir Anthony Farrar-Hockley, *The Army in the Air (The History of the Army Air Corps)* (Dover, N.H.: Alan Sutton Publishing, Inc., 1994), provides a fuller exposition of postwar than wartime developments. His short account of World War II, however, gives the clearest perspective of where the Air-Observation-Post Program fit in terms of the various aviation initiatives that the British Army undertook between 1939 and 1945.

This study may be termed an example of the emerging cultural interpretation of the armed forces, although it places more emphasis on doctrinal differences than on the social milieu of the services. Doctrine is both a prescription for dealing with the chaos of combat and an ingrained world view that can be considered an ideology. The interpretation has emerged from a host of detailed monographic studies that extend back across three generations of scholarship. One of the earliest, and one of the best, is Elting E. Morison, *Admiral Sims and the Modern American Navy* (Boston: Houghton Mifflin and Co., 1942). In this volume, Morison does not so much make a cultural interpretation as provide the materials for one. The same might be said for Peter Karsten, *The Naval Aristocracy: The Golden Age of Annapolis and the Emergence of Modern American Navalism* (New York: Free Press,

1972). Karsten argues that naval officers in the age of Mahan functioned as a self-interested political pressure group, but in the process he provides much interesting information for a cultural interpretation.

Three books might be termed breakthrough volumes. Samuel P. Huntington, *The Soldier and the State: The Theory and Politics of Civil-Military Relations* (New York: Vintage Books, 1957), and Morris Janowitz, *The Professional Soldier: A Social and Political Portrait* (New York: Free Press, 1960), are not so much interested in distinguishing among the services but in differentiating between the military on one hand and the civilian society on the other. Elting E. Morison, *Men, Machines, and Modern Times* (Cambridge: Massachusetts Institute of Technology Press, 1966), by defining a military service as a society organized around a weapons system, made such distinctions possible.

Eight books and one unpublished essay are key to understanding the centrality of a combined arms perspective to the U.S. Army. Perry D. Jamieson, *Crossing the Deadly Ground: United States Army Tactics, 1865–1899* (Tuscaloosa: University of Alabama Press, 1994), states with clarity and concision the tactical dilemma the U.S. Army confronted in a machine-age war and the first steps it took to confront it. Timothy K. Nenninger, *The Leavenworth Schools and the Old Army: Education, Professionalism, and the Officer Corps of the United States Army, 1881–1918*, Contributions in Military History, No. 15 (Westport, Conn.: Greenwood Press, 1978), provides an account of the school that was the intellectual center of professional reform prior to World War I. Harry P. Ball, *Of Responsible Command: A History of the U.S. Army War College* (Carlisle Barracks, Pa.: Alumni Association of the U.S. Army War College, 1983), gives a sophisticated view of the capstone institution for the professional education of the Army. Carol Reardon, *Soldiers and Scholars: The U.S. Army and the Uses of Military History, 1865–1920* (Lawrence: University Press of Kansas, 1990), examines one facet of that professional education. Allan R. Millett, *The General: Robert L. Bullard and Officership in the United States Army, 1881–1925*, Contributions in Military History, no. 10 (Westport, Conn.: Greenwood Press, 1975), provides a life-and-times biography of one of the leading military intellectuals of his generation. Edward M. Coffman, *The Old Army: A Portrait of the American Army in Peacetime, 1784–1898* (New York: Oxford University Press, 1986), describes the social context in which these ideas developed during the nineteenth century. Before Russell Weigley launches into an explication of the details of the campaigns of 1944–1945 in France and Germany, he makes some very perceptive observations about the relationship between unit organization and combat power in *Eisenhower's Lieutenants: The Campaigns of France and Germany, 1944–1945* (Bloomington: Indiana University Press, 1981). The first account to pull this all together is Rand B. Beers, "The Fusion of the Combined Arms Team: The Army Officer Corps, 1898–1950," a paper presented at the U.S. Army Center of Military History on 13 June 1979. A manuscript copy is in the files of the Historical Resources Branch. A combined arms perspective is central to Michael D. Doubler's *Closing with the Enemy: How GIs Fought the War in Europe, 1944–1945* (Lawrence: University Press of Kansas, 1994). There is no American equivalent to Shelford Bidwell and Dominick Graham, *Firepower: British Army Weapons and Theories of War, 1904–1945* (Boston: Allen and Unwin, 1982).

The world view of the Army Air Forces and the Air Force is revealed in DeWitt S. Copp, *A Few Great Captains: The Men and Events That Shaped the Development of U.S.*

Air Power (New York: Doubleday, 1980); his sequel, *Forged in Fire: Strategy and Decisions in the Airwar Over Europe, 1940–1945* (New York: Doubleday, 1982); and James Parton, *"Air Force Spoken Here": General Ira Eaker and the Command of the Air* (Bethesda, Md.: Adler and Adler, 1986). All three studies fall into the category of books that reveal both more and other than what their authors intended. The Parton volume, however, is much more sophisticated and historically important. If Copp and Parton are celebratory, Michael Sherry, *The Rise of American Airpower: The Creation of Armageddon* (New Haven, Conn.: Yale University Press, 1987), is critical. Sherry focuses on the acceptance of airpower theory—and the strategic air campaigns of World War II—by the American public. Sherry is thus concerned about American culture as a whole rather than service culture, but he makes many incisive comments about the latter in passing.

The debate over Department of Defense reform in the early 1980s, culminating in the passage of the Goldwater-Nichols Act in 1986, first brought the cultural interpretation to the fore. The veteran Pentagon correspondent Arthur T. Hadley, *The Straw Giant: Triumph and Failure, America's Armed Forces, A Report from the Field* (New York: Random House, 1986), advanced it to explain differences between the Army and the Navy. The Air Force, however, remained something of a mystery to him. Edgar F. Raines, Jr., and David R. Campbell, *The Army and the Joint Chiefs of Staff: Evolution of Army Ideas on the Command, Control, and Coordination of the U.S. Armed Forces, 1942–1985*, Historical Analysis Series (Washington, D.C.: U.S. Army Center of Military History, 1986), used the combined arms perspective to explain Army views on the creation and subsequent attempts to reform the Joint Chiefs of Staff. Carl H. Builder, *The Masks of War: American Military Styles in Strategy and Analysis*, RAND Corporation Research Study (Baltimore: Johns Hopkins University Press, 1989), provided the first satisfactory explanation of the culture of the three major services. This was the same interpretation that Admiral William J. Crowe and David Chanoff advanced in *The Line of Fire: From Washington to the Gulf, the Politics and Battles of the New Military* (New York: Simon and Schuster, 1993), except that they also had some perceptive things to say about the Marine Corps. Eliot A. Cohen used the same interpretive model as an important subtheme in his 1994 analysis of the future of defense downsizing, "What To Do About National Defense," *Commentary* 58 (November 1994):21–32. Michael R. Gordon and Lt. Gen. (Ret.) Bernard E. Trainor employ the concept of service cultures to explain the U.S. military's conduct of the Gulf War in *The Generals' War: The Inside Story of the Conflict in the Gulf* (Boston: Little, Brown, and Co., 1995).

The growing popularity of the cultural interpretation indicates a much more sophisticated and sympathetic understanding of the military than was conceivable in the not too distant past. The danger of such an interpretation is that mechanistically applied it can become an all-purpose absolution for bureaucratic obstructionism, institutional obscurantism, and command error.

Military Map Symbols

Military Units—Identification

Airborne Infantry	⊠
Armor	⊠
Armored Cavalry	E
Armored Infantry	◯
Engineers	⌀
Infantry	⊠

Size Symbols

Corps	x x x
Division	x x
Brigade	x
Regiment	I I I
Battalion or Armored Cavalry Squadron	I I

Index

Accidents: 309, 314–15
    in European Theater of Operations: 198–99, 208–09
    in Italy: 173, 184
    during landings: 74, 173, 209
    on Okinawa: 314–15
    in Philippines: 260, 263
    reporting system in European Theater: 198–99
    using the Brodie device: 267
Acerno, Italy: 171
Adachi, Lt. Gen. Hatazo: 253
Adams, Lt. Col. John C. L.: 102–03, 110, 111n, 121–22, 235
Adams, Lt. Col. R. H.: 112
Adjutant General of the Army: 63–64
Administrative flights: 166, 173, 174
Aerial evacuation. *See* air ambulances.
Aerial rockets: 298–99
Aeronca Aircraft Corporation: 49, 50, 64, 87–88, 92–93, 95, 111–12, 117, 118
African Americans
    at Department of Air Training: 126, 290, 291
    as mechanics: 290
    as officers: 134
    as pilots: 126, 134, 137, 290, 291
Air ambulances
    HE–1 used at Fort Sill: 127
    L–4s used as, in European Theater: 227
    L–4s used as, in Southwest Pacific Area: 253, 257, 259, 271
    L–5s used as: 259, 261
Air-armor cooperation: 45
Air cavalry: 122
Air Commando, First: 287
Air Corps, Office of the Chief of: 16, 38, 49
Air Corps Act: 14–15
Air Corps Materiel Division: 48
Air Corps Tactical School: 16–18
Air depot groups
    13th: 250
    45th: 200
Air Force Combat Command: 54
Air Force Service Command, XIII: 265
Air Forces
    Fifth: 254, 256–57, 260, 263–64
    Ninth: 192–93, 200
    Twelfth: 156
    Thirteenth: 250
Air-ground communications
    with Army Air Forces fighter-bombers: 183
    balloons: 5, 10
    during column control missions: 213

Air-ground communications—Continued
    and enemy aircraft warnings: 172, 178
    during fire control missions: 212, 224
    by loud speakers: 153
    by message drop: 40
    panels used for: 210, 215
    problems with: 64
    and service test of organic air observation: 65–66
    World War I: 10, 11–12, 13–14
Air-Ground Procedures Board: 36–37, 50, 53
Air Materiel Command: 95, 112, 120
Air Materiel Division: 18–19, 34–35
Air Medal: 251
Air-Observation-Post Program
    Air Staff attack on, early 1944: 273
    Air Staff attack on, November 1942: 103–04
    Army Air Forces criticism of doctrine for: 278
    doctrine for: 40–41, 69, 72–73, 145, 188, 275
    establishment of: 85–86
    expansion beyond Field Artillery: 296–305
    expansion beyond Field Artillery, proposed: 79–80, 102–04, 273–76, 295–96
    institutional development of: 161
    lack of administrative support for: 145, 148, 151–52, 153
    lack of logistical support for overseas units: 145, 156, 188, 244–45, 259–63, 280–82
    lack of unit training: 145, 148, 151–52
    mission: 102–06, 302
    priorities in assignment of air sections: 145
    program management: 87
    research and development: 116
    Seventh Army's proposal to reorganize: 274–76
    size of, during World War II: 307
    War Department policy regarding: 273–80
Air-observation-post schools
    Fifth Army: 152, 157, 307
    II Corps: 151–52, 156, 160, 307
    missions: 152
Air observation posts
    administration of: 145–46, 149, 153–60, 184, 189–93, 223
    for airborne divisions: 117, 118, 120–22
    in attacks on heavy fortifications: 226–28
    battalion control of: 163, 174
    boards of officers for tests of: 70–74, 77–78
    British: 151
    contribution to the war effort: 321, 323–26
    coordination with antiaircraft operations: 40–41, 73, 172–73, 178, 244

Air observation posts—Continued
    in deliberate attacks: 160, 180–82, 231–32, 267–68
    demonstrations of, with 1st Division: 74
    deployment overseas: 145–46
    difficulties integrating with field artillery units: 132–37
    difficulties observing fire for long-range counterbattery missions: 71–72
    and direction of naval fire: 161–63
    doctrine for employing: 69
    doctrine for employing, in airborne operations: 118–19, 204–05
    equipment for units deploying overseas: 112
    in exploitation/pursuit: 182, 183, 187, 212–26, 231, 233–34, 261–62
    Fifth Army: 166
    fired on by U.S. troops: 149–50
    ground crews for, in European Theater: 215
    late arrival of, in Pacific Theater: 240–41
    logistical support for: 112–16, 223, 260–61, 264–65, 266
    logistical support for, in European Theater: 192–93, 200–203
    missions: 69, 136, 162–63, 173, 320
    operational planning for Normandy invasion: 204–05
    opportunities to train with their units: 112
    organization of: 73–74, 86, 163
    personnel assigned to: 100
    priorities in Italy: 181
    security for, in France: 212, 223–24
    security for, in Pacific: 258–59, 263
    service tests of: 63–66, 70
    supplies for: 95
    support for amphibious landings: 161–63, 251–53, 256–57, 259, 265, 267
    support for invasion of Sicily: 161–63
    support for troop movements in jungles: 241, 244–45, 250–51, 253
    tables of organization and equipment: 95, 115–16
    tested against Army Air Forces observation squadrons: 70, 71–72
Air observation posts, centralized vs. decentralized control of
    at Anzio: 178
    in European Theater: 210, 223–24, 231, 235
    in Italy: 174
    on Okinawa: 268, 271
    in Pacific Theater: 240
    in Philippine Islands: 259, 263
    in Sicily: 163
"Air OP Bulletins": 199n
    Third Army: 198
    Fifth Army: 167
Air safety programs
    Army Ground Forces: 127, 128, 276–77
    12th Army Group: 198
    Fifth Army in Italy: 167

Air sections
    assignment of: 129
    composition of: 129–30
    corps artillery: 159
    divisional: 276–77
    personnel transferred to Army Air Forces: 260–61, 264–65
    and tables of organization and equipment: 129–30, 133
    tactical training for: 132–33, 276–77
Air Service Command: 113–14
Air Staff: 54
    attack on Air-Observation-Post Program, November 1942: 103–04
    attack on Air-Observation-Post Program in early 1944: 273
    independent air force becomes priority for: 294, 303, 304, 322–23
    and missions of air forces: 294
    and organic aviation after September 1944: 294–305
    and planning for liaison aircraft in postwar Army Air Forces: 300–301
    and research and development: 284–85, 286–88
Air superiority
    at Anzio: 177–78
    essential for safety of air observation posts: 40–41
    German, in North Africa: 158
    in Italy: 171
    in Philippine Islands: 258
    on Okinawa: 268–69
Air supply offices: 113, 114–15
Air Support Command, XII: 172, 174–75. *See also* tactical air commands.
Air-to-air engagements (L–4s): 234
Air Training Detachment, Field Artillery School: 67–74
Air University: 183n
Airborne Command: 102, 121–22
Airborne Divisions (units)
    11th: 256–57, 258–59, 260, 266, 271–72, 324
    82d: 131, 205, 208
    101st: 205, 208
Airborne Divisions, air observation posts for: 117, 118, 121–22, 131, 208
Airborne Engineer Battalion, 127th: 258
Aircraft. *See also* equipment.
    assembly: 192, 200–201, 205, 241, 245–46
    assigned to air observation posts: 300
    characteristics: 23, 34–35, 52
    commanders' use of: 153, 159, 186–87, 213, 214, 215–17, 219, 220–22, 263, 296, 323
    design: 8, 18–20, 33–34, 72
    destroyed by Japanese infiltrators: 263
    distribution: 110–12, 280
    doctrine for use: 43
    early design: 8
    effects of wrong fuels on: 115

INDEX 355

Aircraft—Continued
    European: 8, 9
    fabric and dope for: 148, 202
    fuels and lubricants
        difficulties obtaining: 115
        effects of wrong fuel on engines: 203, 261
        reserves on board: 197, 204
        shortages of aviation gasoline: 203, 260–61
        use of motor-vehicle gasoline: 23, 203, 261
    guns for: 11
    instrumentation: 23
    light ambulance: 127
    in North Africa: 153
    numbers assigned to units: 33, 274–75, 276, 281–82
    numbers needed by field artillery: 37–38, 88
    owned by military personnel: 67
    performance
        altitude: 18, 23
        carrying capacity: 22, 23, 26
        endurance: 23, 26
        engines: 18, 22–23
        evaluation of: 82
        landing: 23, 52, 117–18
        loiter time: 59
        maneuverability: 19–20, 23, 40–41, 52, 117–18
        range: 18, 23, 197
        speed: 11, 18–20, 23, 34, 59, 117, 118–19, 120n
        takeoff: 23, 26, 33–34, 52, 117–18, 120n
    procurement: 88
    production: 35–36, 110–12, 115, 146–47
    replacement: 197–98, 200, 260–61, 262, 282
    reserves of, in overseas theaters: 153
    rotary-wing. *See* Autogiros; Helicopters.
    salvaging: 290, 292
    service tests
        by Air Corps: 49–50
        by armored units: 47–48
        by Cavalry Board: 50
        at Fort Sill: 48, 52
    shortages of, in prewar period: 33–34
    skis: 201
    for training pilots: 109–12, 146–47
    transport overseas: 156, 161
    warning systems: 41, 172, 178, 223–24, 317
    World War I: 11
Aircraft (by type)
    Auster (British designation for L–2): 151
    B–17 (Boeing): 197
    B–24 (Consolidated): 265
    C–47 (Douglas): 218, 257, 263, 264
    DH–4 (De Havilland): 11, 23
    Fi–156 (Fieseler Storch; German): 23–26, 27, 39, 234
    Fw–190 (Focke-Wulf; German): 171
    HE–1 (Navy designation; also Piper J–5D): 127
    L–2 (also O–57; British Auster; Taylorcraft): 50, 117–18, 151

Aircraft (by type)—Continued
    L–3 (also YO–58; Aeronca): 50, 117–18
    L–4. *See* Aircraft, L–4.
    L–4x. *See* L–14.
    L–5. *See* Aircraft, L–5.
    L–6 (Interstate): 110–11, 276
    L–14 (also L–4x; Piper): 120–22, 286, 299–300
    L–15 (Boeing): 300
    Me–109 (Messerschmidt; German):147
    Me–262 (Messerschmidt; German): 234
    "O" and "L" series designations: 67n
    O–47 (North American): 19–20, 27, 33–35, 38, 39
    O–49 (Stinson, later Vultee): 34–35, 36, 39, 42, 47–48, 49–50, 52, 53, 60
    O–51 (Ryan): 46
    O–52 (Curtiss-Wright): 20n
    O–54 (Stinson): 35, 42, 47–48
    O–57. *See* L–2.
    O–58. *See* L–3.
    O–59. *See* Aircraft, L–4.
    P–39 (Bell): 73
    P–40 (Curtiss-Wright): 183
    P–47 (Republic): 182, 186, 222–23, 229, 234
    P–51 (North American): 175
    Piper Cub J–3 (YO–59; L–4). *See* Aircraft, L–4.
    Piper Cub J–4: 39–40
    Piper Cub J–5D: 120–22, 127
    Rawdon T–1: 120
    Spad XI: 11
    Stinson Model 76. *See* Aircraft, L–5.
    Stinson Model 105. *See* O–54.
    Taylorcraft 9–X: 286
    UC–61 (Fairchild): 127–28
    Wright Flyer: 8
    YG–1B (Kellett): 41–42. *See also* Autogiros.
Aircraft, L–4 (also O–59; Piper J–3 "Cub")
    advantages when pursued: 40–41
    arming of: 197, 228
    and armor exercises at Fort Knox: 48
    availability of replacements: 313
    comparison to L–5: 118, 169, 185–86, 313–14
    comparison to O–49: 49–50, 52, 53
    comparison to YO–54: 48
    delivery from England to Continent: 197–98
    demonstrations of: 48, 49–50
    development of: 22–23
    diverted to Army Air Forces in Pacific Theater: 240
    ground forces requirements for: 277–78
    improvements to: 284
    need for maintenance during transport to theaters: 148
    need for replacement for: 284, 286, 296, 299
    nicknames: 3, 51–52, 147, 158, 257
    pilots' opinions of: 313–14, 320
    pontoons for water landings: 166, 252–53, 291
    production schedules: 35–36, 277–78

Aircraft, L–5 (Stinson Model 76): 39–40, 59, 60
  for air sections in Italy: 169
  arming of: 297–98
  Army Air Forces attitude toward air-observation-post use of: 277
  Army Air Forces pilots and: 222–23
  assignment to non–field artillery units: 295–96
  availability of: 296
  comparison to L–4: 118, 169, 185–86, 313–14
  for corps air sections: 193
  for division air sections: 193
  for Okinawa: 270
  popularity of, in air sections: 202
  procurement of: 299, 321
  production schedule for: 277, 282
  reluctance to use in Air-Observation-Post Program: 284, 286
  testing of: 286
Airframes, maintenance kits for: 95
Airmobility: 235
Airstrips/airfields
  battalion: 223–24
  on beaches: 259, 260
  division: 223, 229
  lack of, in Pacific Theater: 241, 259, 270–71
  lack of suitable sites for, in Italy: 174, 183, 186–87
  marked for night landings: 175
  need for fixed bases for O–47: 33–34
  need for location of, near supported units: 15–16
  in North Africa: 158
  on Okinawa: 269, 270–71
  on OMAHA Beach: 205
  preparation of, in Southwest Pacific Area: 252–53, 256
  prepared by pilots: 229
  priority for construction of, after Pacific landings: 250, 256–57
  during pursuit of Germans in France: 212, 215–17, 229
  roads used as: 259, 260, 265
  security for: 223–24, 229, 259, 263
  site selection for: 257, 260, 265
  in Southwest Pacific Area: 259–60, 263, 265
  World War I: 15–16
Aitape, New Guinea: 253
ALAMO FORCE: 253
Alex, Ralph P.: 120n
Alexander, Field Marshal Harold R. L. G.: 160, 185
Algeria: 147, 150–52
Algiers, Algeria: 147, 150–51
Allcorn, Maj. Ford E.: 96, 148–50, 190–91
Allen, S. Sgt. Claude: 180
Allen, Maj. Gen. Terry de la Mesa: 74
Alley, Richard H.: 67, 68
Allin, Brig. Gen. G. R.: 59, 77
American Expeditionary Forces: 10, 11, 13
  Air Service Board: 16
  Infantry Board: 16
  Superior Board: 16

Amphibious assaults
  air-observation-post support for: 161–63, 166
  in Central Pacific Area: 251–52, 267
  naval support for: 290–91
  Normandy: 203–08
  Salerno: 166
  Sicily: 161–63
  Southern France: 221–22
  Southwest Pacific Area: 252–53, 258–59, 265
Anderson, Maj. Gen. John B.: 232
Anderson, Lt. Col. K. W.: 167, 169
Anderson, Lt. Gen. Kenneth A. N.: 150–51, 158
Andrus, Brig. Gen. Clift: 163
Antiaircraft defenses, coordination of air-observation-post operations with: 172, 178, 317
Antiaircraft warning system, missions: 172, 178, 317
Antiflak missions: 174–75
Antitank rockets for light aircraft: 197, 228
Antitank warnings, air observation posts' role in: 178–80
Anzio, Italy: 3, 121–22, 166, 175, 177–80, 182, 183, 311, 324
Ardennes, Belgium. *See* Bulge, Battle of.
Armies
  First: 33–34, 50–52, 189, 192–93, 200, 201, 202, 204, 208–09, 211, 213, 225, 226, 228–29, 308–09, 311, 313, 314
  Second: 50–52, 136, 264
  Third: 49, 50–52, 136, 190, 193, 198–99, 200, 201–02, 213, 217–18, 219, 221, 225, 226, 229, 232–33, 309n
  Fifth: 152, 153, 156–57, 161, 166–88, 192–93, 202, 277, 278–79, 311, 313, 314
  Sixth: 240, 252, 253, 254, 256, 260–67, 271, 301–02, 314
  Seventh: 161–63, 190, 193, 200, 202, 221, 222, 225, 231, 273–75, 278–79, 285, 309n
  Eighth: 252, 256, 260–67, 271
  Ninth: 190, 193, 198–99, 200, 226, 231–32, 309n
  Tenth: 266–71, 314–15
  Fifteenth: 190, 193, 200
Armor
  organic aerial observation for: 43–47, 79, 131–32
  scouting for: 213
Armored Artillery Regiment, 5th: 133
Armored Corps, I: 161, 162n
Armored Divisions
  1st: 46, 131–32, 157–58, 174, 180, 182, 183, 185
  2d: 46, 50–51, 98, 131–32, 210, 212, 225
  3d: 131
  4th: 213, 228, 235
  5th: 215, 220, 234
  9th: 231
Armored Field Artillery Battalions
  14th: 210, 212
  16th: 231

INDEX 357

Armored Field Artillery Battalions—Continued
 68th: 180
 71st: 214, 234
Armored Force Board: 48
Armored Force Headquarters: 46
Armored Infantry Battalion, 27th: 231
Armored Regiment, 66th: 212
Army Air Corps
 aircraft service tests: 49–50
 arguments for centralized control of aviation: 32, 38
 budget for equipment, 1931: 15
 doctrine: 16–18, 29
 formed: 15
 lighter-than-air program: 20
 mobilization plan of 1936: 26–27
 observation groups: 26–27
 observation squadrons, interwar period: 26–27
 observers: 36
 participation in 1927 maneuvers: 18
 provision of aircraft for testing at Field Artillery School: 42
 refusal to purchase off-the-shelf aircraft for testing: 51
Army Air Corps Enlisted Reserve: 86
Army Air Forces. *See also* Headquarters, Army Air Forces.
 air safety program: 127
 Air Support Party: 213
 Central Air Depot: 201
 competition with Field Artillery for pilots: 96
 cooperation with air observation posts in VI Corps: 222–23
 cooperation with air observation posts in VIII Corps: 229
 failure to provide third-echelon maintenance: 281
 liaison squadrons: 4, 100, 183, 193, 265–66
 light plane squadrons: 54
 missions: 303
 observation squadrons: 54, 100
 Oklahoma Air Depot: 125–26
 Oklahoma City Air Depot: 292
 pursuits used to test Air Training Detachment: 70
 responsible for major repairs for air observation posts: 86
 as source of supplies for air observation posts: 86
 to supply all logistical support for air observation posts: 280–82
 training of Field Artillery pilots: 59
Army Air Forces Board: 299
Army Air Forces Depot Units (Army): 157, 281
 1st: 269–70
 3d: 184
 4th: 193, 202
 5th: 260, 264–65
 6th: 260, 262–63, 264–65
Army Air Forces Flying Training Command: 100–101, 123

Army Air Forces Materiel Command and testing of aircraft: 286
Army Air Forces Primary Flying School: 123
Army Air Forces Training Command: 283–84, 291
Army aviation: 1, 94, 157, 182, 188, 210, 305, 326
Army Ground Forces. *See also* Headquarters, Army Ground Forces.
 Equipment Board: 302
 observers: 276, 283, 296–97
Army Groups
 1st: 189
 6th: 190, 221
 12th: 189, 198, 201, 202, 308
 15th: 184
 21st: 211–12, 231–32
Army-Navy Munitions Assignment Board: 110
Arnold, General of the Army Henry H.
 ability to impose his views: 53–54, 56
 and Air Corps control of aerial observation, 1939: 31–33
 and air support for cavalry divisions: 44
 arguments for return of control of aviation to Army Air Forces: 278–80
 and contracts for short-range observation aircraft: 34–36
 and Danford's 1941 proposal for test detachment: 63
 decline of personal involvement in question of organic aviation: 294
 and distrust of light aircraft: 116–17
 and diversion of L–4s to Army Air Forces in Pacific Theater: 240
 and expansion of organic aviation program: 302–03, 304
 and pilots for Department of Air Training: 100
 and procurement of light aircraft: 110–11
 and proposals for organic aviation for other ground combat arms: 75
 refusal to purchase commercial light aircraft, 1939–1940: 35–36
 and short-range aircraft: 54
 and survivability of slow-speed aircraft: 35
 and War Department approval of air-observation-post concept: 75, 81–83, 318–19
Arracourt, France: 228
Artillery Air Depot (Provisional), Fifth Army: 157, 167, 184, 188, 192, 281
Artillery air officers
 absence of, in higher commands: 145
 on army group staff: 184, 189, 190–91
 on army staffs: 153, 156, 166, 189–90, 252, 266–67, 273–74
 battalion: 224
 on corps staffs: 159, 232, 241, 251–52, 276, 308
 on division staffs: 157, 163, 198, 276
 duties of: 132–33, 153, 189–93, 197–98, 199, 224, 232, 251–52, 264, 276
 not on staff of Central Pacific Area: 251
 not on staff of Southwest Pacific Area: 252
 rank: 132, 276

Artillery air officers—Continued
  in Southwest Pacific Area: 264–66
  theater: 166
Artillery boards
  2d Division: 70, 72, 74, 77
  13th Field Artillery Brigade: 70, 72–73, 74, 77, 78
Artillery Group, 172d: 224
"Artillery Should Carry Its Own OPs": 52–54
Aslito Field, Saipan: 251
Assistant secretary of war for air: 15
Augsburg, Germany: 234
Autogiros: 20, 22, 23, 26, 41–42, 44, 80–81, 116.
  See also Aircraft, YG–1B; Helicopters.
Avranches, France: 215, 217–18

Baer, Brig. Gen. Carl A.: 178
Baetjer, Capt. Edward B.: 171
Baguio, Philippine Islands: 263
Baker, Maj. Thomas S.: 87–88, 90–91, 92, 93, 107, 288
Balloon companies
  Allied armies: 10
  French Army: 4
  German Army: 10
  World War I: 10–11
Balloon Corps: 5
Balloons: 4–8, 10–11, 16, 20, 58
Balmer, Brig. Gen. Jesmond D.: 96, 98, 100, 101, 118, 119
Bamberg, Germany: 234
Barton, Maj. Gen. Raymond O.: 218
Bastogne, Belgium: 229
Bataan, Philippine Islands: 240
Battalion fire-control centers, development of: 28
Battlefield air interdiction: 219
Baybay, Philippine Islands: 259
Beasley, Col. Rex W.: 63, 64, 69, 76
Belgium: 212
Bell, Col. William J.: 278–79, 301
Bennett, Col. John C., Jr.: 301, 305
Berlin, Germany: 234
Bermuda: 148
Biak Island: 253–54
Blair, Lt. Donald: 163
Blakely, Brig. Gen. Harold W.: 204–05
Blohm, Maj. Jack: 202
Board, 1st Lt. Oliver P.: 161–62
BOLERO: 145
Bone, Algeria: 151
Bornstein, Maj. Lloyd M.: 90–91, 125, 281, 294
Bougainville: 241, 245–51, 252
Bowen, Col. William: 254
Bradley, Brig. Gen. J. S.: 303
Bradley, Lt. Gen. Omar N.: 162, 189, 190, 193, 212, 215–16
Bréguet, Louis: 22
Bristol, Col. Delbert L.: 59, 272, 308–09, 314, 325
  and Air Training Detachment: 67, 73
  and Department of Air Training: 90–91

Bristol, Col. Delbert L.—Continued
  and European Theater: 189, 192–93, 197, 198, 201–02, 204–05, 208–09, 229, 299–300
  and North African Theater: 158, 160
  sent to Great Britain: 146
British forces
  First Army: 151, 152, 166
  Second Army: 211–12
  Eighth Army: 160, 181, 182, 185
  XII Corps: 181
British Home Forces: 151
Brodie, 1st Lt. James: 285
Brodie device: 267, 270–71, 272, 284–85, 293–94
Brooks, Maj. Gen. Edward H.: 225
Brooks Field, Tex.: 36, 53, 72
Brown, 2d Lt. Charles M.: 126, 134
Bruce, Maj. Gen. Andrew D.: 79, 105, 258–59
Bryant, Capt. Kenneth: 205
Buckner, Lt. Gen. Simon B., Jr.: 266
Bulge, Battle of the: 228–29
Buna Mission, Philippine Islands: 240
Burma: 287–88, 320
Burr, Capt. George K.: 23, 39–40, 81
Burwell, Col. James B.: 280
Butler, 2d Lt. William H.: 148–49, 150
Byrd, Maj. Jerome W.: 314

Caen, France: 211, 219
Cameras
  for aerial photography: 70–71
  Army Air Forces opposition to air-observation-post use of: 278, 285
  handheld aerial: 176, 247, 285, 300
Camouflage, mission of checking friendly: 136
Camps
  Beauregard, La.: 39–40
  Blanding, Fla.: 70, 72–73, 77
  Bowie, Tex.: 49
Campbell, Col. Boniface: 85–86
Campbell, Brig. Gen. W. A.: 178
Carentan, France: 210
Carolina Maneuvers, 1941. *See* Maneuvers, Carolina.
Carpenter, Maj. Charles C.: 213, 228, 235
Casablanca, French Morocco: 149, 151, 241
Case, S. Sgt. Glenn E.: 244
Case, Thomas A.: 39–40, 48–49
Cassidy, Lt. Col. Robert F.: 72, 124–25, 252, 261, 264–65, 288, 291–92, 299–300
Cassino, Italy: 175
Casualties, pilots
  from accidents: 173, 184, 199
  Department of Air Training: 118
  in European Theater: 198–99, 208–09, 308–09
  from friendly fire: 180, 208
  in Italy: 173, 180, 184
  North African Theater: 160
  in Southwest Pacific Area: 256–57
  statistics on: 173, 308–15
Cavalry, organic aerial observation for: 43–47, 79, 80

INDEX

Cavalry Board: 44, 50, 79
Cavalry Division, 1st: 50–52, 79, 257, 261–62, 295–96
Cavalry Group, 113th: 211
Cavalry reconnaissance squadrons (mechanized): 295–96
Cavalry Regimental Combat Team, 112th: 253, 263–64, 324
Cavalry units, scouting for: 213
Cave warfare: 253–54, 267–68, 298–99
Central Pacific Area: 237, 241, 251–52, 266–71
Central Task Force: 147
Chaffee, Maj. Gen. Adna R., Jr.: 44, 45, 46, 47–49
Chandler, Brig. Gen. Rex E.: 36, 53, 62, 76, 240, 257, 317–18, 323
    and Air Training Detachment: 68
    and Field Artillery's need for aircraft: 41–42, 58, 80
    and Pacific Theater: 240, 257
    and service test of organic air observation: 63–64, 65, 69
Charleroi, Belgium: 200
Chase, Brig. Gen. William C.: 261–62
Cherbourg, France: 211
Chief Signal Officer, Office of the: 9
China-Burma-India Theater: 287–88, 298–99
Christiansen, Maj. Gen. J. G.: 302, 303
Cierva Codorníu, Don Juan de la: 20
Cincinnati Flying Club: 92
Civil Aeronautics Administration: 48, 64–65, 68–69, 92, 307
Civil War, use of balloons: 5, 7–8
Civilian Pilot Training Program: 86, 88, 96, 100–101
Clark, General Mark W.: 77–78, 146, 152–53, 156, 157, 166, 169, 184, 188, 278–79, 317–18, 323
Class Before One: 68, 72, 83, 87–88, 92, 93, 95–96, 98, 107, 123, 136, 146
Cleveland Air Races: 23, 26
Close air support. *See* Forward air control system.
Cochran, Col. Philip G.: 287
Cole, Lt. William: 163
Collins, Maj. Gen. J. Lawton: 219
Collins, Lt. Col. James L.: 223
Column control
    and air observation posts: 136
    and Air Training Detachment test: 70–71
    in European Theater: 212, 213, 220–21
    and Louisiana Maneuvers, 1940: 40
    in Philippine Islands: 261–62
    tests with armored forces: 44, 48
Command and control: 213, 214, 215–17, 219, 220–22, 296, 323
Communications
    air-observation-post pilots with fighter-bomber pilots: 182–83, 213, 219, 229, 263–64
    between airstrips and fire-direction centers: 224
    by wire: 224
Communications flight mission in European Theater: 193. *See also* Liaison mission.
Condon, 1st Lt. David E.: 204–05, 218
Consolidated Aircraft Corporation: 60
Contact missions
    in European Theater: 215–17, 220–21
    in Southwest Pacific Area: 257
    in World War I: 11
Continental Engine Corporation: 22–23, 95
Cook, Maj. Gen. Gilbert R.: 302
Cook Board: 302
Cooke, Lt. Col. E. D.: 46–47
Corlett, Maj. Gen. Charles H.: 211
Corps
    I: 240, 241, 244, 250–51, 254, 266
    II: 96–97, 145–47, 151–52, 157, 159–60, 162, 172, 174, 180
    III: 14
    IV: 39–40, 46, 50–52, 246–47
    V: 204, 205
    VI: 178, 182, 221, 222
    VII: 204, 217–18, 219, 223
    VIII: 228–29
    X: 256, 259, 260, 265
    XII: 192, 229, 232–34, 235
    XIV: 241, 247, 250, 301–02
    XV: 215–17, 219, 220–21, 231
    XVI: 231
    XIX: 211, 212, 226
    XX: 215, 223
    XXIV: 251–52, 256, 259, 267, 270
Corps artillery, service test of organic air observation: 63–66, 70
Coune, Capt. Felix A.: 257, 258
Counterbattery operations
    observation of fire for: 71–72
    photographic support for: 175–77, 181
Counterbattery weapons, L–4s used as
    in Italy: 171, 174–75
    in Sicily: 162–63
    in Southwest Pacific Area: 244
Countermortar fire, air observation posts and: 180
Courier mission. *See also* Liaison mission.
    importance of: 274
    in Italy: 166, 172
    in Sicily: 274
    in Southwest Pacific Area: 257, 263
Cowles, Lt. Col. Stewart L.: 94
Craig, Brig. Gen. Howard A.: 278
Craig, General Malin: 17, 20
Crane, Maj. Gen. John A.: 58, 165–66, 274–75
Crashes
    accidents at Department of Air Training: 118, 127
    causes of: 198–99, 208–09, 263
    escaping German fighters: 158
    in European Theater: 225–26
    fatalities. *See* Casualties.
    due to friendly fire: 150
    midair collisions: 199, 231–32
    North Africa: 150, 158
    in Southwest Pacific Area: 266

Crashes—Continued
    due to terrain: 266
    due to weather: 229
Cuba: 7
Cummings, 1st Lt. Julian W.: 161–62, 170, 289

Dale, 1st Lt. D. F.: 174, 288
Danford, Maj. Gen. Robert M.: 324
    1940 proposal to War Department: 37–39
    1941 proposal to Marshall: 60–62
    1941 proposal to Stimson for organic aviation: 60–62, 80
    and Air-Ground Procedures Board: 36–37
    and air-observation-post concept: 57–59, 80–83, 317–18
    and British air observation: 57–58
    frustration with Army Air Forces: 59
    and organization of aerial observation, 1939: 31–33, 42–43
    and purchase of short-range observation aircraft: 35–36
    and rotary-wing aircraft: 41–42
    and test of air observation detachment at Field Artillery School: 60, 69
    and tests of organic aviation, 1939–1940: 37–43
    and War Department approval of air-observation-post concept: 75–76
Deception plans, air-observation-post role in: 180, 231–33
Decker, Brig. Gen. George H.: 301–02
Delivery missions: 213
Department of Air Training
    air accidents at: 118, 127
    aircraft for: 109–12, 118, 292
    classes, size of: 124, 307
    and doctrine development: 283, 290, 291–92
    Flight Training Division: 122–24
    integration at: 290
    Maintenance Division: 125–26, 292
    maintenance of school's planes: 125–26, 292
    Medical Section: 127
    mission: 122
    need to continue existence of: 282–84
    and night operations: 283–84, 286–87, 291–92, 296–98
    nonteaching contributions of: 283, 290–94
    organization of: 90–95, 124–25, 288–89
    and pilot training: 291, 293–94, 307
    and research and development: 116, 117, 118, 120–22, 290, 292–94, 296–98
    staff for: 288–89, 291
    table of distribution and allowances: 94
    Tactics and Gunnery Division: 124–25
    team sent to Central Pacific Area to train pilots: 267
    and training of aerial observers for the Navy: 290–91
    training mission: 290
Deposito, Philippine Islands: 259

Devers, General Jacob L.: 75, 79, 190–91, 221, 278, 303, 305
Devol, Capt. Breton A., Jr.: 148–49, 150, 161
DeWitt, 2d Lt. Paul A.: 151, 158
Divisions
    1st: 74
    2d: 68, 70, 71–72, 74, 77–78
    36th (Texas National Guard): 39, 49, 81
    Americal: 246, 285
Doctrine
    and aerial observation: 11–12
    development of, as mission of Department of Air Training: 283, 290, 291–92
    on indirect fire: 8, 12–13
    lack of, on air sections: 133
    for tactical employment of aircraft: 133
Donovan, Maj. Gen. William J.: 102
Doolittle, Brig. Gen. James H.: 156
Dorland, Réne: 22
Driniumor River, New Guinea: 253, 324
Drivers for air sections: 130
Dunckel, Brig. Gen. William C.: 246

Eaker, Lt. Gen. Ira C.: 303
Eastern Assault Force: 147, 150–51
Eastern Task Force: 147, 150–51
Edwards, Col. Edmund B.: 266, 268
Edwards, Brig. Gen. Idwal H.: 86, 87, 96, 97–99, 100–101, 104, 106, 123, 129–30, 132, 303
Eichelberger, Lt. Gen. Robert L.: 240, 250–51, 253–54, 256, 264
Eisenhower, General of the Army Dwight D.
    and aircraft for liaison mission: 52, 284, 299–300
    and European Theater: 189
    and field artillery section at theater headquarters: 166
    and Italian campaign: 169
    and North African Theater: 152, 158, 277
    as organic aviation advocate: 76–77, 300, 303, 305, 317–18
    and potential of light aircraft: 49, 51–52
Emmons, Lt. Gen. Delos C.: 54, 76, 79
Engineer operations in Italy, air-observation-post support for: 181
Engines
    Continental A–65: 35, 147, 186
    early problems with: 8
    effects of wrong fuel on: 23, 203, 261
    for light fixed-wing aircraft: 22–23, 317
    Lycoming: 35, 59, 169, 286
    maintenance kits for: 95
    opposed: 22–23
    radial: 35
    spare: 115–16
    stalling of: 23, 117–18
    Warner-Scarab: 127
Equipment. *See also* Aircraft.
    for air sections: 129, 130

INDEX

Equipment—Continued
    for air sections without departure plans: 129
    development of, by Department of Air
        Training: 290, 292–94
    improvement of: 284–85, 286, 290, 292–94,
        296–97
    in-theater fabrication of: 167, 173–74, 197,
        204, 250
    issue of, in European Theater: 192
    repair and replacement in Southwest Pacific
        Area: 260–61, 262–63, 264
Ernest, Maj. Charles: 267
Esch, Luxembourg: 200
European Theater of Operations: 189–235, 300
Evasive maneuvers
    Air Training Detachment tested on: 70, 72–73
    in Italy: 171–72
    training for: 68
Everest, Col. Frank F.: 85–86

Fabric and dope for planes: 148, 202
Falaise Pocket, Battle of: 219–22, 324
Far East Air Force Service Command: 260–61
Far East Air Forces: 256, 260–61, 264–65, 269
Fedala, Morocco: 150
Field army staffs, Field Artillery air positions on: 137
Field Artillery, Office of the Chief of: 318
    and Air-Ground Procedures Board: 36–37
    and branch assignment of aerial observers: 16
    disestablishment of: 117
    and maneuvers of 1940: 39
    and need for organic aircraft: 34n, 37–38
    and Piper Cub demonstrations: 48, 49
    and planning for service test of organic air
        observation: 69
Field Artillery battalions
    commanders' lack of technical knowledge
        about air sections: 133
    need for aircraft: 37
    tables of organization and equipment for: 100
Field Artillery Battalions (units)
    5th: 205
    20th: 218
    29th: 218
    38th: 72
    42d: 218, 228–29
    175th: 151
    202d: 214–15
    208th: 215, 220
    250th: 215
    278th: 199
    344th: 210, 220
    693d: 221, 231
    902d: 259
    957th: 223
    961st: 224–25
    975th: 220
    983d: 265–66
    989th: 220

Field Artillery Board: 38
Field artillery brigade headquarters, air sections for: 129
Field Artillery Brigades
    13th: 58, 68, 70, 71–73, 74, 77–78, 146, 153,
        165–66, 171, 172, 274–75
    18th: 170
    34th: 232
    61st: 39, 49, 200–201
Field artillery doctrine
    between 1929 and 1942: 28
    prior to World War I: 8
    World War I: 11–12
    World War II: 240n, 262
Field Artillery Drill Regulations, 1907: 8
Field Artillery Groups
    6th: 173
    18th: 225
    35th: 175, 178
    194th: 181
    208th: 219, 233–34
    351st: 134
Field Artillery Journal: 9, 40, 43
    and arguments for organic aviation: 33, 40
    articles: 247
Field Artillery Regiments
    1st: 40
    18th: 59
Field Artillery Replacement Center: 125–26, 308
Field Artillery School
    acquisition of light aircraft for: 59
    advance course committees: 52–53
    and aerial firing problems: 36
    Department of Air Training established at:
        87–88, 90–91, 107. *See also* Department
        of Air Training.
    Department of Communications: 58–59
    as home for air-observation-post training pro-
        gram: 89–90
    and indirect fire doctrine and organization: 28
    organization of test air observation detachment
        at: 59–66
    and standard procedures for air sections: 133
Field Manual 6–150, *Organic Field Artillery Air
    Observation*: 291–92
Field Manual 100–20, *Command and Employment
    of Air Power*: 302
Field Service Regulations: 8
Fire control missions
    Air Training Detachment performance of,
        while under air attack: 70, 72–73
    for amphibious operations: 251
    and antitank guns: 178–80
    for Army Air Forces fighter-bombers: 222–23
    centrality to air-observation-post concept: 80,
        81–82
    conducted by pilots: 129
    in European Theater: 218–19, 220, 222–23,
        224, 228–29
    during German withdrawal from St. Lô: 212

Fire control missions—Continued
　　grasshopper tactics for: 158, 162–63
　　in Italy: 170, 175, 178–80, 181
　　lack of training in delivery of indirect fire: 8, 12–13, 15–16
　　and Louisiana Maneuvers: 51–52
　　need for aircraft suitable for: 37
　　at night: 175, 298
　　in Normandy: 208, 209
　　in North African Theater: 158, 160
　　on OMAHA Beach: 204–05
　　in Sicily: 162–63
　　in South Pacific Theater: 246
　　in Southwest Pacific Area: 241, 244, 252–53, 259, 262, 263
　　suitability of light aircraft for: 52
　　training of observers for, by pilots: 134–36
　　training pilots for: 68, 124–25
Flank guard patrol missions: 157, 158
Flight instructors
　　civilian: 64–65, 87–88, 124
　　selected from graduating Department of Air Training classes: 124, 129
Flight pay: 12–13, 90, 153
Flight surgeons: 127, 199–200
Flying gear, cold-weather: 201
Flying techniques: 82, 124
Focke, Heinrich K. J.: 22
Focke-Wulf: 22*n*
Ford, Lt. Col. William W.: 66–67, 318, 323, 324
　　and administrative support for air sections overseas: 146
　　and Air-Observation-Post Program pilot training: 85–86, 88
　　and air safety program: 127
　　and Air Training Detachment: 66–74, 81, 83
　　and airborne divisions: 118
　　and aircraft for Department of Air Training: 117–18, 120–22
　　appointed director of Department of Air Training: 90–91
　　and General Clark: 77
　　continuing influence on Department of Air Training: 290
　　as director of Department of Air Training: 126
　　and helicopters: 119–20
　　leaves Department of Air Training: 288
　　and logistical support for air sections: 115–16
　　and Louisiana Maneuvers, 1940: 40
　　made commander, Air Training Detachment, Field Artillery School: 67
　　and need for air sections to train with their units: 109
　　and Field Artillery's need for aircraft: 40, 41–42, 43, 81
　　and need for L–5s for airborne divisions: 118–19
　　and organization of Department of Air Training: 93–101, 124–25
　　and philosophy of training at Department of Air Training: 93, 95–96, 98, 100–101

Ford, Lt. Col. William W.—Continued
　　proposal for organization of air observation unit at Fort Sill: 59–60
　　and proposed reorganization of Air-Observation-Post Program: 275–76
　　and ratings for pilots: 90
　　and research and development: 116, 120–22
　　and service test of organic air observation: 63–66, 69–74
　　and staff selection: 87–88
　　and startup of Department of Air Training: 88–102, 105–08
　　"Wings for Santa Barbara": 40, 43, 58–59, 64
Fortner, Maj. Marion J.: 90–91, 125–26, 292
Forts
　　Benning, Ga.: 46, 47–48
　　Bliss, Tex.: 50
　　Bragg, N.C.: 20, 38, 58, 70, 121–22
　　Jeanne d'Arc, France: 227
　　Knox, Ky.: 44, 46, 47–48, 79
　　Koenigsmacker, France: 226
　　Logan, Colo.: 7
　　Myer, Va.: 8
　　Riley, Kans.: 8–9
　　Sam Houston, Tex.: 70
　　Sill, Okla.: 8–9, 13, 36, 37, 42, 48, 52, 63–66, 67, 98, 105, 122, 125, 284–85
Forward air control system
　　in European Theater: 222–23
　　in Italy: 183
　　in Southwest Pacific Area: 263–64
France
　　and World War I: 10, 11, 12–13, 15–16, 33
　　and World War II: 47, 199, 203–26
Francis, Lt. Duane: 234
Frazier, Capt. Victor E.: 127, 128
Fredendall, Maj. Gen. Lloyd R.: 146–47, 151–52
Freeman, Maj. Samuel: 162, 200–201
French Army
　　coordination with American air observation posts: 215
　　and French Revolution: 4
　　and organic aviation: 33
　　and World War I: 10, 13, 29
French Expeditionary Corps: 181–82
French forces
　　First Army: 221
　　2d Armored Division: 215
Friendly fire
　　from Army Air Forces: 180, 183, 229
　　avoidance of: 264
　　casualties due to: 180, 208
　　in European Theater: 208
　　in North Africa: 149–50
　　in Southwest Pacific Area: 263–64
Fuchs, Lt. John: 163
Fuddy-Duddies Flying Club: 53, 76, 81, 86, 102, 146
Furuholmen, Lt. Col. Bjarne: 110, 111–12
Futa Pass, Italy: 185, 186

Gall, Capt. John: 234
Gavan, Col. Paul A.: 246
Gerhardt, Maj. Gen. Charles H.: 205
German Army
    Seventh Army: 217–19, 220
    Nineteenth Army: 221–22
    XLVII Panzer Corps: 228
    2d Panzer Division: 212
Germany
    air superiority: 33, 158
    artillery procedures: 170–71
    experience with light aircraft: 39
Gerow, Lt. Gen. Leonard T.: 190
Giffin, Col. Sidney F.: 294–95
Gilbert Islands: 241
Giles, Lt. Gen. Barney M.: 295
Gill, Maj. Gen. William H.: 253
Gillespie, Maj. Eugene P.: 153, 156, 166, 189–90, 276
Glider Field Artillery Battalion, 674th: 258
Goodfellow Field, San Angelo, Tex.: 284
Goodhand, Capt. O. Glenn, Jr.: 175, 178, 222–23
Gothic Line, Italy: 184
Great Britain
    and aerial observation: 57–58
    air depots in: 192–93
    air sections for units deploying to: 129, 145–47
    buildup of U.S. forces in: 96
    experiments with light aircraft: 39*n*
    and invasion of Southern France: 221
    pilot schools in: 146–47
    preparations in, for invasion of Normandy: 189–208
Greely, Maj. Gen. Adolphus W.: 7
Gregorie, Capt. James: 204
Grenoble, France: 200
Grove, Great Britain: 192, 197
Gruenther, Brig. Gen. Alfred M.: 146
Guadalcanal: 250
Guam: 251
Gustav Line, Italy: 171, 175, 180
Guy, S. Sgt. C. N.: 244

Haislip, Maj. Gen. Wade H.: 215–17, 220–21
Hall, Capt. James: 173
Hallstein, Maj. David: 231–32
Halsey, Admiral William F.: 237, 241
Hammond, Col. Elton F.: 274
Handy, Maj. Gen. Thomas T.: 281–82
Harding, Brig. Gen. Horace: 251
Harmon, Maj. Gen. Ernest N.: 183
Harmon, Maj. Gen. Millard F.: 269–70, 271
Harper, Brig. Gen. Arthur M.: 251
Harper, Lt. R. S.: 209
Harper, Maj. Gen. Robert W.: 283
Hart, Brig. Gen. Charles E.: 159, 163, 166, 189, 193, 204
Harte Flying Service: 123
Hawaii: 267
Hawaiian Air Depot: 270

Haynes, Maj. Thomas E.: 192, 197, 228, 232
Headquarters, Army Air Forces: 76
    and Air-Observation-Post Program research and development: 116–17, 120
    and airborne artillery divisions: 118–19
    and aircraft production priorities: 111–12, 115
    and armed light aircraft: 297, 298–99
    attempts to demonstrate feasibility of division flight concept: 104–05
    attempts to reverse War Department decision on air observation posts: 85, 103–06
    attitude toward air observation posts' use of L–5s: 277
    and equipment for Department of Air Training: 94
    and helicopter development: 116–17, 119–20
    and L–5 and L–6 production: 110–11
    and organic aviation for combat arms other than Field Artillery: 103–04
    and pilots for field artillery training program: 88
    provision of J–3 Cubs for service test at Fort Sill: 64
    provision of L–4s for Air Training Detachment: 67
    and ratings for Field Artillery pilots: 90
    refusal to support air-ground training: 99
    sources of antipathy toward Air-Observation-Post Program: 277–78
Headquarters, Army Ground Forces: 76
    and Air-Observation-Post Program: 85–86, 274–75
    and airborne divisions: 118–19
    and aircraft accident reports and statistics: 127
    and aircraft procurement: 110–12, 113–14
    and composition of air sections: 129–30
    and doctrine for Air-Observation-Post Program: 275
    and establishment of Department of Air Training: 89–90
    and expansion of Air-Observation-Post Program beyond Field Artillery: 79–80, 296–98, 301–05
    and light aviation program: 296–303, 324–25
    and planes for Department of Air Training: 118
    and proposal for L–5s for organic aviation: 295–96
    and research and development: 120–22, 284–88, 293–94
    and resupply for air sections: 112
    and training circular on aircraft use: 133*n*
    and unit training: 136
Headquarters, Services of Supply, and ratings for aviation mechanics: 90
Hedgerows: 208
Helicopters: 80–81
    appropriations for the development of: 22, 42, 116, 120
    Bréguet-Dorland 314 Gyroplane Laboratoire: 22

Helicopters—Continued
   demand for: 235, 272
   development of: 20–22, 40–42, 116–17,
      119–20, 188, 286–88
   Fw–61 (Focke-Achgelis; German): 22
   and infantry units: 46–47
   R–1 (Platt-LePage): 42
   R–4 (Sikorsky): 116, 287–88
   R–5 (Sikorsky): 287–88
   R–6 (Sikorsky): 287–88
   Sikorsky: 116, 119–20, 287
   Sikorsky VS–300: 116
Hendrix, Maj. Thomas L.: 166
Hero, Brig. Gen. Andrew, Jr.: 15
Hero Board: 15–16, 33
Herr, Maj. Gen. John K.: 43–44, 45, 47, 58, 75, 79, 80
Hines, Maj. Gen. Ernest: 15
Hitler, Adolph: 33
Hitler Line, Italy: 180
Hodge, Maj. Gen. John R.: 259
Hodges, Lt. Gen. Courtney H.: 46–47, 75, 80, 193
Hoge, Brig. Gen. William M.: 231
Hollandia, New Guinea: 252–53
HORSEFLY: 183, 222–23
Houser, Lt. Edwin F.: 70
Howard, 1st Lt. Alfred R.: 208
Howell, Brig. Gen. Reese M.: 223
Howze, Col. Hamilton H.: 182
Hutchins, 2d Lt. Robert: 133
Hutton, Lt. Col. Carl I.: 210

Ibu, Bougainville: 246
Infantry, organic aerial observation for: 43–47
Infantry Board: 46
Infantry Divisions
   1st: 74n, 157, 160, 163, 205, 209, 211, 225
   2d: 68n, 229
   3d: 148, 161, 178, 221, 231
   4th: 204, 217–18
   5th: 213, 233
   7th: 256, 259, 268–69
   9th: 223
   24th: 252, 256, 265
   28th: 229
   29th: 205, 209, 211
   30th: 202, 215, 217–18
   31st: 265
   32d: 240, 253, 263, 324
   33d: 263–64
   34th: 146, 147, 160
   36th: 39n, 166, 221–22
   37th: 245, 247, 250–51
   38th: 263
   41st: 253
   45th: 162, 180, 221
   75th: 232
   77th: 256, 258–59, 260, 267n
   88th: 182
   90th: 210, 219, 226

Infantry Divisions—Continued
   95th: 227
   99th: 229
   100th: 224
   104th: 246
Infantry Journal: 46
Infantry Regiments
   26th: 163
   120th: 218
   379th: 227
Integration at Department of Air Training: 290
Intelligence mission
   counterintelligence: 70–71
   in European Theater: 210
   in Fifth Army: 172, 175–77
   Operation DIADEM: 180–81
   in Pacific: 247
   in Southern France: 184
   World War I: 11
Irvine, Brig. Gen. Willard W.: 282
"Islands of Safety": 178
Isle of Wight, Great Britain: 204
Italy: 166–88
Iwo Jima, Japan: 266

Japanese antiaircraft activity: 244, 262
Japanese forces
   Eighteenth Army: 253
   Thirty-second Army: 268
Johnson, Maj. Richard A.: 223
Johnson, Lt. Robert: 158
Joint Aircraft Committee: 110–12
Joint Army-Navy Munitions Assignment
   Committee: 121
Jones, Col. Byron Q.: 44–45, 235
Jones, Col. Newton D.: 133
Jungle warfare: 241, 244–45, 250–51, 257, 262, 266, 321, 324

Kasserine Pass, Tunisia: 159
Kellett Autogiro Company: 41–42
Kelly, Lt. Col. Joseph E.: 151
Kenly, Maj. Gen. William L.: 13
Kenney, General George C.: 240, 260, 266–67, 269, 270, 271, 301
Kerr, M. Sgt. James T., Jr.: 68–69, 74, 125, 128
Kesselring, Field Marshal Albert: 184–85
Kiefer, Col. Homer W.: 260, 262, 263, 265
King, Col. George L.: 53
King, Samuel Archer: 7
Knox, 1st Lt. James K.: 293–94
Kreber, Brig. Gen. Leo M.: 245
Kriegsman, Maj. John C.: 259
Krueger, General Walter C.: 49, 51–52, 77–78, 81, 240, 253, 256, 263, 302, 305, 317–18
Kureth, 1st Lt. Charles L.: 214–15

Lake Lanao, Philippine Islands: 265
Landing ships, tank, runways on: 161–62, 166, 221, 267, 291–92

INDEX

Lange, Lt. Clarence: 205
Larkhill, Great Britain: 58, 151
Larson, Lt. Harold E.: 231
Latina, Italy: 173
Le Havre, France: 200
Le Mans, France: 216
Lear, Lt. Gen. Ben: 282–83, 294, 295, 296
Leer, Capt. Edwin H.: 241, 244
Lefever, Lt. Col. Charles W.: 136, 189, 190, 192, 197–98, 201, 203, 204, 299, 305, 308
Leich, Lt. Col. Robert M.: 67, 90–91, 114–16, 120, 122, 125, 190, 198, 275, 305
Lentz, Brig. Gen. John M.: 76, 80, 85–86, 100, 102–03, 104–05, 106–07, 123, 129–30, 274–75, 292–93, 323
LePage, W. Laurence: 42
Lessons learned
    application of: 296, 300, 316
    and Department of Air Training: 291–92
    dissemination of: 283, 297–98
    in North African Theater: 157–58, 160, 161, 241
    in Sicily: 273–74
    World War I: 15–16
Lester, Brig. Gen. James A.: 301–02
Lewis, Brig. Gen. Thomas E.: 76, 80, 86, 96, 146, 152, 153, 156, 188, 323
Leyte, Philippine Islands: 254, 256–66, 267, 324
Liaison mission
    Arnold's perception of, as sole mission for short-range observation aircraft: 38
    in European Theater: 212, 278
    in German Army: 39
    importance of: 323
    in North Africa: 153, 159
    in Philippine Islands: 262, 263
    as secondary concern for Field Artillery: 37
    in Sicily: 161
    in Southwest Pacific Area: 244, 253
    suitability of O–49 for: 52
Liaison Squadrons
    72d: 169, 222
    153d: 193
    aircraft for: 275–76, 286
    Devers' plan to convert to organic air sections: 278
    missions: 193, 275–76, 277, 278, 285, 296, 298–99, 303, 319–20, 321
Liège, Belgium: 200
Light aircraft
    arming of: 45, 296–98
    military characteristics for field artillery: 34–35, 299–300
    missions: 299–300
    need for air superiority of friendly pursuits: 39, 40–41
    procurement of: 109–12, 299
    survivability in battle: 39, 40–41, 57–58, 158, 160, 162–63, 172–73, 316–17
Lineberger, M. Sgt. Paul D.: 125

Lingayen Plain, Philippine Islands: 261
Littauer, Maj. Kenneth P.: 14
Logistical support: 112–16
    for air sections overseas: 156–57
    in the Central Pacific Area: 269–70
    centralized: 174
    in European Theater: 223
    importance of command influence on: 269–70, 271
    in Italian campaign: 174, 184
    lack of ground forces familiarity with Army Air Forces supply system: 87, 95, 115–16, 156–57
    lack of spare parts: 250, 260–61, 262
    in North African Theater: 156–57
    in Philippine Islands: 260–61, 264–65, 266
    planning for: 190–93
    to be provided entirely by Army Air Forces: 280–82
    in South Pacific Area: 250
    in Southwest Pacific Area: 244–45, 260–61, 262, 264–66
Loiata, Italy: 161
Long, Capt. Richard L.: 193, 202
Long-range reconnaissance mission assigned to light bombardment units: 19–20
Losses, German fighters in Italy: 172–73, 178
Losses, planes
    Army Air Forces projections of: 282
    causes of: 308–15
        accidents: 173, 184, 198–99, 208–09, 263, 314–15
        destroyed on the ground: 234, 263, 309
        enemy action: 171–72, 185, 208–09, 269, 309, 311, 314–15
        friendly fire: 263
        small-arms fire: 173, 209
    in European Theater: 208–09
    in Italy: 171–73, 184–85
    on Okinawa: 269
    in Southwest Pacific Area: 254, 256, 260, 262–63
    statistics on: 173, 184–85, 198–99, 208–09, 308–15
Louisiana Maneuvers. *See* Maneuvers, Louisiana.
Lovett, Robert: 49, 50, 62, 77, 116
Low vs. high technology: 81–82, 313–14, 316–17
Lowe, Thaddeus S. C.: 5, 7
Ludendorff Bridge, Germany: 231
Luftwaffe
    aircraft: 23, 26
    ineffective against L–4s: 311
    in Italy: 171–72, 178
    L–4s as primary target of: 171–72, 311
    in North African Theater: 158, 160
Luzon, Philippine Islands: 256–57, 261–64, 265

Maastricht, Holland: 200
MacArthur, General of the Army Douglas: 17, 237, 240, 252, 261–62, 266, 301, 302

McCaw, Lt. Col. Thomas W.: 307
McCloy, John J. ("Blitz"): 53, 60–62, 63, 318
    commitment to air-observation-post concept: 75, 77, 79, 80, 102, 103, 158, 188
    and pilot training: 101, 106, 107–08, 109
    and purchase of light aircraft: 75, 76, 110
McCole, Col. J. C.: 247
McCord, Maj. James: 252, 256, 260, 262, 263
McGinley, Col. Myron E.: 260
McKnight, Maj. Norman E.: 266–67, 269–70
McLain, Brig. Gen. Raymond S.: 210
McNair, Lt. Gen. Lesley J.: 60, 76, 77–78, 212
    and Brodie device: 285
    and Department of Air Training: 96, 97, 98–99
    and Ford's proposal to reorganize Air-Observation-Post Program: 275–76
    frustration with Army Air Forces: 99
    management philosophy: 87, 117
    and research and development: 120–22, 285, 286
    response to Army Air Forces attempt to reverse decision allowing organic aviation: 103, 104–05, 279–80
    support for Air-Observation-Post Program: 98–100, 103, 105–06, 107, 279–80, 284, 321
Madang, New Guinea: 253
Maintenance, advanced
    Air Corps provision of: 38
    Army Air Forces responsibility for: 69, 156, 192–93, 201–02, 281
    in Central Pacific Area: 269–70
    in North African Theater: 156–57
    in Sicily: 161
    unavailable in Southwest Pacific Area: 260, 262, 264–65
Maintenance, routine
    and Air Training Detachment tests, 1942: 74
    difficulties providing in European Theater: 215
    failure of Army Air Forces to provide: 281
    need for simplicity: 37–38
    second echelon performed by Field Artillery mechanics: 69
    in Southwest Pacific Area: 244–45
    training of pilots to perform: 64–65, 67–68, 123, 125–26
Maintenance kits: 95, 115–16, 156
Manarawat, Philippine Islands: 256, 257
Maneuvers
    1940: 64
    1941: 38
    1943: 115
    and aircraft design deficiencies: 33–34
    Carolina, 1941: 50–52
    combined air-ground, 1927: 18
    and development of techniques for employing slow-speed aircraft: 35–36
    Fort Bliss, 1941: 50–52
    German Army, 1937: 23, 26

Maneuvers—Continued
    inadequacy of aerial observation provided by Air Corps: 33–34
    lack of air-ground training for: 99, 100
    and logistical support for air sections: 115
    Louisiana, 1940: 39–40, 46
    Louisiana, 1941: 50–52, 58–59
    Plattsburg, N.Y., 1939: 33–34
    Tennessee, 1941: 50–52
    and testing of aerial observation operations: 39–40
Manila, Philippine Islands: 262, 264
Mantes, France: 221
Manufacturers of light aircraft
    Air Corps attitude toward: 49, 104
    allocation of raw materials to: 110–12
    lobbying by: 47–48, 49, 53, 75, 81
    need for decision on production of light aircraft: 75, 76, 111–12
Map fire: 11
Mapping: 11, 246–47, 254
Mariana Islands: 251
Marine Corps units
    24th Air Group: 265–66
    III Amphibious Corps: 270
    V Amphibious Corps: 251–52
Marinelli, Lt. Col. Jack L.: 174, 180, 184, 186–87, 188, 308
Marshall, General of the Army George C., Jr.: 38, 42, 59, 60–63, 75–76, 79, 221, 279–80, 318–19
Marshall Islands: 241
Martin, Lt. William S.: 234
Mascara, Algeria: 153, 160
Mathews, Capt. William R.: 198–99, 210, 220
Maxfield, Maj. Joseph E.: 7
Maxwell, Maj. Gen. Russell L.: 281, 286, 299
Maxwell Field, Ala.: 16
Mechanics
    African-American: 290
    for air sections: 129, 130
    lack of, in South Pacific Area: 245–46
    for North African Theater: 146, 152–53
    numbers of: 308
    ratings for aviation mechanics: 90
    skill level required: 38
    trained at Air Training Detachment: 68–69
    trained at Department of Air Training: 96–97, 125–26
    trained by field artillery: 86, 89–90
    volunteers for training as: 67, 96–97
Medals and decorations: 163, 180, 251
Medical evacuation: 227, 266, 302, 324
Medical supplies delivered by L–4s: 227, 229, 253, 257, 266
Medjez el Bab, Tunisia: 151
Messina, Italy: 163
Metz, France: 226, 227
Military ballooning: 4–8, 16, 20, 58
Mindanao, Philippine Islands: 265–66

INDEX

Missions, unusual. *See also specific missions and organizations.*
   airdrop: 257
   cargo carriers: 173–74, 257
   laying telephone wires: 173
   radio relays: 173, 246, 257
Mitchell, Brig. Gen. William: 14, 17–18, 31, 32, 45, 81–82
Mobile maintenance organizations: 192–93, 281
Mobile Reclamation and Repair Squadrons
   23d: 193, 197, 201
   27th: 193, 200–201
   43d: 193, 201–02
   50th: 193
Mokmer Airdrome, Biak: 253
Mons, Belgium: 225
Montelimar, France: 222
Montgomery, Field Marshal Bernard L.: 211–12, 231–32
Moore, Maj. Gen. Richard C.: 75
Morgan, John E. P.: 49, 50, 51, 53–54, 81, 323
Morison, Elting E.: 320
Morocco: 147, 149–52
Mortain, France: 217–18
Myer, Brig. Gen. Albert J.: 7

Nancy, France: 226
Naples, Italy: 167
Nassau Bay, New Guinea: 241–42, 262
National Advisory Committee for Aeronautics: 22–23
National Guard observation squadrons: 26, 27
Navy Department
   aerial observers for, trained by Department of Air Training: 290–91
   air observation posts used to mark targets for bombing by: 247, 250
   and Brodie device: 285, 293–94
   and use of air observation posts in Pacific: 240, 241, 256
Nearing, Forrest I.: 125
New Guinea: 240, 241–45, 252–54, 262, 264
Night bombing: 296–98
Night flight: 160, 175, 263, 279, 283–84, 286–87, 291–92, 296–98
Nimitz, Admiral Chester L.: 237, 241, 251, 266–67
Normandy: 188, 203–12
North Africa: 99, 129, 131, 133, 146–60, 240, 241, 275–76
North Pacific Area: 237
Northern Ireland: 146

Oakes, Lt. Col. John C.: 112
Observation flights, pursuit protection for, World War I: 15–16
Observation Group, 3d: 14, 45
Observation squadrons
   Air Corps: 38–39, 47, 275–76
   for armored divisions: 46, 47–48

Observation squadrons—Continued
   British, World War II: 38, 47
   French, World War II: 38, 47
   pilots for: 100
   unsuitability of YO–54s in supporting armor: 47–48
Observation Squadrons (units)
   2d: 27
   5th: 88
   154th: 276*n*
Observed fire missions
   Air Training Detachment tests of: 71–72
   and Field Artillery School: 36, 52–53
   importance of: 274–75, 323
   in Italy: 170
   in North Africa: 149
   on Okinawa: 267, 268–69
   performed by Army Air Forces in German airspace: 172
   service tests of: 39–40, 63–66, 70
   in Southwest Pacific Area: 244
   training for: 8, 12–13, 15–16, 71–72, 86, 89–90, 97, 134–36
   World War I: 10–16
Observers
   assigned to air sections: 129, 130, 134–36
   civilian: 5
   need to be field artillerymen: 13, 34, 52–53
   training
      before 1941: 8, 12–13, 15–16
      by Air Training Detachment: 71–72
      by Field Artillery: 86, 90, 97
      by pilots: 134–36
Office of Strategic Services: 110–11, 285
Okinawa: 267–71, 314–15
Olds, Col. Robert L.: 294
OMAHA Beach: 204, 205–06
Operations
   BOLERO: 96
   DIADEM: 180–81
   OVERLORD: 204
Oran, Algeria: 147
Ordnance Battalion, 737th: 250
Ordnance Corps light aviation companies: 157
Oregon: 246
Organic aviation: 3–4, 16, 32–33, 37–39, 40, 42–44, 45–48, 52–56, 59–60, 63, 64, 69, 76–78, 79–83, 85–86, 87, 94, 99, 102–05, 106–07, 109, 114, 115–16, 118, 122, 127, 129, 133, 136, 137, 145, 151–53, 157, 158, 160, 163, 189, 192, 200, 203, 205, 210, 221, 228, 231, 234–35, 237, 240, 254, 268, 271–72, 273, 275–76, 278–80, 283, 286, 294, 295–96, 298–99, 300–303, 304–05, 307–08, 315, 318–21, 323, 324–25
"Organic Field Artillery Air Observation": 133
Ormoc, Philippine Islands: 256–57, 258–59
Oswalt, Col. John W.: 58*n*, 59*n*, 174–75, 180, 183, 184, 185–86, 188, 314

Overall, 1st Lt. Jesse U., III: 157

Pacific Theater of Operations: 237–72
Panels
    used for air-ground communication: 210, 215
    used for identification from air: 213
Parachute Infantry Battalion, 509th: 167
Parang, Philippine Islands: 265
Parham, Maj. Gen. H. J.: 151n
Patch, Lt. Gen. Alexander M.: 190, 221
Patrick, Maj. Gen. Mason M.: 13, 14
Patrol missions
    in Central Pacific Area: 251–52
    in European Theater: 203
    in Italy: 174, 178, 188
    on Okinawa: 268
    in South Pacific Area: 246
    in Southwest Pacific Area: 244, 262
    with stable fronts: 229
Patterson, Robert P.: 121
Patterson Field, Ohio: 113
Patton, Lt. Gen. George S., Jr.
    and European Theater: 190, 220–21, 232–34
    and invasion of Sicily: 161, 278–79
    and lessons learned from Sicily campaign: 273–74
    and Louisiana Maneuvers, 1940: 40, 46, 51–52
    and Tennessee Maneuvers: 51
    and Western Task Force: 148, 151–52, 159
Pennell, Maj. Gen. Ralph McT.: 286
Perlham Downs, Wiltshire, Great Britain: 146
Pershing, General John J.: 10, 16
Philippine Islands: 26, 27, 240, 254, 256–66, 270
Photograph interpreters: 175–77, 181, 247
Photographic Interpretation Center, Fifth Army: 176–77, 181
Photographic processing units: 300
Photographic reconnaissance mission
    Air Corps proposals for, 1939–1940: 38
    and Air Training Detachment test: 70–71, 81–82
    in Italy: 175–77, 178
    need for: 300, 302
    not fully performed: 296
    proposed use of light bombers for: 38
    World War I: 11
Photographic reconnaissance squadrons: 275–76
Photographs
    aerial, used in training observers: 134
    grid: 176–77
    oblique: 70–71, 176, 181, 213, 246–47, 251–52, 285
    vertical: 71, 176, 181, 247, 251–52
Pillboxes, attacks on: 226–28
Pilot fatigue
    avoidance of: 268
    in European Theater: 198, 199–200, 209, 219
    in Pacific Theater: 252, 263, 264–65
Pilot-mechanics: 64–65, 67–68

Pilots
    African-American: 126, 134, 137, 290, 291
    Air Corps: 54–55, 88
    Army Air Forces: 197–98, 222–23
    assignment to Field Artillery: 88
    briefings and debriefings for: 211, 251–52
    check: 123–24
    used in command and control: 213, 214, 215–17, 219, 220–22
    commissions for enlisted men: 90
    for division artillery headquarters air sections: 129
    at fault in crashes: 198–99, 209
    for field artillery brigade headquarters air sections: 129
    Field Artillery officers: 106, 316
    flight pay for: 90
    flying lessons taken by artillery officers: 59
    health records of: 127
    lack of experience with field artillery battalions: 132–33
    lack of, in Pacific Theater: 240
    medical needs: 199–200
    misassigned as infantry replacements: 146
    need to train with supported artillery units: 16
    numbers of: 307–08
    numbers in training classes: 89–90, 96, 109
    personal pilots for commanders: 153, 159, 186–87, 190–91, 215–17, 263, 323
    ratings for: 90, 100, 153
    recruitment of licensed pilots: 64, 86, 95–96
    replacement of: 166, 197–99, 291
    reserves of, in overseas theaters: 153
    rest camps for: 200
    shortages of: 199, 240
    skill level required: 37–38
    testing of: 70
    to train Field Artillery officers in aerial observation of fire: 97, 134–36
    training: 291, 293–94, 307
        in aircraft maintenance: 64–65, 67–68, 123
        by Army Air Forces: 86, 282–83
        at civilian aviation schools: 123
        controversy, 1942: 97–99
        by Field Artillery: 86, 88, 89–102, 106–08
        in fire direction: 124–25
        in local schools in Great Britain: 146–47, 151
        in local schools in North Africa: 151–53, 160
        matriculation crisis, 1942: 96–97, 100–101
        in tactical employment of air observation posts: 86, 123
        to use the Brodie device: 267
    untrained in making over water flights: 256
Piper, Thomas F.: 67, 87–88
Piper, William T., Sr.: 23, 48–49, 81, 323
Piper Aircraft Corporation: 3, 22–23, 39–40, 48–49, 68–69, 92–93, 95, 111–12, 117–18, 120–21, 157, 313

INDEX

Platt, Harold: 42
Plattsburg, N.Y., maneuvers. *See* Maneuvers, Plattsburg.
Plexiglas: 201
Po River, Italy: 184, 187
Polish forces, II Corps: 181
Portable surgical hospitals (parachute)
    5246th: 257
    5247th: 257
Porter, Maj. Gen. Ray E.: 275–76, 279–80, 283–84, 285–87, 291, 295, 296, 304
Post Field, Fort Sill, Okla.: 88, 122, 125–26
Prisoners of war, German, assessment of American aerial observation: 171
Propellers: 23, 42, 74, 173, 186, 202, 225, 250, 267, 284
Proximity fuzes: 232
"Puff target ranges": 135
Pursuit operations: 212, 214, 225, 231
Pyle, Col. Charles A.: 291

Racism: 126, 134, 137
Radicossa Pass, Italy: 185–86
Radio operators for air sections: 129, 130
Radios
    for air sections: 130, 317
    frequency-modulated: 36–37, 66*n*
    high-frequency: 183
    for observation aircraft: 36–37, 201
    and service test of organic air observation: 65–66
    voice: 28
    weight: 65–66
    World War I: 11, 13–14
Read, Maj. Harold F.: 270
Rear area security. *See* Air observation posts, security for.
Reconnaissance mission
    and Air Training Detachment test: 70–71
    balloon units: 4, 5, 7
    for battalion command groups: 174
    in European Theater: 212, 213, 214, 219, 225, 231
    evaluation of: 300–301
    importance of: 274
    in Italy: 172
    and Louisiana Maneuvers: 51–52
    and mobile operations: 225
    on OMAHA Beach: 205
    as organic aviation mission: 302
    as secondary concern for Field Artillery: 37
    in Sicily: 162–63, 274
    and Signal Corps aerial companies: 8
    in South Pacific Area: 246
    in Southwest Pacific Area: 257
Reconnaissance Troop, 37th: 246
Red Ball Air Express: 227
Red Ball Express: 227*n*
Remagen, Germany: 231
Repair parts kits: 69, 156

Replacement and School Command: 87, 94
Rescue missions: 265–66
Research and development
    and Department of Air Training: 116, 117, 120–22
    of helicopters: 22, 42, 116–17, 119–20
Rhine River, Germany: 204, 231–33
Rhodes, 1st Lt. Wilmot G.: 293–94
Rich, Lt. Oscar: 163, 205, 209, 211
Richardson, Lt. Gen. Robert C., Jr.: 300
Rome, Italy: 182–83
Roosevelt, Franklin D.: 33, 86
Rotary-wing aircraft: 46–47. *See also* Aircraft (by type); Autogiros; Helicopters.
Rouen, France: 200
Roulson, S. Sgt. William T., Jr.: 146
Route reconnaissance missions
    in France: 213, 214, 231
    in Philippine Islands: 261–62
    in Sicily: 162–63
Rover Joe: 183
Royal Air Force: 57–58, 151
Royal Air Force/Royal Artillery Squadron, 651st: 151
Royal Artillery: 57–58, 59, 85, 151
Runways
    on aircraft carriers: 251
    on LSTs: 161–62, 166, 267
    using sand: 250
Ryan, Col. Llewellyn O.: 298
Ryder, Maj. Gen. Charles W.: 147, 150–51

Safety programs. *See* Air safety programs.
St. Lô, France: 211, 212
St. Onge, Lt. Col. V. A.: 112
Saipan: 251–52
Salamaua, New Guinea: 241–42, 262
Salerno, Italy: 166
Salmon, Lt. Col. John D.: 146–47, 152
Salvage replacement parts pools: 157
Salzburg, Austria: 234
Samar Island, Philippine Islands: 256
San Juan Hill, Battle of: 7
San Juan Strait, Philippine Islands: 256, 257
San Pablo Field No. 2, Philippine Islands: 258
Sarko, 1st Lt. John S.: 74
Saville, Brig. Gen. Gordon P.: 222
Schelly, 1st Lt. Kenneth B.: 229
Schirmacher, Capt. Theodore F.: 67, 68, 87–88, 90–91, 92, 93, 107, 288–89
Schlatter, Col. David M.: 103–04, 107
Scriven, Brig. Gen. George P.: 9, 10
Seine River, France: 200, 219, 221, 225
Services of Supply: 112–14, 227*n*. *See also* Army Service Forces.
Shell, 1st Lt. John R.: 148–49, 150, 157–58, 160
Shepard, Maj. Claude L., Jr.: 161, 190, 200, 202, 221, 273–74
Sibert, Maj. Gen. Franklin C.: 265
Sicily: 161–66, 241, 273–74
Sidi Bel Abbés, Algeria: 152–53

Siegfried Line: 226
Sikorsky, Igor: 42, 116, 119–20
Silver Stars: 163, 180
Simpson, Lt. Gen. William H.: 190
Simulation training: 135
Sinon, Maj. Frederick W.: 265–66
Ski Jump: 186–87
Sloan, Maj. Gen. John E.: 182
Smith, Col. Luther S.: 86
Smoke bombs used to mark targets: 247, 250
Snow, Maj. Gen. William J.: 13
Solomon Islands: 250
South Pacific Area: 237, 241, 245–51
Southwest Pacific Area: 237, 240, 241–45, 250, 252–66, 271
Squier, Brig. Gen. George O.: 13–14
Station de Sened, Tunisia: 158
Steiner, Jacob: 5, 7
Stelle, Stanford J.: 67, 68–69
Stephenson, 1st Lt. Hugh K.: 229
Stilwell, General Joseph W.: 298–99, 301, 302, 305
Stimson, Henry L.: 49, 53, 60–62, 318
Stinson Model 76. *See* Aircraft, L–5.
Strategic bombardment as focus of Air Corps: 16–18, 29
Stratemeyer, Maj. Gen. George E.: 103–04
Strok, Capt. Michael J.: 48, 133, 157, 161, 166, 167, 169, 173–74, 175, 184, 188, 202, 308, 309n, 314–15
Survey missions: 246–47
Sutherland, Maj. Gen. Richard K.: 240
Suzuki, Lt. Gen. Sosaku: 256, 258
Swain Field, Okla.: 67
Swenson, Col. J. Elmore: 205, 211, 325
Swift, Maj. Gen. Innis P.: 51–52
Swing, Maj. Gen. Joseph M.: 51–52, 257

Tables of organization
 and aerial companies: 8
 and air sections: 129–30, 133, 307–08
 for airborne divisions: 118–19
 depot units, army: 184
Tactical air commands
 IX: 218–19
 XII: 172, 183, 222
 XIX: 225
Tactical Air Depot, Third: 192, 193, 202
Tactical Air Force (Provisional), First: 200
Tanahmerah Bay, New Guinea: 252–53
Tank Destroyer Center: 104–05
Target-marking missions: 247, 250, 263–64, 298–99
Targets of opportunity, locating: 136, 317
Task Force Howze: 183
Taylor, C. Gilbert: 22–23
Taylor, Maj. Maxwell D.: 62–63
Taylorcraft Aviation Corporation: 49, 50, 95, 111–12, 117
Tennessee Maneuvers, 1941. *See* Maneuvers, Tennessee.

Terrain
 as cause of crashes: 266
 effects on L–4's performance: 120, 160
 effects on types of missions flown: 157, 160
 in Italian campaign: 166, 170, 173, 183, 184–88
 jungle: 241, 244–45, 250–51, 257, 262, 266, 321, 324
 mountains: 120, 160, 162–63, 170, 173, 183, 184–88
 in North African Theater: 157, 160
 in Sicily: 162–63
 in Southwest Pacific Area: 253–54, 256–57, 262
Thionville, France: 226
Thompson, 1st Lt. Don B.: 245–46, 250
Thornton, Maj. Paget W.: 190, 198
Time-on-target technique: 170–71, 221
Tinian, Mariana Islands: 251
Tool kits: 156
Torokino Beachhead, Bougainville: 245
Tournai, Belgium: 225
Training
 of aerial observers for the Navy: 290–91
 air-ground: 99, 100
 air observation posts with supported ground units: 70
 of air sections at local schools overseas: 146–47, 151–53, 160
 aircraft for: 109–12, 291
 at Army Air Forces liaison pilot schools: 282–84
 for Brodie device: 267
 at civilian aviation schools: 123
 demonstration teams: 293–94
 of divisional air sections: 276–77
 of field artillery mechanics: 68–69, 86
 of flight instructors: 124
 in Great Britain: 146–47, 211
 in indirect-fire delivery: 8, 12–13, 15–16
 instructional materials: 146–47
 in L–4s with pontoons: 291
 lack of, in Pacific Theater: 240
 for landings: 68
 in maintenance of planes: 64–65, 123, 125
 manuals: 291–92
 of mechanics by Army Air Forces: 59
 of mechanics by Field Artillery: 59, 86, 89–90, 290
 night-flight: 160, 283–84, 291
 in North African Theater: 151–53
 of observers
  in Air Training Detachment: 71–72
  by Army Air Forces: 59
  by Field Artillery: 59, 86, 90, 97, 134–36
  by pilots: 134–36
 philosophy of, at Air Training Detachment: 68
 philosophy of, at Department of Air Training: 92–93, 107, 122
 of pilot-mechanics: 64–65, 67–68, 123

INDEX

Training—Continued
    of pilots: 282–84, 291, 301
        by Army Air Forces: 59, 98, 100–101
        at Department of Air Training: 93–96, 98–99, 122–28
        by Field Artillery: 59, 86
    responsibility for tactical training of air sections: 132–33
    supervision of: 64–65, 68–69, 153
    for takeoffs: 68
    unit: 129–37, 145, 148, 151–53, 211
Training circulars. *See* War Department Training Circulars.
Training Command, Amphibious Forces, Pacific Fleet: 293–94
Training commands, and training of air sections with their battalions: 136
Transportation, organic, for maintenance units: 192–93
Transportation Corps Army aviation maintenance companies: 157
Transportation of planes
    by landing ship, tank: 161–62, 166, 221, 267, 291–92
    by ship: 156, 256
Troina, Italy: 163
Troop resupply mission
    for advance troops in Italy: 182
    in European Theater: 226–27
    in Italy: 167, 173–74
    in jungle areas: 257, 258, 324
    at Mortain, France: 218
    as organic aviation function: 302, 324
    in Sicily: 163
    in South Pacific Area: 246
    in Southwest Pacific Area: 244, 257–58, 263, 266
Troops delivered by air observation posts: 121–22, 257
Trucks for air sections: 129
Truscott, Lt. Gen. Lucian K., Jr.: 161, 186–87, 221–22
Tunisia: 150–51, 152, 157, 158, 160, 188, 241, 276n, 278
Twaddle, Brig. Gen. Harry L.: 38, 43, 79

Union Army, use of balloons: 5, 7
United Kingdom. *See* Great Britain.
U.S. Army Air Service: 11, 14
U.S. Army Forces in the Far East Board: 301–02
U.S. Army Signal Corps: 5
    aerial companies: 7–8
    and air-ground communication: 28
    Aviation Section: 8, 10, 13
    proposal for aerial messenger companies: 274, 276
    radios: 65–66
USS *Brodie*: 267
USS *Brooklyn*: 149
USS *Ranger*: 148–49

Utah Beach: 204–05

Valencia, Philippine Islands: 259
Van Voorhis, Brig. Gen. Daniel: 44
Vandenberg, Lt. Gen. Hoyt S.: 303
Vaughn, Lt. Frank L.: 231
Vincent, Lt. Col. H. Farley: 293, 297–98
Visibility problems
    caused by weather: 184–86
    caused by windows: 201
Volturno River, Italy: 170
Volunteers
    airplane mechanics: 67, 96–97
    pilot-mechanics: 67
    for pilot training program: 88, 95–96, 100, 101

Wakde Island: 253
Walker, Lt. Col. John T.: 146, 156, 157, 166, 169, 184, 278
Wann, 1st Lt. Henry S.: 49, 51–52, 67, 87–88, 94, 95, 289
War Department
    and air-observation-post supply policies: 156
    aircraft procurement policy: 88
    approval of air-observation-post concept: 75–78, 85–86, 104
    and expansion of Air-Observation-Post Program: 296–305
    G–3 plan for air-observation-post organization: 276
    mobilization planning: 109–10
    policy on aerial observation, 1941: 57–66
    policy on pilots for Field Artillery training program: 88
    policy toward Air-Observation-Post Program, 1943–1944: 273–80
    and priorities for shipping air sections: 240, 241
    and rating of pilots: 90
    reorganization: 76, 77
    and specification of military characteristics for Field Artillery aircraft: 299–300
    and tests of organic aviation: 37
War Department Circular No. 208: 280
War Department General Staff
    Air Corps representation on: 15
    and Air-Observation-Post Program: 85–86
    and assignment of air sections: 131–32
    and doctrine for use of balloons in combat: 8
    and Ford's proposal to reorganize Air-Observation-Post Program: 275
    Operations Division: 129
    Operations Division *Information Bulletin*: 247
    and testing of centralized Air Corps control of aviation: 38–39, 42
War College Division: 9
War Department Training Circulars
    No. 24: 133, 276–77
    No. 132: 127n, 277
War with Spain: 7–8
Washburn, Lt. Col. Israel B.: 214

Water landings (L-4s): 166, 291
Watland, 1st Lt. Lloyd A.: 226
Watson, Capt. Joseph M., Jr.: 23, 39–40, 48, 81, 146–47, 151–53, 289
Weather
    and ability of L-4s to fly missions where Army Air Forces planes failed: 231
    effects on air-observation-post operations in Southwest Pacific Area: 260
    effects on aircraft maintenance: 203
    hazards in European Theater: 228–29, 311
    hazards in Italy: 184–86
Webster, Maj. Thomas J.: 173
Western Task Force: 147–50
Westover, Maj. Gen. Oscar: 20
Weyland, Col. Otto P.: 104
Whiteaker, Brig. Gen. Robert O.: 40, 49, 81
Willems, Col. John M.: 161
Williams, Col. Edward T.: 232–33
Williams, G. P.: 270
Williams, Col. Grant A.: 193
Williams, Lt. Gen. Robert R.: 59, 118–19, 120–21, 305, 325
    and Air Training Detachment: 67, 72
    assigned to Air Staff: 296, 300–301
    and Department of Air Training: 90–91, 94, 95, 107, 127–28, 288, 291–92
    and European Theater: 232

Wilson, Lt. Col. Bryce: 128, 136, 190, 197, 198, 199, 201–02, 204, 226
Windeler, Lt. William G.: 208
"Wings for Santa Barbara": 40, 43, 58–59, 69
Wolf, Col. Gordon J.: 314
    and Air Training Detachment: 69, 70, 72–73
    and artillery air officers: 276–77
    and establishment of Department of Air Training: 87–88, 90–91, 107
    and European and Mediterranean observer mission: 297–98
    as head of Department of Air Training: 288, 290–94, 297–98, 299
    and logistical support for air sections: 115
    and service test of organic air observation: 63–66, 69–70
    and staff for Department of Air Training: 92
    and testing of aircraft: 286
Wood, Maj. Gen. John S.: 213, 222
World War I, use of aviation in: 9–14, 33
World War II, impact on evolution of Army aviation: 324–26
World War II before U.S. entry, massacre of British and French aircrews: 38, 47
Wright Field, Ohio: 19, 94, 95, 261, 262

Yamashita, General Tomoyuki: 262

www.ingramcontent.com/pod-product-compliance
Lightning Source LLC
Chambersburg PA
CBHW082025300426
44117CB00015B/2360